Shakespeare
SUPPRESSED

SHAKESPEARE
SUPPRESSED

The Uncensored Truth About
Shakespeare and His Works

A Book of Evidence and Explanation

by
KATHERINE CHILJAN

FIRST PRINTED EDITION

Published by Faire Editions, San Francisco, CA
Design and layout by Anthony Toy
Manufactured in the United States of America

Library of Congress Control Number: 2011925305
ISBN 978-0-9829405-4-9

shakespearesuppressed.com

THIS WORK IS DEDICATED

To my Father

and

to the Memory of my Mother

Contents

Introduction

THE CONSUMMATE POET, the epitome of high art and culture, the fount of knowledge, the biggest contributor to modern English language, the master dramatist whose 400-year-old plays are performed, read and appreciated today, every day, in many languages, is Shakespeare. The Shakespeare professor or expert, however, would have you believe that a man with scant education, no evidence he could write (other than a crude signature), and no evidence during his lifetime that he was in fact a professional writer, was the same erudite, witty and super-brilliant wordsmith, Shakespeare. Left with so few facts about his personal life and literary career, the very best that the expert can do for the great author, the creator of so many gorgeous verses, and fascinating, lovable and psychologically complex characters, is to make guesses. Nothing but endless speculations and fantasies are offered to explain how England's greatest author reached the pinnacle of literary achievement. But does the professor look at the historical record? Apparently, he does not. If he did, he would see how obvious it is that *his man*, the Stratford Man, was not the great author, Shakespeare. And with only a little extra effort he would also see that the concept of the Stratford Man as Shakespeare is a very old and well-orchestrated fabrication. He would see that the maker of this fabrication or myth was Ben Jonson, directed and sponsored by William Herbert, 3rd Earl of Pembroke, and that their instrument was Shakespeare's First Folio, published in 1623. This book of collected plays suggested for the very first time that "William Shakespeare" and an undistinguished businessman with a similar name who hailed from Stratford-upon-Avon were one and the same. The Stratford Man had been dead for seven years when the book was launched. Jonson and Pembroke's deception remained for the most part undetected for over two centuries. But by the time that unbiased observers were starting to catch on, the Shakespeare professor or expert had evidently become enamored with the idea that a boy with humble origins, little schooling and no connections had transformed himself into a polyglot, a polymath, a master of rhetoric, and a sophisticated, traveled, man of the world who could create timeless literary masterpieces. Any evidence that contradicted this picture was ignored, and that is the situation as it stands to this day.

Numerous good books and articles dispelling the case of the Stratford Man as the true author and showing that "William Shakespeare" was someone's pen name have been written. But no matter how compelling the evidence and the arguments, the Shakespeare professor will entertain not one shred of a doubt about his Shakespeare. He and his peers comprise a tiny, elite minority who have become the rulers of Shakespeare opinion. But there are millions of Shakespeare fans all over the world that read and attend his plays, see the movies, buy biographies, and visit the "birth place," Stratford-upon-Avon. They care about Shakespeare and want to know more about him but they are unaware that the so-called experts are keeping them in the dark. Most devotees of Shakespeare do not know about the numerous problems surrounding his works and the experts' inability to solve them. The experts do not know with certainty when any of the Shakespeare plays were written, their order of composition, or how many he wrote. Many early printed Shakespeare plays have bad text, and the experts are still trying to make sense out of a legion of unclear lines – why were his writings left in such a state? Many printers pirated Shakespeare's works – why was this the case and why did the great author seemingly allow it? How are allusions to Shakespeare's plays in documents and in print before he supposedly wrote them explained? These puzzles are discussed by Shakespeare professors at conferences and written about in academic journals but they have never been adequately explained or even disclosed to the general public. The identities of the people addressed in Shakespeare's very intimate sonnets remain elusive. Who was the boy or young man, today referred to as the "Fair Youth," that he had admired, and what was the nature of their relationship? He was obsessed with the "Dark Lady" – who was she? The experts only put forth theories.

The lack of information about Shakespeare's personal and artistic life is the most frustrating problem of all, and the mystery is not made any clearer by the few facts known about the Stratford Man. No one who knew him in Stratford-upon-Avon ever referred to him as the great author. He and the great author shared the same name but no fact during his lifetime connects him to a literary career. It is believed that he was an actor, and a skilled one, but we do not know when or how he learned his trade or know a single role he played. If the Stratford Man was Shakespeare, then how did he acquire the extensive knowledge displayed in the plays, some of it only obtainable at a university, which the experts admit he never attended? What did the great author look like? Every painting proposed as a Shakespeare portrait is unauthenticated or has been proved a fraud. The two "concrete" images we do have – an engraving by Martin Droeshout and a sculpted bust – are significantly different, and both were rendered after his death. Despite these gaps, discrepancies and frauds, today's Shakespeare experts maintain that there is nothing unusual about his biography. Shakespeare was the most prolific dramatist of his era, and the greatest, and was so acknowledged by his contemporaries – surely there should have been more solid information about him.

Are those who appreciate Shakespeare supposed to just meekly accept that there are no answers to any of these questions? Perhaps they would not if they knew that it is an *unproven theory* that William Shakspere, born in Stratford-upon-Avon in 1564, was the great author, "William Shakespeare." Independent scholars demonstrated over a century ago that this is the case. All documentary evidence gathered about the Stratford Man reveals a successful businessman and property owner with ties to the theater, but that is all. It is pure speculation that he wrote poetry or drama. Shakespeare lovers need to know that the Shakespeare expert or professor has been forced to invent the great author's literary biography and dramatic career due to this lack of hard facts. He calls it biography but any critical reader would classify it as historical fiction. Students of Shakespeare ought to note that, in the classroom, only the literary aspects of the plays are discussed. This is because nothing in the traditional Shakespeare biography is reflected in any of his works. Are we expected to believe that Shakespeare alone among all great poets and dramatists in history did not insert any of his life experiences in thirty-eight or more plays, or in his sonnets, which were written in the first person? This factor alone should raise doubts about the Stratford Man. This book openly presents these problems to the reader and proposes new solutions for them based on contemporary evidence. The Shakespeare professor's case for the Stratford Man as the great author is also examined; the reader will learn that the professor's best evidence is *posthumous*. Meanwhile, the profile of the great author, as revealed in his works and as described by his contemporaries, sharply collides with the factual biography of the Stratford Man. The reader will learn from this book that "William Shakespeare" was the great author's pen name, that he was a nobleman, that he suppressed his authorship during his lifetime and that it continued to be suppressed after his death. The reader will also learn that some in the literary world knew this and very discretely expressed it in print. This book will also attempt to answer the most important question of all – after his death, why was the true identity of the great author deliberately concealed behind the bland face of the Stratford Man?

If the reader is intrigued by this introduction he may wish to know immediately the answer to the other big question: Why didn't the great author, whoever he was, claim or get credit for his own works? The quick response: the great author did not claim authorship during his lifetime because he was a nobleman. Generally speaking, those of high rank who wrote poetry or drama did not seek publication or compensation for what they wrote. After their death, however, the stigma of print would disappear, and their friends or descendants could openly publish their work with their names. But for some reason – some very important and unusual reason – this courtesy was not extended to the great author. The short answer for the Stratford Man is that he never claimed the Shakespeare authorship because he was not the great author. The Shakespeare authorship was "given" to him after his death, or as Shakespeare would say, greatness was thrust upon him, and this book will provide an explanation why. This issue is a complex literary mystery – a series of puzzles – but it can be solved by looking critically and impartially at *contemporary evidence* and by looking at the absence of evidence. *This book will not include as "evidence" the rumors and speculations about the great author that began a generation or more after he lived, many of which have now become accepted as fact.* The Shakespeare problems and absences presented in this book are not controversial – the experts recognize them – but they have not been able to understand or solve them because they have been hampered and constricted by the wrong model, the Stratford Man model, *one that has failed to shed light on any aspect of the great author's works or literary biography.* Only with full information can the reader judge if there is indeed reason to doubt the Stratford Man's authorship of Shakespeare.

After twenty-six years of studying the Shakespeare authorship question, I am certain, "as certain as I know the sun is fire" (*Coriolanus*, 5.4.49), that Edward de Vere, 17th Earl of Oxford (1550-1604), is the nobleman in question behind the pen name, "William Shakespeare." Fourteen years older than the Stratford Man, Oxford's extensive education (private tutors, university and law school attendance), European travel (especially Italy), and involvement in literature and the theater has been preserved in the documentary record. Many details and events of his life are paralleled in the Shakespeare plays, and almost every problem or puzzle associated with Shakespeare can be explained with Oxford as the true author. *This book, however, will not present his case for the Shakespeare authorship.* The question that must be resolved first is about the Stratford Man – is he the great author, aye or nay? There is no point arguing for Oxford, pro or con, until this point has been settled. And if the Stratford Man was not the great author, then why did he get the credit? How and why did the two identities become one? And finally, why was the great author's death not noted in the literary world when it had occurred? The answers to these questions are the keys to unlocking the mysteries surrounding Shakespeare and his works.

I gratefully acknowledge Ramon Jiménez for allowing me to "borrow" some of his Stratford Man eyewitnesses for this book. Ramon, and John Hamill, Dr. Rima Greenhill and Gordon Banchor, also have my special thanks for providing critical commentary on the text.

List of Terms

DNB: *Dictionary of National Biography.*

FIRST FOLIO: Today's nickname of the 1623 edition of collected Shakespeare plays. The book was printed on large folio-sized pages. The second edition, published in 1632, is called the Second Folio. The Third Folio was issued in 1663 and 1664, and the final edition, the Fourth Folio, in 1685. "First Folio" is meant wherever the capitalized word "Folio" appears.

THE GREAT AUTHOR: The creative genius responsible for the poetic and dramatic works credited with the name, "William Shakespeare," which was his pen name.

LORD CHAMBERLAIN: The holder of a high government office that, among other duties, supervised royal entertainment; the Lord Chamberlain also controlled the public theater and play publishing through the Master of the Revels.

LORD CHAMBERLAIN'S MEN: The name of an acting company active from 1594 to 1603 sponsored by the then Lord Chamberlain. After Queen Elizabeth I's death, many of the same members were embraced by King James I to form his own new acting company, The King's Men.

OED: *Oxford English Dictionary.*

QUARTO: The majority of individual Shakespeare plays were first printed in quarto, a page size defined as one quarter of the large sheet of paper used in the printing press.

SHAKESPEARE PROFESSOR OR EXPERT: The representative of the orthodox or Stratfordian position regarding Shakespeare, i.e., that the great author was unquestionably the Stratford Man. There are no Shakespeare professors in the formal sense, only English professors or lecturers who teach Shakespeare; for the sake of convenience, the masculine pronoun only will be applied to them.

SHAKE-SPEARE'S SONNETS AND SHAKESPEARE'S SONNETS: The former term specifically refers to the book published in 1609, reproducing the title exactly as it had appeared. The latter term simply refers to the sonnets of Shakespeare in general and not necessarily the 1609 book.

STATIONERS' REGISTER: The 16th and 17th century logbooks of the Stationers' Company, a guild, in which activities of English printers and publishers were recorded.

STC: *Short-Title Catalogue*. A list of English printed books dated 1475 to 1640; each work has a specific identity number. The Wing Catalogue lists books dated after 1640.

THE STRATFORD MAN (1564-1616): A businessman who hailed from Stratford-upon-Avon (Warwickshire County). His name, William Shakspere, resembled the great author's pen name. Contemporary documents spelled his surname phonetically, and most reflected a pronunciation like "Shackspur." Neither Mr. Shakspere nor his descendants claimed he was the great author. After his death, he was falsely credited as the author known as William Shakespeare.

"WILLIAM SHAKESPEARE" OR "WILLIAM SHAKE-SPEARE": The pen name of the great author. The words "shake" and "speare" are a noun and verb combination that suggests the literal shaking of spears, a much-used expression in the contemporary literature. A hyphen often separated these two words in printed occurrences. Both points suggest the name was an alias. The absence of any personal accounts of a writer named William Shakespeare during his lifetime, or proof of education for a William Shakespeare, substantiates this view.

> *As this is a book of evidence based upon primary sources, many quotations from the period are necessarily included. For the reader's ease, they are presented in modern spelling, with bracketed definitions for unusual or archaic words; italics or capital letters are true to the originally printed text. Underlines in inset quotes, unless otherwise noted, are added for emphasis. Most Shakespeare play citations are based on the Yale Shakespeare.*

PART I

Shakespeare: Greatness & Great Problems

CHAPTER 1

Literary Supreme, Supreme Literary Mystery

SHAKESPEARE'S POEMS AND plays were a sensation in his lifetime and his contemporaries recognized his greatness. In 1598, only five years after the name, "William Shakespeare," first appeared in print, the great author was the subject of an extraordinarily high tribute by a literary critic. Francis Meres wrote that if the Muses, the mythological goddesses that preside over the arts and sciences, spoke English, they "would speak with Shakespeare's fine-filed phrase."[1] Meres also listed Shakespeare's name among the best dramatists of comedy and tragedy, and among the best lyric poets and love poets. Shakespeare was "pleasing the world," wrote poet Richard Barnfield,[2] that same year, and in 1601, Shakespeare was named as one of "the best and chiefest of our modern writers."[3] The high regard for Shakespeare has never waned over the centuries, and probably never will. In the early 20th century, Samuel Clemens, alias Mark Twain, described Shakespeare:

> The author of the Plays was equipped, beyond every other man of his time, with wisdom, erudition, imagination, capaciousness of mind, grace and majesty of expression. Every one has said it, no one doubts it. Also, he had humor, humor in rich abundance, and always wanting to break out.[4]

At the dawning of the 21st century, the British people voted Shakespeare the "Man of the Millennium." Shakespeare's works are perhaps only second to the Bible in the volume of literary scholarship devoted to them, and have inspired numberless derivative works by musicians, painters and other writers over the centuries. Shakespeare was romantic and his love of human beings is often reflected in the politeness, grace and elegance of his characters' language and expression. He loved all types of characters, and was a great observer of character, like Prince Hal in *Henry IV-Part 2*. When the king complained about Prince Hal's "base" company, his brother, the Earl of Warwick, defended him (4.4.67-69):

My gracious lord, you look beyond him quite:
The prince but studies his companions
Like a strange tongue, wherein to gain the language ...

Much wisdom is imparted through Shakespeare's characters, and sympathy – even his villains are presented as real people rather than monsters. Shakespeare often put his characters in unusual or surreal situations, such as an abdicated King Lear wandering upon a field in a storm and Lady Macbeth sleepwalking. A few Shakespeare lines spoken aloud arrests the hearer – they are musical, and one knows it is something different. The super-aware artist who successfully dramatized pride, war, regicide and other complex issues also reinvented with enchantment the mythical world of the fairy.

Beyond his poetic genius, Shakespeare was a scholar, a linguist and a philosopher. He had an extraordinary breadth of knowledge and mastery of many subjects, including the law, classical languages and literature (Latin and Greek), modern languages and literature (Italian, French, etc.), European geography (especially Italy), the Bible, music, heraldry, plants and flowers, and much more. His knowledge was not superficial – he almost always used or expressed it correctly. A multiple-volume study by Geoffrey Bullough is filled with the sources Shakespeare used for his plays, scores of books including foreign-language works not yet translated into English and some works that existed only in manuscript. His knowledge of English history and literature was extensive. Shakespeare was aware of the latest discoveries in science, medicine and astronomy, sometimes alluding to them before they were published, which implies that he was in contact with other intellectuals. With abundant self-confidence, Shakespeare bent the grammar rules to suit his meaning or to fit the poetical meter (like omitting suffixes and prefixes, frequent usage of double and even triple negatives). And if a word did not exist that conveyed his meaning, he would coin one. He turned nouns into verbs, adverbs into adjectives.[5] Shakespeare created at least 1,900 English words,[6] many commonly used today (for example, *successful, lackluster, submerge, employer, lonely, laughable, gloomy*). His vocabulary totaled 31,534 different words, including variations of the same word, according to a study made at Stanford University Department of Statistics;[7] his vocabulary without variations of the same word totaled about 17,000 words.[8] John Milton's vocabulary totaled about 8,000 words, and Christopher Marlowe's about 7,000 words.[9] Shakespeare's play, *Hamlet* is full of phrases routinely said today, like "brevity is the soul of wit," "though this be madness, yet there is method in it" (now said as "there's method in my madness"), "to be or not to be," "frailty thy name is woman," "to the manner born," and "neither a borrower nor a lender be." To summarize his achievement with one of his own phrases, Shakespeare "laid great bases for eternity" (Sonnet 125).

Supreme Literary Mystery

Shakespeare is the most mysterious man in literature. Despite his prolific and incomparable achievement, and recognition by his contemporaries, nothing of a personal nature about him was recorded while he was alive. None of his play manuscripts survive, or personal letters. Exhaustive research by scholars in the environs of Stratford-upon-Avon, the great author's supposed hometown, has failed to illuminate a literary life. The Shakespeare professor usually skips over the mundane facts found there because they shed no light on the great author's poems or plays. These records mostly comprise the Stratford Man's christening (1564), his marriage (1582), his children's christenings (1583, 1585), and his death (1616); sale records of property, grain and stone; records of debts, taxes owed, and other money matters. His name was on a list of grain hoarders during the famine of 1598.[10] The professor refers to the period of 1585 to 1592 as the "The Lost Years" of the Stratford Man's life. This is because the documentary record is nearly blank – only the christening of his twins and interest in his mother's property is recorded. The Stratford Man was aged 21 to 28 during this period. But such blankness has allowed the experts to indulge in fantasies about the Stratford Man's acquisition of culture, knowledge and experience so superbly expressed in the Shakespeare canon. For example, we read that he was a law clerk, a schoolmaster, a soldier. He lived as a servant in the Hesketh household in Lancaster, but his name was "Shakeshafte."[11] No facts support any of these speculations. In the "unlost" years, the first twenty years of the Stratford Man's life (1564-84), nothing recorded is related to education. The professor does not speculate about the Stratford Man's writing career until he can place him in London, the theater center. A scathing remark made by writer Robert Greene in 1592 about an unnamed actor-writer whom he characterized as an "upstart" and a "Shake-scene" is the "fact" that allows the expert to identify him as the Stratford Man. The documentary record *does* place the Stratford Man in London in 1592, *but in an entirely different context*: he made a loan of £7 to John Clayton.[12] The experts usually deny that the moneylender, "Willelmus Shackespere," named on this document was the Stratford Man. Three years will pass before the next *documentary record* in London involving the Stratford Man occurs, a payment to an acting company in 1595. It is the very first document that connects the Stratford Man with the theater: *he was thirty years old.* Four years after this, the Stratford Man bought shares in the Globe Theater (1599) and then in the Blackfriars Theater (1608). In 1603 he was named as an official member of the newly formed King's Men acting company.

Now contrast the above factual summary of the Stratford Man's known life with the emergence of the great author on the London literary scene. In 1593, "William Shakespeare" came out of nowhere and published what would become an instant bestseller, the highly polished narrative poem, *Venus and Adonis*, a story about the love goddess' seduction of a handsome teenager preoccupied with hunting. The Archbishop of Canterbury, John Whitgift, personally ushered the work into print. This outstanding literary debut, a work that inspired much imitation, was matched again the following year with another admired and best-selling poem, *The Rape of Lucrece*. Both of these works were dedicated to one of the most glittering aristocrats of Queen Elizabeth's court, Henry Wriothesley, 3rd Earl of Southampton. Shakespeare's signed dedication letters to this young favorite of the queen, especially the second one, implies a friendship beyond mere acquaintanceship, yet nothing in the documentary record accounts for it. The printer of both of these works, Richard Field, was at the time under the patronage of the queen's top minister, Lord Burghley, printing political propaganda.[13] Field also printed works by several courtier poets, including Sir Philip Sidney, Sir John Harington and Edmund Spenser, as well as the anonymous work of literary criticism, *The Art of English Poesy* (1589), in which Field supplied the dedication letter to Lord Burghley. (Much is made of Field having the same hometown as the Stratford Man; it is possible that they knew each other, but Field left Stratford-upon-Avon permanently in 1579, when the Stratford Man was age 15.) Only a few months after *Lucrece* was released, an anonymous author published a "fiction" (*Willobie His Avisa*) that mocked Shakespeare and Southampton's friendship and hinted at their involvement in an adulterous love triangle. If the Stratford Man were the great author, then his transformation from a barely schooled and unknown moneylender from a small town into a highly educated and refined poet of classical themes, and the close companion of a dazzling courtier, would be nothing less than miraculous. In 1598, the world suddenly learned that the great author, hitherto known only as a poet, had penned twelve or thirteen dramas, one of which, *Love's Labour's Lost*, had been presented before Queen Elizabeth.[14]

Holes in the Historical Record

The reader was given a brief summary of the Stratford Man in the documentary record but much basic information has been left unanswered, if he was the great author. The Shakespeare absences explored below are not only strange but also inconsistent with the historical and literary record left by other poets and playwrights of the same period. Separately, one could perhaps explain away one or two of these absences, but together, they are mystifying. Do not expect the Shakespeare professor to point out these holes in the historical record. He merely accepts them as a lamentable circumstance or denies their relevancy. If evidence to the contrary existed for any of them, then his case for the Stratford Man as the great author would be more plausible.

No evidence of schooling for "Shakespeare"

The majority of poets and dramatists of the period have left behind evidence of schooling. While it is generally accepted that the Stratford Man attended his hometown's grammar school, it cannot be verified because the enrollment records for that period have not survived. Even if he did attend the grammar school, he would not have learned there Greek, rhetoric, the law, etc., subjects that the great author knew well. No other school, university, or the Inns of Court (law schools) recorded a "William Shakespeare" as an attendee. The Stratford Man's parents were illiterate.

No surviving "Shakespeare" handwritten manuscripts of plays, poetry, letters, etc.

Despite an output of almost forty plays, two long poems, and over 150 sonnets, "Shakespeare" left behind not one page of handwritten manuscript, and no diaries, journals, personal letters or notes. Although it is true that most Elizabethan-Jacobean play manuscripts have not survived, Ben Jonson's *The Masque of Queens* exists, despite the fire that he said destroyed his personal library and papers in 1623. Handwritten verses or letters by prominent writers of the period, including Thomas Nashe, Gabriel Harvey, Samuel Daniel, and George Peele, have survived. Many non-famous and "unimportant" Elizabethans and Jacobeans left behind manuscripts. For example, the personal diary of Edward Pudsey, a resident of Warwickshire, survives, and in it Mr. Pudsey copied down Shakespeare phrases.[15]

No authentic image of "Shakespeare"

There are only two "official" portraits of Shakespeare: the engraving displayed on the title page of his collected dramas (First Folio, 1623) and the effigy in the "Shakspeare" monument in the Stratford-upon-Avon church. Neither look like each other and both were rendered posthumously. Upon what likeness were they based? It is not known. Over the past two centuries, numerous portraits have been put forward as Shakespeare's but they either were adjudged as fakes or remain unauthenticated. Many of them are real portraits of the period of other men that were later altered to resemble the two "official" images named above. The Chandos Portrait of Shakespeare at the National Portrait Gallery in London is widely accepted as authentic, yet the experts acknowledge that it "is likely to remain unproven."[16] It is big news when new portraits are claimed as Shakespeare's, but such claims inevitably fizzle due to a lack of hard evidence. Today's publishers of Shakespeare's plays and biographies routinely place unverfied portraits of Shakespeare on their book covers *without qualification*. Shakespeare's personal effects have also not survived. Relics left by Shakespeare's contemporary, the famous actor-producer Edward Alleyn, include an authentic full-length portrait, personal letters, his business diary, a signet ring with his coat of arms, his seal, and a silver-gilt chalice.[17] Alleyn was childless; the Stratford Man had two daughters and a granddaughter who survived him.

No payments to "Shakespeare" as an actor or playwright

No payments for writing to anyone named Shakespeare, or to an unnamed writer of a Shakespeare play, have survived. There is no proof that Shakespeare was compensated for his writing in the form of theater shares. This absence of evidence suggests the great author was not writing for box office receipts. In 1595, William Kemp, William Shakespeare and Richard Burbage received a payment on behalf of the Lord Chamberlain's Men for two play performances. As no other documentary evidence ties "William Shakespeare" to the theater before this document, in what capacity he served this company cannot be ascertained, other than as one of the receivers of a payment (Chapter 5 contains more explanation of this document). The diary of theater owner Philip Henslowe survives, a business journal filled with the names of numerous playwrights and actors, listing loans and payments given to them. The entries are dated between 1592 and 1603, covering roughly the same period that the Shakespeare professor believes the great author was busily penning his plays, but "William Shakespeare" is nowhere named in the diary. Shakespeare play titles, however, are listed, such as *Hamlet* and *Henry VI*.

No personal information written about Shakespeare during his lifetime

"William Shakespeare" was a name renowned in the literary world after the debut of *Venus and Adonis* in 1593, but no one openly published personal details or encounters with him during his lifetime. Dramatist Ben Jonson recorded in his private diary that Shakespeare made a retort to someone said "in the person of Julius Caesar,"[18] but the diary was published after both Shakespeare and Jonson were dead. Contemporary writers did print clues about Shakespeare the man during his lifetime (the subject of Chapter 15) but they are generally unnoticed or unrecognized by the experts.

No notice of "Shakespeare's" death

Within one year of the deaths of the well-known writers, Sir Philip Sidney, Edmund Spenser, Christopher Marlowe, Thomas Nashe, George Chapman and Ben Jonson, notice was taken. Within one year of the death of the supposed Shakespeare in April 1616, there was complete silence, and for four years after that. Dramatist Francis Beaumont also died in 1616 and he was honored with burial in Westminster Abbey, as was poet Edmund Spenser when he died in 1599. "William Shakespeare" died *without any tributes or notice* and he was not buried in Westminster Abbey. Yet Shakespeare's works elicited high praise throughout his life, and were admired by two English monarchs.

The first mention in print that the great author was no longer living occurred in a short verse by John Taylor in 1620; he had listed Shakespeare's name among other famous dead poets (*The Praise of Hempseed*). In 1616, Ben Jonson published over one hundred epigrams to various acquaintances, including writers, but Shakespeare was not among them. Seven years had passed when Jonson printed his first tribute to Shakespeare (in the First Folio), calling him his "beloved." The year of Shakespeare's death was first printed in 1640, and the exact date of death in 1656, when the inscription on the "Shakspeare" monument in Stratford-upon-Avon was reproduced in a book.[19] In 1618, Richard Brathwait published a survey of interesting epitaphs, one of which was located in the church where the Stratford Man was buried.[20] But it was not the Stratford Man's epitaph that caught Brathwait's eye, it was that of John Combe (d. 1614), a "notable usurer." Yet the monument and the gravestone of a notable writer, it is supposed, were only a few feet away. We know that Brathwait had admired Shakespeare because he alluded to his works in his earlier book, *Strappado for the Devil* (1615). The lack of notice upon the decease of England's acclaimed poet and playwright, William Shakespeare, is one of the strangest facts about him.

No direct evidence of patronage for "Shakespeare"

In 1593 and 1594, William Shakespeare dedicated his poems, *Venus and Adonis* and *The Rape of Lucrece*, to Henry Wriothesley, 3ʳᵈ Earl of Southampton. It is logical to assume that Southampton was Shakespeare's patron, but documentary evidence that they knew each other is lacking. Charlotte Stopes, the author of Southampton's first full biography, searched specifically for this evidence but never found it. Subsequent biographers also failed to find it. Documentary evidence of a connection between Shakespeare and his other supposed patron, William Herbert, 3ʳᵈ Earl of Pembroke, is also non-existent.

No evidence of government approval of Shakespeare's English hiStory plays

Any book or play written in Elizabethan and Jacobean times not liked by the Crown could be censored, recalled or eradicated. In November 1589, about the time when the professor believes the Stratford Man commenced his writing career, the Office of the Revels was created to examine the comedies and tragedies of playing companies

> to strike out or reform such part and matters, as they shall find unfit and undecent to be handled in plays both for divinity and state.[21]

In 1599, the printing of plays and histories became subject to control: "That no English histories be printed except they be allowed by some of Her Majesty's Privy Council," and "That no plays be printed except they be allowed by such as have authority."[22] The great author wrote at least ten plays about English history, portraying real English kings and queens, and some of them were not flattering. One play depicts an English king being deposed and murdered (*Richard II*), another poisoned (*King John*), and another as a murderer of adults *and* children (*Richard III*). Apparently the government approved of these plays because there are no records of Shakespeare getting questioned, arrested or disciplined for his writing. As this cannot be said about other prominent writers of the time, including Ben Jonson, Thomas Nashe, and Samuel Daniel, Shakespeare's exemption from interrogation after a public performance of his play, *Richard II*, in 1601 is especially conspicuous. The play was performed the day before the Earl of Essex's rebellion against the government, and was paid for by his supporters. They apparently believed that a showing of this particular drama, in which an English king is successfully deposed, would rouse Londoners in Essex's favor. The deposition scene was so controversial that the first three printed editions of the play (dated 1597 and 1598) had excluded it. After the rebellion, the government questioned actor Augustine Phillips about this production *but not the writer of the play*. Phillips was a member of the Lord Chamberlain's Men; the Shakespeare professor believes that the great author was also a member of this acting company. The government's lack of interest in Shakespeare is even more odd considering his very public association with Essex's co-conspirator, the Earl of Southampton, the dedicatee of his two acclaimed poems. Southampton received a death sentence for his part in the rebellion. Shakespeare's play was also alluded to at Essex and Southampton's treason trial. The prosecuting attorney, Sir Edward Coke, accused them of attempting to capture the queen. Southampton challenged Coke to say what he thought would be done to her if they had. In his reply, Coke asked, "how long lived King Richard the Second after he was surprised in the same manner?"[23] And Essex quoted a Shakespeare line during his sentencing when he said, "I owe God a death"; in *Henry IV-Part 1*, Prince Hal said to Falstaff before a battle, "Thou owest God a death" (5.1.126).[24] Queen Elizabeth also alluded to Shakespeare's *Richard II* six months after the revolt in a conversation with William Lambarde: " ... so her Majesty fell upon the reign of King Richard II, saying, 'I am Richard II. Know ye not that?'" The queen also said, noted Lambarde, "this tragedy was played forty times in open streets and houses." The "tragedy" was Shakespeare's play. If the queen saw herself portrayed as the ill-fated Richard II in Shakespeare's play, wondered Charlton Ogburn, then why did she tolerate forty performances of it?[25] The queen evidently took no offense to its author, and her relationship with the Lord Chamberlain's Men remained unchanged after the rebellion – in fact, they performed before her the night before Essex's execution. Yet, two years before the rebellion had occurred, in 1599, the queen imprisoned John Hayward for publishing his history of Henry IV, which included an account of Richard II's deposition. He was only released after the queen passed away. Hayward may have borrowed Shakespeare's image in *Richard II* (5.2.18-21) of the future Henry IV bareheaded and bowing while greeting crowds for use in his history.[26] Shakespeare was evidently immune to government interference, implying that he had very high connections at court.

No recorded meeting between "Shakespeare" and Queen Elizabeth or King James, yet they liked the Shakespeare plays

Ben Jonson wrote in the First Folio that Elizabeth I, and James I, "delighted" in the Shakespeare plays. *Love's Labour's Lost* and *Merry Wives of Windsor* were performed for Queen Elizabeth (as mentioned on the quarto title pages), yet there is no record that she met Shakespeare. Her encounters with writers Edmund Spenser, George Gascoigne, John Lyly and others were recorded. One and a half years after King James ascended the English throne, six different Shakespeare plays were performed at his court during the Christmas holidays – a tremendous honor. *The Merchant of Venice* was played twice "commanded by the King's Majesty,"[27] but there is no record that Shakespeare was ever present on these occasions. The same is true when several Shakespeare plays were performed at the king's court in 1612-13. The second printed edition of Shakespeare's play, *Hamlet* (1604-05), featured the royal court of arms in an ornament on the first page of text. Printer James Roberts used this particular ornament in only one other publication: *To the Majesty of King James. A Gratulatory Poem* by Michael Drayton (1603). James's consort, Queen Anne, commissioned Samuel Daniel and Ben Jonson to write entertainments for her,[28] but made no commissions for the great Shakespeare.

No eulogy written by "Shakespeare" for his supposed royal sponsors

The Shakespeare professor believes the great author was a member of the Lord Chamberlain's Men, which performed for Elizabeth I, and the King's Men, sponsored by James I. Unlike other writers, the great author apparently could not be bothered to compose a eulogy for Elizabeth at her death (despite promptings by his contemporaries), or a congratulatory verse upon King James's accession, or even a poem upon the death of the 17-year-old Prince Henry in 1612. The prince's death "gave vent to an unprecedented outburst of lamentation," writes Michael Brennan, and within a two-year period, the prince was eulogized in "four university anthologies, two volumes of funeral sermons and over fifty elegies."[29] Shakespeare also never took the trouble to compose a commendatory poem for any of his fellow actors, poets or playwrights.

No evidence "Shakespeare" met Lord Burghley or the 17th Earl of Oxford, both characterized in Hamlet

Scholars have noted that William Cecil, Lord Burghley (d. 1598), was satirized in Shakespeare's *Hamlet* with the character, Corambis; in Latin, this name could mean "double-hearted" (*cor* = heart, *ambo* = both). The name parodied Burghley's family motto, "Cor Unam," Latin for "one-hearted."[30] In one scene, Hamlet called Corambis a fishmonger; Burghley had proposed a law for one fish-eating day per week. These are only two of many coincidences between Burghley, who was the Lord Treasurer of England, and Corambis, who was King Claudius's councilor. The name, Corambis, featured in the play's first printed edition (1603), was changed to Polonius in the second edition (1604-05), which seems to confirm that the name alluded to Lord Burghley. The play was written and performed during Burghley's lifetime (as shown in Chapter 3). These and other negative comments in the play were aimed at the most politically powerful man in England, so how did Shakespeare avoid repercussion? For example, when John Stubbs wrote against the queen's proposed marriage with a French duke, his hand was cut off. This again suggests that the great author had a privileged standing at court or in the government. There is also no evidence that "Shakespeare" met Edward de Vere, 17th Earl of Oxford, whose life in many ways paralleled Hamlet's. Like Oxford, Hamlet was a university student, a traveler, a courtier and an intellectual. Like Oxford, Hamlet was in a ship that was attacked by pirates. Hamlet loved Corambis's daughter, Ophelia; Oxford married Burghley's daughter, Anne, and like Ophelia, she died young. How did Shakespeare know such details in this nobleman's life? There are apparent satires of other courtiers in Shakespeare's works, including Sir Christopher Hatton (Malvolio in *Twelfth Night*), Antonio Perez (Don Armado in *Love's Labour's Lost*), Sir Walter Ralegh (Tarquin in *The Rape of Lucrece*), and Sir Robert Cecil (title character, *Richard III*).[31] If so, then how did the Stratford Man come to know them if he was the great author?

Best Explanation: "William Shakespeare" was a Pen Name

The great author's absence in the full light of the Elizabethan and Jacobean eras, when records, personal letters and diaries abounded, with much still surviving, is best explained if he was writing anonymously or using a pen name. The great author's real name was not "William Shakespeare," which is why, during his lifetime, no one claimed to personally know Shakespeare, why "William Shakespeare" was not named in school or university enrollment lists, why no records of payment to a writer Shakespeare survive, and why Shakespeare was never questioned by the authorities. The first reference to the great author in print hyphenated the name, "Shake-speare" (prefatory poem, *Willobie His Avisa*), and the hyphen was used in about half of all printed occurrences of the name, including the title pages of Shakespeare's plays. The inclusion of the hyphen indicates that the surname's first syllable was pronounced "shake," with a long a, but the majority of records for the Stratford Man's name, which were spelled phonetically, emphasized a short a, like "shack." (Sir George Greenwood noted that a hyphen was never applied to the Stratford Man's name in any surviving document.)[32] The hyphen suggests the literal action of shaking a spear, a noun and verb description. This is pointed out quite openly in Jonson's elegy to Shakespeare in the First Folio in which he punned on the name. Jonson wrote that within Shakespeare's "well turned, and true-filed lines"

> he seems to shake a Lance,
> As brandish'd at the eyes of Ignorance.

Lance is another word for spear. Three others punned on Shakespeare's name. In the play, *Histrio-mastix* (printed 1610), an acting company performs a scene with Troilus and Cressida, characters that were also the subject and title of a Shakespeare play. In an apparent pun on the name of the playwright, Troilus says to Cressida:

> Behold behold thy garter blue
> Thy knight his valiant elbow wears,
> That when he shakes his furious Speare
> Thy foe in shivering fearful sort ... [lines 271-74]

Another pun occurs in *Two Books of Epigrams and Epitaphs* (1639) by Thomas Bancroft in his epigram No. 119 to Shakespeare:

> Thou hast so us'd thy *Pen* (or *shook thy Speare*)
> That Poets startle, nor thy wit come near.

Finally, Thomas Vicars in *Cheiragogia* (1628) did not name Shakespeare in his list of great poets – he described him:

> ... that well-known poet who takes his name from the shaking of a spear ... [33]

Shakespeare used similar expressions of weapon shaking in his works. In *Timon of Athens* (5.1.169), the "savage" Alcibiades

> ... shakes his threatening Sword
>   Against the walls of *Athens*.

All's Well That Ends Well (2.5.95):

> Go thou toward home; where I will never come
> whilst I can shake my sword or hear the drum.

The Tempest (1.2.205):

> ... his [Neptune's] bold waves tremble, yea his dread trident shake.

Henry VI-Part 2 (4.8.19):

> Shake he his weapon at us, and pass by.

In *The Rape of Lucrece* (line 505), the character, Tarquin

> shakes aloft his Roman blade ...

Spear shaking was an often-used expression in the contemporary literature, as demonstrated in excerpts below. (The word "spear" is given as originally spelled, and dates refer to printed editions.) In the gloss to Edmund Spenser's *The Shepherd's Calendar* (1579), E.K. wrote that the fully armed goddess, Pallas Athena,

> shaked her speare at him [Vulcan], and threatened his sauciness.
> ["October"]

In John Lyly's play, *Campaspe* (1584), Hephestion asks Alexander,

> Will you handle the spindle with *Hercules*, when you should <u>shake the speare</u> with *Achilles*? [2.2]

Christopher Marlowe's play, *Tamburlaine the Great-Part 1* (1590):

> Five hundred thousand footmen threat'ning shot,
> <u>Shaking their swords, their speares</u> and iron bills ... [4.1.24-25]

In George Peele's play, *Edward I* (1593), when the Lord of Gallaway is pro-claimed the King of Scotland, Queen Elinor says:

> <u>Shake thy speres</u> in honor of his name ... [scene 3]

Barnabe Barnes's poetry work, *Parthenophil and Parthenophe* (1593):

> When *Mars* return'd from war,
> <u>Shaking his speare</u> afar
> Cupid beheld:
> And him in jest *Mars* <u>shak'd his speare</u> ... [Ode 15]

Edmund Spenser's poem, *The Faerie Queene* (1596):

> With that they 'gan their shivering <u>speares to shake</u> ...
> [Book 4, Canto 2, No. 14]

> He all enrag'd, his shivering <u>speare did shake</u> ...
> [Book 4, Canto 3, No. 10]

Andrew Fairfax's translation, *Godfrey of Bulloigne, or The Recovery of Jerusalem*, by Torquato Tasso (1600):

> [Women, etc.] durst not <u>shake the speare</u>, nor target hold.
> [Book 3, Stanza 11]

> These hands were made to <u>shake sharp spears, and swords</u>.
> [Book 5, Stanza 42]

In light of the name Shakespeare being a descriptive action, in light of the repeated inclusion of a hyphen suggesting it was a made-up name, and in light of the absence of historical evidence of an actual person of this name in relation to literature or education, it is reasonable to assume that "Shake-speare" was a pen name. Shaking spears, swords and other weapons was a common expression that described a warlike action, as shown above by excerpts from the contemporary literature. A spear-shaker also describes a tournament jouster. The great author must have enjoyed this sport or identified himself with soldiery. It was by winning a jousting tournament that the title character in Shakespeare's play, *Pericles, Prince of Tyre*, was able to reverse his fortune after a shipwreck.

The great author himself declared that "William Shakespeare" was a pen name in two instances. The first is found in one line of the dedication letter for his poem, *Venus and Adonis* (1593):

> But if the first heir of my invention prove deformed ...

The "first heir" refers to *Venus and Adonis*, and critics assume that "my invention" means his art or creativity. But unless the great author was lying, *Venus and Adonis* could not have been his first effort at poetry because the piece was too sophisticated. The "invention," therefore, is the *invented* name, "William Shakespeare." *Venus and Adonis* sports the first application of the pen name. It is fact that *Venus and Adonis* was the first occasion that the name, William Shakespeare, appeared in print. In the second example, the great author says in Sonnet 81 that a name attached to a great written work ("such virtue hath my Pen") is assured immortality.

> From hence your memory death cannot take,
> Although in me each part will be forgotten.
> Your name from hence immortal life shall have,
> Though I (once gone) to all the world must die ...
>
> When all the breathers of this world are dead,
> You still shall live (such virtue hath my Pen) ...

The great author is addressing the Fair Youth, so he believes the Fair Youth's name is destined for immortality due to the greatness of his "pen." The Fair Youth's name is not mentioned in any of the sonnets, so his name had to have been already associated with another Shakespeare work. The 3rd Earl of Southampton was the only one to whom Shakespeare made a dedication, in *Venus and Adonis* and *The Rape of Lucrece*. Enormously popular, each edition of these poems carried the names Shakespeare and Southampton. Southampton's immortality, therefore, is assured so long as these works remain in print, says Shakespeare in Sonnet 81, yet in the same sonnet he says his own name "to all the world must die." The only logical explanation for this contradiction is that one name was real (Southampton's) and the other was not (Shakespeare's). The great author's pen name will live forever, *but not his real name,* and this is what he was somberly relating in Sonnet 81. And he was right: after four centuries, almost nothing is known about his personal life or his literary life, just like he had presciently stated, "in me each part will be forgotten."

The Likelihood of His Nobility

Why would a highly acclaimed and popular author need to use a pen name? Answer: politics and social status. If printed material were political or controversial, then anonymity or an invented name would be mandatory. Freedom of speech was not a right in the Elizabethan-Jacobean era. In the case of the great author, however, politics could not have been the main reason initially because the first work published with his alias, *Venus and Adonis*, was poetry based on a classical theme. It enjoyed several printings and was politically approved. John Whitgift, the Archbishop of Canterbury, licensed it for press.[34] Whitgift was a close friend and advisor to Queen Elizabeth. Protection of social status is the other reason for usage of a pen name. The highly ranked avoided public display of their poetry because it would stigmatize them socially. This was clearly explained in *The Art of English Poesy* in 1589:

> Now also of such among the Nobility or gentry as be very well seen in many laudable sciences, and especially in making or Poesy, it is so come to pass that they have no courage to write, & if they have, yet are they loath to be aknown of their skill. So as I know very many notable Gentlemen in the Court that have written commendably, and suppressed it again, or else suffered it to be published without their own names to it: as if it were a discredit for a Gentleman, to seem learned, and to show himself amorous of any good Art. [Book 1, Chapter 8]

Even royalty "take delight in Poets," wrote this author, but "universally it is not so." The "honorable," meaning titled people or the gentry, who are known to be poets, are "infamous" and "subject to scorn and derision," and, "in disdain," they are called "fantastical."

> But in these days (although some learned Princes may take delight in them) yet universally it is not so. For as well Poets and Poesy are despised, and the name become of honorable infamous, subject to scorn and derision, and rather a reproach than a praise to any that useth it, for commonly whoso is studious in the art or shows himself excellent in it, they call him in disdain a "fantastical"; and a light-headed or fantastical man (by conversion) they call a poet. [Book 1, Chapter 8]

The unnamed author of *The Art of English Poesy*, sometimes attributed to John, Lord Lumley,[35] boldly revealed names of poets who were also courtiers:

> And in her Majesty's time that now is are sprung up another crew of <u>Courtly makers Noblemen and Gentlemen</u> of her Majesty's own servants, who have written excellently well as it would appear <u>if their doings could be found out and made public with the rest</u>, of which number is first that noble Gentleman *Edward*, Earl of Oxford. *Thomas* Lord of Buckhurst, when he was young, *Henry* Lord Paget, Sir *Philip Sidney*, Sir *Walter Ralegh*, Master *Edward Dyer*, Master *Fulke Greville*, *Gascoigne*, *Breton*, *Turberville* and a great many other learned Gentlemen ... [Book 1, Chapter 31]

One of high rank could circulate pieces of poetry in manuscript among friends during his lifetime, but printing a poetical work with his own name was socially acceptable only after death. It is on record that the sonnets of Shakespeare were privately circulated in manuscript (Francis Meres, *Palladis Tamia, or Wit's Treasury*, 1598). There are some instances of poems "escaping" into print and credited to the highly ranked, but not whole works with authority. Almost fifty years after *The Art of English Poesy*, John Selden wrote in his book, *Table Talk* (1636), "'Tis ridiculous for a Lord to print verses, 'tis well enough to make them to please himself, but to make them public is foolish." The only way one of high rank could circumvent the stigma of print during his lifetime, if he so desired, would be to print anonymously or with a pen name. Even more stigmatizing – and even scandalous – for a member of the upper class was to write plays that were performed in the public theater. Maintaining the dignity of one's rank and family name was extremely important during this period.

Another reason to suppose that the great author was a man of rank or the nobility is because he had an excellent education. If a child of the upper class displayed signs of genius, he could be immediately accommodated with tutors and a university education. A bright child named William Shakespeare was apparently never brought to the attention of any literate person: not a teacher, tutor, clergyman, mentor, or future patron. The protagonists in Shakespeare's plays were mostly aristocratic men and women, often royalty, and they were realistically portrayed – the "commoner" characters usually served as comic relief. The great author well knew the speech, customs, dress, food and sports (like tennis and falconry) of the nobility. One contemporary wrote that no one could discuss hunting and falconry "in correct technical language unless he was familiar with the sports. It is an easy thing to trip up in one's terms, as Father [Francis] Southwell used to complain."[36] Shakespeare's plays evidently characterized real living courtiers, including the most powerful, Lord Burghley. The great author must have had sufficiently high status to be acquainted with these courtiers and to escape retaliation for alluding to them in his plays, a status the Stratford Man lacked. A nobleman would not be tied down by work obligations to focus upon his art, and would have money and leisure to study and travel (Shakespeare had detailed knowledge of European geography, especially cities in Italy). And a nobleman would not need a patron to sponsor or protect his art. For those who were aware of the great author's nobility, there would have been a natural fear of reprisal had they exposed the pen name. "*Shake-speare* we must be silent in thy praise" was anonymously written in 1640,[37] a generation after Shakespeare lived. This phrase alone is proof that there was something secret about him. Why would silence be necessary if the great author were the Stratford Man, a man with humble beginnings whose art pleased and impressed all classes?

Conclusion

Hungry for knowledge about their hero, Shakespeare enthusiasts keep buying biographies that the experts write. But they are not real biographies of Shakespeare, they are mostly invented ones framed within a description of the age. The paucity of facts *of relevance*, such as Shakespeare's education and his literary life, should long ago have been considered unsatisfactory and suspicious, if not impossible. The lack of personal remembrances by his contemporaries and the nonexistence of his manuscripts or personal letters increases the likelihood that "William Shakespeare" was someone's pen name. The fact that the surname was often hyphenated, a sign of a made-up name, and that spear shaking was a known expression, makes this conclusion nearly absolute – there would be no other reason to apply a hyphen to the name. On the first occasion that the name "William Shakespeare" appeared in print, the great author openly called it his "invention." The great author's primary interest with the upper classes and royalty, their politics and the succession, his complete familiarity with them and their culture, and the extensive learning and experience displayed in the works, inspires the natural conclusion that he himself was from a similarly privileged background. The "nobility or gentry" who wrote poetry were "loath to be aknown of their skill," wrote a contemporary, because it was considered a frivolous or "fantastical" occupation. It was also a social convention of the highly ranked to not publish their creative writing with their names attached while alive; doing so would give the appearance that they were writing for financial gain, which was déclassé. For an aristocrat to be directly involved with the theater and actors was even more socially degrading, and public knowledge of it would certainly mar his reputation, thus the need for anonymity or an alias.

More evidence of the great author's high status was his apparent acquaintance with highly placed people: the first published work signed by Shakespeare had the approbation of the Archbishop of Canterbury and the 3rd Earl of Southampton, two intimates of Queen Elizabeth, and it was issued by a printer who at the time was in the patronage of the Lord Treasurer of England, Lord Burghley. The great author evidently knew Lord Burghley, and his son-in-law, the 17th Earl of Oxford, and by implication, had the government's approval for his dramatic versions of English history. There is no documentary evidence that the Stratford Man was acquainted with any of the aforementioned personages. All of the problems surrounding Shakespeare's biography listed in this chapter are well known to the experts but they ignore the most obvious explanation for them – the name was an alias – because of the existence of another man involved in the theater who was named William Shakespeare. For some reason, it is beyond the experts' comprehension that there could have been two separate people with similar names that had theatrical interest, just like there were two men named John Davies who published poetry and were contemporaries. Although there was an explosion of literary and theatrical activity during this period, it was not an age that one could openly criticize the government, the nobility, or influential people without repercussion. Allegory, symbolism and veiled references in print were the norm, and the reader will learn that such devices were regularly applied when referring to Shakespeare.

CHAPTER 2

A Mess of Genius: Shakespeare's Early Printed Texts

THE SHAKESPEARE PROFESSOR is not only frustrated by the lack of hard facts in great author's biography, but by the appalling state of his literary remains. Shakespeare composed at least 38 plays, 154 sonnets, and more – nearly one million words – and not one page of an original manuscript survives in his handwriting. All that has survived is in printed format and in various states of condition. It is evident that the great author was involved with the publication of his two long narrative poems, *Venus and Adonis* and *The Rape of Lucrece*: both texts have minimal errors, and for each one he provided signed dedication letters to the Earl of Southampton. The state of the great author's theatrical output, however, is another kettle of fish entirely. Most of the earliest printed play editions have messy texts. It was not because the great author was careless but because these texts were mostly, if not entirely, compiled from sources other than the great author's copy. *This is never revealed to the student or the general reader and has never been adequately explained.* These individually printed plays, called the quartos, were evidently pirated editions, and yet, neither the great author nor the acting companies ever openly complained about the thefts. This contradicts the story promoted by the professor that the great author wrote for the theater for profit.

Textual Disorder

Seventeen different Shakespeare plays were printed individually between 1594 and 1622, some with multiple issues. Some of these quarto editions had good texts and some had bad texts, thus the now universal terms "good quartos" and "bad quartos." Each Shakespeare quarto had a different degree of textual accuracy but all were to some extent flawed. Those who printed them knew this, so if the text were subsequently improved, the next edition would often announce it with a phrase like "newly corrected" on the title page. In these cases, some of the text was corrected and even enlarged, but new errors would be introduced. In 1623, thirty-six Shakespeare plays were printed in one large volume, today called "The First Folio," "First" because three others followed, and "Folio" because of the large page size. Twenty of the 36 plays it contained had never before been printed and at least four of them were unknown to the public. Studies have shown that the Folio play texts were also imperfect. In some cases, the Folio featured the quarto version of a play, the good *and* the bad. Even particular passages within the same play vary – sometimes the Folio version is better, sometimes the quarto version is better, with no consistency. Sometimes a given passage will be identical in both the Folio and quarto versions with the exception of one word with no way of knowing which one was the great author's intent. Which version was the authoritative one? Were any? The evidence shows that these early publishers or editors were constantly interpreting and guessing the great author's lines and they often got it wrong. The nature of these imperfections include:

- missing lines (sometimes in the hundreds – *Hamlet*, for example), duplication of lines, lines out of place
- omitted scenes and unclear scene structure
- messy, missing or unclear stage directions
- a character's name changes throughout the text, sometimes within one scene (for example, Queen Eleanor in *King John* is labeled "Elia," "Ele," "Eli," "Queen," "Qu Mo," "Old Queen")[1]
- an actor's name replaces a character's name
- "ghost" characters (a character listed at the beginning of a scene, but has no lines and is never mentioned again)
- words or lines assigned to the wrong character
- prose printed as verse and verse as prose
- verse lines wrongly divided
- misspelling, missing or faulty punctuation, extra or redundant words
- misinterpretation/mishearing of words (for example, "him, most" for "hindmost")
- paraphrased lines, paraphrased speeches, or a synonym replaces the actual word
- lines taken from another play (sometimes not Shakespeare's)

The three earliest editions of *Hamlet* (quartos of 1603 and 1604-05, and the First Folio) are all different. The 1604-05 edition is almost twice as long as the 1603 edition, and the Folio version is 200 lines shorter than the 1604-05 edition. It is not known which edition best represents the great author's final version. The only text that survives for *Macbeth* appeared in the Folio; it is unusually short – about one thousand lines shorter than Shakespeare's other tragedies. Some critics consider it a hacked version of the original. The 1622 quarto edition of *Othello* has thirteen lines or parts of lines that are unique, and the Folio version has 160 unique lines.[2] Many textual errors of

Shakespeare's plays have been fixed by modern editors, but for some lines, there is no remedy. King Lear's final lines in the 1608 quarto, for example, are completely different than those in the Folio version. Ron Rosenbaum called this situation "scandalous" because these lines (comments about Cordelia's death) are considered the key to interpreting King Lear's character for scholars, actors and directors.[3] An example of the Shakespeare editor's dilemma follows. Seeing his father for the first time with his eyes gouged out, Edgar in *King Lear* (4.1.10) says:

> A. "My father poorlie, leed" (quarto, 1608)
> B. "My father parti,eyd."   (quarto, 1619)
> C. "My Father poorely led?" (Folio, 1623)

As pointed out by Michael J.B. Allen and Kenneth Muir, modern editors usually employ B, edited as "my father, parti-eyed."[4] Parti-eyed is supposedly synonymous with parti-colored, describing the colors on the father's mutilated face (blood against flesh). The true phrase will probably never be known.

It is fact that the entire corpus of the Shakespeare plays was left to posterity in imperfect form. It can be inferred then that the great author was not involved in the printing process nor did he provide the printers with the original completed copy of any play. This is supported by the fact that the great author never included a letter to the reader or a dedication page in any edition of his plays. Laudatory verses by friends is also absent in the over forty early Shakespeare quartos that have survived. Such prefatory material was common in play editions. The distorted state of most of these early printed plays implies that *the printers were entirely on their own with the text.* Although the demand for Shakespeare copy was high (added together, there were sixteen printed editions of *Venus and Adonis* and *Lucrece* by 1616), it appears the great author would not authorize the issuing of his plays. The inevitable result was piracy. If the printers did not use the great author's originals, then how did they get the play texts? Shakespeare actors could be paid for a copy of their roles or to recite their lines to a scribe, or stenographers could be placed in the audience during a play performance. This would explain why the bad quartos had wrong or misheard words and phrases, and paraphrases; why verse was printed as regular dialogue and vice-versa, stage directions printed as dialogue, an actor's name replacing a character's name, etc. At least four stenography books were published between 1588 and 1602.[5] It is believed that some Shakespeare text derived from prompt-books, the stage version of the play, which was usually shorter than the author's original. This is possible, but no prompt-book of a Shakespeare play has survived. It is likely that some or all of the above methods were employed to print a Shakespeare play.

These "bad" editions were alluded to in the First Folio's preface, that readers had been

> abused with diverse stolen, and surreptitious copies, maimed, and deformed by the frauds and stealths of injurious imposters, that exposed them.

In 1609, the second issue of Shakespeare's play, *Troilus and Cressida*, featured an anonymous letter to the reader explaining that this play had "escaped" the "grand possessors" for which readers should "thank fortune" – *a bold and defiant admission of piracy.*

"Fair is foul and foul is fair." (*Macbeth*)

To account for the "good quartos" that have decent but still imperfect text, the Shakespeare professor's traditional position is that it derived from the great author's "foul papers" – his first draft, or rough draft, of the play, containing his additions, deletions, and corrections. He further posits that the few plays with cleaner text derived from a "fair copy," the edited version of the "foul papers." The reader must be cautioned that these explanations are *purely hypothetical.* Shakespeare foul or fair copy papers do not exist. The Shakespeare professor asserts with great confidence that the Lord Chamberlain's Men, which the great author was supposedly a member, owned the Shakespeare plays; that they used the great author's "foul papers" and made prompt-books from them which were then given to the printers for profit. *This explanation is also purely hypothetical.* No evidence confirms the Lord Chamberlain's Men or any acting company purchased or owned the Shakespeare plays or sold them to printers. There is not one payment to "Shakespeare" for writing or any indication of an arrangement of profit sharing in lieu of writing services. It is true that the Lord Chamberlain's Men performed some Shakespeare plays, but so did the Lord Pembroke's Men, the Lord Admiral's Men and the Lord Sussex's Men. Who owned what? To this day, it is still not clear to scholars. Even if an acting company owned a Shakespeare play, then why didn't the company provide printers with clean text, or prosecute those who pirated it? And it raises more questions: why would the acting company possess the great author's imperfect foul papers? How could the company act the play with such text? The Lord Chamberlain's Men also performed plays by Ben Jonson, and he evidently published them without this company's involvement.

The professor has no explanation for the Shakespeare piracies and is reluctant to admit that they even occurred, thus the terms "reported text," "memorial reconstruction," "assembled text," and "composite text." All describe

Shakespeare text that is incomplete, imperfect or garbled, indicating deriva-
tion from a source other than the great author. These special phrases still
imply that neither the great author nor the theater company provided printers with a finished copy. Even the First Folio's collection of the Shakespeare
plays, purportedly derived from the great author's "true original copies," used
some text from the bad quartos. As almost every early Shakespeare play text
is imperfect, it is possible that each one was pirated. Phrases like "newly corrected" on several editions indirectly admits that inferior versions preceded
them; the copyists kept improving their product. If the great author were a
man of high social status, then the "stigma of print" would explain why he
was not involved with the publishing of his plays, and he could not prosecute
printers of unauthorized editions in the regular law courts without making known his true identity. Since the Stratford Man sued people to recover
his money, it is hard to believe that he would not have sued for the theft
of his supposed literary property. It is even harder to believe that the great
author was not disturbed seeing his superlative dramas printed in such slip-
shod condition. There are indications, however, that he attempted to stop it.

"Stop Press" Shakespeare

Almost completely unreported to the student and general public is the fact
that some of the earliest publishers of Shakespeare's works were stopped by
authority, and on three occasions their presses were seized. We know this
thanks to the surviving registers of the Stationers' Company. Shortly before
publication, printers would pay a licensing fee to the Company, which was
recorded. Fines and directives from within the Company, and without, were
also recorded. Two possible "stop-press" Shakespeare incidents occurred in
1594. (1) *The Winter's Tale*. On May 22, 1594, publisher Edward White registered "a book entitled, a winters nights pastime,"[6] which evidently never
saw print. The expert would discount this reference because he believes
Shakespeare's play was written in 1610 or 1611, but "a winters nights pastime" is very close to "the winters night tale," an undisputed reference to
Shakespeare's play in 1611 (Appendix A, No. 77). White had also registered
the anonymous play, *King Leir*, the week before, on May 14, 1594.[7] *King Leir*
is considered as the main source of Shakespeare's *King Lear* but it may have
been an early version of the same play. There is no sign that White's edition
of *King Leir* was printed (the first surviving edition was dated 1605 and was
published by others). (2) *Titus Andronicus*. On February 6, 1594, publisher
John Danter registered this play. The one surviving copy was discovered in
Sweden in 1904.[8] (Interestingly, in 1593, a warrant for Danter's arrest was
recorded in the register for an unstated reason.)[9] These incidents of a no-show

and a sole surviving copy could indicate that as early as 1594 the great author was trying to stop unauthorized editions of his plays.

The first confirmed "stop press" Shakespeare involved the first quarto of *Romeo and Juliet*, a notorious piracy. John Danter printed the play during late 1596 or early 1597.[10] Sometime during the period of Lent (February 9 to March 26, 1597), Danter's two presses were seized "by virtue of the decrees of the Star Chamber," and on April 10, 1597 they were ordered to be "defaced and made unserviceable for printing..." Danter's offense was for printing a Catholic work, *Jesus Psalter*, "and other things without authority..."[11] Danter, however, had already been punished for printing *Jesus Psalter* – his press was brought to the Stationers' Company by July 1596, and he evidently went to jail.[12] Although Danter's name alone appeared on the title page as the printer of *Romeo and Juliet*, he only printed sheets A to D – sheets E to K were printed by Edward Allde.[13] *Allde's press was also seized within the same period and also ordered for destruction on April 10.* Allde's recorded offense was for printing the "popish" work, *A Brief Form of Confession*, "without authority license [or] entrance..."[14] Allde was not involved with the printing of *Jesus Psalter*. The inevitable conclusion to be drawn is that Danter and Allde's mutual printing of Shakespeare's *Romeo and Juliet* was the underlying cause of the seizure and destruction of their presses, and that this play must have constituted "other things without authority..." Danter was constantly in trouble with the Stationers' Company before this incident, but this one ended his printing career. Another incident occurred in late 1598 or early 1599. William Jaggard published two editions of *The Passionate Pilgrim*, a poetry work that he ascribed to "W. Shakespeare"; only fragments of the first edition and two complete copies of the second edition have survived. Later testimony by writer Thomas Heywood that this work had upset the great author confirms it was a piracy: "... so the Author I know much offended with *M*. Jaggard (that altogether unknown to him) presumed to make so bold with his name."[15] Thirteen years had elapsed before Jaggard ventured to print a third edition (1612), perhaps an indication of intimidation on the great author's part. On January 3, 1600, printer Eleazar Edgar registered "A book called *Amours* by J.D. with *certain other sonnets* by W.S."[16] Occurring so soon after Jaggard's illicit publication, which had featured the first two Shakespeare sonnets in print, "*certain other sonnets* by W.S." were almost certainly more of Shakespeare's. The work never saw print, perhaps another indication that the great author had intervened.

Publisher James Roberts experienced a rash of "stop press" Shakespeare incidents. The first occurred on July 22, 1598 when he registered *The Merchant of Venice*. Roberts, a 30-year veteran in the publishing trade at the time, was bound by a very unusual condition involving a high government official:

> Provided, that it be not printed by the said James Roberts or any
> other whatsoever without license first had from the right honor-
> able the Lord Chamberlain.[17]

Outside of the monarch and the privy council, the Lord Chamberlain held
the authority over theatrical activity and play publication (George Carey, 2nd
Baron Hunsdon, held this position from 1597 to 1603). Two years passed
with no edition of *Merchant*. Then on October 28, 1600, the play was registered again "with the consent" of Roberts for Thomas Hayes to publish it.[18]
Roberts was still involved, however, as he was listed on the title page as the
printer ("J.R."). It seems that Roberts purposely had transferred his publishing rights to the play to one not specifically bound by a restriction. *Merchant*
was not printed again until 1619. During the year 1600, Roberts tried to
publish six plays, including three by Shakespeare, and all were stayed.[19] He
registered *As You Like It*, *Henry V* and *Much Ado About Nothing* on August 4,
1600. The staying order was made soon after this date because *Henry V* and
Much Ado were reregistered nineteen days later by others and printed that
year;[20] *As You Like It* remained unpublished until the First Folio. The staying
order may have been the consequence of Roberts's reprint of Shakespeare's
Titus Andronicus that same year (1600). Roberts made no attempt to publish
Shakespeare in 1599, but that year two works he wanted to print were stopped
and two more were ordered to be burned.[21] Ever persistent, Roberts registered
another Shakespeare play, *Hamlet*, on July 26, 1602, but Nicholas Ling beat
him to press with the first edition in 1603. (Roberts, however, teamed up
with Ling in late 1604 to print an enlarged version of *Hamlet*.) On February
7, 1603, Roberts again registered a Shakespeare play for publication, which
again required special permission:

> to print when he hath gotten sufficient authority for it, the book of
> *Troilus and Cressida* as it is acted by my Lord Chamberlain's Men.[22]

Roberts never printed *Troilus and Cressida*. In 1606, he sold his business
to William Jaggard. The Shakespeare professor's explanation for Roberts's
frustrations is that he was serving the Lord Chamberlain's Men by registering plays and purposely not printing them on their behalf, that they were
"blocking entries." The unwavering belief that this acting company owned
the Shakespeare plays and that the Lord Chamberlain was protecting them
has led him to this conclusion, but both beliefs are mere assumption. Did
Roberts not have a hand in the publication of *The Merchant of Venice*, *Titus
Andronicus* and *Hamlet*? Could not the Lord Chamberlain have been acting
on someone else's behalf? Perhaps it was the great author or his family that
was trying to stop unauthorized editions of these works, and were people with

enough clout to influence the Lord Chamberlain and the Stationers' Company. Such a scenario is never considered.

Another remarkable incident of "stop press" Shakespeare involved printers Thomas Pavier and William Jaggard. They printed three plays (*Pericles*, *Merry Wives of Windsor* and *A Yorkshire Tragedy*) with the current date of 1619 on the title page and Shakespeare as the author. Then something happened, causing Pavier and Jaggard to print five more plays (*A Midsummer Night's Dream*, *The Merchant of Venice*, *Sir John Oldcastle-Part 1*, *Henry V*, and *King Lear*) with the false dates of 1600 and 1608 on the title pages, and two with no dates (the Contention plays). Two of the falsely dated title pages named a printer who no longer held the copyright.[23] A directive by the Lord Chamberlain to the Stationers' Company in May 1619 was evidently aimed at them for unauthorized printing of Shakespeare's plays.[24] But Pavier and Jaggard circumvented the directive by printing false dates on the title pages to make it appear that these plays were old merchandise, that they were printed long before the Lord Chamberlain's order. This was Jaggard's fourth instance of illicit printing of Shakespeare, preceded by his three editions of *The Passionate Pilgrim*.

Pavier and Jaggard's false dating scheme was apparently inspired by an earlier incident of the same kind in yet another "stop press" Shakespeare. The title page of *Venus and Adonis*, eighth edition (STC 22360), featured the date of 1602, which in the 20th century was proven to be false.[25] This edition had used an ornament that Harry Farr identified as that owned by Robert Raworth, who only began printing in 1606; his career suddenly ended by 1609. The reason why is contained in a 1635 notation in the Stationers' Register: the press owned by Raworth and his partner, John Monger, had been "suppressed (for printing *Venus and Adonis*)."[26] Raworth was not allowed to print for twenty-five years after this incident. More explanation appears on another register page: "Robert Raworth, suppress'd for printing another's Copy."[27] The copyright holder of *Venus and Adonis* at the time was William Leake, a warden of the Stationers' Company (1604-07 and 1610-11). This given reason for putting Raworth out of business gets suspicious when more facts are known. The title page of Raworth's edition of *Venus and Adonis* openly stated that it was "Imprinted at London for William Leake," implying Leake's cooperation. Raworth certainly had Leake's cooperation in 1608, when Leake employed him to print *Two Sermons* by Henry Smith. But what is especially telling is that after the Raworth incident, Leake employed a different printer (Humphrey Lownes) to issue another edition of *Venus and Adonis*, and *it also sported the false date of 1602 on the title page*. A third edition with the 1602 false date was printed, also by Lownes for Leake, but today only the title page survives. As the official owner of the text since June 25, 1596, Leake would have had no reason to use a false date, which means that Raworth's suppression had nothing to do copyright infringement but had everything to do with the author, the text, or the times. Raworth had based his text upon the previous, or seventh, edition of *Venus and Adonis* (STC 22359), which cannot be certainly dated because the sole surviving copy (now at the Bodleian Library) lacks the title page.

When were these three falsely dated editions of *Venus and Adonis* actually printed? Harry Farr conjectured sometime between 1607 and 1610. Raworth started to print books in the latter half of 1606, in which he produced one book; in each of the years 1607 and 1608, he produced about three books. Leake's employment of Raworth to print *Two Sermons* in 1608 shows that they were on friendly terms at that time, and, presumably, the year before (1607). Raworth printed no books with 1609 on the title page. The year 1609 also saw a letter to the reader added to the second issue of *Troilus and Cressida* warning of a coming scarcity of Shakespeare's "comedies." As it happened, no Shakespeare play or poem was openly published in 1610, which seemed to confirm the warning. The year 1611 saw three Shakespeare plays in print (*Titus Andronicus*, *Hamlet* and *Pericles*) so it was evidently safe to print Shakespeare that year, but not in 1610 or part of 1609 (the next edition of *Venus and Adonis* occurred in 1617, after Leake sold his publishing rights). *The Rape of Lucrece* was published in 1607, apparently without incident, but was not published again until 1614. The cumulative evidence strongly suggests that 1609 was the actual printing year of Raworth's falsely dated edition of *Venus and Adonis*; since the two Leake-Lownes editions with false dates followed Raworth's edition, they were likely released in 1609 or 1610. As noted above, Pavier and Jaggard had used earlier false dating on their Shakespeare editions to elude a directive by the Lord Chamberlain. Obviously, something of the same nature must have occurred in 1609, despite the lack of evidence in the official record. Whatever it was, it was extremely serious, enough to destroy Raworth's printing career for his very first offense; the typical punishment for printing another's copy was a fine, usually a small one.[28] Leake and Lownes were apparently unaffected by this incident, but neither involved himself in a Shakespeare printing again. It seems that Raworth took the fall for the evidently unallowed printing of *Venus and Adonis*. Farr detected some "deception."

> If Leake connived at the printing of these editions with a spurious date while taking steps to suppress Raworth for infringing his copyright, we have here a very pretty piece of deception. But his association with Jaggard in the publication of *The Passionate Pilgrim* is some evidence that he was not incapable of it.[29]

One could surmise that Leake ordered Raworth to print *Venus and Adonis* with a false date to avoid the authorities, but when it was discovered, he tried to save his own skin by accusing Raworth of printing it without his permission. But the text must have been much sought after at that time, so Leake took the risk of printing two more editions with the same false date, as if they were more of Raworth's edition. As noted by Farr, Leake's involvement (as bookseller) with the 1598-1599 editions of *The Passionate Pilgrim*, confirmed Shakespeare piracies, indicates that he was "not incapable" of such deception. The year 1609 will prove to be the most critical in the Shakespeare authorship question.

Conclusion

However the expert labels the early editions of the Shakespeare plays, as good or bad quartos, fair or foul copy, the state of these early texts ranges from imperfect to bad. The same is true for the twenty plays that made their print debut in the First Folio, contrary to the Folio's claim that it contained the great author's "true original copies." One can conclude, therefore, that the great author was *not involved in the printing process for any of his plays* and he did not make copies of his complete texts available to acting companies or to printers. The printers apparently obtained Shakespeare play text in many ways: employing stenographers to copy the plays by ear in the audience; paying actors to recite their roles; perhaps obtaining prompt-books and other playhouse working copies of a play, and hiring other writers to fill in the blanks. These patchwork editions of the Shakespeare plays – some close to the original, some butchered, some later improved – are evidence that *most if not all of the early texts were either stolen or unauthorized editions*. As Ernest Honigmann observed regarding Shakespeare, "no other dramatist was honoured by surreptitious publication to anything like the same extent."[30] The Shakespeare professor cannot explain why Shakespeare fell victim to pirates when, if he were the Stratford Man, he would have had every reason to publish his works for his own livelihood and profit, especially since they had such high public demand. These imperfect texts also negate the consistent assumption that the acting companies owned Shakespeare's plays. Even the presumed Folio producers, King's Men actors Heminges and Condell, did not make the claim of Shakespeare play ownership – in their own words, they printed his plays merely as a favor for their "fellow."

The most likely profile of a writer during this era who would allow some of his poetry to be published, albeit with an alias, but who would not publish his dramas, is someone of high rank. Although considered frivolous, writing poetry and circulating it in manuscript was tolerated among the upper class, but writing dramas that eventually got played in the public theater was considered degrading. The substantial evidence that "Shakespeare" was a pen name makes this an inescapable conclusion. The great author did not openly complain about the pirated text of his plays because doing so would publicly expose his true identity. In this scenario, the pirates knew the great author was a nobleman in a "catch-22" situation and fearlessly took advantage. The great author apparently tried to stop this activity, perhaps as early as 1594, but certainly during the years 1597 to 1603, when six Shakespeare plays were stopped from publication. The Lord Chamberlain and officials in the Stationer's Company were apparently acting on the great author's behalf. Why else would two printers get their presses seized for printing *Romeo and Juliet* and another one put out of business for printing *Venus and Adonis* – both love stories with no apparent political content? *Romeo and Juliet* was "often (with great applause) played publicly," according to the title page of its first edition (1597), and the Archbishop of Canterbury originally licensed *Venus and Adonis* for press. Not allowing themselves to be thwarted by the authorities, some publishers of Shakespeare simply took the risk and others resorted to taking unusual steps, such as printing with false dates or no dates. Today's Shakespeare plays are sanitized versions based on centuries of editing work, melding the best texts from the early editions, fixing lines or words to better suit the context or the poetical meter, and correcting evidently misheard or misinterpreted text. The early Shakespeare editions were an imperfect mess, but a mess of genius. The great author's non-cooperation with publishers of his dramas suggests that the original manuscript copies of the plays were kept in his possession, and that they may still exist. If such copies ever get found, then Shakespeare scholarship would be plunged into a whole new world of perfect text, with even more brilliant lines. Has the world yet to read the *real* Shakespeare plays?

CHAPTER 3

Shakespeare Problems the Professor Still Cannot Solve

EARLY MESSY TEXT is only one of many unsolved problems with the Shakespeare plays. What was the first play Shakespeare wrote? The last? When and in what order were the plays written? After 200 or more years of analysis, the Shakespeare professor has no certain answer for any of these questions. The final tally of plays the great author wrote is also guesswork, as is the play that can be rightly proclaimed the first in print. Adding to the confusion are anonymously written plays closely resembling Shakespeare's plays that the professor deems "too early" to have been written by Shakespeare. And plays listed as Queen Elizabeth's entertainment in the 1560s to 1580s with titles similar to or descriptive of Shakespeare's plays are likewise deemed "too early" to have been written by Shakespeare. And references to Shakespeare's plays, or allusions to lines in them, from the 1560s onward are ignored because they are dated "too early" for the professor's consideration. This abundant "too early" evidence does not fit the Stratford Man model, which dates his earliest plays at circa 1590. The constraints imposed by this model, therefore, forces the expert to conclude that the great author was a plagiarist that stole material from many sources. He makes this judgment despite having not *one* firm composition date for any play. One can begin to find solutions to these problems once the Stratford Man model is put aside, which is the approach of this chapter.

A. The Problems of Shakespeare Play Dating and Chronology

The Shakespeare professor usually has to work backward in assessing composition dates for the Shakespeare plays, working with end dates of composition, or *terminus a quo*, based upon the date they were first published, entered in the Stationers' Register, or appeared in Francis Meres's 1598 list of Shakespeare's plays. Less than half of the plays can be dated this way – the rest is based on the writing style or mere guess. The experts have formed an approximate composition dating range of 1590 to 1613 for the complete plays. The starting point is based upon one supposed allusion to Shakespeare as a new writer published in 1592 (Robert Greene's *Groats-worth of Wit*). The end point is based on the morris dance in *The Two Noble Kinsmen* (3.5), which was copied from a masque written by Francis Beaumont in early 1613; it is believed that Shakespeare co-wrote this play with John Fletcher in a state of semi-retirement.[1] In an approximate time frame of twenty-four years, therefore, the Shakespeare professor must find a way to cram thirty-eight or more plays. Accepting "new" plays into the Shakespeare canon, such as *Edward III*, makes this tight model even more unwieldy. Besides the 38 plays solidly attributed to him are plays labeled "Shakespeare Apocrypha," which comprise the seven plays added to the Third Folio (1664 edition). Among them, *Pericles, Prince of Tyre*, is an accepted Shakespeare play, but the authorship of the other six (*The London Prodigal, The Puritan Widow, A Yorkshire Tragedy, The Tragedy of Locrine, The History of Thomas, Lord Cromwell*, and *Sir John Oldcastle*) is doubtful or denied. More plays "to be considered" as Shakespeare's include *Thomas of Woodstock* (or *Richard II–Part 1*), and *Edmund Ironside*. There is also the lost Shakespeare play, *Love's Labour's Won*, that Meres had mentioned; it must have been printed because this title was included in a bookseller's list of items sold in August 1603.[2]

The lack of parallels in the Stratford Man's biography to themes or situations in the Shakespeare plays is a large obstacle in dating them. Meanwhile, allusions in the plays to current historical events that could help them get ignored because they occur too early in the Stratford Man's life. For example, the experts consider it fact that Shakespeare made a contemporary reference to Robert Devereux, 2nd Earl of Essex, in *Henry V* – that he was the "General of our gracious Empress" that Shakespeare had imagined having a triumphant return to London "from Ireland."

> Were now the General of our gracious Empress,
> As in good time he may, from Ireland coming,
> Bringing Rebellion broachèd on his Sword,
> How many would the peaceful City quit,
> To welcome him?   [Act 5, chorus, lines 30-34]

It is true that Queen Elizabeth had sent an army to Ireland in 1599 with Essex as general to put down Irish rebels, but he completely failed in his mission and returned in disgrace. He had set out with an 18,000-man army, and three months later, only 4,000 men were left.[3] The queen ordered Essex to carry on with the war but instead he signed a truce with the rebel leader, the Earl of Tyrone. Then he abandoned his post without permission and hurried back to London. Ramon Jiménez's analysis of this passage shows that Shakespeare had a different general in mind, one that met with a notable success.[4] In 1583, the English forces under general Thomas Butler, 10th Earl of Ormond, caught the Irish rebel, Earl of Desmond. Desmond was decapitated and his head was brought on a sword to Ormond; later the head was brought to the queen. So it was General Ormond who brought "rebellion broachéd on his sword." *Henry V* therefore, should be dated circa 1583-84 rather than circa 1598-99.

B. The Problem of "Too Early" Allusions to Shakespeare's Plays in Other Works

The experts have found numerous examples of phrases or unusual word clusters in Shakespeare's plays that are similar to those in the works of other writers. Since many were written "too early" to be echoes of Shakespeare, the experts are forced to believe that the great author was stealing or "improving" the work of lesser writers, that Shakespeare was "derivative." But as he cannot firmly date any Shakespeare play, it is open to debate as to who borrowed from whom. In many cases, these same "derivative" authors actually borrowed from Shakespeare but this usually goes unnoticed. In fact, the two earliest works in print with Shakespeare's name, *Venus and Adonis* (1593) and *The Rape of Lucrece* (1594), were immediately imitated and plagiarized by several writers.[5] In Appendix A, I have compiled 93 "too early" allusions to 32 different Shakespeare plays made by 30 different writers in 53 different works or sources. Taking this substantial amount of borrowing into account, and the great author's creative genius, it is far more likely that these "derivative" writers were actually imitating, or echoing lines from, Shakespeare's great and already popular plays. If the "too early" allusion to a Shakespeare line does not fall into the derivative or plagiarist categories, then the expert will usually declare it a "commonplace" or proverbial expression first recorded by Shakespeare.

This section will detail twelve "too early" allusions to one of Shakespeare's greatest masterpieces, *Hamlet*, from twelve different sources. They are dated circa 1588 to 1597, yet the Shakespeare professor still believes that Shakespeare's *Hamlet* was written circa 1600-01. One allusion appeared in a letter about the current literary scene by the professional writer, Thomas Nashe. It was so obviously an allusion to Shakespeare's play, and so damaging to the orthodox dating of the entire Shakespeare canon, that a clever excuse was created: Nashe alluded to an earlier, now "lost" play about Hamlet upon which Shakespeare based his play. This theoretical play has been dubbed "Ur-Hamlet." "Ur" means "original." *The "Ur-Hamlet" is a complete invention with no basis in fact.* As most of the twelve "too early" allusions to *Hamlet* have unusual word clusters that mimic those used in Shakespeare's play, the Ur explanation is useless. A few experts believe that the non-existent "Ur-Hamlet" was written by Shakespeare, but even an early version of this intellectually and psychologically complex drama could not be placed near the start of his dramatic output without completely disrupting the currently accepted time-line for the rest of his plays.

On September 7, 1598, *Palladis Tamia, or Wit's Treasury* by Francis Meres was registered for publication. The book listed twelve Shakespeare play titles, including *Henry IV*, which comprises two separate plays. So by September 1598, it cannot be denied that Shakespeare had written thirteen plays. The Shakespeare professor would add another four plays that Meres did not list (all three parts of *Henry VI*, and *Taming of the Shrew*), totaling seventeen plays in an estimated time period of about nine years (1590-98). Contrast this sup-posed output, for example, with that of Christopher Marlowe: seven plays written in a seven or eight year period. The expert attributes Shakespeare's high output of amazing quality in so short a time simply to the "miracle of genius." The evidence compiled in Appendix A explodes this facile explana-tion: sixteen additional Shakespeare plays were alluded to by 1598. With the Stratford Man model, it would mean that he had written thirty-three plays in approximately nine years, among them, two of his greatest tragedies; this does not include the eight separate but early Shakespeare play versions named in Section C, all written by 1594, which, presuming they were written by Shakespeare, would total 41 plays in eight or nine years. Add to this dramatic pile Shakespeare's two popular narrative poems and enough sonnets to war-rant mention by Meres. The Stratford Man model simply cannot contain such a gargantuan effort in so short a period of time. Below are the twelve "too early" allusions to Shakespeare's *Hamlet*; dates in brackets reflect the orthodox dating. The complete compilation of "too early" allusions to Shake-speare's plays is placed in Appendix A, with a summary of the study placed at the end of this chapter.

Twelve "Too Early" Allusions to Shakespeare's *Hamlet*

(1). circa 1588: "Too early" allusion to *Hamlet* [1600-01?].

Thomas Kyd (?), play, *Soliman and Perseda*. Although registered on November 20, 1592, this play can be dated to circa 1588. Editor John J. Murray noted that at this time there was a vogue for plays with Turkish conquerors, like Marlowe's *Tamburlaine* (1587), and complimentary references to the Spanish in the play must have predated the Spanish Armada battle of August 1588.[6]

In *Soliman and Perseda* (4.1.77-78), Soliman compares Perseda's hair to that of a sun god and her forehead to Jove:[7]

Fair <u>locks</u> resembling *Phoebus* [sun god] radiant beams,

> Smooth <u>forehead</u> like the table of high _Jove_ ...

In _Hamlet_ (3.4.57), the title character compares his father's hair to that of a sun god and his forehead to Jove:

> <u>Hyperion's</u> [sun god] <u>curls</u>, the <u>front</u> [forehead] of <u>Jove</u> himself ...

Soliman and Perseda contains "too early" allusions to three more Shakespeare plays, as shown in Appendix A (nos. 31-34).

---

(2). circa 1588: "Too early" allusion to _Hamlet_ [1600-01?].

John Lyly, play, _Mother Bombie_ (registered June 18, 1594 and printed that year). The play definitely dates earlier than the year of registration because it was first performed by the Children of Paul's, a company that was suspended or disbanded in early 1590 for about a decade. Most scholars, including Michael Pincombe, date the play circa 1588.[8]

Mother Bombie:[9]

> the nearer we are in blood, the further we must be from love; and the <u>greater the kindred is, the less the kindness</u> must be. [3.1]

A line in _Hamlet_ (1.2.65), first printed in Quarto 2 (1604-05):

> KING CLAUDIUS
> But now my Cousin _Hamlet_, and my son.
>
> HAMLET
> A little <u>more than kin, and less than kind</u>.

Lyly's play also has a "too early" allusion to _King Lear_ (Appendix A, No. 29).

---

(3). circa 1589: "Too early" allusion to _Hamlet_ [1600-01?].

Anonymous play, _Histrio-mastix, or the Player Whipp'd_ (first printed 1610). This play has no consensus on dating. Roslyn Knutson demonstrated that John Marston was not the play's author, freeing it from the supposed circa 1599 dating, and noted that it contained allusions that were "plausibly topical in 1588-91."[10] E.K. Chambers's latest date for the play was 1591, and believed, like others, that it was an academic play rather than one written for the public theater. _Histrio-mastix_ referred to Marlowe's play, _Tamburlaine_ (ca. 1587), and evidently satirized its lead actor, Edward Alleyn. The line, "O, sweetheart, the Spaniards are come!" (Act 5, line 234), argues for a date after the 1588 Armada invasion. For these reasons, the play is here dated circa 1589.

In *Histrio-mastix* (Act 2, lines 160-61), two characters enter with a dog ("water-spaniel") and a duck:

> VOURCHIER
> One of the goodliest Spaniels I have seen.
>
> LYON-RASH
> And here's the very quintessence of ducks.

Charles Cathcart noted this allusion as a "verbal parody of the speech from *Hamlet*,"[11] where Hamlet ponders man's attributes:

> ... The beauty of the world, the paragon of animals; and yet to me, what is this quintessence of dust? [2.2.315-17]

These lines first appeared in print in Quarto 2 of *Hamlet* (1604-05). Another line in the same speech, "What a piece of work is man," is echoed in *Histrio-mastix* (Act 5, line 246): "O, what a thing is man ..." *Histrio-mastix* also alludes to Shakespeare's play, *Troilus and Cressida* (Appendix A, No. 41).

---

(4). 1589: "Too early" allusion to *Hamlet* [1600-01?].

Thomas Nashe, prefatory letter to Robert Greene's novel, *Menaphon* (registered August 23, 1589).

Nashe's long letter about the current literary scene was addressed to "the Gentlemen Students of Both Universities." In one line he refers to "*Hamlet*" with its "handfuls of tragical speeches" written by "English *Seneca*." Since the Shakespeare professor does not believe that Shakespeare was an established London playwright in 1589, he can only theorize that Nashe's reference was to an earlier play about Hamlet that has been lost – the "Ur-Hamlet." The presence of the word "Kid" two sentences following it, it is further believed, was a punning reference to the playwright, Thomas Kyd: ergo, Kyd was the writer of this "Ur-Hamlet." This explanation has not satisfied many orthodox scholars, including Nashe's editor, Ronald McKerrow, but it has stuck for over two centuries for lack of a better one; today it is treated as fact. Yet Nashe's line can be credibly explained as an allusion to Shakespeare's *Hamlet* when placed into its proper context and if the Stratford Man model is deferred.

In the following passage, Nashe poked fun at writers who translate, with little ability, the Latin works of the ancient Roman writer, Seneca, and use this material for "endeavors of Art," later identified as "stage" writing.

> I'll turn back to my first text, of studies of delight; and talk a little in friendship with a few of our trivial translators. It is a common practice nowadays amongst a sort of shifting companions, that run through every art and thrive by none, to leave the trade of *Noverint* [scrivener/scribe] whereto they are born, and busy themselves with the endeavors of Art, that could scarcely Latinize their neck-verse if they should have need; yet English *Seneca* ...

Nashe makes one exception among those who translate Seneca for play material: a writer of "tragical speeches" whom he calls "English *Seneca*." Nashe clearly separates English Seneca from the "trivial translators" with a semicolon followed by the transition term, "yet."

> yet English *Seneca* read by candlelight yields many good sentences, as *Blood is a Beggar*, and so forth: and if you entreat him fair in a frosty morning, he will afford you whole *Hamlets*, I should say handfuls of tragical speeches. But o grief! [italics original]

Most commentators would say that "English *Seneca*" refers to a book, a translation of Seneca into English. There was such a book printed in 1581, *Seneca His Ten Tragedies*, but the choice sentence, "Blood is a Beggar," is not in it or in any work of Seneca. English Seneca is clearly a person, an English dramatist who writes as well as, or like, Roman Seneca. Nashe recommends these lesser writers to read the work of English Seneca, and that if they "entreat him fair," i.e., ask him nicely, "he will afford" them "handfuls of tragical speeches" from *Hamlet*. Since no English play called *Hamlet* had yet been printed, Nashe was apparently encouraging the "trivial translators" to approach English Seneca personally to see the manuscript copy of his play.

In the lines that follow, Nashe reports that since the "trivial translators" of Latin have translated Seneca "to death" for "our stage" (i.e., the theater), they now (ca. 1589) "leap into a new occupation" of translating Italian authors.

> But o grief! *tempus edax rerum*, what's that will last always? The sea exhaled by drops will in continuance be dry, and *Seneca* let blood line by line and page by page, at length must needs die to <u>our stage</u>: which makes his famished followers to imitate <u>the Kid in Aesop</u>, who enamored with the Fox's newfangles, forsook all hopes of life to leap into a new occupation; and these men renouncing all possibilities of credit or estimation, to intermeddle with <u>Italian translations</u>:

To describe the new vogue among writers of translating Italian works into English, Nashe evokes Aesop's fable about a kid (young goat) and a fox.[12] The fox had tempted the kid out of safety with a new-fangled object and then devoured him. As mentioned above, the Shakespeare professor connects the "kid" reference to writer Thomas Kyd, and this I do concur. Kyd probably wrote the heavily Senecan play, *The Spanish Tragedy*, which was performed circa 1587. In 1588, Kyd translated a prose work by the Italian writer, Torquato Tasso,[13] so one could say that he "leapt into a new occupation." Kyd was also "born" into the trade of "noverint," a scrivener or scribe; this was his father's occupation. Kyd, therefore, could be counted among those "trivial translators" that Nashe was needling, *but he was not English Seneca*, the clear exception among writers. The Shakespeare professor makes the connection between a play called Hamlet and Thomas Kyd merely from the proximity of the two words "Hamlets" and "Kid," not from reading the sense of the passage. This groundless "evidence" is enough to proclaim the existence of Kyd's "Ur-Hamlet," thereby assigning an invented authorship to an invented play.

Instead of theorizing about "Ur-Hamlet" the Shakespeare professor should try to identify English Seneca with the clues that Nashe had provided. First it must be assumed that the identity of English Seneca was already known to university students, the addressees of the letter, otherwise Nashe would not have used this epithet. English Seneca was obviously influenced by Roman Seneca. He wrote a tragedy about Hamlet. Now the Englishman Shakespeare wrote a very famous play called Hamlet, performed at both universities (according to the first printed edition in 1603), and several of his tragedies show a marked influence of Seneca. Indeed, Francis Meres compared Shakespeare with Seneca in 1598.

> As Plautus and Seneca are accounted the best for comedy and tragedy among the Latins: so Shakespeare among the English is the most excellent in both kinds for the stage;
> [*Palladis Tamia, or Wit's Treasury*]

Later, in the First Folio, Ben Jonson compared Shakespeare to six classical writers, including "him of Cordova dead," i.e., Seneca, who hailed from Cordoba, Spain. Considering the conjunction of "English *Seneca*" and "whole *Hamlets*" in the same sentence, it is perhaps not coincidental that the sole mention of Seneca in the entire Shakespeare canon occurs in *Hamlet* (2.2.409): "Seneca cannot be too heavy, nor Plautus too light." So "English *Seneca*" was a fitting name for Shakespeare. (Shakespeare was also called "English Terence" by John Davies of Hereford after Terence, the ancient Roman comedy writer.) Nashe provided a quote from English Seneca in his preface letter: "Blood is a Beggar," which was set apart in the text by italics. Shakespeare may prove to be the only writer of this period to have written a similar phrase, "Beggar'd of blood," published twenty years later in Sonnet 67. Samuel Daniel had also seen Shakespeare's Sonnet 67 – as early as 1592, says Claes Schaar,[14] and had borrowed "phrases and image fragments" from it for his poem, *The Complaint of Rosamond*:

> Such one was I [Rosamond], my <u>beauty</u> was mine own,
> No borrowed blush which <u>banck-rot</u> [bankrupt] <u>beauties seek</u>:
> The new-found shame, a sin to us unknown,
> Th'adulterate <u>beauty</u> of a <u>falsed cheek</u>: [lines 134-37]

Compare with lines in Shakespeare's Sonnet 67:

> Why should <u>false</u> painting imitate his <u>cheek</u>,
> And steal dead seeing of his living hue?
> Why should poor <u>beauty</u> indirectly <u>seek</u>
> Roses of shadow, since his Rose is true?
> Why should he live, now nature <u>bankrout</u> [bankrupt] <u>is</u>,
> Beggar'd of blood to blush through lively veins ...

Another clue points to Shakespeare as English Seneca. When Nashe advised the translators to "entreat him fair," meaning English Seneca, he was employing a favorite Shakespearean expression, one that occurred in five of his plays.[15] In the line after "whole *Hamlets*," Nashe used the Latin phrase, "tempus edax rerum." This line appears in *The Troublesome Reign of John, King of England* (scene 11), a play later attributed to Shakespeare.[16] Nashe's letter in *Menaphon* provides enough evidence to show that English Seneca was Shakespeare and that *Hamlet* had been written as early as 1589. There is no need to presume or invent the existence of an earlier lost play. The additional "too early" allusions to Shakespeare's *Hamlet* in this section, all dated well before the play's orthodox dating of circa 1600-01, fortify this conclusion.

---

(5). circa 1590: "Too early" allusion to *Hamlet* [1600-01?].

George Peele, play, *Edward I* (registered October 8, 1593, published the same year). The consensus for the dating of this play is ca. 1590-91.[17]

In *Edward I*, the title character says to Queen Elinor:

> If any heavenly joy in woman be,
> Sweet of all sweets, sweet Nell it is in thee. [scene 3]

In *Hamlet*, Queen Gertrude throws flowers on Ophelia's grave:

> Sweets to the sweet, farewell! [5.1.245]

Peele's *Edward I* uses the phrase, "mounting mind," to describe Queen Elinor (Scene 1). This same phrase appeared in *Love's Labour's Lost* (4.1.4) as noted by editor A.H. Bullen in *The Works of George Peele* (1888).

———————————

(6). circa 1592: "Too early" allusion to *Hamlet* [1600-01].

Christopher Marlowe, play, *Edward II*.

While Marlowe's character, Young Mortimer, is about to be taken away and executed, he speaks to the queen:

> Farewell, fair Queen; weep not for Mortimer,
> That <u>scorns</u> <u>the world</u>, and as a <u>traveler</u>,
> Goes to <u>discover countries</u> yet <u>un</u>known. [5.6]

Compare the lines above with the two quarto versions of Hamlet's famous soliloquy on suicide. *Hamlet*, Quarto 1 (1603):

> For in that dream of death, when we awake,
> And borne before an everlasting Judge,
> From whence no <u>passenger</u> ever return'd,
> The <u>undiscovered country</u>, and the accurs'd damn'd.
> But for this, the joyful hope of this
> Who'ld bear the <u>scorns</u> and flattery of <u>the world</u>,
> Scorned by the right rich, the rich cursed of the poor? [Scene 18]

Hamlet, Quarto 2 (1604-1605):

> For who would bear the whips and <u>scorns</u> of time ...

> But that the dread of something after death,
> The <u>undiscover'd country</u>, from whose borne
> No <u>traveler</u> returns, puzzles the will ... [Signature G2]

Marlowe's play contains "too early" allusions to three other Shakespeare plays (Appendix A, nos. 60-62). Robert Southwell, in a work that was circulating in manuscript by 1591 (*Saint Peter's Complaint*),[18] used the phrase "The scorn of Time" (Stanza 5).[19]

———————————

(7). 1593: "Too early" allusion to *Hamlet* [1600-01?].

Gabriel Harvey, essay, *A New Letter of Notable Contents* (reg. October 1, 1593).

A New Letter (signature B3):

> May they not surcease to wonder, that wonder how Machiavell can teach a Prince *to be*, and *not to be*, religious? Another question, or two of a sharper edge, were at my tongue's end.

Shakespeare's Prince Hamlet (3.1.56):

> To be, or not to be, that is the Question:

Harvey's italics (with the exception of "and," which was not in Shakespeare's line) indicates a quotation. Harvey mixed Shakespeare's very famous line from Prince Hamlet's very famous soliloquy with an allusion to Machiavelli's treatise, *The Prince*.[20]

---

(8). 1593: "Too early" allusion to *Hamlet* [1600-01?].

Michael Drayton, poem, *Piers Gaveston, Earl of Cornwall* (reg. Dec. 3, 1593).

Piers Gaveston (line 995-96):

> Base <u>dunghill</u> mind, that dost such <u>slavery</u> bring,
> To live a <u>peasant</u>, and be born a King.

Ross D. Waller noted the unusual word cluster of "dunghill," "slavery" and "peasant" in Drayton's lines with one line spoken by Shakespeare's Hamlet.[21] The line in question was transmitted slightly differently in quartos 1 and 2 of *Hamlet* (2.2.560).

Hamlet, Quarto 1 (published 1603):

> Why what a <u>dunghill</u> idiot <u>slave</u> am I?

Hamlet, Quarto 2 (published 1604-05) and Folio versions:

> Oh, what a rogue and <u>peasant</u> <u>slave</u> am I?

---

(9). 1594: "Too early" allusion to *Hamlet* [1600-01?].

Thomas Nashe, essay, *Christ's Tears Over Jerusalem* (2nd edition).

Nashe criticizes Gabriel Harvey in the "Epistle to the Reader":

> His [Harvey's] vainglory (which some take to be <u>his gentlewoman</u>) he hath new <u>painted</u> over <u>an inch thick</u>.

Shakespeare's Hamlet holds the skull of the jester, Yorick, and says to it:

> Now get you to my lady's chamber, and tell her, let her paint an
> inch thick, to this favor she must come. Make her laugh at that.
> [5.1.195-96]

Joseph W. DeMent noted this allusion, and another from *Henry IV-Part 1*
(Appendix A, nos. 75-76), in *Shakespeare Quarterly*.[22]

---

(10). 1594: "Too early" allusion to *Hamlet* [1600-01?].

Diary of Philip Henslowe: "Hamlet," the performance of a play recorded on
June 9, 1594.[23]

---

(11). 1596: "Too early" allusion to *Hamlet* [1600-01?].

Thomas Lodge, pamphlet, *Wit's Misery, and the World's Madness.*

Lodge compared the devil to the ghost in *Hamlet*, which he saw at a playhouse called "The Theatre." The devil is as pale as

> the ghost which cried so miserably at the Theatre, like an oyster
> wife, *Hamlet, revenge*: [p. 56]

The Theatre was built in 1576 and torn down in 1597 (its foundation was discovered in 2008). The 1603 printed edition of Shakespeare's *Hamlet* was registered as "A book called the Revenge of Hamlet, Prince [of] Denmark..."[24]
Thomas Dekker's 1601 play, *Satiro-mastix or the Untrussing of the Humorous
Poet*, also referred to the "revenge" portion of the play's title:

> my name's Hamlet revenge:
> Thou hast been at Paris garden hast not? [4.1.150]

The Paris Garden was the London theater district. *Satiro-mastix* also referred
to other Shakespeare plays: *Anthony and Cleopatra* ("Come, buss thy little
Anthony now, now, my clean Cleopatra") in 3.1.314, Justice Shallow (character in *Henry IV-Part 2* and *Merry Wives of Windsor*) in 2.2, *Timon of Athens*
in 5.2.210, and *The Comedy of Errors* in the 1602 edition's letter to the reader
("behold this short Comedy of Errors").

---

(12). 1597: "Too early" allusion to *Hamlet* [1600-01?].

George Chapman, play, *An Humorous Day's Mirth* (acted May 11, 1597).[25]

An Humorous Day's Mirth (2.2.7):

> A king of clouts [rags], a scarecrow, full of cobwebs ...

Hamlet (1603 edition):

> A king of clouts, of very shreds. [scene 11, line 49]

Scholars know that Chapman borrowed details from Shakespeare's *Hamlet* for his play, *Bussy D'Ambois* (1604): one character says that "faulty apprehensions" form dragons, lions and elephants from clouds (3.1.23-25), and Shakespeare's Hamlet teased Polonius into seeing clouds shaped like a camel, weasel and a whale (3.2.384-90, 1603 ed.). In *The Revenge of Bussy D'Ambois* (c. 1610), Chapman "imitated the closet scene between Hamlet and his mother."[26] Chapman also borrowed "rude mechanicals," from Shakespeare's *A Midsummer Night's Dream* for his translation of Homer's *Odyssey* (1609).[27]

C. The Problem of Early Versions of the Shakespeare Plays

Eight anonymously written plays of the Elizabethan period are directly related to Shakespeare's plays and have similar titles. Most are considered as the source of the corresponding Shakespeare play. Although they are distinctly separate from Shakespeare's plays, they share similar plots and characters, and sometimes similar phrases and metaphors. In some cases, the Shakespeare play and the earlier anonymous play are so closely related that knowledge of the earlier play will explain irregularities in plot or dialogue in the Shakespeare play.[28] The expert's conundrum is how to place the early plays: did the great author plagiarize them, or are they his early versions later rewritten with a more mature hand? Seven of these plays were registered or printed between 1591 and 1595 (five in 1594) and one survived in manuscript only, but not in the author's hand. If Shakespeare did not pen these early plays, then who did? No other author claimed them, or was claimed for them. There is one exception: *The Troublesome Reign of John, King of England* (No. 5 below) which was ascribed to "W. Sh." (1611 edition) and "W. Shakespeare" (1622 edition).

The experts accept that at least portions of *The Contention* (No. 1 below) and the *True Tragedy of Richard, Duke of York* (No. 2 below) were written by Shakespeare, but they do not regard them as early versions of *Henry VI*, parts two and three – they are bad quartos of the plays.[29] But the differences between these two sets of plays, wrote Jane Lee, are too substantial for the bad quarto theory to hold:

> ... we must suppose that some dramatist took [Shakespeare's] stolen copies or his shorthand notes and regularly rewrote them. We

> must suppose that he newly versified the plays; that he introduced
> fresh circumstances; that he added much new and poor matter;
> and that he left out the greatest and most thoughtful passages.
> On no other supposition can the *Contention* and *True Tragedy* be
> imperfect copies of *Henry VI.*, Parts 2 and 3.[30]

The experts cannot accept these two plays as "separate but early" versions by Shakespeare because they are not his top quality and because they would be too early – meaning a composition date outside of the accepted timeline. If they did accept them as early versions, then they would have to likewise accept or seriously consider as Shakespeare's the other similar plays (nos. 3-8 below). And as separate plays, how can they possibly fit into an already overcrowded chronology? If all eight were accepted as "separate but early" Shakespeare plays, then it would push the great author's total output to 46 plays (38 + 8) written during approximately twenty-four years. To see the similarities between these anonymously written plays and Shakespeare's one must study them both, but even a glance at the titles as first published for both works is telling. Although these plays are mostly rejected by the Shakespeare professor as the great author's work, the authorial status of items 3 to 8 below remains undecided. Accepting them all into the Shakespeare canon would force the Shakespeare professor to open his composition dates to the 1580s, when there was no sign of the Stratford Man in London, the theater center. Questionable early play versions are unique to Shakespeare. Making this problem even more acute, Appendix A (nos. 7-8, 12) exposes "too early" allusions to Shakespeare's *Taming of the Shrew* in 1578 and *Timon of Athens* in 1579. This would mean that their corresponding early versions (nos. 4 and 8 below) would have to be dated even earlier than that. *The True Tragedy of Richard the Third* (No. 3 below), a possible early version of Shakespeare's *Richard III*, may have inspired the lost ballad, "A Tragical Report of King Richard the 3," which was registered on August 15, 1586.[31] All of these plays need reevaluation of composition dates *based upon contemporary evidence* rather than trying to fit them within the dubious Stratford Man model. In the list below, the first title is the proposed "early version" play and the second title is the corresponding Shakespeare play. Brackets contain the earliest publication dates.

Early Versions of Shakespeare's Plays

1. *First Part of the Contention Betwixt the Two Famous Houses of York and Lancaster, with the Death of the Good Duke Humphrey*: [1594]

   and

   The Second Part of King Henry the Sixth, with the Death of the Good Duke Humphrey [First Folio, 1623]

2. *The True Tragedy of Richard, Duke of York, and the death of good King Henry the Sixth, with the whole contention between the two houses Lancaster and York* [1595]

   and

   The Third Part of King Henry the Sixth. With the Death of the Duke of York [First Folio, 1623]

3. *The True Tragedy of Richard the Third: Wherein is shown the death of Edward the Fourth, with the smothering of the two young princes in the Tower* [1594]

   and

   The Tragedy of King Richard the Third. Containing, His treacherous plots against his brother Clarence: the pitiful murder of his innocent nephews ... [1597]

4. *A Pleasant Conceited History, called The Taming of A Shrew* [1594]

   and

   The Taming of The Shrew [First Folio, 1623]

5. *The Troublesome Reign of John, King of England, with the discovery of King Richard Cordelion's base son (vulgarly named, The Bastard Falconbridge): also the death of King John at Swinstead Abbey.* [1591, published in two parts]

   and

   The Life and Death of King John [First Folio, 1623]

6. *The Famous Victories of Henry the Fifth: Containing the honorable battle* of Agincourt [registered May 14, 1594; first surviving edition, 1598]

   and

   The Chronicle History of Henry the Fifth, with his battle fought at Agincourt in France ... [1600]

7. *The True Chronicle History of King Leir and His Three Daughters, Gonorill, Ragan, and Cordella* [registered May 14, 1594; first surviving edition, 1605]

   and

   M. William Shak-speare: His True Chronicle History of the Life and Death of King Lear and his Three Daughters. [First recorded performance Dec. 26, 1606; published in 1607]

8. *Timon* [manuscript, circa 1581-1591, Victoria and Albert Museum]

   and

   The Life of Timon of Athens [First Folio, 1623]

D. The Problem of "Too Early" Shakespeare Play References in the Queen's Revels

Possible references to six different Shakespeare plays are contained in the surviving revels accounts, a record of entertainments given before Queen Elizabeth I and her court (she never attended a public theater). They were acted between the years 1566 and 1585 – "too early" to be Shakespeare play references because the Stratford Man was too young or because they fall outside the traditional composition dates. Had they conformed to the Stratford Man model, they would have naturally been considered as the great author's early plays with titles that were later changed. As no Shakespeare play has a certain composition date, this explanation cannot be ruled out. The most obvious parallels are "The History of Error" (1577) with *The Comedy of Errors*, and "The History of Caesar" (1583) with *The Life and Death of Julius Caesar*.

Queen Elizabeth I was acquainted with Shakespeare's plays. She viewed *Love's Labour's Lost* and *Merry Wives of Windsor*, according to the printed editions of 1598 and 1602. Shakespeare's *Twelfth Night, or, What You Will*, was almost certainly the play performed before the queen and her foreign guests of honor in 1601.[32] One of the guests was Virginio Orsino, Duke of Bracciano, and coincidentally, a main character in *Twelfth Night* is Orsino, Duke of Illyria. A similarity of names between a guest of honor and a main character in an entertainment would certainly flatter the guest. The play was acted on the evening of January 5, 1601, which is called Twelfth Night (the eve of the Epiphany, which is twelve days after Christmas). The Shakespeare play makes no reference to Twelfth Night and has no relevance to Twelfth Night, which implies that the title derived from the day it was performed. *What You Will*, the subtitle of this play, may have been the original title. (The first allusion to the double title was a diary entry by John Manningham on February 2, 1602 for a performance he saw at Middle Temple, a law society.)[33] These three Shakespeare plays shown to the queen, added to the six early revels plays listed below, total nine possible Shakespeare plays shown for the queen's entertainment. Accepting them as such is to accept an altered view of the great author's career – that he was initially a dramatist of the royal court and not a common player who later made a stab at writing for the public stage. It would mean that the great author had early access to the royal court and enjoyed Queen Elizabeth's favor for several decades. Listed below are titles that appeared in the records of the queen's revels and the Shakespeare play it could describe, with following. Eva Turner Clark noted most of them in *Hidden Allusions in Shakespeare's Plays* (New York, 1931). The dates in brackets represent the "orthodox" Shakespeare dating according to Sir Edmund Chambers.[34]

DATE	QUEEN'S REVELS PLAY TITLE	CORRESPONDING SHAKESPEARE PLAY
1. 1566 SEPT. 2	*Palamon and Arcyte* by Richard Edwards	*The Two Noble Kinsmen* [1612-13?]
2. 1572 JAN. 1	*Ajax and Ulysses*	*The Tragedy of Troilus and Cressida* [1601-02?]
3. 1577 JAN. 1	*The History of Error*	*The Comedy of Errors* [1592-93?]
4. 1577 FEB. 19	*The History of Titus and Gisippus*	*Two Gentlemen of Verona* [1594-95?]
5. 1579 FEB. 26	*A History of the Duke of Milan and the Marquis of Mantua*	*Two Gentlemen of Verona* [1594-95?]
6. 1583 JAN.	*The History of Caesar*	*The Life and Death of Julius Caesar* [1599-00?]
7. 1583 FEB. 12	*A History of Ariodante and Genevora*	*Much Ado About Nothing* [1598-99?]
8. 1584 DEC. 27	*The History of Agamemnon and Ulysses*	*The Tragedy of Troilus and Cressida* [1601-02?]
9. 1585 JAN. 1	*The History of Felix and Philiomena*	*Two Gentlemen of Verona* [1594-95?]

(1). The "lost" play, "Palamon and Arcite," was performed by students at Oxford University in honor of Queen Elizabeth's visit in 1566. Richard Edwards was the attributed author of this play, and it received smashing reviews by eyewitnesses. Palamon and Arcite are also the main characters in the play, *The Two Noble Kinsmen*, attributed to William Shakespeare and John Fletcher on the first printed edition (1634). Although the text of the Oxford University play has not survived, there is a link between it and a phrase in the prologue of *The Two Noble Kinsmen*.[35]

> If this play do not keep,
> A little dull time from us, we perceive
> <u>Our losses</u> fall so thick, we must needs leave.

The meaning of "Our losses" has baffled scholars but most agree it referred to a current event. Disaster struck shortly before the Oxford University performance: a staircase in the building where the performance was being held had collapsed, killing three people and injuring several more. The show still went on, so acknowledging the tragedy with a few words in the prologue would be expected. The "lost" 1566 play and Shakespeare's play are linked in another way. In *The Two Noble Kinsmen* (5.4.44), Palamon makes this comment at learning that his life has been spared: "Can that be, /When Venus, I have sa is false?" Nowhere in *The Two Noble Kinsmen* did Palamon berate the goddess, *but he did so in the 1566 play*. Spectator John Bereblock, in his summary of the 1566 play, wrote that Palamon had prayed to Venus to win a duel for the hand of Emilia. After he lost, Palamon "casts reproaches upon Venus, saying that he had served her from infancy and that now she had neither desire nor power to help him." The play's conclusion was met with "a tremendous shout and clapping of hands."[36]

Most scholars agree that the main plot of *The Two Noble Kinsmen* was composed by Shakespeare, and that the subplot – the play's majority – was written by Fletcher, explaining why his name topped Shakespeare's on the 1634 title page and why it was excluded from the First Folio. Scholars assume that Shakespeare and Fletcher had collaborated and they date the play circa 1613. They also conclude that Shakespeare's portions of *The Two Noble Kinsmen* were his very last dramatic effort, yet the writing quality is inconsistent with that of his later works. If it were accepted, however, that Shakespeare wrote or co-wrote with Edwards the 1566 play, one could surmise that Fletcher had obtained Shakespeare's portions of the 1566 play and filled it in with his own work several decades later. Another play titled "Palaman and Arcite" had four performances at the Rose Theater in 1594;[37] this may have been a revised version of the 1566 play. Ben Jonson's line, "the Play, *Palemon*," in his play, *Bartholomew Fair* (4.3), written in 1614, probably alluded to *The Two Noble Kinsmen* by its earlier title; the earliest reference to a play titled, *The Two Noble Kinsmen*, occurred on a manuscript dated between 1612 and 1619.[38] Shakespeare was familiar with the work of Richard Edwards, who died in the month following the Oxford University performance. Edwards's poem, "In Commendation of Music" (first printed in *The Paradise of Dainty Devices* in 1576), was quoted in *Romeo and Juliet* (4.4.155-57, 171-72).

(2) and **(8)**. Shakespeare's play, *Troilus and Cressida*, contains characters that were featured in two "lost" revels plays, "The History of Ajax and Ulysses" (1572), and "The History of Agamemnon and Ulysses" (1584). Shakespeare's storyline involving the Grecian leaders, Ajax, Ulysses and Agamemnon, have little intersection with the love story between the Trojan characters, Troilus and Cressida. The two different plots are of similar importance and weight in the play, so theoretically, the "lost" revels play titles are just as fit a title as "Troilus and Cressida," if these plays were essentially the same one by Shakespeare. Allusions to phrases in Shakespeare's *Troilus and Cressida* occurred circa 1588-89, as noted in Appendix A (nos. 24 and 41), even though orthodox dating places it at circa 1601-02.

(3). The January 1577 performance before the queen and her court of the "lost" play, "The History of Error," obviously suggests Shakespeare's play of a similar name, *The Comedy of Errors*, first printed in 1623. On January 6, 1583, there was another performance at court of "A historie of fferrar," and it contained "diverse new thinges As one Citty, one Battlement of canvas ..."[39] which suggests the earlier revels play had been revised. Confirmed references to Shakespeare's play varied the title: "a Comedy of Errors" in 1594, "his Errors" in 1598 (regarding a "comedy" by Shakespeare), and "the Play of Errors" in 1604-05.[40] (A 1580 allusion to Shakespeare's play is noted in Appendix A, No. 18.)

(4), **(5)** and **(9)**. The "lost" revels play, "Titus and Gissippus" (1577), shared its title with a chapter in *The Governour* (1531) by Sir Thomas Elyot. In Elyot's story, Titus, upon learning that his best friend, Gissippus, is in love with his fiancée, willingly hands her over to him. This story has a direct parallel in the final scene of Shakespeare's *Two Gentlemen of Verona*, and is frequently noted by scholars: Valentine surrenders his beloved, Silvia, to his friend, Proteus. (This story also appears in Boccaccio's *The Decameron*, with characters Tito and Gesippo.) Another "lost" revels play title, "The History of the Duke of Milan and the Marquis of Mantua" (1579), resembles characters in Shakespeare's *Two Gentlemen of Verona*. The Duke of Milan in Shakespeare's play banishes Valentine after he attempts elopement with his daughter. After leaving the city in disgrace, Valentine encounters a group of outlaws and eventually becomes their leader; they "work" in the forest of Mantua. As Mantua was a marquisate, Valentine could be described as the "outlaw" Marquis of Mantua who is at odds with the Duke of Milan. The "lost" revels play titled, "The History of Felix and Philiomena" (1585), was probably based on a Spanish story by Jorge de Montemayor called *Diana Enamorada* (1542). In Montemayor's story, Felismena, disguised as a boy, becomes the "page" to her lover, Felix, who employs "him" to woo Celia; a similar situation occurs in *Two Gentlemen* involving the characters Julia, Proteus and Silvia.

(6). The "lost" play, "The History of Caesar," presented at the royal court in January 1583, may have been what was later titled, *The Life and Death of Julius Caesar*, in Shakespeare's First Folio, where it debuted in print. Lines in Shakespeare's play were alluded to as early as 1589 (Appendix A, No. 45), and Henslowe's diary recorded a play about Caesar in two parts in 1594.[41] Over 150 masquers, including one in the costume of Julius Caesar, performed at the royal court on Feb. 1, 1562.[42] The two royal entertainments of 1562 and 1583 may have been related to Shakespeare's play.

(7). The "lost" revels play, "A History of Ariodante and Genevora," presented in 1583, was evidently based upon a story with the same characters in Canto 5 of Ariosto's *Orlando Furioso* (1516). Shakespeare made use of this same canto for his play, *Much Ado About Nothing*. Shakespeare's characters Hero, Claudio and Don John mirror those in Ariosto's story: Ariodante (Hero) is accused of infidelity by Genevora (Claudio), who is made to believe by false testimony (Don John) that he saw her with another man at her bedroom window; Genevora (Claudio) then rejects her. This same plot occurs between the lovers Sir Timbreo and Fenicia in Matteo Bandello's *Novelle* (1554). Scholars believe that "Panecia," another "lost" play acted before the queen on January 1, 1575, was a misspelling of Fenicia, and therefore another possible early source for *Much Ado*. "Panecia," of course, may have been the earliest reference to Shakespeare's *Much Ado*. A "too early" allusion of *Much Ado* occurred in late 1592 (Appendix A, No. 64).

Conclusion

Because the Stratford Man left posterity no clues about his education or his literary biography, or other significant details of his life, the Shakespeare professor cannot provide one solid date of composition for any Shakespeare play, or a solid writing order for the plays in total. Meanwhile he usually ignores "too early" references to the plays and possible early versions of the plays because they do not fit the accepted timeline for the Stratford Man. Or he explains them away by saying the great author plagiarized other writers or that he co-wrote with other writers or that he rewrote or retouched or recast other writers' works, all without proof. He would rather doubt the great author's creative genius than question the Stratford Man's authorship. He even invents early, lost plays that Shakespeare must have based his upon, labeled with the prefix "Ur," to fathom their existence. The great author was evidently connected to the court, as some revels plays descriptive of Shakespeare's plays were performed before Queen Elizabeth in the 1560s to 1580s, decades before the experts believe Shakespeare was writing. The superabundance of "too early" allusions to Shakespeare's plays dated 1562 to 1606 (compiled in Appendix A) would lead any observer without preconceived notions to conclude that almost every Shakespeare play was written earlier than the conventional timeline. The great author did not plagiarize. Many admiring writers were borrowing lines, scenes and subject matter from Shakespeare's plays that he had already made famous – borrowing possibly made in homage. The Shakespeare professor's passionate attachment to the Stratford Man model in light of these allusions defies common sense.

First "Too Early" Allusions to Shakespeare's Plays, Chronological*
(Appendix A)

1562	*Romeo and Juliet*	[1594-95?]
1578	*The Taming of the Shrew*	[1593-94?]
1578	*Measure for Measure*	[1604-05?]
1579	*The Merchant of Venice*	[1596-97?]
1579	*Timon of Athens*	[1607-08?]
1579	*Anthony and Cleopatra*	[1606-07?]
1579	*King John*	[1596-97?]
1579	*Twelfth Night*	[1599-00?]
1579	*Much Ado About Nothing*	[1598-99?]
1579	*Henry IV-Part 2*	[1597-98?]
1583	*Cymbeline*	[1609-10?]
1587	*Henry VI-Part 1*	[1591-92?]
1587	*Richard III*	[1592-93?]
1587	*Julius Caesar*	[1599-00?]
1587	*Merry Wives of Windsor*	[1600-01?]
1588	*Titus Andronicus*	[1593-94?]
1588	*Troilus and Cressida*	[1601-02?]
1588	*Richard II*	[1595-96?]
1588	*King Lear*	[1605-06?]
1588	*Hamlet*	[1600-01?]
1589	*Henry VI-Part 2*	[1590-01?]
1589	*Henry VI-Part 3*	[1590-91?]
1589	*Henry IV-Part 1*	[1597-98?]
1589	*Othello*	[1604-05?]
1592	*As You Like It*	[1599-00?]
1592	*Love's Labour's Lost*	[1594-95?]
1593	*The Tempest*	[1611-12?]
1593	*A Midsummer Night's Dream*	[1595-96?]
1593	*The Winter's Tale*	[1610-11?]
1596	*Macbeth*	[1605-06?]
1601	*Pericles*	[1608-09?]
1606	*The Two Noble Kinsmen*	[1612-13?]

*The plays may have been written before these dates, or revised after these dates. The dates of composition in brackets and question marks are those estimated by E.K. Chambers.

Possible Shakespeare Plays Acted before Queen Elizabeth
(Section D)

1566	*The Two Noble Kinsmen*
1572	*Troilus and Cressida*
1577	*The Comedy of Errors*
1577	*The Two Gentlemen of Verona*
1579	*Twelfth Night*
1583	*Julius Caesar*
1583	*Much Ado About Nothing*

"Early Version" Shakespeare Plays*
(Section C)

Timon [manuscript]
The Troublesome Reign of John, King of England
The Contention Betwixt the Two Famous Houses of York and Lancaster
The True Tragedy of Richard, Duke of York
The True Tragedy of Richard the Third
The Taming of A Shrew
The Famous Victories of Henry the Fifth
The True Chronicle History of King Leir and His Three Daughters

*All written by 1594.

Plays Possibly Written by Shakespeare

Edward III
Edmund Ironside
Thomas of Woodstock (or *The Tragedy of Richard II, Part 1*)

Lost Shakespeare Play

Love's Labour's Won

Shakespeare's Plays Listed in *Palladis Tamia, or Wit's Treasury* (1598)*

The Two Gentlemen of Verona
The Comedy of Errors
Love's Labour's Lost
Love's Labour's Won [lost play]
A Midsummer Night's Dream
The Merchant of Venice
Richard II
Richard III
Henry IV [presumably parts 1 and 2]
King John
Titus Andronicus
Romeo and Juliet

*Listed in the order stated by the author, Francis Meres.

Shakespeare Plays (17) printed before the First Folio (1594-1622)

Hamlet
Henry IV-Part 1
Henry IV-Part 2
Henry V
King Lear
Love's Labour's Lost
The Merchant of Venice
Merry Wives of Windsor
A Midsummer Night's Dream
Much Ado About Nothing
Othello
Pericles
Richard II
Richard III
Romeo and Juliet
Titus Andronicus
Troilus and Cressida

Shakespeare Plays (20) with Print Debut in the First Folio (1623)

All's Well that Ends Well
Anthony and Cleopatra
As You Like It
The Comedy of Errors
Coriolanus
Cymbeline
Henry VI-Part 1
Henry VI-Part 2
Henry VI-Part 3
Henry VIII
Julius Caesar
King John
Macbeth
Measure for Measure
The Taming of the Shrew
The Tempest
Timon of Athens
Twelfth Night
The Two Gentlemen of Verona
The Winter's Tale

Shakespeare Play with Print Debut after the First Folio

The Two Noble Kinsmen (1634)
(with later additions by John Fletcher)

Plays Added to the Third Folio (1664)*

Pericles
The London Prodigal
The History of Thomas, Lord Cromwell
Sir John Oldcastle
The Puritan Widow
A Yorkshire Tragedy
The Tragedy of Locrine

*All but *Pericles* considered apocryphal.

CHAPTER 4

The Sonnets and Other Puzzle-Poems

THE INTROSPECTIVE AUTHOR of Shakespeare's sonnets, which were written in the first person, describes himself as a nobleman with a tarnished reputation. His love and admiration for a younger aristocrat, and his sexual obsession with a dark beauty, his mistress, were also described. This blatantly autobiographical picture clashes spectacularly with the known life of the Stratford Man. The Shakespeare professor, consequently, struggles with every aspect of the sonnets, if he does not outright deny that they were autobiographical. Shakespeare's poem, *A Lover's Complaint*, likewise centered upon a nobleman, and one that had talents similar to those that the great author displayed in his works; it too was written in the first person. *A Lover's Complaint* was evidently an expansion on the theme of a shorter poem written circa 1570 by the 17th Earl of Oxford. Sir George Greenwood described Shakespeare's two poems in *Love's Martyr* as "puzzle-poems."[1] The underlying subject of these morbid but majestic verses may be puzzling, but even more puzzling is why the great author involved himself in a politically dangerous publication, a work that allegorically contradicted the "fact" of Queen Elizabeth's virginity and broached the taboo topic of the succession. *The Passionate Pilgrim* by "W. Shakespeare," a small collection of poems, was a notorious piracy. Although privately this unauthorized publication had "offended" the great author, he never publicly complained about it or took legal recourse against the publisher. The experts dismiss Shakespeare's authorship of eleven of the twenty poems it contained, yet they were never credited to anyone else. Have they been put off by evidence of "too early" dating? This chapter will explore these four Shakespeare poetry works, which, excepting the sonnets, get mild attention by the Shakespeare professor and are generally unknown to readers – in fact, none of these works were openly discussed until several generations after their publication. These poetry works in total support the conclusion that they were authored by a man of high rank and influence who was writing years before conventional belief. Shakespeare's sonnets and his other puzzle-poems need not be mysterious – what they need is examination without pre-conception.

SHAKE-SPEARE'S SONNETS

The reader must excuse this short summary about the sonnets of Shakespeare, the great author's poetic tour de force, and the subject of thousands of books and articles. A sonnet is a fourteen-lined poem, and 154 of them were printed in 1609, titled SHAKE-SPEARE'S SONNETS (three, however, were not strictly sonnets). They differed from other sonnet collections of the period in that they were not addressed to one person, usually a named woman (Aurora, Licia, Delia, et al). The sonnets of Shakespeare were addressed to at least two unnamed people whom he adored, a fair young man, today called the "Fair Youth," and a younger married woman, today called "the Dark Lady." The majority of sonnets were written to or were about the Fair Youth. Who was he and what was his relationship with the poet? Who was the Dark Lady? The publisher, not the author, of SONNETS, signed the dedication. Why was this the case when the presumed "Shakespeare," the Stratford Man, was alive? Who was "Mr W.H.," the dedicatee? Who supplied the manuscript? Was the printed sequence in the actual order that the great author wrote them? Despite two centuries of analysis, all of these questions, and the true story behind the sonnets, remain maddeningly elusive. The reason: these sonnets are the great author's personal ruminations, are strictly autobiographical, and, as far as scholarship has shown, *have nothing to do with the Stratford Man*. This last point has caused some experts to believe, or they are forced to believe, that the sonnets were a mere literary exercise, i.e., fiction. Yet the great author testified that his sonnets were autobiographical: "every word doth almost tell my name" (Sonnet 76); "My life hath in this line some interest /Which for memorial still with thee shall stay" (Sonnet 74); and, in spite of death "I'll live in this poor rhyme" (Sonnet 107). Most experts acknowledge that the sonnet sequence by Sir Philip Sidney, *Astrophel and Stella*, was for the most part autobiographical. Astrophel, which shares a syllable with Philip, represented Sidney; Stella represented the married woman, Penelope Rich, for whom Sidney held an "adulterous passion."[2] When were Shakespeare's sonnets written? The professor only knows that enough existed by 1598 to inspire Francis Meres's comment in *Palladis Tamia, or Wit's Treasury* that Shakespeare's "sugared sonnets" were being "circulated among his private friends."

Presented below are sonnet lines in which the great author describes himself: a man of high rank, older, lame and disgraced. He believed that his works would live forever but his name would not, a contradiction reasonably explained if the great author were writing anonymously or with a pen name. It would also explain his complaint in Sonnet 66: "And art made tongue-ti'd by authority." The following is not interpretation; it is the great author's own first-person testimony. Evidence for the identities of the Dark Lady and the Fair Youth will be given in chapters 14 and 16.

The great author was highly ranked

62_ Methinks no face so gracious is as mine

66_ And gilded honor shamefully misplac'd

88_ Upon thy part I can set down a story /Of faults conceal'd, wherein I am attainted

110_ Alas 'tis true, I have gone here and there, /And made myself a motley to the view

111_ That [Fortune] did not better for my life provide, /Than public means which public manners breeds. /Thence comes it that my name receives a brand, /And almost thence my nature is subdu'd /To what it works in, like the Dyer's hand

125_ Were't aught [anything] to me I bore the canopy, /With my extern the outward honoring ... ?

In Sonnet 62, the great author described his face as "gracious," a word he repeatedly used in the plays to describe royalty and aristocracy ("gracious lord," "gracious lady," "gracious prince," etc.). Gracious is defined as "condescendingly kind, indulgent and beneficent to inferiors" (*OED*). In Sonnet 66, the great author listed many of his personal complaints from which death could release him, including "gilded honor shamefully misplac'd," implying high social status that was compromised. The word "attainted" in Sonnet 88 at the very least meant to lose one's honor (*OED*), and legally, the disbarring of estates and honors due to a crime, which applied only to the highly ranked. In Sonnet 125, the great author said he "bore the canopy," the practice of holding a canopy over the monarch during public occasions, an honor usually performed by courtiers or those with important positions. In Shakespeare's play, *Henry VIII* (5.5), "four noblemen bearing a canopy" was held over the new-born Princess Elizabeth Tudor in the procession to her christening.[3] At the Earl of Hertford's home, Elvetham, an elaborate green satin canopy was created for the queen to sit under while she watched water entertainments. The canopy was "upheld by four worthy Knights" (Sir Henry Grey, Sir Walter Hungerford, Sir James Marvin, and Lord George Carey).[4] The first line of Sonnet 125, "Were't aught to me I bore the canopy ... ?" can be read as, "Did it mean anything to me that I bore the canopy ... ?" These words sound like those of a seasoned courtier bored with superficial shows. Making "myself a motley to the view" (Sonnet 110) appears to be a reference to acting on the public stage, which the great author admits with regret ("Alas"). In Sonnet 111, the great author complained that his name received a brand for accepting public money ("public means"). Both statements make sense if uttered by a nobleman or one of rank but nonsensical if they were the words of a commoner who had profited from the public stage by his acting and writing. The great author's "work," which is writing plays, figuratively stains him as a dyer's work literally stains his hands (Sonnet 111). In Chapter 15, three overlooked remarks about Shakespeare concern staining: "purple robes distain'd" (No. 6), "the stage doth stain pure gentle blood" (No. 10), and "so clear a spring did stain" (No. 12).

The great author wrote with a pen name

66_   And art made tongue-ti'd by authority

72_   Oh lest the world should task you to recite, /What merit liv'd in me that you should love /After my death … /My name be buried where my body is

76_   Why write I still all one, ever the same, /And keep invention in a noted weed, /That every word doth almost tell my name, /Shewing their birth, and where they did proceed?

81_   From hence your memory death cannot take, /Although in me each part will be forgotten. /Your name from hence immortal life shall have, /Though I (once gone) to all the world must die … /You still shall live (such virtue hath my Pen)

Two sonnets demonstrate the great author's belief that his works would live forever, but his name would not, and one pointedly addresses his usage of a pen name. In Sonnet 72, he wrote that "after my death" the world may ask the Fair Youth about his "merit," implying fame from his artistry, yet he believed his own name would "be buried where my body is." He repeats this sentiment in Sonnet 81, predicting immortality for the addressee, because "such virtue hath my pen," while believing that he, "once gone, to all the world must die." As stated in the introduction, this contradiction is explainable if the great author wrote anonymously or with a pen name.

In Sonnet 76, the great author questioned himself: why do I write in the same style, and why do I "keep invention in a noted weed … ?" In the context of this sonnet, "invention" is his creative writing, and "noted weed" can be interpreted as "well-known alias." Weed is another word for garb or clothing. So he specifically asks himself why he bothers to "keep" his "invention" – his plays and poems – in a name that everyone knows is an alias, especially since "every word doth almost tell my name," i.e., every word reveals who he is. Evidently, when he wrote this sonnet, many in the literary world knew that "William Shakespeare" was a pen name. In Sonnet 66, the great author disclosed that "authority" kept him from speaking in his own voice: "And art made tongue-ti'd by authority." He apparently provided more detail in *The Winter's Tale*, as explained in Chapter 13.

The great author was disgraced

25_ Let those who are in favor with their stars, /Of public honor and proud titles boast, /Whilst I whom fortune of such triumph bars

29_ When in disgrace with Fortune and men's eyes, /I all alone beweep my outcast state

37_ So then I am not lame, poor, nor despis'd

66_ And gilded honor shamefully misplac'd ... /And right perfection wrongfully disgrac'd

72_ My name be buried where my body is, /And live no more to shame nor me, nor you. /For I am sham'd by that which I bring forth

111_ Thence comes it that my name receives a brand

112_ Which vulgar scandal stamp'd upon my brow

121_ 'Tis better to be vile than vile esteemed

In Sonnet 66, the great author wrote that he had enjoyed "gilded honor" before "vulgar scandal" (Sonnet 112) ruined it. He is in an "outcast state" (Sonnet 29), and is "vile esteemed" (Sonnet 121) and "despis'd" (Sonnet 37). Sonnet 111 refers to a stigma ("brand") on the great author's name. "Fortune," he wrote, "bars" him from "triumph" of "public honor and proud titles" (Sonnet 25). These statements prove that the great author was a man of high rank with a sterling reputation before scandal ruined it. The list of highly ranked men who were scandalized, and who were also poets, is very short indeed. No evidence exists that the Stratford Man suffered shame or disgrace during his lifetime, and he would have had no reason to feel ashamed if what he had "brought forth" (Sonnet 72) were the Shakespeare plays.

The great author was lame, older and felt death nearing

22_ My glass shall not persuade me I am old

32_ When that churl death my bones with dust shall cover

37_ As a decrepit father takes delight, /To see his active child do deeds of youth, /So I, made lame by Fortune's dearest spite ... /So then I am not lame, poor, nor despis'd

62_ But when my glass shews me myself indeed /Beaten and chopp'd with tann'd antiquity

66_ Tir'd with all these for restful death I cry … And strength by limping sway disabled

71_ No Longer mourn for me when I am dead

72_ After my death (dear love) forget me quite

73_ That time of year thou mayst in me behold, /When yellow leaves, or none, or few, do hang /Upon those boughs, which shake against the cold … /In me thou seest the twilight of such day, /As after Sunset fadeth in the West … /In me thou see'st the glowing of such fire, /That on the ashes of his youth doth lie

74_ But be contented when that fell arrest, /Without all bail shall carry me away, /My life hath in this line some interest, /Which for memorial still with thee shall stay … /So then thou hast but lost the dregs of life, /The prey of worms, my body being dead

81_ Or I shall live your Epitaph to make, /Or you survive when I in earth am rotten, /From hence your memory death cannot take, Although in me each part will be forgotten … /Though I (once gone) to all the world must die, /The earth can yield me but a common grave

89_ Speak of my lameness, and I straight will halt

138_ Thus vainly thinking that she thinks me young, /Although she knows my days are past the best

When the great author penned Sonnet 138, he believed his "days" were "past the best." This sonnet was first published in *The Passionate Pilgrim* in 1598-1599, when the Stratford Man was 34 years old. The great author dwelled on his impending death in several sonnets (66, 71-74, 81). His complaint of lameness in three sonnets (37, 66, 89) cannot be accounted for in the Stratford Man's known biography.

The great author was dead when SHAKE-SPEARE'S SONNETS *was published*

Shakespeare orthodoxy unanimously agrees that the great author was not involved with the 1609 printing of his sonnets – although the text is fairly good, there are numerous misspellings and mistakes. Some scholars even consider it a pirated work despite publisher Thomas Thorpe's very clean record (he published over forty books). More of the author's absence is indicated in the dedication of SHAKE-SPEARE'S SONNETS, which was signed by Thorpe:

> To the only begetter of these ensuing sonnets Mr W.H. all happiness and that eternity promised by our ever-living poet wisheth the well-wishing adventurer in setting forth. T.T.

The great author is described as "our ever-living poet." Ever-living is a term applied to the famous dead. Publisher Thorpe wrote three dedications for books by deceased authors, including one by Christopher Marlowe. The title, SHAKE-SPEARE'S SONNETS, suggests finality, that this edition comprised all of his sonnets. Shakespeare's play, *Troilus and Cressida*, was also printed in 1609; the unsigned letter to the reader added to the second issue of this edition said the play "escaped" the "grand possessors," implying Shakespeare was then not in control of his own works. These five points combined strongly suggest that the great author was dead in 1609, but the Stratford Man was still living. Two overlooked remarks about Shakespeare in Chapter 15 also suggest he was dead by this year. Although the great author expected his sonnets to be published, he apparently did not wish it to occur during his lifetime. As noted in Chapter 2, the great author was "offended" by William Jaggard's issue of *The Passionate Pilgrim*, which featured two of his sonnets, and in 1600, an attempt to publish "certain sonnets by W.S." was evidently blocked. It is slightly problematic that a work of Shakespeare would feature a dedication that implied he was dead, but did not feature tributes by others. It may have been for the same reason that his death was not noted by the literary world when it had occurred.

Conclusion

Because the Shakespeare professor has the wrong man, he will never be able to solve any of the mysteries of the great author's very personal sonnets. Try as he may, *he cannot tie one line among the over two thousand to events in the Stratford Man's known life*. In apparent desperation, however, some experts see a pun on Hathaway, the maiden name of the Stratford Man's wife, in Sonnet 145:

> "I hate," from <u>hate away</u> she threw,
> And sav'd my life saying "not you." [quotation marks added]

It would be less of a strain to see a pun on the 17th Earl of Oxford's name, Edward de Vere, in Sonnet 76: "Every word doth almost tell my name" ("E. Ver.y word … "). The experts conveniently forget that in Sonnet 145 the great author was quoting his lover, the Dark Lady, not his wife. The "will" sonnets (nos. 135, 136, 143) punned on the first name, William, but the meaning would not change a whit if "William Shakespeare" was the great author's pen name. The sonnets would be more understandable if only the experts would take the great author at his own word – that he was a disgraced nobleman cognizant of his literary greatness but "tongue-ti'd by authority" and social convention from revealing himself as writer behind the name Shakespeare.

The great author was dead as of 1609, according to the dedication page of *SONNETS*. As such a picture does not fit with the Stratford Man's factual life, or invented life, such important identifying clues are doubted or never followed.

A LOVER'S COMPLAINT (1609)

Very few Shakespeare fans have read or even know about Shakespeare's poem, *A Lover's Complaint*. Although published along with *SHAKE-SPEARE'S SONNETS* in 1609, both making their print debut, *A Lover's Complaint* is usually left out of modern editions of the sonnets, and in scholarship, it is among Shakespeare's most neglected works. Recently, one English professor tried to expel it from the Shakespeare canon. Why is this the case? Does *A Lover's Complaint* contain biographical elements, like the sonnets? Are these two works connected? There are distinct parallels between the young man of *A Lover's Complaint* and the older poet of the sonnets. If they were the same person, then the great author was a nobleman-courtier who did not spend his youth in a small rustic town.[5]

A Lover's Complaint opens with the poet describing, in the first person "I," a scene he is witnessing in the countryside. A woman is ripping up letters and tossing rings into a river. An old man appears and asks to know her story. The poet is close enough to hear it. Her "complaint" is regret for allowing herself to be seduced by a known womanizer who pleaded true love and later "betrayed" her. The poem gives few details about the woman but her ex-lover is fully described in eight stanzas. He is twice called a "youth," and this is confirmed with line 92, "small show of man was yet upon his chin." He is handsome and very popular.

> O one by nature's outwards so commended,
> That maidens' eyes stuck over all his face. [lines 80-81]

Women obtain his picture and fantasize about being his lover or wife, and they send him gifts of sonnets, pieces of their hair, and jewels, like offerings to a god. He has had numerous conquests including married women, some bearing his children ("his plants in others' orchards grew," line 171). He attracts followers, young and old, "in personal duty." He is also "accomplished." He is an expert horseman, and is a witty and persuasive speaker. In this passage, the woman could easily have been describing Shakespeare's particular gifts:

> So on the tip of his subduing tongue
> All kind of arguments and question deep,

All replication [replies, a legal term] prompt, and reason strong
For his advantage still did wake and sleep,
To make the weeper laugh, the laugher weep
He had the dialect [rhetoric] and different skill,
Catching all passions in his craft of will.   [lines 120-25]

This young man moves in a social circle of moneyed people – those who could afford to buy his portrait and give him expensive presents, and those educated enough to know the sonnet form. He is rich: he gave jewels (of gold and amber) to the woman, and letters tied with silk. Expert horsemanship in so young a man implies that he had the leisure to learn this skill. The phrase, "all replication prompt, and reason strong," and the word "dialect" in the passage above betrays knowledge of law and rhetoric. One of his paramours was a nun who was once wooed by noble courtiers (lines 232-34). The woman's description of a rich, educated and privileged young man, often using the word "grace," indicates that he too is a nobleman. Fully aware of the young man's "falseness" and numerous affairs, the woman initially resisted his seduction, "with safest distance I mine honor shielded" (line 151). Eventually he persuaded her that his love was true, and when he started crying, she "daffed" her "white stole of chastity" (line 297). But "his passion" was only an act – "an art of craft" (line 295). He could blush, cry and turn pale whenever it suited his aims. The poem ends with the woman wondering if she would yield again should he try another seduction. The poet, who opened the poem in his own voice and who was watching the scene and listening to her story, offered no final remarks. He let the deceived lover finish her story without comment. The poet's eavesdropping and his silence at the conclusion of her story suggests that he was the young seducer. Almost certain confirmation of this is in line five, written in the poet's voice:

Ere long [I] espied a fickle maid full pale ...

Even before he heard her story, the poet describes the woman as "fickle," a word of judgment, implying that he already knows her and her personality. In the final two lines of the poem, the woman gives it away herself that the youth had seduced her more than once, and that he

Would yet again betray the fore-betrayed,
And new pervert a reconciled Maid.

"Again" means twice, but "yet again" means three times, so the woman is saying that the youth would attempt to seduce her a third time. Apparently, the woman was hot and cold with the poet, which inspired his "fickle" comment. It is clear, therefore, that the poet of *A Lover's Complaint* was the young seducer of the poem. When one remembers that Shakespeare is the author, and is writing in the first person, one can see that he was poeticizing a personal incident, and by doing so, indirectly revealed his high status. This makes *A Lover's Complaint* a prime piece of anti-Stratfordian evidence, especially when viewed in conjunction with his sonnets.

A Lover's Complaint and SHAKE-SPEARE'S SONNETS debuted at the same time in the same publication, and for each work Shakespeare was separately credited as the author. The works were both written in the first person and all characters involved were unnamed. They both featured one similar character – a young man of high rank, beautiful, admired and sought after. It would be logical to connect the youth of *A Lover's Complaint* with the "Fair Youth" of the sonnets, but there are major differences. The youth of *A Lover's Complaint* is verbally gifted, theatrical, seductive, and is an excellent horseman – qualities Shakespeare never credited to the Fair Youth in over one hundred sonnets to him. But if one compares the profile of the poet of SONNETS, who described himself as older in at least four sonnets, with the young seducer of *A Lover's Complaint*, the only difference is age. As noted above, "grace" was used to describe the youth of *A Lover's Complaint*, a word that often described the nobility or royalty, and in Sonnet 62, the poet wrote, "Methinks no face so gracious is as mine." The poet of SONNETS also uses the phrases, "wherein I am attainted" (Sonnet 88) and "were't aught to me I bore the canopy" (Sonnet 125), implying he was a man of rank and a courtier. In Sonnet 121, the poet admits he has "sportive blood."

> For why should others' false adulterate eyes
> Give salutation to my sportive blood?

The young man of *A Lover's Complaint*, also a man of rank and privilege, said his sensual "offenses"

> Are errors of the blood, none of the mind. [lines 183-84]

The youth of *A Lover's Complaint* had affairs with married women (lines 171-75); the poet of SONNETS, who was married at the time (Sonnet 152), had an affair with the "Dark Lady." The youth of *A Lover's Complaint* was a good actor, and the poet of SONNETS wrote,

> Alas 'tis true, I have gone here and there,
> And made myself a motley to the view ... [Sonnet 110]

indicating with regret that he acted on the stage, most likely the public stage; "motley" refers to "the profession or practice of a jester, clown or (occasionally) actor" (*OED*). There are enough parallels between these two figures to suggest they are the same person at different ages. Regardless, there are *two* Shakespeare works written in the first person using language applicable to noblemen-courtiers. Social convention of the time required noblemen who wrote poetry to do so anonymously or with a pen name, which the hyphen in *SHAKE-SPEARE'S SONNETS* on the title page and throughout the work (in the running titles) seems to imply.

Dating *A Lover's Complaint*

Scholars cannot agree upon a composition date for *A Lover's Complaint* but there are clues. Some words in the poem were archaic by 1600, for example, *eyne* (eyes), *feat* (elegantly), *real* (regal), *sounding* (swooning), *maund* (basket), and *teen* (suffering, hurt). The author invented many new words for this piece (*appertainings, fluxive, impleached, pensived, unexperient, encrimsoned, annexions, blusterer, acture, invised, enpatron,* etc.),[6] so the poem is a strange combination of new and archaic words. The logical explanation for this contradiction is that the archaic words were current when the work was written which would date the poem to before 1600. This is supported by the fact that the vogue of "complaint" poems, some paired with sonnet cycles, was outdated when *SHAKE-SPEARE'S SONNETS* and *A Lover's Complaint* were first printed. The Shakespeare professor routinely says that, for *A Lover's Complaint*, Shakespeare borrowed from Edmund Spenser's poem, *Ruins of Time* (published in *Complaints*, 1591), and from Samuel Daniel's poem, *The Complaint of Rosamond* (1592). But the supposed borrowing did not end there. Lines 123-24 of *A Lover's Complaint*,

> For his advantage still did wake <u>and sleep</u>,
> To make the <u>weeper laugh, the laugher weep</u>

echo those in Thomas Lodge's poetry work, *Phillis* (1593):

> Then lay you down in Phillis' lap <u>and sleep</u>,
> Until she <u>weeping read, and reading weep</u>.   [Induction]

(*Phillis* was accompanied by the poem, *The Tragical Complaint of Elstred*.) Lines from *A Lover's Complaint* and a Shakespeare sonnet also are echoed in *Parthenophil and Parthenophe* (1593) by Barnabe Barnes.

Parthenophil and Parthenophe (Sonnet 49, lines 6-9):

> A <u>Siren</u> which within thy breast doth bath her
> A <u>fiend</u> which doth in <u>graces</u> <u>garments</u> grath [clothe] her,
> A fortress whose force is impregnable:
> <u>From</u> my love's <u>limbeck</u> [distilling device] still <u>still'd</u> <u>tears</u>, oh tears!

Compare the above lines with *A Lover's Complaint* (lines 316-17):[7]

> Thus merely with the <u>garment</u> of a <u>grace</u>,
> The naked and concealed <u>fiend</u> he cover'd ...

And also compare with lines in Shakespeare's Sonnet 119:[8]

> What potions have I drunk of *<u>Siren</u>* <u>tears</u>
> <u>Distill'd</u> <u>from</u> <u>Limbecks</u> foul as hell within ...

Two more lines by Barnes in the same work (Madrigal 1),

> <u>From</u> winds my sighs, from <u>concave</u> rocks and steel,
> My sides and <u>voices</u> <u>Echo</u> ...

recall the opening lines of *A Lover's Complaint*:

> <u>From</u> off a hill whose <u>concave</u> womb <u>reworded</u>,
> A plaintful story from a sist'ring vale
> My spirits t'attend this <u>double</u> <u>voice</u> accorded ...

Echoes of *A Lover's Complaint* and Shakespeare's sonnets in the poetry of others suggest that the two works were circulating together in manuscript in the early 1590s or before and were imitated. Another poem by Spenser, *Ruins of Rome: by Bellay* (1591), contains remarkable parallels with Shakespeare's sonnets. A. Kent Hieatt stated that "the evidence of Shakespeare's verbal recall of *Ruins [of Rome]* is so extensive that the place of this sequence in his imagination is beyond question ... "[9] He noted the following examples:

Spenser's *Ruins of Rome* (Sonnet 7, lines 9-10):

> And though your frames do for a time make war
> 'Gainst time ...

Compare with lines from Shakespeare's sonnets 15 and 16:

> And all in war with Time for love of you ... [15]

> Make war upon this bloody tyrant time ... [16]

Spenser's *Ruins of Rome* (Sonnet 3, line 8):

> The prey of time, which all things doth devour.

Compare with lines from Shakespeare's Sonnet 19:

> Devouring time, blunt thou the Lion's paws,
> And make the earth devour her own sweet brood ...

(Barnabe Barnes also used the phrase, "Devouring time," in a dedicatory poem in his *Parthenophil and Parthenophe*.)[10]

Spenser's *Ruins of Rome* (Sonnet 27, line 6):

> The which injurious time hath quite outworn ...

Compare with a line in Shakespeare's Sonnet 63:

> With time's injurious hand crush'd and o'erworn ...

Sonnet 20 of Spenser's *Ruins of Rome* employed the words "fade" and "vade" just as Shakespeare did in his Sonnet 54. Another poem by Spenser, *Prothalamion or a Spousal Verse* (1596), is so close to *A Lover's Complaint* that Mac-Donald Jackson believes "one poet was unconsciously echoing the other ... "[11] Jackson views Shakespeare as the unconscious borrower, but cumulative evidence suggests the opposite, that Spenser and others were the conscious borrowers of Shakespeare. There is one poem, however, that overshadows all of these supposed influences upon *A Lover's Complaint* that has never been acknowledged by Stratfordians. Edward de Vere, 17th Earl of Oxford, wrote a much shorter poem with a similar subject as *A Lover's Complaint* that dates to circa 1570. Written in the first person, Oxford, as the poet, observes a lady speaking out loud about a "youth" that has captured her heart. An echo reveals Oxford's surname, "Vere."

> Sitting alone upon my thought in melancholy mood,
> In sight of sea, and at my back an ancient hoary wood,
> I saw a fair young lady come, her secret fears to wail,
> Clad all in color of a nun, and covered with a veil;
> Yet (for the day was calm and clear) I might discern her face,
> As one might see a damask rose hid under crystal glass.
>
> Three times, with her soft hand, full hard on her left side she knocks,
> And sigh'd so sore as might have mov'd some pity in the rocks;
> From sighs and shedding amber tears into sweet song she brake,

When thus the echo answered her to every word she spake:

"Oh heavens! who was the first that bred in me this fever? *Vere*
Who was the first that gave the wound whose fear I wear forever? *Vere*
What tyrant, Cupid, to my harm usurps thy golden quiver? *Vere*
What wight [creature] first caught this heart and can from bondage
    it deliver? *Vere*

"Yet who doth most adore this wight, oh hollow caves, tell true?
    You
What nymph deserves his liking best, yet doth in sorrow rue? *You*
What makes him not reward goodwill with some reward or ruth? *Youth*
What makes him show besides his birth, such pride and such
    untruth? *Youth*
May I his favor match with love, if he my love will try? *Aye*
May I requite his birth with faith? Then faithful will I die. *Aye*"

And I, that knew this lady well,
Said, Lord how great a miracle,
To her how echo told the truth,
As true as Phoebus oracle.[12]

In the opening lines of *A Lover's Complaint*, the poet heard echoing sounds coming from a hill, and drawing nearer, saw they emanated from a woman's voice; she was at a river. In Oxford's poem, the poet is "in sight of sea" near woods and observes a lady near rocks speaking out loud which causes echoes. The woman in *A Lover's Complaint* is distressed about her lover and is crying, "often did she heave her napkin to her eyne" (line 15), just as the lady in Oxford's poem is "sighing" and "shedding amber tears" over him. The poet of *A Lover's Complaint*, and Oxford in his poem, eavesdrop on complaining lady lovers, and each knows the woman in question. Both complaining ladies are in love with a young courtier of high birth who is adored by others, who has lied to them, and who does not fully return their love. Oxford's poem only existed in manuscript until modern times.

Conclusion

SHAKE-SPEARE'S SONNETS, and its companion piece, *A Lover's Complaint*, were both written in the first person and published together. Scholars prefer to study these two pieces separately, as if they were unrelated. Yet in both works Shakespeare describes himself as a nobleman-courtier with a busy love life: as a younger man in *A Lover's Complaint* and as an older man in SONNETS. It is reasonable to conclude that both voices were the same person at different ages. Edmund Spenser's poetry work, *Complaints*, registered in 1590 and published in 1591, contains phrases similar to those used in *A Lover's Complaint* and Shakespeare's sonnets. Spenser's work also featured praise of Shakespeare ("our pleasant Willy" in *The Tears of the Muses*), and revealed that he was a nobleman and already an accomplished playwright (Chapter 15). That Shakespeare stole or borrowed lines from Spenser, Samuel Daniel, Thomas Lodge and other writers for *A Lover's Complaint* is impossible to prove because this work has no concrete dating. It is far more likely that "lesser" poets were borrowing and imitating lines from the inventive genius, Shakespeare, rather than the opposite. The archaic words employed in *A Lover's Complaint* accord with this perspective. With Spenser established as the borrower of Shakespeare, one can conclude that *A Lover's Complaint* and some of Shakespeare's sonnets were circulating together in manuscript as early as 1590, and, along with the sonnets of Sir Philip Sidney (first printed in 1591) may have helped set off the ensuing publishing craze of sonnet cycles, works that were often accompanied by "complaint" poems.

LOVE'S MARTYR: OR, ROSALIN'S COMPLAINT (1601)

Shakespeare contributed two beautiful but perplexing poems to a work by Robert Chester titled *Love's Martyr: or, Rosalin's Complaint*. The poems by Shakespeare and others, located in a separate section, titled *Diverse Poetical Essays*, touch upon the same theme as Chester's work, a story about the phoenix – the beautiful bird of myth. The phoenix would would burn itself on a pyre after 500 years of age and from its ashes another phoenix would arise. Comprising a total of 67 lines, Shakespeare's two poems are filled with meaning that has eluded the experts. The first poem, "Let the bird of loudest lay," describes a funeral procession of specially invited birds. The funeral is for the Phoenix and Turtle Dove, mates that had burned together. If one views Shakespeare's poems within the context of the main work by Chester, then it appears the great author and the other contributors were treading on very dangerous ground – the succession of the current monarch, Queen Elizabeth I.

Chester's Phoenix unmistakably symbolized Queen Elizabeth. Numerous works printed throughout her reign and after described her as a phoenix, including Shakespeare in his play, *Henry VIII* (5.5.39). The queen employed the phoenix as her personal symbol. A coin issued in the year of her accession (1558) featured her portrait on one side and a burning phoenix on the reverse.[13] A larger medallion with similar images was created in 1574, today called "The Phoenix Badge" (Plate 2). This medallion most notably featured "ER" (Elizabeth Regina) above the phoenix's head, and a crown above that.[14] Nicholas Hilliard's portrait of the queen, dated circa 1574, is known as the "Phoenix Portrait" (see Plate 3). It features the queen wearing a large jeweled pendant of a phoenix; the piece is placed just above her hand, which holds a red rose, the Tudor emblem. In 1596, a large portrait engraving of the queen was published. She is depicted standing between two columns – atop one column is a burning phoenix, and on the other, a pelican, another symbol of the queen.[15] Posthumously, Queen Elizabeth was depicted in a full-length statue with a phoenix beneath her feet.[16] In the main text of Chester's *Love's Martyr*, and in the poems by the other contributors (Shakespeare, John Marston, George Chapman, Ben Jonson), the phoenix legend was altered to suit the queen: the phoenix was characterized as female but traditionally it is male, and the turtle dove in literature is traditionally female, but it was characterized as male. (Shakespeare's Sonnet 19, probably among those in circulation by this time, also feminized the phoenix, and so did a poem read to Queen Elizabeth at Cowdray in 1591.)[17]

No connection whatsoever existed between the phoenix and a turtle dove before *Love's Martyr*.[18] The title of the work plainly said these two characters were "allegorically shadowed," announcing that they represented real people and their real love story.

> Love's Martyr: or Rosalin's Complaint. *Allegorically shadowing the truth of Love*, in the constant Fate of the Phoenix *and Turtle*.

Chester offered more information that Elizabeth was the phoenix of his work in another title that occurred on the first page of his narrative:

> Rosalin's Complaint, metaphorically applied to Dame Nature at a Parliament held (in the high Star-chamber) by the Gods, for the preservation and increase of *Earth's beauteous Phoenix*.

The "complaint" of Rosalin, or Dame Nature, is presented at "a Parliament" in the "Star Chamber," which was a courtroom in Westminster Palace, the seat of Elizabeth's government. Dame Nature describes the Phoenix, not as a bird, but as a woman: she has hair, forehead, cheeks, chin, lips, teeth, arms, hands, and fingers. In the section titled "Cantos," the Turtle Dove describes the Phoenix several times with the terms rose, queen, and sovereignty. The Turtle Dove chides the Phoenix for her "chasteness," an undisguised reference to Elizabeth's much vaunted virginity. In *Diverse Poetical Essays*, Jonson's two poems about the Phoenix described it as a "Woman" and a "Lady," one with quick wit and "graces," whose "Judgment (adorn'd with Learning) /Doth shine in her discerning," qualities often attributed to Elizabeth (but not usually to mythical birds!). Evidence that the public had understood Chester's phoenix symbolized the queen is contained in *The Mirror of Majesty* (1618), attributed to Sir Henry Goodyere. Goodyere likened Queen Anne, the consort of King James I, to a phoenix. She emerged

> From old Eliza's urn, enriched with fire ... One Phoenix born, another Phoenix burns.

The urn was a direct reference to *Love's Martyr* because it was the first work to associate an urn with the phoenix – in Shakespeare's poem, "Threnos," and in the poem signed Ignoto, both in *Diverse Poetical Essays*.[19] Goodyere had also copied a near-verbatim line from Ignoto's poem:

> Her rare-dead ashes, fill a rare-live urn:
> One *Phoenix* born, another *Phoenix* burn.

Josuah Sylvester also used the phoenix and urn imagery in recalling the late queen Elizabeth in his *Bartas His Divine Weeks and Works* (1605), and extended the image to her successor, King James:

> From Spicy Ashes of the sacred URN
> Of our dead Phoenix (dear ELIZABETH)
> A new true PHAENIX lively flourisheth,
> Whom greater Glories than the First adorn.

The evidence that Queen Elizabeth I was "allegorically shadowed" as the Phoenix in Chester's work is so obvious that it is bewildering that critics rarely consider it, or its implications, in their analysis of Shakespeare's two poems. Perhaps this is the case because hidden behind Chester's allegory was the belief that she had a lover and a grown child, as explained below. To cover himself in case the work offended the queen, Chester proclaimed on the title page that the book was his translation of the "venerable Italian Torquato Caeliano." No writer of this exact name ever existed. Chester evidently invented it by combining the names of the 16th century Italian poets Torquato Tasso (d. 1595) and Livio Caeliano; the latter was the pseudonym of Angelo Grillo (1557-1629). When *Love's Martyr* was rereleased in 1611 (with a new title), the prefatory poem, "The Author's request to the Phoenix," was dropped, presumably because the addressee, Queen Elizabeth I, was dead.

Phoenix-Elizabeth Bore a Child?

The complaint of Rosalin, or Dame Nature, is about the Phoenix's "preservation and increase," which in the context of Queen Elizabeth I could only mean the succession, a topic she reviled and consequently it was illegal to discuss. The name Rosalin is significant because it suggests rose, the symbol of the House of Tudor.[20] The queen was often portrayed with the Tudor Rose. Nicholas Hilliard's "Pelican Portrait" of Elizabeth (circa 1574), for example, prominently displays the figure of a large red rose with a royal crown above it.

Another example is an engraving issued circa 1595 to 1600 which featured a portrait of the queen surrounded by roses and eglantine and the words, "Rosa Electa."[21] Rosalin-Dame Nature fears that the rare and beautiful Phoenix will die childless, i.e., the Tudor ancestors of Elizabeth fear that their dynasty will end unless she produces an heir. The head god, Jove, instructs her to take the Phoenix to the island of Paphos, a place associated with the goddess, Venus. There the Phoenix will find her mate, the Turtle Dove. Just as the Phoenix was described as a woman rather than as a bird, the Turtle Dove was described like a man rather than a bird: "His name is *Liberal honor*" (p. 19) and he has curly hair and a rosy complexion (p. 20). A prayer is made to Christ that the Phoenix will have a child: "Let her not wither Lord without increase, / But bless her with joy's offspring of sweet peace. Amen. Amen." (p. 23). The poem that follows is titled, "To those of light belief," presumably addressing those who may not take the story about to be told seriously, which is described as "Plain honest Truth and Knowledge ... " (p. 23). The story continues. Rosalin-Dame Nature meets the Phoenix, who is sullen and weeping. "Envy" has arisen, the Phoenix says, "A damned Fiend o'er me to tyrannize" (p. 28). Rosalin-Dame Nature replies, "He shall not touch a Feather of thy wing, /Or ever have Authority and power, /As he hath had in his days secret prying ... " As the reader has been warned that this is a true story, it appears that Envy (note the initial E) allegorizes the Earl of Essex, who attempted to "tyrannize" the queen in early 1601, the year of *Love's Martyr*'s issue. Rosalin-Dame Nature banishes Envy and in relief the Phoenix says:

> What is he gone? Is Envy pack'd away?
> Then one foul blot is moved from his Throne,
> That my poor honest Thoughts did seek to slay:
> Away foul grief, and over-heavy Moan,
> That do o'er charge me with continual groans. [p. 29]

Envy wanted "to slay" the Phoenix's "poor honest Thoughts," which also suggests Essex, who wanted "to slay" the queen, or divest her of her "Throne." A line on page 31 clearly refers to the Essex Rebellion: the Phoenix-Queen Elizabeth says that Lady Fortune "did conspire /My downfall" by sending to her "Envy with a Judas kiss ... " Essex was a Judas, a traitor, but it is known that after his execution, the queen would shed tears at the mention of his name. Rosalin-Dame Nature then takes the Phoenix out of Arabia in a flying chariot, and one hundred pages later, they have landed in Paphos. The Turtle Dove sees the "beauteous Phoenix," they pair up, and both commit to "sacrifice" their bodies "to revive one name" (p. 136). In this context, the name that would need reviving is Tudor, which was to expire should Queen Elizabeth die childless. "Of my bones," says the Phoenix, "must the Princely Phoenix rise," a "Creature" that "shall possess both our authority" (pp. 138-39). Chester's allegory has Queen Elizabeth declaring that a child from her own body will rule after her. In the last line of this dialogue, Chester writes: "And thus I end the *Turtle* Dove's true story. Finis. R.C." (p. 139). Chester also wrote a conclusion to this story, or rather an announcement: a new phoenix does arise from the ashes of the Phoenix and Turtle Dove.

> From the sweet fire of perfumed wood,
> Another princely *Phoenix* upright stood:
> Whose feathers purified did yield more light,
> Than her late burned mother out of sight,
> And in her heart rests a perpetual love,
> Sprung from the bosom of the *Turtle-Dove*.
> Long may the new uprising bird increase,
> Some humors and some motions to release,
> And thus to all I offer my devotion,
> Hoping that gentle minds accept my motion.
> Finis. R.C. [p. 142]

Chester offers devotion "to all" – the Turtle Dove, the new "princely Phoenix," and its "late burned mother," the Phoenix. The problem here is that if Chester is allegorically pledging "devotion" to Queen Elizabeth, then he is also pledging devotion to her lover and her child/successor. The reader here must be informed that the traditional phoenix legend has nothing do to with acquiring a mate – it is simply a beautiful rare bird of myth that renews itself every 500 years by self-immolation. Turtle doves are symbolic for loving mates. The Turtle Dove's importance to the Phoenix-Queen Elizabeth is also stressed in the title – he is "Love's Martyr." The Phoenix's "Love" martyred or sacrificed himself by jumping with her on the pyre to produce their child, "Another princely Phoenix." Queen Elizabeth had been specifically called a "princely Phoenix" ten years previously in funeral verses about Sir Christopher Hatton, one of her privy councilors.

> And with our Queen that princely Phenix rare,
> whose like on earth hath seldom times been seen ... [22]

With this clear symbolism, there can be no doubt that Chester and company believed that the queen bore a child. John Marston described this child in *Diverse Poetical Essays* as alive and "grown unto maturity," "wondrous," and "perfection." Shakespeare, conversely, described the Phoenix ("Beauty"), the Turtle Dove ("Truth"), and their child ("Rarity"), as "cinders" lying in an "urn." They are described with the princely term, "grace."

> Beauty, Truth, and Rarity,

Grace in all simplicity,
Here enclosed, in cinders lie …

To this urn let those repair,
That are either true or fair,
For these dead Birds, sigh a prayer. ["Threnos"]

Reference to the living queen as dead, or that she had a grown child, would be treasonous – yet no one involved in the publication was prosecuted. As mentioned above, this book came out in the same year as the Essex Rebellion, which was prompted by, among other issues, the succession question. The earls of Essex and Southampton were convicted of high treason, and sentenced to execution, to be "hanged, bowelled, and quartered."[23] To publish *Love's Martyr* at this time with its political overtones was strangely reckless. Some believe that *Love's Martyr* inspired a bill "specifically to prohibit the writing or publishing of books" about the succession that was drafted (but not passed) in late 1601.[24] The citation is from the Calendar of State Papers dated "October? 1601":

> The preamble to a bill in Parliament, to prohibit the writing and publishing of books about the title to the Crown of this realm, and the authority of the government thereof, subjects being thus lead into false errors and traitorous attempts against the Queen, into private factions, unlawful bonds &c.[25]

The political sensitivity of *Love's Martyr* could explain why pages from the 1601 edition were repackaged with a new title page in 1611. The title was changed to *The Annuals of Great Britain* and no author's (or "translator's") name was given. The repackaging also suggests that the 1601 edition was suppressed. Alexander Grosart was the first to link Queen Elizabeth with Chester's Phoenix. In 1878, he wrote: "The fact that Elizabeth was living when *Love's Martyr* was published fills me indeed with astonishment at the author's audacity in so publishing."[26] Shakespeare's poems in this work provide weighty clues for interpreting his sonnets, which will be discussed in Chapter 16, along with the identity of the Turtle Dove.

Conclusion

In his book, *Love's Martyr*, Robert Chester surely identified the main character, the Phoenix, as Elizabeth I, the then-reigning queen. Chester and the other contributors of this "allegorical shadow," including Shakespeare, betrayed their belief that she had a child by her lover, the Turtle Dove, who was the "Martyr" of the title. They were evidently urging the queen to acknowledge her grown child, "Another princely *Phoenix*," allegory that could be perceived as treasonous, especially in the wake of the Essex Rebellion. For Shakespeare, it was his *second offense in one year* (his play, *Richard II*, was performed on the eve of the revolt, and was sponsored by Essex's supporters). That those involved with *Love's Martyr* were never arrested implies that the work had a powerful protector, possibly the great author himself. (Curiously, four years after *Love's Martyr* was published, contributors Marston, Chapman and Jonson were arrested for writing the play, *Eastward Ho.*) Two centuries passed before critics began analyzing Shakespeare's poems in *Love's Martyr*. Today it is rarely noted how they emerged at such a perilous time in history, or that the book contained such dangerous political allegory. Keeping Shakespeare's poems out of this context perpetuates their mystery.

THE PASSIONATE PILGRIM (1598-1599)

The Passionate Pilgrim is a hornet's nest of problems for the Shakespeare professor that he is yet to master. This small volume is a collection of twenty poems with the name "W. Shakespeare" on the title page. Only fragments of *The Passionate Pilgrim*'s first edition survive; its date is reckoned at late 1598 or the same year as the second edition, 1599. Scholars unanimously agree that the text was pirated. Why it was titled *The Passionate Pilgrim* is unknown. The book may have been publisher William Jaggard's attempt to fulfill public demand for Shakespeare's "sugar'd sonnets circulated among his private friends" that Francis Meres had mentioned in *Palladis Tamia, or Wit's Treasury* (1598). Jaggard somehow acquired two Shakespeare sonnets (slightly different versions of sonnets 138 and 144 in Thomas Thorpe's 1609 edition), and placed them as the first and second poems of the collection. (Although Jaggard did not include the word "sonnet" on the title page, it did occur on a second title page, placed after the fourteenth piece: SONNETS *To Sundry Notes of Music.*) Three additional pieces (nos. 3, 5, 16) were excerpts from Act 4 of Shakespeare's *Love's Labour's Lost*, which was also printed in 1598. A total of five pieces, therefore, were unquestionably by Shakespeare. But attribution to Shakespeare for the rest of the collection has become confused and doubted because of the inclusion of pieces supposedly by other poets. Numbers 8 and 20 were published in Richard Barnfield's *The Encomion of Lady Pecunia: or The Praise of Money* (1598); No. 11 appeared in Bartholomew Griffin's *Fidessa* (1596); and No. 19, "Live with Me and Be My Love," was later attributed to Christopher Marlowe. None of these writers were credited in *The Passionate Pilgrim*. Since the quality of the remaining eleven poems is considered unequal to Shakespeare, the professor has classified their authorship as anonymous even though they were never credited to, or claimed by, anyone else.

The eleven "orphan" poems of *The Passionate Pilgrim*, nos. 4, 6, 7, 9, 10, 12-15, 17 and 18, were long ago dismissed by scholars as works of Shakespeare even though they contain resemblances to his other works. Three of the orphan poems are about Venus and Adonis (nos. 4, 6, 9) and could be regarded as early sketches for Shakespeare's more mature and lengthy poem on the same subject. Orphan No. 6 puts Cytherea (Venus) and Adonis in a setting very similar to a painting of Venus and Adonis described in Shakespeare's *Taming of the Shrew* (1.2.48-53).[27] Orphan No. 6 has the best claim to Shakespeare's authorship, wrote C.H. Hobday, for reasons of vocabulary, subject matter and imagery.[28] Orphan No. 4 also has verbal links to *Taming of the Shrew*, wrote Hobday. Orphan No. 10 resembles Shakespeare's Sonnet 54, and Orphan No. 14 echoes lines in *Romeo and Juliet* (3.5.43-47).[29] Six of the orphan poems (nos. 7, 10, 13, 14, 15, 18) were written in stanzas of six lines, the same format that Shakespeare had used for *Venus and Adonis*.

"Too early" dating of some orphan poems could be behind the experts' denial that they are Shakespeare's compositions. It was noted in the New Variorum edition of Shakespeare's poems that a line in Orphan No. 7 resembled one in Robert Greene's *Mamillia* (1583) and *Perimedes the Blacksmith* (1588),[30] and a line in Orphan No. 13 resembled one in Greene's *Alcida* (1588).[31] Orphan No. 12, "Crabbed age and youth," was most likely the same one printed as a ballad, now lost, in 1591.[32] Orphan No. 18, "When as thine eye hath chose the dame," appeared in the personal notebook of Anne Cornwallis, which contained transcriptions of poems dating to the 1580s and earlier – a time period outside the traditional dating of any Shakespeare work. Now located at the Folger-Shakespeare Library, the notebook (called the Cornwallis-Lysons Manuscript) gets little attention from scholars, yet it contains the earliest handwritten transcription of a work attributed to Shakespeare. The Cornwallis version of Orphan No. 18 is quite different than – and superior to – that printed in *The Passionate Pilgrim*, noted Charles Wisner Barrell, so the poem was not merely copied from the anthology. Had it been so, surely the writer would have ascribed Shakespeare's name to it, but the piece is uncredited.[33] Other manuscript transcriptions of the piece exist, attesting to its popularity. The notebook's owner, according to Arthur Marotti, was the daughter of Sir William Cornwallis, "a man involved in both Elizabethan and Jacobean courtly society" who "hosted visits by Queen Elizabeth on several occasions…"[34] It is not surprising then that a good portion of the 34 pieces in the Cornwallis notebook were compositions by courtier poets, including Richard Edwards, Sir Edward Dyer, Sir Philip Sidney, Sir Walter Ralegh, Sir William Cordell and Edward de Vere, 17th Earl of Oxford. That Shakespeare's anonymous piece was among those of courtier poets written by the 1580s or earlier, and in a volume owned by the daughter of a courtier, is hardly the scenario the Shakespeare professor would envision for the earliest manuscript version of a work attributed to Shakespeare. Another connection between Shakespeare and Orphan No. 18 is the fact that its subject matter – one man's advice to another for success with women – mirrors Canto 47 in *Willobie His Avisa* (1594), a satire that was pointedly directed at Shakespeare and the Earl of Southampton (Chapter 14).

Shakespeare's High Social Status

For his third edition of *The Passionate Pilgrim* (1612), publisher William Jaggard added poems from Thomas Heywood's *Troia Britanica*, a work that Jaggard had issued in 1609. These extra pages doubled the size of the previous edition of *The Passionate Pilgrim* but Jaggard neglected to credit Heywood. Outraged by this and other grievances, Heywood immediately protested with a letter printed in his *An Apology for Actors* (1612) expressing his fear that "the world" would think that he had stolen pieces by Shakespeare. Heywood wrote that his poems were printed

> in a less volume, in the name of another, which may put the world in opinion I might steal them from him; and he to do himself right, hath since published them in his own name: but as I must …

The "less volume" was *The Passionate Pilgrim* "in the name of" William Shakespeare. Heywood believed that people would regard the enlarged third edition of *The Passionate Pilgrim* as Shakespeare's attempt to reclaim stolen property contained in *Troia Britanica*. Jaggard responded to Heywood's complaint by replacing the title page of the remaining copies with one that had omitted Shakespeare's name. What caused Heywood's angst and why did he seemingly care more about Shakespeare's feelings than his own? It is true that Heywood was a Shakespeare imitator (in 1608 he wrote a play titled, *The Rape of Lucrece*), but he apparently feared more than a charge of plagiarism. The answer may be contained in Heywood's claim in the same letter that "the Author" (Shakespeare) was "much offended" with Jaggard. Below is Heywood's passage with brackets providing the identities and subjects behind the confusing usage of pronouns (entire letter in Appendix F):

> but as I must acknowledge my lines [in *Troia Britanica*] not worthy his [the Earl of Worcester's] patronage, under whom [Worcester] he [Jaggard] hath published them [Heywood's lines in *Troia Britanica*], so the Author [Shakespeare] I know much offended with M. *Jaggard* (that altogether unknown to him) presumed to make so bold with his name [for citing Shakespeare as author of *The Passionate Pilgrim*]. These, and the like dishonesties I know you [printer Nicholas Okes] to be clear of …

What has escaped the notice of every interpreter of this passage is the fact that Heywood's *Troia Britanica* was dedicated to and patronized by Edward Somerset, 4th Earl of Worcester, and that Heywood was discretely referring to him to make a point about Jaggard. With this understanding, one can make sense of the passage: Heywood was comparing his own boldness of including the Earl of Worcester's name in the dedication to his "unworthy" *Troia Britanica* with Jaggard's boldness of putting Shakespeare's name to *The Passionate Pilgrim*. But the difference between them was that Heywood's permission to use Worcester's name was implicit because Worcester had paid Jaggard for the book's printing ("his patronage"). This was not the case with Shakespeare. Heywood's comments can be translated like this:

> Jaggard published *The Passionate Pilgrim* in Shakespeare's name without his knowledge, and I know that Shakespeare was much offended with Jaggard for presuming to make so bold with his name. Contrast this with another book published by Jaggard, my *Troia Britanica*: in the preface, I made bold with the Earl of Worcester's name by dedicating the work to him. While I acknowledge the work was unworthy of the Earl of Worcester, the dedication was made with his knowledge, because Jaggard printed it under Worcester's patronage. Jaggard is dishonest.

Presuming to make bold with one's name implies a person of high social status, like the Earl of Worcester. Heywood, therefore, was apparently placing Shakespeare and the Earl of Worcester on a similar social footing. By doing so, Heywood was adding weight to his complaint against Jaggard, but he cautiously avoided naming Worcester, Shakespeare or even the title of the controversial work. Altogether this explains why Heywood was so concerned that others would think him guilty of stealing from Shakespeare – because the property in question was a nobleman's. Heywood's statement also demonstrates that it was apparently well known in the London literary set that Jaggard had "much offended" the great author with *The Passionate Pilgrim*, even though the record shows that he did not openly complain or take legal action. The lapse of thirteen years between the second and third editions of *The Passionate Pilgrim* implies that the great author had personally confronted Jaggard or had paid him to stop printing the work. The great author had to have been an influential person to get this result; and his death no later than 1609 probably emboldened Jaggard to print a third edition (1612).

Jaggard suffered no consequences for the 1598-99 editions, although on October 23, 1600, he and Ralph Blore were fined and nearly imprisoned for printing a pamphlet by Sir Anthony Sherley "without license and contrary to order…"[35] Thomas Judson, printer of the first two editions of *The Passionate Pilgrim*, experienced some trouble after the work was released. His name was among those fourteen printers specifically warned on June 4, 1599 about issuing books forbidden by the Archbishop of Canterbury.[36] The inclusion of his name was probably due to his partial printing of the "treasonous" *The First Part of the Life and Reign of King Henry the Fourth* by John Hayward earlier that year, but Judson's involvement in the unauthorized editions of *The Passionate Pilgrim* may have been a contributing factor. On February 4, 1600, Judson signed a statement with the Stationers' Company that ended his printing career.[37] Richard Field, the Shakespeare-approved printer of *Venus and Adonis* and *The Rape of Lucrece*, was also among those specifically warned by the Archbishop. Why Field's name was on this list, a printer whose only recorded offense with the Stationers' Company had occurred eleven years earlier,[38] is mysterious. Only fifteen days before the list was posted, the Bishop of London (Richard Bancroft) had personally approved a religious work for Field's press.[39] Interestingly, Field had collaborated with Jaggard on a book in early 1598 (*The True Perfection of Cut Works*). Perhaps Field had supplied Jaggard with a few Shakespeare pieces and was found out; Field was certainly in contact with the great author during his printings of *Venus and Adonis* and *Lucrece*.

Who Stole from Whom?

Although *The Passionate Pilgrim* was an unauthorized publication, it does not mean that the eleven "orphan" poems it contained were not penned by Shakespeare. Scholars have deemed them orphans due to William Jaggard's uncredited inclusion of poems by Richard Barnfield, Bartholomew Griffin and Christopher Marlowe, but these author attributions are not as solid as asserted. Perhaps scholars should try a different approach in analyzing *The Passionate Pilgrim* – that Jaggard knew exactly whose work he was printing and that most of the text was truly Shakespeare's. It seems unlikely that the great author would get so upset with Jaggard for printing a mere two sonnets – the three other confirmed Shakespeare pieces were printed in the 1598 edition of *Love's Labour's Lost*. Beginning with Barnfield, the two verses in *The Passionate Pilgrim* (nos. 8 and 20) that first appeared in his *Lady Pecunia* (published by John Jaggard in 1598), were not part of the main work – they were placed in a separate section with a new title page, *Poems: In Diverse Humors*. Barnfield's name did not appear on this title page, leaving open the possibility that some of the nine pieces it contained were not of his composition. A poem in this section that included one of the earliest praises of Shakespeare, "A Remembrance of Some English Poets," was followed by what would become No. 20 of *The Passionate Pilgrim* ("As it fell upon a day"). Number 20 was reprinted in the anthology, *England's Helicon*, in 1600, and was attributed to

"Ignoto" (i.e., unknown); two other poems in *England's Helicon,* however, were correctly credited to Barnfield (No. 8 of *The Passionate Pilgrim* was not featured in *England's Helicon*). *England's Helicon* would have been the perfect vehicle for Barnfield to reassert his authorship of both nos. 8 and 20; instead, *England's Helicon* seemed to confirm Shakespeare's authorship of No. 20 by titling the poem, "Another of the Same Shepherd's," referring to the piece that immediately preceded it, "My flocks feed not," which was No. 17 of *The Passionate Pilgrim* (No. 17, one of the eleven "orphan" poems, was first printed in Thomas Weelkes's *Madrigals to 3, 4, 5 and 6 Voices* in 1597 and without signature). And this poem was immediately preceded by No. 16 of *The Passionate Pilgrim* ("On a day, alack the day," from *Love's Labour's Lost*) and was correctly assigned to "W. Shakespeare." So nos. 16, 17 and 20 of *The Passionate Pilgrim* appeared in a cluster in *England's Helicon*, perhaps so placed to give the impression that they were all by the same author. In 1605, William Jaggard printed a new edition of *Lady Pecunia* without *Poems: In Diverse Humors*, constituting another lost opportunity for both author and publisher to correct the supposed misattributions. The poem from this section that had praised Shakespeare and other writers, however, was retained ("A Remembrance of Some English Poets"). Barnfield never published again.

 England's Helicon, which postdated *The Passionate Pilgrim*, is the sole contemporary source for crediting Christopher Marlowe with the very famous lyric, "Live with Me and Be My Love," No. 19 of *The Passionate Pilgrim*. The text in *England's Helicon* was more complete than that printed by William Jaggard (the actual title was "Come Live with Me and Be My Love"). Scholars have unanimously accepted the anthology's credit of the piece to Marlowe even though at least five of its author attributions have been proven incorrect. *England's Helicon* titled the piece, "The Passionate Shepherd to His Love." Interestingly, the only other piece ascribed to "The Passionate Shepherd" in the anthology is an excerpt from *Love's Labour's Lost*, which was properly credited to "W. Shakespeare" (No. 16 of *The Passionate Pilgrim*). Perhaps the "Passionate" epithet was an intentional reference to *The Passionate Pilgrim*. Another clue tying "Live With Me" to Shakespeare occurs in *Merry Wives of Windsor*, in which a character sings a few lines from this song. Marlowe also made use of this song for two speeches in *Tamburlaine* (parts one and two), and used one line in *The Jew of Malta*.[40] Marlowe borrowed heavily from Shakespeare (as shown in Appendix A), and songs in Marlowe's plays are scarce, if not non-existent, but are plentiful in Shakespeare's plays. With no other contemporary source affirming Marlowe's authorship of "Live with Me," Jaggard's prior claim for Shakespeare cannot be ignored.

 Scholars have long believed that William Jaggard stole Bartholomew Griffin's "Sonnet 3" from *Fidessa, More Chaste Than Kind* (1596) for inclusion in *The Passionate Pilgrim* as No. 11. The two poems share ten lines but four are completely different. Scholars assume that both versions are by Griffin, but this is doubtful knowing that his work was full of borrowed material. In her study of *Fidessa*, "source-hunter" Janet G. Scott concluded that Griffin had plagiarized lines from the sonnets of Sir Philip Sidney, Thomas Watson, Edmund Spenser and Samuel Daniel.[41] Griffin's "Sonnet 15" in *Fidessa* also resembled a passage about sleep in Shakespeare's *Macbeth* (2.2.37-40).[42] Griffin admitted in his preface to *Fidessa* that he was a "young beginner" and that *Fidessa* was "the first fruit of any my writings." If No. 11 of *The Passionate Pilgrim* was Shakespeare's original composition, as Jaggard apparently believed, then it is very likely that Griffin had seen it previously in manuscript and borrowed it for *Fidessa*. To make his Shakespeare theft less apparent, Griffin may have replaced four lines with those of his own composition. Griffin never published again.

Conclusion

The Passionate Pilgrim gets little attention by the Shakespeare professor because he believes that Shakespeare only authored five of the twenty poems. But a cursory examination of the other fifteen suggests that the majority of the work was indeed penned by Shakespeare, that some pieces had circulated in manuscript in the 1580s, and that his admirers were making transcriptions of them and echoing his lines in their own works. (Even the title of the second section, "Sonnets to Sundry Notes of Music," was seemingly echoed in "Sundry sweet Sonnets," the title of the second section of Thomas Lodge's poetry work, *Scylla's Metamorphosis*, in 1589.) The eleven "orphan" poems of the collection – which the Shakespeare professor has classified as of unknown authorship – are a sampling of the great author's early verses, which would explain their not-quite-Shakespearean quality. The evidence that four poems were written by other writers is dubious. The two poems supposedly authored by Richard Barnfield, nos. 8 and 20, were never reclaimed for him, although there was ample opportunity to do so. The poem supposedly written by neophyte poet Bartholomew Griffin (No. 11), first printed in his *Fidessa*, was more than likely Shakespeare's original poem that Griffin borrowed and altered so it would be less noticeable. And there is only a 50-50 chance that the famous song, "Live With Me and Be My Love" (No. 19), was really penned by Christopher Marlowe. That the majority of poems in *The Passionate Pilgrim* were indeed of Shakespeare's composition would explain the great author's ire at publisher William Jaggard for printing his poetry without his authority. Thomas Heywood's letter of complaint about Jaggard indirectly revealed that "the author" of *The Passionate Pilgrim* was a man of high rank. Those of high rank were protective of their names, especially in regard to printing verses. Although the name that Jaggard had abused was only a pseudonym, evidently the literary world knew exactly whom it represented. The Jaggard affair shows that the great author would not openly protest the piracy of his work because it would expose his identity as Shakespeare, and it also shows that he had enough clout to privately influence Jaggard to keep the work out of print for over a decade. This picture is at odds with the experts' belief that the great author was an untitled person who started writing circa 1590 and strictly for profit. With this scenario, there would be no reason for the Stratford Man to be offended by publication of his poetry or usage of his name – rather he would be pleased to take some of the profits. Based upon the Stratford Man's propensity to sue, had he really been "much offended" by Jaggard, he would have undoubtedly seen him in the law courts. Other poetry by Shakespeare, his sonnets and *A Lover's Complaint,* both written in the first person, provided autobiographical clues indicative of the author's nobility. And it appears that Shakespeare's involvement with *Love's Martyr,* a work that almost baldly commented on the royal succession, had shielded all contributors from government prosecution. Perhaps Shakespeare's sonnets would be more solvable, and his other puzzle-poems not so puzzling, if scholars would take these facts into account.

PART II

The Stratford Man as Shakespeare,
Lifetime: The Professor's Evidence

CHAPTER 5

The "Stratford Man": The Faith-based Favorite

EVIDENCE FOR THE Stratford Man's case as the great author *during his life-time* (1564-1616) and evidence *after he died* must be distinguished by the reader. The Shakespeare professor's best evidence is the latter, and is primarily from one source, the First Folio, the subject of Chapter 8. For evidence linking the Stratford Man with the great author during his lifetime, the documentary record is completely blank. There is no "smoking gun" evidence, but the professor has what he regards as proof: three items that have nothing to do with writing. They only suggest that the Stratford Man was an actor and confirm that he was a theater shareholder. *Please take note that the Stratford Man, his family, and his descendants never claimed he was the great author (or actor) "William Shakespeare."* Even the Stratford Man's neighbors took no notice of him in this regard. No fact during his lifetime confirms he was educated or had any interest in education, writing or literature. In the Stratford Man's detailed will there is no mention of books (not even those by Shakespeare) or literary manuscripts (many Shakespeare plays were unpublished when he died, such as *Julius Caesar* and *The Taming of the Shrew*). When the Stratford Man passed away in 1616, no one publicly or privately mentioned that the great author had died, a silence that remained unbroken until 1620.

The first documentary record of the Stratford Man in London, the theater center, occurred when he was 28 years old. On May 22, 1592, "Willelmus Shackspere" loaned £7 to John Clayton;[1] by 1600, the loan was still unpaid, so Shackspere took Clayton to court to recover it. The Shakespeare professor usually ignores this lawsuit or denies that *his* Shakespeare was involved because, if he were, then the first trace of his London presence would be as a moneylender, not as an actor or writer. The professor prefers to focus upon the other "fact" of 1592, an allusion to an actor described as an "upstart Crow" in the book, *Greene's Groats-worth of Wit* (the subject of chapters 6 and 7). Even though he will admit that the Stratford Man was in London in 1592, the Shakespeare professor would rather believe that Clayton got his loan from another man named William Shackspere who lived in Bedfordshire. He will never be able to prove this, so the fact of the Clayton loan cannot be simply ignored. Lending money was in the Stratford Man's family: his father, John, made loans and was accused of usury from 1570 to 1576.[2] The next documented fact of the Stratford Man in London is the Shakespeare professor's Proof No. 1, which also seems to confirm that he was Clayton's moneylender.

Proof No. 1: The Stratford Man as Actor-Member of the Lord Chamberlain's Men (1595)

PROOF: A document dated March 15, 1595 regarding payment for two play performances by the Lord Chamberlain's Men for the queen's Christmastime entertainments. Authorized by the queen's Privy Council, her treasurer recorded a payment of £20 to

> William Kempe William Shakespeare & Richard Burbage servants to the Lord Chamberlain upon the council's warrant dated at Whitehall 15 March 1594 [1595] for two several comedies or interludes shewed by them before her Majesty in Christmas time last past viz. upon St. Stephen's Day and Innocents Day ...[3]

William Shakespeare, presumably the Stratford Man, is named in the document as a "servant" to the Lord Chamberlain along with two actor-members of the Lord Chamberlain's Men, an acting troupe formed in June 1594. The Shakespeare professor claims that the Stratford Man was also an actor-member of this company, but it is questionable.

SUPPORTING EVIDENCE: None. There is no other evidence that "Shakespeare" the man was associated with the Lord Chamberlain's Men during its nine-year existence. "Shakespeare" was not on the initial list of members when this company was formed; this is also true for actor Richard Burbage, but there are records of him acting as early as 1591, contemporary praise of his talent, and knowledge of the roles he played. There is no evidence that the Stratford Man performed for the Lord Chamberlain's Men, or for any other acting company, prior to this document. The treasurer's account books from 1597 to 1616 (1602 is missing) mention actors Heminges, Burbage, Cowley, Bryan and Pope, *but William Shakespeare's name is consistently absent.* The Lord Chamberlain's Men performed at least ten Shakespeare plays but there is no evidence that Shakespeare wrote them specifically for this company. Other acting companies performed Shakespeare's plays, including the Earl of Pembroke's Men, the Earl of Derby's Men, and the Earl of Sussex's Men. As noted in Chapter 1, Shakespeare's name was not even mentioned by the authorities after a controversial performance of his *Richard II* by the Lord Chamberlain's Men.

REALITY: The 1595 document – the second surviving document of the Strat-ford Man's presence in London – *is as one of the receivers of a payment*. It follows neatly upon the first reference to him in London, as Clayton's mon-eylender in 1592. A logical conclusion based upon the documentary record only is that the "William Shakespeare" in the 1595 document served the Lord Chamberlain's Men as a financier, loaning money to the company to cover expenses for these particular performances and was getting back his invest-ment. Someone had to front a substantial sum for the company because the royal household did not pay for these performances for three months; the bill was £20 for two performances, so the productions must have been lavish. It is fact that "Willelmus Shackspere" was a moneylender as early as 1592. *Docu-mentary evidence* shows that financing and investing was a constant theme of the Stratford Man's life, not performing or writing. His service to the Lord Chamberlain was for moneylending and nothing more.

The treasurer's document is crucial to the professor's case for the Stratford Man as the great author because it shows him in association with an acting company in December 1594. If he is an actor, then he must be a writer. This logic has been accepted without corroborating evidence. Thomas W. Baldwin had an unbiased view of the treasurer's payment: "It merely shows that these three were the members deputed to receive the pay for the company. They may or may not themselves have acted in the play."[4] One document alone associates "William Shakespeare" with the Lord Chamberlain's Men, presum-ably as an actor but it is irrelevant because *acting is not writing*.

Proof No. 2: The Stratford Man as Actor-Member of the King's Men (1603)

PROOF: A license for The King's Men acting company, issued on May 19, 1603, under the patronage of the new king, James I. William Shakespeare's name appears among those of eight known actors. The new company embraced the same members (with additions) of the Lord Chamberlain's Men, which became defunct after Queen Elizabeth's death.

> Know ye that We of our special grace, certain knowledge, & mere motion have licensed and authorized and by these presents do license and authorize these our Servants Lawrence Fletcher, Wil-liam Shakespeare, Richard Burbage, Augustyne Phillips, John Hemings, Henrie Condell, William Sly, Robert Armyn, Richard Cowly, and the rest of their Associates freely to use and exercise the Art and <u>faculty</u> of playing Comedies, Tragedies, histories, Inter-ludes, morals, pastorals, Stage plays, and Such others like as they have already studied or hereafter shall use or study, aswell for the recreation of our loving Subjects, as for our Solace and pleasure when we shall think good to see them, during our pleasure ... [5]

SUPPORTING EVIDENCE: None. The name Shakespeare never occurs again in any documentary record associated with the King's Men *in an acting capacity* during the Stratford Man's lifetime. On March 15, 1604, "William Shakespeare" and other King's Men "players" were authorized to receive red cloth, presumably to make garments to be worn during King James's procession through London; it was not for an acting assignment. But it is unlikely that these players took part in the procession because there was no mention of it in contemporary accounts. An expert at the Public Record Office (now the National Archives) believed that the cloth was "probably no more than the customary gift to men connected with the royal service."[6]

REALITY: There is no evidence that Lawrence Fletcher, the first person named on the 1603 license, was active in the King's Men.[7] There is also no evidence that "William Shakespeare" was active in it either. The documentary record shows that from late March to late May 1604 the Stratford Man was busy selling malt and managing his property in Stratford-upon-Avon.[8] Did the king allow him a leave of absence to deal with his personal business? It was about a three-day journey by horseback between Stratford-upon-Avon and London. Two records of payment to the King's Men for acting performances have survived and neither mentions Shakespeare: (1) December 2, 1603, the King's Men were paid £30 for a performance (the piece unnamed) before King James at Wilton House (the seat of the Earl of Pembroke);[9] John Heminges alone was named. (2) August 9-27, 1604, the treasurer of the King's chamber paid King's Men members Augustine Phillips, John Heminges and "ten of their fellows" for their attendance at Somerset House during the visit of a foreign dignitary.[10] During the Christmas season of 1604-05, seven performances of Shakespeare's plays were given before the king and his court; no mention was made of Shakespeare's presence. The same absence of "Shakespeare" occurred during the winter of 1612-13, when several Shakespeare plays were performed during the celebration of Princess Elizabeth's engagement. These royal performances were an outstanding honor for the great author and all occurred while the Stratford Man was still alive. A clue in the wording of the King's Men license could explain these awkward absences: "... to use and exercise the art and faculty of playing Comedies, tragedies ... " Faculty can be defined as "pecuniary ability, means, resources" (*OED*). As the Stratford Man's previous records in London concerned lending money and receiving a payment for performances, his role as a member of the King's Men may have been as their banker or financier. The Stratford Man's physical presence, therefore, would not have been necessary and would explain his post-1603 business activities in Stratford-upon-Avon. Based upon documentary evidence, this explanation is more plausible than his being an actor in this company – but even if he did act for this company, being an actor does not prove one is a writer.

Proof No. 3: The Stratford Man as a Theater Shareholder

Three separate documents confirm the Stratford Man owned a share in the Globe Theater, and one that he owned a share in the Blackfriars Theater. The original ownership papers have not survived, but are referred to in legal documents dated 1615,[11] 1619,[12] and 1635.[13] The Stratford Man, therefore, had a share in the King's Men acting company, and shares in two theaters in which the company acted.

A. The Globe Theater Share: All three documents detail the initial investors of the Globe Theater in February 1599. The investors comprised three parties: brothers Cuthbert and Richard Burbage; Nicholas Brend (the landowner); and William Shakespeare, John Heminges, Augustine Phillips, and Thomas Pope. In the 1635 document, Cuthbert Burbage said that he and his brother

> joined those deserving men, Shakspere, Hemings, Condall, Philips and others partners in the profits of that they call the House ... [14]

"Shakspere" had clearly maintained his ties with members of the Lord Chamberlain's Men after jointly receiving a payment for two of their performances in 1595.

B. The Blackfriars Theater Share: The 1615 document confirms that "William Shakespeare" was a partner in the lease of the Blackfriars Theater, purchased in August 1608. The document names the original investors:

> Ricardo Burbadge prefato Johanni Hemynges & quibusdam Willelmo Shakespeare Cuthberto Burbadge Henrico Condell Thomae Evans de Londonia praedicta generosis ... [15]

SUPPORTING EVIDENCE: In 1613, the Blackfriars Gatehouse, a property located about 600 feet from the Blackfriars Theater, was purchased by "William Shakespeare of Stratford-upon-Avon, Gent.," John Heminges, and two others, from "Henry Walker, minstrel."[16] This document confirms that the Stratford Man was the same person who invested in the Globe and Blackfriars theaters. Interestingly, his share in the Gatehouse property was listed in his will, but not the Blackfriars Theater share (his Globe share was also not listed in his will, but the theater had burned down in 1613).

REALITY: Although these documents clearly prove the Stratford Man's theater involvement, they fail to prove that the Stratford Man was a writer – in fact, one of them implies that he was not the great author. The 1635 document was Cuthbert Burbage's answer to a petition to the Lord Chamberlain, the ruling authority for theatrical matters. Burbage explained his right to own contested theater shares. The Lord Chamberlain at this time was Philip Herbert, 4th Earl of Pembroke and Montgomery, who was one of the dedicatees of the First Folio edition of Shakespeare's plays in 1623. The relevant point is that Burbage referred to "Shakspeare" as an original Globe Theater investor in this document, and that "Shakspeare" was one of the "men players"[17] placed at the Blackfriars Theater after the 1608 lease was signed, but Burbage did not mention him as a playwright. He did not mention that "Shakspeare" was the object of one of the greatest literary tributes in history, the First Folio, dedicated to the same Philip Herbert. Surely Burbage would have called attention to this important and complimentary association if "Shakspeare" were the great author.

Little-Known and Damning Documents

The Shakespeare professor's proofs that the Stratford Man was the great author during his lifetime fail to do so. They neither prove nor suggest that he was a writer. They do, however, prove beyond reasonable doubt that he was involved in the theater and that he was associated with actors. Tangible proof that he actually acted, however, is lacking. There is other evidence that the experts will cite to support their case, but it again only suggests that he was an actor. In his will, the Stratford Man bequeathed to his "fellows" John Heminges, Richard Burbage, and Henry Condell 26 shillings "to buy them rings."[18] All three men were the Stratford Man's colleagues in the King's Men acting company, and his co-partners in two theaters; Richard Burbage was named with the Stratford Man as a receiver of a payment for the Lord Chamberlain's Men. In another will, King's Men actor and Globe theater shareholder, Augustine Phillips, bequeathed 30 shillings each to his "fellows" William Shakespeare, Henry Condell and Christopher Beeston in 1605 (he bequeathed 20 shillings each to five other King's Men actors). Shakespeare is again listed among actors but in a non-acting capacity. There is also the 18th century transcription of a 1602 document naming "Shakespeare" among those who were improperly granted a coat of arms. The document has a sketch of the Stratford Shakespeare's coat of arms, and underneath it, written in a different hand is the phrase, "Shakspear ẙ Player by Garter."[19] The grant was issued to the Stratford Man's father in 1596, so why would the son's name and supposed profession be on this document? Some consider the phrase as an addition made by a modern hand, but forgery or not, all this document could prove is that the Stratford Man was a "player." He was not mentioned as a writer or as a person of credit. The year before this document was written, "Shakespeare" was declared in print as among the "best and chiefest of our modern writers" in *Love's Martyr*.

Other documentary evidence about the Stratford Man during his lifetime is indirectly revealing. The Stratford Man was called as a witness in a lawsuit between Stephen Belott and Christopher Mountjoy, and was deposed in London on May 11, 1612. The signed deposition of "William Shakespeare of Stratford upon Avon in the county of Warwick gentleman" still survives. The Stratford Man testified that, in 1604, while he lodged at the Mountjoy home in London, he had encouraged Stephen Belott to marry Mountjoy's daughter. The marriage took place, but after eight years, Belott claimed that Mountjoy never fulfilled his promise of providing a dowry, etc. By 1612, multiple editions of Shakespeare's poems and plays had been printed and the great author was well known for his literary achievements. The Stratford Man's deposition, however, gives not the slightest hint of his supposed literary or acting career. Humphrey Fludd, another witness deposed for this case, identified himself on his deposition as "one of his Majesty's Trumpeters,"[20] whereas the Stratford Man on his deposition only identified himself as a gentleman. The Stratford Man did not refer to himself as one "of his Majesty's players" or "of the King's Men." The Stratford Man's role in furthering the Belott-Mountjoy marriage was mentioned in the depositions of other witnesses, but they did not associate him with writing or acting. Thus, late in his alleged brilliant writing career, the Stratford Man and the others who testified gave no indication that he was the famous and esteemed writer, William Shakespeare. Another witness in this case was George Wilkins, identified in his deposition as a victualer, a keeper of a restaurant or tavern; Belott and his wife once lodged at his establishment. An occasional writer, Wilkins, it is believed, based his novel, *The Painful Adventures of Pericles, Prince of Tyre* (1608), upon Shakespeare's play, *Pericles, Prince of Tyre*. By way of the Belott connection, Wilkins may have even met the Stratford Man, yet this express admirer of Shakespeare never recorded it.

More insight about the Stratford Man is contained in a document issued by a London law court in November 1596:

> Be it known that William Wayte craves sureties of the peace against William Shakspere, Francis Langley, Dorothy Soer wife of John Soer, and Anne Lee, for fear of death, and so forth.[21]

The Stratford Man, Francis Langley and two women had evidently threatened bodily harm to William Wayte. Court orders of this nature required "the posting of bonds by the defendants as assurances that they would keep the peace for a specified period."[22] The Stratford Man's association with Langley, a moneylender and the owner of the Swan Theater, is telling. The Stratford Man was loaning money as early as 1592, and after this complaint purchased shares in two theaters. It appears that the Stratford Man was following Langley's lead. Langley was neither an actor nor a playwright.

Conclusion

Documentary evidence during the Stratford Man's lifetime identifies him as a seller of grain and stone. It identifies the Stratford Man as a moneylender. It identifies the Stratford Man as a landowner, a husband and a father. It identifies the Stratford Man as a matchmaker and even a bully. It identifies the Stratford Man as a theater investor and an associate or member of two acting companies. But no documentary evidence during his lifetime identifies the Stratford Man as a writer, an educated man, or the author of the Shakespeare works. The most notable actions of the Stratford Man in London *in the documentary record* involved lending money (1592), receiving payment for an acting company (1595), theater investing (1599, 1608), and becoming a charter member of the King's Men acting company (1603). Excluding a name similarity, the Shakespeare professor's evidence for the Stratford Man as the great author during his lifetime consists of a mere leap of faith: he was an actor and a theater shareholder, ergo, he was a writer. The reader should keep this in mind wading through the sea of conjecture that comprises most Shakespeare biographies, which Mark Twain likened to a reconstructed Brontosaur: "nine bones and six hundred barrels of plaster of paris."[23] The experts' best evidence for the Stratford Man occurs years after he had died. But they have one more "proof" – just as insufficient as the others – that has become so crucial to their case that the following two chapters are needed to debunk it.

CHAPTER 6

The "upstart Crow" and the Stratford Man: No Relation

The Professor's Final Proof for the Stratford Man as Shakespeare During His Lifetime

THE INVENTION OF the Stratford Man's early theatrical career by the Shakespeare professor hinges entirely upon one short passage from a 1592 book. It is perhaps his most important proof of all because it puts an end to those long, painfully blank, "lost years" of the Stratford Man, and establishes an approximate starting point for his supposed acting and writing career. This passage is the bridge between them, so it must be analyzed in depth to prove that, when carefully read, and read in context, it has nothing to do with either the Stratford Man or with "Shakespeare" personally. Even the Shakespeare professor would admit that its exact meaning is unclear, yet he is steadfast in his belief that the Stratford Man was the subject of an attack by writer Robert Greene in *Greene's Groats-worth of Wit*. (A groat was a coin worth four pence.) The work was published at Greene's "dying request," according to the title page, which was granted: Greene, age 32, died on September 3, 1592 and his book was registered 17 days later. *Groats-worth* was a novel that contained much of Greene's life story (via the character Roberto), but at the conclusion, Greene added a letter of advice in his own voice to three playwright friends (full text in Appendix B). This is where the passage in question is located. Much of the letter is a diatribe against actors. Greene says that although actors were "beholden" to him, they had "forsaken" him. He singles out one actor, whom he calls the "upstart Crow," for his friends to beware of:

> Yes, trust them not: For there is an upstart Crow, beautified with our feathers, that with his Tiger's heart wrapp'd in a Player's hide, supposes he is as well able to bombast out a blank verse as the best of you: and being an absolute *Johannes factotum*, is in his own conceit the only Shake-scene in a country. O that I might entreat … [original italics]

The experts have entertained various interpretations of this passage, but there is one point upon which they all agree: the Stratford Man was the "upstart Crow." Greene's comment, in their opinion, constitutes evidence of the Stratford Man's involvement in the London theater scene in 1592. Here is their reasoning. Point 1: "Tiger's heart wrapp'd in a player's hide" paraphrases a line later attributed to Shakespeare, "Oh tiger's heart wrapp'd in a woman's hide!" (*Henry VI-Part 3*, 1.4.137). Point 2: "Shake-scene" is a pun on "Shake-speare." Ergo, Shake-scene is Shakespeare, i.e., the Stratford Man. This interpretation is in complete defiance with the documentary record: there is zero evidence the Stratford Man was an actor or playwright in 1592 or before.

The experts usually view the Upstart Crow passage as Greene jealous of an actor who was succeeding in the writing profession, but the passage takes on an entirely different cast when put into its proper context. Greene was ill and dying when he wrote the letter; he was deeply repentant for his immoral behavior and wanted to his friends to heed his advice. Previously an atheist, Greene advised one of them to believe in God, that he was vengeful. He advised another to tone down his satire, which could create enemies, and advised them all to curb their vices. In equally serious terms, Greene warned his writer friends about the Upstart Crow. Shakespeare's line, "Oh tiger's heart wrapp'd in a woman's hide!," was a vicious description of Queen Margaret said by her distraught prisoner, the Duke of York. She had been gloating about her victory and then waved at him a handkerchief dipped in the blood of his murdered teenage son. The "tiger's heart" line was included in York's reaction. By replacing the word "woman's" with "Player's," Greene betrayed his opinion of the Upstart Crow, that he was equally as savage and cold-hearted. And by describing the Upstart Crow as a tiger in player's clothing, like a wolf in sheep's clothing, Greene was saying that he was deceitful. Greene had depended upon the Upstart Crow and was betrayed, and believed he would be ultimately responsible for his death. Greene was warning his friends that the Upstart Crow could ruin their lives, too – this was not jealousy.

Greene also wrote that actors, and therefore, the Upstart Crow, will steal writers' ideas ("admired inventions"), are usurers, and would prove to be "unkind" nurses. In the passage below, Greene purposely used the plural to make his attack on the Upstart Crow less pointed.

> O that I might entreat your rare wits to be employed in more profitable courses: & let those Apes [actors] imitate your past excellence, and never more acquaint them with your admired inventions. I know the best husband of you all will never prove an Usurer, and the kindest of them all will never prove a kind nurse: yet whilst you may, seek you better Masters; for it is pity men of such rare wits [writers], should be subject to the pleasure of such rude grooms.

Greene's advice to his writer friends, "whilst you may, seek you better masters," is an extremely important line in the letter and one that the Shakespeare professor never seems to notice. Greene was railing against an actor who was also Greene's *employer or superior*. Prone to jumping to conclusions, even the Shakespeare professor would not place the Stratford Man as a theatrical boss so early in his supposed career. All of Greene's insults about actors applied to this specific actor-master, or *actor-manager*. Greene repeats this point in the final paragraph.

> ... and when they [actors] soothe you with terms of <u>Mastership</u>, remember Robert Greene, whom they have often so flattered, perishes now for want of comfort ... Trust not then (I beseech ye) to such weak stays: for they are as changeable in mind, as in many attires.

Besides blaming the Upstart Crow for his misery and impending death, Greene was urging his writer friends not to work for him. It is implied then that some or all of them were already doing so. Greene wrote that the Upstart Crow was "beautified with our feathers" – "our" could include the beautiful lines of Greene and the writers he was addressing. Greene's description of the Upstart Crow must have been enough for his friends to know exactly who was meant – otherwise, what would be the point of the warning? Greene was making serious accusations about the Upstart Crow, so he had to be discreet – *it is very unlikely, therefore, that he would have supplied even one syllable of the Upstart Crow's real name or would have parodied a line that he had written.*

Upstart Crow-Player-Ant

Robert Greene's revelation about the Upstart Crow actor being his employer is further supported only a few pages before the letter to his writer friends. Greene's character, Roberto, is a down-on-his-luck scholar who encounters a surprisingly well-dressed "Player" who tells him that he will "be well paid" for "making plays." The Player admits to humble origins, then brags about the £200 worth of playing apparel he owns and that he is wealthy enough to "build a windmill" at his own expense. The Player practically defines the word upstart – one who has newly or suddenly risen in position or importance" and "a parvenu" (OED). The Player also brags that he "thunder'd on the stage," and that he wrote morality plays and dialogue for puppets. Similarly, the Upstart Crow is an actor-writer who "in his own conceit" considers himself the best scene-shaker or stealer ("Shake-scene"), and was Greene's "master" or boss. Greene's "Player" of the previous pages and the "upstart Crow," also called "Player" ("Tiger's heart wrapp'd in a Player's hide"), are one and the same. The Shakespeare professor consistently fails to link the two probably because the Player was Roberto's employer.

Immediately following Greene's letter to his friends was his version of the parable, "The Ant and the Grasshopper," which he applied to his own situation. The pleasure-seeking Grasshopper chastised the Ant for his labors and his thrift. When winter storms came, the Grasshopper "went for succor to the Ant his old acquaintance," who turned him out. "Foodless, helpless and strengthless," the Grasshopper "died comfortless without remedy. Like him, like myself." There is no question that the Player, the Upstart Crow, and the Ant represented one person, who in composite can be described as follows: a successful actor who once was a humble country player; a former writer of puppet shows and morality plays who was now writing plays, some with stolen ideas from Greene; an employer of playwrights (including Greene). He is a bombastic actor ("bombast out a blank verse") who dominates scenes ("Shake-scene"), had forsaken Greene (like the Ant forsook the Grasshopper), and was so heartless that Greene blamed him for "perishing." He is well dressed and rich, and is a jack-of-all-trades ("Johannes factotum"). The Upstart Crow-Player-Ant is not newly arrived on the literary scene – the Shakespeare professor's interpretation – he is newly rich and in a position of power.

Robert Greene's insulting picture of the Upstart Crow-Player-Ant and warning about his devious character makes it unlikely that Greene would make an obvious pun upon this person's real name. To accept this reasoning is to accept that the Upstart Crow was not Shakespeare.

> ... and being an absolute *Johannes factotum*, is in his own conceit the only Shake-scene in a country.

But Greene was definitely punning upon the name "Shakespeare" with "Shake-scene" because of the usage of Shakespeare's "tiger's heart" line. The word "only" in "the only Shake-scene in a country" implies that there was another "Shake-scene," the original one – otherwise the Upstart Crow would not fancifully single himself out as one ("in his own conceit"). It is implied that there was another Shake-scene, one whose reputation was well established before the Upstart Crow started writing dramas. This original, of course, was Shakespeare, so Greene's Upstart Crow conceitedly thought of himself as *another* Shakespeare – that is, the writer – in 1592. As explained in Chapter 3, Thomas Nashe's reference to "English Seneca" and "whole *Hamlets*" in *Menaphon* is evidence that Shakespeare's *Hamlet* had already been written by 1589. *Hamlet* was one of Shakespeare's masterpieces, so he was hardly a new and upcoming writer in 1592. Greene's Upstart Crow was not Shakespeare, he just fancied himself another great writer or scene-shaker – one who could "shake a stage" with terrific plays, as Ben Jonson praised the great author in the First Folio. But Greene also used the word "Shake-scene" literally, which further ties the Upstart Crow with Roberto's employer, the Player, who said he "thunder'd on the stage." Besides "jack of all trades," "Johannes facto-tum" can mean "a person of boundless conceit who thinks himself able to do anything however much beyond the reach of real abilities" (OED). Greene's Upstart Crow conceitedly thought of himself as good a writer as Greene and his friends, and even supposed himself another Shakespeare.

The Stratford Man was not the Upstart Crow. There is no evidence that he was an actor in 1592, and no evidence that he employed Greene or anyone else to write plays at this time. There is no evidence that Greene bore a grudge against the Stratford Man to inspire such a cruel portrayal, or evidence that the Stratford Man bore a grudge against Greene to reject his appeal for help. To discover the Upstart Crow's true identity, one must simply ask, who employed Greene in 1592?

The Real Upstart Crow: Edward Alleyn (1566-1626)

Actor Edward Alleyn's case as the identity behind Robert Greene's Upstart Crow-Player-Ant is strongly supported by his biography and contemporary remarks. The Upstart Crow had to be an actor-manager, one in a superior position to employ writers. Greene's plays, *Friar Bacon and Friar Bungay*, and *Orlando Furioso*, were performed by the Lord Strange's Men, one of the act-ing companies with which Alleyn performed; there were four performances at the Rose Theater from February to May 1592. That year, Alleyn and his com-pany had joined forces with the owner of the Rose Theater, Philip Henslowe (Alleyn also married Henslowe's stepdaughter that year). The DNB noted that "it would appear that he and Alleyn ran the theatre as a shared partnership." This would mean that actor Alleyn was also a theater boss in 1592. But Alleyn was already deeply involved in the business side of acting by January 1589, when he and his brother, also an actor, purchased "playing apparel, play-books, instruments, and other commodities."[1] Presumably they were invest-ing in their company, the Lord Admiral's Men. Alleyn was already a leading actor of this company by circa 1587, when he performed with them the title role of *Tamburlaine the Great* by Christopher Marlowe. It was an enormous success.

By 1592, the year *Groats-worth* was written, Alleyn was wealthy, famous, a box-office draw, and in a position of power. He was such a superstar that the title page of *A Knack to Know a Knave* (a play performed in 1592 but first pub-lished in 1594) included the unprecedented phrase, "as it hath sundry times been played by ED. ALLEN and his Company." Neither the acting company, nor author of the play, was named. Fourteen performances of "harry the vi." by the Lord Strange's Men were recorded during the first half of 1592.[2] Part three of Shakespeare's *Henry VI* contained the famous "tiger's heart" line; it is possible, therefore, that Alleyn had played the Duke of York's role and recited this very line. Although unnamed, the three playwright friends Greene addressed in his letter are usually identified today as Christopher Marlowe, George Peele, and Thomas Nashe. Marlowe and Peele wrote plays for Alleyn's company before *Groats-worth* – so Greene's warning to them, "whilst you may, seek you better Masters," was especially suggestive of Alleyn.

The Upstart Crow actor also wrote plays, and Greene, by implication, had accused him of stealing his play ideas. A.D. Wraight, who believed that Alleyn was the Upstart Crow, gave evidence that he wrote plays. He was paid for *Tambercam*, as noted in Henslowe's diary, and received payments for ten other plays.[3] Most believe that Alleyn was the agent to pay the writers of these now lost plays, but as none of the titles were ever attributed to anyone else, Alleyn's authorship cannot be dismissed. Other actors wrote plays, so it is not unlikely that he did so too. At least one scholar has noted the similarity of plot between the anonymous play, *Fair Em: the Miller's Daughter of Manchester*, and Greene's play, *Friar Bacon and Friar Bungay*. Greene specifically insulted *Fair Em*'s author in the preface to his book, *Farewell to Folly*, printed in 1591, the year before he died:

> And he that cannot write true English without the help of Clerks of parish Churches, will needs make himself the father of interludes. O 'tis a jolly matter when a man hath a familiar style and can indite [write] a whole year and never be beholding to art? but to bring Scripture to prove anything he says, and kill it dead with the text in a trifling subject of love, I tell you is no small piece of cunning. As for example two lovers on the stage arguing one another of unkindness, his Mistress runs over him with this canonical sentence, "A man's conscience is a thousand witnesses," and her knight again excuseth himself with that saying of the Apostle, "Love covereth the multitude of sins." I think this was but simple abusing of the Scripture. [quotation marks added]

Greene's two quotations were paraphrased lines from *Fair Em*.[4] Greene called these lines "blasphemous rhetoric" and their writer a "dunce" and a "witless cockscomb." Wraight argued that Alleyn wrote *Fair Em*, and that Greene revealed this in *Groats-worth*: the Player told Roberto he could build a windmill, which is the setting for one scene in *Fair Em*.[5] Greene had also put down *Tamburlaine the Great* in the same preface, referring to the recently printed version as "unsavory papers"; Tamburlaine was Alleyn's most famous role, another indication that he was targeted.[6] Some "men" stole Greene's material, wrote R.B. in *Greene's Funerals* (1594):

> Nay more the men, that so Eclips'd his fame:
> Purloined his Plumes, can they deny the same?   [Sonnet 9, lines 5-6]

Alleyn and Bombast

Greene's Upstart Crow was a bombastic actor ("supposes he is as well able to bombast out a blank verse as the best of you"), and Edward Alleyn was an actor of bombastic roles. Bombast is "inflated or turgid language" (*OED*). Such was the signature style of Christopher Marlowe, and his *Tamburlaine the Great* could be called the epitome of bombastic plays; Alleyn, as noted above, was its star. Alleyn and Marlowe teamed up to produce a sequel soon after its debut, and they continued to produce similar plays that focused upon one egocentric, larger-than-life character, like *Dr. Faustus* and *The Jew of Malta*. Tamburlaine was a shepherd who transforms himself into a lusty, boasting conqueror bent on world domination. In the excerpts below, Tamburlaine has just captured the Turkish emperor, Bajazet, and has put him in a cage. Referring to Bajazet, he then tells a servant, "Bring out my footstool." Bajazet implores his god to poison Tamburlaine, who responds:

> TAMBURLAINE
> ... But villain! thou that wishest this to me,
> Fall prostrate on the low disdainful earth,
> And be the footstool of great Tamburlaine,
> That I may rise to my royal throne.
>
> BAJAZET
> First shalt thou rip my bowels with thy sword,
> And sacrifice my soul to death and hell,
> Before I yield to such slavery.
>
> TAMBURLAINE
> Base villain, vassal, slave to Tamburlaine!
> Unworthy to embrace or touch the ground,
> That bears the honor of my royal weight;
> Stoop, villain, stoop! – Stoop! for so he bids
> That may command thee piecemeal to be torn,
> Or scattered like the lofty cedar trees
> Struck with the voice of thundering Jupiter.
>
> BAJAZET
> When as I look down to the damned fiends,
> Fiends look on me; and thou dread god of hell
> With ebon scepter strike this hateful earth,

And make it swallow both of us at once.
[*Tamburlaine the Great-Part 1*, 4.2]

In *Tamburlaine*'s sequel, the title character has conquered more Middle Eastern kings. In Act 4, Scene 4 he uses them to draw his chariot, "with bits in their mouths." Tamburlaine shouts these lines at them:

Holla, ye pampered Jades of Asia!
What, can ye draw but twenty miles a day,
And have so proud a chariot at your heels,
And such a Coachman as great Tamburlaine ...

Shakespeare parodied these lines in the mouth of Pistol in *Henry IV-Part 2* (2.4.178):

Shall packhorses,
And hollow pamper'd jades of Asia,
Which cannot go but thirty mile a day,
Compare with Caesars, and with Cannibals,
And Trojan Greeks?

"The pervading sins of Tamburlaine," wrote the 19th century critic, Francis Cunningham,

are so glaring and manifest that he who travels express may read them, but there can be no doubt that it was by virtue of these sins that the plays became so marvelously popular. The bombast and ranting which so grate upon our ears or provoke us to laughter, were in the days of Elizabeth absolutely essential to the conventional idea of an Oriental conqueror.[7]

Marlowe's bombastic language in *Tamburlaine* can be excused, wrote Cunningham, because it was a stereotypical portrayal of an "Oriental conqueror." This may have been partly true, but some of Marlowe's fellow writers panned the play. Thomas Nashe wrote a letter in the preface of Robert Greene's *Menaphon* in which he praised Greene and complained about writers who were imitating the popular bombastic plays, i.e., *Tamburlaine*.[8] But Nashe placed the greatest blame for this trend upon the writers' "idiot art-masters," those who paid them.

But herein I cannot so fully bequeath them [writers] to folly, as their idiot art-masters, that intrude themselves to our ears as the alchemists of eloquence; who (mounted on the stage of arrogance) think to outbrave better pens with the swelling bombast of a bragging blank verse.

Nashe also described the art-masters as actors ("mounted on the stage of arro-gance"). Nashe said that writers were tailoring their works with bombastic verses to please the actor-masters. He characterized this writing as "drum-ming decasyllabon" ("verse that calls attention to itself and panders to the groundlings," says O.B. Hardison, Jr.).[9] The biggest promoter of bombas-tic plays during this period was actor Edward Alleyn – he even later called himself "the fustian king."[10] The similarity of Nashe's line, "swelling bom-bast of a bragging blank verse," and Greene's "bombast out a blank verse" in *Groats-worth*, and the fact that both were describing an actor-master suggests they were blasting the same person, i.e., Alleyn. The wording was so close to Greene's lines in *Groats-worth* that it is no wonder that Nashe was accused of penning *Groats-worth* soon after its release. Thomas Brabine repeated Nashe's sentiments in *Menaphon* in the same preface:

> Come forth you wits [writers] that vaunt the pomp of speech,
> And strive to thunder from a Stage-man's throat:
> View *Menaphon* a note beyond your reach;
> Whose sight will make your drumming descant dote:
> Players avaunt [away], you know not to delight;
> Welcome sweet Shepherd [Greene]; worth a Scholar's sight.

To paraphrase Brabine: "Players, go away! Stop encouraging writers to com-pose loud, pompous, speech for you." Brabine anticipates Greene's Player in *Groats-worth*, who once "thundered on the stage," with the line, "and strive to thunder from a Stage-Man's throat."

Alleyn and Greene

In June 1592, Alleyn and his company took a country tour while the plague was infecting London. At this point, Greene had supplied Alleyn's company with at least two plays that were repeatedly performed. Greene made it very plain in the Ant and the Grasshopper parable that he had asked someone, the Ant, for help, and that he was rejected, which left Grasshopper-Greene "foodless, helpless and strengthless." Greene died in September 1592. Note that Ant and Alleyn share the same initial just like Grasshopper and Greene, perhaps identity clues. Writer Gabriel Harvey referred to Greene as "grass-hopper" in print soon after Greene's death.[11] If Alleyn was the Upstart Crow-Ant, then why did he refuse to help Greene? One reason could be Greene's double dealing. Greene first sold his play, *Orlando Furioso*, to the Queen's Men, and sold it again to Alleyn's company circa 1591-92. The repercussion of the double sale is not known, but Alleyn did play the title role in February 1592 (an original manuscript survives, now at Dulwich College, of Orlando's role with Alleyn's annotations). Jay Hoster, who also believed that Alleyn was the Upstart Crow, surmised that the double sale of *Orlando Furioso* had caused the rift between Alleyn and Greene.[12]

Greene, however, was guilty of other offenses against Alleyn. Before *Groats-worth*, Greene had slammed Alleyn and *Tamburlaine*, his most famous play, at least four times in print. As noted above, Greene referred to the printed edition of *Tamburlaine* as "unsavory papers" and had insulted the writer of *Fair Em*, who was quite possibly Alleyn. Greene belittled *Tamburlaine* in *Perimedes the Blacksmith* (1588); he paraphrased Marlowe's line, "his looks do menace heaven and dare the gods" (1.2):

> I have had it in derision for that I could not make my verses jet upon the stage in tragical buskins, every word filling the mouth like the faburden [legend] of Bow Bell, daring God out of heaven with that atheist Tamburlan.

The "verses" that Greene could not make "jet upon the stage" were probably those he wrote in *Alphonsus, King of Aragon* (c. 1587), a play that tried to rival *Tamburlaine*, but apparently had failed at the box office. Greene took a shot at Alleyn in his *Never Too Late* (1590). Writer-orator Cicero censures actor Roscius for his mistaken conceit: that the applause an actor gets from his audience is really a reaction to good writing.

> Why Roscius, art thou proud with Aesop's Crow, being prank'd with the glory of others feathers? of thyself thou canst say nothing, and if the Cobbler hath taught thee to say *Ave Caesar*, disdain not thy tutor, because thou pratest in a King's chamber: what sentence thou utterest on the stage, flows from the censure of our wits, and what sentence or conceit of the invention the people applaud for excellent, that comes from the secrets of our knowledge. I grant your action, though it be a kind of mechanical labor; yet well done 'tis worthy of praise: but you worthless, if for so small a toy you wax proud.

The "Cobbler" in this quote was Marlowe, who was the son of a shoemaker. Actor Roscius would then be Edward Alleyn – it was the "glory" of Marlowe's dramas, especially *Tamburlaine*, which had catapulted him to stardom. Greene was reminding Alleyn that his success was owed to Marlowe, but he granted him that his "action" on stage was "worthy of praise." Alleyn was especially noted for his action on stage. Thomas Nashe wrote that he outdid the historical Roscius "in action": "Not Roscius nor *Aesop,* those Tragedians admired before Christ was born, could ever perform more in action than famous *Ned Allen*."[13] Greene's "Aesop's Crow," who wore the feathers of other birds, strutting them proudly as if his own, is reminiscent of Greene's "upstart Crow, beautified with our feathers" in *Groats-worth*. In both cases,

Greene was evidently alluding to Alleyn. Greene's history of mocking Alleyn and *Tamburlaine* in print, and his double-dealing, was perhaps just cause for Alleyn to reject Greene in his time of need. Greene retaliated with his most detailed, and final, attack in *Groats-worth*.

The Upstart Crow and Alleyn in Contemporary Literature

In his early days, the Upstart Crow-Player said he was a poor country actor who carried his "playing fardel a footback," meaning he traveled by foot, carrying his acting material. He described some of his roles:

> I am as famous for <u>Delphrigus</u>, and the <u>King of the Fairies</u>, as ever was any of my time. The twelve labors of Hercules have I terribly thundered on the stage, and played three scenes of <u>the devil</u> in the Highway to Heaven …

As a teenager, Alleyn was a member of the Earl of Worcester's Men, a playing company that primarily toured the country. The Upstart Crow-Player was also a "country author":

> I can serve to make a pretty speech, for I was a <u>country author</u>, passing at a moral, for 'twas I that penned the Moral of man's wit, and the Dialogue of <u>Dives</u> and for seven years space was absolute Interpreter to the puppets.

Thomas Nashe used similar words in his prefatory letter in Greene's *Menaphon* (1589). Nashe mentioned country actors who "carried their fardels on footback," "the King of Fairies," and "Delphrigus."

> Sundry other sweet Gentlemen I know that have vaunted their pens in private devices, and tricked up a company of taffeta fools <u>with their feathers</u>, whose beauty if our Poets had not peaked with the supply of their periwigs, they might have anticked it [played clowns] until this time up and down the <u>country</u> with the <u>King of Fairies</u>, and dined every day at the pease porridge ordinaire [a cheap inn] with <u>Delphrigus</u>. But Tolosa [Toulouse] hath forgot that it was sometime sacked, and beggars that ever they carried their <u>fardels on footback</u>:

Nashe said that poets (which would include Greene) have "tricked up" the play material of acting companies; without the writer's beautiful "feathers" – their writing – the players would be clowns touring the country and staying at cheap inns. Nashe's letter had also put down "idiot art masters" who encouraged bombastic writing. Greene's Upstart Crow-Player, a country actor who played Delphrigus and the King of Fairies and who once carried his "playing fardel a footback," and Nashe's country actors who forgot they once "carried their fardels on footback" and who might have played the same roles were clearly describing the same person with a similar story. Nashe's passage continues with the mention of a certain actor, "Roscius," which many commentators believe alluded to Alleyn.

> ... fardels on footback: and in truth no marvel, when as the <u>deserved reputation of one Roscius</u>, is of force to enrich a rabble of counterfeits [writers imitating the fashion of bombastic plays]; yet let subjects [the writers] for all their insolence, dedicate a *De profundis* every morning to the preservation of <u>their Caesar</u> [Roscius], lest their increasing indignities return them ere long to their juggling to mediocrity, and they bewail in weeping blanks the wane of their Monarchy.

Roscius-Alleyn "enriches" the writers of bombastic plays, and they pray for "the preservation of their Caesar," i.e., Roscius-Alleyn. Referring to Alleyn as a Caesar, a leader, means that he was paying writers for bombastic-style plays as early as 1589. These writers "have made Art bankrupt of her ornaments," wrote Nashe; but despite his contempt for this type of writing, he said that Alleyn's reputation for good acting was "deserved."

The allusion to actors who once carried "fardels on footback" appeared again in the play, *The Return from Parnassus-Part 2* (ca. 1601-02), in lines that had unmistakably ridiculed Alleyn. In the passage below, scholars Studioso and Philomusos have abandoned their writing careers, thinking it better to become fiddlers than be in the pay of "glorious vagabonds," i.e., the actors.

STUDIOSO
Better it is 'mongst fiddlers to be chief,
Than at [a] player's trencher [wooden plate] beg relief.
But is't not strange these mimic apes [actors] should prize
Unhappy Scholars at a hireling rate?
Vile world, that lifts them up to high degree,
And treads us down in groveling misery.
England affords those glorious vagabonds,
That carried erst [once] their <u>fardels on their backs</u>,
Coursers [horses] to ride on through the gazing streets,
Sooping [sweeping] it in their glaring Satin suits,
And Pages to attend their masterships:
With mouthing words that better wits have framed
They purchase lands, and now Esquires are named.

PHILOMUSOS
Whate'er they seem being even at the best,
They are but sporting <u>fortune's</u> scornful jest.

STUDIOSO
So merry <u>fortune's</u> wont [apt] from rags to take
Some ragged groom, and him a gallant make.

PHILOMUSOS
The world and <u>fortune's</u> play'd on us [scholar-poets] too long.

STUDIOSO
Now to the world we fiddle must a song. [lines 1916-1934]

The puffed-up actors wear expensive clothes, have servants, and purchase land while they pay scholars a pittance to write plays for them. The final few lines of this passage repeated the word "fortune," a direct allusion to Alleyn and the theater he had recently built named The Fortune. He also had a large share in the Bear Garden (where bear-baiting took place), and was a wealthy landowner. The Player in *Groats-worth* had boasted he could build a windmill. Another allusion to Alleyn in *Parnassus* connects him with the Upstart Crow-Player in *Groats-worth*. The poor scholar-poet Ingenioso says,

It's fine when that Puppet-player *Fortune* must put such a Birchen-lane post in so good a suit, such an Ass in so good a fortune.
[lines 1687-89]

The Upstart Crow, as the Player, said he wrote for puppet shows. The two instances of "fortune" alluded to Alleyn's theater.

The play, *Histrio-mastix, or the Player Whipp'd*, which included a satire on actors, dropped similar clues about Edward Alleyn that also identifies him as Greene's Upstart Crow-Player. Written circa 1589 (see Chapter 3), a main character is Post-Haste, the actor-manager of Sir Oliver Owlet's players. Post-Haste fancies himself as a poet who can perform "extempore"– a word he says twice in the play. His comedy is titled, *The Devil and Dives*, which is described by a lord in the audience as having "most ugly lines," and is "lame stuff indeed." This portrait of an actor-manager who brags about his ability to perform "extempore" and who wrote *The Devil and Dives* specifically describes the Player of *Groats-worth* who "penned" the "Dialogue of Dives," played the devil in another play, and spoke in "plain rhyme extempore" which was so bad that Roberto cut him off. When Sir Oliver Owlet's players are forced into the army, a soldier's remark implies that Post-Haste is Alleyn. Commenting upon how slowly the actors march, the soldier says to one of them, presumably Post-Haste, that he cannot believe that one who once "would rend and tear the Cat /Upon a Stage" marches now "like a drown'd rat." He tells him to "look up and play the *Tamburlaine*, you rogue you" (Act 5, lines 241-43).

Several contemporary references to *Tamburlaine* indicate that Alleyn, who was very tall, acted the title role with gusto and noise, apropos to a scene-shaker or "Shake-scene." Three examples:

> Rampum scrampum, mount tufty Tamburlaine! What rattling thunderclap breaks from his lips?
> [John Marston, *Antonio and Mellida*, 1599, Induction]

> Dost stamp, mad Tamburlaine, dost stamp? Thou thinkst thou hast mortar under thy feet, dost? [T. Dekker, *Satiro-mastix*, 1601, 4.2.210]

> [Re men that "speak all they can"]: And though his language differ from the vulgar somewhat, it shall not fly from all humanity, with the Tamer-lanes, and Tamer-chams of the late age, which had nothing in them but the scenical strutting, and furious vociferation, to warrant them to the ignorant gapers.
> [Ben Jonson, *Timber: or Discoveries*, 1641, p. 100]

Elizabethans considered Tamburlaine as synonymous with "noise and violence," wrote Andrew Gurr.[14] One notable example described "Turkish *Tamburlaine*" on stage:

> The stalking steps of his great personage,
> Graced with huff-cap [blustering] terms, and thund'ring threats,
> That his poor hearers' hair quite upright sets.
> Such soon, as some brave-minded hungry youth,
> Sees fitly frame to his wide-strained mouth,
> He vaunts his voice upon an hired stage,
> With high-set steps, and princely carriage:
> Now sooping inside robes of Royalty,
> That erst [once] did scrub in lousy brokery.
> There if he can with terms Italianate,
> Big-sounding sentences, and words of state,
> Fair patch me up his pure *Iambic* verse,
> He ravishes the gazing Scaffolders:
> [Joseph Hall, *Virgidemiarum*, 1597, lines 8-20]

Rend and tear the cat, rattling thunderclap, stamping, stalking steps, scenical strutting and furious vociferation, thundering threats, high-set steps, etc., all describe how *Tamburlaine* was acted, thus Alleyn's acting style. Through the mouth of Hamlet, Shakespeare was evidently denigrating it:

> Speak the speech I pray you as I pronounc'd it to you, trippingly on the tongue, but if you mouth it as many of our Players do, I had as lief [soon] the town crier spoke my lines, nor do not saw the air too much with your hand thus, but use all gently, for in the very torrent tempest, and as I may say, whirlwind of your passion, you must

> acquire and beget a temperance, that may give it smoothness, O, it
> offends me to the soul, to hear a robustious periwig-pated fellow [a
> wigged actor] tear a passion to tatters, to very rags, to split the ears
> of the groundlings ...
>
> O, there be Players that I have seen play, and heard others prais'd,
> and that highly, not to speak it profanely, that neither having
> th'accent of Christians, nor the gait of Christian, Pagan, nor man,
> have so strutted & bellowed, that I have thought some of Nature's
> Journeymen had made men, and not made them well, they imi-
> tated humanity so abominably. [*Hamlet*, 3.2.1-11, 30-37]

In Thomas Middleton's story, *The Ant and the Nightingale, or Father Hub-
burd's Tales* (1604), the ant is about to relate his adventures to an audience of
other ants and a bird. Middleton describes the ant as a stalking actor:

> the ant began to stalk like a three-quarter sharer, and was not
> afraid to tell tales ...

As "stalking" was descriptive of Alleyn's acting style, it appears that Middleton had associated his ant with Alleyn, doubtless recalling the Ant in *Groats-
worth* that had refused Grasshopper-Greene's plea for help.

Alleyn in Jonson's Works

Ben Jonson also made jabs at Edward Alleyn through the character Histrio in
his play, *Poetaster* (1601). Histrio ("actor" in Latin) passes by Captain Tucca,
who calls him back for insults with another "stalking" reference.

> ... do you hear, you <u>player</u>, rogue, <u>stalker</u>, come back here; no
> respect to men of worship, you slave! what, you are proud, you ras-
> cal, are you proud, ha? you grow rich, do you, and purchase, you
> two-penny <u>tear-mouth</u>? you have <u>FORTUNE</u> ...
>
> come, we must have you turn fiddler again, slave, get a base viol at
> your back, and march in a tawny coat, with one sleeve, to Goose-
> fair ...
>
> what, do you laugh, <u>owlglass</u>! [jester or buffoon] [3.1]

Jonson's Histrio is a "stalking" actor and sometime musician who is now rich
and proud. Actor Alleyn was rich, a musician, and owned the Fortune Theater. Captain Tucca tells Histrio to "cherish" the poetaster, Crispinus, who is
standing next to him.

> Go, he pens high, lofty, in a new stalking strain, bigger than half

the rhymers in the town again: he was born to fill thy mouth, Mino-
taurus, he was, he will teach thee to tear and rand. Rascal, to him,
cherish his muse, go …

Although scholars usually associate Crispinus with John Marston, Captain
Tucca's description of a writer who "pens high, lofty, in a new stalking strain"
particularly applied to Christopher Marlowe (then deceased), whom Alleyn
certainly cherished.

> … he shall write for thee, slave! If he pen for thee once, thou shalt
> not need to travel <u>with thy pumps full of gravel</u> any more, after a
> blind <u>jade and a hamper</u>, and stalk upon boards and barrel heads
> to an old crack'd trumpet. [3.1]

Jonson's phrase, "jade and a hamper," parodied Marlowe's famous line in
Tamburlaine, "Holla, ye pampered jades of Asia!" Jonson also associated
Alleyn with Post-Haste in *Histrio-mastix*. Besides the character's name being
Histrio, the phrase, "pumps full of gravel," echoes the line in the players'
song, "Besides we that travel, with pumps full of gravel…" (Act 2, line 251).
"Owlglass" suggests Post-Haste's acting company, Sir Oliver Owlet's Men.
Captain Tucca said that Histrio was accused of being a usurer and a pimp.
Alleyn was a moneylender, and some of the buildings he owned were for-
merly used as brothels.[15]

Jonson's later epigram, "On Poet-Ape," very much describes Greene's
Upstart Crow-Player. "Ape" is another word for actor. The actor also writes
("poet"), but Jonson has little regard for his writing, calling it "the frippery
of wit." Poet-Ape could also mean one who "apes" poets, implying he really
is not one, like "poetaster." The Poet-Ape is also a "bold thief" of writers'
works, he "makes each man's wit his own"; Greene implied that the Upstart
Crow stole ideas for his plays. The Poet-Ape, like the Upstart Crow-Player,
"brokered" or bought plays, and is wealthy.

> Poor Poet-Ape, that would be thought our chief,
> Whose works are ev'n the frippery of wit,
> From brokage [brokerage] is become so <u>bold a thief</u>
> As we, the robbed, leave rage, and pity it.
> At first he made low shifts, would pick and glean,
> Buy the reversion of old plays; now grown
> To a little wealth and credit in the scene,
> He takes up all, <u>makes each man's wit his own</u>;
> And, told of this, he slights it: Tut, such crimes
> The sluggish <u>gaping auditor</u> devours;
> He marks not whose 'twas first; and after-times
> May judge it to be his as well as ours.
> Fool, as if half-eyes will not know a fleece

From locks of wool, or shreds from the whole piece!
[*Epigrams*, No. 56, 1616]

Jonson's line about the "sluggish gaping auditor," the Poet-Ape's audience, resembles the description of *Tamburlaine*'s audience of "ignorant gapers" that he wrote about in his *Discoveries* (see previous excerpt). Jonson's epigram contained words of clothing – "frippery" (used clothing shop), "fleece," and "locks of wool." At least four records (dated 1589 to 1591) show that Alleyn purchased playing apparel, some of it used.[16] The Upstart Crow-Player bragged that he owned £200 worth of play clothes.

Conclusion

It is pure speculation that the "upstart" actor-writer ridiculed by Robert Greene in his *Groats-worth of Wit* was the Stratford Man, i.e., the professor's Shakespeare. But there is ample evidence in biography and in several contemporary allusions that the Upstart Crow was the successful and nouveau riche actor, Edward Alleyn. The character Roberto, Greene's real-life counterpart, had encountered a player in the story only pages before Greene's letter warning his friends against the Upstart Crow; this player employed him to write plays. In real life, actor Alleyn's company paid Greene for plays. Greene described the Upstart Crow in savage terms, likening him to the cold-hearted Queen Margaret, indifferent to the murder of an innocent teenager (the Shakespeare phrase). It is fact that Greene was ill and living in abject poverty at the time that Alleyn's company had left London for a country tour. As Alleyn was the "actor-master" of the playing company that employed Greene, it is not unlikely that Greene had appealed to Alleyn for a loan or help before his tour and was rejected, leaving him alone to "perish." Greene implied this in the parable of the Ant and the Grasshopper: Ant-Alleyn refused to save Grasshopper-Greene in a time of crisis. Besides blaming him for his coming death, Greene accused the Upstart Crow of stealing his ideas for plays and using them in his own. There is evidence that suggests Alleyn also wrote plays. It was Greene's "dying request" to have *Groats-worth* published – probably to avenge himself of Alleyn.

Greene's plain testimony that the Upstart Crow was Greene's "master" or boss, also related in the main story (the Player employed Roberto), instantly disqualifies the Stratford Man as the Upstart Crow. Greene's usage of the word bombast specifically ties the Upstart Crow to Alleyn, who acted in several of Christopher Marlowe's bombastic plays. The title character of Marlowe's play, *Tamburlaine*, was Alleyn's most celebrated role. "Shake-scene" describes Alleyn's loud, stalking and stamping acting style. Greene's constant put down of Alleyn and *Tamburlaine* in print before *Groats-worth* is all the more reason to believe that Alleyn was the Upstart Crow. Greene's passage in *Groats-worth* also indirectly gave information about Shakespeare. If Alleyn regarded himself as another "Shake-scene," then Shakespeare, the original "Shake-scene," was already a well-established playwright in 1592 – he was not a neophyte.

The Upstart Crow was not the Stratford Man, and not Shakespeare, but was the upstart actor, Edward Alleyn. The loss of this crucial point in the Stratford Man's biography delays the first evidence of his theater involvement to 1595, with the treasurer's payment; the Stratford Man was then 30 years old. The Shakespeare professor's contortion of Greene's lines to suit the Stratford Man does not stop with Greene. He does the same thing with Henry Chettle's lines in his *Kind-heart's Dream*, as explained in the next chapter.

CHAPTER 7

Upstart Crow Uproar, and a Few Hostile Witnesses

ACTOR EDWARD ALLEYN as the real Upstart Crow in Robert Greene's *Groats-worth of Wit* – not Shakespeare – completely ruins the foundation of the professor's invented early theatrical career for the Stratford Man. Greene's attack on the Upstart Crow in *Groats-worth* had evidently caused an uproar, forcing its editor, Henry Chettle, to make a public apology. This apology, which included complimentary remarks to the Upstart Crow, therefore, was not meant for Shakespeare or the Stratford Man, but for Edward Alleyn. Chettle placed the apology in the preface to his novel, *Kind-heart's Dream*, three months after *Groats-worth*'s release. He also included a strong denial that either he or Thomas Nashe had actually penned the work. This reaction confirms that the Upstart Crow had to have been someone powerful enough at the time to inspire the apology and denials. But there were other negative reactions to Greene's work. Chettle wrote in *Kind-heart*'s preface that "one or two" of the playwright friends Greene had addressed in his advice letter were offended by it and had tried to put the blame upon him for its contents. Christopher Marlowe, George Peele, and Thomas Nashe are usually identified as the writers addressed in Greene's letter. Chettle claimed that he was not acquainted with the offended writers, one of whom he cared never to be. In the same line, he mentioned "the other," someone with whom he was acquainted and to whom he wished to apologize, defend and praise as an honest, upright dealer and a gracefully amusing writer. Greene made these points in the reverse sense in his attack of the Upstart Crow. Chettle's "the other," therefore, must have been Edward Alleyn.

> With neither of them that take offense was I acquainted, and with one of them I care not if I never be: <u>The other</u>, whom at that time I did not so much spare, as since I wish I had ...
>
> that I did not, I am as sorry, as if the original fault had been my fault, because myself have seen his demeanor no less civil than he excellent in <u>the quality he professes</u>: Besides, <u>diverse of worship</u> [titled

> people] have reported, his uprightness of dealing, which argues his
> honesty, and his facetious [amusing] grace in writing, that approves
> [proves] his Art.   [Preface, *Kind-heart's Dream* by Henry Chettle]

"Quality" was a word often used to describe the acting profession. Greene's
portrait of Alleyn must have been so obvious and damaging that Chettle
as the editor of *Groats-worth* was compelled to explain himself. The reason
why "one or two" playwrights were offended by Greene's letter then becomes
plain: two of them, Marlowe and Peele, had been writing for Alleyn's company, and probably feared recrimination. They would not have wanted powerful Alleyn to think they had sympathized with Greene or would follow his
advice. Marlowe would have been especially offended by Greene's remark
that he was an atheist, and this allegation against Marlowe may have been the
reason Chettle did not care to meet him (the following year, Marlowe was
interrogated on several charges, including atheism). The third writer, Nashe,
by implication was not offended by Greene's words, most likely because he
agreed with his opinion of Upstart Crow-Alleyn. Nashe, in his preface to
Greene's *Menaphon*, had attacked "idiot art masters" like Alleyn who were
making "Art bankrupt of her ornaments." These previously published statements may be the reason why Nashe was accused of writing *Groats-worth*,
but he immediately took action to counter this charge. In the second issue of
Pierce Penniless, Nashe inserted lines in his letter to the printer denying his
authorship of *Groats-worth*, calling the work "a scald trivial lying pamphlet."

> Other news I am advertised of, that a scald trivial lying pamphlet,
> called Greene's Groatsworth of Wit, is given out to be of my doing.
> God never have care of my soul, but utterly renounce me, if the
> least word or syllable in it proceeded from my pen, or if I were any
> way privy to the writing or printing of it.

Nashe also supplied an alibi in the same letter: "the fear of infection detained
me with my lord in the country." The plague hit London during the summer
of 1592, Robert Greene's last months alive, and the likely time he penned the
advice letter in *Groats-worth*. But at this exact time, Nashe was "detained" by
serving a "lord" in the countryside. (Fortunately for Nashe, the first issue of
Pierce Penniless contained praise of Alleyn, labeled in the margin, "The Due
Commendation of Ned Alleyn.") A few months after *Groats-worth*'s release,
Nashe published *Strange News*, in which he again complimented Alleyn in a
line about poet Edmund Spenser:

> His [Spenser's] very name (as that of Ned Allen on the common
> stage) was able to make an ill matter good.

In *Strange News*, Nashe had also replied to Gabriel Harvey's statements in *Four Letters and Certain Sonnets, Especially Touching Robert Greene* (1592) that Greene had died in poverty. Harvey, Greene's literary adversary, claimed that he had visited Greene's lodging and spoke with his landlady immediately after his death. Nashe accused Harvey of lying about Greene's destitution, an odd point of disagreement.

> For the lousy circumstance of his poverty before his death ... it cannot be but thou liest, learned Gabriel. [*Strange News*, 1592]

Nashe's evidence that Greene did not die poverty-stricken was that he owned some expensive clothing at his death. Alden Brooks theorized that Nashe wanted to give the impression that Greene did not die in penury to cover for the Upstart Crow – that he did not cause, directly or indirectly, Greene's death.[1] In his *Four Letters*, Harvey also mentioned Greene's advice letter in *Groats-worth*, and considered the Upstart Crow more honest than Greene.

> Greene, vile Greene, wouldst thou were'st half so honest, as the worst of the four whom thou upbraidest; or half so learned, as the unlearnedst of the three. Thank other for thy borrowed and filched plumes of some little italianated bravery, and what remaineth but flat impudence and gross detraction, the proper ornaments of thy sweet utterance?

Here Harvey writes that Greene was not even half as honest as the worst of the four he had "upbraided" in *Groats-worth* – the worst meaning the Upstart Crow; he also writes that Greene's learning was far less than the three writers he had addressed. Then Harvey mentions "other," the Upstart Crow. "Thank other for thy borrowed and filched plumes." Harvey here confirms that the Upstart Crow had stolen Greene's ideas, using Greene's exact imagery. Chettle also termed the Upstart Crow as "other" in the *Kind-heart*'s preface in which he had made his apology.

   Henry Chettle's title, *Kind-heart's Dream*, refers to the dream of the character, Mr. Kind-heart. He had encountered five ghosts, one of whom was Robert Greene's, and described him as follows:

> He was of singular pleasance the very supporter, and to no man's disgrace be this intended, the only Comedian of a vulgar writer in this country.

Alden Brooks observed that "comedian" in this passage is defined as a writer of comedies, as Greene was never an actor.[2] To paraphrase Chettle, Greene was the "supporter" or supplier of comedic plays for a "vulgar writer in this country." The "vulgar writer" for whom Greene wrote comedies was his employer, Edward Alleyn. Chettle says he does not mean "vulgar writer" as a "disgrace" or insult, but as a fact that Alleyn wrote entertainments specifically for simple folks. "In this country" also reflects Greene's line, "the only Shake-scene in a country." Greene's ghost also wrote a letter to "Pierce Penniless," referring to Thomas Nashe by one of his book titles. Referring to his "last labors," meaning *Groats-worth*, Greene's ghost wrote, "But for my poverty, methinks wisdom would have bridled that invective" – a specific reference to his attack on the Upstart Crow. Greene's complaint about the Upstart Crow was spurred by his poverty, not by literary jealousy, as the Shakespeare professor views it – this, of course, being the opinion of Chettle, the one who was entrusted with Greene's manuscript. Chettle knew that *Groats-worth* would be controversial: the Stationers' Register noted that the book was entered "upon the peril of Henry Chettle."[3] Chettle must have wanted to fulfill Greene's desire for revenge against Alleyn. But when *Groats-worth* offended several people, including "diverse of worship" in Alleyn's defense, Chettle had to make amends. And he probably did not expect that he and Nashe would be accused of writing *Groats-worth*. Like Nashe, Chettle was an aspiring playwright and it is likely that both feared blacklisting by Alleyn's company. Chettle explained in his apology letter that he had copied Greene's manuscript in his own hand for legibility purposes only.

> To be brief I writ it over, and as near as I could, followed the copy, only in that letter I put something out, but in the whole book not a word in, for I protest it was all *Greene's*, not mine nor *Master Nashe's*, as some unjustly have affirmed.

In the final paragraph of his letter, Chettle again clears Nashe and himself of the *Groats-worth* authorship:

> ... to purge Master *Nashe* of that he did not, as to justify what I did, and withal to confirm what *M. Greene* did:

In conclusion, it can be stated without qualification that Edward Alleyn was the Upstart Crow in Greene's *Groats-worth*, the famous and influential actor-producer of the Elizabethan-Jacobean eras. Greene's invective about Upstart Crow-Alleyn caused trouble for all involved. The work's editor, Henry Chettle, apologized to Upstart Crow-Alleyn in the prefatory letter to his novel, *Kind-heart's Dream*. Chettle wrote that he should have been more discrete about Upstart Crow-Alleyn, that he knew him to be honest, and complimented his acting and writing. Chettle also denied the charge that either he or Thomas Nashe had actually penned *Groats-worth*. Nashe immediately denounced *Groats-worth* in one work, and praised Alleyn *by name* in another work, indirectly revealing his identity as the Upstart Crow. Surely, only an important and powerful person in the theater like Alleyn would have inspired such reactions. The entire contents of the letters of Greene and Chettle are rarely analyzed or reproduced in full – only the relevant sentences are excised and interpreted in isolation. The Shakespeare professor is forced to spin and invent facts so they will agree with the Stratford Man's life, and to ignore other facts and contemporary references that do not – the *Groats-worth* and *Kind-heart* controversies are perhaps the most extreme examples.

A Few Hostile Witnesses

The Shakespeare professor has long relied upon the testimonies of Robert Greene and Henry Chettle to support his fantasy history of the Stratford Man. Yet, with only a little examination, they have proven to be hostile witnesses. But what about those people who directly knew the Stratford Man or his family and were literate? Several such witnesses are available but the experts consistently avoid them because they too would prove hostile to the Stratford Man's case as Shakespeare – none of them ever connected him with the well-known playwright. Ramon Jiménez, author of "Ten Eyewitnesses Who Saw Nothing,"[4] identified several Stratford Man eyewitnesses who left literary remains. A few of Jiménez's eyewitnesses, and his findings about them, are featured below.

William Camden (1551-1623)

Historian and antiquarian William Camden published a book about English history, language and culture titled, *Remains of a Greater Work Concerning Britain* (completed by June 1603, published 1605). Shakespeare's name appeared in Camden's list of eleven modern English poets "whom succeeding ages may justly admire" (in the chapter titled, "Poems"). Two years later, Camden printed his *Britannia* (1607), a tome in Latin describing England's counties and towns and their notable residents; it was his sixth edition, and was much enlarged and updated. In the paragraphs about Stratford-upon-Avon (p. 426), there was no mention that it was Shakespeare's hometown. In the section about Kent, however, it was written that Sir Philip Sidney, another of Camden's admired poets in *Remains*, had a home there. Camden did not mention the Stratford Man's death in his *Annals* of 1616, a work comprised of seven thousand words.[5] His death was not noted in Camden's personal diary, but the deaths of actor Richard Burbage and poet-playwright Samuel Daniel were noted (both died in 1619). Yet this was the same William Camden, who, along with William Dethick, had approved a change to the coat of arms of John Shakspere, the Stratford Man's father, in 1599. Furthermore, a complaint was directed at Camden and Dethick in 1602 for approving twenty-three coats of arms, including John Shakspere's.[6] Although Camden revered the poet, Shakespeare, researched the town of Stratford-upon-Avon, and was certainly cognizant of the Stratford Man's father, he never connected the great author with the Shaksperes of Stratford-upon-Avon.

Michael Drayton (1563-1631)

Poet and playwright Michael Drayton was born and raised in Warwickshire, the same county as the Stratford Man. He wrote plays for the London stage in the late 1590s, the same time the professor believes the Stratford Man was writing the Shakespeare plays. Like Camden, Drayton wrote a book that included histories of English counties, but in verse (*Poly-Olbion*). Drayton described men of note in these counties, but left out Shakespeare in the Warwickshire section. Other English poets, however, did warrant mention in his book, which was published in 1612, when Shakespeare's literary reputation was well established. Drayton was a patient of Dr. John Hall, the Stratford Man's son-in-law. Dr. Hall was the doctor of the wealthy Rainsford family, who lived in Clifford Chambers, only a few miles from Stratford-upon-Avon. Drayton was a friend of the Rainsfords, and during a thirty year period, was a visitor or guest at their home. Yet Drayton's only comment about Shakespeare in his considerable oeuvre was that he was a good comedian and nothing more; and he wrote it over ten years after the Stratford Man's death.

Thomas Greene (d. 1640)

Thomas Greene was the town clerk of Stratford-upon-Avon for over ten years and a London solicitor for the Stratford Corporation. He was an intimate friend of the Stratford Man and his wife, and named his two children, William and Anne, after them. Greene and his family actually lived in the Stratford Man's home for several months (1609-10). Greene mentioned his "cousin" Shakespeare in his diary and letters, but never in the context of literature or the theater. He also failed to note the Stratford Man's death in his diary. Greene was a published poet, and contributed a Shakespearean sonnet to Michael Drayton's work, *The Barons' Wars* (1603).

Dr. John Hall (1575-1635)

Dr. John Hall married the Stratford Man's daughter, Susanna, in 1607, and the couple eventually settled in Stratford-upon-Avon. Hall was educated at Cambridge University (M.A., 1597), knew the French language, and it is believed he studied medicine in Europe. Hall recorded his patients' treatments and noted their personal attributes. Hall described patient Michael Drayton as "an excellent poet." Patient Thomas Holyoak compiled a Latin-English dictionary, noted Dr. Hall. Another patient was John Trap, a schoolmaster at the Stratford-upon-Avon grammar school; Dr. Hall characterized him as remarkably pious and learned, "second to none." It is completely perplexing (even unconscionable!) that Hall had failed to scribble even one line acknowledging his father-in-law as the illustrious author in his patient records. Dr. Hall, described on the printed edition of these records as "very famous" in two counties, was apparently more famous in them than his father-in-law, the Stratford Man.

Dr. James Cooke (1614-1694)

While stationed at Stratford-upon-Avon as an army doctor in 1649, Dr. James Cooke visited Susanna Hall, the Stratford Man's daughter. Dr. Cooke had been acquainted with her late husband, Dr. Hall, and wondered if he had left behind any books or papers. Mrs. Hall showed him two books handwritten in Latin that turned out to be her husband's medical casebooks. Mrs. Hall accepted his offer to buy them. Dr. Cooke subsequently translated them into English and printed them. Ramon Jiménez wrote:

> In his introduction to the book, Cooke described his conversation with Susanna, during which neither of them referred to her supposedly famous father, nor to any books or manuscripts that might have belonged to him. In fact, from Dr. Cooke's report of the meeting, neither Susanna Shakespeare nor the Doctor himself was aware of any literary activity by the William Shakespeare who had lived in the very house they were standing in.[7]

It seems that no one other than Dr. Cooke was interested to meet the daughter of the Stratford Man, but his interest was with her husband, not with her father. Mrs. Hall was willing to sell her husband's unpublished manuscripts, but there is no record of her selling any unpublished play manuscripts supposedly written by her late father.[8] Mrs. Hall died shortly after Dr. Cooke's visit; her daughter, Elizabeth Hall (later Lady Bernard), was the last surviving descendant of the Stratford Man. She lived until 1670, and apparently no one took notice that she was the granddaughter of the great author. In 1655, Shakespeare was described as "The incomparable master of our English poetry" on the title page of *The Rape of Lucrece*, and Shakespeare's Folio was published for the third time in 1663-1664. The Stratford Man's other daughter, Judith Quiney, lived until 1662, having survived her three children. Mrs. Quiney was illiterate – how could the Stratford Man, supposedly the great author, have allowed it? Shakespeare's heroines were literate and well spoken, and he wrote that ignorance is "the curse of God" and knowledge "the wing wherewith we fly to heaven" (*Henry VI-Part 2*, 4.7.77-78). The Stratford Man's younger sister, Joan Hart, died in 1646; her son, Thomas, lived until 1661, and owned the house later known as the Shakespeare birthplace in Stratford-upon-Avon.

Fulke Greville, Lord Brooke (1554-1628)

Fulke Greville was born in Beauchamp Court, less than ten miles from Stratford-upon-Avon. Greville served on a commission that reported recusants, those who refused to attend services of the Church of England. The Stratford Man's father was one of nine recusants listed on his September 1592 report, so there is no doubt that Greville was acquainted with the "Shakspere" name in Stratford-upon-Avon. From 1606 until his death in 1628, Greville held the position of Recorder of Warwick and Stratford-upon-Avon. The recorder had legal knowledge and was appointed by the mayor and aldermen to "record" or keep aware of their court proceedings. Greville was also a poet and playwright and was personally acquainted with many writers, including Ben Jonson and George Chapman – Shakespeare's co-contributors to *Love's Martyr*. But despite Greville's involvement with literature and literati, none of his many surviving letters connect the celebrated poet and playwright Shakespeare with the Stratford Man.

Conclusion

Three more literate eyewitnesses who failed to connect the Stratford Man with the great author could be added to the list above. William Kemp, the actor who was named along with "William Shakespeare" and Richard Burbage to receive a payment for performance in 1595, published a pamphlet in 1600; it included an allusion to *Macbeth* (Appendix A, No. 87). Actor Robert Armin and "William Shakespeare" were both associated with the Lord Chamberlain's Men, and were founding members of the King's Men; a line in one of Armin's plays apparently alluded to *King Lear* (Appendix A, No. 29). George Wilkins, a writer who admired Shakespeare's *Pericles*, was deposed, along with the Stratford Man, for the Belott-Mountjoy case. None of these three writers – two of them actors with some knowledge of Shakespeare's plays – left behind memories of having known the great author.

Each of the first seven chapters of *Shakespeare Suppressed* casts serious doubt that the Stratford Man was the great author, Shakespeare. Chapter 1 demonstrated that "William Shakespeare," a famous obscure writer, was consistently absent in records where he should have been; this absence, and an often hyphenated surname descriptive of spear shaking, a well-used expression during the period, inspires the sensible conclusion that this name was someone's alias. Chapter 2 detailed the compromised condition of early Shakespeare play texts, and several occasions of stopping and seizing of presses involving Shakespeare's works, both points explainable if printers were issuing unauthorized or pirated editions. This evidence suggests that the great author was someone of high rank and influence prevented by custom to publish with his own name, and one who did not wish to broadcast his theater involvement, even with his alias, because it would be socially degrading. Chapter 3 exposed the experts' inability to specifically date or order the Shakespeare plays yet ample evidence is there to help them. For example, there are twelve "too early" allusions to Shakespeare's mature tragedy, *Hamlet*, two as early as circa 1588. Accepting them would not only upset but *explode* the orthodox dating of the complete plays. More evidence suggests that Shakespeare's plays were initially royal court entertainments in the 1560s to 1580s that were later revised and moved to the public theater. Chapter 4 revealed what has been plainly in view for all: in his sonnets and in his poem, *A Lover's Complaint*, Shakespeare gave first-person testimony that he was a nobleman-courtier. Shakespeare contributed verses to *Love's Martyr*, a political allegory about the succession, a very dangerous topic at the time of publication; it could be that his high status at court exempted him (and others) from prosecution. Poet John Heywood attested to the great author's pique at William Jaggard for the unauthorized issue of his verses in *The Passionate Pilgrim*, and for being "bold" with his name. Despite this, the great author never took legal action – a course the Stratford Man favored to resolve his issues – presumably because doing so would cause his own exposure as the person behind the alias, Shakespeare. Chapter 5 supplied the raw data of the Stratford Man's case for the Shakespeare authorship during his lifetime. All it amounts to is an association or membership with two acting companies and theater investing but *not one piece of evidence during his lifetime proves he was a writer*. Chapters 6 and 7 provided a chain of evidence about the Upstart Crow that squarely identifies him as actor Edward Alleyn, *not the Stratford Man*, thus shattering the Shakespeare professor's "rock bed" reality that he was a working actor-writer in 1592. The elimination of this point puts the Stratford Man's first documented association with the theater at 1595, when he was 30 years old. Chapter 7 spotlighted Ramon Jiménez's report of those acquainted with the Stratford Man or his family who left behind written material – none of these "eyewitnesses" even hinted that the Stratford Man was the great author. Each of these chapters can stand on its own to unravel the pretty myth of the Stratford Man, but in unison, his case crumbles to dust. The Shakespeare expert, however, did not start the idea that the Stratford Man was the great author, he merely embellished upon the disinformation and meager scraps deliberately planted in the First Folio and Shakspeare monument, the two pillars supporting the foundation of the Stratford Man myth.

PART III

The Stratford Man as Shakespeare, *Posthumous*: The Professor's Evidence

CHAPTER 8

The First Folio Fraud

ONE OF THE greatest events in literary history was the publication of *Mr William Shakespeare's Histories Comedies and Tragedies* in 1623. Today called the "First Folio," the book contained thirty-six Shakespeare plays, twenty of which had never been printed. It was reissued nine years later, and two times after that. The first sixteen pages of the Folio – the preface – are extremely important to the Shakespeare professor because they contain his best evidence for the Stratford Man as the great author, so much so that *had the First Folio never been published, few or none would have connected the great author with the Stratford Man.* These preliminary pages, therefore, merit close and careful examination – what is said and what is not said. Prior to the First Folio, the great author's person was undefined. "William Shakespeare" was only a name on title pages of his printed works or a name noted by literary critics regarding his works. This fostered the belief among some that the name was a pseudonym, and it seems that the First Folio preface tried to dispel that notion and to fill the personality void. William Shakespeare emerges in the opening pages as a person born with that name and a hint at his origins. He was a natural genius, the fellow of actors, and strictly a man of the theater. The "news" that he was dead was also given, but when or how long ago this had occurred was not given. There was no reason to suspect the book. It had all the trappings of being official: noble patronage (the earls of Pembroke and Montgomery), tributes by people who supposedly knew Shakespeare, and the author's portrait. Twenty new Shakespeare plays appeared along with sixteen previously issued ones. But there is something odd about the preface, and it is not just the strange face put forward as the great author's. Many of the statements made in the preface text are false and contradictory, and much information is left out. The main messages of the preface, as defined below, fostered the illusion that the Stratford Man was the great author, but at the same time, Ben Jonson's prefatory contributions seemed to undermine them. Readers should review the transcription of the Folio's preface in Appendix G for better understanding of the following analysis.

Messages of the Preface

"'William Shakespeare' is the author's real name, and he is a gentleman."

The enormous portrait of a man beneath the title screams to the reader this message: "William Shakespeare is not someone's pen name, he was born with that name, and is thus pictured." The size of the image was unprecedented, covering over half the large page. The large collar worn by the sitter gives the impression of an English gentleman. Even if the reader never ventured beyond the title page, these two points would get conveyed. In this official-looking book, any previously held notion that "William Shakespeare" was someone's pen name would get quashed, upon a first glance.

"William Shakespeare is dead"

After the title page, John Heminges and Henry Condell, noted as Shakespearean actors further into the preface, officially convey the news that William Shakespeare is dead. It can be described as news because only two indifferent remarks preceded it in print: Shakespeare's name was listed among other famous dead poets in a verse by John Taylor in *The Praise of Hempseed* (1620), and printer Thomas Walkley noted in his edition of Shakespeare's *Othello* (1621) that "the Author" was dead.

"Actors Heminges and Condell are Shakespeare's friends and fellows and they produced this book"

Heminges and Condell also wrote that they "collected" the great author's plays and were now acting as their "guardians … only to keep the memory of so worthy a Friend, and Fellow alive, as was our SHAKESPEARE …" The description of Shakespeare as the "friend and fellow" of the actors implies that they had similar social status. In the letter addressed "To the great variety of readers," Heminges and Condell implore the reader to buy the book, implying that it was their own enterprise and were desperate to get their money back.

"William Shakespeare was a 'natural' genius"

Heminges and Condell commented upon the great author's writing habits in their letter to the reader, the very first published. They said he wrote effortlessly, that nearly perfect lines just flowed out of his hand.

> … he was a happy imitator of Nature … His mind and his hand went together: And what he thought, he uttered with that easiness, that we have scarce received from him a blot in his papers.

"William Shakespeare was great and was associated with Avon"

The next two pages contain Ben Jonson's superb and oft-quoted elegy to the great author. Shakespeare's writings are "such, /As neither Man, nor Muse, can praise too much," wrote Jonson, declaring him "Soul of the Age!" Jonson said Shakespeare's talent outshined that of his contemporaries and that of the ancients. In this elegy, Jonson coined the now famous phrase, "Sweet Swan of *Avon*!" Poets were called swans, and Avon is the name of several rivers in England, so this poet Shakespeare presumably lived near a river Avon. It was the first association of Shakespeare with Avon made in print.

"William Shakespeare has a tomb, and a monument in Stratford"

Following Jonson's elegy are poems lamenting Shakespeare's death written by Hugh Holland, James Mabbe and Leonard Digges. The poem by Digges contains the most important line in the entire Folio preface:

> *Shake-speare*, at length thy pious fellows give
> The world thy Works: thy Works, by which, out-live
> <u>Thy Tomb</u>, thy name must, when that stone is rent,
> And time dissolves thy *Stratford* moniment,
> Here we alive shall view thee still.

For the first time in print the great author is associated with "Stratford," where his monument is located, and presumably his tomb. England at the time had at least a dozen towns named Stratford and it was very unlikely that the contemporary reader would have thought of the small town of Stratford-upon-Avon had Jonson not written "Sweet Swan of *Avon*!" on a previous page. This clue about "Stratford" was placed far into the preface, as if not to draw too much attention.

"William Shakespeare was an actor and a man of the theater"

The Folio preface emphasized that Shakespeare was a man of the theater – an actor and a dramatist. Hugh Holland called Shakespeare a "Famous Scenic Poet" in his tribute, and that he has gone to Death's dressing room ("Death's public tiring-house" – "tiring" was short for "attiring"). James Mabbe's tribute offered a similar acting metaphor, that Shakespeare went "From the World's-Stage, to the Grave's-Tiring-room." The Folio's preface also featured a list of "Principal Actors" in Shakespeare's plays, with Shakespeare's name heading it. This was another piece of news hitherto unknown about the great author, i.e., that he acted in his own plays. Prior to the Folio, most Shakespeare commentary was directed at his popular poems. The Folio's neglect of Shakespeare's poetical accomplishment, noted Patrick Cheney, "skews the historical record."[1] Leonard Digges addressed this very point about Shakespeare in a poem printed seventeen years after the Folio was released: "First, that he was a Poet none would doubt."[2]

Unsaid in the First Folio's Preface

The information given in the preliminary pages of the First Folio does not satisfy. It lacks a biography of the great author or more personal information. No birth date or year is given. No death date or year is given or how long he had been dead. No account of where he was born or had died. No account of his career. No mention that he was a member of the Lord Chamberlain's Men or the King's Men acting companies, even though letters in the preface were signed by members of both. (This is also true for the title pages of Shakespeare's printed poems and plays. Actor and poet William Barksted, for example, had described himself as "one of the servants of his Majesty's Revels" on the 1610 title page of his poem, *Hiren: or the Fair Greek*, and actor Robert Armin had described himself as "servant to the King's most excellent Majesty" on the 1609 title page of his play, *The History of the Two Maids of More-clack*.) No mention of the great author's family. Unlike Ben Jonson's collected works, there was no attempt in the Folio to date the Shakespeare plays or give their order of composition. Of the sixteen pages of the preface, five are blank – surely there was enough room for more information. The reader may be surprised to learn that nothing in the Folio preface directly ties the great author to the Stratford Man. The phrase, "Stratford-upon-Avon," does not exist in it. "Stratford" and "Avon" are words on separate pages in verses composed by different people. Robert Brazil observed that the Stratford Man's coat of arms, which appears on his monument, did not appear in the Folio.[3]

Folio Contradictions

The Folio's preface contains contradictions, unverified information, and outright lies. They start on the first page of the Folio's preface, where Ben Jonson advises the reader to ignore the author's portrait on the opposite page, and end on the preface's final page, where Shakespeare is listed among the principal actors in his plays. And there is much in between. Jonson's verses contradicted much of the information in the Folio's preface, and in one instance, he seemingly responds to Heminges and Condell's statement about "the ill fortune" of having to seek patrons for Shakespeare's book: he wrote that Shakespeare was "above the ill fortune of them ... " Jonson metaphorically contradicted Leonard Digges, who referred to Shakespeare's tomb and a "Stratford moniment" in his preface poem; Jonson said to Shakespeare, "Thou art a moniment, without a tomb … " More Folio contradictions, and lies, follow.

Portrait engraving by Martin Droeshout does not depict the great author

On the left side of the title page, a spot often reserved for an author's portrait, is Jonson's verse addressed "To the Reader." It comments upon the huge image, supposedly of the great author, on the page opposite. Jonson tells the reader: "Look /Not on his Picture, but his Book." To paraphrase, the true portrait of the great author is reflected in the plays ("his Book"), so please ignore the supplied image. Jonson repeats this thought in his elegy: "Look how the father's face /Lives in his issue … " Leah Marcus described Jonson's poem, with the large type and high position on the page, as "vying for the reader's attention" in competition with the portrait's direct gaze at the reader.[4]

Acclaimed poets were often pictured with laurel wreaths or bays on their heads, but such was not the case with Droeshout's image of Shakespeare. Hugh Holland and Leonard Digges, however, envisioned Shakespeare with such adornments in their Folio verses:

> That corp's, that coffin now bestick those bays,
> Which crown'd him *Poet* first, then *Poet's* King.

and

> *Shake-speare,* thou can'st never die.
> But crown'd with Laurel, live eternally.

J.L. Nevinson observed that Droeshout could have portrayed Shakespeare as a poet, as a dramatist, or as an actor, but "the image of a gentleman author" won out.[5] It was probably chosen to match the Stratford Man's status of gentleman. The sitter's clothing, however, dated 1610 to 1613,[6] was not in sync with the Stratford Man's age at that time – the sitter looks younger than 46 to 49. This is admittedly a minor point, but it is a major point that the face in the Droeshout engraving does not resemble the effigy's face of "Shakspeare" on the monument in Stratford-upon-Avon. (For years, scholars have wished to exhume the Stratford Man's body to see if there was an actual likeness to the Droeshout engraving or the monument's effigy.) Such details may have been purposely conflicting or carelessly overlooked. The most important point of all, however, is that Droeshout's engraving was a *posthumous* rendition, and one that was not endorsed by Jonson. This raises the question of why it was used at all when it could have been easily changed or improved.

Martin Droeshout's engraving has received mostly negative criticism over the centuries. The figure has an oversized and wooden forehead, and a head out of proportion with the body. From where the likeness derived is unknown. W.W. Greg wrote, "It is not pleasing and has little technical merit."[7] Arthur Hind, in a study of 16th and 17th century prints, called it "lifeless in expression."[8] It appears that a deliberately ugly or grotesque image, and an unclean face (the grizzled mustache and beard), was supplied so it would not inspire worship. But there could have been another objective: to depict the great author as a "rare and accomplished monster, or miracle of nature ..." Jonson added this phrase to the 1616 version of his comedy, *Every Man In His Humor*, in a dialogue addressed to Master Stephen, a character that apparently lampooned the Stratford Man (see Chapter 12):

> let the idea of what you are be portrayed in your face, that men may read in your physiognomy, *here within this place is to be seen the true, rare, and accomplished monster, or miracle of nature,* which is all one. [1.2, original italics]

Master Stephen was a "gull" bent on becoming, or being perceived as, a gentleman. The great author presented as a monster, a freak of nature, was perhaps the only way that the public or posterity would accept such a grand literary achievement coming from someone with the Stratford Man's blank educational background. Alongside this "gentleman-monster" depiction may have been one more message. The double lines under the ear and the "bad hair" could be perceived as a figure wearing a mask – most apropos, as pen names are also masks.

Great author's plays are not "trifles"

In their Folio preface letters, John Heminges and Henry Condell described the great author's plays as "trifles" three times within two lines, and wrote that they expected readers to "censure" or criticize the plays. Ben Jonson's stellar praise of Shakespeare's art, that it was greater than that of his contemporaries and that of the ancients, made the two actors look like cretins. Jonson was so concerned about how the great author should be praised that he devoted the first sixteen lines about it in his Folio elegy, which is paraphrased below.

> I won't envy your name, Shakespeare, although I have much envy for your book and fame; for I confess that neither man nor muse can praise your writings too much. It's true, in all men's collected opinion. But envy and collected opinion are not the ways I mean to praise you. These ways foster silly ignorant comments that are mere echoes of what others say. They foster blind affection that

never advances the truth [i.e., the extent of Shakespeare's achievement]. They foster the crafty malice of those who pretend to praise with the intent to ruin, like an infamous bawd or whore who praises a proper lady – what could hurt her more? But Shakespeare, you are proof against them, and above the ill fortune of them, or the need. I, therefore, will begin.

"William Shakespeare" was not the real name of the great author, and he was born into gentility

Ben Jonson punned on Shakespeare's name twice in his elegy: "Shake a stage" and "shake a lance," the latter an acknowledgement of the descriptive action of the pen name, i.e., spear shaking. The hyphen was applied in five of nineteen occurrences of "Shakespeare" in the Folio's preface. Jonson twice used the phrase, "gentle Shakespeare," in his Folio verses. During this era, the first definition of "gentle" was not "nice," but a well-born person – someone born into the gentry or nobility, which was not the Stratford Man's case.

Great author was not simply a natural genius

Heminges and Condell wrote that Shakespeare's art flowed so naturally from his hands that he barely blotted the paper, as if he were a medium performing automatic writing. Ben Jonson was not so naive, explaining that the great author crafted his talent with hard work.

> Yet must I not give Nature all: Thy Art,
> My gentle *Shakespeare*, must enjoy a part.
> For though the *Poets* matter, Nature be,
> His Art doth give the fashion. And, that he
> Who casts to write a living line, must sweat,
> (such as thine are) and strike the second heat
> Upon the *Muses'* anvil: turn the same,
> (And himself with it) that he thinks to frame;
> Or for the laurel, he may gain a scorn,
> For a good *Poet's* made, as well as born.
> And such wert thou. Look how the father's face
> Lives in his issue, even so, the race
> Of *Shakespeare's* mind, and manners brightly shines
> In his well turned, and true-filed lines:

Like an ironworker, Shakespeare kept "striking" the anvil, or revising, until he produced perfect lines, "sweating" in the process, something like today's expression, "1 percent inspiration, 99 percent perspiration." Heminges and Condell would reverse those figures, that the great author's achievement was merely a "miracle of nature." There is evidence that the natural genius idea was conceived circa 1615, while Jonson was preparing a collection of his own works. It is contained in a manuscript of verses written by "F.B." that was addressed to Jonson.[9]

> ... here I would let slip
> (If I had any in me) scholarship,
> And from all Learning keep these lines as clear
> as Shakespeare's best are, which our heirs [posterity] shall hear
> Preachers [professors] apt to their auditors [students/public] to show
> how far sometimes a mortal man may go
> by the dim light of Nature, 'tis to me
> an help to write of nothing;

"F.B." undoubtedly represented Jonson's dramatist friend, Francis Beaumont, who died in March 1616. In his verse, Beaumont said that Shakespeare's "best" lines are "clear" or free of learning, which implies that Shakespeare had less clear lines that were *full of learning*. He predicted that posterity ("our heirs") will have professors ("preachers") citing Shakespeare as an example to their students ("auditors") of how an uneducated man ("the dim light of Nature") can achieve literary greatness. Beaumont was either psychic or he knew, along with Jonson, that the myth of Shakespeare as a natural uneducated genius was planned as early as circa 1615, *well before the Stratford Man's death*. Proclaiming someone's talent as "natural" halts explanations of how one attains greatness. The Stratford Man's case as the great author would be otherwise untenable. This notion agrees with the apparent depiction of the great author by Droeshout as a freak of nature, a monster.

Folio Lies

LIE: *The First Folio's texts derive from the great author's original manuscripts*

Vaunted on the title page, vaunted by Heminges and Condell in their letter to the readers, and vaunted on the final page of the preface is the claim that the First Folio contains the great author's perfect play texts. This statement is patently false. Several plays contained in the Folio are reprints of flawed quarto editions. There is some good copy too, but there are errors everywhere. The assertion of "true original copy" is one of the biggest lies of the Folio preface. Leah Marcus noted the odd pairing of words: "How can something be both an original and a copy?"[10] Sir George Greenwood showed how Heminges and Condell contradicted themselves about the origin of the play texts: each of their preface letters stated that they took the role of "guardian" of the "orphan" Shakespeare plays, implying that the great author's originals had been entrusted to them for publication. Yet in these same letters they also stated that they "collected" the plays.[11] Greenwood also noted that although

Heminges and Condell were left a small bequest in the Stratford Man's will, nothing in the will hints that he intended them to be his literary executors.[12]

Another lie, as advertised on page 16 of the Folio's preface, is that the Folio contained "all" of Shakespeare's "Comedies, Histories, and Tragedies." *Pericles* and *The Two Noble Kinsmen* were left out, although the latter could be excused because half of the play was written by John Fletcher.

LIE: *Edward Blount was one of the First Folio's printers*

At the bottom of the Folio's title page is the line: "Printed by Isaac Jaggard, and Ed. Blount." Blount was a prominent publisher and bookseller, but never a printer. The Jaggard house printed the Folio. The "and" in this phrase is usually assumed as a misprint for "for."

LIE: *John Heminges and Henry Condell wrote their two Folio preface letters*

Scholars have suspected for over two centuries that both letters signed by Heminges and Condell in the Folio preface were actually written by Ben Jonson. The dedication letter to the brother earls of Pembroke and Montgomery contained language and images taken from the classical writers Pliny and Horace. Heminges and Condell were neither writers nor scholars (after retiring from the stage, we know that Condell worked as a grocer). Jonson was a classical scholar. There are direct parallels between three passages by Horace and Pliny (one from a dedication letter), and one passage in Heminges and Condell's dedication letter.

> Hold out your <u>hands</u>, palms turned to the sky, when the
> New moon is up, my <u>country</u>-bred Phidyle;
> Treat well the Lares [household gods]: bring <u>incense</u>, this year's
> Corn and your greediest pig to please them. ...
>
> Pure, empty <u>hands</u> touch altars as closely as
> Those heaping dear-bought offerings. Simple gifts
> Soothe angry household <u>gods</u>: the poor man's
> Salt that will spit in the fire and plain meal.
> [*Odes* by Horace, Book III, No. 23, stanzas 1 and 4][13]

and

> <u>Country</u> people <u>and many nations</u> offer <u>milk</u> to <u>their gods</u>; and
> they who <u>have not incense obtain their requests with</u> only meal
> and salt; nor was it imputed to any as a <u>fault to</u> worship the <u>gods in</u>
> <u>whatever way they could</u>.
> [*Natural History* by Pliny, dedication letter to Emperor Vespasian][14]

Compare all three passages above with the Folio's dedication letter to the Herbert brothers by Heminges and Condell:

> Country hands reach forth milk, cream, fruits, or what they have: and many Nations (we have heard) that had not gums & incense, obtained their requests with a leavened Cake. It was no fault to approach their Gods, by what means they could: And the most, though meanest, of things are made more precious, when they are dedicated to Temples.

Heminges and Condell's second letter, "To the great Variety of Readers," is a pastiche of phrases found in several of Jonson's works that are too many for coincidence. Below are five Jonson excerpts, two of which are taken from letters to the reader, which resemble lines in Heminges and Condell's letter, "To the great Variety of Readers."[15]

> To the reader in ordinary
>
> The muses forbid that I should restrain your meddling, whom I see already busy with the title, and tricking over the leaves: it is your own. I departed with my right, when I let it first abroad;
> [Jonson, *Cataline His Conspiracy*, 1611]

and

> It is further agreed, that every person here have his or their free-will of censure, to like or dislike at their own charge, the author having now departed with his right: it shall be lawful for any man to judge his six-pen'worth, his twelve-pen'worth, so to his eighteen-pence, two shillings, half a crown, to the value of his place; provided always his place get not above his wit ... as also, that he be fixed and settled in his censure, and what he approves or not approves today, he will do the same tomorrow; and if tomorrow, the next day, and so the next week, if need be, and not to be brought about by any that sits on the bench with him, though they indict and arraign plays daily. [Jonson, Induction, *Bartholomew Fair*, 1614; first published 1631]

and

> To My Bookseller:
>
> Thou that mak'st gain thy end, and wisely well Call'st a book good or bad, as it doth sell ...
> [Jonson, *Epigrams*, No. 3, 1616]

and

> *Suffrages* in Parliament are numbered, not weigh'd: nor can it be otherwise in those public Councils, where nothing is so unequal, as the equality: for there, how odd soever men's brains, or wisdoms are, their power is always even, and the same.
> [Jonson, *Timber, or Discoveries*, p. 95, 1641]

and

The Dedication, <u>To the Reader</u>.

If thou be such [i.e., someone who can read], I make thee my Patron, and dedicate the Piece to thee: If not so much, would I had been at the charge of thy better literature. Howsoever, if thou <u>canst but spell</u> ... [Jonson, *The New Inn, or the Light Heart*, 1628][16]

Now compare the above five Jonson excerpts with the following Folio letter to the reader signed by Heminges and Condell:

<u>To the</u> great Variety of <u>Readers</u>.

From the most able [i.e., able to read], to him that <u>can but spell</u>. There you <u>are number'd</u>. We had rather you were <u>weigh'd</u>. Well! It is now public, & you will stand for your privileges we know: to read, and <u>censure</u>. Do so, but buy it first. That doth best commend <u>a book</u>, the <u>stationer says</u>. Then, <u>how odd soever</u> your <u>brains</u> be, <u>or</u> your <u>wisdoms</u>, make your license <u>the same</u>, and spare not. <u>Judge your six-pen'orth, your shillings worth, your five shillings worth</u> at a time, <u>or higher</u>, so you rise to the just rates, and welcome. But, whatever you do, buy. <u>Censure</u> will not drive a Trade, or make the Jack go. And though you be a Magistrate of wit, and <u>sit on the Stage</u> at *Black-friars*, or the *Cock-pit*, <u>to arraign Plays daily</u>, know, these plays have had their trial already ...

It had been a thing, we confess, worthy to have been wished, that <u>the Author</u> himself had liv'd to have set forth, and overseen his own writings; But since it hath been ordain'd otherwise, and he by death <u>departed from that right</u>, we pray you do not envy his Friends, the office of their care, and pain, to have collected & publish'd them ...

Jonson's *Timber, or Discoveries* (p. 98) contained a passage about Shakespeare:

<u>He was</u> (indeed) honest, and of an open and free <u>nature</u>; had an excellent fantasy, brave notions, and <u>gentle expressions</u>;

Now read Heminges and Condell's letter "To the great Variety of Readers" about Shakespeare:

Who, as <u>he was</u> a happy imitator of <u>Nature</u>, was a most <u>gentle expresser</u> of it.

Scholars are well aware that Jonson borrowed extensively from his own works and from the works of others, increasing the likelihood that he composed Heminges and Condell's letters. For example, read Jonson's verse opposite the Droeshout engraving:

To the Reader.

This Figure, that thou here seest put,

It was for gentle Shakespeare <u>cut</u>;
Wherein the Graver had <u>a strife</u>
<u>with Nature</u>, to out-do <u>the life</u>:
O, could he but have drawn his wit
As well <u>in brass</u>, as he hath hit
His <u>face</u>, the Print would then <u>surpass</u>
All, that was ever writ <u>in brass</u>.
But, since he cannot, Reader, look
Not on his Picture, but his Book.

The theme of Jonson's poem, and the lines, "Wherein the Graver had a strife /with Nature, to outdo the life," were borrowed and paraphrased from lines in Shakespeare's *Venus and Adonis* (1593):

Nature that made thee, with herself at strife [line 11]

Look, when a painter would surpass the life [line 289]

His art with Nature's workmanship at strife [line 291]

Jonson may have even lifted a few words from Thomas Heywood's *An Apology for Actors* (1612), which had expressed the same idea.[17]

The visage is not better <u>cut</u> <u>in brass</u>
Nor can the Carver so express the <u>face</u>
As doth the Poet's Pen whose arts <u>surpass</u>,
To give men's lives and virtues their due grace.

Heminges and Condell's comment that the previous editions of Shakespeare's plays were "maimed, and deformed" echoed a comment by publisher Thomas Walkley. In 1622, Walkley referred to the previous edition of *Philaster* as "maimed and deformed."[18] Even Heminges and Condell's description of Shakespeare as their "Friend, & Fellow" may have been inspired by a line in the play, *The Return to Parnassus-Part 2* (circa 1601-02): the line, "our fellow Shakespeare," was repeated twice by the character, "Kempe," the then-deceased comic actor.[19] This play and the Folio's preface both depicted "ignorant" actors discussing Shakespeare. *Parnassus* may have also contained the first application of the word "master" to Shakespeare in a literary work. (The 1608 quarto edition of *King Lear* is possibly the first instance that "Mr Shakespeare" appeared on a title page.)[20] More phrases in the Folio's preface were evidently borrowed from the dedication letter to *Archaio-ploutos*, a book printed by William Jaggard in 1619. Addressed to the Earl and Countess of Montgomery, the dedication letter opened, "To the most Noble and Twin-like pair ... " Roger Stritmatter first noticed the similar address used in the Folio's dedication to the same Earl of Montgomery and his brother, the Earl of Pembroke: "To the Most Noble and Incomparable Pair of Bretheren."[21] Leah Scragg also found many points of resemblance between Heminges and Condell's dedication letter and one written by Folio publisher Edward Blount in his 1598 edition of Marlowe's *Hero and Leander*.[22]

LIE: *When alive, the great author received the "favor" of the earls of Pembroke and Montgomery, and he was their "servant"*

Absolutely no evidence supports the above statements contained in the dedication letter signed by Heminges and Condell. It is on record that Pembroke's Men performed some Shakespeare plays, but the patron of that acting troupe was the second Earl of Pembroke, not the third. The only person who could claim to be Shakespeare's patron was the Earl of Southampton, to whom the great author dedicated two poems – these poems, and Southampton's name, were left out of the Folio. As mentioned above, the Folio emphasized that Shakespeare was a working man of the theater.

LIE: *"William Shakespeare" was a "principal actor" in his own plays*

One page of the Folio preface lists "principal actors" of the Shakespeare plays. "William Shakespeare" heads the list, his name placed above the celebrated actor, Richard Burbage. There is simply no evidence that "William Shakespeare" was a principal actor in any play. Ben Jonson listed "William Shakespeare" as an actor in two of his plays (*Works*) published shortly after the Stratford Man had died. It is posthumous evidence only that "Shakespeare" acted in the plays of Shakespeare and Jonson, and in both cases, Jonson supplied the "evidence." This Folio "lie" was one of the few not contradicted by Jonson, perhaps because the great author did publicly act in his own plays, making himself "a motley to the view," as he had expressed in Sonnet 110. The scandal that it would have caused to someone of his high status would have made open credit impossible.

LIE: *Jonson "beloved" Shakespeare*

Jonson titled his famous elegy to Shakespeare, "To the memory of my beloved, The Author, Mr. William Shakespeare: And what he hath left us." Jonson never wrote about his "beloved" before the First Folio. A section of Jonson's folio, *Works* (1616), is comprised of 133 epigrams, four of which praised writers John Donne, Sir Henry Goodyere and Josuah Sylvester; Jonson's "beloved" Shakespeare was left out. The Stratford Man died in April 1616, and it is believed that *Works* was printed in the summer of 1616 – plenty of time for Jonson to include a Shakespeare tribute and the perfect occasion to do so.

In 1618, Jonson "censured" several "English Poets" including Shakespeare, in his conversation with William Drummond: "Shakspeer wanted [lacked] art…" Drummond recalled that Jonson also censured Shakespeare for getting it wrong about a shipwreck occurring in Bohemia.[23] After the Folio was published, Jonson called Shakespeare's play, *Pericles*, "a moldy tale" in his play, *The New Inn, or The Light Heart*, written in 1628. In his posthumously published *Timber, or Discoveries*, Jonson seemingly responded to Heminges and Condell's statement that the great author never blotted a line.

> My answer hath been, would he had blotted a thousand. Which they [the actors] thought a malevolent speech. [p. 97]

In the same work, after declaring he "lov'd the man, and do honor his memory (on this side Idolatry) as much as any," Jonson in essence said Shakespeare talked too much. The paragraph ends with a backhanded compliment: "But he redeemed his vices, with his virtues. There was ever more in him to be praised, than to be pardoned" (p. 98). Outside of Jonson's high tribute to Shakespeare in his Folio elegy, the reader may now judge how sincerely Jonson "beloved" Shakespeare.

LIE: *Shakespeare had limited knowledge of classical languages*

> And though thou hadst small *Latin*, and less *Greek*,
> From thence to honor thee, I would not seek
> For names; but call forth thund'ring *Aeschylus*,
> Euripides, and Sophocles <u>to us</u>
> *Pacuvius, Accius*, him of Cordova dead [Seneca],
> <u>To life again</u>, to hear thy buskin tread [ref. to tragedy],
> And shake a stage: Or, when thy socks were on [ref. to comedy],
> Leave thee alone, for the comparison
> Of all, that insolent *Greece*, or haughty *Rome*
> sent forth, or since did from their ashes come.
> Triumph, my *Britain*, thou hast one to show,
> To whom all Scenes of *Europe* homage owe.
> He was not of an age, but for all time!

The traditional interpretation for Ben Jonson's elegy line, "And though thou hadst small *Latin*, and less *Greek*," is that the great author had little knowledge of these languages. Yet this cannot be true because many Shakespeare works display considerable knowledge of both. Shakespeare invented many words based upon Greek and Latin roots.[24] His works are filled with allusions to the works of classical writers, and sometimes he paraphrased their lines. In some cases Shakespeare alluded to or borrowed from a classical work before it had been translated into English. For example, Shakespeare was "indebted" to the Latin play by Plautus, *Menechami*, for his play, *The Comedy of Errors*,[25] yet the experts believe that Shakespeare wrote his play a few years before the first printed English translation in 1595. Charles C. Hower wrote a paper illuminating the true meaning of several Shakespeare lines by applying Latin etymology to the English words.[26] Shakespeare's knowledge of Latin, therefore, was more than "small." Jonson, whose classical reading was extensive, certainly knew this, so what did he mean by his elegy phrase? "Even if" is a valid interpretation of "though." Using this definition, the line would mean, "Even if Shakespeare had small Latin and less Greek," and Jonson would be correctly assessing the great author's knowledge. Yet the Shakespeare professor defends the traditional interpretation, and is perhaps relieved by it, because the Stratford Man's acquisition of Latin at the Stratford grammar school would have been limited (and Greek, not at all), had he in fact attended.

Immediately before the line in question, Jonson said that Shakespeare outshined his contemporaries (John Lyly, Thomas Kyd, Christopher Marlowe). Immediately after it, Jonson listed six classical dramatists (Aeschylus, Euripides, Sophocles, et al) to "honor" Shakespeare. But Jonson said he did not wish to only drop names, he wished to "call forth" these classical dramatists "to us" (Jonson and Shakespeare), and "to life again," so they could witness and "hear" Shakespeare's tragedies and comedies. Jonson said that Shakespeare's works would "triumph" in "the comparison." Presumably Jonson wanted the classical poets to materialize so Shakespeare could hear these dramatists favorably critique his plays – "even if" Shakespeare's understanding of Greek and Latin were limited. Perhaps Jonson had intended the "small *Latin*, and less *Greek*" line to be ambiguous, adding to the idea that the great author was a "natural" unlearned genius. Jonson's contemporary, H. Ramsay, questioned Jonson's elegy line in *Jonsonus Virbius: or, The Memory of Ben* (1638). Ramsay wrote that Jonson had a good command of Latin, "That which your *Shakespeare* scarce could understand?" Jonson did not originate the "small *Latin*, and less *Greek*" line, he borrowed it from the Italian critic, Antonio Minturno, in his *L'Arte Poetica* (1564). In the context of dramatic writing, Minturno wrote about some of his contemporaries who did not properly appreciate the ancients.

> For that reason there are some, who by chance know little of Latin and even less of Greek, who in Tragedy place Seneca, barely known by the Latin writers, before Euripides and Sophocles, who are considered by all to be the princes of Tragic poetry.[27]

Jonson also borrowed from Minturno the names of Sophocles, Euripides and Seneca for his Shakespeare elegy.

Conclusion

The great author's persona first emerged from the preface of the First Folio in 1623. "William Shakespeare" was the great author's born name; he was a gentleman, an actor, a dramatist, a natural genius, and was associated with the place names Avon and Stratford. Some of this information is contradicted within the same pages. This can be explained if the entire preface were geared to two different audiences: the knowing and the unknowing. The knowing audience comprised both those who knew that the great author was a nobleman using a pen name and those who were acquainted with William Shakspere of Stratford-upon-Avon. The Stratford Man could not be openly identified as the great author because many knew it was not true and they could publicly question this identity change and spoil the intention of those who contrived this preface. The unknowing audience, the majority, would make the connection between the great author and Stratford-upon-Avon without question.

Substantial evidence shows that Ben Jonson actually wrote the letters of actors John Heminges and Henry Condell, a "fraud" that taints the entire preface. Jonson styled the letters as he believed actors would write, i.e., ignorantly, for authenticity. They were presented as incapable of recognizing the greatness of Shakespeare's plays by repeatedly calling them "trifles," thus the nonsense lines urging the reader to buy, fearing they would never get their money back. If this was a legitimate concern, then why did they not include Shakespeare's proven top sellers, the poems, *Venus and Adonis* and *The Rape of Lucrece*? His role as poet was instead overlooked. The overemphasis on buying – an entire paragraph – is almost comic and evidently without example. Jonson in his own voice sneers at these actors, and was perhaps trying to distinguish himself from them because at one time he did act. It is unlikely that Heminges and Condell asked Jonson to write their letters because they were so unflattering. And Jonson seemed to use them as scapegoats for the Folio's textual errors, most likely caused from not having the great author's original texts. Meanwhile the Folio's title page put forth the lie that the text was based upon the author's "True Original Copies." The idea that Heminges and Condell were the great author's "friends and fellows," and the Folio their production, was a red herring to help throw the great author's literary identity onto the Stratford Man. It also diverted attention away from the person most responsible for the entire Folio production, the Earl of Pembroke, the subject of the next chapter.

The Shakespeare professor is well aware of Jonson's voice in Heminges and Condell's letters but is reluctant to admit he wrote them because of the implications. If they were fraudulently written, then the veracity of the entire preface is questionable, including Droeshout's image of "Shakespeare." And this preface, in conjunction with the Shakspeare monument in Stratford-upon-Avon, is the professor's best "evidence" that the Stratford Man wrote Shakespeare! The Folio preface was specifically tailored to give the impression that the Stratford Man, a gentleman, was Shakespeare without directly saying so. It was ultimately left to the readers to connect the dots, which they eventually did. Heminges and Condell were chosen as front men because they were colleagues of the Stratford Man in the King's Men acting company, and in other business. Droeshout's engraving of Shakespeare was probably an invented image. The preface was designed to *suggest* that the Stratford Man was the great author, not to blatantly show it. The image was unadorned and imperfect, even deformed, presumably meant to deter public idolization of the Stratford Man, who was the wrong man. This must have been intentional, as none of the other portraits by Droeshout have sitters with faces looking so wooden or artificial. Jonson left posterity the key to understanding Droeshout's bizarre image in lines added to the 1616 edition of *Every Man In His Humor*: the great author is to be depicted as a "rare, and accomplished monster, or miracle of nature ... " Apparently, Jonson believed that the only way the general public and posterity would swallow the idea of the Stratford Man as the great author would be to present him as a freak of nature, a "monster." It is fact that the Stratford Man held the status of gentleman, thus Droeshout's depiction of a gentleman-monster rather than the usual depiction of accomplished poet-dramatists – wearing or holding bay leaves. Readers today are so familiar with Droeshout's image that it may be difficult to see it like this, but one must remember that Jonson composed most of the Folio preface, and that *plans for the identity switch were afoot before the Stratford Man had died* (Beaumont's verses to Jonson). Droeshout's face of Shakespeare was proof enough to convince the masses that the great author was a man born with the name William Shakespeare who was the fellow of actors. But for those who were truly interested in the great author and his works, Jonson provided the voice of truth: the great author is masked, and to discover his true identity, read "his Book" carefully. Below is a summary of the Folio's true and false messages.

The Truth: Ben Jonson in His Own Voice

"Shakespeare" is the greatest dramatic genius ever born, cannot be praised too highly, and "what he hath left us" is something extraordinary. This fact is recognized by the learned and the unlearned. His memory will stay alive so long as his works remain in print. Although certainly inspired with a gift, "Shakespeare" worked hard at his craft, constantly revising. His works "delighted" Queen Elizabeth and her successor, King James. "Shakespeare" was of "gentle" birth, and some noted his dramatic talent with the intent of damaging his reputation/high status. "Shakespeare" is a descriptive pen name ("shake a Lance"). The given "figure" on the title page is not his true image – his works reveal himself best. Shakespeare is "a moniment, without a tomb," i.e., Shakespeare represents a body of writing (one definition of "moniment"), not a human being. (Jonson's reference to Avon in his elegy was not necessarily Stratford-upon-Avon; many towns in England include the word "Avon." Jonson may have been purposely ambiguous on this point, like he was with the line, "small *Latin*, and less *Greek*.")

The False: Jonson in the Voice of John Heminges and Henry Condell

Because Shakespeare died without making arrangements for his own writings, we (Heminges and Condell) have taken it upon ourselves to collect and publish his plays. Despite the "ill fortune" of this task, we do it gladly for our fellow. We hope the earls of Pembroke and Montgomery will patronize this work because they favored Shakespeare, the man and his plays. He was their servant. Unlike previously stolen and false editions of the plays, this book contains Shakespeare's true lines, directly taken from his own clean papers. He was a natural writer, churning out perfect lines as soon as he thought of them. Any errors in the text are due to our limited abilities. It is outside of "our province" to praise these "trifles," so just buy the book. We advise you to read the plays "again, and again … to understand him." If you need more understanding about Shakespeare, "we leave you to other of his Friends," who "can be your guides." ("Friends" James Mabbe, Hugh Holland and Leonard Digges only informed the reader that Shakespeare was dead and had a "Stratford moniment." The best understanding, therefore, comes from "friend" Jonson, the voice of truth.)

Martin Droeshout's Portrait of Shakespeare

Here is the image of the writer, Mr. William Shakespeare. He was actually born with that name. He was a gentleman. He was a rare miracle of nature. He was ugly. Do not worship him. If you're a little skeptical that this image is authentic, you may be right: it could just be a mask covering the identity of the real author.

CHAPTER 9

A Pembroke and Jonson Production

THE LIES AND contradictions contained in the First Folio's preface – and the compelling evidence that Ben Jonson actually wrote the letters signed by John Heminges and Henry Condell – completely discredits it. Outside of Heminges and Condell's signatures, there is no evidence that these two actors initiated the project, paid for it, or were involved with it in any way. Unwilling to see any foul play, the Shakespeare professor apparently likes the idea that Shakespeare's old acting chums spent the time and money to save his "orphans," the plays, from oblivion. It was a matter of fellow actors helping a fellow actor. Their preface letters claim that the Folio was their "enterprise" and twice it was stated that they "publish'd them," meaning the plays, but even this was contradicted by information on the Folio's back page, "Printed at the Charges of W. Jaggard, Ed. Blount, I. Smithweeke, and W. Aspley, 1623." Since the preface was designed to mislead, it follows that the title and back pages were also purposely confusing. Even W.W. Greg thought that the wording, "printed at the charges of," was "rather unusual."[1] Scholars usually view Edward Blount, William Jaggard, and his son, Isaac, as the main Folio investors, with smaller shares owned by William Aspley and John Smethwick (who at the time owned the rights to previous editions of a few Shakespeare plays). These shares were real. When Isaac Jaggard died in 1627, his widow assigned "her part" of the Folio to Thomas Cotes, who printed the Second Folio in 1632 (William Jaggard had died in 1623).[2] Blount assigned his Folio share to Robert Allot in 1630, and Smethwick and Aspley retained their shares for the Second Folio.[3] But did these five actually put up the money to make the Folio happen?

The First Folio was a very expensive production. It comprised 907 large pages printed on better quality paper and it took a long time to print. Exactly how many copies of the Folio were made is not known, but Peter Blayney, the most cited expert on its production, considered 750 total copies a reasonable number – 500 would not be cost effective and 1,200 would be too risky.[4] (The closest example of a production of this type was Jonson's folio of plays and poems, published in 1616; presumably, it was not a big seller since it took twenty-four years to be reprinted.) Blayney's estimated cost of 6 shillings and 8 pence per unit to produce (materials plus labor of compositors and press-men)[5] would put the investment of 750 copies at £250 – an enormous sum during that period. The per-unit cost is based upon the fairly solid evidence that the Folio sold in the bookstore for 15 shillings unbound, and 20 shillings bound (equivalent to £1),[6] and working backward. But this supposed per unit cost for the publisher does not include or even consider pre-production costs: editing and preparing the copy for the compositors, those who set the type for press (as many as nine different compositors were employed on the project). Compositors or typesetters are not editors. Twenty plays in the Folio had never been in print, so they would certainly need editing. The texts of previously issued plays were also used, but they contain enough differences with the Folio's text for one to conclude that they too had been edited for inclusion. Editing and proofreading was evidently performed, therefore, on all thirty-six plays. Several very literate people must have been employed to complete this colossal task.

Unfortunately, records about the Folio's production have not survived. Scholars have reached no consensus as to the identities of the editors, but most would say that Heminges and Condell did not or could not perform the task. If these actors truly considered the Shakespeare plays as "trifles," as repeatedly said in their Folio letters, if they were incapable of recognizing their greatness, then they would not have been capable of preparing them for press. The choice of Leonard Digges, James Mabbe and Hugh Holland as eulogists of Shakespeare in the Folio's preface was peculiar – none of them were associated with the theater or with Shakespeare. They were, however, highly educated men who would have been well qualified to edit Shakespeare's plays. Assuming that this was the case, remuneration for each editor can only be guessed at – perhaps something similar to a schoolmaster's annual salary, approximately £20.[7] Ben Jonson must be included among the editors because of his dominating hand in the preface. ("Some of the character-descriptions are suspiciously Jonsonian," wrote T. J. B. Spencer, about the cast lists of a few plays in the Folio.)[8] The portrait engraving on the title page was also an extra expense. Even more potential costs lay in acquiring the rights to previously published Shakespeare plays, or usage fees, some of which were used in the Folio. And what about the rights to the unpublished plays – would not the great author's family have had an interest? They were not even mentioned in the Folio. Even a conservative addition of £90 to Blayney's estimate to account for some of these "hidden" costs would total £340; the per-unit price for 750 copies, therefore, would have been 9 shillings and 1 pence, well above Blayney's estimate of 6 shillings and 8 pence. Blayney believed that the publishers sold the Folio to booksellers for 10 shillings, which would have been the legal limit if the cheapest version in the bookstores sold for 15 shillings. The point of this brief cost analysis is to show that the Folio was not a moneymaking venture – it was a barely break-even proposition. Blayney described the Folio as "by far the most expensive playbook that had ever been offered to the English public."[9] A huge outlay and a big risk for a very small profit, if any, is hardly an attractive proposition for investors. One must assume, therefore, that a substantial portion of the Folio, if not the entire project, was funded by its dedicatees, the earls of Pembroke and Montgomery.

Pembroke the True Engineer of the First Folio

Dedication letters in books were usually addressed to those likely to sponsor them, and the First Folio was dedicated to William Herbert, 3rd Earl of Pembroke, and his brother, Philip Herbert, Earl of Montgomery. Their role as patrons of the work has never been challenged, *but the possibility that they initiated the Folio project or influenced its production remains unexplored* despite evidence that strongly suggests it. All persons named in the Folio preface were connected to Pembroke, to his protégé, Ben Jonson, or to Montgomery. Pembroke was one of the wealthiest men in England and over one hundred books were dedicated to him.[10] His father patronized a company of actors (Pembroke's Men) that had performed at least five Shakespeare plays. Besides Jonson, Pembroke patronized dramatists Philip Massinger, Thomas Nashe and George Chapman. He hailed from a literary family. His mother, Mary Sidney, Countess of Pembroke, was a respected scholar and writer; her brother was the celebrated poet, Sir Philip Sidney. Pembroke's mistress, Lady Mary Wroth, was a writer of drama, fiction and sonnets; she bore him two illegitimate children.[11] Pembroke, a poet himself, certainly had the literary interest and the money to take on the big project of a Shakespeare play collection. He also had the political power. One of Pembroke's ardent ambitions was to obtain the office of Lord Chamberlain. Under the jurisdiction of this office was the Master of the Revels, who controlled dramatic performance and publication. Pembroke sought this office for several years. One court insider wrote in a January 1614 letter that if Lord Knolles was next appointed to the post of Lord Chamberlain, it

> would be too great a distaste to the earl of Pembroke, who looks duly for it when it falls and if he should fail, would think his long service and diligent waiting ill rewarded.[12]

The Duke of Somerset was awarded the position that year. Six months later, however, Somerset fell into disgrace when his wife was implicated in the murder of Sir Thomas Overbury. Pembroke replaced him in late December 1615, and he was determined to stay there. During Pembroke's eleven-year tenure, King James tried four times to lure him out of this office by offering him others, but four times Pembroke refused. One condition he always held to was that his brother, Montgomery, should succeed him in this office (the new king, Charles I, acceded to this condition upon the fifth offer, so in 1626, Pembroke became the Lord Steward and his brother, the Lord Chamberlain).

Knowing the Earl of Pembroke's background, it may appear surprising that, after he obtained the office of Lord Chamberlain, individual publication of Shakespeare's plays stopped. The years 1616 to 1618 were blank in this regard. Meanwhile, plays by other writers were issued during this period without incident. A breach of Pembroke's unofficial policy, however, occurred in 1619, when Thomas Pavier and William Jaggard printed ten Shakespeare plays (some apocryphal) in an apparent attempt to create a first collected edition. Pembroke took action. He sent a letter to the Stationers' Company with a directive that was summarized in their register on May 3, 1619:

> Upon a letter from the right honorable the Lord Chamberlain. It is thought fit & so ordered that no plays that his Majesty's players do play shall be printed without consent of some of them.[13]

As Pembroke ultimately controlled the plays and players as Lord Chamberlain, the above passage could also mean no printing without *his* consent. The directive resulted in no further Shakespeare play editions for another two years, but not for other dramatists, proving again Pembroke's bias against Shakespeare. Only three of Pavier and Jaggard's ten Shakespeare play editions had the current year on the title pages – five editions displayed earlier false dates, and two had no date. Two editions had false imprints. Evidently, Pavier and Jaggard had printed only three plays before the 1619 directive – all with the current year on the title pages, and then they covertly defied the order by putting false information on the title pages to give the impression that these editions were old stock. The fakery was especially odd because Pavier held the rights to about half of these plays,[14] making it unlikely that he was trying to deceive the King's Men acting company or other publishers. Clearly, it was Pembroke's order that he was trying to evade.

Thomas Pavier and William Jaggard were never prosecuted for their post-directive scheme – on the contrary, they seemed to have prospered after the incident. Within five weeks of Pembroke's directive, Pavier was elected as one of the assistants of the Stationers' Company (June 14, 1619), allowing him to sit on the governing board; it was his first promotion within the company in seven years. In 1622, Pavier was elected underwarden, giving him power to authorize entries in the registers.[15] Pavier never again printed a Shakespeare play. The Jaggard printing house also benefited immediately: *Archaio-Ploutos* in 1619 and Boccaccio's *The Decameron*, registered on March 20, 1620, were books dedicated to Philip Herbert, Earl of Montgomery, the probable sponsor.[16] The First Folio would be the third Jaggard house commission by a Herbert, and its final Shakespeare publication. Considering the benefits that Pavier and Jaggard each received soon after Pembroke's directive, one can surmise that Pembroke privately negotiated with them in return for their cooperation of not printing Shakespeare's plays outside of his authority. To award the Jaggard house with the Folio commission would be otherwise unconscionable: Jaggard's two illicit issues of *The Passionate Pilgrim* in 1598-1599 had incurred the great author's personal contempt for being "so bold with his name," and fully aware of the offense it had caused, Jaggard printed it a third time in 1612. Pembroke was not trying to protect the players and their supposed "property," the Shakespeare plays, with his 1619 directive – he was protecting a plan involving Shakespeare that he wished to enact as soon as he became the Lord Chamberlain. As explained in Chapter 8, Francis Beaumont and Ben Jonson evidently knew about this plan *before* the Stratford Man's death in April 1616, which invalidates Heminges and Condell's "testimony" in their Folio letter of doing a favor to their late colleague. If Pembroke's "diligent waiting" for the office of Lord Chamberlain was primarily to realize this plan, then it was conceived before 1614, or as shown below, as early as 1609.

Shakespeare Play Blackout

The Earl of Pembroke's evident desire to ban individual Shakespeare quarto editions fulfills a prediction made in 1609 about "grand possessors" wanting to do the same thing. Someone calling himself "A never writer" gave "a warning" to readers in the first edition of Shakespeare's *Troilus and Cressida* (1609, second issue) of a coming shortage of published Shakespeare plays:

> And believe this, that when he is gone, and his comedies out of sale, you will scramble for them, and set up a new English Inquisition. Take this for a warning, and at the peril of your pleasure's loss, and Judgment's, refuse not, nor like this the less, for not being sullied, with the smoky breath of the multitude; <u>but thank fortune for the 'scape it hath made amongst you. Since by the grand possessors wills</u> I believe you should have pray'd for them [i.e., printed editions of the plays] rather than been pray'd [i.e., urged to buy them].

According to this anonymous writer, *Troilus and Cressida* "escaped" the "grand possessors" of the Shakespeare plays, for which readers should "thank fortune," implying that the great author was no longer the possessor of his own works in 1609 (entire text in Appendix D). Other evidence, as covered in chapters 4 and 15, suggests that the great author was dead by 1609. Some critics would assert that the phrase, "when he is gone," in the *Troilus* preface letter proves Shakespeare was still alive in 1609, but this line could also mean, "when the printing of Shakespeare's plays ceases" or "when his plays are sold out in bookstores." In an otherwise complimentary letter about the great author's works, "when he is gone" would be a rude way of saying "after his death" had he still been alive.

Scholars speculate about the identity of the "grand possessors." Some think they were the King's Men acting company, but it is unlikely that actors would be termed "grand," and there is no evidence that they owned the Shakespeare plays. The printers and publishers who registered Shakespeare's plays with the Stationers' Company also did not own them; they were registering their versions of the plays, their *pirated versions*, and it was these versions that they held the rights to. It was these versions that they were allowed to transfer or sell to others, but they did not own the Shakespeare plays. If the great author were dead in 1609, then it follows that his family members would be the possessors or owners of his plays. Legally, a possessor is one "who takes, occupies, or holds something without necessarily having ownership, or as distinguished from the owner" (OED). "Grand" implies that they were highly placed. Early printed texts of Shakespeare's plays were imperfect or incomplete, as related in Chapter 2; the escaped *Troilus and Cressida* quarto was no exception, so evidently the grand possessors did not possess the great author's original play manuscripts. They would have possessed, however, the right or the "wills" (the word used in the quote) to publish, or not to publish, the Shakespeare plays. But even so, they still would not have had the authority to stop such publication – only the Lord Chamberlain or the king's privy council could do that. Considering the fact that Pembroke was later responsible for doing this very thing as soon as he obtained the power to do so as Lord Chamberlain, an office for which he "diligently waited"; considering the fact that his nobility would qualify him as "grand"; and considering the fact that Shakespeare's First Folio was dedicated to Pembroke, Pembroke can be confidently identified as one of the grand possessors. As shown throughout this book, the great author was an aristocrat, which increases the possibility that the noble Herbert family were his relations. As the Lord Chamberlain, Pembroke would not allow publication of individual Shakespeare plays, but he did allow the First Folio. The First Folio, therefore, was published with his "will," with his full cooperation. These factors, Pembroke's wealth, and his ties to the Folio preface contributors, as explained at the end of this chapter, make it highly probable that he was the true Folio initiator and financial backer. But there is other indirect evidence of Pembroke's involvement behind the scenes.

The Revels Office and Folio Production

When the presses began to roll for the Folio is not known, but its completion was initially expected to occur by October 1622. We know this because the Folio was advertised in a book fair catalog listing books expected for release between April and October 1622.[17] But as it happened, the Folio would not be completed until November 1623. Obviously, something delayed the production, and those who have studied the forensics of the Folio, including Charlton Hinman, have acknowledged that a major interruption most likely occurred in 1622. The delay was not due to technical reasons, as Jaggard's two presses operated continuously throughout that year printing other books. There were two other Jaggard-printed books advertised in the aforesaid catalog with an expected issue date of 1622. One of them, *Discovery of Errors*, was printed as scheduled. The other, Andre Favyn's *Theater of Honour*, had "1623" on the title page, but was registered on October 23, 1622, meaning it was already completed or near completion. Two books printed by Jaggard in 1622, however, were evidently not scheduled for publication that year: *Description of Leicestershire* and *Christian Dictionary*. Since the Folio delay was not technology-related, then the problem must have been related to the text, causing Jaggard to move projects of his other clients ahead of it (i.e., those two unscheduled ones), shelving it until they were completed. Among Hinman's conjectures are the following:[18]

- First Folio printing began late 1621 or early 1622
- Folio quires A to E were finished by the end of March 1622
- When the printing began for Folio Quire F is uncertain; there was possibly a time interval between the printing of quires E and F (bibliographically, quires A to E differ substantially from all other quires in the book)
- A "major interruption" occurred in Folio printing sometime before October 1622, but the length of the interruption is indeterminable
- Folio printing definitely resumed by October 1622, with a brief interruption in December 1622
- Folio printing was constant from early 1623 to completion in late 1623

While the Folio printing was going well, in early 1622, notice was probably given to the printer of the book fair catalog that the Folio would be finished by October 1622. But then something interrupted these plans, which ultimately resulted in the completion time of November 1623. The Folio was *not listed* in the book fair catalog announcing books to be issued between September 1622 and April 1623, and neither was it listed in the same catalog for publication between April and October 1623. The first sign of confidence that the Folio was nearing completion was its reappearance in the book fair catalog for titles expected during October 1623 to April 1624, the period when it did get released.

The cause of the 1622 interruptions in the Folio's printing may never be known, but they were serious enough to delay the original release date by one year. It is significant, therefore, that at the exact time of the first possible delay, at the end of March 1622, there was a changeover in the Revels Office. The Revels master, Sir George Buc, had gone mad, and Sir John Astley had taken his place. On March 30, 1622, it was reported in a letter:

> Poor Sir George Buck master of the Revels is in his old age fallen stark mad, and his place executed by Sir John Ashley [sic] that had the reversion.[19]

On April 12, Buc was officially declared "insane," and on May 16, his relatives were told to surrender his office. He died on October 31, 1622. During the reign of James I, the Revels Office, which was under the jurisdiction of the Lord Chamberlain, licensed and censored plays for performance and for publication. The supposed interruption in the Folio's printing coinciding with this changeover suggests that Buc was involved with its production. If so, then Pembroke may have arranged for each newly printed Shakespeare play from Jaggard's press to go directly to Buc in the Revels Office to expedite the approval process. Otherwise, had the printed book been given as a whole to the Revels Office, it would have taken a very long time to approve. When Astley took over the Revels Office, there was probably a backlog of plays awaiting approval due to Buc's illness; it is possible that Pembroke ordered Jaggard to stop the Folio's printing until Astley caught up. As late as 1620, Buc was in full control of his mental faculties, because that year "the duke of Buckingham listed [Buc] as one of the scholars best qualified to compose an English Academy" (DNB). On October 6, 1621, however, Buc authorized Thomas Walkley to publish Shakespeare's play, Othello, which was inconsistent with the evident ban of Shakespeare dramatic publication by Pembroke, his superior. Buc may have already been senile at that time, or he may have been influenced by an event that occurred on the day before the Othello permission. On October 5, 1621, Ben Jonson was granted "next in line," i.e., the reversion, for the Revels mastership after Sir John Astley, who held the reversion after Buc. The king raised Jonson's annuity from £66 to £200 at this time, and there were rumors of his getting a knighthood. Perhaps Buc felt that he would soon be replaced and retaliated. Astley may have also feared Jonson's promotion and made a special effort to have his right to succeed Buc verified. When it was officially confirmed on March 29, 1622, Astley replaced the mad Buc. Astley held the mastership of the Revels until July 24, 1623, when he mysteriously leased it to Pembroke's kinsman, Henry Herbert, for £150 per year. (Officially, Astley was still the Revels master because it was a life term.) King James knighted Herbert two weeks later, at Pembroke's estate, Wilton House. One scholar considered it a "buyout" that was "engineered" by Pembroke.[20] In my opinion, Pembroke arranged the buyout because he wanted no complications with the licensing of the First Folio, which at this time was about four months shy of completion. The Folio's sixteen-page preface, which was evidently the last portion to get printed, contained false and misleading information about Shakespeare. Pembroke needed someone he could trust to approve the work for publication quietly and without question. Astley had been granted the reversion to the Revels Office in 1612 by Thomas Howard, Earl of Suffolk, who was the Lord Chamberlain at the time. The Howards were Pembroke's political rivals.

Sir George Buc's approval of Thomas Walkley's quarto of *Othello*, printed in 1622, evidently caused a small explosion of three more Shakespeare play editions that year (*Richard III, Henry IV-Part 1* and *The Troublesome Reign of King John*, which was ascribed to "W. Shakespeare"). The Earl of Pembroke had effectively curtailed Shakespeare dramatic publication for six years (1616 to 1621) excepting those plays issued by Pavier and Jaggard in 1619. On March 3, 1623, Pembroke issued a new order to the Stationers' Company:

> This day a letter from my Lord Chamberlain was openly read to all the master printers concerning the licensing of plays &c. by Sir John Ashley [*sic*].[21]

The letter does not survive, but one can determine its contents by the results: no individual Shakespeare play was openly published between 1623 and 1628, yet at least twelve plays by other writers were printed during this period (one of them, *The Bondman*, 1624, was dedicated to the Earl of Montgomery by author Philip Massinger). Shakespeare's plays were targeted again, with two exceptions: the fourth quarto editions of *Romeo and Juliet* and *Hamlet*, both published by John Smethwick and *both printed with no date on the title pages*. Careful analysis of the paper stock and watermarks by R. Carter Hailey showed "with a high degree of probability" that *Romeo and Juliet* was printed in 1623, and that *Hamlet* could be "demonstrably" dated to 1625.[22] As Pembroke's 1619 order to the Stationers' Company was evidently aimed at Pavier and Jaggard's issue of Shakespeare quartos, it follows that the 1623 order was given for the same reason. Smethwick must have printed *Romeo and Juliet* (Quarto 4) in early 1623, taking a precaution that he may have learned from Pavier and Jaggard – leaving the date off the title page – but was still found out, resulting in Pembroke's March 3rd order to the Stationers' Company.

(Interestingly, Smethwick's edition was issued with two different title pages: one crediting the play to "W. Shakespeare" and one without the author's credit.) There is no evidence that Smethwick was disciplined for this action, but Smethwick did own the rights to *Romeo and Juliet* (Quarto 3, 1609) and *Love's Labour's Lost* (1598) – these particular editions were used in the Folio. Smethwick waited two years after the Folio's release to issue *Hamlet*; this text was not the one used in the Folio.

In August 1626, the Earl of Montgomery became the Lord Chamberlain. An apparent loosening of his brother's Shakespeare policy had occurred in 1629 with one quarto edition of *Richard III* released. Pembroke's health was worsening that same year, and he died on April 10, 1630. Perhaps not coincidently, the year 1630 saw three Shakespeare quartos in print: *Merry Wives of Windsor*, *Pericles* and *Othello*. In 1631, Smethwick published, *with* dates, quarto editions of *Love's Labour's Lost* and *Taming of the Shrew*. Between 1629 and 1639, sixteen editions of individual Shakespeare plays were published. The tight control of Shakespeare play issuance during the years 1616 to 1629 coincides with the appointment of Pembroke to the office of Lord Chamberlain, and a loosening of this control after he died.

The Pembroke-Jonson Connection

Ben Jonson's involvement with the First Folio preface is undisputed, as well as his close alliance to the Earl of Pembroke. "From 1603 to his death in 1630," wrote Pembroke's biographer, Brian O'Farrell, "Pembroke gave employment and protection at court to Jonson, showing his discernment for true talent."[23] While imprisoned in 1605 as one of the writers of the play, *Eastward Ho*, Jonson appealed to Pembroke and the Earl of Montgomery (and others) for assistance. He was released. In 1611, Jonson dedicated his play, *Cataline His Conspiracy*, to Pembroke, and in 1616, two sections of his collected works. Jonson's biographer, David Riggs, noted that all complimentary references to the Howards, Pembroke's political rivals, which were contained in some of Jonson's works, were "carefully expunged" for his folio edition, and concluded that the "ascendancy of Pembroke and his circle is an important motif in [Jonson's] folio as a whole."[24] Dick Taylor observed that "Jonson experienced his best years as a composer of masques under Pembroke's lord chamberlainship," and he "indicated his gratitude by working in salutes to Pembroke in Christmas his Masque, 1616, and in For the Honour of Wales, 1618."[25] Within two months of Pembroke's appointment to this office, Jonson was given a royal grant of 100 marks (about £66) for life.[26] Jonson told William Drummond in 1618 that he was receiving £20 annually from Pembroke expressly to buy books. Pembroke wrote a letter to Oxford University delegates (May 1619) recommending Jonson for an honorary degree, which was granted.

Ben Jonson's *Works* (1616) was the first collection of English dramas printed in England. It was also the first time that dramas appeared in large folio-sized pages, which were usually reserved for the Bible or important reference works. Shakespeare's First Folio evidently was much influenced by Jonson's folio, with a similar amount of pages, actor lists and prefatory tributes. It was probably Jonson's touch to apply the word "works" in reference to the plays on the Folio preface page listing Shakespearean actors. Bibliographic evidence indicates that the printing of Jonson's folio was completed in the summer of 1616,[27] and Riggs believed that Jonson "tinkered" with the text "until the very last minute."[28] Jonson may have added the name, "William Shakespeare," to the cast lists of his plays, *Sejanus*, and *Every Man In His Humor*, after the Stratford Man's death; they were the first published details about Shakespeare's acting career. More new information followed in the First Folio, that Shakespeare acted *in his own plays*. As Jonson's hand is detectable in much of the Folio's preface, and as he was beholden to Pembroke, one can conclude that Jonson was employed by Pembroke to transform the image of the great author from a nobleman using a pen name into a commoner named William Shakespeare, a working actor-playwright whose "fellows" were actors Heminges and Condell. Pembroke apparently wanted to control the public image of Shakespeare and it was a long time in planning. It would not be surprising if Pembroke had agreed to fund Jonson's folio in return for helping with his own project, the collected Shakespeare plays. Jonson was probably one of the Folio editors. The little-known biographies of others named in the Folio's preface (Edward Blount, James Mabbe, Leonard Digges, Hugh Holland, Martin Droeshout) uncovers their ties to the the Herbert brothers, Jonson, or to all three.

First Folio Contributors

Edward Blount: The First Folio's co-publisher, Edward Blount, was erroneously listed as on its title page as printer. Blount's first connection with Shakespeare occurred in 1601 as the publisher of *Love's Martyr*, which featured two new Shakespeare poems, as well as one by Ben Jonson. In May 1608, Blount registered Shakespeare's plays, *Pericles* and *Anthony and Cleopatra*, but he did not publish them. In the previous year (1607), Blount dedicated a translation to the brother earls of Pembroke and Montgomery, stating in the dedication letter that he was "humbly devoted" to them (*Ars Aulica, or the Courtier's Art* by Lorenzo Ducci). Since it is likely that Pembroke was one of the grand possessors of Shakespeare's plays, Blount may have kept these plays out of print at his request (if so, then it is another indication that the great author was dead by this time, i.e., May 1608). In 1609, a different publisher issued *Pericles*, and its corrupt condition suggests it was a pirated copy; *Anthony and Cleopatra* debuted in the Folio.

Blount had no known ties with Heminges and Condell, but he did have ties with others involved in the Folio's production. Blount published Ben Jonson's play, *Sejanus His Fall* (1605), which included a prefatory a poem by Hugh Holland. Blount's edition of John Florio's *New World of Words* (1611) contained a Latin anagram by James Mabbe. In 1622, Blount published *Gerardo, The Unfortunate Spaniard*, a translated work by Leonard Digges that was dedicated to Pembroke and Montgomery, and in 1622-23 Blount published *The Rogue*, a translated work by Mabbe, with preface contributions by Digges and Jonson. Blount's edition of Edward Dering's *Works* (1614) was partially printed by William Jaggard.[29] William Aspley, who was listed on the Folio's back page as a financial contributor, co-published three books with Blount prior to the Folio; in 1600, Aspley also published two Shakespeare plays (*Much Ado About Nothing* and *Henry VI-Part 2*), and was one of the booksellers of SHAKE-SPEARE'S SONNETS (1609).

Blount was known for active involvement in his book projects. In 1620, Blount issued at least three books, but in 1621, he evidently issued none. In 1622, the year of presumed delays in the Folio's printing, Blount issued five books. In 1623, when Folio printing resumed at a continuous pace, Blount published only one title besides the Folio. As his other publishing activity fit neatly with the Folio's printing schedule, Blount may have served as editor or chief editor of the sixteen Shakespeare plays that he registered (with Isaac Jaggard) on November 8, 1623 for the Folio publication. He may have given his full attention to the Folio during 1621 and 1623 and brought in friends Digges and Mabbe to help. (Since Blount already held the rights to *Pericles*, its exclusion from the Folio is interesting.) Blount's publications often included his personal letter to the reader, but this was not the case with the Folio. A notable example is contained in Blount's issue of *Six Court Comedies* (1632), a collection of plays by the then late dramatist, John Lyly. After the Folio, Blount did not publish another book for four years; in his early 60s, he evidently was beginning to retire. William Aspley, in his early 50s, stopped publishing for a seven-year period after the Folio.

Leonard Digges: Digges contributed one poem to Shakespeare in the First Folio preface. Digges was a classical scholar noted for his Latin and Spanish translations. He held a bachelor's and master's degree at Oxford University. The year before the Folio was published, Digges dedicated his translation of a Spanish novel to the earls of Pembroke and Montgomery (*Gerardo, the Unfor-*

tunate Spaniard) with Edward Blount as publisher. Blount also issued Digges's Latin translation of Claudian's *Rape of Proserpine* (1617), and they were life-long friends. Digges was also friends with James Mabbe, and contributed a poem to Mabbe's translation, *The Rogue* (1623), as did Ben Jonson. Thus Digges had direct connections with the brother earls, Jonson, Mabbe and Blount just before the Folio was published. Although he had no known connections with Heminges and Condell, Digges did have an indirect connection with the Stratford Man: his stepfather, Thomas Russell, was the overseer of the Stratford Man's will. Outside of this fact, there is no known intersection between Digges and the Stratford Man, or "William Shakespeare," before the Folio was published. It is very likely that Blount brought in his friend Digges to the Folio project as one of the editors.

Hugh Holland: Holland was a minor poet known today mostly for his sonnet about Shakespeare in the First Folio preface. Holland probably wrote it at the request of his friend, Ben Jonson (Holland's sonnet and the second page of Jonson's elegy face each other in the Folio). In 1603, Jonson contributed a twelve-page ode for Holland's book, *Pancharis*. Holland likewise contributed a poem in the preface of Jonson's play, *Sejanus His Fall* (1605), published by Edward Blount; Holland's poem was reprinted in Jonson's *Works* (1616), which included dedications to the Earl of Pembroke. In 1604, Holland and Jonson both supplied commendatory verses for Thomas Wright's *Passions of the Mind in General*. Holland earned a degree at Cambridge University and has no known connection with John Heminges and Henry Condell, or with Shakespeare. It is very likely he was one of the Folio editors who was brought in by friend Jonson.

James Mabbe: Mabbe is unquestionably the "I.M." who contributed one poem to Shakespeare in the First Folio preface. Mabbe's lines in *The Rogue*,

> a poor kind of comedian that acts his part upon <u>the stage of this world</u> ... when the play is done (which cannot be long) he must presently enter <u>into the tiring house [dressing room] of the grave</u>

resemble lines written by I.M. in the Folio's preface:

> We wondered (*Shake-speare*) that thou went'st so soon
> <u>From the World's Stage, to the Grave's 'Tiring-room.</u>

The Rogue was Mabbe's English translation of a Spanish work, which Edward Blount published in 1622-23; it contained prefatory pieces by Leonard Digges and Ben Jonson. Mabbe was an Oxford University graduate. He was associated with Blount as early as 1611, as a contributor to Blount's publication, *New World of Words*, by John Florio. Blount mentioned Mabbe in some of his surviving letters: in one of them, dated May 30, 1623, Blount called Mabbe "his good friend" and discussed a possible journey with him to Brussels.[30] Mabbe's book, *Christian Policy*, was published by Blount in 1632. Mabbe was associated with Digges as early as circa 1613, when Digges scribbled a remark about him (and also Shakespeare) on a book of sonnets by Lope de Vega. Mabbe has no known connection with Heminges and Condell, or with Shakespeare. He very likely served as one of the Folio editors, along side his friends Blount and Digges.

William and Isaac Jaggard: Father and son printers of the First Folio. William Jaggard's first intersection with Shakespeare occurred in 1598-99 when he published two unauthorized editions of *The Passionate Pilgrim*, and another edition in 1612. In 1619, when Jaggard and Thomas Pavier issued several Shakespeare plays, Lord Chamberlain Pembroke stopped them. In the same year, and the next, the Jaggard house printed two books that were dedicated to Pembroke's brother, the Earl of Montgomery (*Archaio-Ploutos*, *The Decameron*), and a third book in 1623, the First Folio. Favor given to the Jaggards by Pembroke and Montgomery may have been made in exchange for their ceasing to publish Shakespeare outside of their authority. The evidence shows that the Jaggards' interest in the Folio was purely business related. The Jaggards had no hesitation in moving forward two other book projects in 1622, the year that the Folio's printing was delayed, and did not resume the Folio production until these other books were completed. William Jaggard died shortly before the Folio was released.

John Heminges and Henry Condell: Actor-members of the King's Men who signed the First Folio's dedication letter and letter to readers. Lord Chamberlain Pembroke had authority over their acting company. Heminges and Condell performed in Ben Jonson's plays. Since Jonson almost certainly wrote their preface letters in the Folio, their direct involvement in the book's production is doubtful. It is likely that Pembroke compensated them for the use of their signatures, perhaps explaining their mutual retirement from the stage at the time of the Folio's release (although about ten years apart in age). These letters fostered the illusion that they initiated and produced the Folio. The Stratford Man definitely knew Heminges and Condell: he was a member of the King's Men, and they all owned shares in the Globe and Blackfriars theaters. The Stratford Man also left them bequests in his will. Heminges was the Stratford Man's partner in purchasing the Blackfriars gatehouse property.

Martin Droeshout: The engraver of the Folio's image of Shakespeare. There was a controversy as to which Martin Droeshout did the engraving: the Elder, known as a painter, or his nephew, the Younger. Recent evidence by June Schlueter has confirmed that the Younger Droeshout made the Shakespeare portrait.[31] He was twenty-one at the time and apparently inexperienced – no engraving was credited to him before the Folio was published. How did the Younger Droeshout get the Folio commission? Mary Edmond found two documents that associated the Elder Droeshout with the painter, Marcus Gheeraerts.[32] The Earl of Montgomery, who had a keen interest in paintings, was portrayed by Gheeraerts.[33] Gheeraerts, therefore, may have been the link between Droeshout and the Folio commission. A portrait engraving of Montgomery (Plate 10), rendered by Simon de Passe (circa 1620), somewhat resembles Droeshout's Shakespeare, sharing heads disproportionate with bodies and plate-like collars, and perhaps served as Droeshout's model.

It is especially significant that Droeshout, who showed limited ability with his engraved portrait of Shakespeare, made portrait engravings of two members of King James's inner circle: James, 2nd Marquess of Hamilton (Plate 18), and George Villiers, Duke of Buckingham. Hamilton and Buckingham were the king's privy councilors, as was Pembroke. The Hamilton engraving is dated 1623. The undated Buckingham engraving mimics the composition and setting of the Hamilton, and has the same signature ("Martin D. sculpsit"), making it likely that the two were made at the same time. Both the Buckingham and the Hamilton portraits have faces much more natural, or passably human, than the Shakespeare face, yet all three were rendered at approximately the same time. This comparison lends itself to the idea that the Shakespeare portrait was intentionally "monstrous" looking. Christiaan Schuckman discovered that during the period of 1632 to 1635, Droeshout immigrated to Spain. He continued his engraving career, but interestingly, for those works signed with his full name (several were signed with his initials), he had altered his surname to "Droeswood."[34] In 1632, the Second Folio was published, which would have renewed public interest in Droeshout's portrait of Shakespeare – perhaps he was hiding from this association. The only instance that Droeshout signed an engraving with his actual name in full was the most famous one of all, that of Shakespeare.

Conclusion

The nice story believed by the Shakespeare professor that Shakespeare's acting friends produced the First Folio in his honor, perhaps backed by eager investors, is just that: a nice story. Historical evidence in every aspect points to the Earl of Pembroke as the one who initiated and funded the book, with Ben

Jonson as the designer of the misleading Folio preface. For several years, Pembroke sought the position of Lord Chamberlain, which controlled dramatic performances and publication through the Revels Office. When Pembroke finally achieved this position, individual issues of Shakespeare's plays ceased, and he personally halted breaches in this unofficial policy. At about the same time that a new master was installed in the Revels Office, Folio printing was delayed, suggesting that the Revels Office was directly involved with its production. To expedite the approval process of the twenty new Shakespeare plays featured in the Folio, it appears that Pembroke had arranged for each play to be sent to the Revels Office as soon as it was printed. The mental breakdown of the Revels master, Sir George Buc, may have created a backlog of plays for approval, and perhaps caused Pembroke to order a temporary stay in the printing of the Folio plays. Pembroke had attempted to maneuver his protégé, Jonson, into the office as the next master, but failed. Buc's successor, Sir John Astley, eventually "leased" the office to Pembroke's kinsman, Sir Henry Herbert, for reasons still unknown. The changeover occurred about four months before the Folio's release. Pembroke probably wanted a Revels master that he could count on to rubber stamp the First Folio with its false prefatory material.

The history surrounding the Folio's production weakens the long-running assumption that the members of Lord Chamberlain's Men and King's Men acting companies owned Shakespeare's plays; if they had control of them, then why did they allow Thomas Walkley to print *Othello* at about the same time that they were planning to print it themselves in the Folio? Walkley's edition of *Othello* differed substantially from that used in the Folio, so it is certain that the players did not lend him their copy to print. And why would the players also allow John Smethwick to print the fourth edition of *Romeo and Juliet* at a time when its appearance in the Folio was nearing? Did not John Heminges and Henry Condell implore readers to buy the Folio, presumably to get their investment back? Why did Smethwick even bother to print *Romeo and Juliet* separately when he was one of the supposed Folio investors? By doing so, he was in competition with himself. Smethwick printed a quarto edition of *Hamlet* in 1625 without a date on the title page, which was unusual; he may have believed that it was still "unallowed" to openly publish a Shakespeare play, even after the Folio's release. If this was true, then the reason for Pembroke's halting of individually printed Shakespeare plays was not merely because the Folio's release was imminent. Leonard Digges, Hugh Holland and James Mabbe were unlikely choices as eulogists of Shakespeare in a book of his plays: all were university men who were minor poets, not playwrights. But their involvement with the Folio is not surprising since they had ties with the Herbert brothers, Jonson, or Edward Blount. These highly educated men most likely prepared and edited the Folio play texts for publication.

The hitherto unknown engraver, Martin Droeshout the Younger, may have obtained the commission to engrave (and probably invent) Shakespeare's portrait from the Earl of Montgomery via Marcus Gheeraerts, who had painted the earl's portrait. Droeshout's career as a portrait engraver essentially began with the Folio publication, and although his effort was far from commendable, he nevertheless engraved the portraits of two of the king's privy councilors, and in the same year that the Folio was released. The Earl of Pembroke, also a privy councilor, undoubtedly arranged these commissions. A quick comparison of Droeshout's image of Shakespeare with the more life-like image of the Marquess of Hamilton, rendered in 1623, almost proves that the Shakespeare image was intentionally unflattering. The Jaggards did not print the Folio's title page, and it is believed that it and the prefatory material were printed last. Some of the Folio contributors, therefore, may not have known about Droeshout's false image of Shakespeare. Blount performed the role of publisher for the Folio under the direction of Pembroke but was not allowed to draw attention to himself with a letter to the reader, his usual practice. He was credited on the Folio's title page as printer, but this error was purposeful. The Folio preface was meant give the impression that Heminges and Condell, the actual acquaintances or "fellows" of the Stratford Man, were the Folio publishers, so Blount could not be openly named in this capacity. Indeed, Pembroke similarly hid behind the mask of the players in his 1619 directive. For his efforts, Blount was rewarded with half the publishing rights to sixteen Shakespeare plays (the Jaggards held the other half). Pembroke almost certainly was one of the grand possessors who intended to ban individual issues of Shakespeare's plays, as stated in a prefatory letter to *Troilus and Cressida*. This presents a slight contradiction with his authorization of a collected edition of Shakespeare's plays. Pembroke apparently did not want control of the plays per se, *he wanted control of the public's image of the great author*. If it was Pembroke's express intention, money and connections that produced the Folio, *then it was also due to Pembroke that the myth of the Stratford Man as the great author was created and imposed upon the public.* Pembroke did not want independent publishers to reveal the great author's identity before he could get out the "official" image planned for unveiling in the Folio. Evidently, it was something he wanted to do since 1609. Why was this important to him for so long? This is the crux of the Shakespeare authorship question, and an attempt to decipher his reason will be covered in chapters 16 and 17.

CHAPTER 10

The Stratford Monument: Ruse and Reincarnation

THE ENTIRE FIRST Folio preface was a deliberate fraud upon the public, meant to give the impression that the great author was the Stratford Man. The Earl of Pembroke and Ben Jonson were responsible. But the deception was a two-pronged affair, involving not only the Folio preface, but also a monument in Stratford-upon-Avon. The two most important lines in the Folio preface, both addressed to the great author, were: (1) "when that stone is rent,/ And Time dissolves thy Stratford Moniment" (by Leonard Digges), and (2) "Sweet Swan of Avon!" (by Jonson). Taken together, these lines suggested that Stratford-upon-Avon was the location of a monument to the great author. Although this place name does not exist in the Folio's preface, a monument to "Shakspeare" in the Holy Trinity Church of Stratford-upon-Avon did and does exist. These three elements initiated and cemented the idea that this church was the great author's resting place. The Stratford monument, therefore, requires an equally close examination as the Folio's preface.

The Early Stratford Pilgrim

If one were living in late 1623, read Digges's prefatory poem in the First Folio, and were inspired to visit the "Stratford moniment" to Shakespeare in Stratford-upon-Avon, what would one find there? The earliest image of the monument is a July 1634 drawing by Sir William Dugdale; a more detailed version appeared as an engraving in his book, *Antiquities of Warwickshire* (1656).[1] Using Dugdale's book as our guide, and not what is currently in place, the early Stratford pilgrim would find two objects: a monument to "Shakspeare" on the wall in the chancel area, and an unidentified gravestone with only a curse written upon it on the chancel floor. The expectations of the Stratford pilgrim would be fulfilled, at least partly. There was a monument, but the effigy it contained did not resemble Shakespeare's image in the Folio, and it lacked any symbol of writing or literature, like a pen or a book; the effigy figure held a sack. The monument's inscription identified the deceased man as "Shakspeare," not "William Shakespeare," and did not openly characterize him as a poet or playwright. For the grave, the pilgrim would not know which one was Shakespeare's because it did not include his name – there was only a curse. Church personnel must have informed Dugdale which one it was because he featured it in his book.

The monument's inscription (see Plate 11) gives no information about the deceased other than the Stratford Man's death date (today appearing in tiny letters and numbers squeezed in the bottom right corner). The inscription wastes valuable space with these redundancies: the observer is to "read if thou canst," two references that "Shakspeare" is dead, and that his name is on the tomb. The last point is not strictly true – the monument has a name on it, but the tombstone does not. The last two lines on the monument contain the words "writ," "art" and "wit," which suggest a writer, but the overall meaning of these lines is unclear. The English lines do not suggest the deceased was a poet, only the Latin ones, which translate as:

> Judgment of Pylos, genius of Socrates, art of Maro
> The earth encloses. The people grieve. Olympus possesses.

The monument observer would have to be a very literate person to catch the poetry reference. Who else would know that Maro was the cognomen or surname name of the Roman classical poet known as Virgil? Or that Shakspeare's "judgment" was here being compared with King Nestor of Pylos, a minor character in Homer's *Iliad* and *Odyssey*? Why not openly name Nestor and Virgil?[2] Is the Latin inscription supposed to describe Shakespeare? Many have pointed out that Nestor, Socrates and Virgil were inappropriate comparisons. Nestor and Socrates were not writers, and although Virgil was a poet, Shakespeare's "art" was far more influenced by Ovid. Socrates and Shakespeare were geniuses, but that is about all they had in common. Yes, one could say Shakespeare imparted good "judgment" and wisdom in his works, but why would the inscriptionist compare him to King Nestor – a mythological, not an historical, figure? (For example, John Parkhurst's Latin epitaph to the poet, Sir Thomas Wyatt, named "Pylo" among other figures of classical mythology that mourned Wyatt's passing *without* mixing in any historical figures.)[3] As noticed by Diana Price, the statement that "Shakspeare" was "possessed" by Mount Olympus, home of the Greek gods, was odd because poets were traditionally associated with Mount Parnassus.[4] Finally, as the historical record shows, "the people" did not "grieve" or mourn Shakespeare's death until after the Folio's official announcement *seven years* after the Stratford Man had died.

The inscription on the Shakspeare monument contradicts itself about the location of the deceased's body. The second Latin line says the earth enclosed him, implying he was buried. The fourth and fifth English lines say that "death hath placed /within this monument Shakspeare," i.e., he was interred there. Where was "Shakspeare" buried, in the monument or under the gravestone? This confusion had to have been intentional. To understand why, one must return to the Folio preface, and Jonson's elegy lines:

> My Shakespeare, rise; I will not lodge thee by
> Chaucer, or Spenser, or bid Beaumont lie
> A little further, to make thee a room:
> Thou art a moniment, without a tomb ...

Jonson was referring to William Basse's poem (circa 1622) that called for Shakespeare to be buried in Westminster Abbey alongside the other great English writers, Spenser, Chaucer and Beaumont. Basse had asked these dead poets to move a bit closer together to make room for Shakespeare:

> Renowned Spenser lie a thought more nigh
> To learned Chaucer, and rare Beaumont lie
> A little nearer Spenser, to make room
> For Shakespeare in your threefold, fourfold tomb.
> To lodge all four in one bed make a shift ...

Jonson believed Basse's idea was needless because Shakespeare was "a moniment" without a tomb. The official Folio position, therefore, was that the great author's remains should not be moved to Westminster Abbey. The confusion as to where the remains of "Shakspeare" were actually located and the curse on the Stratford Man's gravestone were contrived to prevent this reburial *because the Stratford Man was not the great author.*[5] Neither the monument nor the gravestone inscriptions make overt tribute to a poet and give no information other than a death date. These inscriptions were seemingly written with two goals: hint that the Stratford Man was the great author, but prevent his reburial in the sacred abbey. It seems that the writer of the monument's inscription wanted to refer to Shakspeare as a poet but he did so in the most oblique way, comparing him to a Latin poet that would only be discernible to a Latinist. (Perhaps Virgil was purposely named because of the belief that Virgil sometimes used a pen name.)[6] And although praising Shakspeare with figures of classical Rome and Greece, it seems the inscriptionist purposely chose ones that had little or no association with or influence upon Shakespeare. The English inscription does not honor a poet, playwright or actor, it only makes an obscure reference to "all that he hath writ" which "leaves living art but page to serve his wit." Contrast the inscription on the Shakspeare monument with that of poet Edmund Spenser in Westminster Abbey, erected in 1620 by Lady Anne Clifford:

> Here Lies (Expecting the Second Coming of Our Saviour Christ Jesus) the Body of Edmond Spencer The Prince of Poets in His Time Whose Divine Spirit Needs No Other Witness Than the Works Which He Left Behind Him. He was Born in London in The Year 1553 and Died in the Year 1598.

Adding to the strangeness of the Shakspeare monument's inscription, the curse on his gravestone was completely unusual. Philip Schwyzer, in his *Archaeologies of English Renaissance Literature*, observed how scholars take it for granted that cursed tombstones were "commonplace" at that time; "Nowhere, however, are such remarks accompanied by examples of contemporary epitaphs closely resembling Shakespeare's."[7] The adjoining plots, like that of the Stratford Man's wife, had the full name of the deceased.

> Here lieth interred the body of Anne wife
> of William Shakespeare who departed this life the
> 6th day of August: 1623 being of the age of 67 years.

These three English lines on her gravestone were followed by six Latin ones, which, according to Edgar Fripp, alluded to the biblical books of Matthew and Mark.[8] Notably lacking in her inscription was a reference to her husband as a famous poet, or inclusion of an apt Shakespeare phrase.

Some evidence points to Ben Jonson as the writer of the Shakspeare monument's inscription. Jonson's play, *Poetaster* (1601), featured the poet Virgil as a character (also called Maro in the play), and Virgil was the only poetry reference in the monument's inscription. Some scholars have noted that Jonson's tribute to Virgil in the play could double as a tribute to Shakespeare.[9]

> That which he hath writ
> Is with such judgment labor'd, and distill'd
> Through all the needful uses of our lives,
> That could a man remember but his lines,
> He should not touch at any serious point,
> But he might breathe his spirit out of him. [5.1]

Jonson's apparent association of Virgil with Shakespeare was unique among the literati. Edmund Spenser was regarded as the English Virgil among his contemporaries, such as Thomas Nashe and Charles Fitzgeffrey.[10] Jonson's line, "That which he hath writ," recalls the monument's line, "all that he hath writ." Jonson lauded Virgil's "judgment" in his play, just like Shakspeare's judgment was lauded in the monument's inscription. *Poetaster* also echoed a few Shakespeare phrases and apparently lampooned the Stratford Man (Chapter 12). Jonson's frequent borrowing of Shakespeare may have also extended to the monument's inscription with the phrase, "living art," which occurs in *Love's Labour's Lost* (1.1.19). (Jonson also used the phrase "living line" in his Folio elegy to Shakespeare.) Another point of intersection between Jonson and the monument's inscription, as noted by Charles Isaac Elton, is the coupling of Nature with Shakespeare. Jonson wrote in his Folio elegy to Shakespeare that "Nature herself was proud of his designs, /And joyed to wear the dressing of his lines!" The monument's inscription states, "Shakspeare with whom /Quick nature died."[11] If this evidence is enough to conclude that Jonson wrote the Shakspeare monument's inscription, then one must also conclude that it and the Folio preface were contrived together.

The Inscriptions, and Shakspeare's Monument Originally John's?

Our hypothetical Stratford pilgrim only saw what was in the church in 1634. The earliest record of the Shakspeare monument and gravestone inscriptions are possibly those contained in one copy of the First Folio, now at the Folger-Shakespeare Library (No. 26). Appearing on its back page are three "epitaphs" to Shakespeare in handwriting that is dated circa 1625. All three epitaphs were written very close to each other on the upper half of the page (Plate 13). The first one, titled, "An epitaph of Mr William Shakspeare," contains the six familiar monument lines beginning with "Stay passenger …" The anonymous writer, however, neglected to record the four Latin lines (two lines above the English ones, and two below them). The second epitaph of the three is titled, "Another upon the same," and is otherwise unknown:

> Here Shakespeare lies whom none but Death could Shake
> and here shall lie till judgment all awake;
> when the last trumpet doth unclose his eyes
> the wittiest poet in the world shall rise.[12] [modern spelling]

The third epitaph on the page, titled "An Epitaph (upon his Tomb stone incised)," is the curse on the gravestone. Since the Shakspeare monument and gravestone inscriptions were not yet in print, the circa 1625 writer must have visited the church very soon after the Folio was issued, and evidently saw on the monument not one inscription, but two separate ones. The epitaphs handwritten in Folio 26 have received little notice by scholars, and they have not considered the possibility that the unique second epitaph was originally part of the monument's inscription.

John Weever also visited the church and transcribed the Shakspeare epitaphs. He did so in preparation of his book of epitaphs, published in 1631 (although, interestingly, he did not include them). The year that Weever jotted them down is unknown, but it was certainly before 1631. His monument inscription is similar to today's, including the Latin lines; he did not, however, record the second epitaph noted by the circa 1625 writer. William Dugdale made the third surviving transcription of the Shakspeare epitaphs. In his 1634 drawing, Dugdale recorded the first two words of the Latin lines on the monument, and later printed the full monument and gravestone inscriptions in his 1656 book; they resemble what is there today. If the unique second epitaph to Shakespeare actually appeared on the monument's tablet, it would mean that originally the tablet identified the Shakespeare in Stratford-upon-Avon as "the wittiest poet in the world," but soon after it was wiped out, and the poetry reference buried in an added Latin line. Also wiped out was the cryptic prediction that "the wittiest poet in the world shall rise" when people's judgment is awakened, implying that the public was wrong about Shakespeare's identity, and that one day they will be corrected. The word "judgment" was evidently retained for the next incarnation of the inscription.

Weever and the circa 1625 writer recorded the Shakespeare inscriptions for their personal use. Dugdale's versions, the first in print, were for the public record. Although today's inscriptions are essentially the same as Dugdale's, there are several differences in spelling and format, and one word change: "the tombe" in Dugdale, and "this Tombe" today. Dugdale's inscriptions showed upper and lower case letters, but today's inscriptions are comprised of capital letters, both small and large; Dugdale's inscriptions showed some usage of u for v, but today's inscriptions use v in every case of u and v; Dugdale's inscriptions showed no usage of thorns – a "y" to represent "th" – but today's inscriptions have two thorns on the monument and three on the tombstone. Dugdale did use thorns and all capital letters for other monument inscriptions in the same book.[13] Dugdale's inscription showed one abbreviation on the monument, "wth in" for "within," but today's monument inscription fully spells out "with in." Some words in today's monument inscription have two letters squeezed together to save space, which Dugdale's inscription did not show. Dugdale's rendering of the word "Shakspeare" on the monument was in a larger font size than the other words, and today's monument has "Shakspeare" in a font size consistent with the other words. Today's inscription has three misspelled words (Ganst, Plast, Sieh), unlike Dugdale's version. There are enough differences between the two texts to suggest that the monument and tombstone inscriptions were recut after Dugdale recorded them. But Dugdale's version differs substantially from the circa 1625 version, which

MONUMENT, ANONYMOUS, CA. 1625[1]

Stay passenger why go'st thou by so fast
read if thou Canst, whom enuious death hath plact
within this monument: Shakespeare: with whom
quick nature dy'd; whose name doth deck this toombe
far more then cost; sith all that hee hath writt
leaues liueing art but Page vnto his witt.

Heere Shakespeare lyes whome none but death could shake
and heere shall ly till iudgement all awake;
when the last trumpet doth vnclose his eyes
the wittiest poet in the world shall rise.[2]

GRAVESTONE

Good ffriend for Iesus sake forbeare
To digg the dust inclosed heere
blest bee the man that pau'd these stones
but Cur'sd bee hee that mooues these bones.

JOHN WEEVER, BEFORE 1631[3]

Judcio Pilum, Genio Socratem, Arte Maronem
Terra tegit, populus maeret, Olympus habet.

Stay passenger, why goest thou by so fast
Read if thou Canst whome envious death hath plac't
Within this Monument, Shakespeare with whome
Quick Nature dy'd whose name doth deck his Tombe
far more then cost, sith all Ye hee hath writt
Leaves living Art but page to serve his witt
    ob. Ano̅ do̅i. 1616 aetat. 53. 24 die April.

Good frend for Jesus sake forbeare
To digg the dust enclosed heare
Blest bee Ye man that spares these stones
And curst bee hee that moves my bones.

Shakspeare monument and gravestone inscriptions, transcribed circa 1625 and before 1631.

1. Excerpts from full transcription by Joseph Egert which appears on Plate 13.
2. Note that the appearance of the unique second epitaph on the monument is my conjecture.
3. Society of Antiquaries, SAL MS. 128, Folio 375b, based on complete transcription by Nina Green, © 2009.

MONUMENT, DUGDALE, 1656

Iudicio Pylium genio Socratem, arte Maronem
Terra tegit, populus maret, olympus habet,

Stay passenger why goest thou by soe fast,
Read, if thou can'st whom envious death hath plac't
wᵗʰ in this monument Shakspeare with whome
Quick nature dyed, whose name doth deck the tombe
Far more then cost, sith all that he hath writ
Leaues living art but page to serue his witt.

Obijt Aᵒ Dni, 1616
aet. 53, die 23 Apri:

GRAVESTONE

Good freind for Iesus sake forbeare
To digg the dust inclosed here
Blest be the man that spares these stones
And curst be he that moues my bones

TODAY

IVDICIO PYLIVM GENIO SOCRATEM, ARTE MARONEM,
TERRA TEGIT, POPVLVS MÆRET, OLYMPVS HABET

STAY PASSENGER, WHY GOEST THOV BY SO FAST,
READ IF THOV GANST, WHOM ENVIOVS DEATH HATH PLAST
WITH IN THIS MONVMENT SHAKSPEARE: WITH WHOME
QVICK NATVRE DIDE WHOSE NAME, DOTH DECK Ƴᵉ TOMBE,
FAR MORE, THEN COST: SIEH ALL, Ƴᵗ HE HATH WRITT,
LEAVES LIVING ART, BVT PAGE, TO SERVE HIS WITT.

OBIT ANO DOⁱ 1616.
ÆTATIS · 53, DIE 23 AP.

GOOD FREND FOR IESVS SAKE FORBEARE,
TO DIGG THE DVST ENCLOASED HEARE:
BLESE BE Ƴᵉ MAN Ƴᵗ SPARES THES STONES,
AND CVRST BE HE Ƴᵗ MOVES MY BONES.

Shakspeare monument and gravestone inscriptions, as printed in Dugdale's 1656 book, and today's (see plates 11-12).

suggests that Dugdale's version was not the original. But the circa 1625 version was evidently not the original either.

Dugdale's early drawing and later engraving of the monument's effigy clearly showed a man clutching a sack – something light but firm enough to hold its shape. Richard J. Kennedy's article, "The Woolpack Man," gives strong evidence that the monument's effigy actually depicted John Shakspere, the Stratford Man's father. He died in 1601. Father John traded in wool, so the sack would be a woolsack. Noticeable in Dugdale's drawing and engraving are leopard heads atop the monument's columns on both sides of the effigy. As revealed by Kennedy, the coat of arms for the town of Stratford-upon-Avon featured three leopard heads. It would be right and proper for John Shakspere to have a monument decorated with the town's symbols, observed Kennedy, because he was a former chief bailiff; his son William held no town office.[14] Furthermore, the Stratford Man did not make a provision in his will for a monument to himself; he "committed his body to the earth ... "[15] In late 1622, major work was performed in the chancel area of the church, where the Shakspeare monument and grave are located. A bill dated January 10, 1623, described the work as follows, performed about ten months before the Folio's release:

> Paid the painters for painting the Chancel 20s., Samuel Scriven for glazing the Chancel 20s., to the same glazier 6s. 8d., George Burgess for mending the Chancel walls, 3s.4d., the same for digging two load of stone, 8d., to Hemmings for 7 strike of lime 4s. 8d., Nicholas Tybbotts for 9 strike of hairs 3s.[16]

"Mending the Chancel walls," "digging two load of stone," and purchasing materials for cement ("lime and hair," *OED*) could describe replacement of a monument tablet and gravestone. Perhaps it was John Shakspere's monument tablet, and his son William's gravestone, both with typical funerary inscriptions, that got replaced. Putting only the surname, "Shakspeare," on the monument would suggest either John or William, and for those looking for a monument to a writer Shakespeare, the words "writ" and "wit" would suffice. There never was a monument to William, the Stratford Man – the monument of his father John was evidently reassigned to him.

Fraud upon Fraud upon Fraud

The Stratford monument and the First Folio preface constituted a fraud upon a fraud, one reinforcing the other, but another fraud occurred later that had no connection to Pembroke or Jonson but had unwittingly played into their designs. As shown by Dugdale, the original monument effigy did not depict a writer, pen and paper in either hand both resting upon a cushion, like today's monument – the original effigy clutched a woolsack against its chest. The effigy reincarnated at some point, but besides that and the format of the inscription, it was not the only change made to the monument. Comparing Dugdale's view of the monument with today's monument, one can discern at least thirteen differences with the effigy and the frame and structure that encased it. For example, the aforementioned leopard heads on top of the pillars have disappeared in today's monument. The two angels or boys in the early image sat directly on the ledge, dangled their legs over it, and were situated a good space away from the coat of arms; today the angels sit on mounds, their feet resting on them, and they sit closer to the coat of arms. Originally, the angels held an hourglass and a spade, but today's angels hold an inverted torch and a spade. A skull was added at the base of the right angel. The stained glass windows that surround the monument today were installed in 1891.[17]

The numerous differences between the first documented image of the Shakspeare monument (by Dugdale) and today's monument indicate that the monument proper was changed and the effigy redesigned to show a writer rather than a wool trader. Not surprisingly, Dugdale's engraving of the Shakspeare monument is completely rejected by the Shakespeare professor for the simple reason that it does not agree with today's monument. This circular reasoning flies in the face of the documentary record. After 1634, repairs and "beautifications" were made to the Shakspeare monument, effigy or chancel area of the church in 1649, 1691, 1748, 1790, 1793, 1800, 1835 and 1861.[18] In 1746 it was reported that the Shakspeare monument was "through length of years and other accidents become much impaired and decayed."[19] Money was raised "for repairing and beautifying" it in 1748. These repairs did not last long: in 1814 the effigy was reported by Britton to be "in a decayed and dangerous state."[20] Funds were raised for the repair (£5,000) and carried out in 1835. The Shakespeare scholar, Edmund Malone, arranged for the effigy to be whitewashed in 1793, and in 1861 the white paint was removed and the original colors were restored.[21] The effigy was taken down on several occasions, not only for repair but to have casts made from which reproductions could be made. It is undeniable, therefore, that the Shakspeare monument and its effigy have been tampered with or repaired over the centuries.

To defend the authenticity of today's monument, the Shakespeare professor usually denigrates Dugdale's artistic discernment, but this is hard to do knowing his history. Dugdale was a highly respected historian and antiquarian who wrote several important books. *The Antiquities of Warwickshire*, which contains the engraving of the Shakspeare monument, is considered Dugdale's masterpiece. Four years after he drew the Shakspeare monument, Dugdale

TODAY'S SHAKSPEARE MONUMENT	DUGDALE'S SHAKSPEARE MONUMENT (1634 AND 1656)
ANGELS OR BOYS	
• angels situated close to center box on ledge above effigy	• angels situated on far edges of ledge above effigy
• angels sit upon mounds on the ledge, legs bent	• angels sit directly on ledge, and dangle legs over it (no mounds)
• right angel holds inverted torch, other hand rests on skull	• angel on right holds hourglass, the other hand rests on leg (no skull)
• left angel holds shovel, other hand rests on mound	• left angel holds shovel, other hand rests on leg
EFFIGY	
• effigy's face has upturned mustache and goatee	• effigy's face has long drooping mustache and full beard
• effigy's hands and elbows rest on cushion	• effigy's hands press a woolsack against chest area; effigy's elbows are akimbo, and do not touch woolsack
• effigy's torso is perpendicular to cushion	• effigy's torso and woolsack are parallel
• effigy's hands hold pen and paper	• effigy's hands do not hold pen and paper
STRUCTURAL DETAILS	
• columns: immediately above capitals are four layers of molding that stretch across the monument	• columns: immediately above capitals are leopards' heads (no molding layers)
• arch is one long curve with coffers	• arch curve joins horizontal lines, like bowler hat; no coffers
• side "triangles" on either side of arch: top line almost even with top of capitals	• side "triangles" on either side of arch: top line extends higher than capitals
• brackets at monument's base are rectangular	• brackets at monument's base are trapezoids
• the monument's base layer is even	• the monument's base layer ungulates

Substantive differences between today's Shakspeare Monument and Dugdale's original drawing and engraving (see plates 14-15) was appointed to a paid position in the College of Heralds in London. Later he was appointed Garter king of arms, a very distinguished position, and was knighted. And he was commissioned by an officer of King Charles I to record monuments and epitaphs of London churches, including Westminster Abbey and St. Paul's Cathedral. It is fact that Dugdale visited the Shakspeare monument in person, and to get the full inscription right, he had to have gone very close to make out the tiny letters and numbers of the death date. As Kennedy noted in his article, "Dugdale was *never wrong* regarding the *chief feature* of any of the hundreds of monuments he sketched." Dugdale's book was reissued in 1730, with corrections made by Dr. William Thomas. The section on Stratford-upon-Avon was updated and three pages were added, but the monument's engraving was left untouched. There is no plausible reason why Dugdale would invent the numerous details that differ with today's monument, especially the leopard heads. How could he mistake a short, upturned mustache with a long drooping mustache? Or mistake a torch for an hourglass? Dugdale acknowledged in his book that the Shakspeare monument was to a poet, yet how could he have neglected to insert the pen and paper that turned up on later illustrations of it? Dugdale simply got all these details wrong, says the Shakespeare expert, despite the long history of repairs to the monument and effigy, and despite the absence of documentary proof that Dugdale got it wrong in 1634.

Mustache and Goatee: Keys to the Monument Mystery

When did the extensive changes occur to the monument and effigy that Dugdale had recorded in 1634, and why? The changes were evident by 1721, the date of George Vertue's engraving of it. But whatever the reconstructed effigy face had looked like, Vertue rejected it. Vertue instead inserted the face of the newly discovered Chandos Portrait of Shakespeare in his engraving (later featured in Alexander Pope's edition of the Shakespeare plays, 1723-25). Vertue had engraved the Chandos Portrait two years before, a man with a downturned mustache, full beard, and an earring. A different Shakspeare effigy was certainly in place by 1691, when Gerard Langbaine the Younger wrote that the effigy was "leaning upon a Cushion."[22] Dugdale's figure did not lean upon anything; his hands were holding a woolsack. The date of the monument and effigy redesign can be pushed back even further based upon the effigy's facial hair. Dugdale's effigy showed a man wearing a long drooping mustache and full beard. Today's effigy is of a man with a short upturned mustache and a neatly trimmed and pointed goatee. The mustache is one solid line across the lip that curls up at the ends with a shaved space between it and the nostril. These two mustache and beard depictions are completely different. Putting aside Dugdale's competence, one can easily date production of the face in today's effigy: a time when the upturned mustache and goatee were in fashion. *This style was not in fashion in England during the Stratford Man's lifetime;* he died in 1616, but this style started to emerge circa 1623. Several English portraits from 1625 to 1650 show variations of this combination, which King Charles I wore circa 1630 until his execution in January 1649. The fashion in England waned after 1650.

M.H. Spielmann published three separate articles between 1907 and 1924 (one in *Encyclopedia Britannica*) in which he noted that repair to the Stratford monument was recorded in 1649. Although he did not identify the document, Spielmann wrote, "In 1649 ... the bust was, as it was called, 're-beautified.'"[23] The vestry books of the Stratford-upon-Avon parish confirm that work was done in the chancel area of the church during this time. On November 3, 1648, it was agreed to raise £30 "for the present repairs of the chancel," and on December 15, 1648, £24 and 8 shillings was raised "considered of the decays of the chancel ... "[24] More money "for and towards the repair of the chancel" was needed by June 28, 1650, and another £24 was raised.[25] Between 1634 and 1699, only the years 1648 to 1650 recorded money raised for repair in the chancel area, and it was the only time that the upturned mustache and goatee were in fashion. The probable year of the effigy's first transformation, therefore, is 1649 to 1650, with subsequent repairs and replacements (noted in 1748, etc.) staying fairly close to this *second version*. Supporting evidence for the effigy's reincarnation in 1649 to 1650 is located immediately to the right of it, also on the wall. It is a funeral monument of Judith Combe and her fiancé, Richard Combe, both depicted in effigy (Plate 17). Judith died before their wedding day, on August 17, 1649; Richard erected the monument in her memory. The Combe monument was signed by sculptor Thomas Stanton of Holborn (London area).[26] If the Shakspeare effigy and monument needed to be remade circa 1649, then church funds were available and a funerary sculptor known. Although the Combe monument is larger than the Shakspeare monument, they do have similar design elements.

Dugdale recorded the man with the woolsack, drooping mustache and full beard in 1634 for his book, but it did not get published until 1656. In his "Woolpack Man" article, Richard Kennedy cited Dugdale's dedication letter "To My Honored Friends, the Gentry of Warwickshire," which opens:

> That all things perish by Age and time, or some unhappy accidents, is a thing not to be denied; the consideration whereof, hath not a little incited me to the undertaking of this present work.

In the third paragraph, Dugdale wrote that he was proud to chronicle the tombs of the county's ancestors,

> ... in some sort preserving those Monuments from that fate, which *Time*, if not contingent mischief, might expose them to.

Dugdale's express purpose for this work was to preserve Warwickshire's monuments for the record despite what time, accident, and mischief could do to them. Kennedy suggested that Dugdale had the Shakspeare monument in mind, which, if true, would be more evidence that it had been already changed by 1656. Dugdale certainly revisited the church in 1649 or thereafter: on the same page of his 1634 drawing of the Shakspeare monument were the tombstone inscriptions of the Stratford Man's daughter, Susanna Hall, and her husband, Dr. John Hall.[27] Dr. Hall died in 1635, and Mrs. Hall in 1649. More supporting evidence that the monument and effigy redesign had already occurred when Dugdale's book was published can be seen in an engraving of Shakespeare's face by William Faithorne in the 1655 edition of *The Rape of Lucrece* (Plate 21). It resembled the Droeshout engraving with slight changes: a more distinctly formed mustache, one that was shaven beneath the nostril and had upturned ends. It appears that Faithorne incorporated some features of the new effigy face with Droeshout's engraving. The earliest record of today's effigy face is a painting of the monument by John Hall, who was commissioned to "beautify and repair" the monument in 1748. Unfortunately, the circumstances of its discovery by James Halliwell-Phillips are suspicious and it could be a forgery. Another early record is a drawing of the monument by Josiah Boydell that was made into an engraving by J. Neagle for *Boydell's Folio Edition of Shakespeare* (1802). The very latest limit for the effigy's change in face, therefore, is 1802. That radical changes to the effigy face had occurred during the 18th century is unlikely because the Chandos Portrait with downturned mustache was that century's dominate image of Shakespeare. The Chandos face was the model used for the face of a Shakespeare statue installed in Westminster Abbey (1741). The same is true for the marble statue by Louis-Francois Roubiliac dated 1758 (commissioned by actor David Garrick), and almost every portrait discovered in the 18th century claimed for Shakespeare depicted a man with a downturned mustache.

In July 1634, Dugdale's drawing of the Shakspeare monument showed it was in fairly good condition. Two months later, Lt. Hammond reported in a private manuscript that he saw a "neat monument" to "Shakespeere" during his visit to Stratford-upon-Avon, also implying good condition.

> A neat Monument of that famous English Poet, Mr. William Shakespeere; who was born here.[28]

But fifteen years later, the monument got "re-beautified." The only significant event to occur in Stratford-upon-Avon between 1634 and 1649 was the

English civil war. During the years 1642 to 1646, the town suffered much damage. It was the site of a major battle. The town hall was bombed and the Clopton Bridge was destroyed. Soldiers looted private homes, and documents listing citizen claims for damages still survive. The church was used to house soldiers of both the Royalist and Parliamentary forces. Although the church's exterior did not get damaged, apparently the interior did, creating the need for repairs, as noted above. The entire Shakspeare monument must have been damaged or even destroyed, and such an important monument to the town would eventually have to be repaired or remade. The overall design was fairly close to the original, but some details may have been lost or simply redesigned by the new maker. Another reason for changes to the original monument, especially to the effigy, was perhaps because it was too easy to miss. Tourists eager to visit the Stratford-upon-Avon church to see the monument mentioned in the First Folio may have overlooked the effigy of a wool tradesman identified as "Shakspeare" and not "William Shakespeare." Perhaps the church's personnel were tired of having to direct the tourists, so when the effigy fell into disrepair, something practical was done: refashion it to depict a writer, pen in hand.

Conclusion

Using the First Folio preface and the Shakspeare monument, the 3rd Earl of Pembroke and Ben Jonson evidently pulled off the most successful identity fraud in history. Inclusion of the words "Avon" and "Stratford moniment" in the Folio tributes to the great author planted his origins in Stratford-upon-Avon, a town unrelated to him, but was the hometown of businessman William Shakspere. Already existing in the town church was a monument to John Shakspere, the Stratford Man's father, whose effigy depicted him as a member of the wool trade. To make the Folio reference applicable, the only necessary change to his monument would be a new inscription. The unsuspecting majority took the bait: less than seven years after the Folio's publication the Stratford Man myth was in place. When effects of the English civil war damaged or destroyed the original monument and effigy of the wool dealer, the town replaced it with one more appropriate to a poet, and by doing so, cemented Stratford-upon-Avon's association with the great author. The replacement occurred in 1649 or 1650. The creator of the new effigy face depicted a man sporting a neatly trimmed and upturned mustache and goatee, a fashion contemporaneous to the time but not in fashion during Shakespeare's time. The Shakespeare professor turns a blind eye to the obvious changes that were made not only to the effigy, but also to the monument as a whole, and to the fact that *outside of it and the Folio, nothing ties the*

Stratford Man to the great author. Independently, these two pieces of posthumous "evidence" prove nothing. Had the phrase, "Stratford moniment," not been in the Folio preface, no one would have mistaken the "Shakspeare" monument in Stratford-upon-Avon with the great author because it depicted a wool tradesman. Had the Shakspeare monument not existed, few or none would have associated the great author with Stratford-upon-Avon because that exact place name was not given in the Folio, and many towns in England contained the word "Stratford" (Stratford-at-Bowe and Stratford Langthorne, for example, are towns very near to London). One theory to explain Pembroke and Jonson's use of Stratford-upon-Avon as a decoy will be discussed in chapters 16 and 17.

Conjectured Incarnations of the Stratford Monument and Tomb

The First Incarnation (circa 1601)

John Shakspere died in September 1601, and circa this time a monument was erected with his full name inscribed upon it in the Stratford-upon-Avon church. As his business was the wool trade (later reports said he was a butcher and glove maker, presumably of sheep and sheepskin), John Shakspere's effigy depicted him holding a woolsack. One clue as to when his monument was erected occurs in Ben Jonson's play, *Every Man Out of His Humor*. The character, Sogliardo, which evidently lampooned the Stratford Man, was advised to "build" a tomb in his lifetime.

> SOGLIARDO
> ... and I'll have a tomb, now I think on't; 'tis but so much charges.
>
> CARLO BUFFONE
> Best build it in your lifetime then, your heirs may hap to forget it else.
>
> SOGLIARDO
> Nay, I mean so, I'll not trust to them. [2.1]

The play was written in 1599, two years before John Shakspere had died. Was Jonson mimicking his funeral arrangements? Jonson certainly was aware of the Shakspere coat of arms and motto, which he had mocked in the same play. Richard Brathwait (*Remains After Death*, 1618) claimed that John Combe (d. 1614), the Stratford Man's neighbor, had built his own tomb during his lifetime – perhaps John Shakspere had inspired him. Combe used the same funerary sculptor, "Garat Johnson," according to Sir William Dugdale. There were two Garat Johnsons. The elder founded a sculpture workshop in Southwark, and he described himself as a tombmaker in his will (*DNB*). It is not known if his son, Garrat Johnson the younger, was a sculptor; the record only shows that he made part of fountain, and his birth and death dates are unknown (*DNB*). If the elder Johnson, who died in 1612, made the monument, then it was certainly John Shakspere's monument because his son William died in 1616. The Shakspeare monument may have been based upon that of William Aubrey (d. 1595), in St. Paul's Cathedral, London (Plate 16). After his death in 1616, the Stratford Man was buried within the chancel section of the church under a gravestone that most likely had his full name and usual information.

The Second Incarnation (late 1622)

The Earl of Pembroke and Ben Jonson used John Shakspere's existing monument to suggest that his son, William, was the great author. The monument's inscription tablet was replaced in late 1622, while the Folio was being printed; the effigy of wool trader, John, was unaltered. The Stratford Man's original gravestone was also dug up and replaced with one without his name and with a curse. The unnamed gravestone, and the new line on the monument inscription, "plac't within this monument Shakspeare," encouraged confusion as to the location of the Stratford Man's body. This helped to ensure that his remains would not be mistaken with those of the great author and removed for enshrinement in Westminster Abbey. The fact that Richard Brathwait's epitaph book of 1618 *did not note* the great author's supposed monument in the Stratford-upon-Avon church, or the unusual cursed gravestone, but *did note* Combe's monument nearby them, supports the notion that John Shakspere's monument inscription, and the Stratford Man's gravestone, were replaced after that date. If the two epitaphs recorded circa 1625 were both present on the monument, then Dugdale had recorded the third version of the inscription.

The Third Incarnation (1649-1650)

Soldiers and others taking shelter in the Stratford-upon-Avon church during the English civil war probably caused the destruction of the chancel area, and thus John Shakspere's monument and effigy. After the war, funds were raised, and in 1649-50 the monument was remade and the effigy was completely redesigned to identify the deceased man as a writer. This was meant to accommodate the increasing amount of Shakespeare admirers visiting the church after the publication of the First and Second Folios. The new effigy face sported an upturned mustache with goatee, still *au courant* at that time. The new monument may have been crafted by Thomas Stanton, the London sculptor of the monument to Judith Combe (d. 1649), located on the same wall and only a few feet away from the Shakspeare monument. The Combe and Shakspeare monuments contain similarities with that of William Aubrey in St. Paul's Cathedral (Plate 16). Despite later tampering and subsequent repairs, the monument proper and effigy remained essentially faithful to the second version, with slight changes made to the effigy's facial expression – from "a silly, smiling thing" described by artist Thomas Gainsborough in 1769 (evident in R.B. Wheler's 1806 engraving of the monument),[29] to today's vacant stare.

CHAPTER 11

Folio Feedback

WITH THE SPECTACULAR issuance of the First Folio in late 1623, one would think that an overflow of commentary would erupt from those who could read for the first time Shakespeare's *Anthony and Cleopatra*, *Julius Caesar*, *Macbeth* and seventeen other plays, but the literary world's response was practically mute. It is true that the tome was very expensive – in today's money, it would be priced at over $200, with an estimated "affordability" factor of $2,900[1] – but it sold very well. The only other comparable edition in content, size, and number of pages was Ben Jonson's folio of plays and poems in 1616; a second edition was printed 24 years later. Shakespeare's Second Folio was printed after only nine years, and two more times after that. But despite the Folio's popularity, one decade would pass before the first printed remark about it appeared, and it was not complimentary. The Folio was in its second edition when William Prynne criticized the quality of paper it contained – that it was too good:

> *Some Play-books since I first undertook this subject, are grown from *Quarto* into *Folio*; which yet bear so good a price and sale, that I cannot but with grief relate it, they are now (e) new-printed in far better paper than most Octavo or Quarto *Bibles*, which hardly find such vent as they:
>
> [margin] *Ben-Johnson's, Shackspeer's, and others. (*e*) Shackspeer's Plays are printed in the best Crown paper, far better than most Bibles. [*Histrio-mastix. The Player's Scourge*, 1633]

William Habington, in the following year, suggested that Prynne drink "a plenteous glass" of wine to encourage him to salute rather than criticize Shakespeare, but he did not mention the Folio:

> Of this wine should *Prynne*
> Drink but a plenteous glass, he would begin
> A health to *Shakespeare's* ghost. [*Castara*, 1634]

The next printed mention of the Folio occurred six years later, in a joke book:

> One asked another what Shakespeare's works were worth, all being bound together. He answered, not a farthing. Not worth a farthing! said he; why so? He answered that his plays were worth a great deal of money, but he never heard, that his works were worth anything at all. [R. Chamberlain, *Conceits, Clinches, Flashes* ... (1639)]

The Folio's sales success, contrasted by near silence about it, reflects what the great author experienced in his lifetime: his works were popular and revered, but his personality was ghost-like. The Folio elicited one poetic tribute, perhaps the only, shortly after its release. It is contained in a personal notebook known as the Salisbury Manuscript. The short verse praises Hemings and Condell for performing "noble strains" and for uncovering treasure "raised from the wombs of Earth" that was "manifold" times richer than "gold." For these actors, it could only mean the twenty hitherto unpublished Shakespeare plays. The unidentified writer of this poem did not know "how much" his "good friends" "merited by" the Folio publication.

> To my good friends Mr John Hemings and Henry Condall
>
> To you that Jointly with undaunted pains
> vouchsafed to Chant to us these noble strains,
> how much you merit by it is not said,
> but you have pleased the living, loved the dead,
> Raised from the wombs of Earth a Richer mine
> than Cortez Could with all his Castilian
> Associates, they did but dig for gold,
> But you for Treasure much more manifold.[2]

Despite the lack of printed notice of the Folio, the Shakespeare plays experienced such renewed popularity after its release that the King's Men acting company apparently attempted to stop competitors from performing them. In 1627, John Heminges gave £5 to the Revels Master, Sir Henry Herbert, in the company's behalf "to forbid" the Red Bull Theater from "playing of Shakespeare's plays."[3] This was an odd request coming from one who signed a letter in the Folio urging readers to buy it.

Early Anti-Stratfordians?

The notion that the Stratford Man was the great author was first acknowledged in print seven years after the Folio's release in *Banquet of Jests* (1630). Stratford-upon-Avon was noted as "a town most remarkable for the birth of famous William Shakespeare ... " But the Folio's huge face of a man named "Master William Shakespeare" did not quell entirely the belief that the name was an alias. In 1628, Thomas Vicars added a phrase about Shakespeare in an updated third edition of his *Cheiragogia*, a rhetoric book written in Latin. Vicars mentioned Charles Butler's list of great poets, which included Geoffrey Chaucer, Edmund Spenser, Michael Drayton and George Withers. Vicars wished to add more names to the list, including

> ... that well-known poet who takes his name from the shaking of a spear ... [translation by Prof. Dana Sutton][4]

Shakespeare was only identified by description, not by name, yet Vicars listed the full names of the other admired poets. Fred Schurink translated the line as "that famous poet who takes his name from shaking and spear."[5] Vicars evidently believed that the great author was not born with the name Shakespeare, he "takes" or chooses it, as one would take or choose a pen name or a stage name. A year before the Folio's release, Henry Peacham, Jr. printed a list of the greatest Elizabethan poets in *The Compleat Gentleman* (1622); he did not include Shakespeare. Peacham issued two enlarged editions of his work after the Folio's release, in 1626 and 1627, noted Peter Dickson, but Shakespeare's name was still not included (Peacham lived until 1643).[6] Yet Peacham, or his father, Henry Peacham, Sr., had sketched a scene from Shakespeare's *Titus Andronicus* (now located at Longleat House), presumably indicating some family admiration. Another updated work, Robert Burton's *The Anatomy of Melancholy*, fourth edition (1632), featured revised opening pages resembling those in the First Folio:[7] Burton's portrait was on the title page and opposite it were verses that commented upon it:

> Now last of all to fill a place,
> Presented is the *Author's* face;
> And in that habit which he wears,
> His image to the world appears.
> His mind no art can well express,
> That by his writings you may guess.
> It was not pride, nor yet vainglory,
> (Though others do it commonly)
>
> Made him do this: if you must know,
> The Printer would needs have it so.
> Then do not frown or scoff at it,
> Deride not, or detract a whit.
> For surely as thou dost by him,
> He will do the same again.
> Then look upon't, behold and see,
> As thou likest it, so it likes thee.
>
> And I for it will stand in view,
> Thine to command, *Reader*, Adieu.

Burton said that no art (pictorial) can express the mind, so "deride not" his portrait image; one should "guess" or judge him by his "writings." Ben Jonson's verse opposite the Folio's title page had conveyed a similar message about Droeshout's engraving of Shakespeare. What is even more interesting is that Burton retained usage of his pseudonym, "Democritus Junior," and featured it beneath his portrait. By imitating the Folio, Burton may have been trying to hint that "William Shakespeare" was also a pen name. Burton's line about his image, "do not frown or scoff at it," could also reflect the reaction that Folio readers had to Droeshout's unflattering image.

Hundreds of epitaphs of "eminent persons" were reproduced in the 1631 book, *Ancient Funeral Monuments.* Comprising over 800 pages, the book did not mention the Shakspeare monument or grave in Stratford-upon-Avon. Yet the author, John Weever (d. 1632), was aware of them because he copied both of their inscriptions in his private notebook, which still survives. Next to them he wrote, "Will[ia]m Shakespeare the famous poet."[8] Weever's decision to exclude Shakespeare's epitaph from his book suggests that he later doubted the great author's association with Stratford-upon-Avon. Weever certainly admired Shakespeare: he had printed an epigram of high praise to him in 1599,[9] and his epitaph book featured an anonymous verse ("a Memento for Mortality") that lifted a line from *Hamlet* (5.1.183).[10] In 1638, author William Davenant advised poets *not* to visit "the banks of Avon" to honor Shakespeare. Davenant wrote that Nature had a sickened appearance there; the flowers hang their heads and the trees are stunted and create darkness. The "piteous" Avon river wept so much it is no longer a river but a "shallow brook," wrote Davenant.

> In Remembrance of Master William Shakespeare. Ode.
>
> Beware (delighted Poets!) when you sing
> To welcome nature in the early Spring;
> Your num'rous Feet not tread
> The Banks of Avon; for each Flower
> (As it ne'er knew a Sun or Shower)
> Hangs there, the pensive head.
>
> Each Tree, whose thick and spreading growth hath made
> Rather a Night beneath the Boughs, than Shade,
> (Unwilling now to grow) Looks like the Plume a captive wears,
> Whose rifled *Falls* are steep'd i'th tears
> Which from his last rage flow
>
> The piteous River wept itself away
> Long since (Alas!) to such a swift decay
> That, reach the Map, and look
> If you a River there can spy,
> And for a River your mock'd Eye

Will find a shallow Brook. [*Madagascar*, 1638]

Although this poem was only about "The Banks of Avon," Davenant implied that the town of Stratford-upon-Avon had something to be guilty of.

In 1638, Richard Brome made an intriguing link between Shakespeare and an English earl in his play, *The Antipodes*. Brome's character, Lord Letoy, raves about his players:

> ... These lads can act the Emperors' lives all over
> And Shakespeare's Chronicled histories, to boot.
> And were that *Caesar*, or that English Earl,
> That loved a Play and Players so well, now living,
> I would not be out-vied in my delight [1.5]

Brome, a disciple of Ben Jonson, was describing a real English earl who was known in his lifetime as "Caesar." This had to be the 17th Earl of Oxford, who was described as "a second Caesar, to the view of all that know him" by Anthony Munday, in his novel, *Zelauto* (1580). Munday was Oxford's secretary, and dedicated the work to him. Oxford was a playwright who maintained two acting troupes. Shakespeare had impersonated Caesar in real life, according to Jonson in his then unpublished *Timber, or Discoveries*. Shakespeare, he wrote, jestingly answered someone "in the person of Caesar." Brome's play was influenced by Shakespeare's *Hamlet*, and "fantastic lord" Letoy in many ways resembles Oxford.[11]

In 1639, Thomas Bancroft's epigram to Shakespeare emphasized that the name was descriptive, another hint that it was a pen name:

> Thou hast so us'd thy *Pen*, (or *shook thy Speare*)
> That Poets startle, nor thy wit come near.
> [No. 119, *Two Books of Epigrams and Epitaphs*]

First Folio Mocked

In 1640, John Benson published the small volume, POEMS: WRITTEN BY WIL. SHAKE-SPEARE. *Gent.* It included the first reprint of Thomas Thorpe's 1609 text of the sonnets (all but eight) and *A Lover's Complaint.* The 1612 edition of *The Passionate Pilgrim* and Shakespeare's two poems in *Love's Martyr* were also included. Benson's edition would be the only text of the sonnets available for another seventy years, but it was important for another reason: it contained the first direct criticism of the First Folio's preface by questioning Shakespeare's identity. Opposite the title page was Shakespeare's portrait by William Marshall, an altered version of the Droeshout engraving (Plate 20).

It looks like a spotlight has been aimed at the face. Beneath this image is a poem that opens with a question: "This shadow is renowned Shakespear's?" Using excerpts and paraphrases of lines in Jonson's elegy to Shakespeare in the Folio, Droeshout's engraving was mocked:

> This Shadow is renowned Shakespear's? Soul of th'age.
> The applause? delight? the wonder of the Stage.
> Nature herself, was proud of his designs
> And joy'd to wear the dressing of his lines;
> The learned will Confess, his works are such,
> As neither man, nor Muse, can praise too much.
> Forever live thy fame, the world to tell,
> Thy like, no age, shall ever parallel.

Marshall's engraving resembles a portrait of Ben Jonson by Robert Vaughn (Plate 8) featured in the 1640 reprint of Jonson's *Works*. Both images depicted the author wearing a cloak over one shoulder, and holding or wearing gloves and bay leaves, the latter a symbol of poetic achievement notably absent in Droeshout's image. It seems that Benson chose this image to evoke Jonson's presence and to challenge him: "Droeshout's engraving really represents the great author?" The Jonson challenge continues in this edition's preface with the poem, "Upon Master William Shakespeare, the Deceased author, and his Poems," written by Folio contributor Leonard Digges. But Digges's verse was not about Shakespeare's poetry, it was about Shakespeare's plays, and statements made in the Folio's preface. Digges opened his Shakespeare tribute by throwing a dart at Jonson: "Poets are born not made," a direct response to Jonson's Folio elegy line, "For a good poet's made, as well as born." Digges then recanted the usage of the word "works" in his Folio poem to describe Shakespeare's plays:

> ... I will not say
> Reader his Works for to contrive a play:
> To him 'twas none ...

Digges had used "works" twice in his Folio poem.

> *Shake-speare*, at length thy pious fellows give
> The world thy Works: thy Works, by which, out-live
> Thy tomb, thy name must when that stone is rent,
> And time dissolves thy *Stratford* Moniment ...

Digges may have been ridiculing Jonson, as others had, for titling his collected edition of drama and poems, *Works*. But considering Jonson's fondness for that word, Digges's rejection of it may have been a clue that Jonson had altered his Folio poem – it was this poem that contained the crucial phrase, "Stratford moniment." Digges may also have been insisting that *Shakespeare did not work, that he did not write plays to make a living*; Jonson *did* write plays and masques for his living. Digges continued his carping of Jonson in this poem by writing that Shakespeare's plays outshined Jonson's (*Cataline* was "tedious" and *Sejanus* "irksome") and that audiences much preferred watching Iago, Othello, Falstaff and other Shakespeare characters. Digges also directly referred to the Folio with the phrase, "this whole Book."

> Next Nature only helped him, for look through
> This whole Book, thou shalt find he doth not borrow,
> One phrase from Greeks, nor Latins imitate,
> Nor once from vulgar Languages Translate,
> Nor Plagiari-like from others glean,
> Nor begs he from each witty friend a Scene
> To piece his Acts with, all that he doth write,
> Is pure his own, plot, language exquisite ...

By listing things that Shakespeare *did not do* to write his plays, such as plagiarize, Digges seemed to imply that Jonson *did* do these things. Going out of his way to criticize Jonson and to contradict his signed poem in the Folio preface, Digges apparently was renouncing it. Digges wrote the poem between 1630 and 1634,[12] but it was published posthumously. Digges died in 1635, and Jonson in 1637.

Why would Benson feature a poem covering three pages that so openly denigrated Ben Jonson? That same year (1640), Benson published one volume containing three Jonson works.[13] Although Benson evidently respected Jonson, he may have objected to his part in the First Folio. Benson used the then-deceased Digges as a vehicle to vent his criticism in his edition of Shakespeare's poetry. Benson added insult to injury by including in this edition the poem by William Basse that Jonson had censured in his Folio elegy. Basse had asked Spenser, Chaucer and Beaumont, all buried in Westminster Abbey, to move a little closer to "make room" for Shakespeare. Jonson had belittled the idea, declaring Shakespeare is "alive still, while thy book doth live." Benson inserted one poem that ridiculed Jonson, and another that Jonson had ridiculed. In Benson's edition, Basse's poem was titled "On the death of William Shakespeare, who died in April, Anno Dom. 1616," which accorded with the Stratford Man's death date. It is the only clue in Benson's book linking the great author to the Stratford Man, and it was placed in the back pages of the first section. Benson must have added this title because it did not accompany Basse's verse in its first printed form *(Poems, by J.D.*, 1633); there it was titled, "Epitaph on Shakespeare." Following Basse's piece in Benson's edition was the anonymously written verse, "Elegy on the Death of that Famous Writer and Actor, M. William Shakspeare," a title that reinforced the idea promoted in Jonson's collected works, and afterward in Shakespeare's, that he was a working actor. No other personal information about the great author was given in Benson's edition – not the word Stratford, not the word Avon. Although Benson questioned the Folio's image of the great author, he took the establishment line with the Stratford Man. Benson's edition was printed by Thomas and Richard Cotes, the printers of the Second Folio (1632); perhaps they related inside information to Benson about Shakespeare and the First Folio's production. Benson's bold question about the authenticity of the Folio's image of Shakespeare was not the only unusual statement printed about Shakespeare in 1640. The anonymously written book, *Wit's Recreations*, acknowledged the silence surrounding Shakespeare.

> To Mr. William Shake-spear.
>
> *Shake-speare* we must be silent in thy praise,
> 'Cause our encomiums will but blast thy Bays,
> Which envy could not, that thou didst do well;
> Let thine own histories prove thy Chronicle.   [No. 25]

The writer seems to be saying that by giving praise ("encomiums") to the great author, his garland of "bays" (a prize for excellence) would get blasted off his head. Praising the great author would somehow compromise him. But the anonymous writer *is* praising Shakespeare, and not silently – he is doing so in print. This contradiction is best explained if "Shake-speare" is a pen name – the great author is not being praised *with his real name*. The passage also printed the name twice with a hyphen. Evidently, public praise or commentary of Shakespeare was discouraged, even as late as 1640, after two editions of the Folio. This statement suggests there was something personally or politically troubling about Shakespeare that chilled discussion by fans and critics alike. The *Wit's Recreations* writer ends by saying Shakespeare's works ("histories") will prove his life ("chronicle"), or who he really is, which repeats Jonson's message in the Folio:

> ... Reader, look
> Not on his picture, but his book.

Although printed allusions to Shakespeare's plays continued after 1640, comments that directly or indirectly questioned the image of Shakespeare, as given in the Folio's preface, ended. The rise of Puritanism in politics, which caused the closing of the theaters from 1642 to 1660, evidently stopped them.

Conclusion

Considering the magnitude of its importance, with the print debut of so many dramatic masterpieces, the First Folio of 1623 was publicly received with an eerie and suspicious silence. Although the Folio fostered the impression that the great author was born with the name William Shakespeare in Stratford-upon-Avon, there were signs that members of the literary world were rejecting its both subtle and screaming propaganda. One admirer of Shakespeare declined to print the Shakspeare monument and gravestone inscriptions in his epitaph book, and another insinuated that Stratford-upon-Avon was guilty of something that poets in particular should "beware" of. The idea that "Shakespeare" was someone's alias endured, and a playwright who was close with Ben Jonson evidently believed that Shakespeare was the 17th Earl of Oxford. In 1640, John Benson questioned the veracity of Droeshout's engraving of Shakespeare *in print* and for doing so can be rightly called the father of the Shakespeare authorship question. Benson's edition also included a poem that insulted Ben Jonson, whose material dominated the Folio's preface. Leonard Digges, another Folio contributor, wrote this poem. Also in 1640, the hush about Shakespeare was openly addressed: a poem printed in *Wit's Recreations* said that praising Shakespeare was discouraged, and that only by reading his works will the public really know him. And what did the literary world have to say about the Stratford Man? The next two chapters will explore this question.

PART IV

The Real Stratford Man & The Real Shakespeare

CHAPTER 12

Portrayals of the Stratford Man in Contemporary Comedies (1598 - 1601)

IF THE STRATFORD Man was not the great author, then what part did he play, if any, in the Shakespeare authorship story? Since none of his relatives or acquaintances left memories about him, where can one find more information? Ben Jonson and an anonymous writer at Cambridge University lampooned the Stratford Man in a cluster of comedies performed during 1598 to 1601. All four plays feature one character of this description: an uneducated or naive man who pretends to be or believes he is a gentleman. His pose is seen as ridiculous by the more knowledgeable characters, and in three of four plays he is called a "gull." He pretends to write poetry, but actually he gets it from "brokers," steals it, or hires others to write it. He has money but how he obtained it is not explained. Although some may argue that this is a standard character type, three of the plays describe the gull with characteristics specific to the Stratford Man. It was no accident, then, that the word "gull" was stressed – a pun upon Gulielium – the Latin equivalent of William. In one play, the gull's name is "Gullio," and as he lies prodigiously about his life as a recognized poet, he indirectly reveals a detailed description of the true Shakespeare and how his scholarly admirers received him. The gull character featured in these four plays is completely opposite to the artist who reveals himself in his works: a super-educated, sophisticated, and traveled gentleman who was intimate with the nobility. These plays also contained paraphrases or echoes of Shakespearean lines, and one mentioned Shakespeare by name. In two plays, the gull is fascinated by or concerned with swords; besides its commonality with a spear, "sword" is a simple anagram for "words," as the Ogburns first noted in *This Star of England*.[1] The gull's presence is not just comic relief: he gets the attention of other characters and is important to the plot. These four portrayals do not depict the gull as an actor, and rightly so, for belonging to the acting profession would have been an anathema to a social climbing would-be gentleman. Jonson and the Cambridge University writer evidently knew the Stratford Man and viewed him as an ignorant boor from the country. He was uneducated, greedy, and "bought" gentility. He stole the great author's works by providing a front for pirating printers, exploiting the similarity of his name with the great author's pen name.

EVERY MAN OUT OF HIS HUMOR

(first performed 1599, first published 1600)

The most obvious and pointed portrayal of the Stratford Man was the character Sogliardo in Ben Jonson's comedy, *Every Man Out of His Humor*, with identity clues that even the Shakespeare professor recognizes. Sogliardo's opening line echoes the Stratford Man's financial situation and his desire to improve his social standing:

> I have land and money, my friends left me well, and I will be a gentleman whatsoever it cost me. [1.1]

Sogliardo is "a man of fair revenue" (4.8). The Stratford Man was prosperous enough to purchase one of the largest houses in his hometown in 1597. Sogliardo is ignorant of what defines a gentleman and asks Carlo Buffone,

> If you please to instruct, I am not too good to learn on being a gentleman. [1.1]

Sogliardo's "gifts of the mind" are described as

> nature lent him them, pure, simple, without ... learning and knowledge ...   [4.6]

Evidence that the Stratford Man had any form of education is lacking. "Sogliardo" was translated as "fool" in John Florio's 1598 Italian-English dictionary.[2] Sogliardo obtains a coat of arms not in the ordinary way with proof of gentility or land-owning ancestors, but through purchase:

> I thank God I can write myself gentleman now. Here's my patent. It cost me thirty pound, by this breath. [3.1]

With the then very large sum of £30, Sogliardo may not have been paying only an administrative fee. As "Shakespeare" was listed among those granted a coat of arms improperly by the College of Heralds in 1602 (Chapter 5), bribery may have been involved. Sogliardo describes his coat of arms as a "boar without a head, rampant." Carlo Buffone compliments the College for such apt symbolism:

> I commend the herald's wit, he has deciphered him well: a swine without a head, without brain, wit, anything indeed, ramping to gentility. [3.1]

Sir Puntarvolo mocks Sogliardo's coat of arms as "the most vile, absurd, palpable and ridiculous escutcheon," and for it he suggests the motto, "not without mustard" (3.1). Many consider this a parody of John Shakspere's armorial motto, "Not Without Right." This phrase appears in two separate applications for his coat of arms in 1596, and placed near drawings of the proposed shield. Jonson may have learned about these applications from his former schoolmaster and longtime friend, William Camden, an official at the College of Heralds.

Another connection with the Stratford Man in this play is an allusion to his grain hoarding, which was recorded in February 1598, a famine year. Act 1 scene 1 shows Sogliardo's brother, Sordido, happily planning to hide his grain supply because the almanac predicts bad weather. Several proclamations against this practice were issued from 1587 to 1600.[3] Jonson apparently split characteristics of the Stratford Man between the two brothers to obscure his identity. Another "bad" character, Shift, is introduced in the play posting "bills" (advertisements) on the door of St. Paul's Cathedral. Shift's opening words imply he is engaged in a shady enterprise:

> This is rare. I have set up my bills without discovery. [3.1]

Shift is observed by Sogliardo and others "using action to his rapier" and "expostulating with his rapier." When asked if he would sell his rapier, Carlo Buffone observes,

> He is turned wild upon the question! He looks as he had seen a sergeant. [3.1.354]

A sergeant was a sheriff's officer who could make arrests.[4] Shift replies:

> My rapier? No, sir; my rapier is my guard, my defense, my revenue, my honor. [3.1.396]

Asked if those advertisements on the church door were his, Shift says,

> Sir, if I should deny the manuscripts, I were worthy to be banish'd the middle aisle forever. [3.1.450, 1616 edition]

"Using action to his rapier" and "expostulating with his rapier" is another way of saying shaking swords or spears, or "Shake-speare." The rapier is Shift's "revenue," and if denied "the manuscripts," he would be out of business. Jonson makes it clear that Shift is pirating Shakespeare's plays, the "words" or sword-rapier. Shift brags to Sogliardo of his exploits as a robber. They become fast friends, calling each other "Countenance" and "Resolution." Sogliardo, the Stratford Man, is "Countenance" or a face for Shift, who represents pirating printers. One early meaning of resolution is "the process by which a material thing is reduced" (*OED*). The early printed Shakespeare plays were reduced versions of the originals, because the printers did not have access to them. "Shift" as a verb means to practice or live by fraud, and a "shifter" is a trickster or thief. The Stratford Man had a name that was close enough to the great author's pseudonym for pirates to hide behind. If ever questioned about their source for the plays, the printers could point to the Stratford Man, "William Shakspere." Presumably the Stratford Man was paid to be their "countenance." To emphasize this, Jonson characterized Shift and Sogliardo as "Judas" and "the elder tree he hangs himself upon" (4.5), and puppeteer and puppet. The printer-pirate is a Judas or traitor towards the great author and uses the Stratford Man as his puppet. The grouping of the words "Judas," "elder," and "countenance" also occurred in Shakespeare's *Love's Labour's Lost*, which undoubtedly had inspired Jonson:

> BEROWNE
> Judas was hanged on an elder.
>
> HOLOFERNES
> I will not be put out of countenance.
>
> BEROWNE
> Because thou hast no face ...   [5.2.607-09]

Sir Puntarvolo is a gentleman and courtier described by another character as a great horseman who can "taint a staff well at tilt" (2.1), i.e., he is a good tilter or spear shaker. Jonson was probably hinting that he represented the great author via his pen name. Sir Puntarvolo pays inordinate attention to his greyhound. The dog is kept constantly near him and he is so protective of it he tells a servant,

> If thou losest my dog, thou shalt die a dog's death: I will hang thee.   [3.2]

He uses his dog as collateral for a wager and even describes him as a gem. When Shift, also a tobacconist, tells Sir Puntarvolo he can teach his dog to smoke, Sir Puntarvolo is offended.

My dog shall not eat in his company for a million. [3.6]

Before his visit to the royal court, Sir Puntarvolo leaves the dog with "one that is ignorant of his quality, if I will have him to be safe" (5.1). Upon his return, Sir Puntarvolo is told that Shift stole the dog:

SIR PUNTARVOLO [*to Shift*]
My dog, villain, or I will hang thee! Thou hast confessed robberies and other felonious acts to this gentleman, thy Countenance –

SOGLIARDO
I'll bear no witness.

SIR PUNTARVOLO
And without my dog, I will hang thee for them. [5.3]

Sir Puntarvolo's dog obviously symbolized something more than a pet. If the titled gentleman, Sir Puntarvolo, represents the great author, then his dog must represent the Shakespeare plays. Sogliardo-Stratford Man is an accessory to the crime of stealing the greyhound-plays. When Carlo Buffone taunts Sir Puntarvolo about the now dead dog, Sir Puntarvolo stops him by sealing up his mouth with wax; discussing his involvement with the plays is secret. *Every Man Out of His Humor* alludes to Shakespeare's *Macbeth, Henry VI-Part 2, Julius Caesar*, both parts of *Henry IV, Romeo and Juliet, Othello, Hamlet*, and Sonnet 128.[5]

EVERY MAN IN HIS HUMOR

(first performed 1598, first published 1601)

Ben Jonson's *Every Man Out of His Humor* was clearly a sequel to, or a more explicit version of, his earlier comedy, *Every Man In His Humor*, featuring a similar title and characters. With this perspective, one can see Jonson's first satire of the Stratford Man in the composite of characters Master Stephen and Master Mathew. In Jonson's revised version of the play (published in 1616), he described these characters as "the country gull" (Stephen) and "the town gull" (Mathew) to emphasize they were to be viewed as one entity. The Stratford Man lived in both the country and the city. Although not related in the play, these two gulls share similar character traits. From the very first scene, Stephen is called ridiculous, and throughout the play is repeatedly called a gull, a fool and "stupidity itself" by the other characters. Mathew is not openly called a gull, but his name in the 1601 quarto of the play, Matheo, resembles the Italian word, *matto*, a fool.[6] Stephen and Mathew have pretensions to gentility but lack understanding of what that is. Stephen thinks that reading a book on hunting and hawking and using the proper swear words will make him a gentleman. Mathew's gentlemanly pose is as a melancholy lover who writes sonnets; he is actually a fishmonger's son, who "doth creep and wriggle into acquaintance with all the brave gallants about the town" (1.3). Both Stephen and Mathew are fascinated with swords, just like their counterpart, Sogliardo, in *Every Man Out of His Humor*. The rapier or sword apparently symbolized Shakespeare or his plays. Stephen is inexplicably driven to buy a "rapier," described as "a most pure Toledo." In Mathew's first appearance in the play (3.1), he seeks Captain Bobadill to teach him fencing (also a slang-word for dealing in stolen goods). Besides their interest in swords, Stephen and Mathew both pretend they are poets but spend more time as thieves: Stephen steals a man's cloak and claims it is his, and Mathew steals poetry, obtaining it from "wit brokers" and claims it as his own. Mathew does not specifically steal poetry from Shakespeare, but Shakespeare is definitely present: six of Jonson's characters share names with those in Shakespeare's plays.[7] Mathew openly recites verses that turn out to be garbled lines from *Hero and Leander* by the late Christopher Marlowe. The character Knowell decries it:

> I'll have him free of the wit brokers, he utters nothing but stolen remnants; a filching rogue, hang him! and from the dead! It's worse than sacrilege. [4.1]

Mathew is a plagiarist. "Wit brokers" supplied him with "stolen remnants" from Marlowe. At the end of the play, when all the characters converge in Justice Clement's office (5.1), Mathew's pockets are emptied; they were filled with filched lines from Samuel Daniel's *Delia* sonnets (which was ironic because Daniel was known to plagiarize).

> He carries a whole realm, a commonwealth of paper, in his hose!

After the Justice reads a few lines, he declares, "This is stolen," and burns the lot. Jonson's play debuted one year after the surreptitious printing of Shakespeare's *Romeo and Juliet*.

It appears that Jonson based his character, Master Stephen, upon Stephano, a character from Shakespeare's play, *The Tempest*. Jonson's Master Stephen was originally named Stephano, and Well-Bred in the same play was originally named Prospero, the central character in *The Tempest*. Many scholars accept that Shakespeare's Prospero, a nobleman-magician living in exile on an island, represented the great author. Taking this symbology a step further, the island could be interpreted as the "realm" of the theater.[8] Shakespeare's

Stephano, who was shipwrecked on Prospero's island with others, is egged on by Caliban to murder Prospero. Caliban advised Stephano two times to first "seize" and "possess" Prospero's "books" – the manuscripts of the Shakespeare plays – before he kills Prospero (3.2.95, 98). "Do that good mischief," says Caliban, and it will "make this Island /Thine own forever … " (4.1.217-18). Shakespeare's Stephano was a likely caricature of the Stratford Man. Stealing Prospero's books (i.e., pirating the Shakespeare plays) will make Stephano (the Stratford Man) king of the island (theater). Shakespeare's Stephano, and the jester, Trinculo, fight over a gown in Prospero's wardrobe. As mentioned above, Jonson's Master Stephen steals a man's cloak and claims it is his own.

Jonson may have been speaking to posterity with this prediction about Shakespeare and the Stratford Man through the words of Master Stephen:

> STEPHEN
> I assure you mine uncle here is a man of a thousand a year, Middle-sex land. He has but one son in all the world, I am his next heir, at the common law, Master Stephen, as simple as I stand here, if my cousin die, as there's hope he will: I have a pretty living o' mine own too, beside, hard by here.
>
> SERVINGMAN
> In good time, sir. [1.1]

Master Stephen has "hope" that he will inherit the ownership or author-ship of the Shakespeare plays, "simple" as he is. His "uncle," the real Shake-speare, is a man of "a thousand a year." As explained in Chapter 8, Jonson wrote in the 1616 edition of the play that in Master Stephen's face "*is to be seen the true, rare, and accomplished monster, or miracle of nature*, which is all one" (1.2), a possible hint of what was coming in the First Folio. In the 1601 edition of Jonson's play, the punishment for Mathew's crime of plagiarism was to be bound in the center of the marketplace (5.3), but in the 1616 edi-tion, the justice implies that he will "forgive or forget" (5.1). This may be more evidence of Jonson's insight about the Shakespeare authorship, that the Stratford Man's theft of Shakespeare's plays will not be publicly exposed; he will instead get credited as their author. Perhaps one day the experts will come to the same realization about the Stratford Man that Caliban had about Stephano in *The Tempest*:

> what a thrice-double Ass
> Was I, to take this drunkard for a god?
> And worship this dull fool? [5.1.296-98]

POETASTER

(first performed in 1601, first published in 1602)

The title of Ben Jonson's comedy, *Poetaster, or His Arraignment*, describes the character, Crispinus. Not a poet, Crispinus only "tastes" poetry because he thinks it will make him more like a gentleman. He demonstrates his stupidity with his ludicrous use of language; the second phrase he utters is "I am most strenuously well, I thank you, sir." Snobby Crispinus calls himself a gentleman in the play four times. After Crispinus is asked, "Are you a gentleman born?," he takes out his coat of arms, "for I bear them about me to have them seen" (2.1). Crispinus is also called a plagiary. By this description, Crispinus is kin to Jonson's previous *Every Man* characters, Master Mathew and Sogliardo, the naive posers of gentility who steal poetry. Crispinus is further likened to Sogliardo with his ridiculous escutcheon.

> My name is Crispinus, or Cri-spinas indeed; which is well expressed
> in my arms; a face crying in chief; and beneath it a bloody toe,
> between three thorns pungent. [2.1]

Jonson's choice of the name Crispinus was a daring allusion to Shakespeare. Sir George Greenwood noted that the meaning of the Latin word, *crispo*, is to brandish or shake, an action most applicable to spears and swords.[9] Even more daring was Jonson's revelation that Crispinus uses an alias:

> Crispinus, <u>alias Cri-spinas</u>, poetaster and plagiary. [5.3]

"Cri-spinas" was hyphenated in the first printed text, just as Shakespeare's name was hyphenated about half the time it was printed, reflecting the belief among writers and publishers that it was a descriptive alias. Crispinus and Cri-spinas are names so similar it is as if Jonson was pointing out the name similarity between Shakspere (the Stratford Man) and Shake-speare (the great author). Crispinus is a "gentleman parcel-poet," i.e., a partial poet. "A 'parcel-poet,' wrote Greenwood, "is like a parcel-gilt goblet – he is a poet on the surface only, but inwardly base metal."[10]

Jonson evidently split the identity of Crispinus between the Stratford Man and writer John Marston, especially in the last scene when Crispinus is found guilty of calumniating "the person and writings of" Horace (5.1). Jonson was known as "English Horace" among his peers. It is believed that the character, Brabant Senior, in John Marston's play, *Jack Drum's Entertainment*, written the year before *Poetaster*, was a satirical portrayal of Jonson (*DNB*). In Jonson's opinion, Marston wanted to injure his reputation, so in the play, he put him on trial. Soon after *Poetaster* was performed, a complaint about it reached

Chief Justice Popham. Jonson needed a lawyer to help him explain that the play was not seditious.[11] *Poetaster* alludes to Shakespeare's Sonnet 109, *Romeo and Juliet*, *Twelfth Night*, and *Othello*.[12]

THE RETURN FROM PARNASSUS – PART ONE

(written ca. 1599-1600)

The Stratford Man characters in Ben Jonson's three comedies are doltish social climbers who steal poetry. But the anonymous Cambridge University author of *The Return from Parnassus-Part 1* was even more bold: a similar character is enamored of Shakespeare, steals his works, specifically *Romeo and Juliet*, and impersonates him. There were three "Parnassus" plays written for student entertainment at Cambridge University during 1598 to 1602. The closing lines of the first play, *Pilgrimage to Parnassus*, dropped hints that the second play will have something to do with Shakespeare and a character named "Gullio."

> Let vulgar wits admire the common songs,
> I'll lie with Phoebus by the Muses springs
> Where we will sit free fro' all envy's rage
> And scorn each earthly Gullio of this age.

The first two lines above are a loose translation of the Latin couplet featured on the title page of Shakespeare's *Venus and Adonis* (1593), and the next two lines that Gullio will be the object of "scorn." As noted in the analysis of Jonson's comedies, "gull" was the byword for the Stratford Man characters; "gull" puns on the Latin equivalent of "William" and is another word for stupid or foolish.

The third act of *The Return from Parnassus-Part 1* opens with the scholar, Ingenioso, speaking directly to the audience of Cambridge University students. He introduces Gullio:

> Now gentlemen, you may laugh if you will, for here comes a gull. [line 834]

Gullio is an ignoramus who poses as a gentleman. In his opening line he describes his rapier as "a pure Toledo," instantly recalling *Every Man In His Humor*, when Master Stephen, "the town gull," buys a rapier, "a most pure Toledo." The sophisticated student audience would have made the association with Jonson's fairly recent play. In one revealing passage, Gullio demonstrates how he courted a lady with poetry, while Ingenioso tells the audience where and how he had obtained it.

GULLIO
Pardon, fair lady, though sick-thoughted Gullio makes amain unto thee, and like a bold-faced suitor 'gins to woo thee.

INGENIOSO
We shall have nothing but pure Shakspeare, and shreds of poetry that he hath gathered at the theaters.

GULLIO
Pardon me moy mistressa, ast am a gentleman the moon in comparison of thy bright hue a mere slut, Anthony's Cleopatra a black brow'd milkmaid, Helen a dowdy.

INGENIOSO
Mark Romeo and Juliet: O monstrous theft, I think he will run through a whole book of Samuel Daniels.   [lines 983-94]

In this passage, Gullio first recites paraphrased lines from Shakespeare's *Venus and Adonis* (lines 5-6), and Ingenioso tells the audience that Gullio gathers these and other lines from theaters. Gullio next recites a garbled line from *Romeo and Juliet* (2.3.41-45), and Ingenioso exclaims to the audience Gullio's "monstrous theft" of this play; this was an obvious reference to the pirated quarto edition of the play in 1597, causing the seizure of the printers' presses. After Gullio quotes lines from the play, *The Spanish Tragedy*, Ingenioso remarks to Gullio about his knowledge of English poets. Gullio replies:

> I vouchsafe to take some of their words and apply them to mine own matters by a scholastical imitation.   [lines 1006-08]

Gullio takes other poets' words, including those of Shakespeare, and applies them to his "own matters" by "imitation." Is this not another way of saying pirating for personal gain? To please his lady friend, Gullio asks Ingenioso to write for him original verses in the style of Chaucer, Spenser and Shakespeare as befits a gentleman. Similarly, both Crispinus and Master Stephen went to "wit brokers" or stole poetry to recite in society so they will appear gentlemanly. After Ingenioso provides samples of each, Gullio says he prefers the sample like Shakespeare, whom he "worships."

> Let this duncified world esteem of Spenser and Chaucer, I'll worship sweet Mr. Shakspeare, and to honor him will lay his *Venus and Adonis* under my pillow ... [lines 1200-03]

When Gullio's attempt to impress his lady friend with poetry backfires, he dismisses Ingenioso, who retaliates with choice parting words:

> Farewell gilt ass, farewell base broker's post. [line 1455]

"Base broker's post" – a post being a block of wood – indicates the Stratford Man's stupidity as well as his being a dummy "front" for the "brokers" or printers who pirated Shakespeare's plays. By profiting from Shakespeare in this way, it is no wonder that he "worships" him. Besides being a poser and a thief, Gullio also pretends that he is the great author; he explicitly divulges this in the following passage:

> I am very lately registered in the rolls of fame, in an epigram made by a Cambridge man, one Weaver – fellow [status of a student], I warrant him, else could he never have had such a quick sight into my virtues, howsoever I merit his praise: if I meet with him I will vouchsafe to give him condign [due] thanks. [lines 957-62]

In 1599, John Weever published *Epigrams in the Oldest Cut and Newest Fashion*. Gullio believes that Weever's complimentary epigram to "Gulielmum Shakespear" (Week 4, No. 22) was meant for him, but the joke was that Weever also wrote an insulting epigram to "Gullionis," a criminal:

> Here lies fat Gullio, who capered in a cord
> To highest heav'n for all his huge great weight ... [Week 2, No. 21]

Weever had no "praise" for fat Gullionis, but high praise for "honey-tongu'd Shakespeare" (Jonson similarly described Sogliardo as a "hulk of ignorance").

Gullio recites lines 7 to 12 from Shakespeare's *Venus and Adonis* but with one very notable change. Shakespeare's phrase, "thus she began" (line 7), was altered for Gullio to "thus I began."

> GULLIO
> Thrice fairer than myself, <u>thus I began</u>,
> The gods fair riches, sweet above compare,[13]
> Stain to all nymphs, more lovely than a man,
> More white and red than doves and roses are:
> Nature that made thee, with herself at strife,
> Saith that the world hath ending with thy life.
>
> INGENIOSO
> Sweet Mr Shakspeare. [lines 995-1001]

Alden Brooks first noticed that Gullio was here attributing these Shakespeare lines to himself.[14] But after Gullio's recitation, Ingenioso immediately claims them for "Sweet Mr Shakspeare." Ingenioso constantly tells the audience that all Gullio says is "folly" and that he is a "haberdasher of lies"; it is all pretense

214 | SHAKESPEARE SUPPRESSED

and not to be taken seriously. There is a clear separation between Gullio and Shakespeare: Gullio "worships" Shakespeare, so he cannot actually be Shakespeare. The Cambridge writer makes it very plain that Gullio is imitating and impersonating the great author. With this in mind, it follows that the other "lies" that Gullio advances about himself must be characteristic of the great author. Gullio naively believes that his efforts "to prove a complete gentleman" aroused public admiration.

> Oh Sir, that was my care, to prove a complete gentleman, to be *tam Marti quam Mercurio*, insomuch that I am pointed at for a poet in Paul's churchyard, and in the tilt yard for a champion – nay, every man inquires after my abode: "Gnats are unnoted wheresoe'r they fly, But Eagles waited on with every eye." [lines 929-33]

Gullio has a propensity for reciting Shakespeare's lines, like those quoted above from *Rape of Lucrece* (lines 1014-15, two words excepted), and says he is "pointed at for a poet." Perhaps people mistakenly "pointed at" the Stratford Man as the poet, "William Shakespeare," because of the name similarity. Gullio is also pointed at as a tiltyard champion (or jouster), and "every man inquires after my abode." This suggests that the great author was a champion tilter and lived in an impressive home. (In *Every Man Out of His Humor*, Sir Puntarvolo, who most likely represented the great author, was similarly characterized as an excellent tilter who lived in a castle.) The next lines of Gullio's self-description are especially revealing.

> I had in my days not unfitly been likened to Sir Philip Sidney ... His *Arcadia* was pretty, so are my sonnets; he had been at Paris, I at Padua ... he loved a scholar, I maintain them ...

> [I] also maintain other poetical spirits, that live upon my trenchers [wooden serving dishes]; insomuch I cannot come to my inn in Oxford without a dozen congratulatory orations, made by Genus and Species and his ragged companions. I reward the poor ergoes most bountifully ... [lines 934-39, 952-57]

Gullio brags to Ingenioso that in his earlier days he was compared to poet Sir Philip Sidney and traveled to Italy; he writes sonnets, patronizes scholars and poets, and when he visits Oxford, students celebrate him. Gullio also says he eats gourmet food and socializes with nobility.

> I'll eat a bit of pheasant, and drink a cup of wine in my cellar, and straight to the court I'll go: a countess and two lords expect me today at dinner, they are my very honorable friends, I must not disappoint them. [lines 1036-40]

All of Gullio's boasts, therefore, can be taken as the true characteristics of the true Shakespeare. According to the Cambridge University writer of this play, there was also a man in the late 1590s, an ignoramus named William, who stole from Shakespeare, enjoyed being mistaken with him, and who foolishly tried to imitate or impersonate him. Such a man pretending to be the transcendent literary genius, Shakespeare, was an irresistible subject to parody, especially by those who knew about the real Shakespeare – certainly the Cambridge University audience, for whom the play was written.

Part two of *The Return from Parnassus* (circa 1601-02) contained more evidence of university students' understanding of Shakespeare's identity: that he was a university man and was not the "fellow" of actors. In one scene, two well-known actors, William Kemp and Richard Burbage, are characters speaking about plays written by university men. Kemp says:

> Few of the university pen plays well, they smell too much of that writer *Ovid*, and that writer *Metamorphosis*, and talk too much of *Prosperina & Jupiter*. Why here's <u>our fellow *Shakespeare*</u> puts them all down, aye and *Ben Jonson* too. O that *Ben Jonson* is a pestilent fellow, he brought up *Horace* giving the Poets a pill, but <u>our fellow *Shakespeare*</u> hath given him a purge that made him bewray his credit. [4.3, or lines 1766-73]

Charlton Ogburn wrote that "a special point is being made" of Kemp's ignorance when he refers to "Metamorphosis" as a writer – Metamorphosis is the *title* of a poem by Ovid.[15] Kemp says that plays written by university men "smell too much" of Ovid and include too many classical allusions. Kemp's two misstatements unwittingly describe the real Shakespeare: a writer who was heavily influenced by Ovid and who included numerous classical allusions in his works. By Kemp's definition, therefore, Shakespeare *is* a university man. (Earlier in the play, Act 1, Scene 2, special praise by scholar Judicio was given to "William Shakespeare" for his two Ovid-inspired works: "Who loves not *Adon*'s love, or *Lucrece* rape?") In the next line, Kemp again separates Shakespeare from the university writers: "our fellow Shakespeare puts them all down ... " Kemp is definitely speaking about someone he knows, a "fellow" of himself and Burbage named "Shakespeare" who is not university educated. Ogburn concluded that Kemp was referring to the Stratford Man, and that the play was mocking his identification with the great author. His "fellows," Kemp and Burbage, were members of the Lord Chamberlain's Men, the acting company that the Stratford Man was associated. Both parts of *The Return from Parnassus*, therefore, ridiculed the confusion between the Stratford Man and the great author's pen name.

Conclusion

It was through the "fiction" of plays that the truth about the Stratford Man and the great author could be safely expressed by those in the know – that they were two very different people. The Stratford Man was spoofed in comedies written by Ben Jonson and a Cambridge University writer during a four-year period (1598-1601). Shared characteristics included wanting to be (or posing as) a gentleman, and being a braggart, a liar, an ignoramus and a plagiarizer of poetry. *Every Man Out of His Humor* depicted the Stratford Man in collusion with printers who pirated Shakespeare's plays, serving as their "countenance," or face, with his name, "William Shakspere." Jonson's earlier play, *Every Man In His Humor*, featured a similar character, and in both plays these characters share uncommon interest in swords, a veiled allusion to the Shakespeare plays. The Stratford Man got spoofed a third time in Jonson's play, *Poetaster*. One line blatantly describes him as "Crispinus, alias Cri-spinas, poetaster and plagiary," which can be translated as "a name similarity with someone's alias, a false poet and a thief of poetry." Jonson's three plays contain allusions to Shakespeare's plays, which supports the idea that he was the underlying topic. The Cambridge University writer of the *The Return from Parnassus-Part 1* made a point of distinguishing between the Stratford Man and the great author, including a daring in-depth description of the great author that could not be more opposite than the impression of him given later in the First Folio; but Cambridge University was not the public stage, and this play did not get published until 1886. The play's sequel referred to this mistaken identity through the mouths of "ignorant" actors. Conspicuously absent in all of these plays is the depiction of the Stratford Man character as an actor. If these writers knew about the Stratford Man's folly, then it is certain that the great author did too. The next chapter shows this to be the case.

CHAPTER 13

The Great Author's Portrayal of the Stratford Man

BY EXAMINING SHAKESPEARE'S plays, one can see that the great author was well aware of the Stratford Man, and that he regarded him as a knave, a thief, an imposter and a clown. This is gleaned from evident characterizations of him in four Shakespeare plays. The scenes in which they occur have little or no relation to the main plot, implying a significance that was personal to the great author. The Stratford Man's characters, in most cases, reside in places near Stratford-upon-Avon, and in three cases are named William. In *As You Like It*, the great author interviews the Stratford Man and threatens him to leave his plays alone; in *Henry IV-Part 2*, shady activity by two Williams is tolerated by an authority figure, and in *The Winter's Tale*, the great author explains that he helped the Stratford Man and his father "against his will." And finally, the son of a peddler, a "sly" man who knows the wool trade, is led to believe that he is an English lord just before he watches a performance of Shakespeare's *The Taming of the Shrew*. One of these scenes can be dated to 1598, the year that Ben Jonson started lampooning the Stratford Man in his comedies. In a combination of symbolism and direct identity clues, the great author provided insight about the Shakespeare authorship for posterity in these four plays, as explained in this chapter.

AS YOU LIKE IT

The great author embedded in his comedy, *As You Like It*, an explanation of his relationship with the Stratford Man. The character, William, is a young man from the Forest of Arden, an area mostly enveloped in the county of Warwickshire. William has money but is unlearned, which implies that his wealth was newly acquired. He seeks the hand of the country lass, Audrey (5.1). But earlier in the play, Audrey had agreed to marry Touchstone, a clown who was once a courtier. In one scene, Touchstone has dressed himself like a country peasant to please her. Then he suddenly compares himself to the classical poet, Ovid. Lord Jaques is watching this scene.

> TOUCHSTONE
> … and how, *Audrey,* am I the man yet? Doth my simple feature content you?
>
> AUDREY
> Your features, Lord warrant us: what features?
>
> TOUCHSTONE
> I am here with thee, and thy goats, as the most capricious <u>Poet</u>, <u>honest *Ovid*</u>, was among the Goths.
>
> LORD JAQUES [*hidden, aside*]
> O knowledge ill-inhabited, worse than Jove in a thatch'd house.
>
> TOUCHSTONE
> When a man's verses cannot be understood, nor a man's good wit seconded with the forward child, understanding: it strikes a man more dead than a great reckoning in a little room.   [3.3.2-14]

Touchstone says that the great poetry of Ovid could not be understood or appreciated by the "barbarian" Goths, with whom he lived during his exile. Touchstone then says to Audrey, "Truly, I would the gods had made thee poetical" (3.2.96-97), which she does not understand. It is fair to see symbolism in the Touchstone-Audrey scenes, which otherwise have no relation to the play, and, in the words of Alden Brooks, are "so strangely charged with illogical and irrelevant statements … "[1] Shakespeare was heavily influenced by Ovid, so the witty Touchstone must have been speaking for the great author. Audrey gives us a clue as to what she symbolizes.

> AUDREY
> Well, I am not fair, and therefore I pray the Gods make me honest …
>
> I am not a slut, though I thank the Gods I am foul.
>
> TOUCHSTONE
> Well, praised be the Gods, for thy foulness; sluttishness may come hereafter. But be it, as it may be, I will marry thee: [3.3.32; 37-41]

Audrey describes herself as "foul" and "not fair" – unlikely words coming from a newly engaged woman. Yet a former courtier who values poetry wishes to marry an ugly, foul and ignorant peasant. The public theater was regarded by many as foul during this period, like Henry Crosse: "[it is] like a sink in a town, whereunto all the filth doth run: or a bile in the body that draweth all the ill humors unto it" (*Virtue's Common-wealth*, 1603). Since the Shake-speare plays were performed in public theaters, the great author may have meant that they became foul by association. The former-courtier Touchstone wishes to marry a homely commoner and dresses himself in "simple feature" to content her. Symbolically this could mean that the great author, a noble courtier, is about to wed himself to his "foul" plays with the commoner alias, "William Shakespeare." It would explain Touchstone's regretful lines about a "man's verses" not being "understood." By giving the impression the works were written by a man with "simple feature," a non-courtier, an uneducated peasant like Audrey, by taking them out of context, they will not be com-pletely understood. The observer in this scene, Lord Jaques, phrased it as "knowledge ill-inhabited," and worse than the god Jove living in a hovel.

Touchstone has arranged for Sir Oliver Mar-text to "couple" he and Audrey there in the Forest of Arden. Carrying the symbolism further, Mar-text would then represent pirating printers, who "mar" Shakespeare's "text," or print inferior versions of his works (Mar-text was hyphenated in the original Folio text). The great author perhaps intended to give his works to these printers to "wed" them to the "commoner" alias, William Shakespeare. Lord Jaques then makes himself known to Touchstone, takes off his hat to him and says,

> Will you be married, <u>Motley</u>? ... And will you (<u>being a man of your breeding</u>) be married under a bush like a beggar? [3.3.75; 80-81]

Lord Jaques here emphasizes Touchstone's nobility, "his breeding," and repeats the same thought at the end of the play, addressing the exiled Duke:

> This is the <u>Motley-minded Gentleman</u>, that I have so often met in the Forest: he hath been a <u>Courtier</u> he swears. [5.4.40-42]

The great author had revealed himself as a nobleman-courtier in his sonnets, and said he made himself a "motley to the view" in Sonnet 110, i.e., he acted on the public stage. He is the "Motley-minded Gentleman" who has acting on his brain. Lord Jaques does not want Mar-text to perform the marriage ceremony and Touchstone takes his advice. Mar-text shrugs it off and says,

> 'Tis no matter. Ne'er a fantastical knave of them all shall flout me out of my calling. [3.3.103-04]

Not having the great author's permission to print his plays did not discourage the printers; they found other ways of obtaining his text. Touchstone later described Mar-text as "most wicked" and "most vile" (5.1.5-6).

After establishing Touchstone and Audrey as symbols for himself and his plays, the great author introduces William of the Forest of Arden, the Stratford Man. Touchstone interviews him. In this very short scene, the great author shows the Stratford Man as a pretender to the Shakespeare plays. It is the only appearance or mention of William in *As You Like It*.

> TOUCHSTONE
> But, Audrey, there is a youth here in the Forest lays claim to you.
>
> AUDREY
> Ay, I know who 'tis. He hath no interest in me in the world. Here comes the man you mean. *[enter William]*
>
> TOUCHSTONE
> It is meat and drink to me to see a clown ... [5.1.6-10]

William is immediately described by Touchstone as a "youth," someone younger than himself, and born in the Forest of Arden. He is a "clown," a fool, who "lays claim" to Audrey. The Stratford Man "claims" the Shakespeare plays in competition with the true author; he has no real "interest" in them, other than that of profit. But William shows deference to Touchstone-great author: when they meet, William takes off his hat and speaks to him with respect.

> WILLIAM
> Good ev'n, *Audrey*.
>
> AUDREY
> God ye good ev'n, *William*.
>
> WILLIAM
> And good ev'n to you, Sir.
>
> TOUCHSTONE
> Good ev'n, <u>gentle</u> friend. Cover thy head, cover thy head: Nay prithee be cover'd. How old are you, Friend?
>
> WILLIAM
> Five and twenty, Sir.
>
> TOUCHSTONE
> A ripe age: Is thy name *William*?
>
> WILLIAM
> *William*, sir.

TOUCHSTONE
A fair name. Was't born i' th' Forest here?

WILLIAM
Ay, sir, I thank God.

TOUCHSTONE
"Thank God": A good answer: Art rich?

WILLIAM
'Faith, sir, so-so.

TOUCHSTONE
"So-so" is good, very good, very excellent good: and yet it is not, it is but so-so: Art thou wise?

WILLIAM
Ay, sir, I have a pretty wit.

TOUCHSTONE
Why, thou say'st well. I do now remember a saying: "The Fool doth think he is wise, but the wise man knows himself to be a Fool."

 … You do love this maid?

WILLIAM
I do, sir.

TOUCHSTONE
Give me your hand: Art thou <u>Learned</u>?

WILLIAM
No, sir.

TOUCHSTONE
Then learn this of me, To have is to have. For it is a figure in Rhetoric, that drink being pour'd out of a cup into a glass, by filling the one, doth empty the other. For <u>all your Writers</u> do consent, that *ipse* is he: now you are not *ipse*, <u>for I am he</u>.

WILLIAM
Which he, sir?

TOUCHSTONE
He, sir, that must marry this woman: Therefore, <u>you Clown</u>, abandon: which is in the vulgar, leave, the society: which in the boorish, is company, of this Female: which in the common, is woman: which together, is, <u>abandon the society of this Female, or Clown thou perishest</u>: or to thy better understanding, diest; or (to wit) I kill thee, make thee away, translate thy life into death, thy liberty into bond-

age: I will deal in poison with thee, or in bastinado, or in steel: I will
bandy with thee in faction, I will o'er-run thee with policy: I will kill
thee a hundred and fifty ways, therefore tremble and depart.

AUDREY
Do, good *William*.

WILLIAM
God rest you merry, sir.   [5.1.14-34, 38-63; quotation marks added]

Touchstone refers to William as a clown three times. He calls him "gentle
friend," perhaps a sarcastic reference to the Stratford Man's aspirations to
gentility, or the passage was written after his father officially became a gentleman with the coat-of-arms grant in October 1596.[2] Touchstone's tone
changes when he discusses Audrey or the plays. He says he will speak to William using language for the "vulgar," the "boorish," and the "common" – his
apparent opinion of the Stratford Man.

> For all your Writers do consent that *ipse* is he; now you are not *ipse*,
> for I am he.

The phrase, "all your Writers do consent," leaves no room for doubt that the
great author is speaking for himself about his own property, the Shakespeare
plays. All writers know who is the real author of the plays, "for I am he." The
great author as Touchstone ends this scene with a warning to William – that
he should "abandon" his association with Audrey-the Shakespeare plays. William of Warwickshire was presented without disguise and he was not the great
author – he was the "unlearned" usurper of the plays, or, using the "figure
in rhetoric" of two glasses, "by filling the one doth empty the other." When
Touchstone-the great author asks if William is "rich," he implies that the
Stratford Man has profited from the Shakespeare plays. Touchstone's vio-
lent threats to William to leave alone Audrey-the Shakespeare plays resemble
Sir Puntarvolo's threats to Shift and Sogliardo for hurting his dog, also a
likely symbol of the Shakespeare plays in Ben Jonson's *Every Man Out of His
Humor*.

At the end of *As You Like It*, Touchstone tells the Duke why he wishes to
marry Audrey:

> a poor virgin sir, an ill-favor'd thing sir, but mine own, a poor humor
> of mine sir, to take that that no man else will: rich honesty dwells
> like a miser sir, in a poor house, as your Pearl in your foul oys-
> ter.   [5.4.58-62]

The well-bred former courtier wishes to honestly claim the plays as his own, even if plays are considered "ill-favor'd" and "foul," an association that would taint a nobleman's name. Just before their encounter with William, Touchstone tells Audrey,

> We shall find a time *Audrey*, patience gentle *Audrey*. [5.1.1-2]

Privately, Audrey-the Shakespeare plays is not ugly and foul, but "gentle." There will be a "time" when the Shakespeare plays are recognized as written by a nobleman-courtier, and their "rich honesty" fully understood in context. Until then, Audrey-the Shakespeare plays must have "patience." By referring to Audrey as a "virgin," perhaps the great author was describing the plays as they existed in their purest state, the originals, which never saw print.

In *As You Like It*, the great author wished to describe himself to posterity and to specifically distinguish himself from the Stratford Man. He also conveyed his fear that if he married his plays to an alias, then posterity would not completely understand them and mistakenly believe they were authored by the unlettered "clown," the Stratford Man, an idea that pained him: "it strikes a man more dead than a great reckoning in a little room."

HENRY IV – PART 2

One scene in Shakespeare's history play, *Henry IV-Part 2* (5.1), focuses upon two men named William who are briefly discussed and never mentioned again. Neither appears in the play. Comprised of only 96 lines, this scene is a discussion between Justice Shallow and his servant about things unrelated to the previous four acts. The scene opens with Sir John Falstaff asking Justice Shallow to excuse him for something – for what is not explained.

> SIR JOHN FALSTAFF
> You must excuse me, Master *Robert Shallow*.
>
> JUSTICE SHALLOW
> I will not excuse you: you shall not be excused. Excuses shall not be admitted: there is no excuse shall serve: you shall not be excus'd.
> [5.1.4-6]

In the conversation that follows, it is implied that Falstaff wanted to be excused for not staying for a meal. The justice summons his servant, Davy, and orders him to call his cook, William. While the justice is focused upon the next meal, Davy wishes to address the cook's evident theft of a sack.

JUSTICE SHALLOW
William Cook, bid him come hither. Sir *John*, you shall not be excus'd.

DAVY
Marry, sir, thus; those Precepts cannot be serv'd: and again sir, shall we sow the headland with Wheat?

JUSTICE SHALLOW
With red Wheat, *Davy*. But for *William* Cook: are there no young Pigeons?

DAVY
Yes, Sir. ...
And Sir, do you mean to stop any of *William's* Wages, about the Sack he lost the other day, at Hinckley Fair?

JUSTICE SHALLOW
He shall answer it. Some Pigeons *Davy*, a couple of short-legged Hens: a joint of Mutton, and any petty little tiny Kickshaws, tell *William* Cook.

DAVY [*re Falstaff*]
Doth the man of War, stay all night sir?

JUSTICE SHALLOW
Yes, *Davy*. I will use him well. A Friend i' the Court is better than a penny in purse.   [5.1.11-19, 24-36]

The words William, wheat and pigeon are weaved into the conversation. William the cook lost a "sack" at Hinckley fair – did it contain "red wheat"? The Stratford Man, William, dealt in grain, and was listed as a grain-hoarder in 1598. A precept or petition not getting served appears in the same line about wheat, which could imply that the petition was about hoarding grain. A scene about not "serving precepts," "grain," and a "justice" also occurred in Ben Jonson's *Every Man Out of His Humor* (1599) involving Sordido, the grain hoarder. His servant hands him a "precept."

SORDIDO
Who brought this same, sirrah?

HIND
Marry, sir, <u>one of the justice's men</u>; he says 'tis a <u>precept</u>, and all their hands be at it.

SORDIDO
... But I am wiser than to <u>serve their precepts</u>
Or follow their prescriptions. Here's a device,

> To charge me bring my <u>grain</u> unto the markets:
> Ay, much! when I have neither barn nor garner,
> Nor earth to hide it in, I'll bring 't; [1.3]

As shown in the previous chapter, Sordido and his brother Sogliardo were caricatures of the Stratford Man; it appears that Jonson was enlarging upon clues that the great author had provided. Davy asks the justice if William's wages will be cut for the lost sack. The justice barely acknowledges the question, obviously more concerned about the meal, especially "young pigeons." Besides a bird, a pigeon is a dupe, or as Jonson called the Stratford Man characters in his *Every Man* plays, a gull. In this line, the great author may have been equating William, the Stratford Man, with a "young pigeon."

As Justice Shallow and Davy continue their conversation, another William is mentioned for the first and last time – William Visor of "Woncot." Editors routinely treat Woncot as a misprint for "Wincot" or "Wilmcote," towns near Stratford-upon-Avon.

> DAVY
> I beseech you, sir, to <u>countenance William Visor of Woncot</u> against Clement Perkes o' the hill.
>
> JUSTICE SHALLOW
> There is many <u>complaints, Davy, against that Visor: that Visor is an arrant knave</u>, on my knowledge.
>
> DAVY
> I grant your worship that he is a knave, sir; but yet, God forbid, sir, but a knave should have some countenance at his friend's request. An honest man, sir is able to speak for himself, when a knave is not. I have served your worship truly, sir this eight years; and if I cannot once or twice in a quarter bear out a knave against an honest man, I have but very little credit with your worship. The knave is mine honest friend, sir; therefore, I beseech your worship, let him be countenanced.
>
> JUSTICE SHALLOW
> Go to; I say he shall have no wrong. [5.1, 41-58]

The justice reveals there are "many complaints against that Visor" and that he is "an arrant knave." Davy concedes this point, and contrasts William Visor with "an honest man." As a favor, however, Davy asks his master that Visor be "countenanced" (tolerated), a word he says three times. (Jonson evidently adopted the great author's repetition of the word countenance and applied it to Sogliardo, his most overt portrayal of the Stratford Man, in *Every Man Out of His Humor*.) In this scene's context, authority (Justice Shallow) is asked to tolerate the Stratford Man's (William Visor) theft of the great author's plays for profit. A "visor" is a mask for the face – William Visor was a false front for printers who issued pirated Shakespeare play editions. William the cook was also countenanced: he "lost" or stole a sack of something at Hinckley fair and the justice practically ignored it. Plays were often performed at fairs.

Because this scene stands independently from the rest of the play it is fair to look for contemporary allusions in it. Falstaff's presence is significant. He is described as a man of "the court" or courtier, and wishes the justice to excuse him for something that is linked to the word serve: "no excuse shall serve," and "those Precepts cannot be served." Precept had a definite association with Lord Burghley, Queen Elizabeth's top minister. His list of advice and maxims was published after his death under the title, *Certain Precepts* (1617). Historians have acknowledged that the great author alluded to Burghley's precepts in *Hamlet* (1.3), and that the character Corambis-Polonius satirized Burghley. If Justice Shallow were meant to represent Burghley, then Burghley would not forgive the courtier-great author for this satire, one that appeared on the public stage. Davy, who served him "this eight years," would then represent Burghley's son, Robert Cecil. On May 20, 1590, Cecil was knighted and three months later appointed to the Privy Council. Burghley tried hard to persuade the queen to appoint Cecil as her Principal Secretary, a position that became vacant in April 1590. Although he was not officially appointed until six years later, Cecil performed the duties of this office under his father's direction. When Burghley died in 1598, Cecil had served him in this capacity for eight years. (The name, Davy, may have been inspired by Sir William Davison, the former Principal Secretary who was forced to resign after being made a scapegoat for carrying out the execution order for Mary, Queen of Scots. Although it was expected that the queen would restore Davison's position, Cecil had insinuated himself into it.) This interpretation is apparently confirmed in Shakespeare's play, *Merry Wives of Windsor*. In the opening lines of the play's Folio version, Justice Shallow is complaining about Sir John Falstaff:

> JUSTICE SHALLOW
> Sir *Hugh*, persuade me not: I will make a Star-chamber matter of it, if he were twenty Sir *John Falstaffs*, he shall not abuse *Robert Shallow*, Esquire.
>
> SLENDER
> In the County of *Gloucester*, Justice of Peace and *Coram*.   [1.1.1-6]

Slender's line is a continuation of Justice Shallow's titles, after "esquire." According to the Yale Shakespeare,[3] Slender confused the Latin words *quorum* and *coram*; *quorum* was a title for some justices, and *coram* a term that a justice would use before his name in legal documents. Here *quorum* should have been used instead of *coram*. "Coram" puns on Burghley's motto, "Cor unam." (Corambis was the name of the king's councilor in the first edition of *Hamlet*, but it was changed to Polonius in the second edition.) A few lines later, it is revealed that Falstaff "committed disparagements unto" Justice Shallow, and "wronged" him. Justice Shallow would not excuse the courtier Falstaff, but the thieving cook, William, and the "arrant knave," William Visor, were tolerated. The Stratford Man was allowed to pretend he was the great author, William Shakespeare, for profit, without interference. Satirical portrayals of Burghley and other courtiers in the plays would not be discernable with the Stratford Man perceived as great author.

THE WINTER'S TALE

The Stratford Man and his father seemingly made an appearance in *The Winter's Tale* as Clown and his father, Shepherd. Just like the Stratford Man's father, Shepherd is in the wool trade. Later in the play, Clown fancies himself a "gentleman born," a phrase said six times within eighteen lines. We know that this too was the fancy of the Stratford Man and his father, who had obtained a coat of arms (under questionable circumstances) in 1596, entitling him to the honorific, "gentleman."

> SHEPHERD
> Come Boy, I am past mo'e Children: but thy Sons and Daughters will be all <u>Gentlemen born</u>.
>
> CLOWN [*speaking to Autolycus*]
> You are well met (Sir); you denied to fight with me this other day, because I was no <u>Gentleman born</u>. See you these Clothes? say you see them not, and think me still no <u>Gentleman born</u>: You were best say these Robes are not <u>Gentleman born</u>. Give me the Lie: do, and try whether I am not now a <u>Gentleman born</u>.
>
> AUTOLYCUS
> <u>I know</u> you are now (Sir) a <u>Gentleman born</u>.
>
> CLOWN
> Aye, and have been so any time these four hours.
>
> SHEPHERD
> And so have I, Boy. [5.2.142-154]

The great author has an encounter with the Stratford Man in *The Winter's Tale* just like he does in *As You Like It*. His character, Autolycus, is introduced in Act 4, Scene 3. He is a singing peddler (singing was another word for writing poetry), but was previously a courtier and royal servant who once wore fine velvet ("three-pile").

> I have serv'd Prince *Florizell*, and in my time wore three-pile, but now I am out of service. [4.3.13-14]

(Touchstone, the great author's character in *As You Like It*, was a clown and also a former courtier.) As perceptively noted by the Ogburns,[4] Autolycus-the great author's relationship with Clown-Stratford Man is revealed by their first exchange of lines. To pick the pocket of Clown, Autolycus feigns distress, exhorting

> Oh, that ever I was born.

Clown responds:

> I' th' name of me. [4.3.54-55]

Clown-Stratford Man's line is not merely an expression of surprise. The great author's works were "born" under the "th'name" of William Shakespeare, which also happens to be the Stratford Man's name. By exploiting the similarity, Clown is actually the one who is picking the pocket of the great author. In *As You Like It*, the Stratford Man character, William, was repeatedly called a clown and a fool, yet neither William nor Clown were actual clowns or behaved like them. Since they were only portrayed as somewhat simple men from the country, the use of the words clown and fool must have reflected the great author's personal opinion.

Clown and Shepherd are introduced at the close of Act 3, when Shepherd finds an abandoned baby girl who is swathed in fine linen. The child is a princess, the daughter of the king of Sicillia. Bundled with the child is "Gold, all Gold." The shepherd realizes his amazing fortune and tells his son,

> This is Fairy Gold boy, and 'twill prove so ...
>
> We are lucky (boy); and to be so still requires nothing but secrecy ...
> [3.3.127; 129-30]

If Clown and Shepherd represent the Stratford Man and his father, then the noble child with gold that they discover symbolizes the Shakespeare plays. Holding the child-plays "requires nothing but secrecy," perhaps reflecting their association with unscrupulous printers. The king of Sicillia did not believe the child was his, so he had commanded a nobleman to take her out of his kingdom and abandon her. The nobleman reluctantly did so, and in lines that must express the great author's feelings, says:

> Weep, I cannot,
> But my heart bleeds: and most accurs'd am I
> To be by oath enjoin'd to this. Farewell ... [3.3.50-52]

A bear suddenly appears and the nobleman utters his last line:

> I am gone forever. [3.3.56]

The bear attacks and eats the nobleman. Clown had witnessed the bear-attack but did nothing about it. In this play, "Authority" was defined as "a stubborn Bear" (4.4.835). Authority, therefore, separated the nobleman-great author's true name from his works "by oath enjoin'd ..." The great author is plainly stating that an oath prevented him from openly acknowledging his authorship of Shakespeare, forcing him to abandon the child, his literary works. The child's name, Perdita, meaning lost, reflects the disassociation. (The nobleman's name, Antigonus, may also be a clue to the great author's situation; in the ancient Greek tragedy by Sophocles, Antigone was ordered by a king to be buried alive.) The nobleman-great author's "heart bleeds" and he feels he is "most accurs'd." The bear was still eating the nobleman when Clown reported it to his father.

> CLOWN
> I'll go see if the Bear be gone from the Gentleman, and how much he hath eaten: they are never curs'd but when they are hungry: if there be any of him left, I'll bury it.
>
> SHEPHERD
> That's a good deed: if thou mayest discern by that which is left of him, what he is, fetch me to th'sight of him.
>
> CLOWN
> 'Marry, will I: and you shall help to put him i' th' ground.
>
> SHEPHERD
> 'Tis a lucky day, boy; and we'll do good deeds on 't. [3.3.133-142]

Shepherd and his son were determined to "bury" the nobleman. In the main plot of *The Winter's Tale*, Prince Florizell falls in love with the now grown Perdita, which angers his father, the king of Bohemia, due to her lowly status. After learning that Prince Florizell will marry her anyway, Clown and Shepherd encounter Autolycus. Fearing retribution from the marriage, they wish to tell the story of Perdita's true origins to the king. Autolycus tells them he is a courtier, "Whether it like me, or no, I am a Courtier" (4.4.757), and could get them access. They believe him and treat him with respect.

> CLOWN
> This cannot be but <u>a great Courtier</u> ... He seems to be the more <u>Noble</u>, in being <u>fantastical</u>: <u>A great man</u>, I'll warrant; [4.4.777, 781]

(The courtier-clown Touchstone in *As You Like It* was also described as fantastical.) Clown and Shepherd recognize the worth of Autolycus:

> CLOWN
> <u>We are bless'd, in this man</u>: as I may say, even bless'd.
>
> SHEPHERD
> Let's before, as he bids us: he was provided to do us good. [4.4.864-67]

In the final act, Perdita's true parentage is revealed, as if the great author was imagining the day when his authorship of the plays becomes known and accepted. One gentleman described how the king came to accept Perdita as his lost daughter. It was primarily from the evidence of her "majesty," "nobleness," and "breeding."

> ... the Majesty of the Creature, in resemblance of the Mother: the Affection [inclination] of Nobleness, which Nature shews above her Breeding, and many other Evidences proclaim her, with all certainty, to be the King's Daughter. [5.2.38-44]

Ben Jonson made a similar statement in his Folio elegy about the great author:

> Look how the father's face
> Lives in his issue, even so, the race
> Of *Shakespeare's* mind, and manners brightly shines
> In his well turned, and true-filed lines:

Autolycus called Perdita's true parentage a "Mystery" that had "remained undiscover'd," and a "Secret" (5.2.135-37). When Autolycus encounters Clown and Shepherd again, the great author sums up his feeling about the Stratford Man and his father.

> Here come those I have done good to against my will, and already appearing in the blossoms of their Fortune. [5.2.138-141]

The great author benefited the Stratford Man and his father *against his will*. The nobleman who was forced to abandon Perdita had called her "Blossom" (3.3.45).

As mentioned in the previous chapter, the Stratford Man apparently made a short appearance in *The Tempest* as Stephano, a "drunken Butler," as described in the Folio's dramatis personae. He attempted to kill Prospero, the magician-great author, to become the new king of the island. Another drunken character, Christophero Sly, appears in the opening scenes of *The Taming of the Shrew*, scenes unrelated to the main play. An English lord decides to play a trick on Sly, also called "drunkard" (and "beggar"), by dressing him up in noble attire and putting him in one of the rooms of his manor. He instructs his servants to pretend that the drunkard is the lord. Sly awakens in a state of disbelief:

> What would you make me mad? Am not I *Christopher Slie*, old Slie's son of Burton-heath, by birth a Peddler, by education a Card-maker, by transmutation a Bear-herd, and now by present profession a tinker. Ask *Marrian Hacket* the fat Alewife of Wincot if she know me not ... [1.2.17-22]

Barton-on-the-Heath and Wincot are towns near Stratford-upon-Avon. The Yale Shakespeare edition of the play stated that "A family by the name of Hacket did live in Wincot," and "card" is an instrument for combing wool.[5] Sly ends up believing that he is a lord. In this scene, the great author was apparently mocking a commoner from the environs of Stratford-upon-Avon who impersonates an English lord, the nobleman-author of the Shakespeare plays. Sly, another word for crafty or dishonest, is the son of a peddler who was "educated" in the wool trade. "Bear-herd" in the above passage could relate to Clown, the Stratford Man's character in *The Winter's Tale* who had watched a nobleman get eaten by a bear.

Conclusion

The only place the great author could safely reveal himself and his vexing situation for the record was by dropping clues in his works, which he knew would last through the ages. The great author represented himself in these plays as a courtier, a former courtier, and a nobleman, and in two plays was described as "fantastical." In *As You Like It*, he articulated his fear that posterity would not understand the full meaning of his plays by not knowing their true author, a thought that figuratively struck him dead. The Shakespeare plays were represented as a country lass and an abandoned daughter (Miranda, the daughter of the exiled duke, Prospero, was similarly represented in *The Tempest*).

Both were raised as commoners that former or disguised courtiers wished to marry; secretly, one was "gentle" and the other a princess. The Stratford Man was openly named William in two plays, Clown in another, and his character treated the great author's character with deference. The great author explained the Stratford Man's pretension to the Shakespeare plays – not to steal the credit, but to secretly profit by them. He told us that the Stratford Man's fraud was known and tolerated by the authorities and that this outraged him. In *The Winter's Tale*, the great author told us, through the character, Antigonus, that his anonymity was sworn by an oath that made his "heart bleed." What could have caused the nobleman-courtier to take an oath of silence about his authorship of Shakespeare *forever*, and to whom? Antigonus was commanded by the king of Sicillia to abandon a child that symbolized the Shakespeare plays. In *Henry IV-Part 2*, Justice Shallow and Davy may have represented William Cecil, Lord Burghley, and his son, Sir Robert Cecil. Could the Cecils and the king of Sicillia be linked? A theory involving them will be presented in chapters 16 and 17. One thing is certain: if one can take anyone's word about the Stratford Man and the Shakespeare authorship mystery, then surely one must take the great author's.

THE

Tragicall Historie of

HAMLET

Prince of Denmarke

By William Shake-speare.

As it hath beene diuerse times acted by his Highnesse ser-
uants in the Cittie of London : as also in the two V-
niuersities of Cambridge and Oxford, and else-where

At London printed for N.L. and Iohn Trundell.
1603.

PLATE 1: Shakespeare's play, *Hamlet*, title page of the first printed edition (1603). Shakespeare's name was hyphenated in nearly half of all printed references, suggesting it was an invented name or alias.

255

NVMMVS VOTIVVS

TATUUM REGNI ANGLIAE: CUSUS IN

honorem Reginæ suæ Elisabethæ : partis aliquot
nobilibus, contra Hispanum, victorijs:
circiter Annum Christi

1 5 7 4.

 On omnibus ea Regibus ac Principibus contingit
felicitas: ut subditorum suorum in se amorem stu-
diumque, quale quidem conceptis votis optare pos-
sent, assequantur: sint Aristoni Lacedæmonio simi-
les: pro quo vota publica fiebant; ut filius ei nasce-
retur: ne tam præclara soboles interiret: Octavio
Augusto: cui in publicum prodeunti affatim se populus effundebat, visurus beneficium ac salutare
sydus suum: Vespasiano Cæsari: quem Veneres ac
delicias suas appellabant sceptrum eius agnoscentes. Næ vero horum nu-
mero accensenda Heroina verè Augusta Elisabetha Regina Angliæ, prin-
ceps tum animi, tum corporis dotibus, regiisque virtutibus supra sexum
incomparabilis: quam quod Iustitiam, sapientiam, invictum pectoris robur
mirâ humanitate ac clementiâ temperaret ita efflictim subditi amabant, ut
nummo hoc conquerantur mortalitatis legi, fatiq́, necessitati eam subjectam: nec Phœ-
nicis fortunâ frui: quæ licet igne pereat, ac moriatur: è cineribus attamen suis
similem sibi Phœnicem pariat, atq́, ita in se vivat
perpetuò. Author.

PLATE 2: An English medallion of Queen Elizabeth I and a phoenix (1574) as illustrated in Johann Jacob Luck's *Sylloge Numismatum Elegantiorum* ("A Discourse on the More Beautiful Coins"), Salzburg, 1620.

PLATE 3: The Phoenix Portrait of Elizabeth I by Nicholas Hilliard (c. 1574). Above the queen's hand is a jeweled pendant of a phoenix, her personal symbol, and in her hand is a red rose, the symbol of the royal house of Tudor.

LOVES MARTYR:

OR,

ROSALINS COMPLAINT.

Allegorically shadowing the truth of Loue,
in the constant Fate of the Phœnix
and Turtle.

A Poeme enterlaced with much varietie and raritie;
now first translated out of the venerable Italian Torquato
Cæliano, *by* ROBERT CHESTER.

With the true legend of famous King *Arthur*, the last of the nine
Worthies, being the first *Essay* of a new *Brytish* Poet: collected
out of diuerse Authenticall Records.

To these are added some new compositions, of seuerall moderne Writers
whose names are subscribed to their seuerall workes, vpon the
first Subiect : viz. the Phœnix *and*
Turtle.

Mar: —— *Mutare dominum non potest liber notus.*

LONDON

Imprinted for E. B.

1601.

PLATE 4: *Love's Martyr* (1601), title page.

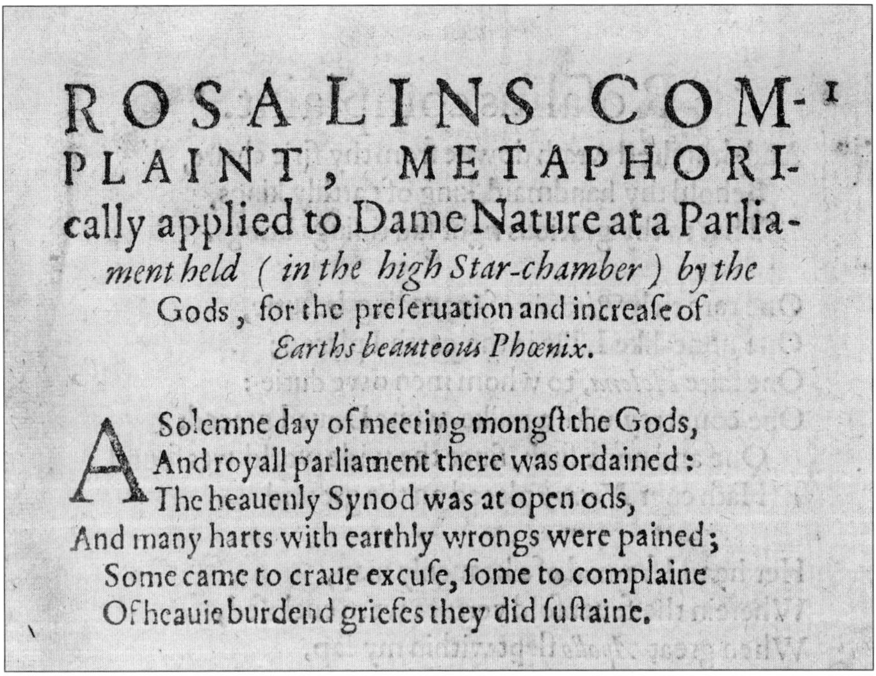

ROSALINS COM-[1]
PLAINT, METAPHORI-
cally applied to Dame Nature at a Parlia-
ment held (in the high Star-chamber) by the
Gods, for the preſeruation and increaſe of
Earths beauteous Phœnix.

A Solemne day of meeting mongſt the Gods,
And royall parliament there was ordained:
The heauenly Synod was at open ods,
And many harts with earthly wrongs were pained;
Some came to craue excuſe, ſome to complaine
Of heauie burdend griefes they did ſuſtaine.

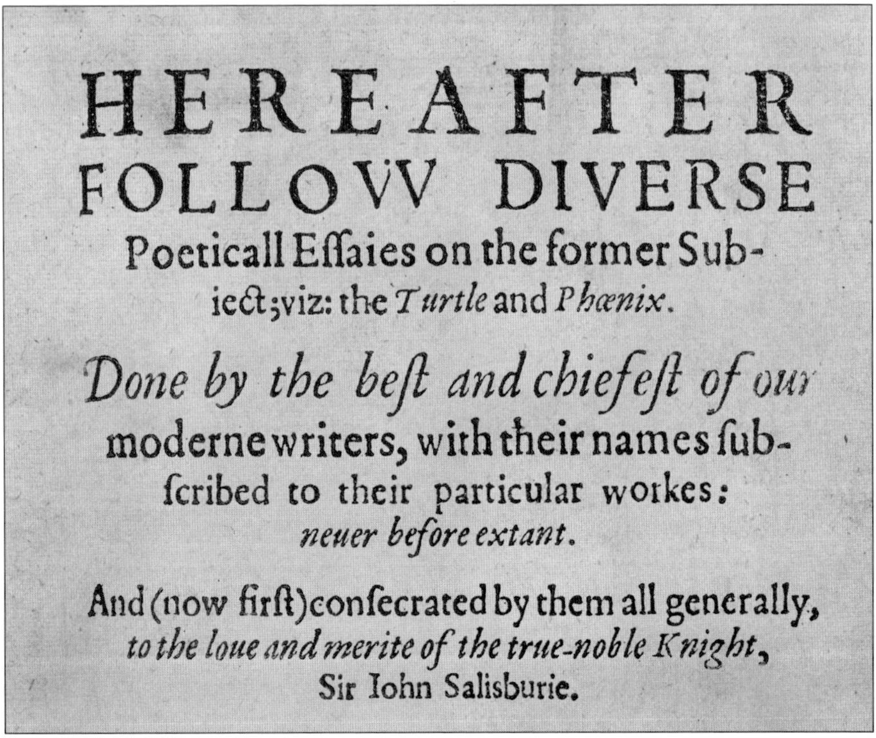

HEREAFTER
FOLLOVV DIVERSE
Poeticall Eſſaies on the former Subiect;viz: the *Turtle* and *Phœnix*.

Done by the beſt and chiefeſt of our
moderne writers, with their names ſub-
ſcribed to their particular workes:
neuer before extant.

And (now firſt) conſecrated by them all generally,
to the loue and merite of the true-noble Knight,
Sir Iohn Salisburie.

By permission of the Folger Shakespeare Library.

PLATES 5 – 6: *Love's Martyr,* first page of text (upper image, detail), and title page of accompanying work, *Diverse Poetical Essays* (lower image, detail), which featured poems about the Phoenix and Turtle Dove by Shakespeare, Ben Jonson, John Marston, George Chapman, and Ignoto.

TAMERLANES TARTARORVM IMPER. POTENTISS. IRA DEI ET TERROR ORBIS APPELLATVS OBIIT ANo 1402
LAWRANCE IOHNSONN. SCVLP.

PLATE 7: The real "upstart Crow" was Edward Alleyn, one of England's earliest superstar actors. Here he is depicted as the character, Tamburlaine the Great, as noted by Martin Holmes (see Other Sources). The engraving is by Lawrance Johnson, and was featured in the 1603 book, *The General History of the Turks*, by Richard Knolles.

VERA EFFIGIES DOCTISSIMI POETARVM ANGLORVM BEN: IOHNSONII.

Ro: Vaughan fecit.

Johnsoni typus, ecce!qui furoris, | Defuncta Pater Eruditionis,
Antistes sacer, Enthei, Camenis, | Et Scenæ veteris novator audax.
Vindex Ingenÿ recens Sepulti, | Nec fœlix minus, aut minus politus
Antiquæ reparator vnus artis, | Cui solus similis, Figura, vivet.
O' could there be an art found out that might
Produce his shape soe lively as to Write. Ab: Holl:

PLATE 8: Ben Jonson, engraving by Robert Vaughn (c. 1622-27). He is wearing laurels, a symbol of poetic achievement.

PLATE 9: Portrait of William Herbert, 3rd Earl of Pembroke, after Daniel Mytens (c. 1625). He holds the staff of the Lord Chamberlain, a position he held from late 1615 to 1626. Shakespeare's First Folio was jointly dedicated to Pembroke and his brother, the Earl of Montgomery (opposite plate).

PLATE 10: Philip Herbert, Earl of Montgomery (later 4th Earl of Pembroke), engraving by Simon de Passe (c. 1620). This image bears a slight resemblance to Droeshout's engraving of Shakespeare.

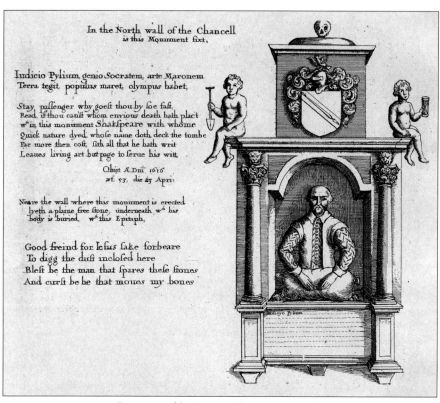

In the North wall of the Chancell is this Monument fixt.

Iudicio Pylium, genio Socratem, arte Maronem
Terra tegit, populus maret, olympus habet,

Stay passenger why goest thou by soe fast,
Read, if thou canst whom envious death hath plact
wth in this monument Shakspeare with whome
Quick nature dyed, whose name doth deck the tombe
Far more then cost, sith all that he hath writ
Leaues living art but page to serue his witt.

Obijt A Dni 1616
æt. 53, die 23 Apri:

Neare the wall where this monument is erected
lyeth a plaine free stone, underneath wth his
body is buried, wth this Epitaph,

Good freind for Iesus sake forbeare
To digg the dust inclosed here
Blest be the man that spares these stones
And curst be he that moues my bones

By permission of the Huntington Library, San Marino, CA.

IVDICIO PYLIVM, GENIO SOCRATEM, ARTE MARONEM,
TERRA TEGIT, POPVLVS MÆRET, OLYMPVS HABET

STAY PASSENGER, WHY GOEST THOV BY SO FAST,
READ IF THOV GANST, WHOM ENVIOVS DEATH HATH PLAST
WITH IN THIS MONVMENT SHAKSPEARE: WITH WHOME,
QVICK NATVRE DIDE WHOSE, NAME, DOTH DECK Y TOMBE,
FAR MORE, THEN COST: SIEH ALL, Y HE, HATH WRITT,
LEAVES LIVING ART, BVT PAGE, TO SERVE HIS WITT.

OBIT ANO DO 1616
ÆTATIS 53 DIE 23 AP:

John Cheal Inspired Images 2010.

PLATE 11 (TOP): The Shakspeare monument in Holy Trinity Church, Stratford-upon-Avon, with inscriptions of the monument and gravestone, as it appeared in *The Antiquities of Warwickshire* by Sir William Dugdale (1656), detail of page 520.

PLATE 12 (BOTTOM): Shakspeare monument inscription today.

By permission of the Folger Shakespeare Library.

An Epitaph ō Mr William Shakspeare

Stay passenger why go'st thou by so fast
read if thou Canst, whom enuious death hath plact
within this monument: Shakespeare: with whom
quick nature dy'd; whose name doth deck this toombe
far more then cost; sith all that hee hath writt
leaues liueing art but Page vnto his witt./

Another vpon the same

Heere Shakespeare lyes whome none but death could shake
and heere shall ly till iudgement all awake;
when the last trumpet doth vnclose his eyes
the wittiest poet in the world shall rise./

an Epitaph (vpon his Toombe stone incised)

Good ffriend for Iesus sake forbeare
To digg the dust inclosed heere
blest bee the man that pau'd these stones
but Cur'sd bee hee that mooues these bones./

PLATE 13: The earliest known transcription of the two (or possibly three) Shakespeare epitaphs in the Stratford-upon-Avon church (detail). It is contained in Folio No. 26 at the Folger-Shakespeare Library. Transcribed by Joseph Egert in his article, *Flying Leaf*, available at SHAKSPER and with PDF figures at HLASM (https://groups.google.com/group/humanitieslitauthorsshakespearemoderated/browse_thead/thread/944bd7139d38e6ba?hl=en).

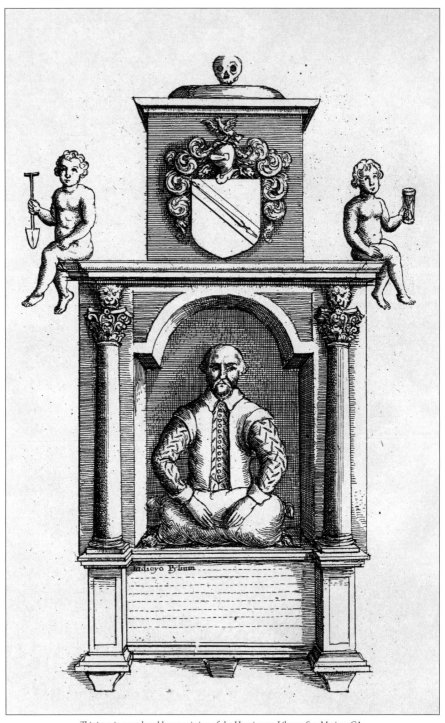

PLATE 14: Shakspeare Monument in Stratford-upon-Avon, engraving (detail) by W. Hollar in *The Antiquities of Warwickshire* (1656) by Sir William Dugdale. The image was based upon a drawing made by Dugdale in 1634.

John Cheal Inspired Images 2010.

PLATE 15: Present Shakspeare Monument, Holy Trinity Church, Stratford-upon-Avon.

PLATE 16: Monument of William Aubrey (d. 1595) as illustrated in Sir William Dugdale's book, *The History of St. Paul's Cathedral in London* (1658). It shares many design elements with the monuments of Shakspeare and Judith Combe (opposite page). The engraving was made by W. Hollar.

John Cheal Inspired Images 2010.

PLATE 17: Monument of Judith Combe (d. 1649) by Thomas Stanton, Holy Trinity Church, Stratford-upon-Avon. If the Shakspeare Monument was remade, then the Combe Monument, located near it on the same wall, may have influenced its design.

© National Portrait Gallery, London.

PLATE 18: James, 2ⁿᵈ Marquess of Hamilton (1623), engraving by Martin Droeshout, and detail.

PLATE 19: Martin Droeshout's portrait engraving of Shakespeare (detail) on the title page of the First Folio (1623).

This Shadowe is renowned Shakeſpear's? Soule of th'age
The applauſe? delight? the wonder of the Stage.
Nature her ſelfe, was proud of his deſignes
And joy'd to weare the droſſing of his lines,
The learned will Confeſs, his works are ſuch,
As neither man, nor Muſe, can prayſe to much.
For ever live thy fame, the world to tell,
Thy like, no age, ſhall ever paralell.

W. M. ſculpſit.

PLATE 20: William Shakespeare, engraving by William Marshall in *POEMS: WRITTEN BY WIL. SHAKE-SPEARE. Gent* (1640). The verse below the image questions the authenticity of Droeshout's portrait of Shakespeare in the First Folio.

The Fates decree, that tis a mighty wrong
To Woemen Kinde, to have more Greife, then Tongue

1655

PLATE 21: William Shakespeare with characters from his poem, *Rape of Lucrece* (1655 ed.) by William Faithhorne. Although Shakespeare's portrait was based on Droeshout's engraving, the mustache changed from a thin line starting at the base of the nose and following the upper lip, to one that is fuller, upraised and shaved near the nose, more like today's monument.

PLATE 22: Portrait miniature of Henry Wriothesley, 3rd Earl of Southampton, age 20, by Nicholas Hilliard (1594). Southampton was the dedicatee of Shakespeare's poems *Venus and Adonis* (1593) and *The Rape of Lucrece* (1594), and was the "Fair Youth" of Shakespeare's sonnets.

Cobbe Collection, Hatchlands Park, England.

PLATE 23: Portrait of Mistress (Anne) Vavasour, attributed to Robert Peake the Elder (c. 1551-1619). Vavasour was probably the "Dark Lady" of Shakespeare's sonnets.

SHAKE-SPEARES

S O N N E T S.

Neuer before Imprinted.

AT LONDON
By *G.* *Eld* for *T. T.* and are
to be solde by *William Aspley.*
1609.

TO.THE.ONLIE.BEGETTER.OF.
THESE.INSVING.SONNETS.
Mʳ.W.H. ALL.HAPPINESSE.
AND.THAT.ETERNITIE.
PROMISED.

BY.

OVR.EVER-LIVING.POET.

WISHETH.

THE.WELL-WISHING.
ADVENTVRER.IN.
SETTING.
FORTH.

T. T.

PLATE 26: Portrait of Edward de Vere, 17th Earl of Oxford, 1581. Several contemporary allusions to William Shakespeare implied that the name was an alias, and three hinted that it was Oxford's alias.

PLATE 27: An Interior with King Charles I, Queen Henrietta Maria, Jeffery Hudson, William Herbert, 3rd Earl of Pembroke and his brother Philip Herbert, later 4th Earl of Pembroke by Hendrick van Steenwyck (c. 1630-35), and detail.

CHAPTER 14

Shakespeare Satirized: *Willobie His Avisa* (1594)

A FEW PLAYS of Shakespeare and those of his contemporaries provided insight about the great author in relation to the Stratford Man. But other literature of the period included contemporary commentary about the great author without reference to the Stratford Man. One of the most revealing examples is contained in *Willobie His Avisa* (registered on September 3, 1594). The book dropped major clues about the great author, as well as clues about two people he addressed in his sonnets, the Fair Youth and the Dark Lady. Anonymously written, the book emerged in the supposed early part of Shakespeare's career. It stated that, in 1594, Shakespeare was an "old player," and implied that "Shake-speare" was the pen name of an aristocrat; it also linked his identity with Edward de Vere, 17th Earl of Oxford. The Fair Youth, according to the *Willobie* writer, was Henry Wriothesley, 3rd Earl of Southampton. The Dark Lady's real name began with A, and it was hinted that she was Anne Vavasour, who was once a lady-in-waiting to the queen. The book was dynamite when it was printed and remained so for decades afterward. Instead of following these major leads to their obvious conclusion, the experts consistently ignore them because they do not fit with their conception of the great author.

In the "poetical fiction" of *Willobie His Avisa*, Avisa is an attractive English woman who meets with various suitors before and after her marriage to an innkeeper. Her chastity and fidelity is so overstated that it is almost suspicious. Henry Willobie, the purported author of the book, is Avisa's fifth and final suitor; Canto 44 marks his first appearance, as well as that of "his familiar friend W.S."

Henrico Willobego. Italo-Hispalensis.

H.W. being suddenly infected with the contagion of a fantastical fit, at the first sight of A., pineth awhile in secret grief, at length not able any longer to endure the burning heat of so fervent a humor, bewrayeth the secrecy of his disease unto his familiar friend W.S. who not long before had tried the courtesy of the like passion, and was now newly recovered of the like infection.

For anyone who kept abreast of poetry at the time, the two sets of initials, W.S. and H.W., would have instantly suggested William Shakespeare and Henry Wriothesley, Earl of Southampton; they were the poet and dedicatee respectively of Shakespeare's famous poems, *Venus and Adonis* (1593) and *The Rape of Lucrece* (1594). In addition, *Willobie His Avisa*, which was printed only a few months after *Lucrece*, specifically invoked Shakespeare in one line of a prefatory poem: "And *Shake-speare*, paints poor *Lucrece* rape." This was the first occasion that the poet's name had appeared in print outside of his two classical poems. A hyphen was placed in the poet's surname, betraying this writer's belief that it was an alias. Another line in this poem coupled Lucrece and Avisa: "Let *Lucres-Avis* be thy name." A third allusion to Shake-speare's poem – "Britain Lucretia" – occurred in the first prefatory letter.

Willobie His Avisa was published six times between 1594 and 1635. The work presented itself as a tale on morality, but G.B. Harrison, who wrote an essay about it, concluded that this was only a pretense: "The initials of Avisa's suitors covered, or rather revealed to contemporaries, persons of great importance; so great, in fact, that the scandals about them were still commercially worth retailing forty years later."[1] In his preface letter to *Willobie*, Hadrian Dorrell claimed the work was from the papers of his roommate, Henry Willobie, and that he published it without his knowledge. He also said that the story of Avisa had "something of truth hidden under this shadow." Dorrell's "historical existence cannot be established" (*DNB*), making it almost certain that it was a false name; the *Short-Title Catalogue* states it was "probably" a pseudonym. *Penelope's Complaint* (1596), another poetry work about a chaste lady, contained a letter to the reader in which it was said that *Willobie His Avisa* had "an unknown author." This shows that "Henry Willobie" was also a false name, but one that purposely suggested Henry Wriothesley, (Southampton). Shadowed truth and false names are indicative of a work with defamatory intent, and the fates of the two subsequent editions seem to confirm it. All that survives of the second edition (1596) is an added poem and prefatory letter that evidently tried hard to undo the damage the first edition had caused. The letter was titled, "The apology, shewing the true meaning of *Willobie his Avisa*," and was signed by Dorrell. He said that "the author intended in this discourse, neither the description or praise of any particular woman; nor the naming or ciphering of any particular man," and that it was a "poetical fiction" written "at least" 35 years before. The added poem, "The victory of English chastity, under the feigned name of Avisa," was signed by "Thomas Willoby," described as "Frater Henrici Willoby nuper defuncti," i.e., the brother of "the lately dead" Henry Willoby. These added "facts" dispel any notion that there was a real person named Henry Willobie who had authored *Willobie His Avisa*. A third edition of *Willobie* emerged in 1599, but by June of that year the title was included in the Archbishop of Canterbury's list of forbidden books; most of these books were satires and ordered to be burned (an event called the "bishop's bonfire").[2] *Willobie* was ordered to be "stayed" and "called in." That *Willobie* was included on the list confirms that it was not only a contemporary satire, but that it had targeted important people that readers had recognized. Needless to say, the record shows no interrogation of a Henry Willobie or a Hadrian Dorrell.

There is more evidence *Willobie His Avisa* had targeted Shakespeare and Southampton. W.S., who had previously courted Avisa with "like passion," advises H.W. (i.e., Henry Willobie) on how to woo her. The *Willobie* writer puts these words into the mouth of W.S., referring to Avisa: "She is no Saint, She is no Nun, /I think in time she may be won" (Canto 47). These lines resemble those in Shakespeare's *Titus Andronicus* (2.1.83), which debuted in print that year: "She is a woman, therefore may be woo'd, /She is a woman, therefore may be won … "[3] They also resemble lines in Sonnet 41 of Shakespeare, in which the great author speaks to the Fair Youth about his mistress, the Dark Lady, that she will try to "woo" him: "Gentle thou art, and therefore to be won, /Beauteous thou art, therefore to be assailed." Scholars have also noted that poem No. 18 in *The Passionate Pilgrim*, a work attributed to Shakespeare, resembles Canto 47 of *Willobie*, both verses with advice about how to court women. The *Willobie* writer also applied theater terms in a passage about W.S.'s certainty that H.W.'s suit to Avisa was futile:

> Thus this miserable comforter [W.S.] comforting his friend [H.W.] with an impossibility, either for that he now would secretly laugh at his friend's folly, or because he would see whether another could play his part better than himself, & in viewing afar off the course of this loving Comedy, he [W.S.] determined to see whether it would sort to a happier end for this new actor [H.W.], than it did for the old player [W.S.]. [Canto 44]

These clues, plus the references to Shakespeare and his poem, *Lucrece*, in *Willobie*'s preface, make it certain that W.S. represented Shakespeare. "Henrico Willobego. Italo-Hispalensis" in the first line of Canto 44 connects Henry Willobie with Southampton. Presumably "Italo-Hispalensis" means that Henry Willobie has interest in Italian and Spanish languages or culture, and this is further demonstrated by the display of Italian mottoes at the foot of his verses to Avisa. In 1594, the Italian language master, John Florio, was employed in Southampton's household,[4] and four years later, Florio dedicated his Italian-English dictionary to Southampton and two other aristocrats. In 1594, Southampton was also saluted in Spanish in a book by Antonio Perez, which suggests he could read this language.[5] H.W. is described as a "headlong youth," and Southampton was just shy of 21 years when *Willobie* was registered. Courtier Sir John Harington associated Avisa with Southampton in a 1596 work: he invented the word, "Avisare," to describe the young grandson of Lord Montagu, who was Southampton's maternal grandfather.[6]

With the identities of W.S. and H.W. firmly established as Shakespeare and Southampton, it means that the *Willobie* writer was basing his satire on real events or reflecting current gossip about them. The *Willobie* writer also alludes to the enigmatic story covered in some of Shakespeare's sonnets: that the poet's mistress, the Dark Lady, had seduced the poet's beloved Fair Youth. The *Willobie* cantos involving W.S., H.W. and Avisa touch upon a similar love triangle between an older man, a younger man, and a married lady (it is revealed in Sonnet 152 that both the Dark Lady and the poet were married to others during their affair, that each were "forsworn"). Another contemporary book, *The Unfortunate Traveler* (1594), by Thomas Nashe, also hinted at a love triangle involving Southampton and Shakespeare. In his dedication letter to Southampton, Nashe wrote

> A dere [*sic*] lover and cherisher you are, as well as the lovers of
> Poets, as of Poets themselves.

R.J.C. Wait concluded, like others, that "Ostensibly this means that Southampton cherishes those who love and appreciate poetry, but can it not also imply that the young Earl is paying his attentions to a poet's mistress?"[7] A glance at Shakespeare's Sonnet 42 tells whose mistress it was:

> That thou hast her it is not all my grief
> And yet it may be said I lov'd her deerely [*sic*]
> That she hath thee is of my wailing chief,
> A loss in love that touches me more nearly.
> Loving offenders thus I will excuse ye,
> Thou dost love her, because thou knowst I love her ...

"Dere lover" in Nashe's dedication to Southampton apparently paraphrased "lov'd her deerely" in Shakespeare's Sonnet 42 – in this sonnet, the great author writes about the Fair Youth's liaison with the Dark Lady. The second edition of *The Unfortunate Traveler* omitted the dedication letter, indicating that Southampton apparently had taken offense to it. Nashe's book was registered on September 17, 1593, indicating his awareness of the Shakespeare-Dark Lady-Southampton love triangle about one year before the publication of *Willobie*. As knowledge of this affair was evidently known in literary circles at the time, *Willobie* should be viewed as an immediately contemporary writer's understanding of the real story hinted in Shakespeare's sonnets (not surprisingly, *Willobie*'s fourth printing in 1609 coincided with the print debut of *SHAKE-SPEARE'S SONNETS*).

Avisa and the Dark Lady

As *Willobie* revealed the correct initials of the great author (i.e., his pen name) and those of the Fair Youth (H.W. or Henry Willobie, a similar-sounding name for Henry Wriothesley), then it follows that the name of the real woman behind the Dark Lady and the Avisa character had the initial A or resembled "Avisa." In fact, the first reference to Avisa in Canto 44 – where the story of her encounter with H.W. begins – she is only identified by the initial A (see first inset quote above). It was the first and only occurrence of her initial in the work's 74 cantos (the "Epistle to the Reader" and "The Author's conclusion" contain three instances of her initial, and in one instance, her initials are "A.D."). The very long opening line of Canto 44 compares H.W.'s passion for A. to a disease, just like Shakespeare described his passion for the Dark Lady in his Sonnet 147 ("My love is as a fever ... "). The cantos that follow are H.W. and W.S.'s discussion of Avisa but her name is not mentioned, and it does not appear until Canto 50, perhaps a clue that the lady discussed is not really named Avisa, but does have the initial A. Another contemporary hint about the real name behind Avisa appeared in an eighteen-lined Latin poem in *Penelope's Complaint*, in which Avisa is compared with the classical figure, Penelope. In line 2, Avisa is called "Anne."

> Why does Avisa seek titles, why does she entice dowries
> Is Anne to be compared to your Penelope?[8]

The writer of this verse, "S.D.," perhaps Samuel Daniel, had a very different view of the personality behind Avisa, that she was not chaste at all but rather was a temptress out for money and titles (Avisa was called "vainglorious" in this work's introductory letter).[9] Avisa was a "chief attendant" of the virgin goddess Diana (*Willobie*, Canto 1), possibly meaning that the real Avisa was a lady-in-waiting to virgin Queen Elizabeth. To summarize, the identity behind the Avisa character is named Anne or has the initial A. She may have been one of the queen's attendants. She has many suitors and is linked with the lady in Shakespeare's Sonnet 147, "the Dark Lady."

The great author describes the Dark Lady as a woman with dark features, including eyes and hair (sonnets 130, 132, 144), and that she has a strong sexual appetite. Her "will [lust] is large and spacious" (Sonnet 135). In Sonnet 137, the poet says that his heart tells him that the Dark Lady is his "property," but he is fully mindful that she is "the wide world's common place." In Sonnet 139, he begs her not to ogle others in his presence, and again in Sonnet

140, asks her to keep her eyes on him "though thy proud heart go wide." Many scholars see a close resemblance between the Dark Lady and the character, Rosaline, in *Love's Labour's Lost*, one of the ladies-in-waiting to Princess Katherine. Like the Dark Lady, Rosaline has "a beauty dark" (5.2.20), and dark eyes (passage below). She is "wanton," i.e., promiscuous.

> A whitely wanton with a velvet brow
> With two pitch balls stuck in her face for eyes.
> Ay, and, by heaven, one that will do the deed [sex act],
> Though Argus [100-eyed giant] were her eunuch and her guard.
> [3.1.198-201]

In the play, Rosaline says the line, "past cure is still past care" (5.2.27-28), which was seemingly taken from Shakespeare's Sonnet 147, "Past cure I am, now reason is past care." As noted above, Sonnet 147 was addressed to the Dark Lady, and was evidently mimicked in Canto 44 of *Willobie His Avisa*. The poet's phrase to the Dark Lady in the same sonnet, "for I have sworn thee fair," is echoed by Rosaline's lover, Berowne, in his defense of her beauty, "I'll prove her fair, or talk till doomsday here" (4.3.274). In lines 248-265 of the same scene, Berowne praises Rosaline's dark features, and in lines 222-228 he uses similar imagery as Shakespeare does in his Sonnet 132 about the Dark Lady. Berowne also wrote a sonnet for Rosaline but it was never read in the play; perhaps it was Shakespeare's Sonnet 147. (Another "dark lady" involved in a love triangle with a "fair youth" occurred in *As You Like It*.)[10]

There was a woman in court circles named Anne that fits the description of Avisa, Rosaline and the Dark Lady of Shakespeare's sonnets. Anne Vavasour, who once served as a lady-in-waiting to Queen Elizabeth, was a notorious femme fatale. While married to another, she openly lived with Sir Henry Lee and bore him a child; after Lee died, she married again while her first husband was still alive, and was fined for bigamy. Her dark brown hair, as shown in existing portraits, certainly qualifies her as a "dark lady" (Plate 23). The name Avisa verbally suggests Anne Vavasour. The letter of apology in the 1596 edition of *Willobie* specifically protested against the idea that Avisa represented a real woman with a similar sounding name, which means that some readers believed it.

> If any man therefore by this, should take occasion to surmise, that the Author meant to note any woman, <u>whose name sounds something like that name</u> [Avisa], it is too childish and too absurd ...

In 1584, it was noted in a book that Vavasour was tempted into a liaison with the Earl of Leicester with jewels and land; Avisa was similarly enticed by a nobleman in the story of her first temptation. The name Avisa is linked to Vavasour in another way. "The Advice" was the title of a poem written by Sir Walter Ralegh addressed to Vavasour regarding her affair with Edward de Vere, 17th Earl of Oxford, which began in the late 1570s.[11] Ralegh had advised Vavasour to "take heed" of "fickle" Oxford. This connection between Ralegh, Vavasour and "Advice" – "avis" means advice in French – seems to confirm G.B. Harrison's theory that *Willobie* was written as a direct riposte at the writer and dedicatee of *Lucrece* (Shakespeare and Southampton) by a Ralegh supporter. In Shakespeare's *Lucrece*, Prince Tarquin raped the title character and was exiled for it. In 1592, courtier Ralegh was involved in a "brutish" scandal involving one of the queen's ladies-in-waiting (Elizabeth Throgmorton), resulting in the queen's wrath and Ralegh's exile from the royal court.[12] After a good length of time, the queen evidently softened her position. In January 1594, it was rumored that Ralegh was expecting an appointment on the queen's Privy Council: "And it is now feared of all honest men that [Ralegh] shall presently come to the Court; yet it is well withstood. God grant some further resistance!"[13] Perhaps *Lucrece*, registered on May 9, 1594, was part of that resistance – as an allegory, it would serve as a timely reminder of Ralegh's scandalous past. *Willobie* was registered only four months after *Lucrece*, and it lampooned Shakespeare and Southampton. In fact, the very title, *Willobie His Avisa*, could also be read as "Willobie his advice," playing on the words of Avisa and advice, because Willobie does get advice from W.S. about the lady Avisa in Canto 47, just like Ralegh had given Vavasour advice about Oxford. Ralegh did return to court, but not for another year.

This theory about Sir Walter Ralegh jibes with another clue in *Willobie*, that the great author, "Shake-speare," was the 17th Earl of Oxford, a courtier poet and playwright known to write anonymously. Lines in two *Willobie* cantos, spoken by W.S., are notably similar to those written by Oxford.

Earl of Oxford poetry excerpt:[14]

> Fain would I sing, but <u>fury</u> makes me <u>fret</u> ...

Willobie His Avisa (Canto 45, excerpt):

> And folly feeds, where <u>fury frets</u> ...

Earl of Oxford poetry excerpt from *The Paradise of Dainty Devices* (1576):[15]

> Then should my sighs to quiet <u>breast</u> retire,
> And shun such signs, as <u>secret</u> thoughts bewray.
> Uncomely love, which now lurks in my <u>breast</u>,

Should cease my <u>grief</u> ... ["Being in love, he complaineth"]

Willobie His Avisa (Canto 45, excerpt):

> So sorrows shrin'd in <u>secret</u> <u>breast</u>,
> Attaint the heart with hotter rage,
> Than <u>griefs</u> that are to friends express'd,
> Whose comfort may some part assuage:

Earl of Oxford poetry excerpt from *The Paradise of Dainty Devices*:[16]

> The <u>trickling tears</u>, that fall along my cheeks,
> The <u>secret sighs</u>, that show my inward grief:
> ["A lover rejected, complaineth."]

Willobie His Avisa (Canto 47, excerpt):

> You must be <u>secret</u>, constant, free,
> Your silent <u>sighs</u> & <u>trickling tears</u>,
> Let her in <u>secret</u> often see ...

Only a few short years before *Willobie* was printed, Southampton seriously considered marriage with Oxford's daughter, Elizabeth Vere (or he was forced to consider it by his guardian, Lord Burghley), so they definitely knew each other. That these two aristocrats were romantically involved with Anne Vavasour at the same time will probably never be proved, but it is fact that Oxford had a lengthy extra-marital love affair with Vavasour while she was single and he estranged from his wife. Their affair resulted in a bastard son, Edward Vere, born in the early months of 1581; the queen punished them with a stay in the Tower. It was a well-known scandal. Although Oxford returned to his wife in late 1581, it is possible that he resumed the affair with Vavasour after his wife's death in June 1588. By this time, Vavasour had a husband; Oxford remarried in late 1591 (Sonnet 152 indicates that the poet and the Dark Lady were married to others at the time of their affair). Associating noble Oxford with Shakespeare in print would no doubt have angered him, as well as associating his former mistress with the character Avisa. The exposure of the Oxford-Vavasour-Southampton love triangle would have been a further embarrassment to all involved.

Conclusion

The personal information and inferences about Shakespeare and the Earl of Southampton divulged by the anonymous *Willobie* writer are well known to the experts but kept at arms length because they do not fit the Stratford Man model. Shakespeare was "old" or an "old player" in 1594 implying that he had been acting a long time or was physically old, or both. In 1594, the Stratford Man was only aged thirty, and his supposed acting career only spanned about four years. *Willobie* contained the first mention in print that the great author also acted, although the word used, "player," also implied he was a player with women, a lothario (like the subject of *A Lover's Complaint*). The *Willobie* writer describes Shakespeare as the "familiar friend" of Southampton and that the two were romantically interested in the same woman, both clues implying that they shared a similar social status – impossible if they represented the Stratford Man and the noble Southampton. Even if this were not implied, it is highly unlikely that a nobleman would socialize with a "lowly" actor-writer at this time. Evidence is also lacking that the Stratford Man knew Southampton or was involved in a love triangle. Meanwhile, the *Willobie* writer hinted that "Shake-speare" was an alias by printing the name with a hyphen in the preface, and by including a character named W.S. whose dialogue was sprinkled with phrases written by the 17th Earl of Oxford. Furthermore, the name Avisa would recall Ralegh's "Advice" poem that had warned Anne Vavasour against Oxford, dredging up the late affair that resulted in their imprisonment by the jealous Queen Elizabeth. These three points, and the reference to a scandalous love triangle, were intended to embarrass this nobleman, the author of *Lucrece*. Ralegh evidently had been embarassed by an association between himself and the rapist, Tarquin, in Shakespeare's poem. The *Willobie* writer gave enough clues to confirm Southampton's identity as H.W.-Henry Willobie; and by placing him in a love triangle with Shakespeare, the *Willobie* writer also revealed his belief that Southampton was the Fair Youth of Shakespeare's sonnets, as Thomas Nashe had believed. The great author being a nobleman would explain the acceptance of his plea to the Fair Youth to father children "for love of me" (Sonnet 10), words that would be otherwise insulting to Southampton coming from the socially inferior Stratford Man.[17] The Dark Lady, the married woman with whom the great author and the Fair Youth were romantically involved, had the initial A, according to the *Willobie* writer, and was named Anne, according to a poem in *Penelope's Complaint*. Oxford's earlier affair with a dark-haired lady named Anne Vavasour, a known wanton at Elizabeth's court, seems to confirm these identities. The Shakespeare experts have shown no interest in following this major clue about the Dark Lady, and are obviously reluctant to place their Shakespeare, i.e., the Stratford Man, in the middle of court romances and politics.

CHAPTER 15

Overlooked Commentary about Shakespeare by His Contemporaries (1589–1614)

THE READER MAY ask, "If Shakespeare was a pen name, or someone other than the Stratford Man, then why didn't anyone of the period mention it?" The literary record shows that at least eleven people – in addition to the author of *Willobie His Avisa* – did mention it in print in fourteen instances, which this chapter will detail. Many of these Shakespeare comments are known but overlooked because what was said does not fit the Stratford Man model, which can be summarized by the following: Shakespeare was born in 1564 and was modestly educated. He was an actor who started his literary career about age 26 and only for monetary gain. He was humbly born and was anxious to raise his social status. He rewrote or "improved" the plays of other writers or was an outright plagiarist. He was indifferent to the ownership of his literary works and to their preservation. He retired to his hometown circa 1613 and died there in 1616. The picture of the great author *made by his contemporaries*, however, differs radically from the Stratford Man model: the great author was a revered poet and playwright well before 1589. He was a generous aristocrat whose compulsion to write plays and to even act in them publicly stained his name and reputation. He wrote anonymously or with a pen name. He was scholarly, well known to students at Oxford and Cambridge universities, and was in Queen Elizabeth's good graces. He was dead by 1607, and in two instances it was hinted that he was the 17th Earl of Oxford. Only one overlooked remark openly identified the subject as "Shakespeare"; the others identified him by initials, by a portion of the pen name, by a descriptive name or phrase, or by inference. This was not as unusual as the reader may think. Most contemporaries alluded to Shakespeare's famous lines or characters – *they did not usually mention his name or give personal information*. Even praise for the great author was often indirect, implying that there was something secret about him. Two commentators said that the great author did not want open acclaim, with which they complied, but after his death other commentators complained about the lack of tributes that were justly due him. Written between 1589 and 1614, these fourteen overlooked comments about Shakespeare *were made years before the First Folio*, which changed the public's perception of him forever. Four of these comments were made even before the name "William Shakespeare" appeared in print. What should be believed: printed statements about Shakespeare made by his contemporaries, or the myths created about him after his death, embellished by the speculations of the experts? *Men of literature and the theater, those who would have had a better understanding of the great author than any modern-day Shakespeare "expert," wrote most of these overlooked Shakespeare comments.* For this reason, the reader is asked to temporarily put aside the Stratford Man model so he can read these statements without bias. (The dates before the title indicate the year of publication, unless stated otherwise.)

---

(1). The English writer of a tragedy about Hamlet, i.e., Shakespeare, is a dramatist well known to university students in 1589; *Hamlet* and at least one Shakespeare sonnet were written by that year.

(1589) Prefatory letter by Thomas Nashe in the book, *Menaphon*, by Robert Greene (registered August 23, 1589). Nashe advised playwrights to read "English *Seneca*," whose writing

> yields many good sentences, as *Blood is a Beggar*, and so forth: and if you entreat him fair in a frosty morning, he will afford you whole *Hamlets*, I should say handfuls of tragical speeches.

English Seneca, an English writer of "tragical speeches" whose works were influenced by the classical dramatist, Seneca, and who wrote a play about Hamlet, describes Shakespeare. For supporting evidence of this identification, Nashe's quotation from English Seneca, "Blood is a Beggar," resembles a line in Shakespeare's Sonnet 67, and to "entreat" someone "fair" was an expression that Shakespeare favored. One can infer from Nashe's letter that in 1589 Shakespeare was a renowned and respected writer, and that his play, *Hamlet*, was already written. Three other allusions to Shakespeare's *Hamlet*, made circa 1588-89, further support this conclusion. Nashe had addressed his letter to the "Gentlemen Students of both Universities." The first printed edition of *Hamlet* (1603) noted that this play had been performed at the universities of Oxford and Cambridge. It is probable then that Nashe's 1589 allusion to Shakespeare's *Hamlet* was topical. Nashe wrote that Shakespeare was approachable and would share his play manuscripts with other writers. This could help explain the numerous allusions to lines in Shakespeare's plays in the works of other writers, as detailed in Appendix A. Shakespeare was apparently sharing manuscripts of his sonnets as well, circa 1589. Nashe's passage is explained in more detail on pp. 52-55.

---

(2). Willy, the learned poet and playwright who wrote *Hamlet*, i.e., Shakespeare, is in a state of retirement; a gentleman, Willy writes plays anonymously, and has been doing so since the 1570s.

(1590) *The Tears of the Muses* by Edmund Spenser (one of nine poetical works published under the title, *Complaints Containing Sundry Small Poems of the World's Vanity*, registered December 29, 1590, published 1591). Each of the nine Muses in Spenser's poem complains about the current state of the arts. The muse of comedy, Thalia, laments the degradation of the comic stage. In the first five stanzas, she says that playwrights at this time aim to please the "vulgar" and that they "despise" the more genteel comedies of old, which filled "with pleasure /the list'ners' eyes, and ears with melody," and that these old plays contained the "sweet delights of learning's treasure." In stanzas 6 to 8, Thalia extols "pleasant *Willy*," one of the writers of the old school:

> And he the man, whom Nature self had made
> To mock herself, and Truth to imitate,
> With kindly [pleasant] counter [countering] under Mimic shade,
> Our pleasant *Willy*, ah is dead of late:
> With whom all joy and jolly merriment
> Is also deaded, and in dolor [sorrow] drent [drenched].
>
> Instead thereof scoffing Scurrility [coarse language],
> And scornful Folly with Contempt is crept,
> Rolling in rhymes of shameless ribaldry
> Without regard, or due Decorum kept,
> Each idle [useless] wit at will presumes to make,
> And doth the Learneds task upon him take.
>
> But that same gentle Spirit, from whose pen
> Large streams of honey and sweet Nectar flow,
> Scorning the boldness of such base-born men,
> Which dare their follies forth so rashly throw;
> Doth rather choose to sit in idle [inactive] Cell,
> Than so himself to mockery to sell.   [lines 205-22]

When Spenser wrote *The Tears of the Muses*, he had recently returned to London for an extended visit (from October 1589 to 1591), after living in Ireland since 1580. The London theaters had apparently changed a great deal in the interim. In Spenser's eyes, the public stage had become rude and foul, with "vain toys" entertaining the "vulgar." No doubt the current vogue for melodramatic plays like Marlowe's *Tamburlaine* had caused Spenser's disgust. Poet

Samuel Daniel in 1592 and 1594 also made references to "barbarism" in the arts, as did W.C. in *Polimanteia* in 1595.[1] The old school playwright, "Our pleasant Willy," must have been writing in the 1570s, before Spenser's relocation to Ireland. This inference is supported by Spenser's line that "large streams of honey and sweet nectar flow" from Willy's pen," i.e., Willy had already written many high quality comedies (Appendix A supplies evidence suggesting the great author had already written over twenty plays by 1590).

Spenser did not disclose Willy's surname, but calls him "the man, whom Nature self had made /to mock herself, and Truth to imitate." In similar words, William Shakespeare's Hamlet tells the actors about the "purpose of playing," which

> was and is, <u>to hold as 'twere, the Mirror up to Nature</u>; to shew Virtue her own Feature, <u>Scorn her own Image</u>, and the very Age and Body of the Time, his form and pressure. [3.2.24]

Willy mocks Nature and imitates truth "With kindly counter under Mimic shade … " Counter here is short for "countering," another word for singing – a poetical way to describe writing in verse. Willy writes "under Mimic shade," i.e., with the mask of a mime, a comic actor. Willy, therefore, writes anonymously. Willy is a "gentle Spirit" and scorns "the boldness of such baseborn men" that write scurrilous and ribald comedies. In this context, "gentle" Willy describes someone of high birth, which explains his need to write "under Mimic shade." The muse laments Willy being "dead of late" – not physically dead in 1590, but "idle" or retired; the experts posit that the Stratford Man's theatrical career *began* circa 1590. Spenser also separates "pleasant Willy" from "each idle wit" – those playwrights who "presume" to write upon "learned" subjects – implying that Willy was very learned.

The great author evidently acknowledged Spenser's poem as "Satire keen and critical" in his play, *A Midsummer Night's Dream*. Theseus is given a list of entertainments from which to choose for his wedding feast, including

> The thrice three Muses mourning for the death
> Of learning, late deceas'd in beggary?
> That is some Satire keen and critical,
> Not sorting with a nuptial ceremony. [5.1.52-54]

A "too early" allusion to this play occurred in 1593 (Appendix A, No. 74). In *The Tears of the Muses*, Spenser alluded to the great author by the first name of his alias; in his next work, he alluded to the last name, as shown below.

(3). The poet with the "heroically sounding" name, i.e., Shakespeare, has the highest social standing among poets.

(1591) *Colin Clout's Come Home Again* by Edmund Spenser. Although this work was first printed in 1595, Spenser left the date on the dedication to Sir Walter Ralegh as December 27, 1591, which was shortly after Spenser had "come home again" to Ireland (he referred to himself as "Colin Clout"). Spenser probably intended the work for publication in 1592, but Ralegh's disastrous fall from the queen's favor that year rendered it impolitic. In this little known passage, Spenser praised twelve poets, including "Aetion":

> And there though last not least is *Aetion*,
> A gentler shepherd may nowhere be found:
> Whose *Muse* full of high thoughts invention,
> Doth like himself Heroically sound.   [lines 444-47]

The phrase, "Doth like himself heroically sound," is a name clue. Aetion's poetry sounds as heroic as "himself." The *Shakspere Allusion-book* (1909) declared that this was a reference to Shakespeare because

> no other heroic poet (i.e., historical dramatist, or chronicler in heroic verse) had a surname of heroic sound. Jonson, Fuller, and Bancroft have similar allusions to our bard's warlike name.[2]

"Shake-speare" is a "warlike name." The line, "A gentler shepherd may nowhere be found," indicates Spenser's belief that Shakespeare had the highest social standing among poets. (The Stratford Man was not even a "gentleman" yet – his father's coat of arms was granted in 1596.) Spenser for the second time, called Shakespeare "gentle." Most of the poets Spenser had admired in this short work have been identified as courtier poets, including Sir Philip Sidney, Sir Walter Ralegh and Samuel Daniel.[3] Circa 1590, the 17th Earl of Oxford held the highest title among courtier poets. The next two overlooked comments about Shakespeare also hint he was Oxford. It is significant that no one referred to the great author by his full pen name until *Venus and Adonis* (1593), where it debuted in print *by his own authority*.

(4). "Gentle Master William," i.e., Shakespeare, is a prolific and idolized poet, a distinguished gentleman of rank, and is a generous patron of scholars. His identity is linked with Edward de Vere, 17th Earl of Oxford.

(1592) *Strange News, of the Intercepting of Certain Letters* by Thomas Nashe (registered on January 12, 1593; the first two issues were dated 1592). Nashe opened his dedication letter to *Strange News* with a description of his dedicatee and a made-up name for him, "Master *Apis lapis*":

> To the most copious Carminist of our time, and famous persecutor
> of *Priscian* his very friend Master *Apis lapis.*

Nashe's dedicatee is a prolific versifier ("most copious Carminist"), one that famously disregards grammar rules ("famous persecutor of Priscian," the Latin grammarian), and is idolized by his fellow writers ("Apis" is "the ox worshipped by the Egyptians as a god"; *lapis* is Latin for "stone").[4] In the next line, Nashe readdresses his dedicatee as "Gentle Master William."

> Gentle M. *William*, that learned writer Rhinish wine & Sugar, in the
> first book of his comment upon Red-Noses, hath this saying ...

In 1944, Charles Wisner Barrell analyzed Nashe's letter and found many Shakespeare associations.[5] William in "Gentle Master William" suggests Shakespeare, and this is confirmed by the phrase, "Rhinish wine & Sugar." Character Sir John Falstaff in Shakespeare's *Henry IV-Part 1* is called "Sir John Sack and Sugar" (1.2.126) – sack being another word for wine. Nashe was apparently associating the wine-loving Falstaff with William Elderton, who was named further into the dedication text; he had written a ballad about London taverns. "Gentle Master William" is also reminiscent of Edmund Spenser's earlier reference to Shakespeare in *The Tears of the Muses* (No. 2 above), where the dramatist is described as "pleasant Willy" and "gentle Spirit." Gentle Master William has a mind full of Chaucer and Terence – two writers who influenced Shakespeare (John Davies of Hereford later dubbed Shakespeare, "English Terence"). Gentle Master William has "pleasant witty humor," and "Grammar rules" were his "special enemies," both lines applicable to Shakespeare. Gentle Master William has a "dudgeon dagger." A dagger was mentioned again within the main text of *Strange News*:

> ... one of my fellows, Will. Monox (hast thou never heard of him and
> his great dagger?)

Nashe's "fellow," Will. Monox, is known for his "great dagger." Nashe's dedicatee, his "very friend," Gentle Master William, has a "dudgeon dagger." These two Williams are the same person, a poet known for his "dagger" or sword-spear, i.e., William Shakespeare. Gentle Master William's other name is "Master Apis lapis"; "ox" is in this name just like "Monox" i.e., "apis," as noted above. "Lapis" occurs only once in the Shakespeare canon, and is connected to the name, William. In *Merry Wives of Windsor* (4.1.33), Sir Hugh Evans tests a boy on his Latin: "What is lapis, William?"

Thomas Nashe's dedication letter also describes Gentle Master William as a man of rank ("your worship") and one who wears a "round cap" (a hat worn by men of distinction). He writes that Gentle Master William has a high regard of John Davies's poem, *Of the Soul of Man.* Although this work was first published in 1599 (with his *Nosce Teipsum),* Davies's *Soul* was completed by July 11, 1592, the date on a surviving manuscript version dedicated to Queen Elizabeth.[6] Davies admired Shakespeare and identified him as a man of rank (No. 7 below). Nashe called Gentle Master William an "infinite Macaenas," or a generous patron, "to learned men" and to "all poor scholars." (Later it was asserted, through the mouth of Gullio, that the great author "maintained" scholars and "other poetical spirits" in *The Return from Parnassus-Part 1.)* Gentle Master William mixes with "grave doctors and men of judgment in both laws every day," says Nashe, showing that he was in constant contact with men in high and distinguished positions. In the first edition of *Strange News* that was dated 1593, Nashe added a line commending Gentle Master William's hospitality, and wrote, "Why should virtue be smothered by blind circumstance?" Nashe may have been commenting upon the emergence in print of the great author's alias in *Venus and Adonis* that same year (registered in April). The great author's "virtue" or his art is "smothered by blind circumstance," the need to use a pseudonym. Nashe's reluctance to openly name the dedicatee of *Strange News* reinforces the other clues he provided of his dedicatee's high status. The courtier poet and playwright, Edward de Vere, 17th Earl of Oxford, qualified as Nashe's dedicatee. He patronized many writers, and was openly named in the main text of *Strange News.* Oxford was known to write plays anonymously. The two "ox" references mentioned above would be punning identity clues. Nashe's phrase, "very friend," in the dedication letter could have punned on Oxford's surname, De Vere.

Gabriel Harvey confirmed that Nashe's "Master Apis lapis" was an important personage in his *Pierce's Supererogation* (1593). Harvey wrote that Nashe, whom he called Shakerley, had "shamefully" criticized his patron, Master Apis Lapis, and others.

> [Shakerley-Nashe] shamefully, and odiously misuseth every friend, or acquaintance, as he hath served some of his favorablest Patrons, (whom for certain respects I am not to name), M. Apis Lapis, Greene, Marlow, Chettle, and whom not?

Harvey placed Master Apis Lapis, as John Rollett noted,[7] in the company of the playwrights Robert Greene, Christopher Marlowe and Henry Chettle. Harvey specifically noted that Master Apis Lapis was not to be named "for certain respects," presumably because he was a man of rank. Harvey, therefore, was deeming Nashe's comical dedication letter to his patron, Gentle Master William-Master Apis Lapis, as especially shameful or disrespectful because of his patron's high status. Perhaps in response to this, the dedication was omitted in one of the issues of *Strange News* (dated 1593).

---

(5). The publication of *Venus and Adonis* with a "muzzle" or alias, i.e., "William Shakespeare," is the hugest and mightiest miracle of 1593. Queen Elizabeth I was involved or responsible. Shakespeare's identity is linked with Edward de Vere, 17th Earl of Oxford.

(1593) *A New Letter of Notable Contents* by Gabriel Harvey (registered October 1, 1593). This essay's concluding piece, "A Strange Sonnet, Entitled Gorgon or the Wonderful Year," told of the "wonders" of 1593. They included a few world events, such as Ruprecht von Eggenberg's defeat of the Turkish pasha in June, and the French King Henry IV's conversion to Catholicism in July.[8] The last wonder noted in this sonnet was an English one: "Weep Paul's, thy Tamberlaine [*sic*] vouchsafes to die." It was the death of Christopher Marlowe (May 30). Although Marlowe was not openly named, Harvey identified him by his most famous play. In the piece that followed, "A Stanza declarative: to the Lovers of admirable Works," another English "wonder" is described, what Harvey called the "hugest" and "mightiest miracle of Ninety Three." It too was literary.

> A Stanza declarative: *to the Lovers of admirable Works*.
>
> Pleased it hath a *Gentlewoman rare*,
> With <u>Phoenix quill</u> in diamond hand of <u>Art</u>,
> <u>To muzzle the redoubtable Bull-bare</u>,
> And play the galliard [valiant] <u>Championesses</u> part.
> Though miracles surcease, yet Wonder see
> *The mightiest miracle of Ninety Three.*
>
> Vis consilii expers, mole ruit sua.[9]

Harvey was providing a news flash to "lovers" or fans of someone with "admirable works." With the previous "wonder" being the death of dramatist Marlowe, and the presence of the words "quill" and "art" in this passage, Harvey's subject was certainly about a writer of admirable works. This writer was "muzzled" in 1593. Harvey dated his book September 16, 1593, so this literary muzzling had occurred earlier that year. Besides Marlowe's death, the only other great literary event in 1593 was the publication of Shakespeare's poem, *Venus and Adonis*, the very first time that the name "William Shakespeare" appeared in print. It was registered on April 18, 1593, and was in circulation by June. In the dedication, Shakespeare wrote that *Venus and Adonis* was the "first heir of my invention," the first printed work to feature his invented name. This presumably was the muzzling that Harvey spoke of. This muzzling pleased "a Gentlewoman rare, /With Phoenix quill," undoubtedly Queen Elizabeth, as the phoenix was her personal device. Harvey's phrase, "galliard Championesses part," supports this identification, a phrase that likely referred to Britomart, "the noble championesse" (Book 3, 12.41) in Edmund Spenser's *Faerie Queene* (1590). The warrior maid, Britomart, was one of several characters that symbolized Queen Elizabeth in Spenser's epic. "Phoenix quill" also appeared in a poem addressed to the queen by Henry Lok: "The sacred dame / ... Whose Phoenix quill /Doth heavenly Crown affect ..." (*Sundry Christian Passions contained in two hundred Sonnets*, registered on May 2, 1593 and published that year). Like his Marlowe reference, Harvey did not name the muzzled writer, he only provided the clue, "redoubtable Bull-bare." A "redoubtable" person is one "to be reverenced or revered, commanding respect" (*OED*), indicating that this writer had a high position or social status. The use of "bull-bare" appears to be another identity clue. Harvey used this unusual word in another work of the previous year. In his *Four Letters, and Certain Sonnets* (1592), Harvey wrote that the 17th Earl of Oxford was told that Harvey's poem, *The Mirror of Tuscanismo*, "was palpably intended against him." Harvey denied this, and said in the passage below that Oxford took the matter lightly:

> But the noble Earl [of Oxford], not disposed to trouble his Jovial mind with such Saturnine paltry still continued, like his magnificent self: and that Fleeting also proved, like the other, a silly bull-beare, a sorry puff of wind, a thing of nothing.

Bull-bear is defined like "bugbear," an imaginary hobgoblin used to scare children, but considering the context, Harvey was also punning on Oxford's name: bull is another word for ox. It seems that Harvey purposely used "Bull-bare" in the Gorgon sonnet to connect the unnamed muzzled writer with his previous passage about Oxford, indicating that Oxford was the "redoubtable Bull-bare." Oxford was a nobleman and poet-dramatist known to write anonymously; he was one of the queen's favorites. Interestingly, in 1578, Harvey had described Oxford with the phrase, "thy will shakes spears" ("vultus tela vibrat") in a Latin speech before the queen and her court at Audley End.[10] Harvey lauded Oxford's poetry and belles lettres in this speech, but suggested he put aside literary pursuits to focus upon military service.

Harvey indicated that the author of *Venus and Adonis* was using a pen name in his previous book, *Pierce's Supererogation*, printed in July 1593. He did so in a passage explaining why his book took so long to see print.

> The stay of the Publication, resteth only at my instance: who can conceive small hope of any possible account, or regard of mine

> own discourses, <u>were that fair body of the sweetest Venus in Print,</u>
> <u>as it is redoubtably armed with the compleat harness of the brav-</u>
> <u>est Minerva</u>. When <u>his necessary defense</u> hath sufficiently acleared
> him, whom it principally concerneth to acquit himself: She shall no
> sooner appear in person, like a new Star in Cassiopea, but every
> eye of capacity will see a conspicuous difference between her, and
> other mirrors of Eloquence: [p. 115]

Harvey wrote that he delayed publication of his *Pierce's Supererogation* because of "the sweetest Venus in Print..." In other words, Harvey would not release *Pierce's Supererogation* while the literary world was caught in the sensation of Shakespeare's poem, *Venus and Adonis*. He felt that there would be little "hope of any possible account," i.e., notice or criticism, of his work. In the same sentence, Harvey openly stated that Shakespeare is a pen name. He wrote that *Venus and Adonis* "is redoubtably armed with the compleat harness of the bravest Minerva." Minerva is the Roman equivalent of the Greek goddess, Athena, who, according to Homer, sprung from the forehead of chief god Zeus in full armor "brandishing her sharp spear."[11] She is usually depicted holding a long spear. The "armor" of *Venus and Adonis*, described in the next sentence as the author's "necessary defense," is the pen name, "William Shakespeare." Harvey's use of "redoubtedly" in this passage is pointedly linked to the muzzling of the "redoubtable bull-bare," Harvey's description of the author of *Venus and Adonis* in the Gorgon sonnet.

Harvey's passage in *Pierce's Supererogation* also relates that *Venus and Adonis* "principally concerneth" a woman ("She") whose depiction will cause others to "see a conspicuous difference" with depictions of her in other works ("mirrors of Eloquence"). But a depiction of the love goddess as a seductress was not out of character.[12] Considering Harvey's commentary in the Gorgon sonnet, he must have associated Shakespeare's Venus with Queen Elizabeth. The queen's portrayal as a seducer would be "conspicuously different" from her depictions in other works as the Virgin Queen. Many scholars have noticed that Venus is often called "queen" in Shakespeare's poem. Harvey was not alone in his association of Shakespeare's Venus with Queen Elizabeth. In a private letter, dated September 21, 1593, William Reynolds wrote:

> Also within these few days there is another book made of Venus
> and Adonis wherein the queen represents the person of Venus ... [13]

Although Harvey never openly praised or mentioned Shakespeare in his printed works, he did allude to a few Shakespeare phrases in *A New Letter of Notable Contents* and *Pierce's Supererogation* (Appendix A, nos. 70-72). Harvey's printed works, as well as those of his nemesis, Thomas Nashe, were ordered for burning in 1599. Although Harvey lived until 1630, *A New Letter* was his last published work, or one that he had claimed authorship.

---

(6). A great poet in the center of the theater world, the one associated with Venus and Adonis, i.e., Shakespeare, is a nobleman. He cannot be publicly praised for his dramatic art because it would "distain" or dishonor him. He was active at the Blackfriars Theater in 1583 or before.

(1593) *Cephalus and Procris* and *Narcissus*, a combined publication by Thomas Edwards (registered October 22, 1593, printed 1595). Edwards's poem, *Cephalus and Procris*, was strongly influenced by Shakespeare's *Venus and Adonis*, as were many other poems.[14] In the epilogue (l'envoy) of the accompanying work, *Narcissus*, Edwards praised poets Edmund Spenser, Samuel Daniel, Thomas Watson and Christopher Marlowe. They were identified not by name but by their works in stanzas 5 to 7. In Stanza 8, Edwards describes Venus and Adonis as characters in a masque performed by actors in luxurious clothing. Adonis is "well-deserved" to get Venus's attention, writes Edwards, but even if she had not tried to seduce him, other nymphs or ladies would have "sent him bays," i.e., given him attention, praise or gifts. Edwards then writes of someone else who deserves attention, a man in the center of the theater world. He wears purple robes, symbolic for royalty or nobility, which are "distained" (defiled, sullied, or dishonored). Edwards says that his powerful talent *should* have made him "the only object and the star" of all English poets. Edwards implies the reason why he is not: he is a nobleman. Public praise of his theatrical talent and activity with his actual name would dishonor him.

> *Adon* deafly masking through,
> Stately troupes rich conceited [costumed],
> Shew'd he well-deserved to,
> Love's [Venus's] delight on him to gaze,
> And had not love [Venus] herself entreated,
> Other nymphs had sent him bays [praise, honors].
>
> Eke [Also] in purple robes distain'd [dishonored],
> Amidst the Center of this clime [realm of the theater],
> I have heard say doth remain,
> One whose power floweth far,
> That should have been of our rhyme [English poetry],
> The only object and the star.
>
> Well could his bewitching pen,
> Done the Muses objects to us [i.e., give inspiration],
> Although he differs much from men,
> Tilting under Friaries,
> Yet his golden art might woo us,

To have honored him with bays.   [stanzas 8-10, l'envoy]

By October 1593, the registry date of Edwards's work, the "star" of English poetry was the author of *Venus and Adonis*, Shakespeare. Since Edwards specifically mentions "Adon" and "Love," i.e., Venus, the goddess of love, surely Shakespeare was the unnamed artist in question. Considering the influence of Shakespeare upon Edwards's work, *Shakespeare had to have been meant* – otherwise, Edwards would have completely neglected to mention a poet whom he obviously had admired. The phrase, "Tilting under Friaries," clinches this identity – tilting is another word for jousting or "spear shaking." "Friaries" most likely referred to Blackfriars, a small theater that catered to the upper class. But when Edwards wrote *Narcissus*, this theater had been closed for a decade. The Blackfriars operated during the years 1576 to 1583; it was closed from 1584 to 1600. By mentioning this theater, Edwards implies that Shakespeare was active there in 1583 or before. Shakespeare "differs much from men" because he is a dramatist and actor who is also a nobleman. Shakespeare's pen seduces and inspires his admirers, just like Adonis inspires the gaze of Venus, but his high status will not suffer direct and open recognition.

---

(7). Admiration for "the Swallow," presumably Shakespeare, a great poet of rank who writes under a shadow.

(1594) *Orchestra or a Poem of Dancing* (registered June 25, 1594, published 1596) by John Davies (knighted in 1603). In the final four stanzas of this poem, Davies expressed his wish to have the talent of certain writers. In the first of these stanzas (No. 128), he refers to poets of the past and present. Davies devotes the entire next stanza (No. 129) to an unidentified poet of great intellect whom he calls "sweet Companion," one who "sings" or writes "under a shadow."

> O could I sweet Companion, sing like you,
> Which of a shadow, under a shadow sing;
> Or like fair *Salues* sad lover true,
> Or like the Bay, the Marigold's darling,
> Whose sudden verse Love covers with his wing:
> O that your brains were mingled all with mine,
> T'enlarge my wit for this great work divine.   [Stanza 129]

In the next stanza, Davies praised two poets that "might one for all suffice." One was Sir Philip Sidney (reference to *Astrophel and Stella*), and the other, a poet whom Davies called "the Swallow."

> Yet *Astrophell* might one for all suffice,

> Whose supple Muse Chameleon-like doth change
> Into all forms of excellent device:
> So might the <u>Swallow</u>, whose swift Muse doth range
> Through rare *Ideas* and inventions strange,
> And ever doth enjoy her joyful spring,
> And sweeter than the Nightingale doth <u>sing</u>. [Stanza 130]

The final stanza of Davies's work is almost delirious praise of the Swallow, also called "the shadow."

> O that I might that <u>singing Swallow hear</u>
> <u>To whom I owe my service and my love</u>,
> <u>His sug'red tunes</u> would so enchant mine ear,
> And in my mind such sacred fury move,
> As I should knock at <u>heav'n's great gate</u> above
> With my proud rhymes, while of this heav'nly state
> I do aspire <u>the shadow to relate</u>. FINIS. [Stanza 131]

Michael Drayton's sonnet cycle, *Idea's Mirror*, was released in 1594, and critics naturally have associated the unnamed Swallow with Drayton because of the phrase, "Through rare *Ideas*," in Stanza 130. But there are reasons to doubt that Drayton was the Swallow. When Davies praised the other poets, he had identified them by their specific poetry works (for example, "Colin" from Edmund Spenser's *Colin Clout's Come Home Again*, "Delia's servant" from Samuel Daniel's *Delia* sonnets). "Swallow" was not associated with Drayton or any other poet. (Drayton's *Idea's Mirror* was actually inspired by the sonnet cycle titled *L'Idée* by the French poet, Claude de Pontoux, who died in 1579.)[15] One modern editor suggested that Davies's friend, Richard Martin, was the Swallow because "a 'martin' is a bird of the swallow family."[16] Martin's poetry, and reputation as a poet, however, is almost non-existent; that his caliber of writing was similar to that of Sidney or Daniel is most unlikely. Shakespeare's association with swallow is likewise unknown, but considering his recent acclaim with *Venus and Adonis* and *Lucrece*, his absence in these stanzas would be otherwise conspicuous. Shakespeare and Swallow do share the initial S. The Swallow is also linked to the unnamed poet in Stanza 129, described as "sweet Companion," and with the words sing and shadow, which he did not use in his praise of the other poets. Davies's lines about the Swallow contain phrase similarity with those written by Shakespeare: (1) Davies's theme of singing birds, and his phrase, "heaven's great gate," resembles lines in Shakespeare's Sonnet 29: "Like to the Lark at break of day arising /From sullen earth sings hymns at Heaven's gate"; there is also an echo with a line in Shakespeare's *Cymbeline* (2.3.31): "Hark, hark, the lark at heaven's gate sings"; (2) Davies's phrase, "inventions strange," and Shakespeare's phrase, "strange invention," in *Macbeth* (3.1.33); (3) Davies's phrase, "sweet companion," and Shakespeare's phrases, "sweet'st companion" in *The Winter's Tale* (5.1.11) and "sweet'st companions" in *Cymbeline* (5.5.350). John Davies of Hereford also used "companion" to describe Shakespeare (No. 13 below).

Davies was bursting to openly speak of this great poet, the shadowed Swallow, but would not certainly identify him. His statement that he owed this poet "service" implies that the Swallow was a man of rank and that Davies did not wish to offend him, thus explaining Davies's discretion. It would have been perfectly respectable for Davies to make a recognizable allusion to Drayton, who held no special rank and who did not write under a shadow, just like he did with Spenser and Daniel. Davies perhaps even alluded to Drayton's work, and to the swallow moniker that has puzzled everyone, to cloud his Shakespeare allusion. Ambiguity in identifying Shakespeare was a constant theme in contemporary references. More puzzling lines in Davies's poem are "fair Salues sad lover true/ ... Whose sudden verse Love covers with his wing" (Stanza 129). Sir Edmund Chambers guessed that "Salues" was a misprint for "Sylues," i.e., Sylve's. If so, then it could allude to the scene in Shakespeare's *Two Gentlemen from Verona* (3.1.140-152) where Valentine's love letter to Sylvia was read aloud.[17] Considering the Swallow's obscurity, the misprint may have been intentional.

When Davies republished *Orchestra* in 1622, he deleted the stanzas containing his praise of poets, but he marked the place of the deletion with the line, "Here are wanting some Stanzas describing Queen Elizabeth." This was a false statement: the excised stanzas were not about the late queen, but about his favorite poets, of which the Swallow had received the highest praise. Apparently, it was not politic to "describe" or praise Shakespeare in 1622, even indirectly.

A third reference in 1594 that implied Shakespeare was a writer who hid his authorship occurred in Thomas Heywood's *Oenone and Paris*, a poem that imitated Shakespeare's *Venus and Adonis*. Shakespeare's dedication letter was also imitated: Heywood described his poem as a first effort, an "unpolished" work, and promised another one to come. But, as noticed by Charlton Ogburn, Heywood added a line saying that he wrote under concealed authorship. Heywood likens himself to the ancient Greek painter, Apelles, who

> having framed any work of worth, would set it openly to the view of all, hiding himself closely in a corner of the work-house, to the end, that if some curious and gaping fellow came to find any fault, he might amend it against the next market. In the publishing of this little poem [*Oenone and Paris*], I have imitated the painter, giving you this poor pamphlet to peruse, lurking in the meanwhile obscurely ...

Heywood was apparently poking fun at the great author for "hiding himself closely in a corner," but, as Ogburn remarked, he "misconstrues the purpose of [Shakespeare's] pseudonymity."[18]

---

(8). Praise of a famous great poet, presumably Shakespeare, could "disparage" him because he was a man of high rank.

(1595) *The First Rape of Fair Helen. Done into Poem* by John Trussell (registered April 16, 1595). Trussell's poem was inspired by Shakespeare's *The Rape of Lucrece*, evidenced by a similar theme and verbal echoes.[19] The poem was also influenced by *Venus and Adonis* and by "complaint" poems that were in vogue at the time (Shakespeare's poem, *A Lover's Complaint*, was in circulation before 1595, as shown in Chapter 4).[20] Trussell seemed to acknowledge Shakespeare's influence upon the work in his prefatory verse titled, "Sonnet." Trussell's "Sonnet" is about his dilemma: should he praise or not praise a certain great poet? He twice says that he is unequal to the task, and believes that the great poet's artistry speaks for him and guarantees his eternal fame. Trussell cites a Latin line, translated as "Who does not praise your lines makes choice of the worse."[21] For this reason he decided to laud the poet, albeit without mentioning his name.

Sonnet.

To praise thy worth or to applaud thy wit,
Or to commend thy pleasing Poetry:
Were but to shew my insufficiency,
Which cannot equal what thyself hast writ.
for thou mayst challenge not unworthily,
true Virtue's merits, Fame's eternity,
Upon thy brows perpetually to sit.
then what need I to laud thy poesy,
(which cannot pen thy praise effectually)
Sith *Phoebus* Laurel will eternize it.
yet though thy own deserts [merits] sufficient be,
to praise thyself without my praising thee.
My praise cannot disparage thee a whit,
Yet since our friendship and our amity,
commanded me as much: (and he,
Qui tua non laudat deteriora dabit)
I have adventur'd, as each eye may see,
to shame myself in seeking praise for thee.   I.T.

Most critics link the admired poet to Shakespeare, but some are unsure because Trussell was so obscure about his identity – there should have been no need with Shakespeare (i.e., the Stratford Man). Trussell's exclusion of the poet's name is explained by the line, "My praise cannot disparage thee a whit," which implied the opposite, that praise *could* disparage him, like Thomas Edwards had said about Shakespeare in his 1593 work (No. 6). This implies that the poet had high social rank, as does the phrase, "commanded me." Trussell claimed friendship with the poet and in a reverent tone. He apparently wished to pay tribute to the writer of *Lucrece, Venus and Adonis,* and *A Lover's Complaint* but obeyed the poet's "command" to not openly do so. This accords with the other veiled references to Shakespeare in this chapter. Trussell never "adventur'd" to praise this poet again.

---

(9). The poet of *The Rape of Lucrece*, i.e., Shakespeare, was well acquainted with Queen Elizabeth and was rewarded by her. He wrote a story with political overtones circa 1588.

(1603) *England's Mourning Garment: worn here by plain shepherds; in memory of their sacred mistress, Elizabeth...* by Henry Chettle (registered April 25, 1603). Chettle called upon several English poets, mostly identified by their works, to write memorial tributes to the late Queen Elizabeth. In the final line of Stanza 6, Chettle alludes to Shakespeare's poem, *The Rape of Lucrece.*

> Nor doth the silver tongued *Melicert*,
> Drop from his honeyed muse one sable tear
> To mourn her death that graced his desert [merit],
> And to his lays [poetry] open'd her Royal ear.
>   Shepherd remember our *Elizabeth*.
>   And sing her Rape, done by that *Tarquin*, Death.

The poet-shepherd, "silver tongued Melicert," is, therefore, Shakespeare. The queen "graced" Shakespeare's merit, and "open'd her Royal ear" to him, wrote Chettle, implying that they knew each other well and that she somehow had rewarded him (in Sonnet 111, the great author mentioned "public means," perhaps that he received funds from the queen's treasury). But this was not the only notice of Shakespeare in Chettle's work. "Smooth tongued Melicert" was mentioned earlier in the text (signature B3). Characters Thenot and Colin discussed Queen Elizabeth and King Philip II of Spain, that some believed she was the first to break the truce between their countries, but this, said Colin, was not true: she had "suffered many wrongs before she left off the league." Colin was speaking of the period before the Spanish Armada invasion in 1588. Thenot asked Colin to explain further, based on his own experience and on the poetry of the time (Philsides was probably Sir Philip Sidney, d. 1587):

... for thou has heard the songs of that warlike Poet *Philsides* good

> *Meloebee*, and smooth tongued *Melicert*: tell us what thou has observed in their saws, seen in thy own experience, and heard of undoubted truths touching those accidents.

Melicert-Shakespeare evidently wrote a "saw" or story about the Spanish that helped justify English "accidents" or aggression towards the Spanish before the Armada attack. Chettle was possibly referring to Shakespeare's play, *Othello*; historian Lilian Winstanley demonstrated that the title character, the jealous untamed Moor, symbolized Spain-Philip II, and the good and gentle Desdemona symbolized Venice.[22] But circa the Armada invasion, Desdemona would be perceived as symbolic of England-Queen Elizabeth. A "too early allusion" to *Othello* occurred circa 1589 (Appendix A, No. 40).

In 1589, another shepherd with a similar name, Melicertus, figured in Robert Greene's romance, *Menaphon*. This character was also a poet, and three of his pieces, one of which was called a sonnet, were featured in the book. At the end of the story, it was revealed that Melicertus was actually the nobleman, Lord Maximus. Interestingly, Greene's book featured one unascribed poem titled, "Sonetto." The piece was later credited to the 17th Earl of Oxford (*England's Parnassus*, 1600).

---

(10). Shakespeare's acting and writing is not his profession – it is his "pastime" or hobby; he is a nobleman whose acting on the public stage "stains" his reputation; Fortune has "refused" recognition of Shakespeare's poetry in his actual name.

(1603) *Microcosmos. The Discovery of the Little World, with Government Thereof*, by John Davies of Hereford. Davies wrote a short passage about his admiration for actors, especially those who used their spare time practicing other arts. He singled out William Shakespeare and Richard Burbage (by their initials), noting that, in their "pastime," one was a poet and the other a painter. Davies called "Fortune" cruel for "refusing" them, presumably for recognition of these other talents. Burbage was not renowned for his painting, it is true, but Shakespeare *was much renowned* for his poetry. It can only mean that Davies believed "Shakespeare" was a pen name – that the great author was not getting due recognition for his poetry *in his true name*. Fortune "refus'd" them "for better uses," wrote Davies, without further explanation. The great author wrote he was in "disgrace" with Fortune, and Fortune chided him, spited him, and barred him from triumph in sonnets 25, 29, 37, 90 and 111.

> *Players*, I love ye, and your *Quality*,
> As ye are Men, *that* pass-time not abus'd:
> And **c**some I love for **d**painting, poesy,
> And say fell [cruel] *Fortune cannot be excus'd*;

> That hath for better *uses* you refus'd:
> *Wit, Courage, good shape, good parts,* and all *good,*
> As long as all these *goods* are no *worse* us'd,
> And though the *stage* doth stain pure gentle *blood,*
> Yet **e**generous ye are in *mind* and *mood.* [p. 215]

  c W.S. R.B.
  d Simonides saith, that painting is a dumb Poesy, & Poesy, a speaking painting.
  e Roscius was said for his excellency in his quality [acting], to be only worthy to come on the stage, and for his honesty to be more worthy than to come thereon.

One line in Davies's verse stated that the stage "stains" players with "pure gentle blood," meaning it was socially degrading for nobility to act on the public stage. Burbage did not have "gentle" blood, but as this chapter shows, many overlooked remarks about Shakespeare say or imply that he was an aristocrat. The last two lines, therefore, were meant for Shakespeare only; these lines contained a footnote that mentioned the dilemma of the ancient Roman actor, Roscius: his acting ability was worthy enough for the stage, but his honesty made him too worthy to appear on it. Similarly, Shakespeare is "generous" for deigning to appear on the public stage, which "stains" his nobility. This recalls Shakespeare's Sonnet 110, where the poet regretted his public acting, making himself "a motley to the view." Davies evidently believed that Shakespeare was a nobleman who acted and wrote poetry as a *pastime*, not for his livelihood. *Microcosmos* was among the first books that praised the Earl of Southampton after his 1603 release from the Tower.

In 1609, Davies again coupled Shakespeare and Burbage as actors who were not rewarded or compensated ("guerdon'd") by Lady Fortune, not as they had deserved ("deserts"), in his *Humors Heav'n on Earth* (Stanza 76):

> Yet some she [Lady Fortune] guerdon'd [rewarded] not, to their* deserts;
> Who while they acted ill, ill stayed behind ...
>   * W.S. R.B.

This statement concurred with others made about Shakespeare, that he could not be openly praised or credited, but this was not true for Burbage.

---

(11). The Muses "lov'd" Shakespeare but public recognition of "his art and wit" is still "due to him"; he was dead by 1607.

(1607) *Mirrha, the Mother of Adonis* by William Barksted. Barksted was a member of the King's Revel's acting company when he published a long poem about Mirrha, the mother of Adonis. Inspired by the poem, *Venus and Adonis*, Barksted ended his work with a tribute to its author, Shakespeare. Four lines before the passage in question, Venus speaks to Adonis about his mother. But Barksted interrupts their conversation ("stay my Muse") because that is Shakespeare's story, one that he told in his superlative poem. In the final lines of his poem, Barksted addresses his muse.

> But stay my Muse in thine own confines keep,
> & wage not war with so dear lov'd a neighbor [Shakespeare]
> But having sung thy day song, rest & sleep
> preserve thy small fame and his [Shakespeare's] greater favor:
> His song was worthy merit (Shakspeare)[;] he
> sung the fair blossom [Adonis], thou [Barksted's muse] the
>   withered tree [Mirrha]
> *Laurel* is due to him [Shakespeare], his art and wit
> hath purchased it, *Cypress* thy [Barksted's muse] brow will fit.
> FINIS.

Barksted bade his muse not to compete ("wage not war") with Shakespeare, "so dear lov'd a neighbor." This line implies that Shakespeare was no longer mortal, that he was the "neighbor" of a muse – the Muses were goddesses in Greek mythology. Barksted also referred to Shakespeare in the past tense ("His song was worthy merit"). These two references combined imply that Shakespeare was dead by 1607. (In 1609, the publisher of SHAKE-SPEARE'S SON-NETS, Thomas Thorpe, made a similar inference with the phrase, "our ever-living poet.") Barksted said his muse sang about the "withered tree" (reference to Mirrha, who was turned into a tree) and is fit to wear cypress, symbolic for mourning. Conversely, Shakespeare meritoriously wrote about Adonis, "the fair blossom," and deserves to be wearing laurels. The overall meaning of Barksted's passage is that the great Shakespeare is dead, but tributes to him are still lacking ("*Laurel* is due to him"). It is true that whatever year the great author had died, no tributes marked the occasion.

---

(12). Shakespeare was dead ca. 1609, but his "verses live" under a pen name. "Dispraise" about him in print had stained his reputation. Although Shakespeare is famous and admired, the lack of tributes in his real name will cause his ultimate obscurity.

(ca. 1609) *Envy's Scourge, and Virtue's Honor* by M.L. The author of this poetical work eludes identification, but the following lines indicate that he had written something shameful about "a reverend wit" that he later felt was undeserved and begged his pardon.

> Myself instead <u>a reverend wit have blamed</u>
> <u>Without desert [deserving], whereof I am ashamed</u>. [St. 24, lines 5-6]

> Pardon <u>sweet wit</u> (which hast a liberal part

> of pure infusion in thy happy brain)
> My sorrowing sobs have bloodless left my heart,
> that giddy rage so <u>clear a spring did stain</u>.
> Let worthless lines be scattered here and there,
> <u>But verses live supported by a speare</u>.   [Stanza 25]
>
> Now I do praise that I disprais'd of late,
> and hold thy favorites in high admire;   [Stanza 26, lines 1-2]

M.L. did not provide the "sweet wit's" name, but even the experts acknowledge the pun on Shakespeare's name in the line, "But verses live supported by a speare."[23] M.L. was not just making a pun – he was openly saying that Shakespeare's verses exist because they are "supported" by a pen name. M.L. also wrote that his "worthless lines" had wrongly "stained" Shakespeare, implying that he had done so in a printed work. (The association of "stain" with Shakespeare was also made in nos. 6 and 10.) The lines, "Now I do praise that I disprais'd of late /and hold thy favorites in high admire," indicates that M.L. had recently seen "verses" by Shakespeare about his "favorites" that had inspired a new appreciation of them or cleared a misunderstanding. Which Shakespeare verses could they have been?

Only one copy of *Envy's Scourge* has survived (Robert H. Taylor Collection, Princeton University Library), and the title page, which usually contains a date, was lost. A printing expert dated the work 1605 to 1615.[24] Given this time frame, M.L. had to have been alluding to the 1609 joint publication of SHAKE-SPEARE'S SONNETS and *A Lover's Complaint*, which were the final poetry "verses" by Shakespeare to be published. It had to have been a Shakespeare work that M.L. had not seen before that had changed his attitude about the great author and his "favorites." This conclusion is suported by Stanza 21, in which M.L. complained to Atropos, one of the Fates, about the death of a great poet.

> Why so untimely didst thou [Atropos] dim the light
> of him that sweetest lays [poems] did chant of late
> The dear bemoaner of his honored friend
> Which got much honor when his life did end.   [Stanza 21, lines 3-6]

The "honored friend" of the "dear bemoaner" seems to describe the Fair Youth and the great poet of SHAKE-SPEARE'S SONNETS. These two figures had been "shamefully" treated in only one publication, *Willobie His Avisa* (the subject of Chapter 14), which was printed for the fifth time in 1609. M.L.'s remorse makes him a good candidate for the identity of the anonymous *Willobie* writer. (Arthur Acheson was the first to attribute the authorship of *Willobie* to Matthew Roydon, which accords with one of M.L.'s initials.)[25] He may have read *SHAKE-SPEARE'S SONNETS* in 1609 and come to a new understanding of the great author's relationship with the Fair Youth; he felt "ashamed," regretting his ridicule of them in *Willobie*. In *Envy's Scourge*, he publicly begged the great author's pardon, lamented his "untimely" death, and "now" holds "thy favorites in high admire." The plural, "favorites," was a simple device to make the reference to the Fair Youth less pointed. Since *Willobie* clearly indicated the Fair Youth was the Earl of Southampton, it would mean that Shakespeare had died circa 1603-04, the period when "his honored friend /… got much honor …" By July 1603, James I created Southampton Knight of the Garter and recreated his title; an act of Parliament in April 1604 fully restored his rights. M.L.'s lament of the great author's death agrees with William Barksted's reference to Shakespeare as non-mortal in 1607, and Thomas Thorpe's "ever-living" clue in 1609.

Having established that Shakespeare was an underlying topic of *Envy's Scourge*, one can see more revelatory comments about him mixed in stanzas 15 to 26. Shakespeare is a "delicious" poet who is "despis'd, disgrac'd" and defamed (Stanza 15). M.L. wishes to commend his "power" and to defend him (Stanza 18). The poet is a "buried man" (Stanza 19). There are forces that would "divorce" "all praise" from this "learned" wit, "and shut" him "in obscurest vaults below"; M.L. calls upon Astraea, the goddess of justice, to overthrow these forces (Stanza 20). Shakespeare placed "ripe knowledge" in the "hearts" of the ignorant, and although he is in a "grave," his "fame yet lives of all the earth admir'd" (Stanza 22). In Stanza 23, M.L. addresses the great author:

> Let the divine perfection of thy mind,
> as it was chief so have the chiefest place.
> Let thy beams shine as far as farthest Inde,
> that it may vanquish every black disgrace;
> Let Reason censure of thy virtue's beauty,
> And cause all hearts to honor thee of <u>duty</u>. [Stanza 23]

In conclusion, when M.L. read the newly published *SHAKE-SPEARE'S SON-NETS*, he learned the truth behind the great author's relationship with the Fair Youth. Now ashamed for publishing a satire about them (*Willobie His Avisa*), he wished to make amends to the great author with a poetry work about envy. He revealed that although the great author is famous and admired, he is also despised and disgraced. The lack of tributes at his death was unjust and will destine him to obscurity. M.L. hopes that this will not happen to one who has given so much enlightenment to the masses. He wishes that worldwide fame of the great author's achievement will "vanquish every black disgrace" that touched him, and that it will "cause all hearts to honor" him "of duty."

(13). Shakespeare is the pen name of a nobleman-dramatist who acted for "sport"; he had close relations with royalty.

(1610) *The Scourge of Folly, consisting of Satirical Epigrams and others* by John Davies of Hereford (registered October 8, 1610, published 1611). In his Epigram No. 159, Davies described Shakespeare as "our English Terence."

> *To our English Terence Mr.* Will: Shake-speare
>
> Some say (good *Will*) which I, in sport, do sing
> <u>Hadst thou not played some Kingly parts in sport,</u>
> <u>Thou hadst been a companion for a *King*</u>;
> And, been a King among the meaner sort.
> Some others rail; but, rail as they think fit,
> Thou hast no railing, but, a reigning Wit:
> *And* honestly *thou sow'st*, which they do reap;
> *So, to increase their* Stock *which they do keep.*

In 16th and 17th century England and Europe it was believed that the ancient Roman aristocrats, Scipio and Laelius, wrote some plays under the name of a former slave, Terence (185-159 BC).[26] By describing "Mr. Will: Shake-speare" as "our English Terence," and by including a hyphen in his surname, Davies was openly saying that Shakespeare was the pseudonym of a nobleman-dramatist. Davies also wrote that had "Shake-speare" not acted upon the public stage, he may have been "a companion for a King," implying either a marriage or a special position or status. This agrees with Davies's other Shakespeare comment about the stage staining actors who are aristocrats (No. 10). There are recorded instances of nobility performing before Queen Elizabeth and King James on private occasions, which was acceptable; nobility performing on the public stage, however, was considered déclassé. Davies also said that had the "mean" or lower class spectators in the audience known Shakespeare's true identity, he would have been their king, too ("And, been a King among the meaner sort"). The experts are still puzzled about this freely addressed comment to Shakespeare because it is so inapplicable to the Stratford Man, whom the experts believe acted for his living, not for sport. To summarize Davies's comments about Shakespeare (including No. 10): "William Shake-speare" was the pen name of a nobleman, whose appearances on the public stage stained him; he did this knowingly, which showed his generosity; had he not appeared on the public stage, he may have held a high office; he was never rewarded or recognized for his art by his real name; those who "rail" against him (i.e., criticize, perhaps because he was a nobleman who acted before commoners) also "reap" the benefits of his "stock," the plays.

An anecdote recorded in 1825 seems to agree with Davies's statement that Shakespeare was a nobleman who "played some Kingly parts." If there is any truth to it, then the great author was well known to Queen Elizabeth and may have been her relative. It relates an incident on stage when "Shakspeare himself was personating the part of a King."[27] The queen stepped on the stage while he was performing. He took no notice of her and continued with his role. Bent on getting his attention, the queen dropped her glove in front of him just before he exited the stage. Noticing this, he improvised these lines:

> And though now bent on this high embassy,
> Yet *stoop* we to take up our *Cousin's* glove!

As the queen never attended the public theater, this alleged incident would have occurred during a private performance. Although the above lines were uttered in the character of a king, it still would have been daring and presumptuous for a commoner to call the queen his cousin. The comment would have been acceptable, however, had the actor been a nobleman. Even in 1825, when the great author was unquestionably the Stratford Man, this anecdote endured.

---

(14). People should "praise" and not "detract" the great poet who immortalized Richard III, i.e., Shakespeare.

(1614) *The Ghost of Richard the Third. Expressing himself in these three parts* by C.B. This book featured King Richard III's ghost speaking about himself. Part two opens with Richard praising a great writer whose work raised him out of oblivion. He did not name him.

> To him that Imp'd [implanted] my Fame with *Clio's* [Muse] *Quill*;
> Whose *Magic* rais'd me from *Oblivion's* den;
> That writ my *Story* on the *Muses Hill*;
> And with my *Actions* Dignifi'd his *Pen*:
> He that from *Helicon* sends many a *Rill* [a small brook];
> Whose *Nectared Veins*, are drunk by thirsty *Men*:
> Crown'd be his *Style* [literary], with *Fame*; his *Head*, with *Bays*;
> And none detract [disparage], but gratulate [hail] his *Praise*.
>
> Yet if his *Scenes* have not engross'd all *Grace*,
> The much fam'd Action could extend on *Stage* ...

Shakespeare and his very popular play, *Richard III*, were surely intended in this passage, and this is supported by phrases from Shakespeare's play occurring in other parts of the book.[28] C.B. wanted no one to "detract" the great author, "but gratulate his Praise." This shows that people were disparaging Shakespeare – why would they at a time when his works were universally acclaimed? Was the true author, a nobleman, getting disparaging remarks because he wrote plays that appeared on the public stage, and because he also acted in them? The line also shows that the great author was not getting proper praise for his excellent works, rivers of "nectar" that are "drunk by thirsty men." It agrees with the other overlooked comments that said Shakespeare was not adequately praised or recognized because doing so in his real name would "stain" him.

In another 1614 work, *Run, and a Great Cast* (combined with *Rub, and A Great Cast*), writer Thomas Freeman was also concerned about "Master W. Shakespeare" getting "deserved bays" or praise:

> Then let thine own works thine own worth upraise,
> And help t'adorn thee with deserved Bays.   [Epigram 92, lines 13-14]

The words of C.B., Freeman and others demonstrate how Shakespeare's contemporaries were struggling with the dilemma of wanting to celebrate the great author by his real name but having to comply with the need to keep it secret. This thought was repeated as late as 1640:

> To Mr. William Shake-spear.
>
> _Shake-speare we must be silent in thy praise_,
> 'Cause our encomiums will but blast thy Bays,
> Which envy could not, that thou didst do well;
> Let thine own histories prove thy Chronicle.   [*Wit's Recreations*, No. 25]

Conclusion

Years before the First Folio created the myth of the Stratford Man as Shakespeare, literary contemporaries were describing the great author as a very different person: a nobleman who wrote plays and poetry anonymously or with a pseudonym; a supreme poet who could not be publicly recognized or acknowledged by his actual name, or even by his pen name in some cases; a patron of writers who idolized him. He wrote as a pastime, not as work. His dramatic career and reputation had been long established by 1590, a time the Shakespeare professor believes was his starting point. One of Shakespeare's contemporaries called the public adoption of the pen name, William Shakespeare, the greatest miracle of 1593, and that Queen Elizabeth was involved. Another contemporary wrote that the queen and Shakespeare were well acquainted and that she had graced him with rewards. The great author's theatrical activities, including acting on the public stage, stained his reputation, and after his death, his real name and accomplishments continued to be suppressed. He was dead by 1607. It is certainly true that whenever the great author had died his passing occurred without public acknowledgment. It follows then, that an aristocrat-poet of the time who had died without notice by his admirers could be identified as the great author. Such was the case for the 17th Earl of Oxford, who was linked with the great author's identity in two overlooked remarks, and in *Willobie His Avisa*. Some refused to stay silent, however, and did praise Shakespeare in print, but did so almost in code. Those who indirectly referred to him after 1593 perhaps did so out of a refusal to identify him by his alias. The greatest instance of open praise of the great author after his death occurred under controlled circumstances in the First Folio, and at the same time, directed it at someone else, i.e., the Stratford Man. None of these overlooked references to the great author, or any other Shakespeare allusion before 1623, associated him with Stratford-upon-Avon or the county of Warwickshire. The great author was surely someone else.

PART V

Conjectures and Dares

CHAPTER 16

The Deliberate Mix-up: the Great Author
with the Stratford Man. Why?

BASED UPON THE evidence presented thus far, the name "William Shakespeare" should have been recognized long ago as the pseudonym of a nobleman, and the Stratford Man as a red herring. But the red herring has endured, in my opinion, because of the absence of a common sense explanation for it – that "William Shakespeare" was not just a pseudonym, it was an identity switch. A credible explanation is needed to cover the following questions. Why did the 3rd Earl of Pembroke, the presumed engineer of the First Folio of Shakespeare's plays, authorize the extra step of putting flesh to the pseudonym in the book? Why did he wish to merge the great author's literary identity with that of the Stratford Man? Why was the great author's pseudonym not enough to cover whatever needed covering, even after his death? What exactly was being covered? Why was the great author's passing not openly noted when it had occurred, and for many years after it? A theory answering these questions will be presented in this chapter and the next and should be regarded by the reader as separate from the rest of this book. Although it is conjecture – but based upon historical evidence – this attempt at the ultimate solution to the authorship puzzle should in no way lessen or negate the evidence presented in the previous chapters that disproves the Stratford Man as the great author and proves that "William Shakespeare" was the pen name of a nobleman. Those with closed minds who are intent on maintaining the Stratfordian myth may call this solution – and therefore, the entire book – ridiculous. Casting aspersions upon doubters of the accepted Shakespeare is the best stratagem that the upholders of the Stratford Man myth possess. This is because they lack direct proof of his authorship of Shakespeare *during his lifetime*. Repeating the tired phrase, "His name is on the book," is simply not enough to bestow the laurels of one of humanity's greatest artistic geniuses upon a complete unknown.

The Ultimate Puzzle

History has shown that arguments disproving the Stratford Man as the great author – and arguments proving that the great author was another person – have not been adequate enough to change the minds of the experts or the general public. Trying to resolve the issue with either of these approaches has resulted in a standoff that has allowed the Stratford Man myth to prevail. Neither of these arguments addresses the real question, the one that, if answered plausibly, would change everyone's minds: If the Stratford Man was not the great author, then why was false evidence planted in the First Folio and the Shakspeare monument in Stratford-upon-Avon to suggest that he was? The reason must have been something extremely important to go to such lengths. Evidence that "William Shakespeare" was a pen name, contemporary testimony, and the Shakespeare works themselves – especially those two written in the first person – all confirm that the great author was a nobleman. During his lifetime, he desired anonymity, or society required it. It was undignified for those of high rank to publish poetry works during their lifetimes, and even more so for plays. Hence the reference by Meres that the great author circulated his "sugar'd sonnets among his private friends." This was done on handwritten manuscript, an accepted form for the highly ranked to share writing. Circulation in print, however, suggested commercialism, hence profit, which was beneath the dignity of such gentlemen. This social norm explains why the great author never provided clean finished copy of his dramas to any printer. But demand for Shakespeare was high, leaving unscrupulous printers no choice but to print pirated texts, and often corrupt ones. In the case of the poems, *Venus and Adonis* and *Lucrece*, the great author stepped outside of social custom and allowed them to be printed, but he employed a pseudonym. It was acceptable, however, for those of high rank to have literary works published and fully credited to them after their deaths. If the First Folio producers were still a little nervous about putting the great author's real name to the Shakespeare plays, then usage of the pen name should have sufficed. But they took the extra step of displaying an image of a gentleman, and providing testimony that he was the "fellow" of "lowly," ignorant actors, plus two place names, to insinuate that the great author was the Stratford Man.

This added step taken to permanently change the great author's literary identity in the public's mind implies that there was something dangerous or scandalous about him that needed covering up. The complete blackout of notice of the great author's death whenever it had occurred supports this notion. Something that needs hiding from the public is usually political. If the Shakespeare plays were politically scandalous or dangerous to the Crown, then it would have been impossible that the Earl of Pembroke, one of the king's most trusted servants and ardent supporters, would have sponsored the

Folio or allowed his name to be in it. Obviously, he would not have promoted anything that would disturb the king or endanger his position. Moreover, King James approved of the Shakespeare plays: they were performed many times at court and publicly throughout his reign. One must conclude that the Shakespeare plays were not politically sensitive at the time of the Folio's issue. Most notably, however, the Folio did not contain Shakespeare's major works of poetry. *Venus and Adonis* and *Lucrece* were excluded, yet they were praised at the time of their publication and printed repeatedly during the reigns of both Elizabeth and James. The contents of SHAKE-SPEARE'S SONNETS were also excluded, even though its publisher, Thomas Thorpe, had been professionally associated with the Folio publishers and partners, Edward Blount and William Aspley. The Folio preface laid great stress upon Shakespeare as an actor and dramatist and downplayed his accomplishment as a poet. Among Shakespeare's three major poetry works, only his sonnets, first published in 1609, went unnoticed by critics, yet the sonnets contained some of the most sublime poetry in the English language. *There was absolutely no public commentary about Shakespeare's sonnets specifically for over one hundred years after the first edition.* This quiet raises a red flag and is the most logical lead to follow in the quest to find something politically problematic with Shakespeare.

The Fair Youth of the Sonnets: the Earl of Southampton

SHAKE-SPEARE'S SONNETS (1609) was not a mere gathering of poems about various topics that were printed. Nearly every sonnet was about specific but unnamed people. The Fair Youth sonnets comprise over 75 percent of the collection. The great author lavished praise and allegiance to this young man repeatedly in them. He even told the Fair Youth not to call his love and devotion "idolatry." In the 1640 edition, some Fair Youth sonnets were altered to make it appear that the author was addressing a woman instead of a man. To find anything politically sensitive or scandalous about the sonnets, one must first focus upon and conclusively identify the Fair Youth.

The Fair Youth was a male of fair or light complexion and a feminine face. He was beautiful, more beautiful than Adonis and Helen of Troy (Sonnet 53), and his eyes were exceptional: "If I could write the beauty of your eyes" (Sonnet 17). The Fair Youth was "gazed on" by the public (Sonnet 2), was the "world's fresh ornament" (Sonnet 1), and was much sought after by women. His nobility was emphasized. The great author believed that after his death the world would ask the Fair Youth about him (Sonnet 72), implying that their association was well known. Henry Wriothesley, 3rd Earl of Southampton, matches all of these points, indeed, for the last one Southampton is the only person who qualifies. His name was the only one associated with a Shakespeare work, on the dedications to *Venus and Adonis* and *Lucrece*. Southampton, therefore, was the person addressed in Sonnet 81:

> Your name from hence immortal life shall have,
> Though I (once gone) to all the world must die.

By dedicating two works to Southampton, the great author conferred immortality upon him – as long these works live, so will Southampton's name. This sonnet also indirectly proves that Shakespeare was a pen name. The name Shakespeare will live, but not the great author's real name, which "to all the world must die." If posterity wished to know about the great author, then they would ask Southampton. For these reasons, Southampton has been and still is the lead candidate for the Fair Youth's identity. That this issue is still considered unresolved, despite the solid evidence contained in *Willobie His Avisa* (see Chapter 14), is to deny the obvious, but additional evidence proves that Southampton was the Fair Youth – "fair" meaning both beautiful and light colored. Southampton's existing portraits show that he was light complexioned with auburn hair that in his teens and twenties was worn long past his shoulders. In 1591, a poem about Narcissus, a beautiful youth of Greek myth, was dedicated to Southampton. In 1592, he was praised as "nobody more handsome" ("formosior") in a public speech;[1] in 1593, his eyes were described as "gracious" and "heavenly lamps";[2] in 1594, Southampton was called "beautiful" ("lindo") in Spanish by Antonio Perez.[3] In 1595, a sonnet addressed to Southampton by Gervase Markham evidently acknowledged Shakespeare's judgment of his eyes:

> Thou glorious Laurel of the Muses hill,
> Whose eyes doth crown the most victorious pen.[4]

Southampton's "eyes doth crown" the works of Shakespeare, "the most victorious pen." As a beautiful young courtier, and favorite of the queen since age seventeen, Southampton could certainly be described as "the world's fresh ornament" (Sonnet 1). A line in Sonnet 20 describing the Fair Youth, "A man in hew all *Hews* in his controlling," apparently punned on Southampton's name (HEnry Wriothesley).[5] The capital H and italics (*Hews*) was in the original 1609 text. Southampton was a devotee of the theater, and in 1604 entertained Queen Anne at his home with a performance of Shakespeare's play, *Love's Labour's Lost*.[6] This fact strongly suggests that Shakespeare and Southampton were still friendly a decade after *Venus and Adonis* and *Lucrece*. Despite the overwhelming evidence for Southampton as the Fair Youth, the experts have found no evidence that Shakespeare and Southampton knew each other. It is another "unsolvable" mystery. Their task would be made easier if they would accept that William Shakespeare was the great author's pen name, and not the gentleman from a small town with a similar name. The two Southampton-dedicated works, and the sonnets, presumably dedicated to Southampton, were omitted from the First Folio. Southampton was not even mentioned in it. What follows, therefore, is an examination of Southampton's life and career in the search for something scandalous or politically dangerous about him that needed hiding from the general public.

The record shows that from the beginning of his adulthood, Southampton was eager for military power. He shared this yearning with the 2nd Earl of Essex, and the two were linked from 1596 onward, when Southampton joined Essex on military missions. Although Essex enjoyed great favoritism by Queen Elizabeth, he and his followers were in competition for power with Sir Robert Cecil after the death of his father, the great Lord Burghley, in 1598. Eventually Essex and Southampton incited a rebellion that failed, and both were sentenced to death. Essex was duly executed, but miraculously, Southampton was never sent to the block. And even more miraculously, Southampton was set free shortly after the queen's death by order of the new king, James I. His pardon was issued even before James left Scotland to take his place on the English throne. Within the first two years of James's reign, Southampton's titles and lands were fully restored, he was appointed Knight of the Garter (a very high honor), given several estates, and awarded a few minor posts, such as the king and queen's master of game, and the queen's councilor. Southampton was present at most important court events. Why was the king so especially generous, both financially and at court, to a convicted traitor of England whom he could have justifiably left in prison to rot?

Based on the evidence about to be presented, one can surmise that King James and others, including Shakespeare, believed that he was the natural child of Queen Elizabeth and was her potential successor. It is not a new theory, but it is one that is not usually supported by historical evidence. It is not the purpose of this book to disprove the virginity of Queen Elizabeth or to prove that she had a child. Indeed, to expect to find documentary proof of a hidden birth would be unrealistic; such an event would not be recorded and only the queen's most trusted servants would know about it. As noted by Simon Adams, the queen's Privy Chamber was "an inner sanctum impenetrable to most of the Court."[7] To make such a claim about the queen during this period was a treasonable offense. Despite this, rumors of the queen bearing children spread outside of the court, with many such claims made throughout her reign.[8] A reading "between the lines" of historical and literary documents of the period suggests that Southampton was the queen's child, a prince, and with this perspective, it will be demonstrated how this ultimately influenced the Shakespeare authorship.

Southampton Thought a Prince

When Southampton's father, the second earl, died in 1581, the nearly eight-year-old Henry was made a ward of Queen Elizabeth and eventually was placed in the guardianship of her top minister, Lord Burghley, in London. His career as a courtier started very early and met with immediate favor by the queen. In his eighteenth year, the queen honored him with a visit to his home at Titchfield (late August-early September 1591), which followed upon her visit to the home of his grandfather, Lord Montagu, at Cowdray.[9] The year 1591 also saw the first book dedicated to Southampton, a poem titled, *Narcissus*. In the dedication letter, author John Clapham described the teenager Southampton as "most famous" and "most distinguished."[10] One year later (September 1592), Southampton was among those lauded in verses by John Sanford during the queen's visit to Oxford University.[11] Sanford called Southampton a prince in his speech, according to the Latin translation by John Rollett:

> After him there follows a hereditary Prince [*dynasta*] of illustrious lineage, whom as a great hero the rich House of Southampton lawfully lays claim to as one of its own.[12]

Sanford used the Latin word "dynasta" to describe Southampton. As explained by Rollett, the 16th century definition of this word was "a lord of great power, a prince, a ruler"; and the English counterpart of dynasta, "dynasty," was only used in reference to royalty, to a line of kings or princes, and not to nobility or to a line of earls. (Southampton's biographer, Charlotte Stopes, also translated *dynasta* as "prince.")[13] Why would Sanford call Southampton "a hereditary prince" in a public speech before the queen, and describe the unproven teenager as "a great hero"? And was it only by "law" that the house of Southampton "claimed" Southampton "as one of its own"? Rollett concluded that this open allusion to Southampton's princely status indicated that it was known at the time, and that his being an Oxford graduate would "bring credit to the University if he ever became King." Sanford's verses were printed soon after the event and evidently without any trouble.

The prince references about Southampton peaked in 1593. In a letter written in May 1593, Philip Gawdy wrote that Southampton was nominated for the Knight of the Garter – one of England's most prestigious honors usually given to those of outstanding achievement or service to the Crown.[14] The 19-year-old Southampton had achieved nothing and had rendered no service to the Crown. Neither was he romantically involved with the queen. Although Southampton received no votes that year, his biographers have found it remarkable that he was even considered for the honor at that age, being one not of royal blood.[15] Henry Percy, 9th Earl of Northumberland, was awarded the honor that year, and was installed in June. George Peele wrote celebratory verses for this occasion, but oddly, at one point in the text he diverted from his subject to laud Southampton, expressing his hope that the queen will notice him as a "star" in her court.

> Gentle Wriothesley, South-Hampton's star,
> I wish all fortune that in Cynthia's eye
> Cynthia the glory of the Western world,
> With all the stars in her fair firmament,
> Bright may he rise and shine immortally.[16]

Queen Elizabeth was often referred to as Cynthia or the moon, and was considered "the glory of the Western world," so Peele was wishing for Southampton's immortality along with the queen's. Shakespeare was similarly anxious that his verse would confer immortality upon the Fair Youth, as repeatedly written in his sonnets, some of which were circulating at this time. Shakespeare described Southampton as "the world's hopeful expectation" in his dedication letter to *Venus and Adonis* (registered April 1593). In early 1593, Thomas Nashe dedicated a very bawdy poem, *The Choosing of Valentines*, to "Lord S.a.," presumably Southampton. Two lines in Nashe's dedication verses show that he associated "Lord S.a." with the Fair Youth of the sonnets, and evidently believed the queen was his mother.

> Pardon, sweet flower of matchless poetry,
> And fairest bud the red rose ever bore.

The "matchless" poet, Shakespeare, constantly employed the words sweet, fair, flower, and bud to describe the Fair Youth in his sonnets. The "red rose" unmistakably symbolized Queen Elizabeth. In Nashe's words, Southampton ("sweet flower"), the subject of Shakespeare's sonnets ("matchless poetry"), was the prettiest child ("the fairest bud") that the queen ("the red rose") gave birth to ("ever bore"). Although Nashe's poem was only circulating in manuscript at the time (it remained unpublished until the 20th century), it was censured for its subject matter (a man's visit to a brothel) and sexual explicitness. Perhaps to save his writing career, Nashe subsequently published his first religious work, *Christ's Tears Over Jerusalem,* registered on September 8, 1593. Shortly afterward, Gabriel Harvey joked in print about Nashe's two very diverse works, one of "rankest villainy" and the other of "ripest divinity" written within months of each other:

> What say you to a Spring of rankest *Villainy* in February: and a Harvest of ripest *Divinity* in May? May they not surcease to wonder,

that wonder how Machiavell can teach a Prince *to be*, and *not to be*, religious?[17] [italics original]

Harvey "wondered" in his book, *A New Letter of Notable Contents*, how within a few months Nashe could "teach a Prince *to be*, and *not to be*, religious," with his *Christ's Tears* and *Valentines*. Since *Valentines* was dedicated to Fair Youth-Southampton, then he is the "Prince" that Harvey spoke of, albeit couched within an allusion to Machiavelli's treatise, *The Prince* (*Christ's Tears* was dedicated to Elizabeth, wife of Sir George Carey). But to make Southampton's identification plain, Harvey threw in an allusion to one of the most famous lines in Shakespeare's *Hamlet*, "To be or not to be," even italicizing these words with the exception of "and," which was not in Shakespeare's line. The association between Shakespeare and Southampton was public knowledge at this time. Harvey was terming Southampton a prince, and associating him with Prince Hamlet, a character who was in line for the succession. Perhaps significantly, Harvey never published in his own name again after *A New Letter*. Nine days after Nashe registered *Christ's Tears*, he registered *The Unfortunate Traveler*; Nashe dedicated the book to Southampton, and called him "the large spreading branch of renown."

"Prince" Southampton also happened to be a very eligible bachelor. The rich and politically powerful Lord Burghley tried for a few years (circa 1590) to match Southampton with his granddaughter, Lady Elizabeth Vere. As Southampton's guardian, Burghley had the right to arrange his marriage. But Southampton refused the match, and rumor had it that Burghley fined him £5,000 (perhaps he thought it would change his mind). Eventually Burghley succeeded in matching his granddaughter with the 6th Earl of Derby, one of the richest men in England, far richer than Southampton. Derby's family was older than Southampton's and had a better loyalty record, and even had a claim to the throne (it was discussed in the book, *A Conference About the Next Succession to the Crown of England*, in 1594), yet Southampton was Burghley's first choice. It has been suggested that Burghley commissioned his secretary, John Clapham, to shame or rebuke Southampton with his poem, *Narcissus* – that it was his narcissism that caused him to reject the Vere match.[18] In 1595, Southampton received four votes in the election for Knight of the Garter, and in 1596 he received ten out of twelve votes.[19] Although the queen did not appoint him, it was still a tremendous honor to receive so many votes with nothing to recommend him. In February 1598, Southampton accompanied Sir Robert Cecil, the queen's principal secretary, on an official visit to France. According to Stopes, "they were received with great honour when they reached the Court," and "Southampton was specially presented" to the French king by Cecil.[20]

In light of these princely hints about the 3rd Earl of Southampton, it is fair to take a more critical view of his origins. He was the only surviving son of Henry Wriothesley, 2nd Earl of Southampton. There was evidently a longstanding belief that the 3rd Earl was his second son, and Sidney Lee and A.F. Pollard treated it as fact in separate entries in the DNB (1900 edition); biographer Stopes wrote that it lacked authority. Stopes, however, thought it "strange" that no record of the 3rd Earl's christening was preserved,[21] and she could not find any reference to his having godparents. Prior to the 3rd Earl's birth, his father experienced imprisonments for his Catholic intrigues and for doubts about his loyalty to the queen. By July 1573, the 2nd Earl of Southampton was free. In October 1573, he happily reported in a letter that his wife delivered a boy. His good fortune continued – on July 12, 1574, he was appointed to the Commission of the Peace. But a letter written to Lord Burghley by one of his spies in Europe, dated September 3, 1574, stated that the 2nd Earl of Southampton "had fled to Spain."[22] This cannot be otherwise confirmed, but reportage of the 17th Earl of Oxford's "flying" out of England appeared in the same sentence. Since other documents confirm that Oxford had indeed fled England for Flanders in July 1574,[23] the information about the 2nd Earl was probably reliable. By late September 1574, the 2nd Earl was back in England and acknowledged the queen's "manifold graciousness" toward him in a letter.[24] One can only speculate about the reason why the 2nd Earl fled the country for Spain, but his return and quick forgiveness by the queen may have been conditional: accept a royal bastard child as his son and heir to his earldom. If this were the case, then it would mean that the identity of his own son, who was born in October 1573 and named Henry, would have been switched with that of the royal bastard. This would account for the belief that the 3rd Earl was the second son. The 2nd Earl's sister, Lady Katherine Cornwallis, was one of the queen's ladies-in-waiting at that time and would serve her faithfully for thirty years.[25] In 1577, the 2nd Earl separated himself from his wife, taking his son and daughter with him, and in 1581 he died. Young Henry, now the 3rd Earl of Southampton, became a royal ward under the guardianship of Lord Burghley, "with only occasional visits allowed to his mother and grandfather."[26]

Shakespeare Believed Southampton was a Royal Heir to the Throne?

Shakespeare's sonnets, it will be shown, demonstrate the great author's belief that the Fair Youth, the 3rd Earl of Southampton, was a prince and presumptive heir to the throne. These references were not direct, of course, but contained in imagery, some of which can be illuminated by reading Shakespeare's two poems about the Phoenix and the Turtle Dove in Love's Martyr (Appendix E). The phoenix, a beautiful bird of myth, was a recognized symbol of Queen Elizabeth during her lifetime, as detailed in Chapter 4. Shakespeare's two poems in *Love's Martyr* referred to the Phoenix as "Queen" and "Beauty," and the Turtle Dove as "Truth." In Shakespeare's Sonnet No. 1, "beauty's *Rose*" describes the Fair Youth, the "rose" of "Beauty." "Beauty's rose" also described Queen Elizabeth in at least two sources. One was contained in a book of verses about the queen written by John Davies in 1599 (*Hymns of Astraea in Acrostic Verse*). Hymn 7 was titled, "To the Rose."

> R ose of the Queen of Love belov'd;
> E ngland's great Kings divinely mov'd,
> G ave Roses in their Banner;
> I t shewed that <u>Beauty's Rose</u> indeed,
> <u>N ow in this age should them succeed</u>,
> A nd reign in more sweet manner.

The queen was also called "Beauty's rose" in verses addressed to her during entertainments at Harefield House (1602).

> <u>Beauty's rose</u> and Virtue's book, Angel's mind and angel's look ... [27]

The Fair Youth also has "beauty" and is "beauteous" (words that occur in more than seventy instances in the sonnets), a quality he inherited from his mother, Beauty-Queen Elizabeth. He is explicitly called a rose, the symbol of the Tudors, in sonnets 54, 67 and 109. Rose also identifies the Fair Youth as Southampton. As noted by Martin Green and many scholars before him, his surname, Wriothesley, may have been pronounced "Rosely," the "th" not pronounced when before "s," like in "clothes." A printed eulogy for the 2nd Earl of Southampton spelled the surname "Wrisley," without the "th," as did the baptism record for "Thomas Wryosley," the son of "Henry and Eliz. Wroseley, [3rd] Earl and Countess of Southampton."[28] In Sonnet 95, explained Green, "thy budding name" revealed that the Fair Youth's name "is like a flower." Green also noted that the coat of arms for the city of Southampton featured three roses.[29]

In Sonnet 101, Shakespeare says that the Fair Youth is the personification of Truth and Beauty ("truth in beauty dy'd"), and that "Both truth and beauty" depend upon him. This is not an impersonal abstraction: the queen-Beauty-Phoenix and Truth-Turtle Dove depend upon him to marry and produce a son to perpetuate the royal line, which is the subject of the first seventeen sonnets. Shakespeare's line in Sonnet 127, "Beauty slander'd with a bastard shame," describes the slander of Beauty-Queen Elizabeth having a bastard. As the Fair Youth is the majority subject of the sonnets, and as the great author constantly describes him in terms of kingship (succession, king, sun, crown, etc.), it is logical to identify him as the royal bastard. Robert Chester also wrote in *Love's Martyr* that the Phoenix-Queen Elizabeth had a child, "another princely Phoenix," that was fathered by the Turtle Dove. This child would be Southampton.

> From the sweet fire of perfumed wood,
> Another princely *Phoenix* upright stood:
> Whose feathers purified did yield more light,
> Than her late burned mother out of sight,
> And in her heart rests a perpetual love,
> Sprung from the bosom of the *Turtle-Dove*.
> Long may the new uprising bird increase ...

Chester's "princely Phoenix" is also an "uprising bird," probably referring to the February 1601 Essex Rebellion or "uprising" in which Southampton took part. *Love's Martyr* was published soon after the rebellion, so it is almost certain that Shakespeare composed his Phoenix and Turtle Dove poems while his beloved Southampton was in prison as a convicted traitor. This circumstance perhaps inspired Shakespeare's line in his *Love's Martyr* poem that "Beauty, Truth and Rarity" were dead, and "in cinders lie." Rarity would then represent Beauty and Truth's child, Southampton, who at this point was figuratively dead in the Tower.

> Beauty, Truth, and Rarity,
> Grace in all simplicity,
> Here enclosed, in cinders lie.
>
> Death is now the *Phoenix* nest,
> And the *Turtle's* loyal breast
> To eternity doth rest.
>
> Leaving no posterity ...
>
> Truth and Beauty buried be.

The above Shakespeare lines were counter to the phoenix myth – a new phoenix is *not* born out of the ashes, there is no posterity. Not only did the failed Essex Rebellion threaten "prince" Southampton's life, it left his chances to succeed the queen "in cinders," effectively ending the House of Tudor. This was probably the underlying theme of Shakespeare's two funereal poems in *Love's Martyr*. The death of a dynasty could account for the poet's choice of the words "session," "interdict," and "tyrant" in lines 9 and 10 of the first poem, which "suggests judicial and executive power."[30] The post-rebellion dating of these poems can be confirmed by the book's dedication to "Sir

John Salusbury," who was knighted in June 1601 specifically for his loyalty to the queen during the rebellion (*DNB*). The *Love's Martyr* title page advertised that "some new compositions, of several Writers" were in the book, which included those by Shakespeare.

Identity of the Turtle Dove

The identity behind the Turtle Dove-Truth in *Love's Martyr* – the allegorical lover of Phoenix-Queen Elizabeth – has never been conclusively determined. Some have viewed him as the Earl of Essex, but this is unlikely since *Love's Martyr* was dedicated to a man who helped suppress his rebellion and was knighted for it. Furthermore, Anthea Hume found evidence that Salusbury "belonged to the anti-Essex faction in Denbighshire."[31] Chester certainly would not dedicate a work to his patron, Salusbury, had it idealized Essex as the martyred Turtle Dove. His anti-Essex stance was probably the reason why he was chosen as the dedicatee for this work, and again separately for the section titled, *Diverse Poetical Essays*, which contained the poems by Shakespeare and others. Chester also made a special appeal to the queen in prefatory verses titled, "The Author's request to the Phoenix." Chester calls her "Phoenix of beauty" and asks her to not only "accept" her Turtle Dove, but to accept Chester's "home-writ praises" of him. This appeal disqualifies the recently executed Essex as the Turtle Dove.

> The Author's request to the Phoenix
>
> Phoenix of beauty, beauteous Bird of any
> To thee I do entitle all my labor,
> More precious in mine eye by far than many,
> That feedst all earthly senses with thy savor:
> Accept my home-writ praises of thy love,
> And kind acceptance of thy *Turtle-dove*. [Stanza 1]

Chester's "home-writ praises" of the Turtle Dove immediately follow in the second stanza. The Turtle Dove is a famous scholarly poet of "wit-enchanting verse" who "should sing" or compose a work about Phoenix-Queen Elizabeth. Shakespeare, who contributed two poems to Chester's work, certainly fits this description.

> Some deep-read Scholar <u>fam'd for Poetry</u>,
> <u>Whose wit-enchanting verse deserveth fame</u>,
> Should sing of thy [the Phoenix-queen] perfections passing <u>beauty</u>,
> And elevate thy famous worthy name:
> Yet I [Chester] the least, and meanest in degree,
> Endeavored have to please in praising thee.
> R. Chester [Stanza 2]

Chester even alluded to Shakespeare in connection with the Turtle Dove in the section titled, "Cantos," which are the Turtle Dove's verses to the "fair Phoenix." The opening line of the first canto, "A Hill, a Hill, a *Phoenix* seeks a Hill," obviously echoes the line, "A Horse, a Horse, my Kingdom for a Horse," in Shakespeare's play, *Richard III* (5.4.7). This line was already in print, famous, and much copied.[32] The canto ends with the Turtle Dove saying he will love the Phoenix in secret:

> Ah, be my *Phoenix*, I will be thy *Dove*,
> And thou and I in secrecy will love.

In Shakespeare's *Love's Martyr* poems, the "Turtle and his queen" are "co-supremes," "stars of love," and "love shined between them." The Turtle Dove is "loyal" to "his Queen," which R.J.C. Wait observed means "he is not a king, but a subject."[33] The great author being a nobleman increases the possibility that he was the Queen's lover and that they had a lovechild. Shakespeare describes the Phoenix and the Turtle Dove as "married chastity," implying that they were joined together by something – perhaps by their child – but lived apart. Chester apparently believed that the great author, Shakespeare, was the Turtle Dove, and that the "princely Phoenix," i.e., Southampton, was the child of Turtle Dove-Shakespeare and Phoenix-Queen Elizabeth.

In his sonnets, the great author expressed an affection for the Fair Youth-Southampton that went beyond friendship. His love may have been that of a father for his son, or homosexual. For the latter viewpoint, one of the most persuasive lines, "thou Master Mistress of my passion," said to the Fair Youth, occurs in Sonnet 20:

> A Woman's face with nature's own hand painted,
> Hast thou the Master Mistress of my passion …

It is true that young Southampton's feminine face, beautiful eyes, and long hair may have attracted the poet, but another credible explanation for these lines can be found by reviewing lines in Sonnet 3:

> Thou art thy mother's glass and she in thee
> Calls back the lovely April of her prime …

By so much resembling his mother ("thy mother's glass"), the Fair Youth is both master and mistress of the poet's "passion." "Passion" was also another word for love poem, "hence implying the sonnets," wrote the Ogburns.[34] (The great author may also have been revealing in Sonnet 20 that the Fair Youth's mother was his mistress.) So Sonnet 20 can be explained without homosexual overtones. Also, it must be noted that male friends calling one another love or lover in the literary world during this period was a social convention reflecting the Renaissance ideal of friendship, without sexual innuendo. For example, Ben Jonson signed his printed dedications to William Camden, Richard Martin, and Sir Francis Stuart with the line, "your true lover" (*Works*, 1616).

The sonnets also related the great author's painful discovery that his mistress, the Dark Lady, with whom he had been having an adulterous affair, was also having an affair with the Fair Youth. Both men were in the claws of the Dark Lady at the same time. That the great author was sexually obsessed by her and pained by her roving eye weakens the notion that concurrently he was lusting after the Fair Youth. Furthermore, the great author considered his love of the Dark Lady as sinful (sonnets 141, 142), and like a disease (Sonnet 147), and described her as his "bad angel" (Sonnet 144), yet he expressed no qualms about the nature of his love for the Fair Youth. Adultery was considered sinful in those days, but so was the act of sodomy or a man's feeling of erotic love for another man. The great author did not describe his love of the Fair Youth as bad or sinful. He considered the Fair Youth as his "good angel" and "saint" (Sonnet 144). The great author intended his sonnets to be the Fair Youth's "monument" (sonnets 81, 107), a lasting tribute to his memory. In Sonnet 55, the great author wrote that the Fair Youth will "shine more bright in these contents / Than unswept stone, besmeared with sluttish time." But how could he if those very contents also carried the taint of homosexuality? Had homosexuality been so blatant in the sonnets they probably would not have been published, needlessly endangering the reputations of the great author and Southampton (and the reputations of the publisher, printer and booksellers named on the title page). These factors contradict the theory of homosexual longing or affair in Shakespeare's sonnets.

The view that the great author's love of the Fair Youth in his sonnets was *parental* rarely gets considered – this is due, in part, to the constraints imposed by the Stratford Man model. The great author makes a clear class distinction between himself and the Fair Youth, so it would be unlikely that a man with low social status, like the Stratford Man, would beget an aristocrat. Relieved of the Stratford Man model, however, one could interpret the great author's intense love for the Fair Youth as a proud aristocrat father for his son, a son that he believed was a prince and above him in social status, but a son that he could not openly recognize because of his bastardy. The theme of the first seventeen sonnets, in which the great author urges the Fair Youth to marry and beget children, is especially suggestive of a parental relationship and inconsistent with a homosexual one. The great author urges the Fair Youth to give his "sweet semblance to some other" to marry and have children (Sonnet 13). He implies in Sonnet 3 that he knew the Fair Youth's mother as a younger woman, indicating a substantial age difference between this pair and the Fair Youth. The great author as father would explain his description of the Fair Youth as "my next self" in Sonnet 133, "that other mine" in Sonnet 134, and "'Tis thee (my self)" in Sonnet 62. In this last sonnet, the great author says that he and the Fair Youth look alike. It opens with the great author chiding his own narcissism, his sin of self-love, and then he arrives at an explanation for it: the "beauty" he sees in the mirror is the same as the Fair Youth's, albeit an older version.

> But when my glass shews me my self indeed
> Beated and chopp'd with tann'd antiquity,
> Mine own self love quite contrary I read
> Self so self loving were iniquity [sin],
> 'Tis thee (my self) that for my self I praise,
> Painting my age with beauty of thy days. [Sonnet 62, lines 9-14]

These statements written by the great author in his sonnets, and the references to the Fair Youth's bastardy in sonnets 33, 70 and 127, imply that he was his father. The nobleman-poet yearned for the queen's open acknowledgement of their son so he could be her successor. A similar appeal was also conveyed, allegorically, in *Love's Martyr*.

Although it would be unusual for a bastard to succeed the throne, the queen seemed to legally prepare for it. A 1571 law prohibited discussion of candidates for the succession *excepting* those who were the "natural issue of her Majesty's Body."[35] This law was harshly criticized the following year in *A Treatise of Treasons Against Queen Elizabeth, and the Crown of England* (1572). The author believed that the law's usage of the phrase, "natural issue," indicated that the unmarried queen already had, or intended to have, a bastard.

> For, in the prohibition of any Heir to be named, they except only the Issue of her body, with the term and addition of *Natural*, which Term being in your Statutes and Judicial writings strange and unwonted, and in all other languages signifying plain Bastards: and they, now purposely forsaking the accustomed words of your Law in such cases, by changing lawful, for Natural: and by leaving the old usual words of lawful Heir, lawful Children, or Children lawfully begotten, for the new term of Natural Issue, that in all languages signifieth Bastardy: what other can be gathered of this (being spoken of your Queen, that is unmarried) but that they would thereby covertly insinuate unto the world, that she hath, or mindeth to have children Natural, and not lawful. [pp. 112-13]

Up until the queen's death, there was no definite candidate to succeed her. The field was open even though Sir Robert Cecil worked in secret on behalf of

King James of Scotland after the Essex Rebellion. Before the rebellion, there was a chance that her natural issue could succeed her, and this possibility evidently fired the great author's imagination and inspired many of his sonnets. On the queen's deathbed, Cecil claimed that she acknowledged James as her successor. No will ever came to light.

Princely References in the Sonnets

The following sonnet excerpts demonstrate the great author's apparent view that the Fair Youth-Southampton was Queen Elizabeth's bastard son and successor. As explained above, it appears that the great author, a nobleman, was his father. He consistently describes the Fair Youth as having higher social status than himself, and it is implied that it is royal: he often compares him to the sun, a symbol of royalty, and a rose, the emblem of the Tudors, and he uses several royal terms, like sovereign, crown and succession. In two sonnets (76, 105), the armorial mottos of Queen Elizabeth and the Earl of Southampton were merged into one line. The great author's belief that Southampton was a prince is why he "idolized" him and felt bound to him in "duty." Referring to the Fair Youth as his "friend" in several sonnets instead of son can be explained if he intended the sonnets to be circulated in manuscript, which on the evidence of echoed lines in Spenser's *Complaints* and in other works, occurred as early as 1589. (That the sonnets had been in circulation for at least 20 years could explain the line, "Never before Imprinted," on the 1609 title page of *SONNETS*.) Because of the political implications of such a revelation, discretion and ambiguity was a likely necessity. This view is supported in Sonnet 36 – the great author says that he cannot publicly acknowledge the Fair Youth, presumably as his bastard son, that they must live in separation:

> I may not ever-more acknowledge thee,
> Lest my bewailed guilt should do thee shame.

In sonnets 70 and 127, the great author reveals that the Fair Youth was suspected by those in his social circle as being a royal bastard. Sonnet 126 could be dated soon after the Essex Rebellion, when Fair Youth-Southampton was in the Tower; he had been sentenced to death for high treason and could be executed at any time. The great author believed that the "sovereign mistress," Queen Elizabeth, would eventually release him.

"Princely" References to the Fair Youth
in Shakespeare's Sonnets (excerpts)

SONNETS 1, 10

The first two lines of Sonnet 1 explain the theme of the first seventeen, the poet's urging of the Fair Youth to marry and produce children.

> From <u>fairest</u> creatures we desire increase,
> That thereby <u>beauty's *Rose* might never die</u> ...

"Beauty" represents the Phoenix-Queen Elizabeth in Shakespeare's *Love's Martyr* poem. The rose is the symbol of the Tudor dynasty. The "fairest creature" is the Fair Youth. The poet calls upon the Fair Youth, therefore, to have children to continue the Tudor line, so "beauty's Rose might never die." This same idea is expressed in Sonnet 10:

> Make thee [the Fair Youth] <u>another self</u> for love of me,
> That <u>beauty still may live</u> in thine or thee.

SONNETS 2, 63

In Sonnet 2, the poet wishes the Fair Youth to think about the future, when his beauty is faded or gone. By having a child, the Fair Youth's beauty will become the child's "by succession," a royal term.

> Proving his <u>beauty by succession</u> thine.

In Sonnet 63, the poet wishes to preserve in verse "all those beauties" of the Fair Youth, "whereof now he's King."

SONNET 6

The poet urges the Fair Youth to marry and have children so "beauty's treasure," the "treasure" or child of Queen Elizabeth, will not "kill" or end her royal line.

> treasure thou some place,
> With <u>beauty's treasure ere it be self kill'd</u>:

SONNETS 37, 69, 114

In sonnets 37 and 69, the poet uses "crown" imagery to describe the Fair Youth:

> For whether beauty, birth, or wealth, or wit,
> Or any of these all, or all, or more
> Entitled in their parts, do <u>crowned</u> sit ...
> [Sonnet 37]

> Thy outward thus with outward praise is <u>crown'd</u> ...
> [Sonnet 69]

In Sonnet 113, the poet says that his mind causes his eyes to see a resemblance of the Fair Youth in all objects. In the next sonnet (114), the poet wonders if this "flattery" is caused by his mind being drunk with the Fair Youth, or if he is seeing accurately. He uses royal imagery to express this idea.

> Or whether doth my mind being <u>crown'd</u> with you
> Drink up the <u>monarch's</u> plague this flattery?
> Or whether shall I say mine eye saith true ... ?

> Oh 'tis the first, 'tis flatt'ry in my seeing,
> And my great mind most <u>kingly</u> drinks it up ... [Sonnet 114]

SONNETS 7, 33, 34, 49

In Sonnet 7, the Fair Youth is compared to "the gracious light," the sun, a common symbol of royalty. The poet says all eyes below (on earth) pay "homage" to the Fair Youth, "Serving with looks his sacred majesty."

In Sonnet 33, the Fair Youth is again compared to the sun "with sovereign eye."

> Full many a glorious morning have I seen,
> Flatter the mountaintops with <u>sovereign</u> eye,
> Kissing with golden face the meadows green ...

The final six lines of Sonnet 33 seem to describe the Fair Youth as the great author's bastard son. He wrote, "my sun one early morn did shine," i.e., his son was born. He called this event his "triumphant splendor," but his joy was very brief. He said the child was "but one hour mine."

> Even so my Sun one early morn did shine,
> With all triumphant splendor on my brow,
> But out alack, he was but one hour mine,
> The region cloud hath mask'd him from me now.
> Yet him for this, my love no whit disdaineth,
> Suns of the world may stain, when heaven's sun staineth.

The Ogburns noted that "region" in the line, "The region cloud hath mask'd him from me now," puns on regina or queen. The queen "mask'd" or covered the child, the Fair Youth, because he was a bastard,[36] a royal "stain" ("heaven's sun staineth"). The queen apparently did not keep or acknowledge the baby.

Sonnet 34's opening lines again speak to the Fair Youth as the sun, and that his greatness ["bravery"] was being hidden, like in the previous sonnet, by a cloud.

> Why didst thou promise such a <u>beauteous day</u>,
> And make me travail forth without my cloak,
> To let base <u>clouds</u> o'er-take me in my way,
> <u>Hiding thy brav'ry</u> [the sun's rays] in their rotten smoke [?]

In Sonnet 49, the great author foresees a time when the Fair Youth shall "strangely pass" him by, "And scarcely greet me with that sun thine eye" for "reasons" of "settled gravity," i.e., the need to maintain royal decorum.

SONNET 14

Looking into the Fair Youth's eyes, the poet predicts in Sonnet 14 that "Truth and beauty shall together thrive" should he produce children; if he does not, then the poet predicts "Truth and Beauty's doom and date."

> But from thine eyes my knowledge I derive,
> And constant stars in them I read such art
> As truth and beauty shall together thrive
> If from thyself, to store thou wouldst convert:
> Or else of thee this I prognosticate,
> Thy end is Truth's and Beauty's doom and date.

These lines directly parallel Shakespeare's poems in *Love's Martyr*, where Beauty and Truth symbolize the Phoenix and the Turtle Dove. If the child of the Phoenix-Beauty-Queen Elizabeth does not reproduce, then the Tudor monarchy is "doomed." Shakespeare's poems in *Love's Martyr* also described the Phoenix and Turtle Dove as "Love and Constancy" and "co-supremes and stars of love," thus reflected in Sonnet 14's phrase, "constant stars."

SONNET 26

In Sonnet 26, the poet speaks to the Fair Youth like a subject would to his sovereign. He uses the word "duty" three times, as well as "vassalage" and "embassage," the latter a message entrusted to an ambassador. These terms are applicable to a ruler or king.

> Lord of my love, to whom in vassalage
> Thy merit hath my duty strongly knit;
> To thee I send this written embassage
> To witness duty, not to shew my wit.
> Duty so great ...

"Duty" was echoed in the dedications of Shakespeare's *Venus and Adonis* and *Lucrece* to Southampton: "Your Honor's in all duty" and "Your Lordship's in all duty."

SONNETS 54, 70, 127

In the opening two lines of Sonnet 54, Beauty-Queen Elizabeth's "sweet ornament" is the Fair Youth, "given" or fathered by "truth," the Turtle Dove-Shakespeare.

> Oh how much more doth <u>beauty</u> beauteous seem,
> By that <u>sweet ornament which truth doth give,</u>
> <u>The Rose looks fair</u>, but fairer we it deem ...

(Sonnet 1 described the Fair Youth as "the world's fresh ornament" and "Beauty's rose.") In the rest of Sonnet 54, the "beauteous and lovely youth" is compared to roses, those that do have scent ("Sweet Roses") and those that do not ("cankers" or wild roses). The Fair Youth is a true sweet-smelling rose, i.e., he is a true member of the Tudor royal family.

In Sonnet 70, "The ornament of beauty," the Fair Youth, "is suspect" and is "slandered." He is suspected by society of being the bastard child of Queen Elizabeth, "beauty."

> That thou art blam'd shall not be thy defect,
> For <u>slander's mark</u> was ever yet the fair,
> <u>The ornament of beauty is suspect,</u>
> <u>A Crow that flies in heaven's sweetest air</u> ...
>
> If some <u>suspect</u> of ill mask'd not thy show,
> Then thou alone <u>kingdoms</u> of hearts shouldst owe.

The Fair Youth is the "Crow" or black bird that "flies in heaven's sweetest air," heaven representing the highest social stratum, the queen and her court. Had this suspicion of bastardy not surrounded the Fair Youth, then "kingdoms of hearts" would be owed to him, presumably as an acknowledged prince.

The imagery of blackness and bastardy is carried in Sonnet 127:

> In the old age <u>black</u> was not counted <u>fair</u>,

> Or if it were <u>it bore not beauty's name</u>:
> <u>But now is black beauty's successive heir,</u>
> <u>And Beauty slander'd with a bastard shame</u>,
> For since each hand hath put on Nature's power,
> Fairing the foul with Art's false borrow'd face,
> <u>Sweet beauty hath no name</u> no holy bower,
> <u>But is profan'd</u> [debased], <u>if not lives in disgrace</u>.
> Therefore my Mistress' eyes are Raven black
> Her eyes so suited, and they mourners seem,
> At such who not born fair no beauty lack,
> Sland'ring Creation with a false esteem ... [Sonnet 127]

Beauty, the queen, is "slander'd with a bastard shame." Her "successive heir" is "black," meaning he is soiled or stained, i.e., he is a bastard. "Sweet beauty," the Fair Youth, "hath no name," he does not bear her royal name and "lives in disgrace." This sonnet very openly says that the Fair Youth-Southampton was the queen's unacknowledged bastard child, and also her "heir" to the "succession" of England as her natural issue. This sonnet is usually classified as one about the "Dark Lady," but the great author writes that his mistress' eyes are only theoretically black, not actually black ("<u>Therefore</u> my Mistress' eyes are Raven black"). Shakespeare used the phrase, "successive heir," in one other instance. In *Henry VI-Part 2*, it was said that Humphrey, Duke of Gloucester, reputed himself "As next the King, he was successive Heir ... " (3.1.49).[37]

SONNETS 57, 58, 87

In Sonnet 57, the poet calls the Fair Youth "my sovereign." In Sonnet 58, the poet says he is the Fair Youth's "vassal," and in both sonnets, his "slave," a total of three times. Leslie Hotson noted that in sonnets 58 and 87 the poet employed terms "peculiar to a king: power to grant charters of privilege and letters patent, power to pardon crimes – in short, the exclusively royal prerogative."[38]

> Be where you list, your <u>charter</u> is so strong,
> That you yourself may <u>privilege</u> your time
> To what you will, to you it doth belong,
> Yourself to <u>pardon</u> of self-doing crime. [Sonnet 58]

The first definition of charter is "a written document delivered by the sovereign or legislature" (OED).

> The <u>Charter</u> of thy worth gives thee releasing:
> My <u>bonds</u> in thee are all determinate
> For how do I hold thee but by <u>thy granting</u> ...
>
> And so my <u>patent</u> back again is swerving. [Sonnet 87]

SONNETS 55, 59

In Sonnet 59, the poet imagines the Fair Youth's image as being featured in 500-year-old history books, "five hundredth courses of the Sun." The Fair Youth's immortality will occur not only because he is the subject of great poetry, but also because, as the poet believes, he will become a king. Numerous sonnets attest to the poet's desire that his verse will confer immortality upon the Fair Youth, like the "monument, /Of Princes" in Sonnet 55:

> Not marble, nor the gilded <u>monument</u>,
> <u>Of Princes</u> shall outlive this powerful rhyme ...

SONNETS 67, 68

In Sonnet 67, the poet posits, why should "poor beauty," Queen Elizabeth, "indirectly seek" the Fair Youth, her "shadow" ("Roses of shadow")? The Fair Youth is truly her child ("his Rose is true"), and she has no other heir or treasure ("exchequer") but him. By keeping her child in shadow – by not acknowledging him – the queen is "Nature" bankrupt. She makes herself a "beggar" of her own royal "blood."

> Why should poor <u>beauty</u> indirectly seek
> <u>Roses of shadow</u>, since <u>his Rose is true</u>?
> Why should he live, now <u>nature</u> bankrout [bankrupt] is,
> Beggar'd of blood to blush through lively veins,
> For she hath no exchequer [treasure] now but his ...

In Sonnet 68, the poet writes how much the Fair Youth looks like Beauty-Queen Elizabeth. Her beauty "of yore," before her "bastard" was "born," is stored in him like a map.

> Thus is his cheek the map of day's outworn,
> When <u>beauty liv'd</u> and died as flowers do now,
> Before these <u>bastard signs of fair were born</u> ...
>
> And him as for a map <u>doth Nature store</u>,
> To shew false Art what <u>beauty was of yore</u>.[Sonnet 68]

Elsewhere in the sonnets, "nature" refers to the queen, especially in Sonnet 20, where the Fair Youth's resemblance to her is noted: "A Woman's face with nature's own hand painted..." It is also mentioned in Sonnet 126 below. (In Sonnet 62, the great author noted the Fair Youth's resemblance to himself.)

SONNETS 76, 105

In Sonnet 76, the line, "Why write I still all one, ever the same," merges Southampton's family motto, "one for all, all for one" (*Ung par tout, tout par ung*) and Queen Elizabeth's motto, "always the same" (*Semper eadem*); in another line, the poet compares his love for the Fair Youth with "the Sun."

In Sonnet 105, the reason why the poet's love of the Fair Youth should "not be call'd idolatry" is because he lauds Southampton ("to one, of one," his motto) and the queen ("still such and ever so," her motto) and not false gods:

> Let not my love be call'd <u>Idolatry</u>,
> Nor my beloved as an Idol show,
> Since <u>all alike</u> my songs and praises be
> <u>To one, of one, still such, and ever so</u>.

SONNET 126

The poet in this sonnet gives the Fair Youth advice about "Nature" or Queen Elizabeth, "sovereign mistress over wrack." Southampton's "wrack" or wreck was his death sentence for his part in the Essex Rebellion in 1601. Although his sentence was not immediately carried out, the Queen-Nature could at any time enforce it. The poet advises the Fair Youth-Southampton, presumably while he was still in the Tower, to "fear her." The Fair Youth is "her treasure" but her delayed "audit," i.e., her delayed judgment of what to do with Southampton, must be given. The great author believed that her settlement, "quietus," will be to restore him.

> If Nature (sovereign mistress over wrack)
> As thou goest onwards still will pluck thee back ...
>
> Yet fear her [Nature] O thou minion of her pleasure,
> She may detain, but not still keep her treasure!
> Her *Audit* (though delay'd) answer'd must be,
> And her *Quietus* [settlement] is to render [restore] thee.
> (   )
> (   )

The great author defined "treasure" as a child in Sonnet 2:

> Then being ask'd, where all thy beauty lies,
> Where all the treasure of thy lusty days [?] ...
>
> If thou couldst answer "this fair child of mine
> Shall sum my count ... "[quotation marks added]

Sonnet 126 lacked two lines, but empty parentheses were printed, as if to indicate to the reader that these lines exist, but were purposely left out.

Another Light on the Essex Rebellion

Adding to the historical and literary revelations about the Earl of Southampton's "princely" status is the fact that he had involved himself in a rebellion that was focused on the succession. On February 8, 1601, Robert Devereux, 2nd Earl of Essex, and his chief supporter, Southampton, led an attempted coupe d'état against Queen Elizabeth and her council. A combination of poor planning, Sir Robert Cecil's advance knowledge of the plan and bad luck contributed to its failure.[39] Essex clearly desired the queen's dethronement: the day before, his supporters paid for a special performance at the Globe Theater of Shakespeare's *Richard II*. Actor Augustine Phillips testified that they spoke to him and other actors "to have the play of the deposing and killing of King Richard the Second," and Sir Francis Bacon likewise printed that they "had procured to be played before them, the Play of deposing King Richard the second."[40] The deposition scene in *Richard II* was so politically charged that the first three printings of the play (1597-1598) had omitted it (the next issue occurred in 1608). The queen herself admitted to William Lambarde of her resemblance to Richard II when she made this post-Rebellion remark: "Know ye not I am Richard?" Many of the investigated confederates reported that Essex had planned to call a parliament as soon as he secured the city and the royal court, perhaps another indication of a change in rulers or installing a regent. Had the rebellion succeeded, then whomever Essex and Southampton promoted to succeed the queen would have been in effect the new ruler.

Some said that it was Essex himself who wanted the throne. When the trial opened, the "effect of the indictment" was that Essex sought "to disinherit the queen of her crown and dignity."[41] The prosecuting attorney, Sir Edward Coke, said during the trial, "But now in God's most just judgment, he of his earldom shall be Robert the Last, that of a kingdom thought to be Robert the First."[42] Cecil repeated this idea at the trial after Essex accused him of promoting the Spanish princess for the succession. "I have said the king of Scots is a competitor, and the king of Spain a competitor, and you I have said are a competitor: you would depose the queen, you would be king of England, and call a parliament."[43] The week before the trial, in a discussion of the rebellion in the Star Chamber, Cecil said that Essex "had been devising five or six years to be King of England."[44] The queen herself was aware of Essex's ambition for the English throne; she had warned him two years before his revolt, according to French ambassador Harlay, who recorded this conversation with her:

> ... she had warned the said Count [Earl of Essex] more than two years before that since he took every occasion of displeasing her and insolently despising her person, he should be careful not to touch her scepter, so that she would be compelled to punish him according to the laws of England and not according to her own, which he

had found too gentle and favorable to fear that they would ever do him harm.[45]

Since contemporaries said that Essex eyed the English throne, it is possible that he was the queen's child by the Earl of Leicester. This would explain the elderly queen's affection for him, his extraordinary advancement as a young man, their constant companionship, and her consistent toleration of his recalcitrance, disobedience and even insults.[46] Essex was named after Leicester, who was his godfather, and later, his stepfather. Essex's mother, Lettice, was the queen's first cousin once-removed. The *DNB* cites Sir Henry Wotton's commentary that Essex's father, Walter Devereux, doubted his son's paternity, and "preferred his younger son and namesake."

If the Earl of Essex did not try to take the throne for himself, then he may have intended it for "prince" Southampton, which would explain his participation in Essex's treasonous and suicidal scheme. Their willingness to risk everything would be completely irrational unless they felt that they had a "right" to do so. Queen Elizabeth was 68 years old at the time – quite aged in those days – and she refused to name her successor. Meanwhile the two earls believed that Cecil was secretly making arrangements for the succession of the Catholic Spanish princess. On February 19, both earls were found guilty of high treason and sentenced to death. The next day, the queen signed the execution warrant for Essex, which was carried out five days later; the warrant still exists at the British Library.[47] But what does not exist, and probably never did exist, was a warrant for the execution of Southampton. As the queen's principal secretary, and the de facto ruler of England, Cecil was the one in charge of getting such a document to the queen for her signature; and indeed, as Southampton's enemy, Cecil should have done so without delay, but evidently no such warrant ever materialized. Why Southampton's death sentence was not carried out was never explained in any contemporary document and still remains unexplained. Cecil's position was clear two days after the rebellion: he was convinced that Essex, Southampton and others "shall have lost their heads" by the time his letter to Sir George Carew reached him in Ireland.[48] But his opinion about Southampton changed very rapidly. In a letter to the same man written only one month later, Cecil wrote that he was among those trying to save "the poor young Earl of Southampton, who merely for the love of the Earl hath been drawn into this action…"[49] Considering Essex and Southampton's open accusation of Cecil's treasonous activity, it was a remarkable turnaround. Southampton's meager defense for his crime, that he was ignorant of the law and only wanted to help Essex, does not seem substantial enough to have softened the unscrupulous Cecil. The Lord High Steward (Thomas Sackville, Lord Buckhurst), had pronounced a sentence of execution for both earls ("hanged, bowelled, and quartered"),[50] so Cecil should have at least prepared Southampton's execution warrant, and left the decision to the queen whether or not to sign it. The queen's acceptance of Essex's guilt and punishment was a given, otherwise she would not have signed his warrant; it should have been no different with Southampton, who, after he married without the queen's approval, was less of a favorite than Essex. Since Cecil inexplicably "interested himself in securing a commutation of Southampton's sentence" (DNB), it means that a third party was able to change Cecil's mind almost instantly. Other than the queen, only Cecil had the power to delay a death sentence. Since some Essex supporters regarded Cecil as "chiefly responsible for the Queen's decision to execute" Essex,[51] it follows that he was similarly responsible for Southampton's reprieve. Southampton's status circa June 1601 was indicated on Cecil's list of those implicated in the rebellion, his name appearing under the category, "Persons living that are condemned."[52]

Was the nobleman writing under the pen name, Shakespeare, the one who dealt with Cecil to save his loved one's life? As discussed in Chapter 13, the great author seemed to reveal in *The Winter's Tale* that he was "enjoin'd by oath" to permanent (i.e., posthumous) secrecy about his authorship of Shakespeare. If so, then he did so for some very compelling reason. In the play, the oath was made between a nobleman and the King of Sicillia. The name similarity between Sicillia and Cecil makes it almost certain that the deal was made with Cecil, whose family members were characterized in some Shakespeare plays, in exchange for Southampton's life. Cecil's father, Lord Burghley, was lampooned in *Hamlet* as Corambis-Polonius, and by extension, his daughter Anne, who had an early death, was tragically portrayed as Ophelia. Contemporaries were also connecting Sir Robert Cecil with Shakespeare's character, King Richard III. Although the Earl of Leicester, Sir Nicholas Bacon and Lord Burghley had been likened to the evil king in books of the 1570s and 1580s,[53] the association crystallized with Cecil from the 1590s and onward. Such a comparison was especially inviting and irresistible to make considering they had shared (or it was believed that they had shared) a physical deformity – a hunchback. Lily Campbell observed that King Richard III was, "at least by 1572, accepted as the archetype of Machiavellianism, his activities being made the pattern by which to interpret the doings of political aspirants. And he continued to be so used."[54] Cecil's father, Lord Burghley, practiced out of *Machiavill*," wrote one critic in 1592, and warned that he was grooming his "second crooked cub," Robert Cecil, in the like manner.[55] Cecil had been knighted and appointed to the Privy Council in the previous year. Margaret Hotine wrote about the timing coincidence of Cecil's long anticipated appointment as the queen's principal secretary on July 5, 1596 and the first publication of Shakespeare's play in 1597. Although the experts believe the play was written as early as 1592, Hotine suggested that "some event had occurred that made it topical, prompting a revival in the theatre."[56] She also suggested that the next three editions of the play (1598, 1602 and 1605) were issued not only due to the play's popularity but also because of its "continued topicality" as the world watched Cecil's power grow. In 1612, Shakespeare's *Richard III* was printed for the fifth time, the year of Cecil's death; presumably no longer topical, the play would not be printed again for ten years.

Parallels between Cecil and Shakespeare's Richard III included the fact that they were both called devil, toad and elf.[57] A poetry work about Richard III by Sir William Cornwallis, which had only been circulating in manuscript, was intercepted by the Essex faction and revised, pre-Rebellion, in an apparent attack on Cecil.[58] The alterations and additions to Cornwallis's original text specifically dispraised Richard III, and in many cases changed Cornwallis's intent. Cecil had aroused such hatred, which was necessarily suppressed during his lifetime, that at his death he was publicly execrated. John Chamberlain wrote

> The memory of the late Lord Treasurer [Cecil] grows daily worse and worse and more libels come as it were continually.[59]

A satirical epitaph on Cecil survives in a contemporary manuscript:

> Here lies little Crookback
> Who justly was reckon'd
> Richard the 3rd and Judas the second,
> In life they agreed,
> But in death they did alter
> Great pity the pox prevented the halter.[60]

As the public connected Cecil with Shakespeare's Richard III, had it become generally known that Shakespeare was a nobleman intimate with powerful players at court, then Cecil and Shakespeare's self-consciously evil Richard III would be forever linked. If anyone had a motive, therefore, to permanently separate the great author's real name with his plays, it would be Sir Robert Cecil for his own sake and for that of his family. Southampton's life was in Cecil's hands, and this could have been the condition that Cecil demanded from the great author to save him. It would certainly explain why the great author was convinced that the Fair Youth-Southampton would be immortalized by his verse but that his own name, his real name, would be forever buried. The great author, whose love for Southampton was so strongly expressed in his sonnets, exchanged his posthumous claim to authorship of the incomparable Shakespeare works for Southampton's life – a selfless act certainly characteristic of a father saving his child. The only other Essex conspirator besides Southampton who was not executed but not freed while the queen lived was Sir Henry Neville. Besides being Cecil's cousin, Neville's life was spared apparently because he had the means to pay a huge fine, initially set at £10,000.[61] Other members of the nobility and knights connected with the rebellion were fined and eventually released. Southampton was not fined.

Sometime between June and December 1601 was published *Love's Martyr* by Robert Chester, which urged the Phoenix-Queen Elizabeth to accept the new "princely Phoenix" that arose from the ashes of the Phoenix and Turtle Dove. Chester wrote:

> Long may the new uprising bird increase,
> Some humors and some motions to release,
> And thus to all I offer my devotion,
> Hoping that gentle minds accept my motion.
> Finis. R.C.

Chester hoped that "gentle minds" will "accept" his "motion," which in this sense is "a proposal, suggestion, or petition" (*OED*). As Southampton was the only person in England whose princely status was hinted at publicly and in print, one could reasonably conclude that Chester was appealing to the queen "to release" her imprisoned child, Southampton. It may be significant that Shakespeare signed his poems in *Love's Martyr* with a hyphen, "William Shake-speare," unlike his signatures on the dedication letters in *Venus and Adonis* and *Lucrece*. Post the Essex Rebellion, and post his oath to "authority," the great author may have wished it to be broadly known that "William Shakespeare" was actually his pen name. All three of the above named poetry works were printed by Richard Field and contained Shakespeare's clean text and apparent approval. Field's involvement in *Love's Martyr* could indicate that the great author's role was not merely as a contributor to the work, but as a fosterer, and as one who shared in Chester's appeal to the queen. No other Shakespeare work, new or old, was printed in 1601. It was a notable ceasing of a steady flow of his works since 1593; the previous year (1600) saw seven different Shakespeare works in print. It appears that publishers had trepidations about printing Shakespeare in the year of the Essex Rebellion.

Queen Elizabeth never did release Southampton, but it may be telling that he was not treated as a horrible traitor. He was lodged in an apartment with two rooms, near the Queen's Gallery, which were specially repaired and painted for him. When he was ill, the queen sent a physician to him. He was allowed visitors including his wife and mother. He apparently was allowed to send letters: Edward Bruce mentioned in his letter to Lord Henry Howard that Southampton had written King James "an earnest letter for a warrant of his liberty immediately upon [Elizabeth's] death…"[62] Remarkably, this is what happened. Shakespeare's Sonnet 107 almost certainly commented upon this miraculous event.

> Not mine own fears, nor the prophetic soul,
> Of the wide world, dreaming on things to come,
> Can yet the lease of my true love control,
> Suppos'd as forfeit to a confin'd doom.
> The mortal Moon hath her eclipse endur'd,
> And the sad Augurs mock their own presage,
> Incertainties now crown themselves assur'd,
> And peace proclaims Olives of endless age …

The "crown" passed peacefully from Queen Elizabeth ("the mortal Moon") to James I on March 24, 1603. To the poet's immense relief, the Fair Youth-Southampton survived the queen, and was freed. He had "supposed" that Southampton's life was "forfeit" to a prison sentence ("confin'd doom").

> … Now with the drops of this most balmy time,
> My love looks fresh, and death to me subscribes [submits],
> Since spite of him I'll live in this poor rhyme,
> While he insults o'er dull and speechless tribes.
> And thou in this shalt find thy monument,
> When tyrant's crests and tombs of brass are spent.

The great author's sacrifice of claiming his artistic works in his own name stopped Southampton's execution: "Death" submitted to him. He was the "Martyr" for his "Love." But despite his deal with Death, says the great author, "I'll live in this poor rhyme," his sonnets, his "monument" to Southampton.

James sent his order to release Southampton on April 5, but on March 26 "bills reversing the attainders of the Earls of Southampton and Essex were read a first time"[63] in the House of Lords, according to Essex's biographer, Walter Bourchier Devereux. This introduction of a bill to restore their noble status occurred a mere two days after Queen Elizabeth's death. "James must, therefore, have given instructions before he became King," wrote Devereux, "or else his wishes were so well known to Cecyll that he ventured to forestall them thus; a remarkable circumstance whichever way it is viewed." The other explanation could be that the queen had privately commanded that Southampton be released and his titles restored immediately after her death. Shakespeare seemed to note this in Sonnet 126, probably written while Southampton was still in the Tower: "and her Quietus is to render thee" (the queen will restore you). Although it is known that Southampton's release occurred on April 10, it was rumored on March 27 that he was already "at liberty," and had voiced his support for Lord Beauchamp as king after it was proclaimed for the king of Scotland. A man listening to a conversation with actors reported the rumor.[64] The succession question seemed to follow Southampton. Meanwhile two requests in print for Shakespeare's eulogy of the queen were ignored. Could it be that he bore some personal grudge?

Conclusion

After determining that the Stratford Man was not the great author, Shakespeare, the true deciding question of the Shakespeare Authorship is: why did he get the credit (posthumously), or why did the sponsors of the First Folio want the public to believe that another man, one not of the nobility, was the great author? The other crucial question is why no one remarked upon the great author's death whenever it had occurred. There must have been something terribly wrong with Shakespeare for everyone in the literary world to completely ignore the death of so celebrated a poet and dramatist. He was dead no later than 1609, with no formal acknowledgment for fourteen years after that. Robert Chester's poetry work, *Love's Martyr*, published in 1601, apparently related a love affair between Queen Elizabeth and the great author through the symbolism of the Phoenix and the Turtle Dove, and that they produced a child, "another princely Phoenix." Shakespeare's poems in the work personified these birds as Beauty and Truth, terms also contained in his sonnets. Chester appealed to the Phoenix-Queen Elizabeth to recognize the Turtle Dove, hinted at as Shakespeare, and their child, the "princely Phoenix," the bird involved in the "uprising," i.e., Southampton. Shakespeare's involvement with this work implies that he also wished the queen to recognize Southampton. Those in the literary world who had read manuscript copies of the great author's sonnets, with its prince-royal imagery of the Fair Youth, would have connected the Fair Youth and the "princely Phoenix" of *Love's Martyr* with Southampton (and possibly even the "changeling" boy that the Fairy King in Shakespeare's *A Midsummer Night's Dream* wanted to take from the Fairy Queen, a character solidly associated with Queen Elizabeth). Shakespeare's view about the succession, therefore, was broadly advertised in *Love's Martyr*, and in his long circulating sonnets, and his choice of candidate was not King James VI of Scotland, who eventually succeeded. How could anyone praise the great author at the time of his passing with this unchangeable and impolitic fact?

The earls of Essex and Southampton made a last-ditch effort in a bid for power against their political adversary, Sir Robert Cecil. They proved no match for Cecil, who practically orchestrated their downfall. The earls were convicted of high treason and sentenced to death. Essex was beheaded soon afterward but Southampton's execution was never carried out. For some still unexplained reason, Cecil stopped it, and surely he was rewarded for his pains. Such a reward may have been the severing of links between satirical portrayals of Cecil and his father, Lord Burghley, in the popular Shakespeare plays, especially in *Richard III* and *Hamlet*. Although *Hamlet* had not yet been printed at the time of the supposed agreement, Cecil shrewdly recognized that Shakespeare's works were destined for immortality. If the nobleman-writer behind these plays agreed to forever keep his real name off of them, then this link would vanish. The great author deeply loved the Earl of Southampton, was probably his father, and desperately wanted to save him from execution. This could have been the deal, or the "oath," related in *The Winter's Tale*, between a nobleman and the King of Sicillia (i.e., Sir Robert Cecil) that silenced the great author and his family about his Shakespeare authorship forever. But another crisis came later that ultimately required, as a political safeguard, the deliberate mix-up between Shakespeare and the Stratford Man: the publication of SHAKE-SPEARE'S SONNETS in 1609.

CHAPTER 17

"Simple Truth Suppress'd": A Unified Solution

ONE OF THE earliest acts of James I as the new king of England was the freeing of the Earl of Southampton. One line of hearsay seems to be the only modern explanation for this act: some time after James was crowned the English king, he called the Earl of Essex his "martyr" in a private conversation.[1] If Essex was James's martyr, then so was his co-conspirator, Southampton, and nothing more need be said. Although shortly before his execution, Essex said that his rebellion was to take the throne for King James of Scotland, it seems illogical. Essex risked treason and death to force the succession onto James before the queen's passing (she was not ill) and without James's involvement? It is true that Essex had been in correspondence with James about two years before his rebellion, but it was only just before that he had asked James to send an ambassador to England – not troops, not money. It appears that Essex wanted James's diplomatic support only after he had enacted a change of regime. An ambassador was sent, as requested, but he conveniently appeared *after* both the rebellion and Essex's beheading. Obviously, at that point, James did not want to get involved with convicted traitors. It was immediately after Essex's execution that Sir Robert Cecil opened negotiations with James to become the queen's successor via secret correspondence. But if both Essex and Cecil had wanted a Scottish succession all along, then why were they enemies? Essex and Southampton's exposure of Cecil as a promoter of the Catholic Spanish princess for England's throne, true or not, may have ruined Cecil's plans, requiring him to seek another "king" to make. Historians have acknowledged that Cecil received a pension from the Spanish government during the reign of James I, and think it not unlikely that it had originated in Queen Elizabeth's reign.[2]

Southampton James's Martyr?

Evidence shows that Essex did not wish King James VI of Scotland to be the next English king, nor did James sincerely regard Essex as his martyr.

Firstly, one and a half years before his rebellion, Essex was warned about King James's regard of him by Thomas Wenman, who learned of a conversation between the king and an agent named Ashfield. Wenman, in his letter to Essex, reported that Ashfield told the king that Essex was his only "obstacle" to the English throne, which took "deep root in the King's heart"; the king then was resolved to contrive Essex's "utter ruin and final overthrow," and hoped that his mission in Ireland would fail.

> [Ashfield had] proposed your lordship [Essex] as the only likely obstacle to withstand and resist the intended Scottish title: which suggestion has taken so deep root in the King's heart that he is resolutely determined to work by all possible means your utter ruin and final overthrow, the which I think he will endeavor to effect rather by the fox's craft than the lion's strength. ... He [James] desires nothing more than the ill success of the Irish wars in general or of your own person in particular (God prevent both.)
> [Aug. 18, 1599; underlines are original][3]

Another letter, written shortly after the Essex Rebellion, reported that "inwardly [James] is one way sorry for it and another pleased with it."[4] Another post-Rebellion report, but pre-Elizabeth's death, reveals the true feelings that Essex and James had toward each other. Henry Percy, 9th Earl of Northumberland, wrote to James that Essex thought it would be "scandalous to our nation that a stranger should be our king." James would be considered a "stranger" because he was not born in England. And when Essex learned that Northumberland supported James as Queen Elizabeth's successor, Essex "cancelled his familiarity" with him. Northumberland was Essex's brother-in-law, and he offered further insights about Essex's aims in a circa 1601-1602 letter: that he wanted the English crown for many years and only offered James his "service" just before his revolt, "at the last push."

> How often have I [Northumberland] heard that he [Essex] inveighed against you [James] amongst such as he conceived to be birds of his own fortune? Did his soldiers followers dream or speak anything but of his being king of England? ... Did he ever offer you this service but in his declining time, and at the last push? ... Well, to conclude, he [Essex] wore the crown of England in his heart these many years, and therefore far from setting it upon your head if it had been in his power. [5]

(Sir Robert Cecil believed that Essex "had been devising five or six years to be king of England.")[6] Northumberland also referred to the comments that James made about Essex in his previous letter:

> ... your Majesty's judgment of Essex to be a noble gentleman, but that you lost no great friend by him, leads me on the rather to this discourse; to confirm therefore your Majesty's censure, I must say justly, that although he was a man endued with good gifts, yet was his loss the happiest chance for your Majesty and England that could befall us ... [7]

Evidently, James had written to Northumberland that he had "lost no great friend" in regard to Essex's death. Had James thought Essex his great friend, then perhaps he would have intervened on his behalf before his execution.

More evidence of James's dubious feelings for Essex was revealed in a letter written by the Dean of Limerick to Sir Robert Cecil about a month after the execution. He wrote that James's "displeasure" about it was "greater show than sorrow."[8] Furthermore, the notion that Essex was not a traitor was *not* tolerated after James became the king of England. During Sir Walter Ralegh's treason trial in 1603, the king's attorney general, Sir Edward Coke, said these words about Essex:

> He died indeed for his offense. The king himself spake these words;
> "He that shall say, Essex died not for treason, is punishable."[9]

Shortly after Southampton's prison release, Thomas Powell dedicated a book to him (*A Welsh Bait to Spare Provender*, 1603). Powell declared in a prefatory verse that Southampton was not a traitor:

> *Ever*
> Whoso beholds this Leaf, therein shall read,
> A faithful subject's name, he shall indeed:
> The gray-eyed morn in noontide clouds may steep,
> But traitor and his name shall never meet.
> *Never.*

Valentine Simmes was fined for printing Powell's work "without license" on December 5, 1603, and was ordered not to sell or print it again.[10] In the third line of the above verse, Powell had lifted a phrase from Shakespeare's play, *Romeo and Juliet* (2.1.230), and the words "Ever" and "Never" that bound the verse seemed to prefigure the anonymous letter, "A never writer, to an ever reader," contained in the 1609 edition of Shakespeare's play, *Troilus and Cressida*. Robert Pricket's poem, *Honor's Fame in Triumph Riding* (1604), had lauded Essex, and included the line, "He died for treason; yet no traitor." The book was dedicated to three former Essex supporters, including Southampton. Soon after its release, the book was recalled, the publisher was interrogated, and Pricket was jailed.[11] In early 1605, Samuel Daniel's play,

The Tragedy of Philotas, was performed before the king. The *DNB* states that "Daniel was immediately called before the Privy Council to answer the charge that his treatment of the subject – the downfall of Philotas, a favourite of Alexander the Great – was a seditious comment on the trial and execution of Robert, earl of Essex, in 1601." Daniel naturally denied the resemblance of the hero Philotas to Essex, but scholars today think it obvious (Pauline Croft noted that the "treacherous dwarf" in the play probably represented Robert Cecil).[12] It is hardly likely that Powell, Pricket and Daniel would have written sympathetically about Essex and Southampton knowing that it would offend the king.

Putting aside the one supposed martyr remark and looking at the hard facts, one can justly conclude that James's immediate pardon and release of Southampton was odd and needs some justification – even more so since James did more than just free him. Within the first year of Southampton's release, James reinstated his titles, gave him land and lucrative offices, and even gave his mother £600; her name topped the list titled, "Free Gifts out of the Exchequer." Southampton's step-father, Sir William Harvey, was granted the reversion for the office of Remembrancer of the First Fruits and Tithes.[13] Southampton was also given the prestigious title of Knight of the Garter in 1603, along with members of the royal circle – Prince Henry, the King of Denmark, and Ludovick, Duke of Lennox. The Earl of Mar, who was the prince's custodian, also received this honor, as did a new favorite, the Earl of Pembroke. Interestingly, of the two English Knights of the Garter appointed that year, Southampton was a key conspirator of the Essex Rebellion, and Pembroke had declared it a "wicked action" in a letter to Cecil only days after it had occurred.[14] Essex conspirator Sir Henry Neville was released along with Southampton, but he was given no honors or offices. Margot Heinemann observed that King James did not promote followers of Essex to important positions, "but found places in the separate household and mini-court of Queen Anne of Denmark, as well as that of Henry Prince of Wales."[15]

King James did, however, show immediate favor to Essex's eldest son and heir. When the king met the 12-year old Robert during his journey to London to claim the English throne, he kissed him and "loudly" declared him "the son of the most noble knight the English had ever begotten," wrote the Venetian ambassador.[16] The king appointed Robert to hold the sword in his coronation procession, restored his title as the 3rd Earl of Essex, and named him as the companion of Prince Henry. The 3rd Earl's biographer, Vernon Snow, believed that these actions were calculated because the Essex Rebellion was "more closely related" to the succession question "than the official accounts indicated." Snow concluded that the 3rd Earl was so treated to "repay a political debt" and "to appease the masses who had idolized" the 2nd Earl of Essex and his former supporters. When the 3rd Earl married, at age 15, the king's wedding gift was £1,000 in gold and silver. But despite this outward favor, in 1610, during an argument on the tennis court, Prince Henry called the 3rd Earl "the son of a traitor." Surely such a remark must have reflected the sentiments of those who influenced him – his father, the king, and those in the court. The 3rd Earl responded by slamming his racquet on the prince, which drew blood. The 3rd Earl was not punished – in fact, later the same year, the king granted him a sum of £3,000, based upon a claim that his father had placed with the late queen.[17]

James's letter of pardon for the Earl of Southampton (April 5, 1603) made no mention of martyrdom or even gratitude to him for support of any kind. The release occurred because Queen Elizabeth "was moved to exempt [him] from the stroke of justice," states the pardon, and because the Tower was an uncomfortable place.

> Although we are now resolved, as well in regard of the great and honest affection borne unto us by the Earl of Southampton as in respect of his good parts enabling him for the service of us, and the state, to extend our grace and favor towards him, whom we perceive also the late Queen our sister, notwithstanding his fault towards her, was moved to exempt from the stroke of justice ... Because the place [Tower] is unwholesome and dolorous to him to whose body and mind we would give present comfort, intending unto him much further grace and favor, we have written to the Lieutenant of the Tower to deliver him out of prison ...[18]

The king's actions throughout his English reign also did not reflect one who considered Southampton his martyr, hero or even ally. Outside of the honors and the perks, James was reluctant to give Southampton any real power, and regarded him with suspicion. James confined or imprisoned Southampton on three occasions, the first one shortly after his release from the Tower. On July 3, 1603, it was reported that Southampton and Lord Grey "dared, and belied one another,"[19] and "renewed old quarrels" about the Essex Rebellion in the presence of Queen Anne.

> The Queen bade them remember where they were, and soon after sent them to their lodgings, to which they were committed with guards upon them. The next day they were brought out and heard before the Council, and condemned to the Tower.[20]

Why would Southampton be so quickly returned to the Tower for a mere quarrel – a man who, within the span of three months, was released from prison by a special pardon from the king, granted restitution to his title and property, and awarded the highest honor in the land? His second imprisonment occurred one year later. Southampton and four others (including former Essex supporters, Lord Henry Danvers and Sir Henry Neville) were put into the Tower late in the evening of June 24, 1604. Southampton was interrogated and his papers were seized. Not recorded in the English state papers, the incident was separately reported by two different ambassadors. Historians still do not know the cause. Southampton's biographer, G.P.V. Akrigg, summarized the French ambassador's report: "James had gone into a complete panic and could not sleep that night even though he had a guard of his Scots posted around his quarters. Presumably to protect his heir, he sent orders to Prince Henry that he must not stir out of his chamber."[21] For some reason, King James suddenly felt threatened by Southampton and former Essex supporters, and feared for his heir's safety. Evidently, he felt that Southampton was plotting regicide; one wonders who he thought would be his replacement? Southampton and the others were released the next day, and the following month the king gifted him four properties in four counties. Akrigg viewed it as compensation "for the humiliation and shock"[22] from this incident, but six months later another disturbing event would occur. In January 1605, John Chamberlain reported that "above two hundredth pounds worth of popish books" were taken out of Southampton House "and burned in Paul's Churchyard";[23] Southampton had only recently resettled there. But all was well again by March 1605, when the king stood as godfather to Southampton's newborn son, James, who was baptized in the Chapel Royal. The subsequent years, however, proved disappointing for Southampton. The king appointed others to offices he was qualified for and military commands in Europe were denied him. It was later in his reign (1617) when James promised Southampton a seat on his Privy Council, but it took him two years to fulfill it (in contrast, the Earl of Pembroke, who had denounced the Essex Rebellion within days of its occurrence, was appointed to the Privy Council in 1611). Southampton's third imprisonment by James, a ten-week confinement at his home, occurred while he was a privy councilor (1621). Among the charges against him was that he was trying to undermine the king's authority in Parliament, and that he was conspiring with the exiled King and Queen of Bohemia (the latter was James's daughter, Princess Elizabeth).[24] In 1624, Southampton was authorized to command an army in the Netherlands to regain lands lost to Spain, a commission that perhaps not coincidentally resulted in his death.

James's ambivalent feelings about the Earl of Essex, and his constant suspicion of the Earl of Southampton during his reign makes it highly doubtful that he ever considered either earl "his martyr." Perhaps it was a public relations tactic to leak the "martyr" remark since Essex's popularity endured after his death. It may have also served as an excuse for Southampton's release, and subsequent honors and benefits that perhaps were given in exchange for his renouncing any claim to the throne. James's disfavor of Southampton – multiple imprisonments and denying him political power for years – can then be interpreted as his fear that "prince" Southampton would one day try to take the throne away from him or his heir, as he and Essex had tried to do with Queen Elizabeth. There is no doubt that James *indirectly* benefited by the Essex Rebellion because it destroyed Essex, who apparently wanted the throne for himself or Southampton. The Essex Rebellion narrowed the field of potential successors, so Essex could certainly be called his martyr *after the fact*. James was insecure about his English throne from the start. He took his time coming to London because he was not sure how his new subjects would receive him. On his coronation day, James created about 450 knights, and within his first year in power, nearly one thousand in total.[25] The true reason of James's generosity to Southampton – compensation for not getting the Crown – could not be publicly acknowledged.

Southampton Published *SHAKE-SPEARE'S SONNETS*

Five years into the reign of James I, Southampton had the king's favor, attending him at most major events, and hosting him at his country home, but his only political advancements were two minor posts: Captain of the Isle of Wight, and a lieutenancy (shared with the Earl of Devonshire) of the county and town of Southampton and city of Winchester.[26] His appointment as the queen's councilor was practically insignificant. Conversely, Sir Robert Cecil's positions of Principal Secretary and Master of the Court of Wards during Elizabeth's reign were retained, and, in addition, he was appointed the Lord Treasurer on May 6, 1608. This must have been viewed as an alarming and appalling consolidation of power by courtiers such as Southampton and members of the Privy Council. (Cecil was also created Baron Essendon in 1603, Viscount Cranborne in 1604, the Earl of Salisbury in 1605, and Knight of the Garter in 1606.) At Christmas-time, 1608, a strange power play occurred while the king was on progress. Prince Henry ordered Southampton and the Earl of Pembroke to vacate their lodgings so he could be situated closer to his father. Such an order coming from a 14-year-old prince did not sit well with the two elder earls. When they refused to leave, Prince Henry forced them out with his attendants. This action may have soured the Christmas spirit at court. One observer wrote it was "a dull and heavy Christmas hitherto (like the weather), no manner of delight or lightsome news: only there have been plays at court."[27] This latest insult to Southampton, and made by a child, compounded with two earlier imprisonments on no recorded charges, and the burning of his library, may have inspired a backlash.

With this previous history in mind, one can take a better view of the emergence of *SHAKE-SPEARE'S SONNETS,* registered for publication on May 20, 1609. The book's dedication, signed by publisher Thomas Thorpe, described "Mr W.H." as "the only begetter" of the sonnets:

> To the only begetter of <u>these ensuing sonnets</u> Mr W.H. <u>all happiness</u> and that eternity promised by our ever-living poet <u>wisheth</u> the <u>well-wishing adventurer</u> in setting forth. T.T.

Begetter can mean inspirer, and it can mean source, but it appears that both definitions were intended. The line, "and that eternity promised by our ever-living poet," connects "Mr W.H." with the Fair Youth of the sonnets. It was only the Fair Youth whom the great author believed would be eternized in his sonnets, terming them as his "monument" to him. The Fair Youth certainly inspired the sonnets. As over 75 percent concern him, one can justly surmise that he owned a manuscript copy. The great author even testified that "this line," i.e., his sonnets, were in the Fair Youth's possession:

> My life hath in this line some interest,
> Which for memorial still with thee shall stay ...
>
> The worth of that, is that which it contains,
> And that is this, and this with thee remains.   [Sonnet 74]

The great author also imagined the Fair Youth reading the sonnets after his death: "And shalt by fortune once more resurvey: /These poor rude lines of thy deceased Lover ... " (Sonnet 32). As detailed in the last chapter, evidence that Henry Wriothesley, 3rd Earl of Southampton, was the "Fair Youth" is overwhelming. What has prevented the experts' conclusive identification of Southampton with "Mr W.H." is the reversal of his initials, and the title, "Master," which would have been inappropriate for an earl. A light disguise such as this may have been necessary because of the implication in the sonnets that the Fair Youth was Queen Elizabeth's child, and "begetter" could be read as the source of the manuscript. The reversal of initials in print was not unprecedented.[28] The reemergence of *Willobie His Avisa* in 1609 (after a four-year lapse) clinches the identity of Southampton with "Mr W.H." because this work had lampooned Shakespeare and Southampton in the context of the sonnets. The *Willobie* publisher had apparently associated "Mr W.H." with "H.W." the young friend of "W.S.," in the book, and thought the public would too. The other candidate for "Mr W.H." is William Herbert, 3rd Earl of Pembroke, whose initials matched perfectly and who was one of the First Folio dedicatees. If the dedication were meant to be straightforward and without disguise, however, then Thorpe would not have addressed Pembroke as simply "Master" but as "My lord," befitting his noble title. Pembroke's portraits also depict a man with dark, rather than fair, hair color. A third candidate put forward as "Mr W.H." is publisher William Hall. As begetting manuscripts was Hall's business, it is a reasonable identification, but it is not reasonable to assume that Hall was the Fair Youth, the recipient of "that eternity promised" by the great author, when a relationship of any kind between Hall and Shakespeare has yet to be established.

It is largely unknown that the Earl of Southampton was associated with Thomas Thorpe in a professional capacity before, and after, *SHAKE-SPEARE'S SONNETS* was published. In 1604, Southampton was the dedicatee of a combined volume of two works written by Thomas Wright, one of which, *A Succinct Philosophical Declaration of the Nature of Climacterical Years, Occasioned by the Death of Queen Elizabeth*, was published by Thorpe.[29] Evidently, Southampton sponsored the volume. In 1616, Thorpe published *The Praise of King Richard the Third* by Sir William Cornwallis.[30] It was the first printed edition, but manuscript versions had circulated earlier. The particular manuscript that Thorpe used predated the Essex Rebellion. It contained revisions not original to Cornwallis's manuscript that put Richard III in a negative light. The person responsible for this altered version was "Hen. W.," the person who signed the manuscript's dedication letter to Sir Henry Neville.

> I am bold to adventure to your honor's view this small portion of my private Labors, as an earnest penny of my love, being a mere Paradox in praise of a most blameworthy, and condemned prince king Richard the third ... [31]

"Hen. W." was Southampton, suggested editors J.A. Ramsden and A.N. Kincaid, and he used Cornwallis's work "for his own political purposes,"[32] i.e., to persuade Neville to join the Essex faction against Sir Robert Cecil. As previously stated, the public associated Cecil with Richard III, the hunchbacked tyrant, and Neville was his kinsman. Both Cecil and Cornwallis were deceased when this manuscript was printed. The dedication letter by "Hen. W." was not included, and Thorpe did not credit Cornwallis. Southampton's open patronage of one work published by Thorpe, and his being the evident supplier of the manuscript of another work published by Thorpe, strengthens his case as the source, the begetter, of *SHAKE-SPEARE'S SONNETS*.

The Dedication

The dedication of *SONNETS* is hardly easy to understand, especially the line after Mr W.H. is wished happiness and eternity: "wisheth the well-wishing adventurer in setting forth." It is not clear who is wishing the adventurer, or what he is wishing him; it seems that a word is missing after "adventurer." And *who* is the adventurer? The OED interprets the adventurer in this dedication as "Mr W.H.," that he was a commercial speculator about to take a trip or make an investment, but this is a mere guess. As the reader of the dedication is also someone who is about to read the sonnets, it is logical to equate the reader with the "adventurer," and to define him as one "who seeks adventure or engages in hazardous enterprise" (OED). The dedication would then be hinting to the reader that the sonnets contain an important, and possibly dangerous, hidden meaning, and he is being wished "luck" – perhaps the missing word – with understanding it, or perhaps for even holding a copy of it. And oddly, the adventurer is described as well-wishing: a person about to take an adventure is usually the one who is wished well. A notable example is contained in the pamphlet, *A Good Speed to Virginia* (1609). Author Robert Gray wrote a prefatory letter to the Council of Virginia, whom he described as "adventurers," and wished them well in their enterprise to colonize Virginia.

> To the Right Noble and Honorable Earls, Barons and Lords, and to the Right Worshipful Knights, Merchants and Gentlemen, Adventurers for the plantation of *Virginia*, all happy and prosperous success, which may either augment your glory, or increase your wealth, or purchase your eternity ...
>
> Your Honors and Worships in all affectionate well wishing, R.G.

Did Thomas Thorpe actually write the dedication of *SONNETS*? There is evidence that other writers were echoing portions of it before it was published. Robert Gray, as noted above, used the words "adventurer," "well wishing," "all happy" and "eternity," in the address and signature of his preface letter. The letter was dated April 28, 1609, which was about three weeks before *SONNETS* was registered. After the address, Gray opened his letter, "Time the devourer of his own brood consumes both man and his memory." This line was directly based on lines in Shakespeare's then unpublished Sonnet 19: "Devouring time blunt thou the Lion's paws, /And make the earth devour her own sweet brood ... " Much earlier echoes of the dedication of *SONNETS* occurred in other works. *Saint Peter's Complaint* by Robert Southwell had been circulating in manuscript no later than 1591.[33] In his prefatory verses, Southwell, a Jesuit, complained that most poets of the time were writing upon classical themes rather than upon Christian ones. In the following excerpt, he seemed to be reacting to Shakespeare's "pagan" poem, *Venus and Adonis*, at least two years before it was printed.

> Still finest wits are 'stilling [distilling] Venus' rose,
> In Paynim [pagan] toys the sweetest veins are spent;

> To Christian works few have their talents lent.

Saint Peter's Complaint was written in the same meter as *Venus and Adonis*,[34] and Shakespeare could certainly be counted among "finest wits" that compose in "sweetest veins." Southwell was alluding to Shakespeare. A few lines later is a striking echo of the SONNETS' dedication phrase, "wisheth the well-wishing adventurer":

> Favor my <u>wish, well-wishing</u> works no ill;

Peter Milward wrote that with this phrase Southwell was "foreshadowing" the dedication of SONNETS about seventeen years before it was printed.[35] Michael Drayton apparently answered Southwell's plea for Christian poetry with *The Harmony of the Church* (1591). Drayton employed the word "well-wisher" in the dedication letter to Lady Jane Devoreux of Merivale (dated Feb. 10, 1591).

> Then (good Lady) myself, as an admirer of your many virtues, and a <u>well-wisher</u> unto your <u>happy and</u> desired estate, do here present the fruits of my labors ...

The great author used "wish" twice in one line of his dedication letter to the Earl of Southampton in *Venus and Adonis* (1593). The word "adventured" showed up in the dedication letter to the Countess of Shrewsbury in Thomas Lodge's sonnet cycle, *Phillis* (1593). The word also appeared in John Trussell's work, *The First Rape of Fair Helen* (1595), in a prefatory poem titled "Sonnet" that was almost certainly addressed to Shakespeare (Chapter 15). The phrase, "these ensuing sonnets," occurred in the letter to readers in Henry Constable's sonnet sequence, *Diana*, in 1592. And "All happiness" in the dedication of SONNETS was a phrase the great author used in his dedication letter to Southampton in *Lucrece* (1594). These seven examples were either printed or circulated in manuscript between circa 1591 and 1595 and all occurred in the preface or dedication of a poetry work. As some of Shakespeare's sonnets were circulating in manuscript circa 1590 and thereafter (Chapter 4), it is conceivable that a dedication page written by the great author had accompanied it. These readers – his "private friends," as Meres described them – more than likely were "well-wishers" or supporters of the Fair Youth-Southampton, thus the "well-wishing adventurer." The dedication page of SONNETS is actually a combination of a dedication to Mr W.H. and a note to the reader (the adventurer). Thorpe evidently merged two separate prefatory pieces into one. The author's initials (or name), usually present in such pieces, were lost in the process – with Thorpe replacing them with his own. The original dedication page may have read: "To the only begetter of these ensuing sonnets, Mr. W.H., all happiness and that eternity promised. W.S." The original note to the reader-adventurer may have read, "W.S. wisheth [well?] the well-wishing adventurer in setting forth." As the great author was dead when SONNETS was printed, Thorpe may have inserted "our ever-living poet" between the two pieces.

The cumulative evidence suggests that the sonnets of Shakespeare were circulating privately circa 1590, and with a dedication and note to the reader worded very close to what was later printed; it suggests that Southampton was Mr W.H., and that he authorized Thorpe to publish his copy of the sonnets after the great author's death. Why would Southampton wish to publish Shakespeare's sonnets, and why in 1609? In light of his position in late 1608, this action may have been specifically directed to King James and his son to remind them of his royal blood. The French ambassador to England, the Comte de Beaumont, had observed that King James's popularity, especially among the nobility, started to wane not long after his coronation.[36] Perhaps Southampton was still eyeing the throne and wished to enlighten the public of his true status, or reaffirm it to those who already knew. Southampton was no stranger to taking risks.

Thomas Thorpe must have anticipated big sales of SONNETS because he distributed the book through two different vendors, yet the world received these incomparable verses with utter silence. Those in the English literary set, however, considered SONNETS "the supreme achievement in contemporary poetry," according to Paul Morgan,[37] within five years of its release. Morgan's statement was based upon a handwritten inscription contained in one copy of Lope de Vega's sonnets, *Rimas* (1613 edition), now at Balliol College, Oxford.

> Knowing that Mr Mab: was to send you this Book of sonnets, which with Spaniards here is accounted of [esteemed or valued] their Lope de Vega as in England we should of our: Will Shakespeare. I could not but insert thus much to you, that if you like him not, you must never never read Spanish Poet.

The English *should* value the sonnets of Shakespeare, wrote Leonard Digges to Will Baker, as much as the Spanish value the sonnets of De Vega, which was very high. Digges added that if Baker did not like *Rimas* by De Vega – who was one of Spain's most admired poet-playwrights at that time – then there would be no point of him reading any Spanish poetry. Digges, therefore, had a very high assessment of the sonnets of Shakespeare. "Mr Mab" was James Mabbe, who later wrote a verse, like Digges, for the First Folio's preface. Although the English did not openly express it, they *did* value Shakespeare's sonnets – many copied down their favorite pieces. About twenty-five manuscript versions of individual Shakespeare sonnets have survived, some dating to the 1660s.[38] The contradiction of readers' favor of Shakespeare's sonnets and muted commentary about them after they were printed suggests that the book was suppressed, despite the lack of official action in the record. An extraordinary prediction made about Shakespeare play publication in 1609 supports this view. An anonymous letter to the reader was inserted in the second issue of Shakespeare's play, *Troilus and Cressida*. It predicted a coming shortage of printed Shakespeare plays by the "wills" of the "grand possessors." The first issue of the play was released after January 28, the registration date. The second issue more than likely was released later in the year, *after* the release of SHAKE-SPEARE'S SONNETS (the first surviving record of purchase was in June 1609). Something important involving Shakespeare must have happened that year to inspire such an unusual warning. It is notable that the printer of SONNETS, George Eld, also printed both issues of *Troilus and Cressida*. As an interested party, perhaps it was Eld who had written the anonymous letter to the reader, titled, "A never writer, to an ever reader. News." Eld was a printer, not a writer, thus "A never writer." Whoever he was, his warning was on the mark because no Shakespeare play or poem was issued – or issued openly – in 1610. But it was probably not the "grand possessor's wills" that caused it, it was fear among publishers. They knew that the sonnets clearly identified the great author with a certain nobleman, and that they revealed the Fair Youth was his son by Queen Elizabeth. The publication of SONNETS suddenly politicized Shakespeare.

Charles Fitzgeffrey evidently believed that Shakespeare's sonnets were dangerous before they were printed. In the year of the Essex Rebellion (1601), he published several verses in Latin praising the top writers of the day. Shakespeare's name was absent, but Mark Anderson (*Shakespeare By Another Name*) suggested that two verses addressed to "Bardum" or bard were meant for him. One line translates as, "You have been cautious, saying, 'I will publish verses after my death,'" and another line, "Let the letter never be handed over, O Bard, be silent."[39] Anderson posited that "verses" and "the letter" referred to Shakespeare's unpublished sonnets. If one accepts Fitzgeffrey as a witness, then the great author intended his sonnets to be published after his death – his expectation that they would become immortal (sonnets 63 and 81, for example) assumes it. Fitzgeffrey's warning to the great author may have been sparked after reading *Love's Martyr*, which was printed the same year.

Thorpe Offended the "Grand Possessors"?

Thomas Thorpe's career took a downward turn immediately after SHAKE-SPEARE'S SONNETS was published, which also suggests the work was suppressed. Thorpe had successfully published poetry and drama between 1600 and 1609, including works by acclaimed writers such as Christopher Marlowe. He published Ben Jonson's masques and plays for four straight years (1605 to 1608). Thorpe, however, transferred his rights to Jonson's two plays, *Sejanus* and *Volpone*, to another publisher in October 1610, and their association ended.[40] It is possible that Jonson's allegiance to the Earl of Pembroke may have caused his professional break from Thorpe. The warning letter in the 1609 edition of *Troilus and Cressida* made it clear that the grand possessors of Shakespeare's works were not happy that year, undoubtedly because of SONNETS, and evidence points to Pembroke as one of them (Chapter 9). SONNETS was Thorpe's only publication in 1609, yet early that year he had registered *The Discovery of a New World* by Joseph Hall. The work was printed in 1609, but not by Thorpe: he evidently transferred it to his friend, Edward Blount, and W. Barrett, who were named as publishers on the title page. The book featured a fawning dedication letter to its patron, the Earl of Pembroke, by the work's translator, John Healey.

Thorpe's first publication after SONNETS was probably *Epictetus, His Manual,* in 1610, another translation by Healey. Thorpe's name was on the title page as publisher, but a variant edition dated the same year lists Blount and Barrett as the publishers. Both editions featured a dedication letter to John Florio written by Thorpe in which he reveals his unfortunate state in 1610.[41] Thorpe characterizes himself as "distressed Sostratus" and as Florio's "poor friend," and that Florio was the "more fortunate Arius." Thorpe was alluding to the story of Sostratus (also known as Philostratus), who had angered Augustus Caesar; a ragged Sostratus badgered his friend, Arius, a philosopher much esteemed by Caesar, to be the mediator between them to obtain his pardon.

> Sir, as distressed *Sostratus* spake to more fortunate *Arius*, to make him his mediator to *Augustus*, "The learned love the learned, if they be rightly learned": So this your poor friend though he have found much of you, yet doth still follow you for as much more: that as his *Maecenas* you would write to *Augustus* ... [quotation marks added]

Thorpe then mentions in his letter that it was Florio who had "procured" the patronage of Healey's *The Discovery* ("his apprentice's essay"), and hoped he would get the same patron for the present work. As noted above, that patron was the Earl of Pembroke.

> ... For his apprentice's essay you [Florio] procured (God thank you) an impregnable protection: He now prays the same Patron (most worthy of all praise) for his journeyman's Masterpiece:

Pembroke evidently chose not to patronize this work (*Epictetus, His Manual*), which was initially Thorpe's property. Knowing that Pembroke was the subtext of Thorpe's dedication letter to Florio, it appears that a "distressed" and "poor" Thorpe-Sostratus was also hoping that "fortunate" Florio-Arius would mediate on his behalf to obtain a pardon from Pembroke-Augustus. For what did Thorpe need a pardon? Since Thorpe's fortunes fell soon after *SONNETS*, this work may have angered "grand possessor" Pembroke, a man influential enough to block sponsorship or protection of Thorpe's publications. Thorpe's career did not end after 1609, but Clinton Heylin suggests that Thorpe's transfers of literary property in 1609-10 may have been due to financial difficulty, that *SONNETS* "predicated the collapse of Thorpe's publishing dreams..."[42] Interestingly, in 1610, Thorpe dedicated *St. Augustine, Of the City of God*, another Healey translation, to Pembroke, and wrote a servile dedication letter to him. Thorpe, again characterizing himself as "poor," figuratively lays the book at Pembroke's feet.

> Wherefore his legacy laid at your Honor's feet, is rather here delivered to your Honor's humbly thrice-kissed hands by his poor delegate. Your lordship's true-devoted, Th. Th.

It appears that Thorpe did more than express his humility to please Pembroke. In 1612, Thorpe published *A Funeral Elegy in Memory of the Late Virtuous Master William Peter of Whipton near Exeter*. Peter was murdered on January 25, 1612, at age thirty. The author's initials, "W.S.," were prominently featured on the title page. The dedication letter to Peter's brother, also signed "W.S.," was especially reminiscent of Shakespeare's dedication letter to the Earl of Southampton in *The Rape of Lucrece*. The letter by W.S. begins, "The love I bore to your brother," and Shakespeare's letter to Southampton begins, "The love I dedicate to your Lordship..." W.S. wrote "yet whatsoever is here done, is done to him," and Shakespeare wrote, "What I have done is yours, what I have to do is yours..." W.S. said his elegy to Peter was "this last duty of a friend" and Shakespeare signed his letter to Southampton "in all duty." Like *SONNETS*, George Eld was *Elegy*'s printer. Such similarities would encourage the reader to believe that William Shakespeare wrote *Elegy* for his late friend, William Peter. Thorpe's name was not on the title page, but he registered the work for publication. Recent scholarship by Richard Kennedy and others strongly suggests that John Ford was the elegy's true author, so why were false initials given? In my opinion, Thorpe was trying to give the impression that Shakespeare was still alive in 1612, to counter that given in the dedication of *SONNETS* ("our ever-living poet"), and more importantly, it *would give the impression that William Peter was the Fair Youth, and not Southampton*. William Peter as the Fair Youth would decontextualize – and depoliticize – Shakespeare's sonnets because Peter was not a nobleman; the theme of the sonnets, therefore, would not involve the succession. In 1616,

Thorpe dedicated another book to Pembroke with another over-humble dedication letter. The book was the second edition of *Epictetus His Manual*, with Edward Blount listed as publisher. Thorpe's letter contained six instances of "Your Lordship" and twice craved Pembroke's pardon for dedicating the work to him.

> ... pardon my presumption, great Lord, from so mean a man, to so great a person: I could not without some impiety present it to any other ... in the hope of this honorable pardon and acceptance I will ever rest your lordship's humble devoted, T. Th.

After 1616, Thorpe's publishing activities slowed considerably. By late 1623 he was receiving money out of the "poor fund" of the Stationers' Company (*DNB*); it continued for two years. Considering his financial situation at this time, it is odd that Thorpe did not reprint the sonnets, or sell them to another. His publishing career was over by 1625. On December 3, 1635, government papers noted that Thomas Thorpe was granted an "almsroom" in the hospital of Ewelme.[43] If this man was Thorpe the publisher, then the government was keeping its eyes on him.

Thirty-one years passed before the sonnets of Shakespeare were printed a second time. Scholars have confirmed that John Benson's text of the sonnets (1640) almost mirrored that in Thomas Thorpe's edition, but Benson did everything he could to distinguish – or disguise – his edition from Thorpe's. It started with the book's small size (octavo, half the size of Thorpe's quarto), and with the title, *POEMS: WRITTEN BY WIL. SHAKE-SPEARE. Gent.* Benson never used the word "sonnets," they were "Shakespeare's Poems," the phrase he used to register the work.[44] Benson's edition featured all but eight of the sonnets contained in Thorpe's edition, and were mixed with Shakespeare's poems from *The Passionate Pilgrim* (Thomas Heywood's verses from the 1612 edition were also included but not mixed with Shakespeare's). Shakespeare's two poems in *Love's Martyr* were also reprinted there for the first time, as well as *A Lover's Complaint*. Only about thirty sonnets were printed separately – the rest were clumped together in groups of two to five and their order was rearranged. And for each individual sonnet or sonnet grouping Benson added titles, as if the great author was ruminating on various themes instead of expressing his feelings for specific people. Benson changed pronouns from he to she in some sonnets giving the impression that they were addressed to a woman instead of a man (the Fair Youth). One feature that Benson had adopted from Thorpe's edition was printing "Shakespeare" in all capitals, and inserting a hyphen, which hinted that the name was an alias. Benson's edition also included an altered version of Droeshout's engraving of Shakespeare and questioned its veracity, as noted in Chapter 11.

Unlike Thorpe in his edition of the sonnets, Benson did not include a dedication letter, and made no allusion to "Mr W.H.," the "begetter" of SONNETS. Instead he boldly stated in the first line, with a large and decorated capital I, that the book was his own production: "I here presume ... "

> To the Reader.
>
> I here presume (under favor) to present to your view, some excellent and sweetly composed Poems, of Master *William Shakespeare*, Which in themselves appear of the same purity, the Author himself then living avouched; they had not the fortune by reason of their Infancy in his death, to have the due accommodation of proportionable glory, with the rest of his ever-living Works, yet the lines of themselves will afford you a more authentic approbation [proof] than my assurance any way can, to invite your allowance [approval]; In your perusal ...

Benson's letter to the reader resembled the letters of Heminges and Condell in the First Folio's preface. Speaking of Shakespeare's "poems," really meaning the sonnets, Benson wrote that the great author had "avouched" the "purity" or integrity of the enclosed text. Heminges and Condell had similarly claimed the Folio version of the plays were the author's "true original copies," distinguished from the "stol'n and surreptitious" versions. Benson claimed the great author had died before he had a chance to get the poems-sonnets properly printed ("due accommodation"), and likened them to orphaned children, as Heminges and Condell had said about the plays in the Folio. And like the Folio, both points were questionable or false. Thorpe had long ago taken care of the "orphaned" sonnets with his 1609 edition. Although never mentioning Thorpe's edition, Benson seemed to imply its existence – he had no reason to avouch purity unless another less pure version preceded it. Benson's phrase, "his ever-living works," directly recalls Thorpe's reference to "our ever-living poet" in the dedication of SONNETS, as does the phrase "these ensuing lines" (see below) with "these ensuing sonnets."[45]

> In your perusal you shall find them *Serene*, clear and elegantly plain, such gentle strains as shall recreate and not perplex your brain, no intricate or cloudy stuff to puzzle intellect, but perfect eloquence; such as will raise your admiration to his praise: this assurance I know will be seconded by the sufficiency of <u>these ensuing Lines</u>; I have been somewhat solicitous to bring this forth to the perfect view of all men; and in so doing, glad to be serviceable for the continuance of glory to the deserved Author in these his Poems.   I.B.

Benson's letter to the reader featured the first printed commentary (post 1609) about Shakespeare's sonnets, but it was indirect – the "poems" are "excellent and sweetly composed" and "perfect eloquence." Benson also said they did not receive praise that was "proportionable" to their "glory." Benson served as another eyewitness (like Digges in his note to Will Baker) that the 1609 edition of the sonnets had lacked open public acclaim. Benson's final lines conveyed a sense of mission and "service" to the "deserved" great author and to "all men": to give the world Shakespeare's "poems," i.e., the sonnets. John Warren's poem in the preface added that Benson's "love" of Shakespeare inspired the publication (see Appendix H). Benson's edition did not mention the Earl of Southampton, the main subject of the sonnets, and excluded Shakespeare's openly dedicated poems to Southampton, *Venus and Adonis* and *Lucrece*, just like the First Folio had. It seems that Southampton was the problem for both the Folio and Benson's edition. Benson was evidently cautioning the reader not to delve into the meaning of the "poems" by claiming that they were clear and not puzzling or perplexing. This pretense, the obvious changes made to disguise Thorpe's edition, and a nod to the Stratford Man by printing the year of his death (as noted in Chapter 11), was perhaps the only way Benson could republish and preserve Shakespeare's sonnets. It suggests that the sonnets were still politically dangerous in 1640, even with the mask of the Stratford Man. What else could have been Benson's reason for disguising Thorpe's edition, when Thorpe had been dead for five years? Benson's fervent desire to preserve the "glorious" sonnets of Shakespeare outweighed the obvious risk he was taking by reprinting them; his publishing output did slow temporarily after this edition (for about six years). Benson did not reprint this edition, and the sonnets would not be seen in print again for seventy years.

After-Effects of *SONNETS*

King James's behavior after the publication of *SHAKE-SPEARE'S SONNETS* can be viewed as a peculiar combination of fear and favor to Southampton. On July 9, 1609, Southampton was ordered to receive £300 from the Crown's treasury to repair castles on the Isle of Wight, where he was captain. Southampton did not receive the money, so he wrote a letter in the same month to Sir Robert Cecil (now the Earl of Salisbury) saying he would advance the funds himself. Cecil had sent the money *but evidently not to Southampton.* This may have prompted Southampton's letter of October 7 saying it were "better that he should deal with the contractors himself."[46] On October 19, a warrant was issued to reimburse Southampton for the £300, but it again was not forthcoming (he finally received it on March 20, 1610).[47] Another incident occurred in August 1609, shortly before the king's yearly summer stay at Southampton's country home, Beaulieu. The king commanded an extra guard for the visit:

> twenty-four able and sufficient men, well furnished with bills, halberds, and other fit and convenient weapons, to guard his Majesty's person.[48]

The order was not directed to Southampton, who was the king's host, but to the mayor and aldermen of the city of Southampton. Charlotte Stopes wrote, "This was thought a very strange request and strangely couched."[49] Was it merely coincidence that after June 1609 until 1613, Southampton had no new books dedicated to him? If it was not his choice, then authors were not seeking his patronage at this time. There were no editions of *Venus and Adonis* dated 1603 to 1616, and *Lucrece* between 1608 and 1615. These two poems contained laudatory dedications to Southampton by William Shakespeare. *Venus and Adonis* was a very popular work and there were no problems with its publication until the eighth, ninth and tenth editions, which were falsely dated. As explained in Chapter 2, the printer of the eighth edition, Robert Raworth, had no publications dated 1609 or thereafter for twenty-five years. His press had been "suppressed" for printing *Venus and Adonis*. Considering the sensitive political climate surrounding Southampton in 1609, it is very likely that 1609 was the actual publishing date of the falsely dated editions. The authorities evidently did not tolerate praise of Southampton in print at this time. Yet in 1609 Southampton finally achieved a position of power: he was appointed a vice-admiral. Two years later, he was granted a £2,000 annuity from customs on sweet wines. *SONNETS* may have inspired this largess: James was apparently following a normal royal necessity of appeasing or paying off nobles in exchange for their loyalty. Sir John Salusbury, the dedicatee of the seemingly pro-Southampton work, *Love's Martyr*, also experienced trouble in 1609. His biographer, Carleton Brown, wrote that Salusbury "appears to have been harassed about this time by petty creditors and his enemies eagerly seized upon these embarrassments to discredit him to the King." Brown cited Salusbury's letter to Cecil, dated June 26, 1609, one month after *SHAKE-SPEARE'S SONNETS* was registered.

> I have been informed that some Adversaries of mine (to wreak their malice against me) have (of late) practiced to incense the King's most excellent majesty of some disobedience in me to processes in law upon some matters of suits for small debts, purposing thereby to procure his highness' indignation against me.[50]

Reasonable offers to these creditors were made, wrote Salusbury, "but nothing will be accepted." Salusbury, who was Queen Elizabeth I's officer of the body and who was knighted for his service during the Essex Rebellion, fully expected an appointment by the new king and pressed Cecil for it. But such an appointment never came. Perhaps the king and Cecil did not want any potential Southampton supporters in government positions. For a period in 1609, the Privy Council banned all public plays in London; it is believed that plague inspired the ban, but this was not mentioned in the order.[51]

On September 29, 1609, about four months after *SONNETS* was released, it was decided that a new parliamentary session (the fourth) would be set for February 9, 1610.[52] The theme of this session was evidently to reaffirm James as the undoubted sovereign of England and to enforce the loyalty of his subjects. Only days before the opening of this session, *A Book of Proclamations* was published and released by the king's official printer, Robert Barker. The book listed every proclamation of the king since the start of his English reign. Page one reprinted "A Proclamation, declaring the undoubted Right of our Sovereign Lord King James, to the Crown of the Realms of England, France and Ireland." The entire text of this March 24, 1603 document was included, and the upper half of page 3 displayed in large type the noblemen and high officers of Queen Elizabeth's government who had signed it. On February 17, 1610, at the House of Lords, Sir Robert Cecil (Earl of Salisbury) announced "the causes of calling this Parliament."[53] The first stated reason was to have Henry created the Crown Prince of Wales. Cecil had been in discussion with the 16-year-old prince about this as early as October 1609.[54] This was approved, and his investiture took place on June 4, 1610; at the ensuing banquet, the Earl of Southampton "acted as the prince's carver, to the pleasure of the king" (*DNB*). Some members had questioned the idea of holding the ceremony during parliament, noted Pauline Croft, during which time "all business was halted for a week." Croft added that the "pageantry at Westminster, which was followed at court by days of fireworks, masques and tilting, was deliberately designed to produce a surge of loyal affection towards the already popular young prince."[55] The second stated reason to call Parliament was to ask for more money for the royal household. Cecil said that the king and the prince would be at "great peril and danger if either of them should want means sufficient for their maintenance."[56] And significantly, very early into the session, a new Oath of Allegiance was proposed for adoption: not only Catholics were required to recognize the king's sovereignty by reciting an oath, *but now all peers and members of parliament would be required to do so*. It passed by the end of the session.[57] It is interesting to note that the earls of Montgomery and Southampton had a major altercation during a tennis match in April 1610, less than one year after the release of *SHAKE-SPEARE'S SON-*

NETS. They "flung their rackets" at each other and had intended to duel, but were stopped by the king.[58]

James used the parliament of 1610 to legally strengthen his and his successor's royal position, perhaps due to a perceived threat from the publication of *SONNETS*. Evidently, this was not enough. The work's underground success may have prompted James's supporters to find a way of permanently separating the Fair Youth's identity from Southampton: they wanted to erase any public "knowledge" about Southampton as the natural child of Queen Elizabeth to ensure a smooth succession for the next Stuart king. The royal dislodge could be accomplished by reassigning the great author's literary identity onto someone who was not a nobleman or a royal court insider. Enter the Stratford Man and the First Folio, where his identification with Shakespeare originated, sponsored by the brother earls, William and Philip Herbert. The opening pages overemphasized the idea that Shakespeare was the fellow or equal of common players. The sonnets and the Southampton-dedicated poems, *Venus and Adonis* and *Lucrece*, were purposely excluded from the Folio and Southampton was not mentioned. William Herbert, 3rd Earl of Pembroke received high favor from King James from the start of his English reign. Pembroke was immediately created a Knight of the Garter; later he was appointed Steward of the Duchy of Cornwall, Lord Warden of the Stanneries of Devon and Cornwall, and Lord Lieutenant of Cornwall, which, according to Michael Brennan, gave him "administrative and military power over a large part of the South-West of England."[59] In 1611, Pembroke became a member of the king's Privy Council. His brother, Philip Herbert, was appointed Gentleman of the king's Privy Chamber in 1603 and two years later was created Baron Herbert of Shurland and Earl of Montgomery; in 1608, he was made a Knight of the Garter, and he received "lavish" land grants from the king (*OED*). The Herbert brothers naturally wanted their high favor to continue with James's successor. As soon as he was appointed Lord Chamberlain in December 1615, Pembroke evidently forwarded his plans to control the identity of the great author in the public's mind. Ben Jonson was editing his own collected works at this time, and may have suggested to Pembroke that a similar edition of Shakespeare's plays would be the perfect vehicle to reinvent the great author's literary identity. Jonson knew the Stratford Man as early as 1598-1599, the years he wrote plays lampooning him and his father. Jonson was aware that the Stratford Man had served as a mask for printers that pirated Shakespeare's plays, and that the authorities had tolerated it. Jonson had inserted in his own collected works the new information that "William Shakespeare" acted in two of Jonson's plays. Preparation for the Shakespeare folio most likely began in the second half of 1616, after Jonson saw his own folio into print. Jonson was granted a pension from the Crown earlier that year. The printing of Shakespeare's folio probably began in late 1621, after taking approximately five years to prepare the text. Although this may seem like a long time, there were 36 plays to gather and edit *without the great author's originals*. The Folio was released in late 1623. King James died in March 1625, and his son, Charles I, succeeded him. The Earl of Pembroke carried the crown at his coronation.

Southampton Murdered?

The Earl of Southampton became a privy councilor in April 1619, but two years later, on June 15, 1621, the king wrote to the Privy Council that he "thought fit to restrain for some time the person of the Earl of Southampton."[60] He was placed under house arrest and not allowed to communicate with anyone for ten weeks. Interrogation records imply that the king and the royal favorite, the Duke of Buckingham, had suspected Southampton of raising discontent in Parliament. The Venetian ambassador reported the confinement in a letter, and described Southampton as

> a leading nobleman, very popular throughout the country, and is considered here to be almost the only person capable of commanding an army.[61]

There had been discussion in parliament about sending an army to the Netherlands to defend the Dutch against the Spanish. Southampton supported this action. When Parliament convened in November, Southampton was advised not to attend. The Venetian ambassador wrote, "Southampton and some others abstained from appearing for fear that they could not express their opinions safely."[62] By the summer of 1624, however, the political landscape had changed. Military action in the Netherlands was approved, and Southampton was sent there as a commander of an army. His eldest son, James, accompanied him on active duty. On November 5th, his son fell ill and died. Immediately, Southampton traveled with his son's body to the port of Bergen to sail home to England, but on November 10th, he too fell ill and died. One report of the cause of their deaths was "lethargy," and another, "fevers with convulsions."[63] A letter written by Southampton's servant, William Beeston, dated November 7, 1624, reported that Southampton was well until Dr. Samuel Turner administered to him a clyster, an enema.

> Since my Lord of Southampton's departure from Rosendael his Lordship both in his own apprehension & opinion of them about him & judgment of the physicians grew much better than he last was when he parted from your Lordship [3rd Earl of Essex] till this afternoon at 4 a clock, which immediately upon a clyster given him by Dr. Turner he fell heavy & sleepy & slept some 4 hours through

with much disquiet & troubled passions. After his awaking he fell
extremely ill & could not speak to any of us.[64]

There is no evidence of an investigation made regarding the sudden deaths of
the two Wriothesleys. Certainly the elder's death was suspicious since he took
an immediate turn for the worse after receiving the clyster, a known method
of giving poison. This was how Sir Thomas Overbury was murdered in 1613:
"At length by a poison'd Clister given him under pretense of curing him, he
was dispatch'd . . . "[65] King James's physician, George Eglisham, believed that
Buckingham, the royal favorite and de facto ruler of England at the time, was
behind Southampton's death. He printed a pamphlet in 1626 accusing him
of poisoning King James and the Marquess of Hamilton (both died in 1625
within weeks of each other, Hamilton was aged 36), and that Southampton's name was on Buckingham's hit list. The pamphlet, apparently printed
abroad, emerged while members of the House of Commons were airing their
grievances against Buckingham. Interestingly, Dr. Turner, a member of parliament, was among the most vocal. (Dr. Turner "probably" owed his parliament seat to the earls of Pembroke and Montgomery, according to the DNB.)
A private letter, dated May 2, 1626, discussed Eglisham's pamphlet.

> The Duke [of Buckingham] is surely an unhappy man, for here are
> books sent over from Bruxelles to some of the Lords from one Dr.
> Ecclestone [Eglisham], a physician to King James, but a papist, by
> which he chargeth the Duke that he absolutely and resolutely did
> poison the King, the Duke of Richmond, the Marquises of Ham-
> ilton, Southampton, and Dorset, and speaks of other lords that
> were to have been poisoned. This makes a hue and cry, the rather
> because Ecclestone [Eglisham] offers to come and prove it, if he may
> come and go safely.   [Nicholas Herman to the Earl of Middlesex][66]

Charles I abruptly dissolved this session of parliament to save Buckingham, and himself, further embarrassment. Buckingham was assassinated in
1628. He was so generally hated that his murderer, apparently influenced by
Eglisham, believed he was ridding England of a tyrant. Eglisham's accusations
about Buckingham as a multiple murderer resurfaced in a book printed in
1652 by Sir Edward Peyton, so this belief endured for many years.[67] Whether
or not Southampton and his son were poisoned by agents of Buckingham,
their deaths were politically expedient, if they indeed had royal blood. One
of Southampton's eulogists, Sir John Beaumont, also suspected foul play in
his death. In a poem, dated 1624, Beaumont expressed his belief that it was
not war that killed Southampton, but "treachery" by someone "close" to him.

But Death, who durst not meet him in the field,

In private by close treach'ry made him yield.[68]

Southampton and his son's death went completely unacknowledged by King James or the government, but it inspired numerous printed tributes by others. Not one of them, however, mentioned Southampton's association with one of England's greatest poets, Shakespeare, who little more than a year before had been honored by the publication of an extraordinary book of his collected plays. Yet their association was so well known that Shakespeare himself believed posterity would ask Southampton (as the Fair Youth) about him:

> Oh lest the world should task you to recite,
> What merit liv'd in me that you should love
> After my death (dear love) forget me quite ... [Sonnet 72]

Without mentioning Shakespeare, Francis Beale made an allusion to *Henry VI-Part 1* in his eulogy of Southampton and his son in *The Tears of the Isle of Wight* (1625).

> Naught is Immortal underneath the Sun,
> We all are subject to Death's restless date,
> We end our lives before they are begun,
> And mark'd in the Eternal Book of Fate.
> But for thy Self [Southampton], and Heir one thread was spun
> And cut: like *Talbot's* and his valiant Son.

In Shakespeare's play, "valiant" John Talbot dies in the arms of his father, Lord Talbot, after a battle. But Lord Talbot also was mortally injured, and expired after his son, uttering his final line, "Now my old arms are young *John Talbot's* grave." Beale had placed in the margin, "H.6.32.1454," or "Henry the Sixth, 32, 1454."[69] Beale's phrase, "death's restless date," sounds like a phrase in Shakespeare's Sonnet 30, "death's dateless night." In the same book, "Ar. Price" ended his poem to Southampton with the line, "And Phoenix-like, you burn, and die, and live," a possible allusion to *Love's Martyr*, which featured poems by Shakespeare. These three literary allusions were the closest that any contemporary made about Southampton's famous link to Shakespeare after their deaths. One month after Southampton died, his vacant seat on the king's Privy Council was granted to the Earl of Montgomery.

Conclusion

Coincident with the Earl of Southampton's debut at the royal court of Queen Elizabeth I (circa 1590), the sonnets of Shakespeare were circulated in manuscript. They featured praise of Southampton, "the Fair Youth," and celebrated him in royal imagery and language, serving as an unofficial announcement of his true status as a royal prince and possibly the queen's successor. Other writers followed suit by honoring Southampton in public and in print, and some expressed their belief that he was a prince. This belief evidently inspired his consideration for the high honor of Knight of the Garter at such a young age. To further promote and add prestige to the young "prince" Southampton, the great author, a nobleman, stepped outside of social custom by publishing two of his poems in 1593 and 1594. In order to dedicate them to Southampton with laudatory letters, the great author needed to employ a signature, thus the pen name, "William Shakespeare." (He had already been using this pen name by 1590-1591, as seen in the works of Edmund Spenser.) These poems, *Venus and Adonis* and *The Rape of Lucrece*, were highly regarded and he achieved his purpose. By this time many in the literary world already knew that "Shakespeare" was a nobleman's pen name and cryptically alluded to it, wanting to praise him openly but respecting the convention of anonymity for nobility that wrote poetry or were involved with the theater. In February 1601, Southampton involved himself in the disastrous Essex Rebellion, possibly to place the Earl of Essex, or himself, on the throne, or as the queen's regent. With Southampton's death sentence for his treason imminent, the great author was able to intervene and agreed to forever disassociate his real name with the Shakespeare works in exchange for Southampton's life and eventual freedom. The deal was made with the queen's principal secretary, Sir Robert Cecil, whom the public had come to associate with the corrupt king, Richard III, in Shakespeare's play; Cecil's father, Lord Burghley, was also satirized in *Hamlet* (as "double-hearted" Corambis), and possibly in other plays. Had it been publicly known after the great author's death that "William Shakespeare" was a noble courtier's pen name, then the allusions to the Cecil family in the plays would be unmistakable to the public and to posterity. Later the same year, "William Shake-speare" contributed two poems to *Love's Martyr*, a book by Robert Chester that made an allegorical plea to the queen to recognize Southampton as her natural issue and successor to the Tudor dynasty, which would otherwise end upon her death. Shakespeare's involvement with this book advertised his position on the succession, and his candidate was not the King of Scotland, who eventually did succeed Queen Elizabeth due to Cecil's efforts. Southampton was released immediately after the queen's death and the bargain was fulfilled. The king evidently deferred to kingmaker Cecil; otherwise, he would have had no reason to release Southampton, whom he evidently viewed as a constant threat to the succession. It is possible that it was not King James who released Southampton, but Queen Elizabeth herself as revealed in Shakespeare's Sonnet 126. She may have privately commanded that he be released at the time of her death.

As evidenced in Sonnet 107, the great author lived to see the release of Southampton from the Tower in 1603, and James's peaceful accession to the English throne. He was dead, however, when his sonnets were published in 1609. Whenever his death had occurred, no one either privately or publicly noted it. His high status should not have prevented literary eulogies at the time of his passing. The wholesale avoidance of such tributes for many years was most likely due to political fear – that anyone who openly praised "Shakespeare" or the great author's real name post *Love's Martyr*, and post James's succession, would be viewed as a Southampton supporter and thus a potential traitor. Other contributors to *Love's Martyr* – George Chapman, John Marston and Ben Jonson – were arrested in 1605 for writing a play deemed offensive to the Crown, perhaps already having been suspected as unsympathetic to the new king. Mutilation was their intended punishment but it was not carried out. This incident could indicate that the great author was already dead, and that these writers no longer had his protection. The play in question, *Eastward Ho*, included several allusions to Shakespeare's *Hamlet*. Its writers "seem to have gone out of their way to call attention to their borrowings" from Shakespeare's play, noted editor Richard Horwich.[70] The play featured a minor character named Hamlet that was introduced in Act 3, Scene 2; in the same scene, Gertrude, another character name from *Hamlet*, sings this song:

> His <u>head</u> as <u>white as</u> milk,
> <u>All flaxen was his</u> hair;
> But now <u>he is dead</u>,
> And laid in his <u>bed</u>,
> <u>And never will come again</u>.
>
> <u>God be</u> at your labor.

The above song resembles the one that mad Ophelia sang about her dead father in *Hamlet* (4.5.189-200):

> <u>And will he not come again?</u>
> <u>And will he not come again?</u>
> No, no, <u>he is dead</u>,
> Go to thy death-<u>bed</u>,
> <u>never will come again</u>.
> His beard was <u>white as</u> snow,
> <u>All flaxen was his poll</u> [head];
> He is gone, he is gone,
> And we cast away moan;
> God ha' mercy on his soul!

And of all Christian souls, I pray God. <u>God be</u> wi' you!

As Gertrude's song in *Eastward Ho* was unrelated to the plot, it may have been a veiled memorial to the great author. Touchstone is another character in *Eastward Ho*. Although his trade is jewelry, Touchstone's apprentices are more concerned about crafting poetry lines. "Touchstone," his surname, is a verb and noun construct like "Shake-speare," and his first name is William. Touchstone was also the name of the courtier-clown in *As You Like It* who had a meaningful encounter with William of the Forest of Arden, who represented the Stratford Man. *Eastward Ho* also alluded to Shakespeare's *The Merry Wives of Windsor, Henry IV-Part 2*, and *Richard III*.[71]

The 1609 publication of SHAKE-SPEARE'S SONNETS, in which the Earl of Southampton was revealed through imagery as the child of Queen Elizabeth and the nobleman-great author, was viewed by those in power as a potential threat to King James and the Stuart line. A coming scarcity of Shakespeare printing by the "wills" of the "grand possessors," one of them being the Earl of Pembroke, was predicted that same year. As a precaution, Pembroke employed Ben Jonson to control public awareness of the great author in a book of his collected plays, a "deceit bred by necessity" (*Henry VI-Part 3*). The preface of this book, now called the First Folio, transformed "Shakespeare" from a nobleman author using a pen name into a common player from Stratford-upon-Avon born with that name – a man with no known ties to Southampton. Deliberately excluded from the Folio was Southampton's name and the three Shakespeare poetry works dedicated to him. One may ask, if the Folio's preface was a fraud, then why did the earls of Pembroke and Montgomery allow their names to be so openly emblazoned in it? Why not keep their involvement secret? The answer could be that in order to make their obliteration of Southampton's connection with Shakespeare complete, they needed to reinvent his past patronage. The 1640 line from *Wit's Recreations*, "*Shake-speare* we must be silent in thy praise," implied that something about Shakespeare was political. Only politics could impose a general public silence about England's most celebrated poet-playwright twenty-four years after his supposed death. As the Pembroke-sponsored Folio contained the Shakespeare plays, one can infer that the plays were not problematic (Sir Robert Cecil had been dead eleven years when the Folio was published) – it was the *excluded works* dedicated to Southampton that were problematic. Southampton was active and influential in politics, was popular, and held the king's suspicion throughout his reign; the unpopular Duke of Buckingham, the royal favorite, may have been behind Southampton's death in November 1624. King James died four months later, and Prince Charles's succession went smoothly. Royal favor for the Herbert brothers continued, which was memorialized in an unusual painting featuring the brother earls alongside the monarch and his queen (Plate 27).

The disembodiment of the great author with his vast literary output, including multiple masterpieces, was intertwined with the succession to the crown of England. The Stratford Man profited from the Shakespeare plays by providing a face for those who pirated them, and as an investor in theaters that performed them, but he was not responsible for posterity's mistake. Although the great author knew the Stratford Man, he did not use him as a front, rather he took pains in his plays to show that they were two separate people. The Earl of Pembroke may have committed an unforgivable crime against the great author after his death by changing his literary identity, merging it with that of the Stratford Man, but the printing and preservation of twenty new Shakespeare plays in the Folio was an immeasurable gift to humanity. Malice toward the great author was not behind Pembroke's deception, it was politics: he could have still fulfilled his aims with a less elaborate and expensive production. The great author may have agreed to silence himself forever about his authorship of Shakespeare to save his beloved son Southampton from execution, but ironically it was his own sonnets, published by Southampton, that caused his ultimate anonymity. Had Southampton never done so there may never have been a Shakespeare authorship question; but his boldness preserved for us some of Shakespeare's greatest verses. After the great author agreed to Sir Robert Cecil's heartless scheme, he deliberately inserted clues about it, and the Stratford Man, in some of his plays for posterity's sake, which has unfortunately fallen upon the deaf ears of Shakespeare academics. "Truth will out" (*The Merchant of Venice*, 2.2.83) may have been the great author's personal philosophy. He probably died believing that his works would carry his pseudonym and that eventually posterity would realize this and figure out his true identity.

In the final conclusion, the great author was suppressed, and is still being suppressed, for several reasons. During his lifetime, he suppressed his claim to the Shakespeare authorship for social convention to protect his noble name for his own sake and that of his family; he later agreed to a permanent (i.e., posthumous) suppression to save his son, the Earl of Southampton, from execution. When the great author died, writers in the know were silenced because it was politically dangerous to laud a nobleman who evidently wanted Southampton on the throne instead of James, advertised in his long circulating sonnets and in *Love's Martyr*. The Earl of Pembroke suppressed the great author's identity to preserve the Stuart family on the royal throne, which in turn preserved his own wealth and political power. Today the Shakespeare expert is evidently suppressing Shakespeare to preserve his own career and reputation, or maybe cannot be troubled with the truth. Independent scholars, those outside of the experts' coterie who have looked at the evidence for the Stratford Man as Shakespeare, and doubt it, are ignored or belittled by them; thus the great author's loving public is kept in the dark.

In the epilogue to *The Tempest*, the great author wrote that his "strength" was "most faint" and his creative powers spent ("my Charms are all o'er-thrown"), presumably written at the end of his life. Speaking through the character of the exiled duke and magician, Prospero, the great author spoke directly to his admirers. Prospero says that his "Dukedom" has been returned to him and that he has "pardon'd the deceiver," but he says that it is up to his admirers ("confin'd by you") whether or not he remains on "this bare Island."

> Now my Charms are all o'er-thrown
> And what strength I have 's mine own
> Which is most faint: now 'tis true
> I must be here confin'd by you,
> Or sent to Naples, Let me not
> Since I have my Dukedom got,
> And pardon'd the deceiver, dwell
> In this bare Island, by your Spell,
> But release me from my bands
> With the help of your good hands:
> Gentle breath of yours, my Sails
> Must fill, or else my project fails,
> Which was to please:

Were his "bands" the permanent suppression of his authorship of Shakespeare? If so, then he was telling his admirers that he will remain in exile, i.e., remain anonymous, unless they help him, otherwise his "ending is despair."

> Now I want [lack]
> Spirits to enforce: Art to enchant,
> And my ending is despair,
> Unless I be reliev'd by prayer
> Which pierces so, that it assaults
> Mercy itself, and frees all faults.

In the final lines of *The Tempest*, the great author begs us for our "indulgence" in this matter.

> As you from crimes would pardon'd be,
> Let your indulgence set me free.

CHAPTER 18

Dare the Shakespeare Professor

THE SHAKESPEARE PROFESSOR – with few exceptions – is not interested in following the evidence about Shakespeare, and not interested in knowing the truth about Shakespeare, in my opinion. If either of these points were not true, then he would not use fiction to fill a Shakespeare biography, or resort to name calling those who doubt the Stratford Man was the great author. He apparently prefers fantasy and ridicule rather than investigation. As shown in chapters 14 and 15, there is plenty of revealing commentary about the great author made by his contemporaries that the professor mostly skips over because it does not match his preconceived notions.

In the mid-19th century, legitimate arguments against the Stratford Man's authorship of Shakespeare emerged. Many prominent writers, lawyers, judges and politicians participated in the debate. But the emergence of "evidence" based upon cryptograms, like Ignatius Donnelly's book promoting Sir Francis Bacon as Shakespeare in 1881, started to elicit ridicule about the authorship question, and rightly so in Donnelly's case, but it tarred with the same brush the otherwise very credible doubts about the Stratford Man. That is when the insults began. "The upholders of the Stratford-Shakespeare superstition call *us* the hardest names they can think of, and they keep doing it all the time,"[1] wrote Mark Twain in 1909. One century later, the "crazy" slur still holds, with or without cryptograms, no matter how many reasonable and impartial questions are put to the professor. He can get away with this insulting non-answer, even on national television, because he is considered the expert. It is his opinion and his work that is sought from book publishers, academic journals, and the media. Thus the problem gets perpetuated, but the old canard of "crazy" is wearing thin. In 2007, the Declaration of Reasonable Doubt was launched (doubtaboutwill.org), a document stating reasons to doubt the Stratford Man's authorship of Shakespeare without naming an alternative candidate. Within only six months, over 1200 signatures were garnered, with one third of the signatories holding academically high degrees.

As this list increases, it will be harder for the professor to attack the character of doubters.

Another reason for the Shakespeare professor's apparent blindness, in my opinion, is because he is primarily a literary critic and does not usually delve into the Stratford Man's history. He also places all credibility upon the First Folio and Shakspeare monument, i.e., posthumous evidence, and upon those who started Shakespeare's biography over a generation after the Stratford Man's death. His confidence in the Stratford Man is also bolstered by the majority opinion of "professionals," those whose opinions "matter," i.e., his colleagues in the English departments. The doubts and questions raised by outsiders do not matter. But consensus of opinion is still only opinion, not fact. It is time for the professors, lecturers and experts to reacquaint themselves with the problems surrounding their subject, Shakespeare. It is time that they prove the Stratford Man was the great author with evidence *during his lifetime*, outside of a name similarity, and outside of the Folio's contrivance, and if they cannot, to admit that there is reason to doubt it. This is the only way that Shakespeare research can get on the right path, one that will undoubtedly lead to new and significant discoveries.

Shakespeare professors or experts often discourage Stratford Man doubters with the following:

- personal attacks or name-calling to the challenger, such as "crazy," "amateur" and "snob"
- present speculation as if fact, without qualification
- explain away problems with probabilities
- explain away problems with facts about Shakespeare's contemporaries, but not facts about Shakespeare
- say that there is no problem with Shakespeare's biography
- say that he is the expert and only he is qualified to answer questions about Shakespeare
- express disdain for conspiracy theories
- change the argument

Provided below is a list of charges and countercharges meant to assist those willing to dare the experts with questions about the authorship of Shakespeare.

(1). The "crazy" charge. Those who raise the Shakespeare authorship question are "crazy." This is a common defense tactic, i.e., attack your opponent's character instead of addressing the issue. A discussion or debate is over when the name-calling starts, but this is frequently the expert's first move – a first resort instead of last resort. Reply: "Crazy" is a personal slur. Please address the issue with facts and evidence.

(2). The "amateurs" charge. Those who challenge the Shakespeare authorship are amateurs, not professionals like the English professor. This is another personal attack instead of addressing the question. "Amateurs," in his opinion, are those without doctorates in English literature and are therefore unqualified to have an opinion about Shakespeare. Reply: By this definition, many respected figures in Shakespeare scholarship were amateurs. E.K. Chambers, Edmund Malone, George Steevens, Alexander Grosart, Sidney Lee, Edgar Fripp, and James Halliwell-Phillipps were not English professors. The concept of literary or historical authority being exclusive to academics solidified in the 20th century.

(3). The "no evidence" that someone else wrote Shakespeare charge. This charge is a simple changing of the argument. Reply: The issue is about the Stratford Man. Please provide evidence that he was the great author during his lifetime, then address the case of the other candidate(s).

(4). The "snob" charge, i.e., anti-Stratfordians are snobs because they believe only a nobleman could write great literature. The person who wrote Shakespeare's plays was very familiar with the culture of the aristocracy, and many contemporary remarks about him imply that he was highly ranked. There is no direct proof that the Stratford Man had exposure to the aristocracy. Reply: "snob" is a personal attack. Please address the issue with facts.

(5). The "he existed" charge. Another old trick used by the experts is to pretend that the authorship question is really about whether or not the Stratford Man actually existed, and then asserting that a plethora of records proves that he did. Anti-Stratfordians do not question the Stratford Man's existence, only his authorship of Shakespeare. Among the "plethora" of records about the Stratford Man during his lifetime not one is related to education, writing, or interest in literature. To question the Stratford Man's existence is wrong, but to question his authorship of Shakespeare is reasonable. Reply: We accept that the Stratford Man existed; we will not accept that he wrote Shakespeare until clear proof during his lifetime is given, outside of the name similarity. Other proofs, i.e., the First Folio and the Shakspeare monument, are posthumous.

(6). The "he was an actor" charge. "William Shakespeare" was named in one document along with two known actors as a receiver of a payment for two play performances (1595), and another names him as a founding member of the King's Men acting company (1603). No other evidence during the Stratford Man's lifetime substantiates the experts' claim that he was an actor. Counter-reply: Even if proof existed that the Stratford Man actually acted, it does not prove that he was a dramatist.

(7). The "conspiracy theory" charge. The idea that keeping Shakespeare's true identity secret would have been impossible. This charge is another diversion. Conspiracies have occurred in the past, and still do occur, especially in politics. In 1640, an anonymous person wrote, "*Shake-speare*, we must be silent in thy praise," which indicates that there was something secret about Shakespeare. Reply: If it was open and common knowledge that the Stratford Man was the great author, then please explain the conspiracy of silence by his friends, relatives and neighbors about it. Please explain the conspiracy of silence by those in the literary world when the Stratford Man died in 1616, and for seven years after that? The great author was associated with Stratford *for the very first time in 1623*, in the preface of the First Folio.

(8). The "we know more about Shakespeare than any other dramatist of the time, except Ben Jonson" charge. Researchers have found much mundane information about the Stratford Man, such as owing taxes and business documents, but not one document during his lifetime indicates that he was the famous dramatist, William Shakespeare. Over two centuries of research by armies of scholars proves that the Stratford Man was a businessman, not an artist. Reply: We might have more information about "Shakespeare" than any other dramatist except Jonson, but we know less about Shakespeare's education and writing career than any other dramatist of the time. One wonders why universities or Shakespeare institutions do not put more money – or any money – into documentary research with the aim of finding out more. The National Archives in England still has hundreds of manuscripts of the Elizabethan and Jacobean periods that have yet to be examined or catalogued. It is quite possible that more information about Shakespeare or the Stratford Man exists.

(9). The "there is no Shakespeare authorship problem" charge, or "this issue is not discussed academically" charge. The academics do not acknowledge an authorship problem so consequently it does not get discussed academically, but that does not invalidate the issue. Three Supreme Court justices in 1987 thought the authorship question worthy of discussion by presiding over a debate. In 2009, Supreme Court Justices Stevens and Scalia expressed their belief that the 17th Earl of Oxford was the real Shakespeare, and Justice Ginsberg named John Florio as a possible candidate.[2] The *Tennessee Law Review* (Fall 2004) devoted an entire issue to the Shakespeare authorship question. Many famous writers like Ralph Waldo Emerson, Mark Twain, Sigmund Freud, and others were doubters of the Stratford Man's authorship. Shakespearean actors Orson Welles, John Gielgud, Michael York, Jeremy Irons and others have also openly declared their doubt. Reply: If Shakespeare professors do not discuss the authorship problem, or provide documentary proof during the Stratford Man's lifetime, then criticism and dissent will never go away. All the vexing problems about Shakespeare's life and works will never get resolved until they do.

(10). The "his name is on the book" charge. Here the Shakespeare professor refers to the First Folio, his primary evidence. Reply: Yes, the name

William Shakespeare is credited with the plays contained in the First Folio, and with some quartos, but overwhelming evidence suggests that this name was the great author's pen name. A man was born with the name "William Shakspere" in Stratford-upon-Avon but facts during his lifetime proving that he was the great author are non-existent. Another man born with this name was listed as a soldier in Warwickshire in 1605.[3] Were these two Warwickshire natives the same man or were there a few men with this name? This is why name similarity is not enough to award the Stratford Man with the unmatchable Shakespeare works. Even the inscription on the "Shakspeare" monument in Stratford-upon-Avon does not explicitly identify the deceased as a poet, dramatist or actor.

(11). Dare the Shakespeare professor about the Stratford Man's acquisition of detailed knowledge displayed in the Shakespeare poems and plays. The usual reply is either a probability or a denial that Shakespeare had this knowledge. If all else fails, the professor will employ one of his favorite expressions: "He was a genius." As Sir George Greenwood explained, "Genius may give the power of acquiring knowledge with marvelous facility; but genius is not knowledge."[4] Here are the experts' typical responses to such questions:

Q: How can you account for the Stratford Man's knowledge of law?
A: He probably was a law clerk.

Q: How can you account for his knowledge of soldiery?
A: He probably was in the army.

Q: How can you account for his knowledge of European geography?
A: He was wrong about Bohemia.

Q: How can you account for his knowledge of French language?
A: He probably learned it in tavern talk.

Every alternate candidate proposed as the true Shakespeare has education and life experiences that can be verified. For example, knowledge of law, soldiery, European geography, French and Latin language can be accounted for with documentary evidence for the 17th Earl of Oxford. And Shakespeare was not wrong about Bohemia.

(12). Dare the Shakespeare professor about the dating of *The Tempest*. The professor is adamant that *The Tempest* was based upon the 1609 shipwreck in Bermuda, and constantly brings up this point at authorship debates. This year serves him well because the lead candidate, the 17th Earl of Oxford, died in 1604. There were several written accounts of shipwrecks during Elizabethan and Jacobean times, but no one can say with certainty upon which real "tempest," if any, the great author had based his play. Moreover, the account of the Bermuda shipwreck was written on July 15, 1610 in a private letter, and it was published after the Stratford Man's death. *The Tempest* was evidently written by 1593, as shown in Appendix A (No. 66).

(13). The "what does it matter who wrote the plays?" charge. This is the Shakespeare professor's admission of utter defeat. The authorship matters immensely to him because if he got the authorship wrong, then his books and articles and doctorates would be wrong, and his slavish devotion to the status quo will be ridiculed by succeeding generations. The Shakespeare professor always craves for new biographical information about the great author, and is probably dreading the day when either public consensus discredits the Stratford Man model, or a Shakespeare play manuscript turns up in the handwriting of a known personage. Reply (a): If the true biography of one of the greatest minds of Western civilization does not matter, then whose does? (b): Knowing the identity of the real Shakespeare would shed much needed light on many "unsolvable" problems about Shakespeare and his works (as detailed in the first four chapters of this book). (c): Knowing the true author would add a new depth of understanding to the plays and would help to demystify obscure passages. (d): If you authored a highly acclaimed comedy or drama, would it not matter to you if someone else got the credit? (e): We can learn from the truth.

(14). The "Shakespeare plays and poems are not autobiographical" charge. This is latest defense by the experts, one that they have been forced to adopt because the Shakespeare works, especially the sonnets, have no relation with the Stratford Man's documentary life – a clear example of circular reasoning. Every creative writer draws upon his life experiences for his material, yet the experts would have you believe that Shakespeare intentionally divorced himself from detection in about forty plays, and 154 sonnets written in the first person. Reply: The great author testified that his sonnets were autobiographical: "every word doth almost tell my name" (Sonnet 76); "My life hath in this line some interest /Which for memorial still with thee shall stay" (Sonnet 74); and, in spite of death "I'll live in this poor rhyme" (Sonnet 107). Most experts acknowledge that the sonnet sequence by the Elizabethan poet, Sir Philip Sidney, titled *Astrophel and Stella*, was mostly autobiographical, as were the sonnets of William Alexander, titled *Aurora, containing the first fancies of the author's youth* (1604). Sidney's sonnets centered upon his frustrated love for Penelope Rich ("Stella"), a real person. There is no logical reason to doubt that Shakespeare's sonnets reflected his personal feelings about real people and events in his life. Most experts agree that the Fair Youth and Dark Lady were real people and not a figment of the great author's imagination.

(15). The "no one questioned the Shakespeare authorship for 200 years" charge. Reply: Not true. On the opening page of John Benson's 1640 edition of Shakespeare's sonnets and other poetry was an altered image of the Droeshout engraving. A line of disbelief was placed immediately below this image: "This Shadow is renowned Shakespear's?" (Plate 20).

Conclusion

An English professor offered this advice to "defenders" of the traditional Shakespeare in lieu of direct evidence:

> All we need to prove is that such a man from Stratford could have written the plays, not that he did so.[5]

If this professor's opinion represents the majority, then Shakespeare academics do not feel the need to prove the Stratford Man wrote Shakespeare, only that he *could have*. This keeps his authorship firmly in the realm of theory and *out of the realm of fact and evidence*. In the realm of theory one can invent any scenario without the need for proof. Meanwhile, those who question the accepted model, the Stratford Man – a model that has failed to enlighten any aspect of Shakespeare study – are discouraged. Upon this model are based thousands of books and articles, doctorates and grants. A good portion of this scholarship will become compromised or invalidated when this model is dropped. If Shakespeare admirers are ever to have the fullest comprehension of one of the greatest literary achievements in the history of mankind, then they must openly challenge the experts' case of the Stratford Man as Shakespeare. This book, I hope, will help them to do so.

93 "Too Early" Allusions to Shakespeare's Plays (1562 to 1606)

FOR OVER A CENTURY, orthodox Shakespeare scholars have been finding unusual word clusters or phrases in the Shakespeare works that are mirrored in the works of his contemporaries; many were written years or decades before it is believed that a given Shakespeare work was written. To suit the Stratford Man model, these other works are necessarily labeled as Shakespeare's sources. The preponderance of evidence given in this appendix points to the opposite conclusion, that Shakespeare was the originator – the source from which other writers were drawing. This appendix compiles 93 instances of "too early" allusions to 32 different Shakespeare plays. They were made by 30 different writers (some neither poets nor dramatists) and occurred in 53 different sources. This extensive and detailed compilation should put the Shakespeare expert into a dilemma: either the great author was a serial plagiarist and therefore was not a creative genius, or his works were written far earlier than supposed. The former conclusion contradicts itself and the latter would seal the doom of the Stratford Man as the great author. This study does not assign the actual composition date of a given Shakespeare play, it only shows that a given Shakespeare play – or at least one version of it – had been written by a given date. Scores of other "too early" allusions will be discovered when the experts finally toss out the Stratford Man model. In the compilation below, the date of the "too early" allusion is given first, followed by the Shakespeare play and its orthodox dating by Sir Edmund Chambers (in brackets with question marks), and then the specific allusion. The play dating estimated by professors Stanley Wells and Gary Taylor (*William Shakespeare, A Textual Companion*, 1997 edition) differs only slightly with Chambers's dating, but does not upset the list below (with the exception of No. 58, which is addressed). The dating of Christopher Marlowe's plays is based on the opinions of John Bakeless and *The Reader's Encyclopedia*. The "too early" allusions to *Hamlet* featured in Chapter 3 are included but abbreviated.

---

(1)-(6). 1562: "Too early" allusion to *Romeo and Juliet* [1594-95?].

Arthur Brooke, poem, *The Tragical History of Romeus and Juliet* ("November 19, 1562" was printed on the last page). Brooke's poem is always cited as one of Shakespeare's sources for his play, *Romeo and Juliet*. Yet Brooke wrote in his preface that he had seen "lately" a drama about Romeo and Juliet that was "better set forth" than his poem – in other words, this earlier drama was his inspiration.

> Though I saw the same argument [subject of *Romeo and Juliet*] lately set forth on stage with more commendation, than I can look for (being there much better set forth than I have or can do) yet the same matter penned as it is, may serve to like good effect, if the readers do bring with them like good minds, to consider it.

The play that Brooke had seen, perhaps the very first dramatization of the famous lovers in England (and possibly in Europe), is now "lost." Yet it was so good and so popular that it inspired not only Brooke's work, but Bernard Garter's *The Tragical and True History which Happened between Two English Lovers* (1563), and the story, "Rhomeo and Julietta," which appeared in William Painter's *Palace of Pleasure* (1567) – interestingly, the story that immediately followed was titled, "Two Gentlemen of Venice" (Shakespeare wrote a play titled, *Two Gentlemen of Verona*). Brooke's poem was based upon the French story by Pierre Boaistuau (who had based his work upon the Italian, Matteo Bandello), but Sir Sidney Lee noted that Brooke did "not adhere very closely to his French original: he develops the character of the Nurse and alters the concluding scene in many important points, in all of which he is followed by Shakespeare."[1] More similarities between Brooke's poem and Shakespeare's play follow, as noted by Kenneth Muir.[2]

(1). Brooke's apothecary describes the poison he gives to Romeus as "the speeding gear" (line 2585). Shakespeare's Romeo, while speaking to the apothecary, referred to the poison he sought as "some soon-speeding gear" (5.1.60).

---

(2). In both works, the nurse answers Juliet's question about the identity of Romeus/Romeo:

His name is Romeus (said she) a Montegewe ... *Romeus and Juliet* [line 353]

His name is Romeo, and a Montague ...   *Romeo and Juliet* [1.4.253]

---

(3). In both works, Romeus/Romeo and Juliet have just fallen in love, at which point they are similarly described:

Through them [Juliet's eyes] he [Romeus] swalloweth down love's sweet empoison'd bait ...
Romeus and Juliet [line 219]

And she [Juliet] steal Love's sweet bait from fearful hooks.
Romeus and Juliet [1.4.269, Chorus]

---

(4). In both works, Juliet asks the nurse a question about Romeus/Romeo:

But of our marriage say at once, what answer have you brought?
Romeus and Juliet [line 684]

What says he of our marriage? what of that?
Romeo and Juliet [2.4.48]

---

(5). In Brooke's poem (lines 1353-54, 1358), the friar scolds Romeus:

Art thou quoth he a man? Thy shape saith so thou art.
Thy crying and thy weeping eyes, denote a woman's heart ...
If thou a man, or woman wert or else a brutish beast.

In Shakespeare's play (3.3.109-112), the friar scolds Romeo:

> Art thou <u>a man? thy form</u> cries out <u>thou art</u> –
> <u>Thy tears</u> are <u>wom'nish</u>, thy wild acts denote
> Th'unreasonable fury of <u>a beast</u>.
> Unseemly <u>woman</u> in a seeming <u>man</u>,
> And ill-beseeming <u>beast</u> in seeming both …

_____

(6). In both works, Juliet asks the friar a question:

> Where is my Romeus?   *Romeus and Juliet* [line 2710]
> … where is my Romeo?   *Romeo and Juliet* [5.3.150]

More shared phrases between Brooke's poem and Shakespeare's play, as found by Robert Adger Law, include "no inconstant toy," "lamentable day," "field-bed," and "To cease thy suit" ("your suit" in Brooke).[3] The only reason that Shakespeare is considered as the borrower of Brooke, and indirectly, the "lost" play that Brooke had viewed, circa 1562, is because the Stratford Man was not yet born. The play about Romeo and Juliet that Brooke had viewed was most likely the earliest version of Shakespeare's play – it was never lost. More allusions to Shakespeare's play occurred in 1589, 1592 and 1593 – all well before the orthodox dating – and are included in this study.

_____

(7)-(9). 1578: "Too early" allusions to *The Taming of the Shrew* [1593-94] and *Measure for Measure* [1604-05?].

John Lyly, novel, *Euphues. The Anatomy of Wit* (registered December 2, 1578).

(7). The title character, Euphues, characterizes a few philosophers:[4]

> Aristippus a <u>Philosopher</u>, yet who more courtly? Diogenes a Philosopher, yet who more carterly [boorish]? Who more popular than Plato retaining always good company? Who more envious than <u>Timon</u>, denouncing all human society? Who so severe as the *Stoics*, which like <u>stocks</u> [wooden posts] were moved with no melody? [p. 5]

Euphues repeats the pun on Stoics about twenty pages later:

> Thought he him a *Stoic* that he would not be moved, or a <u>stock</u> that he could not? [p. 16v]

In *The Taming of the Shrew* (1.3.31), Tranio speaks to Lucentio about some philosophers and similarly puns on Stoics:

> Glad that you thus continue your resolve,
> To suck the sweets of sweet <u>Philosophy</u>.
> Only (good master) while we do admire
> This virtue, and this moral discipline,
> Let's be no *Stoics*, nor no <u>stocks</u>, I pray,

> Or so devote to _Aristotle_'s checks
> As _Ovid_; be an outcast quite abjur'd:

Lyly also mentioned Timon in his passage, another "outcast" like Ovid in Shakespeare's passage. That Lyly was referring to Shakespeare's play, _Timon of Athens_, is very likely considering the allusion to it that appeared in 1579 (see No. 12 below).

---

(8). In the second allusion to _The Taming of the Shrew_, Euphues thinks women's defects should not be covered with nice language by their boyfriends:[5]

> be she never so comely call her counterfeit, be she never so straight think her crooked. And wrest all parts of her body to the worst, be she never so worthy. If she be well set, then call her a Boss [fat woman], if slender, a Hazel twig, if Nut-brown, as black as coal; if well colored, a painted wall; if she be pleasant, then is she a wanton; if sullen, a clown; if honest, then she is coy; [p. 43v]

In _The Taming of the Shrew_ (2.1.236-37, 246-49), Petruchio describes the shrewish Kate, his future fiancée, in complimentary terms:

> I find you passing gentle.
> 'Twas told me you were rough and coy and sullen,
> And now I find report a very liar ...
>
> Why doth the world report that _Kate_ doth limp?
> O sland'rous world: _Kate_ like the hazel-twig
> Is straight, and slender, and as brown in hue
> As hazelnuts, and sweeter than the kernels:

The Taming of the Shrew featured the expression "cold comfort" (3.3.29). Michael Macrone (_Brush Up Your Shakespeare!_) cited Arthur Golding for first usage of the phrase in his translation of Jean Calvin in 1571 (_The Psalms of David and Others_). Since _Taming_ was evidently written in the 1570s, perhaps Shakespeare did coin it.[6]

---

(9). A passage in Lyly's _Euphues_ discusses prostitutes as thieves:[7]

> The Parthians, to cause their youth to loathe the alluring trains of women's wiles and deceitful enticements, had most curiously carved in their houses, a young man blind, besides whom was adjoined a woman so exquisite, that in some men's judgment Pygmalion's Image was not half so excellent, having one hand in his pocket as noting her theft, and holding a knife in the other hand to cut his throat. [p. 3v]

In Shakespeare's _Measure for Measure_ (3.1.317-21), Pompey the pimp is being taken to jail. Lucio jokingly asks him where the thieving prostitutes have gone:

> What is there none of _Pygmalion's_ Images newly made woman to be had now, for putting the hand in the pocket, and extracting clutch'd?

George Whetstone's play, *Promos and Cassandra*, is often cited as the main source for *Measure for Measure*; like *Euphues*, it was written in 1578. But this "crude, awkward play,"[8] wrote Naseeb Shaheen, was never performed, so Whetstone rewrote it as prose and included it in a book of collected stories; it was printed in 1582. It seems that Whetstone and Lyly were both borrowing from Shakespeare.

---

(10). 1579: "Too early" allusion to *The Taming of the Shrew* [1593-94].

Thomas Churchyard, miscellany, *A General Rehearsal of Wars, or Churchyard's Choice* (registered August 3, 1579).

In *A General Rehearsal of Wars*, Churchyard used the phrase, "thereby hangs a tale," in a story involving a horse.[9]

> For stubborn Colt, in teeth had got the bit.
>
> He let me run, o'er hedge, o'er hill and dale,
> And would not pluck, the reins of bridle back:
> I could tell why, but thereby hangs a tale ... [sig. Y4v]

In *The Taming of the Shrew* (3.3.50-54, 71-76), Grumio recalls a mishap involving himself, Petruchio, Kate and a horse.

> GRUMIO
> First, know my horse is tired; my master and mistress fallen out.
>
> CURTIS
> How?
>
> GRUMIO
> Out of their saddles into the dirt – and thereby hangs a tale ... how he beat me because her horse stumbled; how she waded through the dirt to pluck him off me ... how her bridle was burst ...

---

(11). 1579: "Too early" allusion to *The Merchant of Venice* [1596-97].

Stephan Gosson, essay, *The School of Abuse ... a pleasant invective against Poets, Pipers, Players, Jesters, and such like Caterpillars of a Commonwealth* (pub. 1579).

One of the few plays commended by Gosson was

> The Jew, and Ptolome, shown at the Bull [a theater]; the one representing the greediness of worldly choosers, and bloody minds of usurers ... [p. 22v]

Gosson's description of "The Jew" is so close to the theme of *The Merchant of Venice* that some scholars believe it was another "Ur," a "lost" Shakespeare source.[10] But Shakespeare's *Merchant* was also known as "The Jew of Venice," according to the Stationers' Register (entry dated July 22, 1598): "a book of the Merchant of Venice or otherwise called the Jew of Venice ... " Edmund Spenser's private letter to Gabriel Harvey in 1579 probably alluded to Shakespeare's *Merchant*; it was signed, "He that is fast bound unto thee in more obligations than any merchant in Italy to any Jew there." Edward Scott, who discovered the letter at the British Museum (Sloane Ms. 93, folio 42), believed that Spenser, Harvey and Gosson all viewed the same play in 1579 (*Letter-Book of Gabriel Harvey*, London, 1884, p. 78). The court performance of "The history of Portio and demorantes" in February 1580, added Charlton Ogburn (*The Mysterious William Shakespeare*, 1984, p. 615), may have been an earlier title for Shakespeare's play, referring to heroine, Portia, and "the merchants," which was mistranscribed.

---

(12). 1579: "Too early" allusion to *Timon of Athens* [1607-08?].

Sir Thomas North, translation, *The Lives of the Noble Grecians and Romans* by Plutarch (registered April 6, 1579).

Plutarch's chapter on Marcus Antonius included two epitaphs for the misanthrope, Timon of Athens, but North replaced them with completely different text:

> Here lies a wretched corse [corpse], of wretched soul bereft:
> Seek not my name: a plague consume you wicked wretches left ...

> Here lie I Timon, who alive all living men did hate:
> Pass by and curse thy fill: but pass, and stay not here thy gate.[11]

North's epitaph (pp. 1003-4) mirrored the one given in Shakespeare's play, *Timon of Athens* (5.4.70-74), with the exception of the word "wretches," which replaced "caitiffs" (villains). Similarly phrased lines in North's text occur in Shakespeare's *Coriolanus*, *Anthony and Cleopatra*, and *Julius Caesar*. Eva Turner Clark suggested that the court performance of "The History of the Solitary Knight" on February 17, 1577 was *Timon of Athens*.[12] Another play, *Timon*, dated circa 1581-90, was possibly an early version of Shakespeare's play (p. 61).

---

(13)-(18). 1579: "Too early" allusions to *Anthony and Cleopatra* [1606-07?], *The Merchant of Venice* [1596-97?], *King John* [1596-97?], *Twelfth Night* [1599-1600?], *Much Ado About Nothing* [1598-99?], and *Henry IV-Part 2* [1597-98?].

John Lyly, novel, *Euphues and His England* (reg. July 24, 1579, pub. 1580).

(13). Euphues says that the goddess of love, Venus, and ladies in Italy, use tricks to disguise themselves so men will not know their true natures. Then he mentions "the Egyptian," presumably the famous seductress, Cleopatra, and that she played "fast or loose" to make men love her:[13]

> Thus with the *Egyptian* thou playest fast or loose, so that there is nothing more certain, than that thou wilt love ... [p. 53]

In *Anthony and Cleopatra* (4.8.24, 39-43), Marc Antony speaks of the betrayal of his lover, Cleopatra, the Egyptian queen, and that she "beguil'd" him like a gypsy "hath at fast and loose."

> This foul <u>Egyptian</u> betrayed me ...
>
> O this false soul of Egypt! This grave charm,
> Whose eye beck'd forth my wars, and call'd them home,
> Whose bosom was my crownet [coronet], my chief end,
> Like a right gypsy hath at <u>fast and loose</u>
> Beguil'd me to the very heart of loss.

The phrase, "man of men," in *Anthony and Cleopatra* (1.5.72), also occurs in Marlowe's play, *Dido, Queen of Carthage* (3.3),[14] written circa 1587.

_____

(14). In *Euphues and His England* (p. 38v), the title character speaks of love:[15]

> For as by Basil the Scorpion <u>is engendered</u>, and by means of the
> same herb destroyed: so love, which by time and <u>fancy is bred</u> <u>in</u>
> an idle <u>head</u>, is by time and <u>fancy</u> banished from <u>the heart</u>: or as
> the *Salamander* which being a long space <u>nourished</u> in the fire ...

In *The Merchant of Venice* (3.2.69-75), Bassanio ponders which casket to choose
that will win him Portia's hand in marriage:

> Tell me where <u>is fancy bred</u>,
> Or <u>in</u> <u>the heart</u>, or in the <u>head</u>:
> How begot, how <u>nourished</u>. Reply, reply.
> It <u>is engender'd</u> in the eyes,
> With gazing fed, and <u>Fancy</u> dies,
> In the cradle where it lies:
> Let us all ring <u>Fancy's</u> knell.

_____

(15). *Euphues and His England* (p. 18v) contains an allusion to Hercules's shoe:[16]

> And therefore me thinketh the time were but lost, in pulleying
> <u>Hercules</u> <u>shoe upon an</u> Infant's foot, or in setting *Atlas* <u>burthen</u>
> on a child's <u>shoulder</u>, or to bruise <u>your backs</u> with the <u>burthen</u> of
> a whole kingdom.

In *King John*, the Bastard Falconbridge alludes to the shoes of Alcides (Hercules).

> ... As great <u>Alcides' shoes upon an</u> Ass:
> But Ass, I'll take that <u>burthen</u> from <u>your back</u>,
> Or lay on that shall make your <u>shoulders</u> crack. [2.1.143-46]

In *King John* (2.3.175), Shakespeare described criminal politicians as "The Caterpillars of the Commonwealth." In *Euphues and His England*, Lyly described 300
senators as "thieves and caterpillars in the commonwealth." Both Lyly and Shakespeare applied the expression to politicians. In 1577, Rafael Holinshed referred to
beggars as "thieves and caterpillars in the commonwealth," and in 1579, Stephen
Gosson described poets and entertainers as "Caterpillars of a Commonwealth" in
the subtitle of his *School of Abuse*.[17]

(16). In *Euphues and His England* (p. 30), a nobleman in Sienna gives his opinion of a gentlewoman's beauty and stature in a dialogue with her:[18]

> "I know not how I should commend your beauty, because it is somewhat <u>too brown</u>, nor your stature being somewhat <u>too low</u>, & of your wit I cannot judge." "No" quoth she "I believe you, for none can judge of wit, but they that have it." "Why then" quoth he, "<u>dost thou think</u> me a <u>fool</u>?" "<u>Thought is free</u>, my Lord" quoth she, "I will not take you at your word." [punctuation marks added]

In *Much Ado About Nothing* (1.1.178-84), a nobleman of Padua gives his opinion a gentlewoman's beauty and stature:

> Why i' faith methinks she's <u>too low</u> for a high praise, <u>too brown</u> for a fair praise, and too little for a great praise ...

The expression, "as sound as a bell," occurs in *Much Ado About Nothing* (3.2.12-13) when Don Pedro says of Benedick: "He hath a heart as sound as bell, and his tongue is the clapper ... " The OED cites first usage of this expression in Thomas Newton's *The Touchstone of Complexions* (1576).[19] Queen Elizabeth I viewed a play in February 1583 that may have been Shakespeare's *Much Ado* (Ch. 3).

---

(17). The dialogue above from *Euphues and his England* is echoed in Shakespeare's *Twelfth Night*:[20]

> SIR ANDREW AGUECHEEK
> Fair Lady, <u>do you think</u> you have <u>fools</u> in hand?
>
> MARIA
> Sir, I have not you by th'hand.
>
> SIR ANDREW AGUECHEEK
> Marry but you shall have, and here's my hand.
>
> MARIA
> Now, sir, <u>thought is free</u>. [1.3.64-69]

---

(18). *Euphues and His England* (p. 49v):[21]

> With what face Euphues canst thou return to thy <u>vomit</u>, seeming with the greedy <u>hound</u> to lap up that which thou didst <u>cast up</u>.

Henry IV-Part 2 (1.3.95-99):

> Thou, beastly feeder, art so full of him,
> That thou provok'st thyself to <u>cast</u> him <u>up</u>.
> So, so, thou common <u>dog</u>, didst thou disgorge
> Thy glutton bosom of the royal Richard,
> And now thou wouldst eat thy dead <u>vomit</u> up ...

Another apparent allusion to Shakespeare in Lyly's *Euphues and His England* occurs in his dedication letter to the 17th Earl of Oxford: "the Lapwing, who fearing her young ones to be destroyed by passengers, flyeth with a false cry far from their nest." This line resembles, "Far from her nest the lapwing cries away,"[22] in Shakespeare's *The Comedy of Errors* (4.2.27).

---

(19). 1583: "Too early" allusion to *Cymbeline* [1609-10?].

John Lyly, play, *Campaspe* (performed at Whitehall on Jan. 1, 1584, pub. 1584).[23]

In *Campaspe*, Trico sings a song at Sylvius's request:

> ... Who is't now we hear?
> None but <u>the Lark</u> so shrill and clear.
> How <u>at heaven's gates</u> she claps her wings,
> The morn not waking 'til she <u>sings</u>.
> <u>Hark, hark</u>, with what a pretty throat ... [5.1.39-44]

In *Cymbeline*, as noted by H.R.D. Anders,[24] Cloten requests musicians to play a song, excerpted below:

> <u>Hark, hark!</u> <u>the lark</u> <u>at heaven's gate</u> <u>sings</u>,
> And Phoebus [the sun] 'gins arise ... [2.3.22-23]

An even earlier date for *Cymbeline* may be detected from the phrase, "at last gasp" (1.5.53). A 1577 book by Meredith Hamner employs a similar phrase, "a valiant and invincible mind unto the last gasp," which the OED credits as its first usage.[25] Eva Turner Clark suggested that the queen's revels play, "An history of the cruelty of A Stepmother," shown on December 28, 1578, but now lost, was Shakespeare's *Cymbeline*.[26] Shakespeare's protagonist, Imogene, was victim to the machinations of her stepmother. It is believed that Shakespeare's principal source of the story about Belarius in *Cymbeline* was derived from the play, *The Rare Triumphs of Love and Fortune*, shown to the queen in December 1582;[27] it was probably the other way around. The very unusual expression, "How creeps acquaintance?" in *Cymbeline* (1.4.26), occurred in only one other work, Robert Greene's *A Quip For An Upstart Courtier* (1592): "to be brief, the end of all being, as to know God, And not as your worship good master velvet breeches wrests to creep into acquaintance."[28] In 1594, John Davies echoed two lines from *Cymbeline* in his poem, *Orchestra* (Ch. 15, No. 7).

---

(20)-(22). ca. 1587: "Too early" allusions to *Henry VI-Part 1* [1591-92?], *Richard III* [1592-93?], and *Julius Caesar* [1599-1600?].

Christopher Marlowe, play, *Tamburlaine the Great*, Parts 1 and 2.

(20). *Tamburlaine the Great-Part 1* (5.1.140-41), as noted by Anders:[29]

> And, like to Flora in her morning pride,
> <u>Shaking her silver tresses in the air</u> ...

Henry VI-Part 1 (1.1.1-2):

> Comets, importing change of times and states,

Brandish your crystal tresses in the sky ...

------

(21). In *Tamburlaine-Part 1* (5.1.239-44), Zabina, the wife of the imprisoned sultan, Bajazet, hopes for a grizzly death of conqueror Tamburlaine. Bajazet tells her their situation is hopeless, and she replies:[30]

> Then is there left no Mahomet, no God,
> No fiend, no fortune, nor no hope of end
> To our famous, monstrous slaveries.
> Gape earth, and let the fiends internal view
> A hell as hopeless and as full of fear
> As are the blasted banks of Erebus ...

In Shakespeare's *Richard III* (4.4.75-77), Queen Margaret, widow of King Henry VI, prays for King Richard III's death:

> Earth gapes, hell burns, fiends roar, saints pray,
> To have him suddenly convey'd from hence.
> Cancel his bond of life, dear God!

Another possible early allusion to *Richard III* occurs in Robert Greene's play, *The Scottish History of James IV* (ca. 1590): "Some then will yield, when I am dead for hope" (5.6). Compare this line with, "yield thy breath. I died for hope ere I could lend thee aid,"[31] in *Richard III* (5.3.173-74). The character name, "Menaphon," a Persian captain in *Tamburlaine-Part 1*, may have been inspired by a line in *The Comedy of Errors* (5.1.369-70): "Brought to this town by that most famous warrior /Duke Menaphon, your most renowned uncle." (Robert Greene titled his fiction work, *Menaphon*, in 1589.)

------

(22). The sequel to *Tamburlaine* (4.1.140), also dated circa 1587, contains an apparent allusion to *Julius Caesar*.[32] One character predicts blood and fire dropping from heaven on Tamburlaine's head:

> Thy [Tamburlaine] victories are grown so violent,
> That shortly heaven, filled with the meteors
> Of blood and fire thy tyrannies have made,
> Will pour down blood and fire on thy head,
> Whose scalding drops will pierce thy seething brains ...

In *Julius Caesar* (2.2.24-26), Calpurnia relates various omens to Caesar, including blood dropping from the clouds:

> Fierce fiery Warriors fight upon the Clouds
> In ranks and Squadrons, and right form of War
> Which drizzl'd blood upon the Capitol:

It is believed that Shakespeare borrowed a description of an omen in Tacitus for this passage, but the concept of blood from a battle in heaven dropping onto Earth was unique to Shakespeare.[33] A play titled "The History of Caesar" was acted before Queen Elizabeth in January 1583.

(23). 1587: "Too early" allusion to *The Merry Wives of Windsor* [1600-01?].

John Lyly, play, *Endimion* (reg. October 4, 1591, and printed the same year). The play was first performed Feb. 2, 1588, and presumably written the previous year.[34]

In *Endimion*, fairies sing a song about pinching the "mortal" Corsites:[35]

> Pinch him, <u>pinch him</u>, black and blue,
> Saucy mortals must not view
> What the Queen of <u>Stars</u> is doing,
> Nor pry into our <u>Fairy</u> wooing. [4.3.28-31]

In *The Merry Wives of Windsor* (5.5.105-08), fairies sing a song about pinching the "mortal" Falstaff:

> Pinch him, <u>fairies</u>, mutually
> <u>Pinch him</u> for his villainy
> Pinch him, and burn him, and turn him about,
> Till candles and <u>star</u>light and moonshine be out.

---

(24)-(25). circa 1588: "Too early" allusions to *Troilus and Cressida* [1601-02?] and *Richard II* [1595-96?].

Christopher Marlowe, play, *Dr. Faustus*.

(24). Marlowe's Dr. Faustus makes this remark upon beholding Helen of Troy:

> <u>Was this the face that</u> <u>launched</u> <u>a thousand ships</u>,
> And burnt the topless towers of Ilium! [5.1.92-93]

Helen of Troy is discussed in *Troilus and Cressida* (2.2.81):

> Is she worth keeping? Why she is a pearl
> Whose price hath <u>launch'd</u> above <u>a thousand ships</u> ...

The above parallel, and No. 25 below, were noted by Robert A. Logan.[36]

---

(25). The title character in *Richard II* repeats the phrase, "Was this the face that" (4.1.281-86) while looking in a mirror:

> <u>Was this face, the face</u>
> <u>That</u> every day, under his household roof,
> Did keep ten <u>thousand</u> men? <u>Was this the face</u>,
> <u>That</u> like the sun, did make beholders wink?
> <u>Is this the face</u>, which fac'd so many follies,
> That was at last outfac'd by *Bolingbroke*?

The revels plays, "Ajax and Ulysses" (January 1572) and "The History of Agamemnon and Ulysses (December 1584), may have been early versions of *Troilus and Cressida* (p. 64).

(26)-(28). 1588: "Too early" allusions to *King Lear* [1605-06?], *Richard III* [1592-93?], and *Titus Andronicus* [1593-94?].

George Peele (?), play, *The Battle of Alcazar* (pub. 1594). The "most likely date of composition" for this play is late 1588, wrote editor Charles Edelman.[37]

(26). In the presence of King Sebastian, who has just redirected his war plans from Ireland to Africa, Tom Stukeley in *The Battle of Alcazar* says:[38]

> Saint George for England! and Ireland now <u>adieu</u>,
> For here Tom Stukeley <u>shapes his course</u> anew. [2.4.166-67]

In *King Lear* (1.1.189-90), the Earl of Kent takes his leave from the king after being declared a banished man:

> Thus Kent, O princes, bids you all <u>adieu</u>:
> He'll <u>shape his</u> old <u>course</u> in a country <u>new</u>.

The line in the anonymous sonnet cycle, *Zepheria* (1594), "And veil thy face with <u>frowns</u> as with a <u>frontlet</u>" (Canzonet 27), resembles lines said by the title character in *King Lear* (1.4.182-3): "How now, daughter? What makes that <u>frontlet</u> on? / Methinks you are too much of late i' th' <u>frown</u>."[39] *Zepheria* also echoes lines in Shakespeare's sonnets.[40] The anonymous play, *King Leir*, published in 1594, is regarded as Shakespeare's source for his *King Lear*.

(27). Just defeated in battle, the Moor, a lord who tried to take the throne from his uncle, the rightful King of Morocco, says (*The Battle of Alcazar*, 5.1.96):

> A horse, a horse, villain, a horse.

At the climax of the Battle of Bosworth Field, a nearly defeated Richard III shouts (*Richard III*, 5.4.10):

> A Horse, A Horse, my Kingdom for a Horse.

As noted by Ramon Jiménez, this phrase was probably a reworking of King Richard's line, "A horse! A horse! A fresh horse!" in the earlier play, *The True Tragedy of Richard the Third*.[41]

(28). In *The Battle of Alcazar* (2.3.3), the Moor says:[42]

> The fatal poison of my swelling heart!

In *Titus Andronicus* (5.3.13), Aaron the Moor says:

> The venomous malice of my swelling heart!

On the authority of Ben Jonson, *Titus Andronicus* was a 25 or 30-year-old play in 1614, which would date it to circa 1584-89.

> He that will swear, *Jeronimo*, or *Andronicus* are the best plays,
> yet, shall pass unexpected at, here, as a man whose judgment
> shews it is constant, and hath stood still, these five and twenty,
> or thirty years ... [*Bartholomew Fair*, Induction]

An earlier dating for *Titus Andronicus* is supported by an extant manuscript depicting a scene from this play (now at Longleat House), accompanied by some of the text. Signed "Henry Peacham," the manuscript was dated using Latin abbreviations instead of regular numbers. David Roper concluded that the Latin notation corresponded to the year 1574, which would identify the artist as Henry Peacham the Elder, and not, as it is believed, his son, Henry Peacham the Younger.[43] *A Shakespeare Companion* explains that a play noted in Philip Henslowe's diary, "Titus & Vespasia," was probably Shakespeare's *Titus Andronicus*; it was performed on April 11, 1592 and several times during that season. In the German version of Shakespeare's play, printed in 1620, Titus's son, Lucius, is named Vespasianus. Lucius is important to the plot because he revenges injuries made to his father.[44]

---

(29)-(30). circa 1588: "Too early" allusions to *King Lear* [1605-06?] and *Hamlet* [1600-01?].

John Lyly, play, *Mother Bombie* (registered June 18, 1594 and printed that year). The composition date is explained in Chapter 3 (p. 51).

(29). In *Mother Bombie* (4.2.28), the "half-witted Silena" mistakes Accius for a stool (piece of furniture), saying:[45]

> I cry you mercy, I took you for a join'd stool.

In *King Lear* (3.6.49-51), the title character mistakes a stool for his daughter, Goneril. The Fool speaks to it:

> FOOL
> Come hither, mistress. Is your name Goneril?
>
> LEAR
> She cannot deny it.
>
> FOOL
> Cry you mercy, I took you for a joint-stool.

The "join'd stool" line occurred in Robert Armin's comedy, *The History of the Two Maids of More-clacke*. The clown, Tutch, is asked if a certain lady "will continue firm?" The clown replies, "Firm sir, yes, unless you take her for a join stool" (STC 773, sig. D2 verso). Both *Lear* and *Two Maids* featured lines said by fools about a joined stool being mistaken with a lady. *Two Maids* was written circa 1597-1602, then revised in 1605-06 and published in 1609.[46] It is believed that the clown, Tutch, was modeled upon the clown, Touchstone in *As You Like It*. More supporting evidence for an earlier dating for *King Lear*: Philip Henslowe noted a performance of "King Lear" on April 6, 1594 by the Earl of Sussex's Men,[47] and "I for sorrow sung" in the Fool's song in *King Lear* (1.4.180) was evidently echoed in Thomas Nashe's 1596 letter to William Cotton: "some men for sorrow sing ..."[48]

_____

(30). *Mother Bombie* (3.1):

> the nearer we are in blood, the further we must be from love; and
> the <u>greater the kindred</u> is, the <u>less the kindness</u> must be.

The following line in *Hamlet* (1.2.65) was first printed in Quarto 2 (1604-05):

KING CLAUDIUS
But now my Cousin *Hamlet*, and my son.

HAMLET
A little <u>more</u> than <u>kin</u>, and <u>less</u> than <u>kind</u>.

A line from a song in *Mother Bombie*, "To whit to whoo, the Owl does cry ..." (3.4) resembles the refrain in the song that closes *Love's Labour's Lost*: "Then nightly sings the staring Owl /'Tu-whit to-who.'"[49]

_____

(31)-(35). circa 1588: "Too early" allusions to *King John* [1596-97?], *The Merchant of Venice* [1596-97?], *Romeo and Juliet* [1594-95?], and *Hamlet* [1600-01?].

Thomas Kyd (?), play, *Soliman and Perseda* (see p. 50 for dating).

(31). In *Soliman and Perseda* (1.3), Piston comically asks the bragging knight, Basilisco, to swear upon his dagger that he will attend a tilting match with him. Basilisco repeats Piston's oath with a slight addition:

PISTON
I, the aforesaid Basilisco –

BASILISCO
I, the aforesaid Basilisco – Knight, good fellow, Knight, Knight –

PISTON
Knave, good fellow, Knave, Knave ...

In *King John* (1.1.242-44), the Bastard Faulconbridge asks his mother who was his real father. She replies:

LADY FAULCONBRIDGE
What means this scorn, thou most untoward knave?

BASTARD FAULCONBRIDGE
Knight, knight, good mother, Basilisco-like.
What! I am dubb'd! I have it on my shoulder.

For the "Basilisco-like" reference in *King John*, orthodox scholars routinely say that Shakespeare was parodying the lines of Basilisco in *Soliman and Perseda*. But reading Shakespeare's lines in the proper context, it was clearly the opposite. Just before the lines in question, the Bastard Faulconbridge had been renamed "Richard Plantagenet" and knighted by King John, in recognition of his being the natural son of the late king, Richard I, known as "Coeur-de-lion" or "Lion Heart." In *King John*, the name "Richard Cordelion" was mentioned five times. Since ancient times, the brightest star in the constellation Leo, Alpha Leonis, was known as "Cor Leonis," the "Lion's Heart." In the 16th century, however, "Cor Leonis" was renamed "Basiliscus."[50] The Bastard Faulconbridge alludes to the new name of this star to emphasize his new name and high parentage, although it was anachronistic. Shakespeare, therefore, was alluding to astronomy and not to the character in *Soliman and Perseda*, a play critics unanimously regard as unremarkable. This interpretation was dismissed as a "curious coincidence" in the *New Variorum* edition of *King John* in 1919[51] and has not been discussed since.

---

(32). A second parallel allusion between *Soliman and Perseda* and *King John* was noted by E.A.J. Honigmann.[52] In *Soliman and Perseda* (1.5.16-17), the Turkish emperor, Soliman, speaks of attacking the island of Rhodes, which is being protected by Christians:

> Till it [the proposed attack] have prick'd the heart of <u>Christendom</u>,
> Which now that <u>paltry</u> Island [Rhodes] keeps from <u>scathe</u> [harm].

In *King John*, the king of France of the coming English invasion:

> Then turn your forces from this <u>paltry</u> siege
> And stir them up against a mightier task.
> England, impatient of your just demands,
> Hath put himself in arms ...
>
> To do offense and <u>scathe</u> in <u>Christendom</u>. [2.1.54-57, 75]

---

(33). In *Soliman and Perseda* (1.3.51-55), the Turkish colonel, Brusor, speaks of his military experience:[53]

> Against <u>the Sophy</u> [the Shah of Persia] <u>in three</u> pitched <u>fields</u>,
> Under the conduct of great <u>Soliman</u>,
> Have I been chief commander of an host,
> And put the flint heart <u>Persians</u> to the <u>sword</u> ...

In *The Merchant of Venice*, the Prince of Morocco speaks of his sword's exploits:

> By this <u>scimitar</u> [curved sword]
> That slew <u>the Sophy</u> and a <u>Persian</u> prince
> That won <u>three fields</u> of Sultan <u>Soliman</u> ... [2.1.24-27]

---

(34). An exact phrase in *Soliman and Perseda* (2.1.231) also appears in Shakespeare's *Romeo and Juliet*, and in a similar context.[54] Lucina plays a game with gentlemen wearing masks; when it is over, she asks them to remove their masks to thank them "For <u>this</u> so courteous and <u>unlook'd for sport</u>." In *Romeo and Juliet* (1.4.145), Old Capulet makes a remark about the masked dancers at his party: "<u>this</u> <u>unlook'd for sport</u> comes well."

(35). In *Soliman and Perseda* (4.1.77-78), Soliman compares Perseda's hair to that of a sun god and her forehead to Jove:

> Fair <u>locks</u> resembling *Phoebus* [sun god] radiant beams,
> Smooth <u>forehead</u> like the table of high *Jove* ...

In *Hamlet* (3.4.57), the title character compares his father's hair to that of a sun god and his forehead to Jove:

> <u>Hyperion's</u> [sun god] <u>curls</u>, the <u>front</u> [forehead] of <u>Jove</u> himself ...

---

(36)-(40). circa 1589: "Too early" allusions to *The Merchant of Venice* [1596-67?], *Romeo and Juliet* [1594-95?], *Othello* [1604-05?] and *Henry VI-Part 3* [1590-91?].

Christopher Marlowe, play, *The Jew of Malta*.

(36). In *The Jew of Malta*, the daughter of Barabas, the Jew of the title, recovers her father's hidden fortune by sneaking into their old house. While she drops the moneybags down to him, he exclaims:[55]

> O my girl,
> My gold, my fortune, my felicity! ...
>
> O girl, O gold, O beauty, O my bliss!
> [2.1.50-51, 57]

Barabas's daughter loved a Christian man.

In *The Merchant of Venice*, the daughter of the Jew, Shylock, stole some of her father's money and jewels. She tossed down a casket of his ducats through the window to her waiting lover, a Christian, before they eloped. Shylock's reaction:

> My daughter! O my ducats! O my daughter!
> Fled with a Christian! O my Christian ducats!
> Justice! the law! my ducats, and my daughter! [2.8.15-17]

---

(37). In *The Jew of Malta*, the Jew, Barabas, speaks how he bears the insults of Christians:[56]

> I learned in Florence how to kiss my hand,
> <u>Heave up my shoulders</u> when they <u>call me dog</u> ... [2.3.23-24]

In *The Merchant of Venice*, the Jew, Shylock, speaks how he bears the insults of Christians:

> Still I have borne it with a patient <u>shrug</u>,
> (For sufferance is the badge of all our Tribe.)
> You <u>call me</u> misbeliever, cutthroat <u>dog</u> ... [1.3.113-15]

A 1588 book included the phrase, "Merchant of Venice," in its subtitle: *The Voyage and Travail: of M. Caesar Frederick, Merchant of Venice, into the East India, the*

Indies, and beyond the Indies. This was Thomas Hickock's English translation of the Italian work by Cesare Federici, published in 1587. The original title of Federici's book did not include "Merchant of Venice" (*Viagge de M. Cesare de i Federici, nell'India Orientale, et oltra l'India…*). Perhaps the phrase was added because it already had name recognition from Shakespeare's play and would add to the book's attractiveness. *The Merchant of Venice* may also have been the play referred to in Henslowe's diary, dated August 25, 1594: "The Venetian Comedy."[57] The First Folio classified *Merchant* as a comedy, and the second page of the first quarto (1600) gives the title as "The comical History of the Merchant of Venice." Shylock's comment upon his daughter's choice of husband in *Merchant* (4.1.297-98), "Would any of the stock of Barabbas /Had been her husband rather than a Christian," may have inspired the character name, Barabas, in Marlowe's play.

---

(38). The next three parallels were noted by John Bakeless. In *The Jew of Malta* (2.1.41-42), at night, Barabas sees his daughter, Abigail, and says:

> But stay, what star shines yonder in the east?
> The loadstar of my life, if Abigail.

In *Romeo and Juliet* (2.1.44-45), at night Romeo sees Juliet at the balcony.[58]

> But soft, what light through yonder window breaks?
> It is the East and Juliet is the sun.

In the 1581 play, *The Three Ladies of London*, Lady Lucre says to Dissimulation: "Thou art very pleasant full of thy ropery" (sig. B1, 1584 ed.). In *Romeo and Juliet* (2.3.146), the nurse asks Romeo about Mercutio: "I pray you, sir, what saucy merchant was this, that was so full of his ropery?"[59] *Three Ladies* (by Robert Wilson) resembles Shakespeare's *Merchant of Venice*: an Italian merchant becomes indebted to a Jew for 3000 ducats in 3 months, and there is a trial scene (*DNB*).

---

(39). In *The Jew of Malta* (3.2), Ferneze makes this exclamation upon discovering his dead son:[60]

> What sight is this? my Lodowico slain!
> These arms of mine shall be thy sepulcher.

In *Henry VI-Part 3* (2.5.114-5), a father who has accidently killed his son in battle says to him:

> These arms of mine shall be thy winding-sheet;
> My heart, sweet boy, shall be thy sepulcher.

---

(40). In *The Jew of Malta* (5.1.82-84), Barabas says:[61]

> I drank of poppy and cold mandrake juice,
> And being asleep, belike they thought me dead
> And threw me o'er the walls.

In *Othello* (3.3.330-33), Iago says to the title character:

> Not <u>poppy</u>, nor <u>mandragora</u>,
> Nor all the drowsy syrups of the world,
> Shall ever medicine thee to that sweet <u>sleep</u>
> Which thou ow'dst yesterday.

John Weever may have incorporated lines from both Marlowe and Shakespeare for his poem about Sir John Oldcastle, printed in 1601:[62]

> Of <u>Mandrake</u>, <u>Poppy</u>, evergreen did flourish,
> With herbs whose <u>juice</u> the <u>drowsy</u> sense would nourish.

---

(41)-(42). circa 1589: "Too early" allusions to *Troilus and Cressida* [1601-02?] and *Hamlet* [1600-01?].

Anonymous play, *Histrio-mastix, or the Player Whipp'd* (for dating, see p. 51).

(41). In *Histrio-mastix*, a traveling acting company performs a scene with characters Troilus and Cressida. Before he goes to battle, the Troilus actor puts Cressida's garter on his elbow for luck. He also openly alludes to Shakespeare.

> Behold, behold thy garter blue
> Thy knight his valiant elbow wears,
> That when he shakes his furious Speare
> The foe, in shivering fearful sort
> May lay him down in death to snort ...

The Cressida actor gives her scarf to Troilus, and tells him to wear it in his helmet:

> Here take my screen [probably a scarf], wear it for grace;
> Within thy helmet put the same,
> Therewith to make thy enemies lame.
> [Act 2, lines 271-75, 277-79]

In Act 4 of Shakespeare's *Troilus and Cressida*, Troilus gives Cressida his sleeve, and Cressida gives Troilus her glove, and both pledge fidelity to each other before a battle. But in the next act, Cressida gives Troilus' sleeve to her other suitor, Diomedes, who says he will wear it on his helmet to provoke its owner (5.2.101). This is a key moment in the drama: Troilus, who was observing this scene, learns of Cressida's falseness.

In *Histrio-mastix*, just before the play within a play, a character named "Prologue" introduces the play. This is another allusion to Shakespeare's *Troilus and Cressida*: the prologue features an actor dressed in war costume who tells the audience that he is "a Prologue arm'd," but not so-dressed to defend the author. Ben Jonson evidently copied the idea for the prologue of *Poetaster* (1601), as did John Marston for the epilogue of *Antonio and Mellida* (published 1602).[63]

(42). In *Histrio-mastix*, two characters enter with a dog and a duck:

> VOURCHIER
> One of the goodliest Spaniels I have seen.
>
> LYON-RASH
> And here's the very quintessence of ducks. [Act 2, lines 160-61]

Shakespeare's Hamlet ponders man's attributes:

> The beauty of the world, the paragon of animals; and yet to me,
> what is this quintessence of dust? [2.2.315]

---

(43). 1589: "Too early" allusion to *Henry VI-Part 2* [1590-91?].

George Peele, poem, *A Farewell*, reg. Feb. 23, 1589 (T. Baldwin, *On the Compositional Genetics of The Comedy of Errors*, Urbana, IL, 1965, p. 227).

Peele wrote verses on the occasion of Norris and Drake's anti-Spanish naval mission: "Bid England's shore and Albion's chalky cliffs /Farewell:" (lines 3-4).

In *Henry VI-Part 2*, Queen Margaret recalls her sea voyage to England. The winds twice blew her back towards France, so she "bid them blow towards England's blessed shore"; in the storm she could barely discern its "chalky cliffs" (3.2.90, 101).

---

(44). 1589: "Too early" allusion to *Hamlet* [1600-01?].

Thomas Nashe, preface to Robert Greene's novel, *Menaphon* (registered August 23, 1589). See full explanation on pp. 52-55.

> ... yet English *Seneca* read by candlelight yields many good sentences, as *Blood is a Beggar*, and so forth: and if you entreat him fair in a frosty morning, he will afford you whole *Hamlets*, I should say handfuls of tragical speeches.

---

(45). 1589: "Too early" allusion to *Julius Caesar* [1599-1600?].

Edmund Spenser, poem, *The Faerie Queene* (reg. Dec. 1, 1589, pub. 1590).

In Spenser's famous epic, "youths" at night muse about victory while being overtaken by the "leaden mace" of Morpheus or sleep, as noted by P.C. Bayley:[64]

> But whenas *Morpheus* had with leaden mace
> Arrested all that courtly company,
> Up-rose *Duessa* from her resting place ... [Book 1, 4, 44]

At night before the battle at Philipi in *Julius Caesar* (4.3.266-68), Brutus asks his young servant to play music. When he soon falls asleep, Brutus remarks:

> This is a sleepy tune: O murderous slumber,
> Lay'st thou thy leaden mace upon my boy,

That plays thee music? Gentle knave, good night;

---

(46). 1589: "Too early" allusion to *Henry IV-Part 1* [1597-98?].

Anon. pamphlet (John Lyly?), *Pap with an Hatchet. Alias, A Fig for My Godson.*

The OED lists the expression, "give the devil his due," as first occurring in *Pap.*[65]

> O but be not partial, <u>give</u> them <u>their due</u> though they were <u>devils</u>, so <u>will</u> I, and excuse them for taking any money at interest. [D2]

In *Henry IV-Part 1* (1.2.120-22), Prince Hal says of Falstaff,

> Sir John stands to his word. The devil shall have his bargain, for he was never yet a breaker of proverbs: He <u>will</u> <u>give</u> the <u>devil</u> <u>his</u> <u>due</u>.

---

(47). circa 1589: "Too early" allusion to *The Merry Wives of Windsor* [1600-01?].

Robert Greene, play, *Friar Bacon and Friar Bungay.*

Friar Bacon tests Miles on his Latin:[66]

> FRIAR BACON
> <u>Come on, sirrah</u>, what part of speech is *Ego*?
>
> MILES
> *Ego*, that is "I"; marry, <u>*nomen*</u> *substantivo*. [Scene 5, lines 29-30]

In *The Merry Wives of Windsor*, Sir Hugh Evans tests William on his Latin:

> MISTRESS PAGE
> <u>Come on, sirrah</u>; hold up your head; answer your master, be not afraid ...
>
> EVANS
> What is he, William, that does lend articles?
>
> WILLIAM
> Articles are borrowed of the pronoun, and be thus declined, *Singulariter, <u>nominativo</u>, hic, hoec, hoc*. [4.1.22-22, 40-44]

The *Merry Wives* character, Dr. Caius, "doctor of physic," was based on the real-life physician, Dr. John Caius, an instructor at Cambridge University. Caius's known eccentric behavior is paralleled in Shakespeare's character; he died in 1573.

---

(48). circa 1590: "Too early" allusion to *Hamlet* [1600-01?].

George Peele, play, *Edward I* (registered October 8, 1593).

King Edward I says to Queen Elinor:

> If any heavenly joy in woman be,

> Sweet of all sweets, sweet Nell it is in thee. [scene 3]

In *Hamlet* (5.1.245), Queen Gertrude throws flowers on Ophelia's grave and says:

> Sweets to the sweet, farewell!

---

(49). 1590: "Too early" allusion to *Titus Andronicus* [1593-94?].

Anonymous fiction, *The Cobbler of Canterbury* (published in 1590).

In *The Cobbler of Canterbury* ("The Cobbler's Tale"), the prior and the smith's wife are having an affair. The smith did not

> suspect anything, for the blind eats many a fly, and much <u>water</u>
> runs <u>by the mill</u> that <u>the miller wots</u> [knows] not on. [p. 8]

The prior learned that the smith's wife slept with another man, one who

> had <u>cut a shive</u> [slice] on his <u>loaf</u> ... [p. 8]

In *Titus Andronicus* (2.1.85-89), Demetrius says he will seduce the newly married Lavinia and make a cuckold of her husband.[67]

> What man, more <u>water</u> glideth <u>by the Mill</u>
> Than <u>wots the Miller</u> of, and easy it is
> Of <u>a cut loaf</u> to steal <u>a shive</u>, we know:

The excerpts from *The Cobbler of Canterbury* – evidently two different proverbial expressions – occurred on the same page. Only in Shakespeare's *Titus Andronicus* do they occur in two consecutive lines and with similar wording.
    Another phrase in *The Cobbler of Canterbury*, "bestowed the Mariners under hatches" ("The Scholar's Tale"), resembles a Shakespeare phrase, "The mariners all under hatches stowed ... " (*The Tempest*, 1.2.230).[68]

---

(50)-(51). 1591: "Too early" allusions to *Titus Andronicus* [1593-94?] and *King John* [1596-97?].

George Peele, poem, *Descensus Astraea* (published 1591).

(50). Peele's opening speech describes Queen Elizabeth's ascension to the throne with the image of Time making the moon and sun "gallop the zodiac."[69]

> ... behold
> How Time hath turn'd his restless wheel about,
> And made the silver moon and heaven's bright eye
> <u>Gallop the zodiac</u>, and end the year ... [lines 1-4]

In *Titus Andronicus*, Aaron describes the "new-made empress" of Rome, Tamora (also the Queen of Goths), with the image of the sun galloping the zodiac.

> As when the golden sun salutes the morn,

And, having gilt the ocean with his beams,
<u>Gallops the zodiac</u> in his glistering coach,
And overlooks the highest-peering hills; [2.1.5-8]

Peele apparently borrowed several unusual words from Shakespeare's *Titus Andronicus* for his poem, *Honour of the Garter* (written by June 26, 1593): *palliament, Enceladus, re-salute*, and phrases, "virtue consecrate," "House of Fame," "to whom my thoughts are humble" ("humbled" in *Titus*), and "rich ornaments" ("ornament" in *Titus*). The phrase in *Titus Andronicus*, "Laden with honor's spoils," appeared almost exactly in line 89 of Peele's *An Eclogue... Robert Earl of Essex* (1589). Shakespeare wrote "spoils" and Peele wrote "spoil."[70]

———

(51). *Descensus Astraea* describes Fortune working against Queen Elizabeth:

While <u>Fortune</u> for her service and her sake
<u>With golden hands</u> doth strengthen and enrich
The Web that they for fair Astraea [Elizabeth] weave. [lines 35-37]

In *King John* (3.1.54-58), "corrupted" Fortune works against France:

... But <u>Fortune</u>, O,
She is corrupted, changed, and won from thee.
She adulterates hourly with thine uncle John,
And <u>with</u> her <u>golden hand</u> hath pluck'd on France
To tread down fair respect of sovereignty.

———

(52). 1591 or earlier: "Too early" allusion to *Timon of Athens* [1607-08?].

Robert Southwell, poem, *Saint Peter's Complaint*. This work was circulating in manuscript by 1591 (*Reader's Encyclopedia*), and printed in the year of Southwell's execution, 1595. His literary writing ended in June 1592, when he was imprisoned for his Jesuit activities.

In Stanza 42, Southwell describes a "stormy place":[71]

Where fear, my thoughts <u>candied with icy cold</u>:
<u>Heat</u>, did my tongue to perjuries unfold.

Timon of Athens (4.3.226-27):

Will the <u>cold</u> brook,
<u>Candied with ice, caudle</u> [give warmth] thy morning taste,
To cure the o'er-night's surfeit?

———

(53)-(56). 1592: "Too early" allusions to *King John* [1596-97?], *Love's Labour's Lost* [1594-95?], *Henry IV-Part 2* [1597-98?], and *Romeo and Juliet* [1594-95?].

Samuel Daniel, poem, *The Complaint of Rosamond* (registered February 4, 1592).

(53). *The Complaint of Rosamond*, as noted by Honigmann:[72]

> My <u>birth</u> had honor, and my beauty fame:
> <u>Nature and Fortune join'd to make</u> me blest ... [lines 79-80]

King John (2.2.52-53):

> But thou art fair, and at thy <u>birth</u>, dear boy,
> <u>Nature and fortune join'd to make</u> thee great:

———

(54). The next two parallels were noted by Robert Law (after Anders).[73]

The Complaint of Rosamond (lines 120-21):

> Ah beauty Siren, fair enchanting good,
> Sweet silent <u>Rhetoric of persuading eyes</u>:

In *Love's Labour's Lost* (4.3.60-62), Longaville reads a sonnet aloud:

> "Did not the heavenly <u>rhetoric of</u> thine <u>eye</u>
> 'Gainst whom the world cannot hold argument,
> <u>Persuade</u> my heart to this false perjury?"

Berowne's line in *Love's Labour's Lost*, "Well set thee down sorrow" (4.3.4), perhaps alluded to "Come sorrow, come set thee down," a song with a dating limit of c. 1585. John Florio may have alluded to the play in *First Fruits* (1576): "We need not speak so much of love, all books are full of love, with so many authors, that it were labour lost to speak of Love."[74]

———

(55). *The Complaint of Rosamond* (lines 232-33):

> Dost thou not see how that <u>Thy King thy Jove</u>,
> Lightens forth glory on thy dark estate:

In *Henry IV-Part 2* (5.5.50), Falstaff says to the new King Henry V:

> <u>My King! My Jove</u>! I speak to thee, my heart!

———

(56). In *The Complaint of Rosamond*, the king describes his dead love:[75]

> And naught-respecting <u>death</u> (the last of pains)
> Plac'd his <u>pale</u> colors (th'<u>ensign</u> of his might)
> Upon his new-got spoil before his right. [lines 605-08]

In *Romeo and Juliet* (5.3.94-96), Romeo describes his dead love, Juliet:

> Thou art not conquer'd – Beauty's <u>ensign</u> yet
> Is crimson in thy lips and in thy cheeks,
> And <u>Death's pale</u> flag is not advanced there.

Daniel's poem also shared word clusters with Shakespeare's *Lucrece* (1594).[76]

The Complaint of Rosamond (lines 432-33):

> Com'd was the <u>night, mother of</u> sleep <u>and fear,</u>
> Who with her <u>sable</u> mantle friendly covers ...

Lucrece (lines 117-18):

> Till <u>sable Night, mother of</u> dread <u>and Fear,</u>
> Upon the world dim darkness doth display ...

Since Daniel probably borrowed lines from Shakespeare's Sonnet 67 for *Rosamond* (see p. 55), it's likely he did the same with Shakespeare's *The Two Gentlemen of Verona* (Chambers dates 1594-95?, Wells and Taylor, 1590-91?).

The Complaint of Rosamond (lines 370-71):

> With costly <u>Jewels</u> Orators of Love:
> Which (ah too well men know) <u>do women move.</u>

The Two Gentlemen of Verona (3.1.89-91):

> Win her with gifts, if she respect not words:
> Dumb <u>jewels</u> often in their silent kind
> More than quick words <u>do move</u> a <u>woman</u>'s mind.

Scholars have noted that Daniel borrowed from Shakespeare's *Anthony and Cleopatra* for the revised version of his *The Tragedy of Cleopatra* (1607).[77] Unlike Shakespeare, contemporaries regarded Daniel as a plagiarist: John Harington's epigram to Daniel was titled, "Of honest theft, to my good friend Master Samuel Daniel,"[78] and the play, *The Return From Parnassus-Part 2*, contained this passage:

> Only let him [Daniel] more sparingly make use
> Of others' wit, and use his own the more,
> That well may scorn base imitation. [lines 238-40][79]

---

(57). 1592: "Too early" allusion to *Twelfth Night* [1599-1600?].

Samuel Daniel, sonnet cycle, *Delia* (reg. Feb. 4, 1592).

In his Sonnet 5, Daniel writes about the rejection of his love.

> [She] Cast water-cold disdain upon my face
> Which <u>turn'd</u> my sport <u>into a Hart</u>'s [deer] despair,
> Which still is chas'd, while I have any breath,
> By <u>mine</u> own thoughts, set on me by my Fair:
> <u>My thoughts</u> (<u>like Hounds</u>) <u>pursue me</u> to my death.

In *Twelfth Night* (1.1.19-23), the Duke is reminded of his unrequited love of Olivia when asked if he will go deer-hunting:[80]

> O, when <u>mine</u> eyes did see Olivia first,
> <u>Methought</u> she purged the air of pestilence.
> That instant was I <u>turn'd into a hart</u>;
> And my desires, <u>like</u> fell and cruel <u>hounds,</u>
> E'er since <u>pursue me.</u>

Daniel's *Delia* sonnets and Shakespeare's sonnets share similar lines, as noted below.[81]

Daniel's *Delia* Sonnet 13:

> I figured on the table of mine heart
> The fairest form that all the world admires ...

Compare with Shakespeare's Sonnet 24:

> Mine eye hath play'd the painter and hath steel'd,
> Thy beauty's form in table of my heart ...

Daniel's *Delia* Sonnet 36:

> Must yield up all to tyrant Time's desire;

Compare with Shakespeare's Sonnet 16:

> Make war upon this bloody tyrant time?

Daniel's *Delia* Sonnet 36:

> When golden hairs shall change to silver wire ...

Compare with Shakespeare's Sonnet 130:

> If hairs be wires, black wires grow on her head:

---

(58). 1592: "Too early" allusion to *Titus Andronicus* [1593-94?].

Anonymous play, *A Knack to Know a Knave* (performed June 10, 1592, as noted in Henslowe's diary, and first printed in 1594).

A Knack to Know a Knave:

> My gracious Lord, as welcome shall you be,
> To me, my Daughter, and my son-in-law,
> As *Titus* was unto the Roman Senators,
> When he had made a conquest on the <u>Goths</u>:
> That in requital of his service done,
> Did offer him the imperial Diadem:
> As they in *Titus*, we in your Grace still find,
> The perfect figure of a Princely mind.   [lines 1488-95]

The phrase, "As they in *Titus*," with Titus in italics, indicates the reference was to a literary or dramatic work. "Shakespeare's play is the only known version of the story with Goths instead of Moors," according to *A Shakespeare Companion*. Wells and Taylor called it "an apparent allusion" to Shakespeare's play.[82]

---

(59)-(62). circa 1592: "Too early" allusions to *Hamlet* [1600-01?], *King John* [1596-97?], *Romeo and Juliet* [1594-95?], and *Henry IV-Part 1* [1597-98?].

Christopher Marlowe, play, *Edward II*.

(59). In *Edward II*, Young Mortimer, who is about to be taken away and executed, speaks to the queen:

> Farewell, fair Queen; weep not for Mortimer,
> That <u>scorns</u> <u>the world</u>, and as a <u>traveler</u>,
> Goes to <u>discover countries</u> yet <u>unknown</u>. [5.6.64-66]

Compare the above passage with the two quarto versions of *Hamlet* of the famous soliloquy on suicide (below).

Hamlet, Quarto 1 (1603):

> For in that dream of death, when we awake,
> And borne before an everlasting Judge,
> From whence no <u>passenger</u> ever return'd,
> The <u>undiscovered country</u>, and the accurs'd damn'd.
> But for this, the joyful hope of this
> Who'ld bear the <u>scorns</u> and flattery of <u>the world</u>,
> Scorned by the right rich, the rich cursed of the poor? [Scene 18]

Hamlet, Quarto 2 (1604-05):

> For who would bear the whips and <u>scorns</u> of time ...

> But that the dread of something after death,
> The <u>undiscover'd country</u>, from whose borne
> No <u>traveler</u> returns, puzzles the will ... [Signature G2]

———

(60). Marlowe's *Edward II* (3.2.208-09), as noted by Honigmann:[83]

> Away, base upstart, brav'st thou nobles thus?

King John (4.3.87):

> Out, dunghill! dar'st thou brave a nobleman?

———

(61). In Marlowe's *Edward II* (4.3.63-66), the title character waits for day to come, as noted by Anders:[84]

> <u>Gallop apace</u>, bright <u>Phoebus</u>, through the sky,
> And dusky <u>night</u>, in rusty iron car,
> Between you both shorten the time, I pray,
> That I may see that most desired day ...

In *Romeo and Juliet* (3.2.1-4), Juliet waits for night to come:

> <u>Gallop apace</u>, you fiery-footed steeds,
> Towards <u>Phoebus</u>' lodging: such a wagoner
> As Phaeton would whip you to the west,
> And bring in cloudy <u>night</u> immediately.

(62). In *Edward II* (2.2.127-130), Mortimer Junior wants to shout at the king for his refusal to ransom his uncle, Mortimer Senior.[85]

> MORTIMER JUNIOR
> Cousin, and if <u>he will not ransom</u> him
> I'll thunder such a peal <u>into his ears</u>
> As never subject did unto a king.
>
> LANCASTER
> Content, <u>I'll</u> bear my part – <u>holloa</u>! Who's there?

In *Henry IV-Part 1* (1.3.219-22, 227), Hotspur wants to shout at the king for his refusal to ransom his kinsman, Edmund Mortimer:

> HOTSPUR
> He said <u>he will not ransom</u> <u>Mortimer</u>,
> Forbade my tongue to speak of Mortimer.
> But I will find him when he lies asleep,
> And <u>in his ear</u> <u>I'll holla</u> "Mortimer!"
>
> WORCESTER
> Hear you, <u>cousin</u>.

The exact title of Marlowe's *Edward II*, as printed in 1594, was *The Troublesome Reign and Lamentable Death of Edward the Second, King of England*. It appears that Marlowe, or printers, also borrowed part of this title from *The Troublesome Reign of John, King of England*, a play printed in 1591 and later ascribed to Shakespeare.[86]

---

(63)-(64). 1592: "Too early" allusions to *As You Like It* [1599-1600?] and *Much Ado About Nothing* [1598-99?].

Thomas Nashe, pamphlet, *Strange News, of the Intercepting of Certain Letters* (registered on January 12, 1593; the first two issues were dated 1592).

(63). Nashe comments upon verses written by Gabriel Harvey:[87]

> I would trot a <u>false gallop</u> through the rest <u>of</u> his ragged <u>Verses</u>, but that if I should retort his rhyme doggerel aright, I must make my verses (as he doth his) run hobbling like a Brewer's Cart upon the stones, and observe no length in their feet; which were *absurdum per absurdius*, to <u>infect</u> my vein <u>with</u> his imitation. [sig. Dv]

In *As You Like It* (3.2.112), Touchstone criticizes Orlando's verses to Rosalind:

> This is the very <u>false gallop of verses</u>. Why do you <u>infect</u> yourself <u>with</u> them?

"False gallop," also appeared in Shakespeare's *Much Ado About Nothing* (3.4.94).

(64). In *Strange News*, Nashe writes about his own character:[88]

> For the order of my life, it is as civil as a civil orange; I lurk in no corners, but converse in a house of credit … [sig. L4]

In *Much Ado About Nothing*, Beatrice comments on Count Claudio's character:

> The count [Claudio] is neither sad, nor sick, nor merry, nor well; but civil, count, as civil as an orange, and something of that jealous complexion. [2.1.305-08]

"Civil" was a pun on "Seville." Two exact phrases in *Strange News* also occur in *The Comedy of Errors*, as noted by J. Dover Wilson.[89] *Strange News*: "… heart and goodwill, but never a rag of money" (sig. G4v). *The Comedy of Errors*: "Money by me! heart and goodwill you might; /But surely, master, not a rag of money" (4.4.84-85).

Thomas Lodge's book, *Euphues' Shadow*, which preceded *Strange News* by almost a year, contained the phrase, "but never a rag of money" (sig. L4v). If Nashe and Lodge were borrowing from Shakespeare, then it would then push back the dating of *The Comedy of Errors* to at least 1591. But *Errors* was probably written by 1577, when a play with a similar title was shown to the queen (see p. 63). *Strange News* evidently alluded to *Henry IV-Part 1* and *The Merry Wives of Windsor* (Chapter 15, No. 4).

---

(65). circa 1593: "Too early" allusion to *Julius Caesar* [1599-1600?].

Christopher Marlowe (d. May 30, 1593), play, *The Massacre at Paris*.[90]

After being warned of a possible attack on his life, Marlowe's character, the Duke of Guise, says:

> Yet *Caesar* shall go forth
> Let mean conceits, and baser men fear death:
> Tut, they are peasants; I am Duke of Guise;
> And princes with their looks engender fear.

The Duke is immediately attacked, and says:

> Thus *Caesar* did go forth, and thus he dies. [3.2]

In Shakespeare's *Julius Caesar* (2.2.10-13, 28), the title character is undisturbed by his wife's dream of his murder, and leaving his house, says to her:

> *Caesar* shall forth; the things that threaten'd me,
> Ne'er look'd but on my back: When they shall see
> The face of *Caesar*, they are vanished.
> …
> Yet *Caesar* shall go forth;

He is assassinated shortly afterward.

Scholars routinely say that Shakespeare borrowed from Marlowe, but they rarely mention that Marlowe borrowed two lines from Shakespeare's *Henry VI-Part 3* (1590-91?) for *The Massacre at Paris*, as cited in *Reader's Encyclopedia*:[91]

The Massacre at Paris by Marlowe:

> Sweet Duke of Guise, our prop to lean upon
> Now thou art dead, here is no stay for us. [3.3]

Shakespeare's *Henry VI-Part 3*:

> Sweet Duke of York, our prop to lean upon,
> Now thou art gone, we have no staff, no stay. [2.1.68-69]

Another line in *The Massacre at Paris* (2.6), "And we are graced with wreaths of victory," appears exactly in *Henry VI-Part 3* (5.3.2).

---

(66)-(68). 1593: "Too early" allusions to *The Tempest* [1611-12?], *Romeo and Juliet* [1594-95?], and *The Winter's Tale* [1610-11?].

Christopher Marlowe (d. May 30, 1593), poem, *Hero and Leander*. Similar phrasings of Marlowe's poem with three Shakespeare plays follow (Anders noted nos. 66-67).[92]

(66). *Hero and Leander* (Sestaid 1, lines 346-48):

> Far from the town (where all is <u>whist</u> [quiet] and still),
> Save that the sea, playing on <u>yellow sand</u> ...

Ariel sings a song in *The Tempest* (1.2.376-79):

> Come unto these <u>yellow sands</u>,
> And then take hands:
> Curtsied when you have, and kiss'd
> The wild waves <u>whist</u>,
> Foot it featly [gracefully] here and there ...

"Foot it featly" was an unusual expression that occurred in only one other work, Thomas Lodge's *Scylla's Metamorphosis* ("Footing it featly on the grassy ground," sig. A2v), printed in 1589.[93] German dramatist, Jakob Ayrer, wrote *The Comedy of the Beautiful Sidea* (circa 1595); this play resembles Shakespeare's *The Tempest*, so much so that some scholars believe they share a common source that has been lost (another "Ur" play). Ayrer wrote plays circa 1593 until his death in March 1605, a time period when English actors were performing English plays in Germany. That Ayrer's plays were influenced by English plays is well accepted.[94] Ben Jonson evidently borrowed Shakespeare's character, Stephano, in *The Tempest*, for his comedy, *Every Man In His Humor*, first performed in 1598 (Ch. 12).

---

(67). *Hero and Leander* (Sestaid 2, lines 1-4):

> By this, sad Hero, with love unacquainted,

> Viewing Leander's face, fell down and fainted.
> He <u>kiss'd</u> her, <u>and breath'd</u> <u>life</u> <u>into</u> her <u>lips</u>
> Wherewith, as one displeased, away she trips;

In *Romeo and Juliet* (5.1.6-9), Romeo says:

> I dreamt my lady came and found me dead
> (Strange dream, that gives a dead man leave to think!)
> <u>And breath'd</u> such <u>life</u> with <u>kisses</u> <u>in</u> my <u>lips</u>,
> That I reviv'd, and was an emperor.

---

(68). The unusual image of "peeping blood" occurs in *Hero and Leander*:

> <u>Through</u> whose white skin, softer than soundest sleep,
> With damask eyes <u>the</u> ruby <u>blood</u> doth <u>peep</u>. [Sestaid 3, lines 39-40]

Shakespeare's *The Winter's Tale* (4.4.170-71):[95]

>   ... but that your youth
> And <u>the</u> true <u>blood</u> which <u>peeps</u> fairly <u>through</u>'t ...

---

(69). 1593: "Too early" allusion to *Romeo and Juliet* [1594-95?].

Barnabe Barnes, poetry, *Parthenophil and Parthenophe* (printed May 1593).

Parthenophil and Parthenophe (Sonnet 63), as noted by Victor Doyno:[96]

> Would <u>I were</u> chang'd but to my mistress <u>gloves</u>,
> That those white lovely fingers I might hide,
> <u>That I might</u> kiss those <u>hands</u>, which mine heart loves ...

Romeo and Juliet (2.1.66-67):

> O that <u>I were</u> a <u>glove</u> upon that <u>hand</u>
> <u>That I might</u> touch that cheek.

Parthenophil and Parthenophe also contained similar lines with Shakespeare's Sonnet 119 and *A Lover's Complaint* (Chapter 4).

---

(70)-(71). 1593: "Too early" allusions to *Love's Labour's Lost* [1594-95?].

Gabriel Harvey, essay, *Pierce's Supererogation or a New Praise of the Old Ass* (printed July 1593). Rupert Taylor noted the following two parallel word clusters with *Love's Labour's Lost*.[97]

(70). In *Pierce's Supererogation*, letter to the reader, Harvey writes of "the excellent Gentlewoman,"

> ... my Patroness, or rather Championess in this quarrel, is meeter by nature, fitter by nurture, to be an enchanting Angel with her <u>white quill</u>, than a tormenting Fury with her <u>black ink</u>.

In *Love's Labour's Lost* (1.1.243-45), Armado writes a letter to his lady love about an event

> that draweth from my snow-white pen the ebon-colored ink, which here thou viewest ...

____

(71). In *Pierce's Supererogation* (p. 45), Harvey alludes to Thomas Nashe's book, *Pierce Penniless*:

> She knew what she said, that entitled Pierce, the hogshead of wit ...

In *Love's Labour's Lost,* the schoolmaster, Holofernes, breaks down the word, parson, into "pierce" and "one." He asks, "If one should be pierced, which is the one?" Costard replies, "Marry, Master schoolmaster, he that is likest to a hogshead." Holofernes replies,

> Of piercing a hogshead! ... 'tis pretty; it is well. [4.2.89-90]

Nashe's phrase, "mutton and porridge," in *Strange News* (1592) also occurred in *Love's Labour's Lost* (1.1.285): "I had rather pray a month with mutton and porridge."[98]

____

(72). 1593: "Too early" allusion to *Hamlet* [1600-01?].

Gabriel Harvey, essay, *A New Letter of Notable Contents* (reg. October 1, 1593).

> May they not surcease to wonder, that wonder how Machiavell can teach a Prince *to be*, and *not to be*, religious? Another question, or two of a sharper edge, were at my tongue's end. [sig. B3]

Shakespeare's Prince Hamlet (3.1.56):

> To be, or not to be, that is the Question:

____

(73). 1593: "Too early" allusion to *Hamlet* [1600-01?].

Michael Drayton, poem, *Piers Gaveston, Earl of Cornwall* (registered Dec. 3, 1593).

Piers Gaveston (lines 995-96):

> Base dunghill mind, that dost such slavery bring,
> To live a peasant, and be born a King.

Compare Drayton's lines with a line in Shakespeare's *Hamlet* (2.2.560) that was transmitted slightly differently in Quartos 1 and 2:

Hamlet, Quarto 1 (published 1603):

> Why what a dunghill idiot slave am I?

Hamlet, Quarto 2 (published 1604-05) and Folio versions:

> Oh, what a rogue and <u>peasant</u> <u>slave</u> am I?

---

(74). 1593: "Too early" allusion to *A Midsummer Night's Dream* [1595-96?].

Anonymous poet, anthology, *Arbor of Amorous Devices* (reg. January 7, 1594, first surviving edition 1597).

Arbor of Amorous Devices ("A Poem of a Maid Forsaken"):[99]

> <u>The Lark</u>, the Thrush and Nightingale,
> The Linnets sweet, and eke the Turtles <u>true</u>,
> The chattering Pie, the Jay, and eke the Quail,
> <u>The Throstle</u>-<u>Cock</u> that was <u>so black of hue</u>. [Poem 3, lines 25-28]

In *A Midsummer Night's Dream* (3.1.131-34, 137), Bottom sings a song:

> <u>The</u> ouzel-<u>cock, so black of hue</u>,
> With orange-tawny bill,
> <u>The throstle</u> with his note so <u>true</u>,
> The wren with little quill ...
>
> The finch, the sparrow, and <u>the lark</u> ...

---

(75)-(76). 1594: "Too early" allusions to *Hamlet* [1600-01?] and *Henry IV-Part 1* [1597-98?].

Thomas Nashe, essay, *Christ's Tears Over Jerusalem* (2nd edition).

(75). Nashe comments about Gabriel Harvey in the "Epistle to the Reader":

> His [Harvey's] <u>vainglory</u> (which some take to be his <u>gentlewoman</u>) he hath new <u>painted</u> over <u>an inch thick</u>. Some few crumbs of my book he hath confuted, all the rest of his invention is nothing but an <u>ox with</u> a <u>pudding in his belly</u>, not fit for anything else, save only to feast the dull ears of ironmongers, ploughmen, carpenters, and porters.

Shakespeare's Hamlet holds the skull of the jester, Yorick, and says to it:

> Now get you to my <u>lady's</u> chamber, and tell her, let her <u>paint an inch thick</u>, to this favor she must come. Make her laugh at that. [5.1.195-96]

---

(76). The second Shakespeare allusion in Nashe's passage is to a line in *Henry IV-Part 1* (2.4.457-58) in which Prince Henry describes Sir John Falstaff:

> ... that roasted Manningtree <u>ox with</u> the <u>pudding in his belly</u> ...

(77). 1594: "Too early" allusion to *The Winter's Tale* [1610-11?].

Stationers' Register, entry dated May 22, 1594:

> Edward White. Entered for his copy under the hands of both the wardens, a book entitled, *a winters nights pastime*.[100]

No book with the title, "a winters nights pastime," has survived, but "a play called *the winters nights tale*," recorded on November 5, 1611, is an undisputed reference to Shakespeare's *The Winter's Tale*.[101] The phrase, "a winter's tale," occurs in Christopher Marlowe's play, *The Tragedy of Dido, Queen of Carthage* (3.4): "Who would not undergo all kind of toil, / To be well stor'd with such a winter's tale?" Posthumously printed (1594), *Dido* is considered one of Marlowe's earliest plays, probably circa 1587. George Peele used the phrase, "a merry winter's tale," in his comedy, *The Old Wives Tale*, registered on April 16, 1595.

(78). 1594: "Too early" allusion to *Hamlet* [1600-01?].

Henslowe's Diary, "Hamlet," the performance of a play recorded on June 9, 1594.

(79)-(80). 1594: "Too early" allusions to *Henry IV-Part 1* and *Henry IV-Part 2* [both plays 1597-98?].

Samuel Daniel, poem, *The First Four Books of the Civil Wars Between the Two Houses of Lancaster and York* (registered October 11, 1594, published 1595).

(79). In Daniel's *Civil Wars* (Book 2, Stanza 57), King Richard II says, "<u>Base-pickthank</u> [sycophant] *Flattery* ... "[102]

In Shakespeare's *Henry IV-Part 1* (3.2.23, 25), Prince Hal spoke to his father, King Henry IV, deposer of Richard II, of "many Tales devis'd" about him "By smiling <u>Pick-thanks</u>, and <u>base</u> News-mongers ... "

(80). In *Civil Wars*, Daniel describes the nearly dead King Henry IV:

> Wearing <u>the wall so thin that</u> now the <u>mind</u>
> Might well <u>look through, and</u> his frailty find. [Book 3, Stanza 116]

In Shakespeare's *Henry IV-Part 2* (4.4.135-38), the title character has just fainted; his son, Thomas, Duke of Clarence, thinks he is near death:[103]

> No, no, he cannot long hold out: these pangs,
> Th'incessant care, and labor of his <u>Mind</u>,
> Hath wrought <u>the Mure</u> [wall], <u>that</u> should confine it in,
> <u>So thin, that</u> Life <u>looks through, and</u> will break out.

Daniel's epic covers the same historical period as Shakespeare's Henry IV plays.

(81). 1596: "Too early" allusion to *Othello* [1604-05?].

Edmund Spenser, poem, *The Faerie Queene* (Part 2, registered January 20, 1596).

In *The Faerie Queene*, the "words" of Slander are described in Book 4 (8.26):[104]

> Which passing through the ears, would pierce the heart,
> And wound the soul itself with grief unkind:

In *Othello* (1.3.214-19), Brabantio hears that Othello has stolen his daughter, Desdemona, and has married her. The report was only half true, the marriage was consensual, but this knowledge does not console him:

> But he bears both the sentence and the sorrow
> That, to pay grief, must of poor patience borrow.
> But words are words; I never yet did hear
> That the bruis'd heart was pierced through the ear.

(82). 1596: "Too early" allusion to *Hamlet* [1600-01?].

Thomas Lodge, pamphlet, *Wit's Misery, and the World's Madness* (pub. 1596).

Lodge compared the devil to the ghost in *Hamlet*, which he saw at a playhouse called "The Theatre." The devil is as pale as

> the ghost which cried so miserably at the Theatre, like an oyster wife, "Hamlet, revenge." [p. 56]

(83). 1596: "Too early" allusion to *Macbeth* [1605-06?].

Bartholomew Griffin, sonnet cycle, *Fidessa, More Chaste Than Kind* (pub. 1596).[105]

Griffin devotes one sonnet to sleep, that it eases worries, is a balm, restores the worker, and is man's "chief felicity."

> Care-charmer sleep, sweet ease in restless misery,
> The captive's liberty, and his freedoms song:
> Balm of the bruised heart, man's chief felicity,
> Brother of quiet death, when life is too too long.
> A Comedy it is, and now an History,
> What is not sleep unto the feeble mind?
> It easeth him that toils, and him that's sorry:
> It makes the deaf to hear, to see the blind.
> Ungentle sleep, thou helpest all but me,
> For when I sleep my soul is vexed most: [Sonnet 15]

Macbeth's passage on sleep covers the same points as Griffin's sonnet:

> *Macbeth* doth murder Sleep, the innocent Sleep,
> Sleep that knits up the ravel'd [frayed] Sleave [thread of silk] of Care,
> The death of each day's Life, sore Labor's Bath,
> Balm of hurt Minds, great Nature's second Course,
> Chief nourisher in Life's Feast. [2.2.36-46]

As mentioned in Chapter 4 (*The Passionate Pilgrim*), Griffin plagiarized material from several writers for *Fidessa*. For example, Griffin's opening phrase, "Care-charmer sleep," was lifted from Sonnet 52 of Samuel Daniel's *Delia* (1592).

(84). 1597: "Too early" allusion to *Hamlet* [1600-01?].

George Chapman, play, *An Humorous Day's Mirth* (performed May 11, 1597).

An Humorous Day's Mirth (2.2.7):

> A king of clouts [rags], a scarecrow, full of cobwebs ...

Hamlet (1603 edition, scene 11, line 49):

> A king of clouts, of very shreds.

(85). circa 1597: "Too early" allusion to *King Lear* [1605-06?].

Ben Jonson, comedy, *The Case is Altered* (first published in 1609). This play has a "likely" composition date of 1597, according to Anne Barton.[106]

To treat an injury on Onion's head, Jonson's character, Juniper, says:

> Go, get a white of an egg, and a little flax, and close the breach of the head ... [2.4]

In *King Lear* (3.7.104-06), a servant uses a similar treatment for the savagely blinded Earl of Gloucester:[107]

> Go thou. I'll fetch some flax and whites of eggs
> To apply to his bleeding face. Now, heaven help him!

Early critics noted that Jonson's naming of this specific treatment for a "comic" injury may have been a "sneer" at Shakespeare because his character called for a light remedy to treat a catastrophic injury.

(86). 1599: "Too early" allusion to *Othello* [1604-05?].

Ben Jonson, comedy, *Every Man Out of His Humor* (performed 1599, pub. 1600).

Jonson's character, Sogliardo, takes a lady's hand and says:[108]

> How does my sweet lady? hot and moist? beautiful and lusty? [5.2]

In *Othello* (3.4.36, 38-40), the title character asks Desdemona, "Give me your hand." Suspecting her infidelity, he remarks

> This hand is moist my Lady ...

> This argues fruitfulness, and liberal heart:
> Hot, hot, and moist. This hand of yours requires
> A sequester from Liberty ...

The expression, "hot and moist," appeared as a chapter heading in the 1576 medical book, *The Touchstone of Complexions*, translated by Thomas Newton: "Of a Hot and Moist Complexion" (p. 88). The previous chapter was titled, "Of a Cold and Moist Complexion."

---

(87). 1600: "Too early" allusion to *Macbeth* [1605-06?].

William Kemp, pamphlet, *Nine Days' Wonder* (registered April 22, 1600).

Comic actor Kemp writes:

> I met a proper upright youth … a penny Poet whose first making was the miserable stolen story of Macdoel, or Macdobeth, or Macsomewhat: for I am sure a Mac it was, though I never had the maw [stomach] to see it. [sig. D3v]

As noted in the New Variorum Edition of Shakespeare's *Macbeth*,[109] the words, "to see it," coming from an actor implies the work referred to was dramatic. The "penny Poet's" story was "stolen," and its title sounded like Macbeth. Kemp did not have the stomach ("maw") to see the play; he must have assumed that this stolen story resembled Shakespeare's very bloody play.

---

(88). 1601: "Too early" allusion to *Pericles* [1608-09?].

Thomas Wright, psychology book, *The Passions of the Mind in General* (registered June 12, 1601). Wright's title was apparently taken from a passage in Shakespeare's *Pericles* where Pericles explained how his mind and emotions worked:

> Yet neither pleasure's art can joy my spirits,
> Nor yet the other's distance comfort me.
> Then it is thus: the passions of the mind,
> That have their first conception by mis-dread,
> Have after-nourishment and life by care; [1.2.9-13]

The 1604 edition of this book was dedicated to the 3rd Earl of Southampton.

---

(89). 1601: "Too early" allusion to *Othello* [1604-05?].

Ben Jonson, comedy, *Poetaster, or His Arraignment* (acted 1601, printed 1602).

In *Poetaster* (3.1), Captain Tucca encounters the actor, Histrio. Tucca tells his pages to perform before Histrio, so they recite lines from a few contemporary plays. One page says, "you shall see me do the *Moor*: Master, lend me your scarf a little." The identity of the play is obvious: the handkerchief in Shakespeare's *Othello* was the key evidence that convinced Othello the Moor that his wife was unfaithful, ultimately provoking him to murder her.[110] Jonson's 1599 play, *Every Man Out of His Humor*, shared a phrase with *Othello* (see No. 86 above).

(90). 1601 or earlier: "Too early" allusion to *The Tempest* [1611-12?].

William Alexander, play, *The Tragedy of Darius* (pub. 1603).[111]

King Darius says:

> And let this worldly pomp our wits enchant.
> All <u>fades</u>, and scarcely <u>leaves</u> <u>behind</u> a token.
> Those golden <u>Palaces</u>, those <u>gorgeous</u> halls,
> With furniture superfluously fair:
> Those stately Courts, those sky-encount'ring walls
> Evanish [dissipate] all like vapors <u>in the air</u>. [4.2]

In *The Tempest* (4.1.148-156), Prospero, the former Duke of Milan, says:

> These our actors,
> As I foretold you, were all spirits and
> Are melted <u>into</u> <u>air</u>, into thin air:
> And, like the baseless fabric of this vision,
> The cloud-capp'd towers, the <u>gorgeous</u> <u>palaces</u>,
> The solemn temples, the great globe itself,
> Yea, all which it will inherit, shall dissolve
> And, like this insubstantial pageant <u>faded</u>,
> <u>Leave</u> not a rack <u>behind</u>.

Ben Jonson alluded to *Darius* in 1601: in Act 3 of *Poetaster*, Captain Tucca ordered his servants to "speak in King Darius's doleful strain" to impress the actor, Histrio. Tucca's servants performed excerpts from contemporary plays in this scene.

---

(91)-(92). 1603: "Too early" allusions to *King Lear* [1605-06?].

Samuel Harsnett, *A Declaration of Egregious Popish Impostures* (reg. Mar. 16, 1603).

(91). Harsnett's 1603 book was an expose of exorcism by Catholic priests based upon a case that occurred in 1585-1586. A Jesuit named Edmunds, alias Weston, performed exorcism on three chambermaids who were supposedly possessed by multiple devils at once. Harsnett commented upon the Catholic priests' reaction to sounds coming from one of the chambermaids' belly:[112]

> One time she remembreth, that she having the said <u>croaking</u> in her <u>belly</u>, or making of herself some such noise in her bed, they said it was the <u>devil</u> that was about the bed, that spake with <u>the voice of a</u> Toad. [p. 195]

In *King Lear* (3.6.29-32), Edgar remarks about a fiend in the Fool's belly:

> The foul fiend haunts poor Tom in <u>the voice of a</u> nightingale.
> Hoppedance cries in Tom's <u>belly</u> for two white herring. <u>Croak</u> not,
> <u>black angel</u>; I have no food for thee.

(92). In *King Lear* (4.1.58-63), Edgar names "five fiends" that possess poor Tom:

> Five fiends have been in poor Tom at once: of lust, as Obidicut; Hobbididance, prince of dumbness; Mahu, of stealing; Modo, of murder; Flibbertigibbet, of mopping and mowing, who since possesses chambermaids and waiting-women.

F.W. Brownlow observed that the names of the five fiends only occur in Harsnett's book and Shakespeare's play.[113] As a "too early" allusion to *Lear* occurred in 1588 (No. 29 above), Shakespeare's line about devils possessing chambermaids was evidently topical. The two works also share many unusual words, noted Kenneth Muir, such as *intelligences, yoke-fellow, pestilent, pernicious, auricular, asquint, gaster, propinquity,* and *apish.*[114] More words or phrases exclusive to *King Lear* and Harsnett's book are: "play at bo-peep," "meiny," "hysterica passio," and "vaunt-courier." Muir also noted that Harsnett's work contains detailed knowledge of the theater.

---

(93). 1606: "Too early" allusion to *The Two Noble Kinsmen* [1612-13?].

Barnabe Barnes, treatise, *Four Books of Offices: Enabling Private Persons for the Special Service of All Good Princes and Policies* (registered February 3, 1606).

Barnes wrote about war:

> It is the noble <u>corrector of</u> all prodigal <u>states</u>, a skillful <u>blood</u> letter against all dangerous obstructions and <u>pleurisies of</u> peace, the most sovereign purgation of all superfluous and spreading humors or leprosies, which can breed in any general politic body. [p. 161]

The above passage echoes Arcite's prayer to the war god, Mars, in *The Two Noble Kinsmen* (5.1.62-66), as noted by Paul Bertram:[115]

> O Great <u>Corrector of</u> enormous times,
> Shaker of o'er-rank <u>States</u>, thou grand decider
> Of dusty and old titles, that heal'st with <u>blood</u>
> The earth when it is sick, and cur'st the world
> O'th' <u>pleurisy of</u> people ...

"Too Early" Shakespeare Play Allusions by Year*

1562 *Romeo and Juliet* (6)

1578 *Taming of the Shrew* (2), *Measure for Measure*

1579 *Taming of the Shrew, The Merchant of Venice* (2), *Timon of Athens, Anthony and Cleopatra, King John, Twelfth Night, Much Ado About Nothing, Henry IV-Part 2*

1583 *Cymbeline*

1587 *Henry VI-Part 1, Richard III, Julius Caesar, Merry Wives of Windsor*

1588 *Troilus and Cressida, Richard II, Richard III, King Lear* (2), *King John* (2), *Romeo and Juliet, The Merchant of Venice, Hamlet* (2), *Titus Andronicus*

1589 *Hamlet* (2), *The Merchant of Venice* (2), *Romeo and Juliet, Othello, Henry VI-Part 2, Henry VI-Part 3, Troilus and Cressida, Julius Caesar, Henry IV-Part 1, Merry Wives of Windsor*

1590 *Hamlet, Titus Andronicus*

1591 *Titus Andronicus, King John, Timon of Athens*

1592 *Hamlet, Titus Andronicus, King John* (2), *Romeo and Juliet* (2), *Love's Labour's Lost, Henry IV-Part 1, Henry IV-Part 2, Twelfth Night, As You Like It, Much Ado About Nothing*

1593 *Hamlet* (2), *Julius Caesar, The Tempest, Romeo and Juliet* (2), *Love's Labour's Lost* (2), *The Winter's Tale, A Midsummer Night's Dream*

1594 *Hamlet* (2), *Henry IV-Part 1* (2), *Henry IV-Part 2, The Winter's Tale*

1596 *Hamlet, Macbeth, Othello*

1597 *Hamlet, King Lear*

1599 *Othello*

1600 *Macbeth*

1601 *Pericles, Othello, The Tempest*

1603 *King Lear* (2)

1606 *The Two Noble Kinsmen*

*Multiple allusions indicated in parentheses.

First "Too Early" Allusions to Shakespeare's Plays, Alphabetical*

1579 *Anthony and Cleopatra* [1606-07?]
1592 *As You Like It* [1599-00?]
1583 *Cymbeline* [1609-10?]
1588 *Hamlet* [1600-01?]
1589 *Henry IV-Part 1* [1597-98?]
1579 *Henry IV-Part 2* [1597-98?]
1587 *Henry VI-Part 1* [1591-92?]
1589 *Henry VI-Part 2* [1590-91?]
1589 *Henry VI-Part 3* [1590-91?]
1587 *Julius Caesar* [1599-00?]
1579 *King John* [1596-97?]
1588 *King Lear* [1605-06?]
1592 *Love's Labour's Lost* [1594-95?]
1596 *Macbeth* [1605-06?]
1578 *Measure for Measure* [1604-05?]
1579 *The Merchant of Venice* [1596-97?]
1587 *Merry Wives of Windsor* [1600-01?]
1593 *A Midsummer Night's Dream* [1595-96?]
1579 *Much Ado About Nothing* [1598-99?]
1589 *Othello* [1604-05?]
1601 *Pericles* [1608-09?]
1588 *Richard II* [1595-96?]
1587 *Richard III* [1592-93?]
1562 *Romeo and Juliet* [1594-95?]
1578 *The Taming of the Shrew* [1593-94?]
1593 *The Tempest* [1611-12?]
1579 *Timon of Athens* [1607-08?]
1588 *Titus Andronicus* [1593-94?]
1588 *Troilus and Cressida* [1601-02?]
1579 *Twelfth Night* [1599-00?]
1606 *The Two Noble Kinsmen* [1612-13?]
1593 *The Winter's Tale* [1610-11?]

*Orthodox dating in brackets.

APPENDIX B

Greene's Groats-worth of Wit (1592)

Here (Gentlemen) break I off *Roberto*'s speech; whose life in most parts agreeing with mine, found oneself punishment as I have done. Hereafter suppose me the said *Roberto*, and I will go on with that he promised: Greene will send you now his groat's-worth of wit, that never shewed a mite's-worth in his life: yet ere I die I will by my repentance endeavor to do all men good.

. . .

To those Gentleman his Quondam acquaintance that spend their wits in making plays, R.G. wisheth a better exercise, and wisdom to prevent his extremities.

If woeful experience may move you (Gentlemen) to beware, or unheard of wretchedness entreat you to take heed: I doubt not but you will look back with sorrow on your time past, and endeavor with repentance to spend that which is to come.

Wonder not, (for with thee will I first begin) thou famous gracer of Tragedians, that Greene, who hath said with thee (like the fool in his heart) There is no God, should now give glory unto his greatness: For penetrating is his power, his hand lies heavy upon me, he hath spoken unto me with a voice of thunder, and I have felt he is a God that can punish enemies. Why should thy excellent wit, his gift, be so blinded, that thou shouldst give no glory to the giver? Is it pestilent Machiavellian policy that thou hast studied? O peevish folly! What are his rules but mere confused mockeries, able to extirpate in small time the generation of mankind. For if *Sic volo, sic jubeo*, hold in those that are able to command: and if it be lawful *Fas & nefa*s to do anything that is beneficial; only Tyrants should possess the earth, and they striving to exceed in tyranny, should each to other be a slaughter man; till the mightiest outliving all, one stroke were left for Death, that in one age man's life should end. The broker of this Diabolical Atheism is dead, and in his life had never the felicity he aimed at: but as he began in craft; lived in fear, and ended in despair. Quam inscrutabilia sunt Dei judicia? This murderer of many brethren, had his conscience seared like *Cain*: this betrayer of him that gave his life for him, inherited the portion of *Judas*: this Apostata perished as ill as *Julian*: and wilt thou my friend be his disciple? Look but to me, by him persuaded to that liberty, and thou shalt find it an infernal bondage. I know the least of my demerits merit this miserable death, but willful striving against known truth, exceedeth all the terrors of my soul. Defer not (with me) till this last point of extremity; for little knowst thou how in the end thou shalt be visited.

With thee I join young *Juvenal,* that biting Satirist, that lastly with me together writ a Comedy. Sweet boy, might I advise thee, be advised, and get not many enemies by bitter words: inveigh against vain men, for thou canst do it, no man better, no man so well: thou hast a liberty to reprove all, and name none; for one being spoken to, all are offended; none being blamed no man is injured. Stop shallow water still running, it will rage, or tread on a worm and it will turn: then blame not Scholars vexed with sharp lines, if they reprove thy too much liberty of reproof.

And thou no less deserving than the other two, in some things rarer, in nothing inferior; driven (as myself) to extreme shifts, a little have I to say to thee: and were it not an idolatrous oath, I would swear by sweet S. George, thou art unworthy better hap, sith thou dependest on so mean a stay.

Base minded men all three of you, if by my misery you be not warned: for unto none of you (like me) sought those burrs to cleave: those Puppets (I mean) that spake from our mouths, those Antics garnished in our colors. Is it not strange, that I, to whom they all have been beholding: is it not like that you, to whom they all have been beholding, shall (were ye in that case as I am now) be both at once of them forsaken? Yes, trust them not: For there is an upstart Crow, beautified with our feathers, that with his *Tiger's heart wrapped in a Player's hide,* supposes he is as well able to bombast out a blank verse as the best of you: and being an absolute *Johannes factotum,* is in his own conceit the only Shake-scene in a country. O that I might entreat your rare wits to be employed in more profitable courses: & let those Apes imitate your past excellence, and never more acquaint them with your admired inventions. I know the best husband of you all will never prove an Usurer, and the kindest of them all will never prove a kind nurse: yet whilst you may, seek you better Masters; for it is pity men of such rare wits, should be subject to the pleasure of such rude grooms.

In this I might insert two more, that both have writ against these buckram Gentlemen: but let their own works serve to witness against their own wickedness, if they persevere to maintain anymore such peasants. For other newcomers, I leave them to the mercy of these painted monsters, who (I doubt not) will drive the best minded to despise them: for the rest, it skills not though they make a jest at them.

But now return I again to you three, knowing my misery is to you no news: and let me heartily entreat you to be warned by my harms. Delight not (as I have done) in irreligious oaths; for from the blasphemer's house, a curse shall not depart. Despise drunkenness, which wasteth the wit, and maketh men all equal unto beasts. Fly lust, as the deathsman of the soul, and defile not the Temple of the holy Ghost. Abhor those Epicures, whose loose life hath made religion loathsome to your ears: and when they soothe you with terms of Mastership, remember Robert Greene, whom they have often so flattered, perishes now for want of comfort. Remember Gentlemen, your lives are like so many lighted Tapers, that are with care delivered to all of you to maintain: these with wind-puffed wrath may be extinguished, which drunkenness put out, which negligence let fall: for man's time is not of itself so short, but it is more shortened by sin. The fire of my light is now at the last snuff, and for want of wherewith to sustain it, there is no substance left for life to feed on. Trust not then (I beseech ye) to such weak stays: for they are as changeable in mind, as in many attires. Well, my hand is tired, and I am forced to leave where I would begin: for a whole book cannot contain their wrongs, which I am forced to knit up in some few lines of words.

Desirous that you should live, though himself be dying:
Robert Greene.

APPENDIX C

Kind-heart's Dream (1592) by Henry Chettle – PREFACE LETTER

To the Gentlemen Readers.

It hath been a custom Gentle men (in my mind commendable) among former Authors (whose works are no less beautified with eloquent phrase, than garnished with excellent example) to begin an exordium to the Readers of their time, much more convenient I take it, should the writers in these days (wherein that gravity of indicting by the elder exercised, is not observ'd, nor that modest decorum kept, which they continued) submit their labors to the favorable censures of their learned overseers. For seeing nothing can be said that hath not been before said, the singularity of some men's conceits, (otherways excellent well deserving) are no more to be soothed, than the peremptory posies of two very sufficient Translators commended. To come in print is not to seek praise, but to crave pardon: I am urged to the one; and bold to beg the other, he that offends being forced, is more excusable than the willful faulty, though both be guilty, there is difference in the guilt. To observe custom, and avoid as I may cavil, opposing your favors against my fear, I'll shew reason for my present writing, and after proceed to sue for pardon.

About three months since died *M. Robert Greene*, leaving many papers in sundry booksellers hands, among other his Groats-worth of wit, in which a letter written to diverse play-makers, is offensively by one or two of them taken, and because on the dead they cannot be avenged, they willfully forge in their conceits a living Author: and after tossing it two and fro, no remedy, but it must light on me. How I have all the time of my conversing in printing hindered the bitter inveighing against scholars, it hath been very well known, and how in that I dealt I can sufficiently prove. With neither of them that take offense was I acquainted, and with one of them I care not if I never be: the other, whom at that time I did not so much spare, as since I wish I had, for that as I have moderated the heat of living writers, and might have used my own discretion (especially in such a case) the Author being dead, that I did not, I am as sorry as if the original fault had been my fault, because myself have seen his demeanor no less civil than he excellent in the quality he professes: Besides, diverse of worship have reported, his uprightness of dealing, which argues his honesty, and his facetious grace in writing, that approves his art.

For the first, whose learning I reverence, and at the perusing of *Greene's* Book, struck out what then in conscience I thought he in some displeasure writ: or had it been true, yet to publish it, was intolerable: him I would wish to use me no worse than I deserve. I had only in the copy this share, it was ill written, as sometime *Greene's* hand was none of the best, licensed it must be, ere it could be printed which could never be if it might not be read. To be brief I writ it over, and as near as I could, followed the copy, only in that letter I put something out, but in the whole book not a word in, for I protest it was all *Greene's*, not mine nor *Master Nashe's,* as some unjustly have affirmed. Neither was he the writer of an Epistle to the second part of Gerileon, though by the workman's error T. N. were set to the end: that I confess to be mine and repent it not.

Thus Gentlemen, having noted the private causes, that made me nominate myself in print; being as well to purge Master *Nashe* of that he did not, as to justify what I did, and withal to confirm what M. *Greene* did: I beseech ye accept the public cause, which is both the desire of your delight, and common benefit: for though the toy be shadowed under the Title of *Kind-heart's Dream*, it discovers the false hearts of diverse that wake to commit mischief.

Had not the former reasons been, it had come forth without a father: and then should I have had no cause to fear offending, or reason to sue for favor. Now am I in doubt of the one, though I hope of the other; which if I obtain, you shall bind me hereafter to be silent, till I can present ye with something more acceptable.

Henrie Chettle

APPENDIX D

Troilus and Cressida (1609, second issue) – LETTER TO THE READER (Anonymous)

A never writer, to an ever reader. News.

Eternal reader, you have here a new play, never stal'd with the Stage, never clapper-claw'd with the palms of the vulgar, and yet passing full of the palm comical; for it is a birth of your brain, that never undertook anything comical, vainly: And were but the vain names of comedies changed for the titles of Commodities, or of Plays for Pleas; you should see all those grand censors [critics], that now style them such vanities, flock to them for the main grace of their gravities: especially this author's Comedies, that are so fram'd to the life, that they serve for the most common Commentaries, of all the actions of our lives, shewing such a dexterity, and power of wit, that the most displeased with Plays, are pleas'd with his Comedies. And all such dull and heavy-witted worldlings, as were never capable of the wit of a Comedy, coming by report of them to his representations, have found that wit there, that they never found in themselves, and have parted better wittied than they came: feeling an edge of wit set upon them, more than ever they dream'd they had brain to grind it on.

So much and such savored salt of wit is in his Comedies, that they seem (for their height of pleasure) to be borne in that sea that brought forth *Venus*. Amongst all there is none more witty than this: And had I time I would comment upon it, though I know it needs not, (for so much as will make you think your testern [sixpence coin] well bestow'd) but for so much worth, as even poor I know to be stuffed in it. It deserves such a labor, as well as the best Comedy in *Terence* or *Plautus*.

And believe this, that when he is gone, and his Comedies out of sale, you will scramble for them, and set up a new English Inquisition. Take this for a warning, and at the peril of your pleasure's loss, and Judgment's, refuse not, nor like this the less, for not being sullied, with the smoky breath of the multitude; but thank fortune for the 'scape it hath made amongst you. Since by the grand possessors' wills I believe you should have pray'd for them [Shakespeare's plays] rather than been pray'd [to buy them]. And so I leave all such to be pray'd for (for the states of their wits healths) that will not praise it. *Vale*.

[Paragraph breaks added. Note that Shakespeare's name was not mentioned. He was referred to as "this author," just as Heywood and Walkley did in their letters to the reader.]

APPENDIX E

Shakespeare's Two Poems in *Love's Martyr* (1601)

Let the bird of loudest lay,
On the sole *Arabian* tree,
Herald sad and trumpet be:
To whose sound chaste wings obey.

But thou shrieking harbinger,
Foul precurrer [precursor] of the fiend,
Augur of the fever's end,
To this troop come thou not near.

From this Session interdict
Every fowl of tyrant wing,
Save the Eagle feath'red king,
Keep the obsequy so strict.

Let the Priest in Surplice white,
That defunctive Music can,
Be the death-divining Swan,
Lest the *Requiem* lack his right.

And thou treble-dated Crow,
That thy sable gender mak'st,
With the breath thou giv'st and tak'st,
'Mongst our mourners shalt thou go.

Here the Anthem doth commence,
Love and Constancy is dead,
Phoenix and the *Turtle* fled,
In a mutual flame from hence.

So they loved as love in twain,
Had the essence but in one,
Two distincts, Division none,
Number there in love was slain.

Hearts remote, yet not asunder;
Distance and no space was seen,
'Twixt this *Turtle* and his Queen;
But in them it were a wonder.

So between them Love did shine,
That the *Turtle* saw his right,
Flaming in the *Phoenix* sight;
Either was the other's mine.

Property was thus appalled,
That the self was not the same:
Single Natures double name,
Neither two nor one was called.

Reason in itself confounded,
Saw Division grow together,
To themselves yet either neither,
Simple were so well compounded.

That it cried, "How true a twain,
Seemeth this concordant one,
Love hath Reason, Reason none,
If what parts, can so remain."

Whereupon it made this *Threne*,
To the *Phoenix* and the *Dove*,
Co-supremes and stars of Love,
As *Chorus* to their Tragic Scene.

Threnos.

Beauty, Truth, and Rarity,
Grace in all simplicity,
Here enclosed, in cinders lie.

Death is now the *Phoenix* nest,
And the *Turtle's* loyal breast,
To eternity doth rest.

Leaving no posterity,
'Twas not their infirmity,
It was married Chastity.

Truth may seem, but cannot be,
Beauty brag, but 'tis not she,
Truth and Beauty buried be.

To this urn let those repair,
That are either true or fair,
For these dead Birds, sigh a prayer.

William Shake-speare.

APPENDIX F

An Apology for Actors (1612) by Thomas Heywood – PREFACE LETTER

To my approved good Friend, Mr. *Nicholas Okes.*

The infinite faults escaped in my book of *Britain's Troy*, by the negligence of the Printer, as the misquotations, mistaking of syllables, misplacing half lines, coining of strange and never heard of words. These being without number, when I would have taken a particular account of the *Errata*, the Printer answered me, he would not publish his own disworkmanship, but rather let his own fault lie upon the neck of the Author: and being fearful that others of his quality, had been of the same nature, and condition, and finding you on the contrary, so careful, and industrious, so serious and laborious to do the Author all the rights of the press, I could not choose but gratulate your honest endeavors with this short remembrance. Here likewise, I must necessarily insert a manifest injury done me in that work, by taking the two Epistles of *Paris* to *Helen*, and *Helen* to *Paris*, and printing them in a less volume, under the name of another, which may put the world in opinion I might steal them from him; and he to do himself right, hath since published them in his own name: but as I must acknowledge my lines not worthy his patronage, under whom he hath published them, so the Author I know much offended with M. *Jaggard* (that altogether unknown to him) presumed to make so bold with his name. These, and the like dishonesties I know you to be clear of; and I could wish but to be the happy Author of so worthy a work as I could willingly commit to your care and workmanship.

Yours ever
Thomas Heywood.

[The "less volume" referred to *The Passionate Pilgrim* (1598-99 edition), and "the Author" referred to Shakespeare.]

APPENDIX G

First Folio preface, page 1

To the Reader.

This Figure, that thou here feeſt put,
    It vvas for gentle Shakeſpeare cut;
Wherein the Grauer had a ſtrife
    with Nature, to out-doo the life :
O, could he but haue dravvne his vvit
    As vvell in braſſe, as he hath hit
His face ; the Print vvould then ſurpaſſe
    All, that vvas euer vvrit in braſſe.
But, ſince he cannot, Reader, looke
    Not on his Picture, but his Booke.

B. I.

First Folio preface, page 2

First Folio preface, page 3

First Folio preface, page 4

TO THE MOST NOBLE

A N D

INCOMPARABLE PAIR
OF BRETHREN.

W I L L I A M
Earle of Pembroke, &c.   Lord Chamberlain to the
King's most Excellent Majesty.

AND

P H I L I P
Earl of Montgomery, &c. Gentleman of his Majesty's
Bed-Chamber. Both Knights of the most Noble Order
of the Garter, and our singular good
L O R D S.

Right Honorable,

Whilst we study to be thankful in our particular, for the many favors we
have received from your L.L. we are fall'n upon the ill fortune, to mingle
two the most diverse things that can be, fear, and rashness; rashness in the
enterprise, and fear of the success. For, when we value the places your H.H.
sustain, we cannot but know their dignity greater, than to descend to the
reading of these trifles: and, while we name them trifles, we have depriv'd
ourselves of the defense of our Dedication. But since your L.L. have been
pleas'd to think these trifles some-thing, heretofore; and have prosecuted
both them, and their Author living, with so much favor: we hope, that
(they out-living him, and he not having the fate, common with some, to
be executor to his own writings) you will use the like indulgence toward
them, you have done

First Folio preface, page 5

The Epistle Dedicatory.

unto their parent. There is a great difference, whether any Book choose his Patrons, or find them: This hath done both. For, so much were your L.L. likings of the several parts, when they were acted, as before they were published, the Volume ask'd to be yours. We have but collected them, and done an office to the dead, to procure his Orphans, Guardians; without ambition either of self-profit, or fame: only to keep the memory of so worthy a Friend, & Fellow alive, as was our *SHAKESPEARE*, by humble offer of his plays, to your most noble patronage. Wherein, as we have justly observed, no man to come near your L.L. but with a kind of religious address; it hath been the height of our care, who are the Presenters, to make the present worthy of your H.H. by the perfection. But, there we must also crave our abilities to be consider'd, my Lords. We cannot go beyond our own powers. Country hands reach forth milk, cream, fruits, or what they have : and many Nations (we have heard) that had not gums & incense, obtained their requests with a leavened Cake. It was no fault to approach their Gods, by what means they could: And the most, though meanest, of things are made more precious, when they are dedicated to Temples. In that name therefore, we most humbly consecrate to your H.H. these remains of your servant *Shakespeare*; that what delight is in them, may be ever your L.L. the reputation his, & the faults ours, if any be committed, by a pair so careful to shew their gratitude both to the living, and the dead, as is

Your Lordships most bounden,

JOHN HEMINGE.

HENRY CONDELL.

First Folio preface, page 6

To the great Variety of Readers.

From the most able, to him that can but spell. There you are number'd. We had rather you were weigh'd. Especially, when the fate of all Books depends upon your capacities : and not of your heads alone, but of your purses. Well! It is now public, & you will stand for your privileges we know : to read, and censure. Do so, but buy it first. That doth best commend a Book, the Stationer says. Then, how odd soever your brains be, or your wisdoms, make your license the same, and spare not. Judge your six-pen'orth, your shillings worth, your five shillings worth at a time, or higher, so you rise to the just rates, and welcome. But, whatever you do, Buy. Censure will not drive a Trade, or make the Jack go. And though you be a Magistrate of wit, and sit on the Stage at *Black-Friars*, or the *Cock-pit*, to arraign Plays daily, know, these Plays have had their trial already, and stood out all Appeals ; and do now come forth quitted rather by a Decree of Court, than any purchas'd Letters of commendation.

    It had been a thing, we confess, worthy to have been wished, that the Author himself had liv'd to have set forth, and overseen his own writings; But since it hath been ordain'd otherwise, and he by death departed from that right, we pray you do not envy his Friends, the office of their care, and pain, to have collected & publish'd them; and so to have publish'd them, as where (before) you were abus'd with diverse stolen, and surreptitious copies, maimed, and deformed by the frauds and stealths of injurious impostors, that expos'd them: even those, are now offer'd to your view cur'd, and perfect of their limbs; and all the rest, absolute in their numbers, as he conceived them. Who, as he was a happy imitator of Nature, was a most gentle expresser of it. His mind and hand went together: And what he thought, he uttered with that easiness, that we have scarce received from him a blot in his papers. But it is not our province, who only gather his works, and give them you, to praise him. It is yours that read him. And there we hope, to your diverse capacities, you will find enough, both to draw, and hold you: for his wit can no more lie hid, than it could be lost. Read him, therefore; and again, and again: And if then you do not like him, surely you are in some manifest danger, not to understand him. And so we leave you to other of his Friends, whom if you need, can be your guides: if you need them not, you can lead your selves, and others. And such Readers we wish him.

John Heminge.
Henrie Condell.

First Folio preface, page 7

First Folio preface, page 8

To the memory of my beloved,
The AUTHOR
MR. WILLIAM SHAKESPEARE:
AND
what he hath left us.

To draw no envy (*Shakespeare*) on thy name,
  Am I thus ample to thy Book, and Fame;
While I confess thy writings to be such,
  As neither *Man*, nor *Muse*, can praise too much.
'Tis true, and all men's suffrage.   But these ways
  Were not the paths I meant unto thy praise;
For seeliest Ignorance on these may light,
  Which, when it sounds at best, but echo's right;
Or blind Affection, which doth ne'er advance
  The truth, but gropes, and urgeth all by chance;
Or crafty Malice, might pretend this praise,
  And think to ruin, where it seem'd to raise.
These are, as some infamous Bawd, or Whore,
  Should praise a Matron. What could hurt her more?
But thou art proof against them, and indeed
  Above th' ill fortune of them, or the need.
I, therefore will begin.   Soul of the Age !
  The applause ! delight ! the wonder of our Stage !
My *Shakespeare*, rise; I will not lodge thee by
  Chaucer, or *Spenser*, or bid *Beaumont* lie
A little further, to make thee a room :
  Thou art a Moniment, without a tomb,
And art alive still, while thy Book doth live,
  And we have wits to read, and praise to give.
That I not mix thee so, my brain excuses ;
  I mean with great, but disproportion'd *Muses* :
For, if I thought my judgment were of years,
  I should commit thee surely with thy peers,
And tell, how far thou didst our *Lily* outshine,
  Or sporting *Kid*, or *Marlowe's* mighty line.
And though thou hadst small *Latin*, and less *Greek*,
  From thence to honor thee, I would not seek
For names; but call forth thund'ring *Aeschilus*,
  Euripides, and *Sophocles* to us,
Pacuvius, *Accius*, him of *Cordova* dead,
  To life again, to hear thy Buskin tread,
And shake a Stage : Or, when thy Socks were on,
  Leave thee alone, for the comparison

First Folio preface, page 9

Of all, that insolent *Greece*, or haughty *Rome*
  sent forth, or since did from their ashes come.
Triumph, my *Britain*, thou hast one to show,
  To whom all Scenes of *Europe* homage owe.
He was not of an age, but for all time !
  And all the *Muses* still were in their prime,
When like *Apollo* he came forth to warm
  Our ears, or like a *Mercury* to charm !
Nature herself was proud of his designs,
  And joy'd to wear the dressing of his lines !
Which were so richly spun, and woven so fit,
  As, since, she will vouchsafe no other Wit.
The merry *Greek*, tart *Aristophanes*,
  Neat *Terence*, witty *Plautus*, now not please;
But antiquated, and deserted lie
  As they were not of Nature's family.
Yet must I not give Nature all: Thy Art,
  My gentle *Shakespeare*, must enjoy a part.
For though the *Poets* matter, Nature be,
  His Art doth give the fashion. And, that he,
Who casts to write a living line, must sweat,
  (such as thine are) and strike the second heat
Upon the *Muses* anvil : turn the same,
  (And himself with it) that he thinks to frame;
Or for the laurel, he may gain a scorn,
  For a good *Poet's* made, as well as born.
And such wert thou. Look how the father's face
  Lives in his issue, even so, the race
Of *Shakespeare's* mind, and manners brightly shines
  In his well turned, and true-filed lines :
In each of which, he seems to shake a Lance,
  As brandish'd at the eyes of Ignorance.
Sweet Swan of *Avon!* what a sight it were
  To see thee in our waters yet appear,
And make those flights upon the banks of *Thames*,
  That so did take *Eliza*, and our *James* !
But stay, I see thee in the *Hemisphere*
  Advanc'd, and made a Constellation there !
Shine forth, thou Star of *Poets*, and with rage,
  Or influence, chide, or cheer the drooping Stage;
Which, since thy flight from hence, hath mourn'd like
  night,
  And despairs day, but for thy Volume's light.

                         BEN: JONSON.

First Folio preface, page 10

Upon the Lines and Life of the Famous
Scenic Poet, Master WILLIAM
SHAKESPEARE.

Those hands, which you so clapp'd, go now, and wring
You *Britains* brave; for done are *Shakespeare's* days :
His days are done, that made the dainty Plays,
Which made the Globe of heav'n and earth to ring.
Dri'd is that vein, dri'd is the *Thespian* Spring,
Turn'd all to tears, and *Phoebus* clouds his rays :
That corp's, that coffin now bestick those bays,
Which crown'd him *Poet* first, then *Poet's* King.
If *Tragedies* might any *Prologue* have,
All those he made, would scarce make one to this :
Where *Fame*, now that he gone is to the grave
(Death's public tiring-house) the *Nuncius* is.
  For though his line of life went soon about,
  The life yet of his lines shall never out.

HUGH HOLLAND.

First Folio preface, page 11

First Folio preface, page 12

A CATALOGUE
of the several Comedies, Histories, and Tragedies contained in this Volume.

COMEDIES.

The Tempest.

The two Gentlemen of Verona.

The Merry Wives of Windsor.

Measure for Measure.

The Comedy of Errors.

Much ado about Nothing.

Love's Labour lost.

Midsummer Night's Dream.

The Merchant of Venice.

As you Like it.

The Taming of the Shrew.

All is well, that Ends well.

Twelfth-Night, or what you will.

The Winter's Tale.

HISTORIES.

The Life and Death of King John.

The Life & death of Richard the second.

The First part of King Henry the fourth.

The Second part of K. Henry the fourth.

The Life of King Henry the Fift.

The First part of King Henry the Sixt.

The Second part of King Hen. the Sixt.

The Third part of King Henry the Sixt.

The Life & Death of Richard the Third.

The Life of King Henry the Eight.

TRAGEDIES.

The Tragedy of Coriolanus.

Titus Andronicus.

Romeo and Juliet.

Timon of Athens.

The Life and death of Julius Caesar.

The Tragedy of Macbeth.

The Tragedy of Hamlet.

King Lear.

Othello, the Moor of Venice.

Anthony and Cleopater.

Cymbeline King of Britain.

[NOTE: Page numbers excluded.]

First Folio preface, page 13

First Folio preface, page 14

TO THE MEMORY
of the deceased Author Master
W. SHAKESPEARE.

Shake-speare, at length thy pious fellows give
The world thy Works : thy Works, by which, out-live
Thy Tomb, thy name must · when that stone is rent,
And Time dissolves thy *Stratford* Moniment,
Here we alive shall view thee still. This Book,
When Brass and Marble fade, shall make thee look
Fresh to all Ages: when Posterity
Shall loath what's new, think all is prodigy
That is not *Shake-speare's*; ev'ry Line, each Verse
Here shall revive, redeem thee from thy Hearse.
Nor Fire, nor cank'ring Age, as *Naso* said,
Of his, thy wit-fraught Book shall once invade.
Nor shall I e'er believe, or think thee dead
(Though miss'd) until our bankrout Stage be sped
(Impossible) with some new strain t'out-do
Passions of *Juliet*, and her *Romeo* ;
Or till I hear a Scene more nobly take,
Than when thy half-Sword parleying *Romans* spake.
Till these, till any of thy Volumes rest
Shall with more fire, more feeling be express'd,
Be sure, our *Shake-speare*, thou canst never die,
But crown'd with Laurel, live eternally.

L[eonard]. Digges.

To the memory of M. *W. Shakes-speare.*

We wond'red (*Shake-speare*) that thou went'st so soon
From the World's-Stage, to the Grave's-Tiring-room.
We thought thee dead, but this thy printed worth,
Tells thy Spectators, that thou went'st but forth
To enter with applause.   An Actors Art,
Can die, and live, to act a second part.
That's but an *Exit* of Mortality;
This, a Re-entrance to a Plaudite.

J. M. [James Mabbe]

First Folio preface, page 15

First Folio preface, page 16

The Works of William Shakespeare,
containing all his Comedies, Histories, and
Tragedies: Truly set forth, according to their first
O R I G I N A L.

The Names of the Principal Actors
in all these Plays.

William Shakespeare.	Samuel Gilburne.
Richard Burbadge.	Robert Armin.
John Hemmings.	William Ostler.
Augustine Phillips.	Nathan Field.
William Kempt.	John Underwood.
Thomas Poope.	Nicholas Tooley.
George Bryan.	William Ecclestone.
Henry Condell.	Joseph Taylor.
William Slye.	Robert Benfield.
Richard Cowly.	Robert Goughe.
John Lowine.	Richard Robinson.
Samuell Crosse.	John Shancke.
Alexander Cooke.	John Rice.

APPENDIX H

Upon Master William Shakespeare, the Deceased Author, and his Poems.

Poets are born not made, when I would prove
This truth, the glad remembrance I must love
Of never dying *Shakespeare*, who alone,
Is argument enough to make that one.
First, that he was a Poet none would doubt,
That heard th'applause of what he sees set out
Imprinted; where thou hast (I will not say
Reader his Works for to contrive a Play:
To him 'twas none) the pattern of all wit,
Art without Art unparalleled as yet.
Next Nature only help'd him, for look through
This whole Book, thou shalt find he doth not borrow,
One phrase from Greeks, nor Latins imitate,
Nor once from vulgar Languages Translate,
Nor Plagiari-like from others glean,
Nor begs he from each witty friend a Scene
To piece his Acts with, all that he doth write,
Is pure his own, plot, language exquisite,
But oh! what praise more powerful can we give
The dead, than that by him the King's Men live,
His Players, which should they but have shar'd the Fate,
All else expir'd within the short Term's date;
How could the Globe have prospered, since through want
Of change, the Plays and Poems had grown scant.
But happy Verse thou shalt be sung and heard,
When hungry quills shall be such honor barr'd.
Then vanish upstart Writers to each Stage,
You needy Poetasters of this Age,
Where *Shakespeare* liv'd or spake, Vermin forbear,
Lest with your froth you spot them, come not near;
But if you needs must write, if poverty
So pinch, that otherwise you starve and die,
On God's name may the Bull or Cockpit have
Your lame blank Verse, to keep you from the grave:
Or let new Fortunes younger brethren see,
What they can pick from your lean industry.
I do not wonder when you offer at
Black-Friars, that you suffer: 'tis the fate
Of richer veins, prime judgments that have far'd
The worse, with this deceased man compar'd.
So have I seen, when Cesar would appear,
And on the Stage at half-sword parley were,
Brutus and *Cassius*: oh how the Audience

Were ravish'd, with what wonder they went thence,
When some new day they would not brook a line,
Of tedious (though well labored) *Catalines*;
Sejanus too was irksome, they priz'd more
Honest *Iago*, or the jealous Moor.
And though the Fox and subtle Alchemist,
Long intermitted could not quite be miss'd,
Though these have sham'd all the Ancients, and might raise,
Their Author's merit with a crown of Bays.
Yet these sometimes, even at a friend's desire
Acted, have scarce defray'd the Seacoal fire
And doorkeepers: when let but *Falstaff* come,
Hal, Poins, the rest you scarce shall have a room
All is so pester'd: let but *Beatrice*
And *Benedick* be seen, lo in a trice
The Cockpit Galleries, Boxes, all are full
To hear *Malvoglio*, that cross garterer'd Gull.
Brief, there is nothing in his wit fraught Book,
Whose sound we would not hear, on whose worth look
Like old coin'd gold, whose lines in every page,
Shall pass true current to succeeding age.
But why do I dead *Sheakspeare's* praise recite,
Some second *Shakespeare* must of *Shakespeare* write;
For me 'tis needless, since an host of men,
Will pay to clap his praise, to free my Pen.

Leon. Digges.

Of Mr. *William Shakespeare.*

What, lofty Shakespeare, art again reviv'd?
And Virbius like now show'st thyself twice liv'd,
'Tis love that thus to thee is shown,
The labors his, the glory still thine own.
These learned Poems amongst thine after-birth,
That makes thy name immortal on the earth,
Will make the learned still admire to see,
The Muses gifts so fully infus'd on thee.
Let Carping Momus bark and bite his fill,
And ignorant Davus slight thy learned skill:
Yet those who know the worth of thy desert,
And with true judgment can discern thy Art,
Will be admirers of thy high tun'd strain,
Amongst whose number let me still remain.

John Warren.

Notes

Abbreviated Citations

ARBER: *A Transcript of the Registers of the Company of Stationers of London (1554-1640)*, ed. Edward Arber, London, 1876

CHAMBERS: Edmund K. Chambers, *William Shakespeare, A Study of Facts and Problems*, Oxford, 1930

GREENWOOD's *Restated*: Sir George Greenwood, *The Shakespeare Problem Restated*, London, 1908

GREENWOOD's *Problem*: Sir George Greenwood, *Is There A Shakespeare Problem?* London, 1916

OGBURN's *Mysterious*: Charlton Ogburn, Jr., *The Mysterious William Shakespeare: The Myth and the Reality*, New York, 1984

PMLA: *Publications of the Modern Language Association*

PRICE: Diana Price, *Shakespeare's Unorthodox Biography*, Greenwood Press, Westport, CT, 2001

Reader's Encyclopedia: *The Reader's Encyclopedia of Shakespeare*, ed. Oscar James Campbell, New York, 1966

STOPES's *Southampton*: Charlotte C. Stopes, *The Life of Henry, Third Earl of Southampton, Shakespeare's Patron*, Cambridge Univ. Press, 1922

Chapter 1. Literary Supreme, Supreme Literary Mystery

1. "As Epius Stolo said, that the Muses would speak with Plautus' tongue if they would speak Latin, so I say that the Muses would speak with Shakespeare's fine-filed phrase, if they would speak English." Francis Meres, *Palladis Tamia, or Wit's Treasury*, 1598.
2. Richard Barnfield, *The Encomion of Lady Pecunia or The Praise of Money*, 1598.
3. Robert Chester, *Love's Martyr, Or, Rosalin's Complaint*, 1601.
4. Mark Twain, *Is Shakespeare Dead?* New York, 1909, p. 116.
5. Alexander Schmidt, *Shakespeare-Lexicon, A Complete Dictionary of All the English Words, Phrases and Constructions in the Works of the Poet*, revised edition by Gregor Sarrazin, Berlin, 1962 (reprint), vol. 2, pp. 1413-24.
6. PRICE, p. 235.
7. Bradley Efron and Ronald Thisted, "Estimating the Number of Unseen Species: How Many Words Did Shakespeare Know?" *Biometrika*, vol. 63, no. 3 (Dec. 1976), p. 435.
8. Alfred Hart, "The Growth of Shakespeare's Vocabulary," *Review of English Studies*, vol. 19, no. 75 (July 1943), p. 242.
9. OGBURN's *Mysterious*, p. 290, crediting Alfred Hart.
10. For a "concise" summary of facts about the Stratford Man, see PRICE, pp. 14-19.
11. E.A.J. Honigmann, *Shakespeare: "The Lost Years,"* Totowa, New Jersey, 1985.
12. PRICE, pp. 20-21.

13. Denis B. Woodfield, *Surreptitious Printing in England (1550-1640)*, New York, 1973, p. 35. Lord Burghley patronized Field to print political works from 1588 until 1598, the year Burghley died.

14. Meres, *Palladis Tamia, or Wit's Treasury*, 1598; the title page on *Love's Labour's Lost* (1598).

15. Ramon Jiménez, "Shakespeare in Stratford and London: Five More Eyewitnesses Who Saw Nothing," *Shakespeare-Oxford Newsletter*, Winter 2005, p. 4.

16. Tarnya Cooper, *Searching for Shakespeare*, National Portrait Gallery, Yale Univ. Press, 2006, p. 54.

17. S.P. Cerasano, "Tamburlaine and Edward Alleyn's Ring," *Shakespeare Survey 47*, Cambridge Univ. Press, 1994, p. 171.

18. Ben Jonson, *Timber: or Discoveries Made Upon Men and Matter*, 1641, p. 98.

19. The month and year of Shakespeare's death were first printed in POEMS: WRITTEN BY WIL. SHAKE-SPEARE. *Gent* (1640), and the exact date in Dugdale's *Antiquities of Warwickshire Illustrated* (1656).

20. Richard Brathwait, *Remains After Death*, 1618 (combined publication with *A Happy Husband, or Directions for a Maid to Choose her Mate* by Patrick Hannay, STC 12747).

21. Virginia Gildersleeve, *Government Regulation of the Elizabethan Drama*, New York, 1908, p. 18.

22. ARBER, vol. 3, p. 677.

23. STOPES's *Southampton*, p. 210.

24. Martin Green, *Wriothesley's Roses*, Baltimore, MD, 1993, p. 214.

25. OGBURN's *Mysterious*, p. 10.

26. Margaret Dowling, "Sir John Hayward's Troubles Over His *Life of Henry IV*," *The Library*, 4th series, vol. 11, no. 2 (Sept. 1930), pp. 219-20.

27. *Reader's Encyclopedia*, p. 683.

28. David Riggs, *Ben Jonson, A Life*, Harvard Univ. Press, 1989, p. 118.

29. Michael Brennan, *Literary Patronage in the English Renaissance: The Pembroke Family*, New York, ca. 1988, p. 127.

30. One of the earliest writers to make the connection between Corambis-Polonius and Lord Burghley was George Russell French in *Shakespeareana Genealogica*, London, 1869, pp. 301-05. Michael Cecil, the 18th Baron Burghley, said that the name Corambis in *Hamlet* was a "pretty obvious swipe at our family motto" (paper presented at the 2010 Shakespeare-Oxford Society/Shakespeare Fellowship Conference).

31. Sir Christopher Hatton as Malvolio in *Twelfth Night*: OGBURN's *Mysterious*, p. 634; Antonio Perez as Armado in *Love's Labour's Lost*: Gustav Ungerer, *A Spaniard in Elizabethan England: The Correspondence of Antonio Perez's Exile*, London, c. 1974, vol. 2, pp. 377-98; Sir Walter Ralegh and Tarquin in *Lucrece*: *Willobie His Avisa*, ed. G.B. Harrison, London, 1926, p. 230; Sir Robert Cecil and *Richard III*: Margaret Hotine, "*Richard III* and *Macbeth* – Studies in Tudor Tyranny?" *Notes and Queries*, Dec. 1991, pp. 480-86.

32. GREENWOOD's *Problem*, pp. 220-21.

33. Thomas Vicars, *Cheiragogia, Manuductio ad Artem Rhetoricam*, 3rd ed. (1628); translated by Dana Sutton, The Philological Museum, www.philological.bham.ac.uk.

34. W.W. Greg, *Licensers for the Press, &c. to 1640*, Oxford Univ. Press, 1962, p. 20.

35. B.M. Ward, "The Authorship of the *Arte of English Poesie*: A Suggestion," *Review of English Studies*, vol. 1, no. 3 (July 1925), pp. 284-308.

36. *John Gerard, The Autobiography of an Elizabethan*, tr. Philip Caraman, London, 1951, p. 15.

37. *Wit's Recreations*, 1640 (STC 25870).

Chapter 2. A Mess of Genius: Shakespeare's Early Printed Texts

1. *King John*, The Arden Edition of the Works of Shakespeare, ed. E.A.J. Honigmann, Harvard Univ. Press, 1954, reprinted 1965, intro., p. 34.

2. *Shakespeare's Plays in Quarto, Facsimile Editions of Copies Primarily from the Henry E. Huntington Library*, eds. Michael J.B. Allen, Kenneth Muir, Univ. of California Press, Berkeley, 1981, intro., p. 18.

3. Ron Rosenbaum, *The Shakespeare Wars*, Random House, New York, 2006, p. 114.

4. *Shakespeare's Plays in Quarto*, eds. Allen and Muir, intro., p. 21.

5. CHAMBERS, vol. 1, p. 159.

6. ARBER, vol. 2, p. 650.

7. ARBER, vol. 2, p. 649.

8. *Reader's Encyclopedia*, p. 880. The quarto is now at the Folger-Shakespeare Library.

9. Cyril B. Judge, *Elizabethan Book-Pirates*, Harvard Univ. Press, 1934, p. 135; ARBER, vol. 1, p. 561.

10. Chiaki Hanabusa, "A Neglected Misdate and *Romeo and Juliet* Q1 (1597)," *Notes and Queries*, June 1999, pp. 229-30.

11. *Records of the Court of the Stationers' Company, 1576 to 1602, from Register B*, eds. W.W. Greg and E. Boswell, London, 1930, p. 56. The "decrees of the Star Chamber" were probably those issued in June 1586, which gave powers to the Stationer's Company to regulate and punish printers.

12. Judge, *Elizabethan Book-Pirates*, p. 136; ARBER, vol. 1, p. 580.

13. Harry R. Hoppe, *The Bad Quarto of Romeo and Juliet: A Bibliographical and Textual Study*, Cornell Univ. Press, New York, 1948, p. 3; Standish Henning, *Papers of the Bibliographical Society of America*, vol. 60, 1966, p. 363-64; J.A. Lavin, "John Danter's Ornamental Stock," *Papers of the Bibliographical Society*, 1970, pp. 21-34.

14. *Records of the Court of the Stationers' Company, 1576 to 1602*, eds. Greg and Boswell, p. 57.

15. Thomas Heywood, *An Apology for Actors*, 1612.

16. ARBER, vol. 3, p. 153.

17. ARBER, vol. 3, p. 122.

18. ARBER, vol. 3, p. 175.

19. *As You Like It*, A New Variorum Edition of Shakespeare (vol. 8), ed. H.H. Furness, Philadelphia, 1890, p. 297. On May 27, 1600, *A Moral of Cloth Breeches and Velvet Hose* was stayed, and two days later, another play, *Allarum to London*, was not to be printed "without further and better authority." Two months later, Roberts's attempt to publish three Shakespeare plays and one by Ben Jonson was stayed.

20. ARBER, vol. 3, p. 170.

21. A translation of Herodotus was stayed and *The History of Don Frederigo* was to be limited to one copy and a donation to charity. On June 4, 1599, Roberts's issue of two satires by John Marston were ordered to be burned (along with books by others) by the Archbishop of Canterbury.

22. ARBER, vol. 3, p. 226.

23. Sonia Massai, *Shakespeare and the Rise of the Editor*, Cambridge Univ. Press, 2007, p. 107.

24. *Records of the Court of the Stationers' Company, 1602 to 1640 (Court-Book B)*, ed. William A. Jackson, London, 1957, p. 110. In 1909, W.W. Greg proved that the Pavier-Jaggard quartos were falsely dated.

25. Harry Farr, "Notes on Shakespeare's Printers and Publishers with Special Reference to the Poems and *Hamlet*," *The Library*, 4ᵗʰ series, vol. 3, no. 4 (March 1, 1923).

26. ARBER, vol. 3, p. 701.

27. *Ibid*, p. 703.

28. William White was fined 2 shillings, 6 denari for printing Harrison's copy of "Master Gentes Sermons" on Sept. 14, 1603 (ARBER, vol. 2, p. 835). On the same day, Valentine Simmes was fined 13 shillings, 4 denari for printing "a ballad belonging to Mistress Aldee." Matthew Law was fined 20 shillings for printing *England's Mourning Garment* "being Thomas Millington's copy" on June 7, 1603 (ARBER, vol. 2, p. 836). A 1619 order by the Stationers' Company: "Mr Eld and Mr Flesher shall pay to Mr Jackson 6 shillings, 8 denari for imprinting the book called Madmen of Gotam which was formerly entered to the said Mr Jackson" (*Records of the Court of the Stationers' Company*, ed. William A. Jackson, p. 110).

29. Farr, "Notes on Shakespeare's Printers and Publishers," p. 245.

30. E.A.J. Honigmann, *Shakespeare's Impact on His Contemporaries*, London, 1982, p. 47.

Chapter 3. Shakespeare Problems the Professor Still Cannot Solve

1. *Reader's Encyclopedia*, p. 914. Fletcher later collaborated with Beaumont on dozens of plays.

2. *The Norton Shakespeare*, 2ⁿᵈ ed., ed. Stephen Greenblatt, New York, 2008, p. 837.

3. Catherine Drinker Bowen, *The Lion and the Throne: The Life and Times of Sir Edward Coke (1552-1634)*, Boston, 1957, p. 128.

4. Ramon Jiménez, "'Rebellion broachéd upon his sword': New Evidence of an Early Date for *Henry V*," *The Shakespeare Oxford Newsletter*, Fall 2001, pp. 8-11.

5. These works include *A Discourse of Horsemanship* (1593), *Cephalus and Procris* (1593), *The First Rape of Fair Helen* (1595), *The Ghost of Lucrece* (1600), "The Shepherd's Song of Venus and Adonis" in *England's Helicon* (1600), and *Acolastus, His After-wit* (1600), the latter work containing many "unashamed plagiarisms of lines" from Shakespeare's two poems (*Reader's Encyclopedia*, p. 1). Sir George Greenwood (*Restated*, pp. 59-60) noted the resemblance between the horse description in *Venus and Adonis* and a passage in Josuah Sylvester's translation of Guillaume Du Bartas, *The Second Week* (1598).

6. *The Tragedy of Solyman and Perseda Edited from the Original Texts*, ed. John J. Murray, New York, 1991, p. xii; T.W. Baldwin, "On the Chronology of Thomas Kyd's Plays," *Modern Language Notes*, vol. 40, no. 6 (June 1925), pp. 343-49.

7. Albert S. Cook, "Shakespeare, *Hamlet* 3.4.56," *Modern Language Notes*, vol. 20, no. 7 (Nov. 1905), pp. 216-17.

8. Michael Pincombe, *The Plays of John Lyly: Eros and Eliza*, Manchester Univ. Press, 1996, p. 171.

9. *Hamlet*, A New Variorum Edition of Shakespeare (vol. 3), ed. Horace H. Furness, Philadelphia, 1877, vol. 1, p. 33.

10. Roslyn Knutson, *Playing Companies and Commerce in Shakespeare's Time*, Cambridge Univ. Press, 2001, p. 96; E.K. Chambers, *The Elizabethan Stage*, Oxford, 1923, vol. 4, p. 18.

11. Charles Cathcart, "*Histriomastix*, *Hamlet*, and the 'Quintessence of Duckes,'" *Notes and Queries*, Dec. 2003, p. 429.

12. The reference to the kid was probably taken from Edmund Spenser's *The Shepherd's Calendar* (1579), May eclogue (Andrew Hadfield, "The Ur-Hamlet and the Fable of the Kid," *Notes and Queries*, March 2006, p. 47).

13. *The Householder's Philosophy* by T.K., an English translation of Torquato Tasso's *Il Padre di Famiglia*, registered on Feb. 6, 1588 (STC 23702.5).

14. Claes Schaar, *Elizabethan Sonnet Themes*, Lund Studies in English, no. 32, Copenhagen, 1962, reprint AMS Press, New York, 1973, p. 66. Nashe also echoed a line in Shakespeare's Sonnet 6, "Be not self-will'd," in *Have With You to Saffron-Walden* (1596), see Penny McCarthy, *Pseudonymous Shakespeare: Rioting Language in the Sidney Circle*, Ashgate Publishing Ltd., Aldershot, Hampshire, U.K., 2006, p. 152.

15. "My gracious lord, entreat him, speak him fair" (*Henry VI-Part 2*, 4.1.120); "I'll write unto them, and entreat them fair" (*Henry VI-Part 3*, 1.1.271); "be patient, and entreat me fair" (*Richard III*, 4.4.151); "Entreat her fair" (*Troilus and Cressida*, 4.4.111); "And with our fair entreaties haste them on" (*Coriolanus*, 5.1.74).

16. E.B. Everitt, *The Young Shakespeare*, Anglistica, vol. 2, Copenhagen, 1954, p. 28.

17. Dora Jean Ashe, "The Text of Peele's *Edward I*," *Studies in Bibliography*, vol. 7, 1955, p. 153.

18. *Reader's Encyclopedia*, p. 816.

19. *Hamlet*, Variorum Edition, ed. Furness, vol. 1, p. 211. An allusion to *Timon of Athens* also occurred in *Saint Peter's Complaint* (see Appendix A, No. 52).

20. Alden Brooks in *Will Shakspere and The Dyer's Hand* (New York, 1943, p. 190) cited the passage where this line occurred but did not note the *Hamlet* allusion.

21. Ross D. Waller, "Dunghill: Peasant: Slave," *Times Literary Supplement*, Nov. 17, 1932, p. 859.

22. Joseph W. DeMent, "A Possible 1594 Reference to *Hamlet*," *Shakespeare Quarterly*, vol. 15, no. 4 (Autumn 1964), pp. 446-47.

23. *Henslowe's Diary*, ed. R.A. Foakes, Cambridge Univ. Press, 2002 (2nd ed.), p. 21.

24. ARBER, vol. 3, p. 212 (July 26, 1602).

25. *The Plays of George Chapman: The Comedies, A Critical Edition*, ed. Allan Holaday, Univ. of Illinois Press, 1970, p. 59.

26. *Reader's Encyclopedia*, pp. 105-06.

27. Richard F. Kennedy, *Notes and Queries,* London, Dec. 2000, p. 464.

28. Ramon Jiménez, "Who Was the Author of Five Plays that Shakespeare Rewrote as His Own?" *Shakespeare Oxford Newsletter*, Winter 2008, pp. 13-20.

29. *William Shakespeare: A Textual Companion*, eds. Stanley Wells and Gary Taylor, W.W. Norton, New York, reprint, 1997, pp. 111-12.

30. *The True Tragedy. The First Quarto. 1595 Facsimile with Introduction*, eds. Charles Praetorius, Thomas Tyler, London, 1891, citing *The New Shakspere Society's Transactions*, 1875-1876, p. 229.

31. E.K. Chambers, *The Elizabethan Stage*, Oxford, 1923, vol. 4, p. 44; ARBER, vol. 2, p. 454.

32. Leslie Hotson, *The First Night of Twelfth Night*, New York, 1954; Katherine Chiljan, "The Earl of Oxford's Annuity to Robert Hales," *Shakespeare Oxford Newsletter*, Fall 2005, pp. 7-9.

33. *The Diary of John Manningham of the Middle Temple 1602-1603*, ed. Robert Parker Sorlien, Hanover, NH, 1976, p. 48. John Marston wrote a play titled *What You Will*, written presumably after Shakespeare's play became known as, or retitled, *Twelfth Night*.

34. CHAMBERS, vol. 1, pp. 270-71.

35. Katherine Chiljan, "Oxford and the 1566 play, *Palamon and Arcite*," *Shakespeare Oxford Newsletter*, Spring 1999, pp. 10-13.

36. W.Y. Durand, "Notes on Richard Edwards," *Journal of Germanic Philology*, vol. 4, no. 3, 1902, p. 361 (both quotes from Bereblock). Edwards died in October 1566.

37. *Henslowe's Diary*, ed. R.A. Foakes, p. 24.

38. Sir George Buc used some waste paper from the Revels Office to write his manuscript, *The History of Richard the Third*. The reverse side of one page listed "The 2 Noble Kinsmen," "The Winter's Tale," and two other plays. Buc was the Revels Master from 1612 to 1622; the manuscript was dated 1619. See E.K. Chambers's book review of *The King's Office of the Revels (1610-1622)* by Frank Marcham, *Review of English Studies*, vol. 1, no. 4 (October 1925), p. 480.

39. Steele, Mary Susan, *Plays and Masques at Court during the Reigns of Elizabeth, James and Charles*, New York, 1926, p. 87.

40. 1594 reference: *Gesta Grayorum* (1688), p. 22; 1598: *Palladis Tamia, or Wit's Treasury* by Francis Meres; 1604-05: King's Revels accounts, *Reader's Encyclopedia*, p. 683.

41. *Reader's Encyclopedia*, p. 411.

42. *The Diary of Henry Machyn, Citizen and Merchant-Taylor of London, from A.D. 1550 to A.D. 1563*, ed. John Gough Nichols, 1848, reprint AMS Press, New York, p. 276.

Chapter 4. The Sonnets and Other Puzzle-Poems

1. GREENWOOD's *Restated*, p. 199.

2. *Sir Philip Sidney's* An Apology for Poetry *and* Astrophil and Stella: *Texts and Contexts*, ed. Peter C. Herman, College Publishing, Glen Allen, VA, 2001, intro., p. 44.

3. Noted by Nina Green on the online scholarly discussion group, Phaeton. See www.Oxford-Shakespeare.com.

4. John Nichols, *The Progresses and Public Processions of Queen Elizabeth*, London, 1823, vol. 3, p. 110. The event occurred in 1591.

5. This essay is based upon my article, "Complaints about *A Lover's Complaint*," *Shakespeare Oxford Newsletter*, Winter 2008.

6. *William Shakespeare, The Complete Sonnets and Poems*, ed. Colin Burrow, Oxford Univ. Press, 2002, pp. 696-710 (footnotes).

7. *Ibid*, p. 716.

8. *Barnabe Barnes, Parthenophil and Parthenophe, A Critical Edition*, ed. Victor A. Doyno, Southern Illinois Univ. Press, 1971, p. 156.

9. A. Kent Hieatt, "The Genesis of Shakespeare's *Sonnets*: Spenser's *Ruines of Rome: by Bellay*," *PMLA*, vol. 98, no. 5 (October 1983), p. 802; E. De Selincourt stated that Spenser transformed Du Bellay's text into the Shakespeare sonnet form (*The Poetical Works of Edmund Spenser*, Oxford Univ. Press, 1942 reprint, intro., p. 31).

10. Noted by Gary Schmidgall, letter to the editor, *PMLA*, March 1984, p. 244.

11. MacDonald P. Jackson, "Echoes of Spenser's *Prothalamion* as Evidence Against an Early Date for Shakespeare's *A Lover's Complaint*," *Notes and Queries*, June 1990, pp. 180-82.

12. *Letters and Poems of Edward, Earl of Oxford*, ed. Katherine Chiljan, San Francisco, 1998, p. 183. Five manuscript versions of this poem survive – two ascribe authorship to Oxford, two ascribe it to Oxford's mistress, Anne Vavasour, and one labels it as "Verses of" Oxford and Vavasour. That the lady in the poem was Vavasour is unlikely

because she complains about a "youth," and expresses her wish to "match" with him; Oxford was in his late 20s-early 30s during his affair with Vavasour, and was married.

13. Edward Hawkins, *Medallic Illustrations of the History of Great Britain and Ireland*, eds. Augustus Franks, Herbert Grueber, London, 1885, vol. 1, pp. 90-91. Three slightly different versions of the coin were made.

14. *Ibid*, pp. 124-25. The badge contained Latin inscriptions, translated by Hawkins as "Alas! that virtue endued with so much beauty, should not uninjured enjoy perpetual life," and "Happy Arabs whose only Phoenix reproduces by its death a new Phoenix. Wretched English whose only Phoenix becomes, unhappy fate, the last in our country." The former inscription was a verse by Walter Haddon (*Poemata*, 1567).

15. Roy C. Strong, *Portraits of Queen Elizabeth I*, Oxford, 1963, p. 113; Francis A. Yates, *Astraea, The Imperial Theme in the Sixteenth Century*, London, 1975, plate 6b. The engraving is attributed to Crispin de Passe, Sr. and was published by John Woutneel.

16. Roy C. Strong, *Portraits of Queen Elizabeth I*, p. 156. The statue (by Nicholas Stone) was finished in March 1623.

17. "There is a bird that builds her nest with spice, /and built, the Sun to ashes doth her burn, /Out of whose cinders doth another rise. /& she by scorching beams to dust doth turn: /Thus life a death, and death a life doth prove, /The rarest thing on earth except my love." *The Speeches and Honorable Entertainment given to the Queen's Majesty in Progress, at Cowdrey in Sussex, by the Right Honorable the Lord Montecute* (1591) (STC 3907.7). According to Nichol's *Progresses* (vol. 2, p. 143), "At the Queen's reception in Norwich in August, 1578, a gateway was ornamented with the Tudor roses and her arms, under which were these verses, 'Division kindled strife /Blest Union quench'd the flame. / Thence sprang our noble Phoenix dear / The peerless Prince of Fame.'"

18. T.W. Baldwin, *On the Literary Genetics of Shakspere's Poems and Sonnets*, Univ. of Illinois Press, 1950, p. 374.

19. William H. Matchett, *The Phoenix and the Turtle*, The Hague, 1965, pp. 182-83.

20. *Robert Chester's Love's Martyr*, ed. Alexander Grosart, *New Shakspere Society*, London, 1878, intro., p. 45.

21. Strong, *Portraits of Queen Elizabeth I*, p. 114; Yates, *Astraea*, plate 8b. The engraving was by William Rogers.

22. John Phillips, *A Commemoration on the Life and Death of the Right Honorable, Sir Christopher Hatton*, 1591.

23. T.B. Howell, *A Complete Collection of State Trials and proceedings for high treason and other crimes and misdemeanors*, London, 1816, p. 1357.

24. Anthea Hume, "*Love's Martyr*, 'The Phoenix and the Turtle,' and the Aftermath of the Essex Rebellion," *Review of English Studies*, New Series, vol. 40, no. 157 (Feb. 1989), p. 65. The documentary record for Chester ends January 1604 (*DNB*).

25. *Calendar of State Papers, Domestic Series, of the Reign of Elizabeth*, ed. Mary Anne Everett Green, London, 1870, vol. 6 (1601-1603 with addenda), pp. 115-16.

26. *Robert Chester's Love's Martyr*, ed. Grosart, intro., p. 46.

27. *The Poems*, A New Variorum Edition of Shakespeare (vol. 22), ed. Hyder E. Rollins, Philadelphia, 1938, p. 278.

28. C.H. Hobday, "Shakespeare's Venus and Adonis Sonnets," *Shakespeare Survey 26*, Cambridge Univ. Press, 1973, pp. 103-09.

29. *The Poems*, Variorum Edition, ed. Rollins, p. 296.

30. *Ibid*, p. 281.

31. *Ibid*, p. 292.

32. *Ibid*, p. 547. The anthology, *The Garland of Goodwill* (first surviving edition, 1631), featured this poem as the first stanza of a longer poem titled "A maiden's choice twixt age and youth." A ballad called "The maiden's choice," was registered for publication on August 26, 1591. *The Garden of Goodwill*, presumably *The Garland of Goodwill*, was registered on March 5, 1593; Thomas Nashe mentioned *Garland* in 1596.

33. Charles Wisner Barrell, "Early Authenticated 'Shakespeare' Transcript Found with Oxford's Personal Poems," *The Shakespeare Fellowship Quarterly*, April 1945, p. 24.

34. Arthur F. Marotti, "The Cultural and Textual Importance of Folger MS V.a.89," *English Manuscript Studies (1100-1700)*, eds. Peter Beal and Grace Ioppolo, London, 2002, vol. 11, p. 71.

35. Edwin E. Willoughby, *A Printer of Shakespeare: The Books and Times of William Jaggard*, London, 1934, p. 59; ARBER, vol. 2, p. 831.

36. *DNB*, 1888 edition. The fourteen printers named on the list: John Windet, Gabriel Simpson, Richard Braddock, Felix Kingston, William White, Ralph Blore, Thomas Judson, Peter Short, Adam Islip, Richard Field, Edmund Bollifant, Thomas Creed, Edward Allde, Valentine Simmes (ARBER, vol. 3, p. 678). The printers were ordered to take "especial" notice of the Archbishop's "Commandments."

37. *The Passionate Pilgrim*, ed. Joseph Quincy Adams, New York, 1939, intro., p. 25. John Wolfe, publisher of Hayward's book, was questioned and briefly imprisoned for his part. The names of both printers of Hayward's book, Edward Allde and Thomas Judson, were included on the Archbishop's list.

38. A.E.M. Kirwood, "Richard Field, Printer, 1589-1624," *The Library*, 4th series, vol. 12, no. 1 (June 1931), p. 8.

39. *The Sacred Shield of All Christian Soldiers* by John Gibson; ARBER, vol. 3, p. 145.

40. John Bakeless, *The Tragicall History of Christopher Marlowe*, Westport, CT, 1942, vol. 2, p. 153; Frederick W. Steinfeld and Mary Joiner Chan, "Come Live With Me and Be My Love," *Comparative Literature*, vol. 22, no. 2 (Spring 1970), p. 174.

41. Janet G. Scott, "Minor Elizabethan Sonneteers and their Great Predecessors," *Review of English Studies*, vol. 2, no. 8 (October 1926), pp. 424-25. Griffin evidently borrowed from Shakespeare's *Macbeth* (see Appendix A, No. 83).

42. C.J. Rawson, "Macbeth on Sleep: Two Parallels," *Shakespeare Quarterly*, vol. 14, no. 4 (Autumn 1963), pp. 484-85.

Chapter 5. The "Stratford Man": The Faith-Based Favorite

1. PRICE, pp. 15, 16, 20-21.

2. Bill Bryson, *Shakespeare, The World as Stage*, Atlas Books/HarperCollins, New York, 2007, pp. 11, 35-36.

3. Samuel Schoenbaum, *Shakespeare, A Documentary Life,* New York, 1975, p. 136. Public Record Office, Declared Accounts, E351/542, f. 107b (Lord Chamberlain's payment document). The 1595 document is not the original, but a copy of it written a few years later. No record besides this indicates the queen had entertainments on those dates. The original books of the queen's treasurer, and those of the Privy Council, are lost for the years 1594-95.

4. T.W. Baldwin, *Organization and Personnel of the Shakespearean Company*, Princeton Univ. Press, 1927, p. 39.

5. Schoenbaum, *Shakespeare, A Documentary Life*, p. 197.

6. *Shakespeare in the Public Records*, Public Record Office Handbooks, No. 5, ed. N.E. Evans, London, 1964, p. 21.
7. *Reader's Encyclopedia*, p. 103.
8. PRICE, pp. 33-35.
9. *Reader's Encyclopedia*, p. 620.
10. Schoenbaum, *Shakespeare, A Documentary Life*, p. 199.
11. 1615 document: Thomasina Ostler vs. Heminges, Oct. 9 (?), 1615, CHAMBERS, vol. 2, p. 58 (Ostler was daughter of John Heminges, and widow of actor Will Ostler).
12. 1619 document: Witter vs. Heminges and Condell (April 28, 1619), CHAMBERS, vol. 2, p. 52.
13. 1635 document: Answer of Cuthbert Burbage, et al to Robert Benfield et al, to the Lord Chamberlain (Aug. 1, 1635), CHAMBERS, vol. 2, p. 65-66.
14. Roland B. Lewis, *The Shakespeare Documents*, Stanford Univ. Press, 1941, vol. 2, p. 519.
15. Charles William Wallace, *Advance Sheets from Shakespeare, The Globe, and Blackfriars*, Stratford-upon-Avon, 1909, p. 5.
16. Schoenbaum, *Shakespeare, A Documentary Life*, pp. 220-21.
17. Cuthbert Burbage said that he and his brother "purchased the lease remaining from Evans with our money, and placed men players, which were Hemings, Condall, Shakspeare, &c." Lewis, *The Shakespeare Documents*, vol. 2, p. 520.
18. Schoenbaum, *Shakespeare, A Documentary Life*, p. 247.
19. PRICE, p. 104; Schoenbaum, *Shakespeare, A Documentary Life*, p. 172.
20. Charles Nicholl, *The Lodger Shakespeare: His Life on Silver Street*, Viking, New York, 2008, p. 294.
21. Leslie Hotson, *Shakespeare Versus Shallow*, Boston, 1931, p. 9; Court of King's Bench, KB 29/234.
22. *Reader's Encyclopedia*, p. 938.
23. Mark Twain, *Is Shakespeare Dead?* New York, 1909, p. 49.

Chapter 6. The "upstart Crow" and the Stratford Man: No Relation

1. S.P. Cerasano, "Edward Alleyn: 1566-1626," *Edward Alleyn, Elizabethan Actor, Jacobean Gentleman*, eds. Aileen Reed, Robert Maniura, Dulwich, U.K., 1994, p. 13.
2. *Henslowe's Diary*, ed. R.A. Foakes, Cambridge Univ. Press, 2002 (2nd ed.), pp. 16-19.
3. A.D. Wraight, *Christopher Marlowe and Edward Alleyn*, Chichester, reissue, 1993, p. 218.
4. *Fair Em*, Malone Society reprints, ed. W.W. Greg, Oxford Univ. Press, 1927, intro., p. 7.
5. *Fair Em: A Critical Edition*, ed. Standish Henning, New York, 1980, pp. 113-14.
6. In the preface letter to his *Farewell to Folly*, Greene said that his previous work, *Greene's Mourning Garment*, was sold out: "…the Printer hath passed them all out of his shop, and the peddler found them too dear for his pack, that he was fain to bargain for the life of Tomliuclin to wrap up his sweet powders in those unsavory papers." Greene purposely misspelled Tamburlaine as "Tomliuclin," presumably close enough to identify but different enough to avoid libel.
7. *Works of Christopher Marlowe*, ed. Francis Cunningham, London, 1870, intro., p. 11.
8. The object of Nashe's letter was "to pour contempt on Marlowe and the Tamburlaine circle, and to contrast them to their disadvantage with the illustrious scholars associ-

ated with Saint John's College, Cambridge…" wrote J. Churton Collins (editor), *The Plays and Poems of Robert Greene*, Oxford, 1905, vol. 1, p. 41. *Tamburlaine* was mentioned in the text of Greene's *Menaphon*. One character said that she read about "mighty Tamberlaine…"

9. O.B. Hardison, Jr., "Speaking the Speech," *Shakespeare Quarterly*, vol. 34, no. 2 (Summer 1983), p. 139.

10. Andrew Gurr, *The Shakespearean Stage*, 1574-1642, Cambridge Univ. Press, 1970, p. 67.

11. Gabriel Harvey, *Four Letters and Certain Sonnets, Especially Touching Robert Greene and other parties by him abused* (1592), as noted by Donald J. McGinn in "Nashe's Share in the Marprelate Controversy," *PMLA*, vol. 59, no. 4 (Dec. 1944), p. 956.

12. Jay Hoster, *Tiger's Heart: What Really Happened in the Groats-worth of Wit Controversy of 1592*, Columbus, Ohio, 1993.

13. Thomas Nashe, *Pierce Penniless His Supplication to the Devil*, 1592.

14. Andrew J. Gurr, "Who Strutted and Bellowed?" *Shakespeare Survey 16*, 1963, pp. 95-101.

15. S.P. Cerasano, "Edward Alleyn: His Brothel's Keeper?" *Medieval and Renaissance Drama in England*, 2001, vol. 13, p. 93.

16. E.K. Chambers, *The Elizabethan Stage*, Oxford, 1923, vol. 2, p. 137.

Chapter 7. Upstart Crow Uproar, and a Few Hostile Witnesses

1. Alden Brooks, *Will Shakspere and the Dyer's Hand*, New York, 1943, p. 41.

2. *Ibid*, p. 46.

3. ARBER, vol. 2, p. 620.

4. Ramon Jiménez's article, "Ten Eyewitnesses Who Saw Nothing," appeared in two parts in the *Shakespeare Oxford Newsletter*, Fall 2002 and Winter 2003.

5. Dorothy Ogburn, Charlton Ogburn, Jr., *Shakespeare: the Man Behind the Name*, New York, 1962, pp. 35-36.

6. Samuel Schoenbaum, *William Shakespeare, A Compact Documentary Life*, Oxford Univ. Press, 1977, p. 231.

7. Ramon Jiménez, "Ten Eyewitnesses Who Saw Nothing," *Shakespeare Oxford Newsletter*, Fall 2002, p. 15.

8. GREENWOOD's *Problem*, 1916, pp. 314-15.

Chapter 8. The First Folio Fraud

1. Patrick Cheney, *Shakespeare, National Poet-Playwright*, Cambridge Univ. Press, 2004, p. 69.

2. *POEMS: WRITTEN BY WIL. SHAKE-SPEARE. Gent*, 1640 (STC 22344); see Appendix H.

3. Researcher Robert Brazil in 2005 first noted the absence of the Shakespeare arms in the First Folio preface in the online scholarly discussion group, Elizaforum.

4. Leah S. Marcus, *Puzzling Shakespeare: Local Reading and Its Discontents*, U.C. Press, Berkeley, 1988, p. 19.

5. J.L. Nevinson, "Shakespeare's Dress in His Portraits," *Shakespeare Quarterly*, vol. 18, no. 2 (Spring 1967), p. 106.

6. Tarnya Cooper, *Searching for Shakespeare*, National Portrait Gallery, London, 2006, p. 48.

7. W.W. Greg, *The Shakespeare First Folio, Its Bibliographical and Textual History*, Oxford, 1955, p. 451.

8. Arthur M. Hind, *Engraving in England in the 16th and 17th Centuries, Part 2 (Reign of James I)*, Cambridge Univ. Press, 1955, p. 357.

9. CHAMBERS, vol. 2, p. 224.

10. Marcus, *Puzzling Shakespeare*, p. 19.

11. GREENWOOD's *Restated*, p. 291.

12. GREENWOOD's *Problem*, p. 314.

13. *The Odes of Horace*, translated by James Michie, New York, 1963, p. 235.

14. Translation by C.M. Ingleby in *Shakspere Allusion-Book*, London, Oxford Univ. Press, 1932, vol. 1, p. 314.

15. Many of these parallels were noted in an article by Prof. W. Dinsmore Briggs, "Ben Jonson and the First Folio of Shakespeare," *Times Literary Supplement*, Thursday, Nov. 12, 1914, p. 502, and *Ben Jonson*, ed. C.H. Herford and Percy and Evelyn Simpson, Oxford, 1952, vol. 11, pp. 140-44.

16. GREENWOOD's *Restated*, p. 265.

17. Cooper, *Searching for Shakespeare*, p. 50.

18. Francis Beaumont and John Fletcher, *Philaster*, 1622, letter to reader.

19. *The Return from Parnassus, Part 2* (4.3); see J.B. Leishman, *The Three Parnassus Plays (1598-1601)*, London, 1949, p. 337.

20. *M. William Shak-speare, His True Chronicle History of the Life and Death of King Lear and His Three Daughters*, 1608 (STC 22292).

21. Roger Stritmatter, "Bestow how, and when you list," *Shakespeare Oxford Newsletter*, Fall 1998, pp. 18-19; *Archaio-Ploutos… the former Treasury of Ancient and Modern Times*, 1619 (STC 17936.5).

22. Leah Scragg, "Edward Blount and the Prefatory Material to the First Folio of Shakespeare," *Bulletin of the John Rylands Univ. Library of Manchester*, vol. 79, no. 1 (Spring 1997).

23. *Notes of Conversations with Ben Jonson made by William Drummond of Hawthornden, January 1619*, ed. G.B. Harrison, New York, 1923, pp. 3-4.

24. Edwin Reed (*Francis Bacon, Our Shake-Speare*, London, 1902, pp. 144-69) listed many words with Latin roots that Shakespeare coined. For example, *abruption, circummure, conflux, credent, deracinate, empiricutic, festinate, fluxive, iterance, sanctuarize*.

25. *Reader's Encyclopedia*, p. 635.

26. Charles C. Hower, "The Importance of a Knowledge of Latin for Understanding the Language of Shakespeare," *The Classical Journal*, vol. 46, no. 5 (Feb. 1951), pp. 221-27.

27. Antonio Minturno, *L'Arte Poetica*, Venice, 1564, p. 158. This passage was noted in *Ben Jonson*, eds. C.H. Herford, Evelyn and Percy Simpson, Oxford, 1952, vol. 11, p. 145. Excerpt translated by Elizabeth Coggshalle (doctoral candidate, Stanford Univ.).

Chapter 9. A Pembroke and Jonson Production

1. W.W. Greg, *The Shakespeare First Folio, Its Bibliographical and Textual History*, Oxford, 1955, p. 5.

2. ARBER, vol. 4, p. 182.

3. ARBER, vol. 4, p. 243 (entry dated Nov. 16, 1630).

4. Peter W.M. Blayney, *The First Folio of Shakespeare*, Folger Library Publications, Washington D.C., 1991, p. 2.

5. *Ibid*, p. 26.

6. *Ibid*, pp. 25-26.

7. Bill Bryson, *Shakespeare, The World As Stage*, Atlas Books/HarperCollins, New York, 2007, p. 37.

8. T.J.B. Spencer, "Ben Jonson on his beloved, The Author Mr. William Shakespeare," *The Elizabethan Theatre IV*, ed. G.R. Hibbard, Hamden, CT, 1974, p. 27.

9. Peter W.M. Blayney, "Introduction to the Second Edition," *The Norton Facsimile: The First Folio of Shakespeare based on Folios in the Folger Shakespeare Library Collection*, 2nd ed., New York, 1996, intro., p. 29. Folio production costs of appx. £340 would translate to almost $1 million today, according to "affordability" based on average earnings (measuringworth.com).

10. Brian O'Farrell, *Politician Patron Poet: William Herbert, The Earl of Pembroke*, unpublished dissertation, Univ. of California, Los Angeles, 1966 (list of book dedications on pp. 332-38).

11. Michael Brennan, *Literary Patronage in the English Renaissance: The Pembroke Family*, London, ca. 1988, p. 157.

12. *The Letters of John Chamberlain*, ed. Norman Egbert McClure, Memoirs of the American Philosophical Society, Philadelphia, 1939, vol. 1, p. 536.

13. *Records of the Court of the Stationers' Company, 1602 to 1640 (Court-Book B)*, ed. William A. Jackson, London, 1957, p. 110. "Henry Hemings" was listed in the margin next to this entry, which Jackson noted could have been a relation of King Men's member, John Heminges.

14. Sonia Massai, *Shakespeare and the Rise of the Editor*, Cambridge Univ. Press, 2007, p. 113.

15. Gerald D. Johnson, "Thomas Pavier, Publisher," *The Library, the Transactions of the Bibliographical Society*, series 6, 1992, p. 22.

16. *Archaio-Ploutos…the former Treasury of Ancient and Modern Times*, 1619 (STC 17936.5); *The Decameron* [anonymous translation of Boccaccio, possibly by John Florio], 1620 (STC 3172).

17. *Catalogus Universalis* printed by John Bill. See F.P. Wilson, "The Jaggards and the First Folio of Shakespeare," *Times Literary Supplement*, Thursday, Nov. 5, 1925, p. 737.

18. Charlton Hinman, *The Printing and Proof-reading of the First Folio of Shakespeare*, Oxford, 1963, vol. 1, pp. 342-63.

19. *The Letters of John Chamberlain*, ed. McClure, vol. 1, p. 430.

20. Richard Dutton, *Mastering the Revels: The Regulation and Censorship of English Renaissance Drama*, Univ. of Iowa Press, 1991.

21. *Records of the Court of the Stationers' Company 1602-1640*, ed. W.A. Jackson, p. 155.

22. R. Carter Hailey, "The Dating Game: New Evidence for the Dates of Q4 *Romeo and Juliet* and Q4 *Hamlet*," *Shakespeare Quarterly*, vol. 58, no. 3 (Fall 2007), p. 372. Smethwick's edition of *Romeo and Juliet*, Quarto 4, is STC 22325, and *Hamlet*, Quarto 4, is STC 22278.

23. O'Farrell, *Politician, Patron, Poet*, p. 271.

24. David Riggs, *Ben Jonson, A Life*, Harvard Univ. Press, 1989, p. 226.

25. Dick Taylor, Jr., "The Masque and the Lance: The Earl of Pembroke in Jacobean Court Entertainments," *Tulane Studies in English*, 1958, vol. 8, p. 28.

26. Riggs, *Ben Jonson*, p. 220.

27. Johan Gerritsen, "Stansby and Jonson Produce a Folio," *English Studies: A Journal of English Letters and Philology*, Feb. 1959.

28. Riggs, *Ben Jonson*, p. 221.

29. Edwin E. Willoughby, *A Printer of Shakespeare: the Books and Times of William Jaggard*, London, 1934, p. 105. Jaggard printed the section titled, "A Brief and Necessary Catechism or Instruction ... " (STC 6682.3).

30. E.A.J. Honigmann, *The Texts of Othello and Shakespearean Revision*, New York, 1996, p. 35.

31. June Schlueter, "Martin Droeshout *Redivivus*: Reassessing the Folio Engraving of Shakespeare," *Shakespeare Survey*, vol. 60, Cambridge Univ. Press, 2007.

32. Mary Edmond, "It was for Gentle Shakespeare Cut," *Shakespeare Quarterly*, vol. 42, no. 3 (Autumn 1991), pp. 339-44.

33. Gheeraerts painted "Portrait of a Man in Classical Dress, probably Philip Herbert, 4th Earl of Pembroke, circa 1610," at Tate Britain (T03466); although "probably" Herbert, the face matches a confirmed portrait of him by William Larkin (Audley End House, Essex). Gheeraerts also painted a similar portrait of a man in classical dress "probably William Herbert, 3rd Earl of Pembroke, circa 1610" (Stanford Univ.). See both portraits in *Marcus Gheeraerts II, Elizabethan Artist* by Karen Hearn, Tate Publishing, London, 2002, pp. 26-27.

34. Christiaan Schuckman, "The Engraver of the First Folio Portrait of William Shakespeare," *Print Quarterly*, vol. 8, no. 1 (March 1991), London, pp. 40-43.

Chapter 10. The Stratford Monument: Ruse and Reincarnation

1. Sir William Dugdale, *Antiquities of Warwickshire*, London, 1656. W. Hollar made the engraving. Dugdale's early drawing is featured in PRICE, p. 156.

2. For example, John Lyly referred to Nestor in a letter as "Nestorem." *The Complete Works of John Lyly*, ed. R. Warwick Bond, Oxford, 1902, vol. 1, p. 15.

3. Hoyt H. Hudson, *The Epigram in the English Renaissance*, Princeton Univ. Press, 1947, pp. 98-99.

4. PRICE, p. 162.

5. Sir George Greenwood (*Problem*, pp. 316-17) noted William Hall's 1694 letter about his visit to the Stratford-upon-Avon church. Regarding Shakespeare's tomb, Hall wrote: " ... they have laid him full seventeen feet deep, deep enough to secure him." Rumor or true, either would discourage removal of the Stratford Man's remains.

6. According to a note in Edmund Spenser's *The Shepherd's Calendar* (1579), the French poet, Marot, used the name Colin "to secretly shadoweth himself, as sometime did Virgil under the name of Tityrus ... " ("January"); Patrick Cheney noted this in *Shakespeare's Literary Authorship*, Cambridge Univ. Press, 2008, p. 100.

7. Philip Schwyzer, *Archaeologies of English Renaissance Literature*, Oxford Univ. Press, 2007, p. 117.

8. Edgar Fripp, *Shakespeare: Man and Artist*, Oxford Univ. Press, 1938 (1964 reprint), vol. 2, p. 854.

9. For example, see Margaret Tudeau-Clayton, *Jonson, Shakespeare and Early Modern Virgil*, Cambridge Univ. Press, 1998, pp. 1-5, and *The Works of Ben Jonson*, ed. W. Gifford, vol. 2, London, 1875, p. 475.

10. Charles Fitzgeffrey, *Caroli Fitzgeofrida Affaniae: Sive Epigrammatum Libri Tres*, Oxford, 1601, in Book 2, No. 13: "To Edmund Spenser: You call Chaucer our Virgil. Ill done, if you can do anything amiss. For he is our Ennius, but you our Virgil." Translated by Dana Sutton in the Philological Museum (www.philological.bham. ac.uk); Nashe in *Strange News* (1592): "Chaucer and Spenser, the Homer and Virgil of England ... "

11. Charles Isaac Elton, *William Shakespeare His Family and Friends*, London, 1904, pp. 238-39.

12. Robert C. Evans, "'Whome None But Death Could Shake': An Unreported Epitaph on Shakespeare," *Shakespeare Quarterly*, vol. 39, no. 1 (Spring 1988), p. 60.

13. For example, see Dugdale, *Antiquities of Warwickshire*, pp. 790-91.

14. Richard J. Kennedy, *The Woolpack Man: John Shakspere's Monument in Holy Trinity Church*, Stratford-on-Avon, Stairway Press, Newport, OR, 2005, webpages.charter. net/stairway/ woolpackman.htm/.

15. E.A.J. Honigmann and Susan Brock, *Playhouse Wills*, 1558-1642, Manchester Univ. Press, 1993, p. 105.

16. Fripp, *Shakespeare: Man and Artist*, vol. 2, p. 849.

17. Philip B. Chatwin, "The Later Monumental Effigies of the County of Warwick," *Birmingham Archaeological Society Transactions and Proceedings*, 1935, vol. 57, p. 126.

18. *The Vestry Minute-Book of the Parish of Stratford-on-Avon, From 1617 to 1699 AD*, ed. George Arbuthnot, London, ca. 1890, AMS Press, reprint, 1971.

19. Richard Whalen, "The Stratford Bust: A Monumental Fraud," *The Oxfordian*, vol. 8 (October 2005), p. 16; Hildegard Hammerschmidt-Hummel, *The True Face of William Shakespeare*, transl. Alan Bance, Chaucer Press, London, 2006, p. 121.

20. Charlotte C. Stopes, "The True Story of the Stratford Bust," *The Monthly Review*, no. 43 (April 1904), p. 121.

21. Chatwin, "The Later Monumental Effigies," p. 124.

22. Gerard Langbaine, *An Account of the English Dramatic Poets*, Oxford, 1691, p. 469.

23. *Encyclopedia Britannica*, 11th edition, New York, 1911, vol. 24, p. 787; *The Title-Page of the First Folio of Shakespeare's Plays. A Comparative Study of the Droeshout Portrait and the Stratford Monument*, London, 1924, p. 23; *The Works of William Shakespeare*, ed. Bullen, 1907, vol. 10 (Stratford-upon-Avon), p. 380.

24. *Vestry Minute-Book*, ed. George Arbuthnot, pp. 64-65.

25. *Ibid*, p. 69.

26. Chatwin, "The Later Monumental Effigies," p. 150.

27. GREENWOOD's *Problem*, p. 564.

28. CHAMBERS, vol. 2, pp. 242-43. The manuscript was titled, "A Relation of a Short Survey of 26 Counties." Chambers stated that Lt. Hammond arrived in Stratford-upon-Avon about Sept. 9, 1634.

29. Whalen, "The Stratford Bust," p. 17; R.B. Wheler, *History and Antiquities of Stratford-upon-Avon*, Stratford-upon-Avon, 1806, opposite p. 71.

Chapter 11. Folio Feedback

1. Today's equivalent of £1 in 1623 is £130.53 according to the retail price index on measuringworth.com/. The Folio's affordability for the average person at that time, based on average earnings, today would be £1,880, or $2,895, according to the same source.

2. *Reader's Encyclopedia*, p. 735.

3. *The Dramatic Records of Sir Henry Herbert, Master of the Revels, 1623-1673*, ed. Joseph Quincy Adams, Yale Univ. Press, 1917, p. 64. The Red Bull Theater was also notorious for undignified productions.

4. Dana Sutton, Philological Museum, www.philological.bham.ac.uk/.

5. Fred Schurink, "An Unnoticed Early Reference to Shakespeare," *Notes and Queries*, March 2006, p. 72-73.

6. Peter W. Dickson, "Henry Peacham on Oxford and Shakespeare," *Shakespeare Oxford Newsletter*, Fall 1998.

7. William H. Edwards in *Shaksper Not Shakespeare* (1900) was probably the first to write about the similarities between Burton's work and the First Folio.

8. Society of Antiquaries, SAL MS. 128, Folio 375b, as transcribed by Nina Green, ©2009 (Oxford-Shakespeare.com/).

9. John Weever, *Epigrams in the Oldest Cut, and Newest Fashion*, 1599.

10. John Weever, *Ancient Funeral Monuments within the United Monarchy of Great Britain, Ireland, and the Islands Adjacent*, 1631, pp. 492-93.

11. Katherine Chiljan, "Richard Brome's *The Antipodes* and English Earle," *Shakespeare Oxford Society Newsletter*, Spring 1994.

12. John Freehafer, "Leonard Digges, Ben Jonson, and the Beginning of Shakespeare Idolatry," *Shakespeare Quarterly*, vol. 20, no. 1 (Winter 1970), p. 64.

13. *Masque of Gypsies, Epigrams of Noble Personages*, and Horace's *Art of Poetry* (translation).

Chapter 12. Portrayals of the Stratford Man in Contemporary Comedies

1. Dorothy and Charlton Ogburn, *This Star of England*, New York, 1952, p. 489.

2. *Every Man Out of His Humour / Ben Jonson*, ed. Helen Ostovich, Manchester Univ. Press, New York, 2001, p. 107.

3. Samuel Schoenbaum, *Shakespeare, A Documentary Life*, New York, 1975, p. 179; Lucy de Bruyn, *Mob Rule and Riots, the Present Mirrored in the Past*, London, 1981, pp. 56-57.

4. *Every Man Out of His Humour*, ed. Ostovich, p. 239.

5. Farmer Sordido's hanging himself "with expectation /Of rotten weather" (1.3) seems to parody the Porter's line in *Macbeth* (2.3.4-5), "Here's a farmer that hang'd himself on th'expectation of plenty." The line, "Some stray, some stray … the lord of the soil has all wefts and strays here, has he not?" (1.2), echoes one in *Henry VI-Part 2* (4.10.26-28), "Here's the lord of the soil come to seize me for a stray, for entering his fee-simple …" The line, "Reason long since is fled to animals" (3.1), is echoed in *Julius Caesar* (3.2.110-11): "O judgment, thou art fled to brutish beasts, /And men have lost their reason." Both Jonson's play (4.3) and *Henry IV-Part 1* (1.2) discuss robberies at Gadshill. Jonson's play has a love scene at a balcony (2.2), like *Romeo and Juliet*. Jonson's play refers to Shakespeare's characters, Justice Silence (5.2), and Sir John Falstaff (5.4). Jonson's character, Shift, is called "Apple John" (3.1), as the prince in *Henry IV-Part 2* (2.4.5-6) referred to apple johns as Sir Johns (i.e., Falstaff). Jonson's line, "the strumpet Fortune" (1.3), and the lines in *Hamlet*, "Jonson's line about a lady's "sweet fingers" on the viol, "she tickles it so" (3.3) and Shakespeare's Sonnet 128 about his lady playing the virginal with "sweet fingers" that "so tickled" the keys, both observed by men who envy the instrument. For the *Othello* allusion, see Appendix A (No. 86).

6. *Every Man in his Humour / Ben Jonson*, ed. Robert S. Miola, Manchester Univ. Press, 2000, p. 81.

7. Lorenzo (*The Merchant of Venice*), Prospero (*The Tempest*), Stephano (*The Tempest*), Biancha (*Othello*), Thorello (anagram for Othello, with added "r"), and Peto (*Henry IV*, parts 1 and 2). Jonson changed these names in his 1616 folio edition of the play, with the exception of Stephano, which was merely anglicized to Stephen.

8. Ogburns, *This Star of England*, pp. 558-60.

9. GREENWOOD's *Problem*, p. 376.

10. GREENWOOD's *Restated*, p. 460. The Latin word *crispo*, to brandish, was "so frequently used by Virgil, and other writers, of a spear …"

11. David Riggs, *Ben Jonson, A Life*, Harvard Univ. Press, 1989, p. 80.

12. *Poetaster*: "And let me breathe <u>my soul</u> <u>in thy breast</u>" (4.10) and Shakespeare's Sonnet 109: "As from <u>my soul</u> which <u>in thy breast</u> doth lie." *Poetaster* (4.9) has a balcony scene with lovers, one named Julia, like *Romeo and Juliet*. *Poetaster* (2.2): " … <u>at your ladyship's service</u>. I got that speech by seeing <u>a play last day</u>," and *Twelfth Night* (1.5.301): "Here, <u>madam, at your service</u>." *Poetaster* (4.5): "I have read in a book that <u>to play the fool wisely</u> is high wisdom" and *Twelfth Night* (3.1.62): "This fellow is <u>wise</u> enough <u>to play the fool</u>." For the *Othello* allusion, see Appendix A (No. 89).

13. *Venus and Adonis*, line 8 reads, "The field's sweet flower, sweet above compare."

14. Alden Brooks, *Will Shakspere and The Dyer's Hand*, New York, 1943, p. 253.

15. OGBURN's *Mysterious*, pp. 106-08.

Chapter 13. The Great Author's Portrayal of the Stratford Man

1. Alden Brooks, *Will Shakspere and The Dyer's Hand*, New York, 1943, p. 621.

2. *Reader's Encyclopedia*, pp. 121-22.

3. *The Merry Wives of Windsor*, Yale Shakespeare, ed. George Van Santvoord, Yale Univ. Press, 1922, p. 109.

4. Dorothy and Charlton Ogburn, *This Star of England*, New York, 1952, p. 995.

5. *The Taming of the Shrew*, The Yale Shakespeare, ed. Thomas G. Bergin, Yale Univ. Press, revised ed., 1954, pp. 8, 112.

Chapter 14. Shakespeare Satirized: *Willobie His Avisa* (1594)

1. *Willobie His Avisa*, ed. G.B. Harrison, London, 1926, p. 186.

2. *Reader's Encyclopedia*, p. 948.

3. *Ibid*. Similar lines occur in *Henry VI-Part 1* (5.3.78-79) and *Richard III* (1.2.228-29). *Titus Andronicus* was registered on Feb. 6, 1594, and *Willobie His Avisa* on Sept. 3, 1594.

4. STOPES's *Southampton*, p. 69.

5. Antonio Perez, *Pedacos de historia, ô Relaçiones*, 1594 (STC 19624.5) printed by Richard Field.

6. C. Creighton, "Willobie His Avisa," *Atheneum*, no. 4053, July 1, 1905, p. 19. Creighton cited a passage from *An Apologie, Metamorphosis of Ajax* (1596) by Sir John Harington. Referring to Cowdray, the seat of Anthony Browne, Viscount Montagu, Harington wrote: " …the young Lord I hear doth *patrysare*, or rather I should say *Avisare* (and that is a good word, if he will mark it)." As a grandson of Viscount Montagu, Southampton could be identified as the "young Lord." "Patrisso" in Latin means resembling one's father; "Avisare" puns on the Latin "avitis," taking after one's

grandfather. Harington remarked that Avisare was an invented word, clearly alluding to the then infamous *Willobie His Avisa*.

7. R.J.C. Wait, *The Background to Shakespeare's Sonnets*, New York, 1972, p. 79.

8. Translated by Duncan Harrington, L.H.G., F.S.A., F.S.G., www.historyresearch. co.uk/; *Penelope's Complaint* by Peter Colse, 1596.

9. It is believed that the *Willobie* writer borrowed from Robert Greene's story, "The Conversion of an English Courtesan," in *A Disputation Between a He Conny-catcher, and a She Coney-catcher* (1592). An attractive and talented young woman runs away with her lover, who then leaves her alone at an inn while he visits her parents for permission to marry. When word gets out of her presence there, she is besot by suitors, and in her own words, "began I to affection these new-come guests…"

10. Silvius, a shepherd (byword for poet), loves Phoebe, a lady with black hair and eyes; Phoebe loves Ganymede (Rosalind disguised as a man), once called "fair youth." Phoebe says she hates Silvius, just as the Dark Lady said she hated the great author (Sonnet 145). "Fair youth" Ganymede says, "I'll sauce [Phoebe] with bitter words" (3.5.68-9), and "bitter sauces" occurs in Dark Lady Sonnet 118. Silvius asks Phoebe to "pity me" like the great author entreats the Dark Lady (sonnets 132, 142, 143). (Ogburns, *This Star of England*, 1952, p. 899.)

11. *The Poems of Sir Walter Ralegh*, ed. Agnes M.C. Latham, Cambridge, MA, 1962, pp. 14-15, 110.

12. *Willobie His Avisa*, ed. G.B. Harrison, p. 202. Arthur Acheson in *Mistress Davenant, the Dark Lady of Shakespeare's Sonnets* (1913), was the first to propose Matthew Roydon as the *Willobie* author; Harrison concurred in his edition of *Willobie* (p. 227) and C.S. Lewis thought it "not improbable" (*DNB*, Roydon).

13. William Stebbing, *Sir Walter Ralegh, A Biography*, Oxford, 1899, p. 108. The quotation was from Nicholas Faunt's letter to Anthony Bacon.

14. *Letters and Poems of Edward, Earl of Oxford*, ed. Katherine Chiljan, San Francisco, 1998, pp. 186, 199 (Tanner MS 306, f. 115, Bodleian Library, Oxford).

15. *Ibid*, p. 165.

16. *Ibid*, p. 166.

17. GREENWOOD's *Restated*, p. 83.

Chapter 15. Overlooked Commentary About Shakespeare by His Contemporaries (1589-1614)

1. Harold Stein, *Spenser's Complaints*, Oxford Univ. Press, New York, 1934, pp. 49-50. Spenser's passage was "likely a gibe at Marlowe and the University Wits, who turned their university learning to profit by writing plays and pamphlets to suit vulgar taste," wrote Patrick Cheney, *Marlowe's Counterfeit Profession: Ovid, Spenser, Counter-Nationhood* (1997), pp. 167-69.

2. *The Shakspere Allusion Book: A Collection of Allusions to Shakspere from 1591 to 1700*, ed. C.M. Ingleby, et al, Oxford Univ. Press, reissued 1932, vol. 1, p. 1.

3. Stein, *Spenser's Complaints*, p. 51.

4. *Cassell's New Latin Dictionary*, ed. D.P. Simpson, New York, 1960, p. 51.

5. Charles Wisner Barrell, "New Milestone in Shakespeare Research; Contemporary Proof that the Poet Earl of Oxford's Literary Nickname Was 'Gentle Master William,'" *The Shakespeare Fellowship Quarterly*, October 1944.

6. J.R. Brink, "The Composition Date of Sir John Davies's *Nosce Teipsum*," *Huntington Library Quarterly*, vol. 37, no. 1 (Nov. 1973), pp. 19-32.

7. Feb. 14, 2010 email on the online scholarly discussion group, Elizaforum.

8. Virginia F. Stern, *Gabriel Harvey, His Life, Marginalia and Library*, Oxford Univ. Press, 1979, pp. 116-17; Sally E. Mosher, *People and their Contexts: A Chronology of the 16th Century World*, (Xlibris), 2001, p. 220.

9. "Power without good sense comes crashing down under its own weight," *Horace Odes and Epigrams*, ed. Niall Rudd, Harvard Univ. Press, 2004, p. 157.

10. Andrew Hannas, "Gabriel Harvey and the Genesis of 'William Shakespeare,'" *Shakespeare Oxford Newsletter*, Winter 1993.

11. Mark P.O. Morford and Robert J. Lenardon, *Classical Mythology*, 2nd edition, 1977, p. 98 (Homeric Hymn, no. 28).

12. João Froes, "Shakespeare's Venus and the Venus of Classical Mythology," *Venus and Adonis, Critical Essays*, ed. Philip C. Kolin, New York, 1997, pp. 301-06.

13. Katherine Duncan-Jones, "Much Ado with Red and White: The Earliest Readers of Shakespeare's *Venus and Adonis* (1593)," *The Review of English Studies*, New Series, vol. 44, no. 176 (Nov. 1993), p. 488. Queen Elizabeth was symbolically depicted as Venus in coins issued in the Netherlands in 1580 and 1587; see *Elizabethan Silent Language* (Univ. of Nebraska Press, 2000) by Mary E. Hazard, pp. 126-27, and figures 24-25.

14. Duncan-Jones, "Much Ado with Red and White," pp. 479-501. See note 5, Ch.3 for a partial list.

15. *Elizabethan Sonnets*, ed. Sidney Lee, Westminster, 1904, (reprint, New York, 1964), vol. 1, intro., p. 88.

16. *The Poems of Sir John Davies*, ed. Robert Krueger, Oxford Univ. Press, 1975, p. 376.

17. *The Oxford Book of Sixteenth Century Verse*, ed. E.K. Chambers, Oxford, 1932 (corrected edition, 1970), p. 885.

18. OGBURN's *Mysterious*, p. 96.

19. Other published works with this theme were Richard Barnfield's short poem in *The Affectionate Shepherd* in 1594 (which was also inspired by Shakespeare's poems) and Thomas Watson's Latin translation of the Greek by Coluthus, *Raptus Helenae* (1586).

20. M.A. Shaaber, "The First Rape of Faire Hellen by John Trussell," *Shakespeare Quarterly*, vol. 8, no. 4, (Autumn 1957), pp. 414-15.

21. *Ibid*, p. 446.

22. Lilian Winstanley, *"Othello" as the Tragedy of Italy*, London, 1924.

23. R.C. Horne, "Two Unrecorded Contemporary References to Shakespeare," *Notes and Queries*, June 1984, p. 219.

24. Katherine F. Panzer, as quoted in an article by Thomas P. Roche, Jr., "Enuies Scourge, and Vertues Honour, A Literary Mystery," *Princeton Univ. Library Chronicle*, vol. 47, no. 2 (Winter 1986), p. 148.

25. Arthur Acheson, *Mistress Davenant, The Dark Lady of the Sonnets*, London, 1913; *Willobie His Avisa*, ed. G.B. Harrison, p. 226.

26. PRICE, p. 63.

27. CHAMBERS, vol. 1, p. 300, in chapter titled, "The Shakespeare-Mythos."

28. *The Shakspere Allusion-Book*, vol. 1, p. 250.

Chapter 16. The Deliberate Mix-up: The Great Author with the Stratford Man. Why?

1. John Sanford, *Apollinis et Musarum euktika eidyllia, in serenissimae reginae Elizabethae auspicatissimum Oxoniam*, Oxford, 1592 (STC 21733); Duncan Harrington translated "formosior" as "handsome." The word has also been translated as "beautiful," "fair," and "comely."

2. Barnabe Barnes, *Parthenophil and Parthenophe*, 1593.

3. John Hamill, "A Spaniard in the Elizabethan Court: Don Antonio Perez," *Shakespeare Oxford Newsletter*, June 2009, p. 20; Antonio Perez, *Pedacos de historia, ô Relaçiones*, London, 1594 (STC 19624.5); reprinted as *Las Obras y Relaciones de Ant. Perez*, Geneva, 1644, p. 531.

4. Gervase Markham, *The Most Honorable Tragedy of Sir Richard Grenville, Knight*, 1595.

5. Dorothy and Charlton Ogburn, *This Star of England*, New York, 1952, p. 878.

6. *Calendar of the Manuscripts of the Most Honorable the Marquess of Salisbury Preserved at Hatfield House, Hertfordshire*, Historical Manuscripts Commission, ed. M.S. Guseppi, London, 1933, vol. 16, p. 415.

7. Simon Adams, "Eliza Enthroned? The Court and its Politics," *The Reign of Elizabeth*, ed. Christopher Haigh, Univ. of Georgia Press, 1985, p. 73.

8. Carole Levin, "'We shall never have a merry world while the Queene Lyveth,' Gender, Monarchy and the Power of Seditious Words," *Dissing Elizabeth: Negative Representations of Gloriana*, ed. Julia M. Walker, Duke Univ. Press, 1998, pp. 88-90. One of the most extraordinary claims that Queen Elizabeth bore a child was the case of Arthur Dudley. In 1588, Dudley told the English Ambassador in Spain that he was the child of the queen and Sir Robert Dudley, born in 1562, but given to a servant of Katherine Ashley, the queen's personal servant. His claim was evidently never refuted.

9. John Nichols, *The Progresses and Public Processions of Queen Elizabeth*, London, 1823, vol. 3, pp. 90, 98. The progress at Cowdray was on August 15.

10. Charles Martindale and Colin Burrow, "Clapham's Narcissus: A Pre-Text for Shakespeare's Venus and Adonis?" *English Literary Renaissance*, vol. 22, no. 2 (Spring 1992), p. 157.

11. Sanford, *Apollinis et Musarum*.

12. John M. Rollett, "Was Southampton Regarded as the Son of the Queen? (Part 2)," *De Vere Society Newsletter*, July 2000.

13. STOPES's *Southampton*, p. 50: "After him followed a Prince of a distinguished race, whom (rich in her right) Southampton blazons as a great hero. No youth there present was more beautiful or more brilliant in the learned arts…" The translation by Duncan Harrington reads: "After this follows a prince of a famous line, a rich man in his own right to whom Southampton lays claim as a great hero. Nobody more handsome or more distinguished in learned skills stood before him …"

14. *Letters of Philip Gawdy*, ed. Isaac Herbert Jeayes, London, 1906, p. 70 (May 13, 1593).

15. STOPES's *Southampton*, p. 55; Sir Sidney Lee, *A Life of William Shakespeare*, 4th edition, London, 1925, p. 660.

16. George Peele, *The Honour of the Garter: displayed in a poem gratulatory*, [1593].

17. Gabriel Harvey, *A New Letter of Notable Contents*, 1593 (registered October 1, 1593).

18. Martindale, Burrow, "Clapham's *Narcissus*," p. 150.

19. The Garter tally of votes was related to me in private email by John Rollett, who cited the Liber Caeruleus in the British Library as his source.

20. STOPES's *Southampton*, p. 117, quoting a letter by Rowland Whyte.

21. *Ibid*, p. 2.

22. *Ibid*, p. 519.

23. Alan H. Nelson, *Monstrous Adversary, The Life of Edward de Vere, 17th Earl of Oxford*, Liverpool Univ. Press, 2003, pp. 110-12.

24. STOPES's *Southampton*, p. 519.

25. John Rollett, via private email, 2010.

26. STOPES's *Southampton*, p. 17.

27. "The Song of St. Swithin," possibly by Sir John Davies, *Davison's Poetical Rhapsody*, ed. A.H. Bullen, London, 1891, vol. 2, pp. 177-78.

28. John Phillip, *Epitaph on the Death, of the Right Honorable and Virtuous Lord Henry Wrisley, the Noble Earl of Southampton*, 1581; STOPES's *Southampton*, p. 313.

29. Martin Green, *Wriothesley's Roses*, Baltimore, MD, 1993, pp. 18-21.

30. John Finnis and Patrick Martin, "Another turn for the Turtle," *Times Literary Supplement*, April 18, 2003, p. 12.

31. Anthea Hume, "Love's Martyr, 'The Phoenix and the Turtle,' and the Aftermath of the Essex Rebellion," *Review of English Studies*, New Series, vol. 40, no. 157 (Feb. 1989), p. 64.

32. *Richard III* was first printed in 1597. Two parodies of this famous line follow: "A man, a man, a kingdom for a man!" John Marston, *The Scourge of Villainy*, 1598 (Satire 7); "A boat, a boat, a boat, a full hundred marks for a boat!" (3.4), Jonson, Marston, Chapman, *Eastward Ho* (1605).

33. R.J.C. Wait, *The Background to Shakespeare's Sonnets*, New York, 1972, p. 148.

34. Dorothy and Charlton Ogburn, *The Renaissance Man of England*, New York, 1955 (revised ed.), p. 51.

35. *The Statutes of the Realm (1225-1713)*, London, 1819, vol. 4, p. 527.

36. Ogburns, *This Star of England*, p. 663.

37. J.A. Fort, *A Time Scheme for Shakespeare's Sonnets*, London, 1929, p. 142.

38. Leslie Hotson, *Mr W.H.*, New York, 1964, p. 32.

39. Paul E.J. Hammer, "Shakespeare's *Richard II*, the Play of 7 February 1601, and the Essex Rising," *Shakespeare Quarterly*, vol. 59, no. 1 (Spring, 2008), p. 14.

40. *The Bedford Companion to Shakespeare: An Introduction with Documents*, ed. Russ McDonald, Boston, 1996, p. 71; Sir Francis Bacon, *A Declaration of the Practices and Treasons Attempted and Committed by Robert late Earl of Essex, and his complices, against her Majesty...* (1601), Sig. K3. Essex had evidently seen a performance of Shakespeare's *Richard II* as arranged by Sir Robert Cecil. In Sir Walter Ralegh's 1597 letter to Cecil, he wrote that Essex was "wonderful merry at your conceit of Richard the Second"; the line before it was about "entertainment." See Edward Edwards, *The Life of Sir Walter Ralegh*, London, 1868, vol. 2, p. 169.

41. T.B. Howell, *A Complete Collection of State Trials and proceedings for high treason and other crimes and misdemeanors*, London, 1816, vol. 1, p. 1336.

42. *Ibid*, p. 1339.

43. *Ibid*, p. 1351.

44. *Calendar of State Papers Domestic Series of the Reign of Elizabeth (1598-1601)*, ed. Mary Anne Everett Green, London, 1869, p. 554.

45. A letter dated June 10, 1602 from the French Ambassador, Christophe de Harlay, Comte de Beaumont, to King Henri IV, was translated by Frederick Chamberlin in *The Private Character of Queen Elizabeth*, New York, 1922, p. 152.

46. In 1559, it was reported by a Spanish ambassador that Queen Elizabeth and Sir Robert Dudley (future Earl of Leicester) were lovers. From 1560 onwards, "the first of a long line of offenders" were sent to prison "for asserting" that the queen was with child by Dudley (*DNB*). In 1561, the queen and Dudley enlisted the aid of the Spanish for support of their marriage. The Earl of Essex was born in 1565. After he was beheaded for treason in 1601, he was buried in the Royal Chapel of St. Peter ad Vincula (Tower of London), the same resting place of Ann Boleyn, Queen Elizabeth's mother, who was also executed. According to Walter Bourchier Devereux, after Essex's execution, "the Queen ordered that the banner and hatchment of the Earl of Essex as Knight of the Garter should not be removed from St. George's Chapel." *Lives and Letters of the Devereux, Earls of Essex*, London, 1853, vol. 2, p. 190.

47. A.J. Collins, "The Death-Warrant of Robert Earl of Essex," *The British Museum Quarterly*, vol. 16, no. 2 (April 1951), pp. 37-38.

48. *Letters from Sir Robert Cecil to Sir George Carew*, ed. John Maclean (Camden Society No. 88), London, 1864, p. 66.

49. *Ibid*, p. 74.

50. Howell, *State Trials*, p. 1357.

51. Michael Brennan, *Literary Patronage in the English Renaissance: The Pembroke Family*, London, ca. 1988, p. 116.

52. *Calendar of the Manuscripts of the Most Honorable The Marquis of Salisbury*, Dublin, 1906, vol. 11, p. 214.

53. *The Treatise of Treasons*, Louvain, 1572 (STC 7601); *A Copy of a Letter, Written by a Master of Art of Cambridge, to his Friend in London*, [Paris], 1584 (STC 5742.9), later known as *Leicester's Commonwealth*.

54. Lily Campbell, *Shakespeare's Histories, Mirrors of Elizabethan Policy*, 6th ed., The Huntington Library, San Marino, CA, 1978, p. 326.

55. *Ibid*, p. 332. Quotations from *A Declaration of the True Causes of the Great Troubles, Presupposed to be Intended Against the Realm of England*, [Antwerp], 1592 (STC 10005), and *An Advertisement Written to a Secretary of My Lord Treasurer's of England*, [Antwerp], 1592, p. 60 (STC 19885).

56. Margaret Hotine, "*Richard III* and *Macbeth* – Studies in Tudor Tyranny?" *Notes and Queries*, Dec. 1991, p. 480.

57. Clare Asquith, *Shadowplay: The Hidden Beliefs and Coded Politics of William Shakespeare*, PublicAffairs, New York, c. 2005, p. 80.

58. Michelle O'Callaghan, "Talking Politics: Tyranny, Parliament and Christopher Brooke's Ghost of Richard the Third (1614)," *The Historical Journal*, vol. 4, no. 1 (March 1998), p. 112.

59. Hotine, "*Richard III* and *Macbeth* – Studies in Tudor Tyranny?," p. 480.

60. G.P.V. Akrigg, *Jacobean Pageant, or the Court of King James I*, Harvard Univ. Press, 1962, p. 110 (citing Folger MS. 452.1 at Folger-Shakespeare Library).

61. Brenda James and William D. Rubinstein, *The Truth Will Out: Unmasking the Real Shakespeare*, Pearson Longman, Harlow, England, 2005, p. 146.

62. *Correspondence of King James VI of Scotland with Sir Robert Cecil and Others in England, during the Reign of Elizabeth*, ed. John Bruce, Camden Society, 1861, p. 51.

63. Walter Bourchier Devereux, *Lives and Letters of the Devereux, Earls of Essex*, London, 1853, vol. 2, p. 221.

64. STOPES's *Southampton*, p. 258, citing *The Thirteenth Report of the Royal Commission on Historical Manuscripts*, Appendix 4 (Manuscripts of Rye and Hereford Corporations), London, 1892, p. 126.

Chapter 17. "Simple Truth Suppress'd": A Unified Solution

1. Margot Heinemann, "Rebel Lords, Popular Playwrights, and Political Culture: Notes on the Jacobean Patronage of the Earl of Southampton," *The Yearbook of English Studies*, vol. 21 (1991), p. 70. The "martyr" reference is frequently mentioned by scholars, but I have yet to see the original source cited.

2. *Letters from Sir Robert Cecil to Sir George Carew*, ed. John Maclean, Camden Society (no. 88), London, 1864, p. 68, note B.

3. *Calendar of the Manuscripts of the Most Honorable the Marquess of Salisbury*, Historical Manuscripts Commission, Part 9, London, 1902, pp. 307-08.

4. P.M. Handover, *The Second Cecil: The Rise to Power 1563-1604*, London, 1959, p. 234, quoting from Salisbury Manuscripts, vol. 14, London, 1923, p. 172. The letter was addressed to Cecil but the writer is unknown.

5. *Correspondence of King James VI of Scotland with Sir Robert Cecil and Others in England, During the Reign of Elizabeth*, ed. John Bruce, Camden Society, 1861, p. 66.

6. Handover, *The Second Cecil*, p. 224.

7. *Correspondence of King James VI*, ed. Bruce, p. 65.

8. Maureen King, "The Essex Myth in Jacobean England," *The Accession of James I: Historical and Cultural Consequences*, eds. Glenn Burgess, Rowland Wymer, and Jason Lawrence, Palgrave, Macmillan, Handmills, Hampshire, 2006, p. 178. Dionise Campbell, Dean of Limerick, to Sir Robert Cecil, March 27, 1601.

9. *Ibid*, p. 182.

10. ARBER, vol. 3, p. 249.

11. G.P.V. Akrigg, *Shakespeare and the Earl of Southampton*, Harvard Univ. Press, 1968, p. 139.

12. Pauline Croft, "The Reputation of Robert Cecil: Libels, Political Opinion and Popular Awareness in the Early Seventeenth Century," *Transactions of the Royal Historical Society*, 6th series, 1991, vol. 1, p. 48.

13. STOPES's *Southampton*, p. 265, and John Nichols, *The Progresses, Processions, and Magnificent Festivities, of King James the First*, London, 1828, vol. 1, p. 426.

14. *Calendar of the Manuscripts of the Most Honorable The Marquis of Salisbury*, Part 11, Dublin, 1906, p. 40.

15. Heinemann, "Rebel Lords, Popular Playwrights, and Political Culture," p. 71.

16. Vernon F. Snow, *Essex the Rebel, The Life of Robert Devereux, the Third Earl of Essex (1591-1646)*, Univ. of Nebraska Press, Lincoln, 1970, p. 21.

17. *Ibid*, pp. 29, 39.

18. STOPES's *Southampton*, p. 259.

19. *Dudley Carleton to John Chamberlain, 1603-1624*, ed. Maurice Lee, Jr., Rutgers Univ. Press, 1972, p. 35.

20. STOPES's *Southampton*, p. 267, citing Dudley Carleton.

21. Akrigg, *Shakespeare and the Earl of Southampton*, pp. 140-42; the letter of the Venetian ambassador, Nicolo Molin, occurs in *Calendar of State Papers and Manuscripts relating to English Affairs, existing in the Archives and collections of Venice*, ed. Horatio F. Brown, London, 1900, vol. 10 (1603-09), p. 165.

22. Akrigg, *Shakespeare and the Earl of Southampton*, p. 142.

23. *Ibid*, p. 181, citing Chamberlain's *Letters*, ed. McClure, 1939, vol. 1, p. 202.

24. Robert Zaller, *The Parliament of 1621: A Study in Constitutional Conflict*, U.C. Press, Berkeley, 1971, p. 139.

25. William A. Shaw, *The Knights of England: A Complete Record from the Earliest Time to the Present Day*... London, 1906, vol. 2, pp. 100-31.

26. *Calendar of State Papers Domestic Series of the Reign of James I (1603-1610)*, ed. Mary Anne Everett Greene, London, 1857, vol. 8, p. 89.

27. *The Letters of John Chamberlain*, ed. Norman Egbert McClure, Memoirs of the American Philosophical Society, Philadelphia, 1939, vol. 1, p. 279.

28. Reversed initials occurred in Anthony Munday's dedication letter for his play, *Fedele and Fortunio* (1585), see Richard Hosley, *A Critical Edition of Anthony Munday's Fedele and Fortunio*, New York, 1981, p. 17; Nicholas Ling's reversed initials appear on his letter to the reader in *England's Helicon* (1600).

29. Leona Rostenberg, "Thomas Thorpe, Publisher of 'Shake-Speare's Sonnets,'" *Papers of the Bibliographical Society of America*, vol. 54, First Quarter, 1960, p. 21.

30. *The Praise of King Richard the Third* was contained in a combined publication titled, *Essays of Certain Paradoxes*, 1616 (STC 5779).

31. British Library, Additional MS 29307.

32. *The Encomium of Richard III by Sir William Cornwallis the Younger*, ed. A.N. Kincaid, London, 1977, intro., p. 7.

33. *Reader's Encyclopedia*, p. 816.

34. Mario Praz, "Robert Southwell's 'Saint Peter's Complaint' and Its Italian Source," *Modern Language Review*, vol. 19, no. 3 (July 1924), p. 288. The only books Southwell had requested in prison, noted Praz, were the Bible and the works of Saint Bernard.

35. Peter Milward, *Shakespeare's Religious Background*, Indiana Univ. Press, 1973, pp. 55-58.

36. Margaret Hotine, "*Richard III* and *Macbeth* – Studies in Tudor Tyranny?" *Notes and Queries*, Dec. 1991, p. 485.

37. Paul Morgan, "'Our Will Shakespeare' and Lope de Vega: An unrecorded contemporary document," *Shakespeare Survey 16*, Cambridge Univ. Press, 1963, pp. 118-120.

38. *William Shakespeare, The Complete Sonnets and Poems*, Oxford World's Classics, ed. Colin Burrow, Oxford Univ. Press, 2002, p. 106. Over half of the sonnets recorded by individuals in commonplace books appear without ascription to Shakespeare, and many vary with Thorpe's 1609 text; this suggests they were copied from manuscripts circulating before Thorpe's edition. See Marcy L. North, "Rehearsing the Absent Name: Reading Shakespeare's Sonnets Through Anonymity," *The Faces of Anonymity: Anonymous and Pseudonymous Publication from the Sixteenth to the Twentieth Century*, ed. Robert J. Griffin, Palgrave Macmillan, 2003, pp. 19-21.

39. Mark Anderson, *Shakespeare By Another Name*, Gotham Books, New York, 2005, p. 337.

40. Rostenberg, "Thomas Thorpe," p. 34; ARBER, vol. 3. p. 445.

41. Clinton Heylin, *So Long as Men Can Breathe: The Untold Story of Shakespeare's Sonnets*, Da Capo Press, 2009, p. 92; Frances A. Yates, John Florio, *The Life of an Italian in Shakespeare's England*, New York, 1968, pp. 283-84. The Sostratus story appears in *The Apophthegmes of Erasmus*, 1564 (STC 10444), reprint, Boston, Lincolnshire, 1877, p. 266.

42. Heylin, *So Long as Men Can Breathe*, p. 91-92.

43. *Calendar of State Papers Domestic Series, of the Reign of Charles I*, ed. John Bruce, London, 1865, vol. 8, p. 527.

44. *"An Addition of some excellent Poems to Shakespeare's Poems* by other gentlemen" (Nov. 4, 1639), ARBER, vol. 4, p. 487.

45. John Michel, *Who Wrote Shakespeare?*, London, 1996, p. 182.

46. STOPES's *Southampton*, p. 347.

47. *Calendar of State Papers Domestic*, ed. Greene, vol. 8, p. 551.

48. August 3, 1609; John Nichols, *The Progresses, Processions and Magnificent Festivities of King James the First*, London, 1828, vol. 2, p. 263.

49. STOPES's *Southampton*, p. 345.

50. *Poems by Sir John Salusbury and Robert Chester*, ed. Carleton Brown, London, 1914, intro., p. 25.

51. "Orders concerning loose persons and idle assemblies. That all plays bearbaitings games singing of ballads buckler play or such like causes of assemblies be utterly prohibited and the parties offending severely punished by any Alderman or Justice of the Peace." The exact month that the 1609 order was issued is unknown, but W.W. Greg dated it "? May." *Collections*, The Malone Society, ed. W.W. Greg, Oxford Univ. Press, 1931, vol. 2, part 3, p. 319.

52. *A Collection of Several Speeches and Treatises of the late Lord Treasurer Cecil*, ed. Pauline Croft, Camden Miscellany, vol. 29 (Camden 4th Series, vol. 34), London, 1987, p. 266. The first Parliament of James I comprised five sessions during the years 1604 to 1610. The third session occurred in 1606-07; the fourth, Feb. 9 to July 23, 1610; the fifth, October 16 to Dec. 6, 1610 (Prof. Johann Sommerville, Univ. of Wisconsin-Madison, "The Emergence of Britain," http://faculty.history.wisc.edu/sommerville/).

53. *Parliamentary Debates in 1610*, ed. Samuel Gardiner, Camden Society (vol. 81), 1862, p. 2.

54. Pauline Croft, "Robert Cecil and the Early Jacobean Court," *The Mental World of the Jacobean Court*, ed. Linda Levy Peck, Cambridge Univ. Press, 1991, p. 141.

55. *Ibid*, pp. 141-42.

56. *Parliamentary Debates in 1610*, ed. Gardiner, p. 3.

57. *Proceedings in Parliament 1610*, ed. Elizabeth Read Foster, Yale Univ. Press, 1966, vol. 1 (House of Lords), p. 164.

58. *Report on the Manuscripts of the Marquess of Downshire preserved at Easthampstead Park, Berkshire*, Historical Manuscripts Commission, vol. 2 (The Papers of William Trumbell the Elder, 1605-1610), ed. E.K. Purnell and A.B. Hinds, London, 1936, pp. 279-80.

59. Michael Brennan, *Literary Patronage in the English Renaissance: The Pembroke Family*, New York, ca. 1988, p. 122.

60. STOPES's *Southampton*, p. 405.

61. *Ibid*.

62. STOPES's *Southampton*, p. 414.

63. "Lethargy" in Vernon F. Snow, "New Light on the Last Days and Death of Henry Wriothesley, Earl of Southampton," *Huntington Library Quarterly*, vol. 37, no. 1 (Nov. 1973); "fevers and convulsions" in *Dudley Carleton to John Chamberlain, 1603-1624*, ed. Maurice Lee, Jr., Rutgers Univ. Press, 1972, p. 317.

64. Snow, "New Light on the ... Death of ... Southampton," p. 62.

65. Anthony Wood, *Athenae Oxonienses. An exact history of all the writers and bishops who have had their education in the ... University of Oxford*, 1691, pp. 330-31 (Wing 3382).

66. *Fourth Report of the Royal Commission on Historical Manuscripts, Part 1: The Manuscripts of the Right Honorable the Earl de la Warr at Knole Park, Co. Kent*, London, 1874, p. 289.

67. Sir Edward Peyton, *The Divine Catastrophe of the Kingly Family of the House of Stuarts*, 1652, p. 37.

68. STOPES's *Southampton*, p. 468. Beaumont's poem was first published in *Bosworth Field: with a taste of the variety of other poems, left by Sir John Beaumont, baronet, deceased*, 1629, p. 178. His younger brother was the dramatist, Francis Beaumont.

69. The historic Lord Talbot (John Talbot, Earl of Shrewsbury) died in 1453. The number "32" in the margin could refer to line 32 in the First Folio edition of *Henry VI, Part 1*, (pp. 113-14 of the histories section). Lord Talbot's final words occur in Act 4, Scene 7.

70. Richard Horwich, "*Hamlet* and *Eastward Ho*," *Studies in English Literature, 1500-1900*, vol. 11, no. 2 (Spring 1971), p. 231.

71. See notes in *Eastward Ho*, ed. R.Q. Van Fossen, Manchester Univ. Press, 1979.

Chapter 18. Dare the Shakespeare Professor

1. Mark Twain, *Is Shakespeare Dead?* New York, 1909, p. 102.

2. *Wall Street Journal*, April 18-19, 2009.

3. *Calendar of State Papers of the Reign of James I, 1603-1610, Domestic Series*, ed. Mary Anne Everett Green, London, 1857, p. 234.

4. GREENWOOD's *Problem*, p. 284.

5. Gail Kern Paster in "The Ghosts of Shakespeare," *Harper's Magazine*, April 1999, p. 39.

Appendix A. 93 "Too Early" Allusions to Shakespeare's Plays (1562-1606)

1. *DNB*, 1885 edition.

2. Kenneth Muir, *Shakespeare's Sources*, London, 1957 (1961 reprint), vol. 1, pp. 26-27.

3. Robert Adger Law, "On Shakespeare's Changes of his Source Material in *Romeo and Juliet*," *Studies in English*, Bulletin, Univ. of Texas, vol. 9 (July 8, 1929), pp. 97-98.

4. William Lowes Rushton, *Shakespeare's Euphuism*, London, 1871, pp. 2-3; *Complete Works of John Lyly*, ed. R. Warwick Bond, Oxford, 1902, vol. 1, pp. 190, 210.

5. *Complete Works of John Lyly*, ed. Bond, vol. 1, p. 254, lines 15-18.

6. Michael Macrone, *Brush Up Your Shakespeare!*, New York, 1990, p. 206. All references to Macrone in these notes or in the main text are taken from his chapter titled, "Faux Shakespeare: Phrases Often Misattributed to Shakespeare"; Arthur Golding, *The Psalms of David and Others*, 1571, p. 35 (verso), a translation of Jean Calvin (STC 4395): "And yet we receive but cold comfort of whatsoever the scripture speaketh concerning God's power and justice."

7. Rushton, *Shakespeare's Euphuism*, p. 19.

8. Naseeb Shaheen, "Shakespeare's Knowledge of Italian," *Shakespeare Survey*, vol. 47, Cambridge Univ. Press, 1994, p. 167.

9. Macrone, *Brush Up Your Shakespeare!*, p. 209.

10. Sigurd Burckhardt, "*The Merchant of Venice*: The Gentle Bond," *English Literary History*, vol. 29, no. 3 (Sept. 1962), p. 249.

11. *Shakespeare's Plutarch ... Containing the Main Sources of Anthony & Cleopatra and of Coriolanus*, ed. C.F. Tucker Brooke, New York, 1966, vol. 2, pp. 112-13. North's work

was a translation of *Les Vies des Hommes Illustres Grecs et Romains* (Paris, 1559) by Jacques Amyot, a French translation of the Greek book by Plutarch.

12. Eva Turner Clark, *Hidden Allusions in Shakespeare's Plays*, New York, 1931, p. 75.

13. *Complete Works of John Lyly*, ed. Bond, vol. 1, p. 174.

14. Robert A. Logan, *Shakespeare's Marlowe: The Influence of Christopher Marlowe on Shakespeare's Artistry*, Ashgate Publishing, Aldershot, U.K., 2007, p. 170

15. *The Merchant of Venice*, A New Variorum Edition of Shakespeare (vol. 7), ed. Horace H. Furness, Philadelphia, 1888, p. 141.

16. W.L. Rushton, "Parallel Passages," *Notes and Queries*, 4th series, October 18, 1873, p. 304.

17. *The Life and Death of King John*, A New Variorum Edition of Shakespeare (vol. 19), ed. Horace H. Furness, Jr., Philadelphia, 1919, p. 170.

18. Rushton, *Shakespeare's Euphuism*, pp. 103-04.

19. Macrone, *Brush Up Your Shakespeare!*, p. 206; Thomas Newton (translator), *The Touchstone of Complexions*, 1576 (STC 15456): "... they be people commonly healthy, and as sound as a Bell," p. 110 (verso).

20. *The Tempest*, A New Variorum Edition of Shakespeare (vol. 8), ed. H.H. Furness, Philadelphia, 1892, p. 170.

21. Rushton, *Shakespeare's Euphuism*, p. 44.

22. *The Comedy of Errors*, Arden Edition, ed. R.A. Foakes, Harvard Univ. Press, revised ed., 1962, p. 68.

23. Michael Pincombe, *The Plays of John Lyly: Eros and Eliza*, Manchester Univ. Press, 1996, intro., p. 13.

24. H.R.D. Anders, *Shakespeare's Books: A Dissertation on Shakespeare's Reading and the Immediate Sources of His Works*, 1904, reprint AMS Press, New York, 1965, p. 133.

25. Meredith Hamner, *The Ancient Ecclesiastical Histories of the First Six Hundred Years After Christ*, 1577, p. 147, as noted by Macrone, *Brush Up Your Shakespeare!*, p. 207.

26. Clark, *Hidden Allusions in Shakespeare's Plays*, p. 30.

27. *Reader's Encyclopedia*, p. 167.

28. *The Tragedie of Cymbeline*, A New Variorum Edition of Shakespeare (vol. 18), ed. H.H. Furness, Philadelphia, 1913, p. 47.

29. Anders, *Shakespeare's Books*, pp. 121-22.

30. Logan, *Shakespeare's Marlowe*, p. 39.

31. *The Tragedy of Richard the Third*, A New Variorum Edition of Shakespeare (vol. 16), ed. H.H. Furness, Philadelphia, 1908, p. 400.

32. *The Tragedie of Julius Caesar*, A New Variorum Edition of Shakespeare (vol. 17), ed. H.H. Furness, Jr., Philadelphia, 1913, p. 114.

33. *Tacitus, The Histories*, translated by Clifford H. Moore, London, 1931, vol. 2, pp. 197-99 (Book 5, Chapter 13).

34. Josephine Waters Bennett, "Oxford and Endimion," *PMLA*, vol. 57, No. 2 (June 1942), p. 363.

35. Anders, *Shakespeare's Books*, pp. 132-33.

36. Logan, *Shakespeare's Marlowe*, pp. 15, 27.

37. *The Stukeley Plays: The Battle of Alcazar by George Peele, The Famous History of the Life and Death of Captain Thomas Stukeley*, ed. Charles Edelman, Manchester Univ. Press, 2005, p. 19.

38. Anders, *Shakespeare's Books*, p. 135.

39. *King Lear*, A New Variorum Edition of Shakespeare (vol. 5), ed. H.H. Furness, Philadelphia, 1880, p. 76.

40. Margaret Christian, "Zepheria (1594; STC 26124): A Critical Edition," *Studies in Philology*, vol. 100, no. 2 (Spring 2003), pp. 195-243.

41. *The Tragedy of Richard the Third*, Variorum Edition, ed. Furness, p. 421; Ramon Jiménez, "'The True Tragedy of Richard the Third': Another Early History Play by Edward de Vere," *The Oxfordian*, 2004, vol. 7, p. 128.

42. J.M. Robertson, *An Introduction to the Study of the Shakespeare Canon*, London, 1924, p. 185.

43. David Roper, "The Peacham Chronogram," *Shakespeare-Oxford Newsletter*, Fall 2001.

44. F.E. Halliday, *A Shakespeare Companion (1550-1950)*, New York, 1952, p. 654. The German version of Shakespeare's *Titus Andronicus* was titled, "Tragoedia von Tito Andronico," and was printed in *Englische Comedien und Tragedien* (1620).

45. Anders, *Shakespeare's Books*, p. 134.

46. Charles Felver, "Robert Armin, Shakespeare's Source for Touchstone," *Shakespeare Quarterly*, Winter 1956, pp. 135-37.

47. *Henslowe's*, ed. R.A. Foakes, p. 21.

48. *The Works of Thomas Nashe*, eds. Ronald B. McKerrow, F.P. Wilson, Oxford, 1958, vol. 5, p. 196.

49. *The Life and Death of King John*, Variorum Edition, ed. Furness, p. 318.

50. Richard Hinckley Allen, *Star Names and Their Meanings*, New York, 1889, p. 256.

51. *The Life and Death of King John*, Variorum Edition, ed. Furness, p. 64.

52. *King John*, The Arden Edition of the Works of Shakespeare, ed. E.A.J. Honigmann, Harvard Univ. Press, 1965 (reprint), p. 25.

53. Anders, *Shakespeare's Books*, p. 131.

54. *The Tragedy of Solyman and Perseda*, ed. Murray, p. 46.

55. Logan, *Shakespeare's Marlowe*, pp. 117-18.

56. *The Merchant of Venice*, Variorum Edition, ed. Furness, p. 46.

57. *Henslowe's Diary*, ed. R.A. Foakes, Cambridge Univ. Press, 2002 (2nd edition), p. 23.

58. John Bakeless, *The Tragicall History of Christopher Marlowe*, Westport, CT, 1942, reprint Harvard Univ. Press, 1970, vol. 2, p. 266.

59. *Romeo and Juliet*, A New Variorum Edition of Shakespeare (vol. 1), ed. H.H. Furness, Philadelphia, 1913, p. 134; *The Three Ladies of London*, 1584 (STC 25784, sig. B1).

60. Bakeless, *Christopher Marlowe*, vol. 2, p. 211.

61. *Ibid.*

62. John Weever, *The Mirror of Martyrs or The Life and Death of that Thrice Valiant Captain, and Most Godly Martyr, Sir John Old-castle, Knight, Lord Cobham*, 1601, sig. A8v.

63. *Troilus and Cressida*, A New Variorum of Shakespeare (vol. 26), ed. Harold N. Hillebrand, Philadelphia, 1953, pp. 4-5.

64. *The Faerie Queene*, ed. P.C. Bayley, Oxford Univ. Press, 1965, vol. 1, p. 288.

65. Macrone, *Brush Up Your Shakespeare!*, p. 206; *Pap with an Hatchet* (STC 17463).

66. H.H. Holland, *Shakespeare, Oxford and Elizabethan Times*, London (1933), reprint, Folcroft Library Editions, 1974, p. 133; the play was dated 1589 in *Friar Bacon and Friar Bungay*, ed. J.A. Lavin, London, 1969, p. 28.

67. *The Tragedy of Titus Andronicus*, The Yale Shakespeare, ed. A.M. Witherspoon, Yale Univ. Press, 1926, p. 99.

68. Robert Ralston Cawley, "Shakspere's Use of the Voyagers in *The Tempest*," *PMLA*, vol. 41, no. 3 (Sept. 1926), p. 693.

69. T.W. Baldwin, *On the Literary Genetics of Shakespeare's Poems and Sonnets*, Univ. of Illinois Press, Urbana, 1950, p. 7.

70. Charles Crawford, "The Date and Authenticity of Titus Andronicus," *Shakespeare Jahrbuch*, Berlin, 1900, vol. 36, pp. 114-18; J.M. Robertson, *An Introduction to the Study of the Shakespeare Canon*, London, 1924, p. 179.

71. *The Complete Poems of Robert Southwell, S.J.*, ed. Alexander Grosart, The Fuller Worthies' Library, London, 1872 (AMS Press, New York, reprint 1971), p. 21.

72. *King John*, Arden Edition, ed. Honigmann, p. 53.

73. Robert Adger Law, "Daniel's *Rosamond* and Shakespeare," *Studies in English*, Univ. of Texas, 1947, vol. 26, pp. 42-48.

74. *Henry Stanford's Anthology*, ed., Steven W. May, New York, 1988, pp. 76, 276-77; the song was printed in Thomas Morley's *The First Book of Airs* (1600). The quote by Florio was noted by Frances A. Yates, *John Florio*, New York, 1968 (reprint), p. 35.

75. Anders, *Shakespeare's Books*, p. 87.

76. *Ibid*, p. 86.

77. *Reader's Encyclopedia*, p. 24.

78. Noted by Claes Schaar, *Elizabethan Sonnet Themes and the Dating of Shakespeare's Sonnets*, Copenhagen, 1962, reprint New York, 1973, p. 70.

79. Noted by Paula Glatzer, *The Complaint of the Poet, The Parnassus Plays: A Critical Study of the Trilogy Performed at St. John's College, Cambridge, 1598/99 – 1601/02, Authors Anonymous*, Salzburg, 1977, p. 258.

80. Anders, *Shakespeare's Books*, p. 88.

81. Claes Schaar, *An Elizabethan Sonnet Problem*, Copenhagen, 1960, pp. 158-59.

82. *A Shakespeare Companion (1550-1950)*, ed. F.E. Halliday, New York, 1952, p. 344; *William Shakespeare, A Textual Companion*, eds. Stanley Wells, Gary Taylor, New York, 1997, p. 113.

83. *King John*, Arden Edition, ed. Honigmann, p. 113.

84. Anders, *Shakespeare's Books*, pp. 125-26.

85. Noted by Edmund Malone (Meredith Skura,"Marlowe's *Edward II*: Penetrating Language in Shakespeare's *Richard II*," Shakespeare Survey 50, 1997, p. 46.

86. *The Troublesome Reign and Lamentable Death of Edward the Second, King of England*, 1594 (STC 17437); *The Troublesome Reign of John, King of England*, 1591 (STC 14644).

87. *As You Like It*, The Works of Shakespeare, eds. Sir Arthur Quiller-Couch, John Dover Wilson, Cambridge Univ. Press, 1926, pp. 106-07.

88. *The Works of Thomas Nashe*, eds. McKerrow, Wilson, vol. 3, p. 24.

89. *Ibid*, vol. 3, p. 301, citing J. Dover Wilson. Thomas Lodge's line occurs in "The Deaf Man's Dialogue," *Euphues Shadow* (1592).

90. Bakeless, *Christopher Marlowe*, vol. 2, p. 85.

91. *Reader's Encyclopedia*, p. 505.

92. Anders, *Shakespeare's Books*, p. 97.

93. *The Tempest*, Variorum Edition, ed. Furness, p. 79.

94. Albert Cohn, *Shakespeare in Germany in the Sixteenth and Seventeenth Centuries*, London, 1865, part 1, pp. 68-71, part 2, p. 1.

95. *The Winter's Tale*, A New Variorum Edition of Shakespeare (vol. 11), ed. H.H. Furness, Philadelphia, 1898, p. 6.

96. *Barnabe Barnes, Parthenophil and Parthenophe, A Critical Edition*, ed. Victor A. Doyno, Southern Illinois Univ. Press, 1971, p. 163.

97. Rupert Taylor, *The Date of Love's Labour's Lost*, Columbia Univ. Press, New York, 1932, pp. 95, 108.

98. *The Works of Thomas Nashe*, eds. McKerrow, Wilson, vol. 3, p. 24.

99. Frank Howland McCloskey, "The Date of *A Midsummer Night's Dream*," *Modern Language Notes*, vol. 46, no. 6 (June 1931), pp. 389-90.

100. ARBER, vol. 2, p. 652.

101. *Reader's Encyclopedia*, p. 951.

102. *Henry the Fourth, Part 1*, A New Variorum Edition of Shakespeare (vol. 21), ed. Samuel B. Hemingway, Philadelphia, 1936, p. 365.

103. *The Second Part of Henry the Fourth*, A New Variorum Edition of Shakespeare (vol. 23), ed. Matthias A. Shaaber, Philadelphia, 1940, p. 353.

104. *Othello*, A New Variorum Edition of Shakespeare (vol. 6), ed. H.H. Furness, Philadelphia, 1886, p. 66.

105. C.J. Rawson, "Macbeth on Sleep: Two Parallels," *Shakespeare Quarterly*, vol. 14, no. 4 (Autumn 1963), pp. 484-85.

106. Anne Barton, *Ben Jonson, Dramatist*, Cambridge Univ. Press, 1984, p. 31.

107. *King Lear*, Variorum Edition, ed. Furness, p. 229.

108. *Every Man Out of His Humour / Ben Jonson*, ed. Helen Ostovich, Manchester Univ. Press, New York, 2001, p. 326.

109. *Macbeth*, A New Variorum Edition of Shakespeare (vol. 2), ed. H.H. Furness, Philadelphia, 1873, pp. 359-60; William Kemp, *Nine Days' Wonder*, 1600.

110. Charles W. Barrell, "Creative Calendar: An Illuminating Shaw-Shakespeare Parallel with Ben Jonson's Testimony," *Shakespeare Fellowship News-Letter*, June 1943, p. 46.

111. Anders, *Shakespeare's Books*, p. 139; Alexander was later created Earl of Sterling.

112. Kenneth Muir, "Samuel Harsnett and *King Lear*," *Review of English Studies*, New Series, vol. 2, no. 5 (Jan. 1951), p. 19.

113. F.W. Brownlow, *Shakespeare, Harsnett, and the Devils of Denham*, Univ. of Delaware Press, 1993, p. 110 (note).

114. *King Lear*, The Arden Edition of the Works of Shakespeare, ed. Kenneth Muir, Harvard Univ. Press, reprinted with corrections, 1963, pp. 253-56.

115. Paul Bertram, *Shakespeare and the Two Noble Kinsmen*, Rutgers Univ. Press, 1965, p. 258 (note).

Other Sources

Advice to a Son, ed. Louis B. Wright, Ithaca, NY, 1962.

Albright, Evelyn May, "Shakespeare's Richard II and the Essex Conspiracy," *PMLA*, vol. 42, no. 3, (Sept. 1927).

Albright, Evelyn May, *Dramatic Publication in England, 1580-1640; A Study of Conditions Affecting Content and Form of Drama*, New York, 1927.

Alden, Raymond MacDonald, "The 1640 Text of Shakespeare's Sonnets," *Modern Philology*, vol. 14, no. 1 (May 1916).

Altick, Richard D., *The Scholar Adventurers*, New York, 1960, pp. 190-95.

The Applause First Folio of Shakespeare in Modern Type, ed. Neil Freeman, Folio Scripts, Vancouver, Canada, 2001.

Armstrong, William A., "Shakespeare and the Acting of Edward Alleyn," *Shakespeare Survey*, vol. 7, 1954.

Astington, John H., "Sir John Astley and Court Culture," *Shakespeare Studies*, vol. 30, 2002.

Baskervill, Charles Read, *English Elements in Jonson's Early Comedy*, 1911, reprint, New York, 1967.

Ben Jonson Poems, ed. Ian Donaldson, Oxford Univ. Press, 1975.

Bentley, Gerald Edes, *The Jacobean and Caroline Stage Dramatic Companies and Players*, Oxford, 1941.

Bergeron, David M., *Textual Patronage in English Drama (1570-1640)*, Ashgate Publishing Ltd., Aldershot, Hampshire, U.K., 2006.

Bertram, Paul and Cossa, Frank, "'Willm Shakespeare 1609': The Flower Portrait Revisited," *Shakespeare Quarterly*, vol. 37, no. 1 (Spring, 1986).

Bloom, J. Harvey, *Shakespeare's Church,* London, 1902.

Bowen, Gwynneth, "The Incomparable Pair and 'The Works of William Shakespeare,'" *Shakespearean Authorship Review*, Autumn 1961.

Bradbrook, M.C., *The Rise of the Common Player*, Cambridge, MA, 1962.

Brooks, Alden, *This Side of Shakespeare*, New York, 1964.

Cadwallader, Laura H., *The Career of the Earl of Essex 1597-1601*, Philadelphia, 1923, p. 83.

Cairncross, Andrew S., "Shakespeare and the 'Staying Entries,'" *Shakespeare in the Southwest: Some New Directions*, ed. T.J. Stafford, Univ. of Texas at El Paso, 1969, pp. 80-93.

Carroll, D. Allen, *Greene's Groatsworth of Wit*, Medieval and Renaissance Texts and Studies, vol. 114, Binghamton, NY, 1994.

Collier, J. Payne, *Bibliographical and Critical Account of the Rarest Books in the English Language*, New York, 1866, vol. 4.

The Complete Works of Thomas Watson, ed. Dana F. Sutton, Lewiston, NY, 1997, vol. 2.

Craik, George L., *Spenser and His Poetry*, London, 1871, vol. 3.

Deelman, Christian, *The Great Shakespeare Jubilee*, New York, 1964.

The Dictionary of Art, ed. Jane Turner, Macmillan Publishers, 1996 (Thomas Stanton).

Duncan-Jones, Katherine, "Was the 1609 Sonnets Really Unauthorized?" *Review of English Studies*, New Series, vol. 34, no. 134 (May 1983).

Dutton, Richard, *Ben Jonson: Authority: Criticism*, New York, 1996.

Edwards, S.J., Francis, *Plots and Plotters in the Reign of Elizabeth I*, Four Courts Press, Portland, OR, 2002.

England's Helicon, 1600, 1614, ed. Hyder E. Rollins, Harvard Univ. Press, 1935, 2 vols.

Esdaile, Katharine A., "A Seventeenth-Century Model of an English Monument," *The Burlington Magazine for Connoisseurs*, vol. 55, no. 319 (October 1929).

Esdaile, Mrs. Arundell, "The Stantons of Holborn," *The Archaeological Journal*, vol. 85 (March-Dec. 1928), London, 1930, p. 153.

Esdaile, Katharine A., *English Church Monuments 1510-1840*, London, 1946.

Foster, Donald W., "Master W.H., R.I.P.," *PMLA*, vol. 102, no. 1 (Jan. 1987).

Foster, Donald W., *Elegy by W.S., A Study in Attribution*, Univ. of Delaware Press, 1989.

Friswell, J. Hain, *Life Portraits of William Shakspeare*, London, 1864.

George, M. Dorothy, "Notes on the Origin of the Declared Account," *The English Historical Review*, vol. 31, no. 121 (Jan. 1916).

Gollancz, Sir Israel, "Contemporary Lines to Heminge and Condell," *Times Literary Supplement*, Thursday, Jan. 26, 1922, p. 56.

Gray, Arthur, "Spenser's Aetion," *Times Literary Supplement*, Jan. 24, 1935, p. 48.

Greenwood, Sir George, *The Stratford Bust and the Droeshout Engraving*, London, 1925.

Greg, W.W., "Edward Alleyn," *A Series of Papers on Shakespeare and the Theatre*, London, 1927.

Greg, W.W., *The Editorial Problem in Shakespeare*, Oxford, 1942, pp. 225-27.

Greg, W.W., "The Copyright of Hero and Leander," *The Library: Transactions of the Bibliographical Society*, vol. 24, nos. 3-4 (Dec. 1943 – March 1944).

Gurr, Andrew, *The Shakespearean Stage (1574-1642)*, Cambridge Univ. Press, 1970.

Hart, Alfred, *Stolne and Surreptitious Copies: a Comparative Study of Shakespeare's Bad Quartos*, Melbourne Univ. Press, 1942.

Hieatt, A.K. et al, "Shakespeare's Rare Words: 'Lover's Complaint,' *Cymbeline*, and *Sonnets*," *Notes and Queries*, June 1987, p. 219.

Holmes, Martin, "An Unrecorded Portrait of Edward Alleyn," *Theatre Notebook V*, 1950.

Honigmann, E.A.J., "Shakespeare and London's Immigrant Community Circa 1600," *Elizabethan and Modern Studies Presented to Professor Willem Schrickx*, ed. J.P. Vander Motten, Gent, 1985.

Honigmann, E.A.J., *The Stability of Shakespeare's Text*, Univ. of Nebraska, Lincoln, 1965.

Honigmann, E.A.J., *John Weever, A Biography of a Literary Associate of Shakespeare and Jonson*, Manchester Univ. Press, 1987.

Hosking, G.L., *The Life and Times of Edward Alleyn,* London, 1952.

Hotson, Leslie, *I, William Shakespeare, Do Appoint Thomas Russell, Esq.*, London, 1937.

Ingram, William, *A London Life in the Brazen Age: Francis Langley (1548-1602)*, Harvard Univ. Press, 1978.

Jackson, W.A., "The Funeral Procession of Queen Elizabeth," *The Library (Transactions of the Bibliographical Society)*, vol. 26, no. 4 (March 1946).

John Marston, What You Will, ed. M.R. Woodhead, Nottingham Univ. Press, 1980.

Kay, W. David, *Ben Jonson: A Literary Life*, New York, 1995.

Kirschbaum, Leo, *Shakespeare and the Stationers*, Ohio State Univ. Press, 1955.

Knight, Charles, *William Shakspere; A Biography*, London, 1843.

Knutson, Roslyn L., "*Histrio-Mastix*: Not by John Marston," *Studies in Philology*, Univ. of North Carolina Press, Chapel Hill, 2001.

Mackail, J.W., "A Lover's Complaint," *Essays and Studies by Members of the English Association*, ed. W.P. Ker, Oxford, 1912, vol. 3.

Mathew, Frank, *An Image of Shakespeare*, New York, 1923, pp. 112-15.

Memorials of the Affairs of State in the Reigns of Queen Elizabeth and King James I collected chiefly from the original papers of the Rt. Hon. Sir Ralph Winwood, Kt (1563-1617), ed. E. Sawyer, 1725, vol. 3.

Monroe, Robert D., "Notes on a Unique Engraving and 'Lost' Portrait of Shakespeare," *Shakespeare Quarterly*, Summer 1961.

Norris, J. Parker, *The Portraits of Shakespeare*, Philadelphia, 1885.

Oakeshott, Walter, "Love's Martyr," *Huntington Library Quarterly*, vol. 39, no. 1 (Nov. 1975), pp. 47-49.

The Old Taming of A Shrew, upon which Shakespeare Founded His Comedy, ed. Thomas Amyot, London, 1844.

Othello, New Cambridge Shakespeare, ed. Scott McMillin, Cambridge Univ. Press, 2001.

The Passionate Pilgrim by William Shakespeare, The Third Edition, 1612, ed. Hyder E. Rollins, New York, 1940.

The Passions of the Mind in General by Thomas Wright, ed. William Webster Newbold, The Renaissance Imagination, vol. 15, New York, 1986.

Phillips, G.W., *Lord Burghley in Shakespeare*, London, 1936.

Piper, David, *Catalogue of 17th-Century Portraits in the NPG 1625-1714*, Cambridge Univ. Press, 1963.

Piper, David, *The English Face*, National Portrait Gallery, London, 1978.

Piper, David, *Sweet Mr. Shakespeare, I'll Have His Picture, The Changing Image of Shakespeare's Person, 1600-1800*, National Portrait Gallery, London, 1964.

Piper, Ferdinand, *Mythologie der christlichen Kunst*, Weimar, 1847, p. 469.

The Plays and Poems of Philip Massinger, eds. Philip Edwards, Colin Gibson, Oxford Univ. Press, 1976.

The Poems of Sir John Beaumont, Bart, ed. Alexander Grosart, Lancashire, 1869.

Poetaster by Ben Jonson, ed. Josiah H. Penniman, Boston, 1913.

Pohl, Frederick J., "The Death-Mask," *Shakespeare Quarterly*, vol. 12, no. 2 (Spring 1961).

Pollard, Alfred W., *Shakespeare Folios and Quartos: A Study in the Bibliography of Shakespeare's Plays (1594-1685)*, London, 1909.

Price, Diana, "Reconsidering Shakespeare's Monument," *Review of English Studies*, New Series, vol. 48, no. 190 (May 1997).

Rendall, Gerald H., *Ben Jonson and The First Folio Edition of Shakespeare's Plays*, 1939, reprint, 1970.

Rhodes, R. Crompton, *Shakespeare's First Folio*, Oxford, 1923.

Riddell, William Renwick, "The Death of King James I. A Medico-Legal Study," *Journal of the American Institute of Criminal Law and Criminology*, vol. 19, no. 1 (May 1928).

Robertson, J.M., *Shakespeare and Chapman*, London, 1917.

Secord, Arthur W., "I.M. of the First Folio of Shakespeare and Other Mabbe Problems," *Journal of English and Germanic Philology*, vol. 47, no. 4 (October 1948).

Shakespeare Cross-Examination: A Compilation of Articles first appearing in the American Bar Association Journal, ed. Tappan Gregory, Chicago, 1961.

Shakespeare's Sonnets, eds. Louis B. Wright, Virginia A. LaMar, New York, 1967.

Sir William Davenant, The Shorter Poems, and Songs from the Plays and Masques, ed. A.M. Gibbs, Oxford, 1972.

Smith, Hallett, "'No Cloudy Stuffe to Puzzell Intellect': A Testimonial Misapplied to Shakespeare," *Shakespeare Quarterly*, vol. 1, no. 1 (Jan. 1950).

Smith, Hallett, *Tension of the Lyre, Poetry in Shakespeare's Sonnets*, Huntington Library, San Marino, 1981.

Smith, Irwin, *Shakespeare's Blackfriars Playhouse*, New York Univ. Press, 1964.

The Sonnets, A New Variorum Edition of Shakespeare (vols. 24-25), ed. Hyder E. Rollins, Philadelphia, 1944.

Spence, Richard T., *Lady Anne Clifford*, Thrupp, Gloucestershire, 1997.

Stopes, Charlotte C., *Shakespeare's Environment*, London, 1914.

Studies in the First Folio, ed. Sir Israel Gollancz, London, 1924.

Summers, Claude, and Pebworth, Ted-Larry, *Ben Jonson Revised*, New York, 1999.

Talbert, Ernest William, "The Purpose and Technique of Jonson's *Poetaster*," *Studies in Philology*, vol. 42, no. 2 (April 1945).

Taylor, Dick, "The Earl of Montgomery and the Dedicatory Epistle of Shakespeare's First Folio," *Shakespeare Quarterly*, Winter 1959.

Taylor, Jr., Dick, "The Third Earl of Pembroke as a Patron of Poetry," *Tulane Studies in English*, 1955.

Taylor, Jr., Dick, "The Earl of Pembroke and the Youth of Shakespeare's Sonnets: An Essay in Rehabilitation," *Studies in Philology*, Jan. 1959.

Tennant, Philip, "Stratford-upon-Avon in the Civil War," *History of an English Borough, Stratford-upon-Avon*, ed. Robert Bearman, Stroud, U.K., 1997.

Thomas Nashe, The Unfortunate Traveller and Other Works, ed. J.B. Steane, Penguin (reprint), New York, 1985 (*The Choosing of Valentines*).

Thompson, Anthony B., "Licensing the Press: The Career of G.R. Weckherlin during the Personal Rule of Charles I," *The Historical Journal*, vol. 41, no. 3 (Sept. 1998).

Timon, eds. J.C. Bulman, M. Nosworthy, Malone Society Reprints, Oxford Univ. Press, 1980.

Tricomi, A.H., "Philip, Earl of Pembroke, and the Analogical Way of Reading Political Tragedy," *Journal of English and Germanic Philology*, vol. 85 no. 3 (July 1986).

The Triumphs Over Death by The Venerable Robert Southwell, S.J., ed. John William Trotman, St. Louis, MO, 1914.

Walker, Alice, *Textual Problems of The First Folio*, Cambridge Univ. Press, 1953.

Wallace, Charles W., "Shakespeare and His London Associates as Revealed in Recently Discovered Documents," *University Studies of the University of Nebraska*, 1909, vol. 9.

A Warning for Faire Women: A Critical Edition, ed. Charles Dale Cannon, The Hague, 1975.

Webb, Judge Thomas E., *The Mystery of William Shakespeare: A Summary of Evidence*, London, 1902.

Whinney, Margaret, *Sculpture in Britain, 1530 to 1830*, Baltimore, MD, 1964.

Williams, Robin P., *Sweet Swan of Avon. Did a Woman Write Shakespeare?*, Peachpit Press, Berkeley, CA, 2006.

Williamson, Hugh Ross, *George Villiers, First Duke of Buckingham. Study for a Biography*, London, 1940.

Wilson, J. Dover, *An Introduction to Shakespeare's Sonnets for Historians and Others*, Cambridge Univ. Press, 1964.

Wivell, Abraham, *An Inquiry into the History, Authenticity, and Characteristics of the Shakspere Portraits*, London, 1847.

Wolff, Max J., "Zum Phoenix and Turtle," *Englische Studien*, ed. Johannes Hoops, Leipzig, 1932-33, p. 159.

The Works of Ben Jonson, eds. W. Gifford, Francis Cunningham, London, 1875.

The Works of Spenser, Variorum Edition, ed. Charles G. Osgood, et al, Baltimore, MD, 1932-1949, vols. 7-8.

Wraight, A.D., *The Story That the Sonnets Tell*, London, 1994.

Index